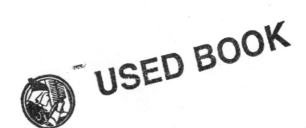

Psychology and Work Today

■ ■ ■

Psychology and Work Today

An Introduction to Industrial and Organizational Psychology

■ ■ ■

EIGHTH EDITION

Duane P. Schultz

University of South Florida

Sydney Ellen Schultz

Upper Saddle River, New Jersey 07458

Library of Congress Cataloging-in-Publication Data

Schultz, Duane P.
　　Psychology and work today : an introduction to industrial and organizational
psychology / Duane P. Schultz, Sydney Ellen Schultz.—8th ed.
　　　p.　cm.
　　Includes bibliographical references and index.
　　ISBN 0–13–034131–2
　　　1. Psychology, Industrial.　I. Schultz, Sydney Ellen.　II. Title.

HF5548.8.S356　2001
158.7—dc21

2001032118

Executive Editor: Stephanie Johnson
Managing Editor (Editorial): Sharon Rheinhardt
Editorial Assistant: Katie Fox
AVP, Director of Manufacturing and Production: Barbara Kittle
Sr. Managing Editor (Production): Mary Rottino
Production Liaison: Fran Russello
Project Manager: Jessica Balch (Pine Tree Composition, Inc.)
Marketing Manufacturer: Nick Sklitsis
Prepress and Manufacturing Buyer: Tricia Kenny
Creative Design Director: Leslie Osher
Cover Designer: Robert Farrar-Wagner
Cover Art: Chad Baker/Photo Disc, Inc.
Director, Image Resource Center: Melinda Lee Reo
Manager, Rights & Permissions: Kay Dellosa
Interior Image Specialist: Beth Boyd
Photo Researcher: Kathy Ringrose
Marketing Manager: Jeff Hester

This book was set in 10/12 Meridien by Pine Tree Composition, Inc.,
and was printed and bound by Courier Kendallville. The cover was printed
by Phoenix Color Corp.

Earlier editions, entitled *Psychology and Industry Today: An Introduction
to Industrial and Organizational Psychology,* copyright © 1973, 1977, and 1982
by Duane P. Schultz; copyright © 1986, 1990, and 1994 by Duane P. Schultz
and Sydney Ellen Schultz.

 Published by Pearson Education, Inc.
Upper Saddle River, New Jersey 07458

Printed in the United States of America
10 9 8 7 6 5 4 3

ISBN 0-13-034131-2

Pearson Education Ltd., *London*
Pearson Education Australia Pte, Limited, *Sydney*
Pearson Education Singapore, Pte. Ltd.
Pearson Education North Asia Ltd., *Hong Kong*
Pearson Education Canada, Ltd., *Toronto*
Pearson Educación de Mexico, S.A. de C.V.
Pearson Education—Japan, *Tokyo*
Pearson Education Malaysia, Pte. Ltd.
Pearson Education, *Upper Saddle River, New Jersey*

Brief Contents

Contents

5 ■ Performance Appraisal   126

6 ■ Training and Development   159

PART THREE

ORGANIZATIONAL PSYCHOLOGY 189

7 ■ Leadership 191

8 ■ Motivation, Job Satisfaction, and Job Involvement   223

PART FIVE

ENGINEERING PSYCHOLOGY   383

13 ■ Engineering Psychology   385

PART SIX

CONSUMER PSYCHOLOGY   421

Preface

Most of the students taking this introductory course in industrial-organizational (I-O) psychology will work for some kind of organization. Many are already employed while attending college. Our goal in this book is to show them how I-O psychology will directly influence their lives as job applicants, trainees, employees, managers, and consumers. In brief, we are teaching students about the nature of work in modern society.

Our focus is on the practical and the applied rather than the scientific ideal. For example, we believe that students must be introduced to topics such as training needs analysis, but they also should know that, in the reality of the workplace, training needs analyses are rarely conducted because companies are reluctant to spend money on them.

It is important that students learn about the major theories, models, research techniques, and findings of the science of I-O psychology, so that they can develop an understanding of the aims and goals of the field. However, students must also be aware that I-O psychology in practice is tempered by the conditions and demands of organizational life. Therefore, we have chosen to discuss theories, methods, and research results within the framework of actual work situations and job-related problems rather than as academic exercises.

Most of the research we cite deals with employees on the job, not college students performing simulated work tasks in the psychology department laboratory. We describe I-O psychology programs in action, showing how they are developed and implemented in a variety of organizational settings, using diverse groups of workers from many countries throughout the world.

Thus, the eighth edition of *Psychology and Work Today* continues to present I-O psychology within the context in which work actually takes place. We recognize the growing ethnic diversity of the workforce, the impact of changing economic conditions, and the effects of twenty-first-century technology.

We have written this text primarily for students who are not psychology majors and who have little background in the field. These students make up the majority of the enrollment in courses in I-O psychology, business psychology, personnel psychology, and applied psychology in psychology departments and business schools at the community college, college, and university levels.

The changes in this edition mirror the dynamic nature of the field. Chapters have been rewritten and reorganized to incorporate current research studies and management techniques. We acknowledge the importance of computer technology in several new sections on virtual reality—such as virtual workplaces, research laboratories, meetings, and self-managing work teams. Related to this phenomenon is the use of online technology for recruiting, employee selection, interviewing, polling, and psychological testing. Internet-based training and electronic monitoring for performance appraisal are covered, along with problems of Internet addiction and social isolation.

Other topics new to this edition include the failures of fair employment (anti-discrimination) legislation, discrimination based on genetic testing, ethnic harassment, executive coaching, career self-management, organizational justice, occupational health psychology, safety issues for home offices, and management hoteling (private offices on demand).

Some topics from the previous editions given expanded coverage are the Big Five personality factors as predictors of job success, electronic performance monitoring, 360-degree feedback, women in management, gender and sexual harassment, and telecommuting.

The chapters include outlines, summaries, annotated reading lists, and key terms in boldface type. Definitions for the key terms are presented in the margins and are cumulated in a glossary at the back of the book. Chapters 3 through 14 contain case problems (*Case in Point*), which are descriptions of current on-the-job research to illustrate specific topics and research approaches. *Think About It* questions challenge students to analyze material from the chapter in evaluating the cases. The questions are also suitable for class discussion and written assignments. The popular *Newsbreak* feature has been expanded. These brief sections offer informal discussions of real-world job issues, such as casual dress in the office, how *not* to interview, power napping, workplace violence, and anonymity in rating one's boss. Web-based resources are provided throughout the book in a feature called *Online!* All addresses are current as of the time of publication. An instructor's manual and test bank to accompany the text has been prepared by Tom Meriwether of the Virginia Military Institute.

We would like to thank the many students and colleagues who wrote to us about the book and who offered valuable suggestions for the new edition. In addition, several reviewers provided perceptive feedback on the manuscript, and we are appreciative of their efforts. They include Jessica M. Sterling, State University of New York–Albany; Ken Gray, College of Dupage; and Lori Rosenthal, Emerson College.

Duane P. Schultz
Sydney Ellen Schultz

The Practice of Industrial-Organizational Psychology

The work of industrial-organizational (I-O) psychologists will affect your behavior and emotional well being, both on and off the job, whether you are seeking your first job, advancing in your career, or planning for your retirement. In Chapter 1 we describe the scope of I-O psychology. In Chapter 2 we review the research methods I-O psychologists use to collect data, draw conclusions, and make recommendations to management, thus applying their findings to all facets of organizational life.

Principles, Practices, and Problems

CHAPTER 1

IS WORK A FOUR-LETTER WORD?

Not for Tom Gau, it isn't. He's one of the lucky few. This 40-something financial planner from Torrance, California, absolutely, positively enjoys his work. He talks about it with passion. "I love my job," he told an interviewer.

I love my job. I'm a workaholic. I get here at 6 or 7 in the morning. I get out at 9 at night. I manage a lot of money. I'm one of the top producers in the nation. But . . . I'm not here because of that. I'm here to help people. I love helping people. I don't have to work anymore. I'm financially independent. So why am I working these long hours? Because I love helping people (Gladwell, 2000, p. 71).

What about you? Would you work if you didn't need the money? Suppose you won $50 million in the state lottery. Would you still spend most of your adult life doing some kind of work for long hours 5 days a week like Tom Gau? Many people say they would. We're not talking about athletes or performers or superstar musicians. No, we're talking about people in traditional jobs who continue to work hard even though they have more than enough money to live comfortably for the rest of their days.

Think about the CEOs of large corporations, many of whom receive salaries that top $1 million a week. Yet they keep working. Or young venture capitalists and dot.com billionaires who rarely take vacations and who put in the same long hours, driven by the same intensity, as they did before they became so successful.

Many surveys have been taken of the rest of us, the people working at less glamorous jobs such as teacher, computer programmer, lab technician, or auto mechanic. The results consistently show that more than three out of four people questioned would continue to work even if they suddenly became financially secure and no longer needed the salary from their job.

People receive much more from their jobs than just a paycheck. Those who are fortunate enough to have found the type of work that suits their abilities will experience personal satisfaction, fulfillment, and the pride of accomplishment. These feelings provide their own reward, distinct from income. Thus, work is related not only to economic well being but also to emotional security, self-esteem, and contentment. For these people, work is definitely not a four-letter word. And it doesn't have to be for you, either.

Your job can offer a sense of identity and status, defining for you and for others who and what you are. Your work can give you the chance to learn new skills and master new challenges. It can bring positive social experiences, satisfying your need to belong to a group and providing the security that comes from being an accepted and valued member of a team. A job can furnish the opportunity to form friendships and to meet people of diverse backgrounds.

On the other hand, your job can be tedious, monotonous, and even hazardous to your health. Some work environments pose physical dangers; others can produce stress, anxiety, and dissatisfaction. If you are bored with your job, thwarted in your plans for advancement, or angry with your boss, you may bring your discontent home at the end of the workday and foist these negative

Your work helps to define your identity and contributes to your sense of self-esteem.

feelings on your family and friends. Then you may indeed think that work is a four-letter word.

Long-term research has linked work-related stressors with physical and emotional health. The single most reliable predictor of a long life is satisfaction with one's job. People who are satisfied with their work tend to live longer than people who are dissatisfied with their work.

Selecting the job that is compatible with your interests, skills, and temperament is among the most significant decisions you will ever make. For that reason, this course in industrial-organizational (I-O) psychology may be the most personally relevant of your college career. You will find that I-O psychology will have an impact on your future from the day you apply for your first job until the day you announce your retirement.

The findings and practices of I-O psychologists, second to your own skills and motivation, will determine the positions for which you are hired, the way you are expected to perform your job duties, your rank and compensation, your ultimate level of responsibility, and the personal happiness you derive from your work.

INDUSTRIAL-ORGANIZATIONAL PSYCHOLOGY ON THE JOB

I-O psychologists working in the area of human resources, or employee selection, help initially with the difficult task of choosing a job. Your first formal contacts with I-O psychology outside the classroom are likely to be with recruitment Web sites, application blanks, interviews, psychological tests, and other employee selection measures I-O psychologists have devised to help employers determine whether you are the right person for their job, and whether that job is the most suitable one for you.

After you have satisfied yourself and the organization that the position is appropriate, your advancement will depend on your performance in training programs and on the job, using assessment criteria developed by I-O psychologists.

Because of your college training, it is likely that you will qualify for management positions within the corporate hierarchy. These jobs require that you be aware of and sensitive to the diverse motivational factors and personal concerns that affect the people who work for you. To learn how to lead and motivate your subordinates to put forth their best efforts, you will need to be aware of the research of I-O psychologists on these factors.

Even if you have no direct subordinates—if, for example, you are an engineer, programmer, or accountant, or are self-employed—you would still benefit from a knowledge of human relations skills. Knowing how to get along with others can mean the difference between failure and success.

Ideally, you will feel some commitment to your employing organization and will want to see it prosper so that it continues to provide opportunities for your own advancement. The company's output must be produced efficiently and at a high level of quality. The physical plant, equipment, and working conditions should foster a productive working climate. I-O psychologists help design manufacturing and office environments to maximize productivity. In addition, a company's output must be effectively packaged, advertised, and marketed. Psychologists play a role in all these activities.

Thus, at all levels of modern organizational life, psychologists provide essential services to both employees and employers. I-O psychology serves these two masters—you and your company. As it benefits one, it automatically benefits the other.

We offer a note of caution, however. As vital as I-O psychology is, as influential as it will be throughout your working career, it is primarily a tool. And any tool is only as valuable as the skill of the person using it. If the methods and findings of I-O psychology are used improperly by management or are misunderstood by employees, they can do more harm than good. Therefore, it is important for you to know something about I-O psychology, if only for self-defense.

INDUSTRIAL-ORGANIZATIONAL PSYCHOLOGY IN EVERYDAY LIFE

There is more to I-O psychology than its application to the workday world. It also affects your attitudes and your behavior in other areas of life. Consider how you started your day. What governed your choice of toothpaste or bath soap? Why did you choose a particular brand of breakfast cereal this morning? Most likely your decisions were influenced by the psychological image created for the product, by the perceived attractiveness of the package, or by the emotional need a particular brand was intended to satisfy. Did an ad or a slogan tell you that you would be more popular or successful if you wore these jeans or drove that car? I-O psychologists have helped develop advertising and marketing techniques to create, identify, and influence these needs.

Similar psychological techniques are used to promote and sell political candidates. Opinion polls and focus groups are used to inform political leaders about how voters feel about the candidates' public stands on various issues. Polling techniques are also used to determine ratings for television programs.

I-O psychologists assist engineers in the design and layout of displays and controls, such as those on the instrument panel of your car or in various consumer appliances. Psychologists ensure that the controls are comfortable to operate and that the visual displays are easy to interpret. The shape and color of familiar highway signs resulted from I-O psychology research. Psychologists have been involved in the design of aircraft cockpits, cell phones, microwave ovens, and computer monitors and keyboards to make them user-friendly and efficient.

WHAT I-O PSYCHOLOGY MEANS TO YOUR EMPLOYER

Why are the services of I-O psychologists used by so many different types of organizations? Because they work. They promote efficiency, improve morale, and increase corporate profits. Consider the problem of employee absenteeism. Workers who fail to show up cost the company money. Techniques devised and applied by I-O psychologists to reduce absenteeism can result in substantial savings. A bank in Canada with 30,000 employees estimated that it saved $7 million in 1 year by heeding a consulting psychologist's advice to install a computerized absentee reporting system. The psychologist's fee and the cost of the system were considerably less than the amount saved.

Another costly problem in organizations is turnover. When employees quit, the company loses the investment made in recruiting, selecting, and training them. Then it must hire and train replacements. At one financial brokerage house in New York, the loss for each employee who quit exceeded $10,000. An I-O psychologist studied the situation and suggested ways to deal with the high incidence of quitting. Implementing these recommendations led to a 10% reduction in turnover and a cost saving of $100,000 within the first year.

Enhancing job satisfaction is a major concern in business today. Corporate leaders call on I-O psychologists to improve the attitudes of the work force toward their jobs and their organizations. Enhanced satisfaction with work can reduce grievances and other labor disputes and decrease absenteeism, turnover, work slowdowns, faulty products, and accidents.

Appropriate employee selection methods, such as psychological tests, designed and monitored by I-O psychologists help ensure that the most qualified applicants are hired. For example, researchers compared federal government employees who were hired on the basis of their cognitive ability (intelligence) test scores with employees hired on the basis of level of education and work experience. The tests were found to be far superior for selecting better and more productive workers, and the cost savings were substantial.

These examples indicate the importance of the work of I-O psychologists to all types of employing organizations. I-O psychology contributes to organizational efficiency and improves the bottom line on the company's financial report.

THE SCOPE AND HISTORICAL DEVELOPMENT OF I-O PSYCHOLOGY

I-O psychology The application of the methods, facts, and principles of the science of psychology to people at work.

Psychology is the science of behavior and cognitive processes. **Industrial-organizational psychology** involves the application of the methods, facts, and principles of psychology to people at work. That fact that psychology is a science tells us how it operates. A science deals with observable facts that can be seen, heard, touched, measured, and recorded. Hence, a science is empirical, which means that it relies on verifiable observation, experimentation, and experience, not on opinions, hunches, pet notions, or private prejudices. A science is objective in its approaches and results.

It is important to remember that a science is defined by its methods, not by its subject matter. In methods and procedures, I-O psychology attempts to be just as scientific as physics or chemistry. When psychologists observe the behavior of people at work, they do so in the best traditions of science: objectively, dispassionately, and systematically.

The subject matter of I-O psychology is also objective. Psychologists observe and analyze overt human behavior, such as our movements, speech, writings and other creative works, to analyze and understand the people who are the focus of these observations. These overt behaviors are the only aspects of human existence that can be objectively seen, heard, measured, and recorded. Something more must be involved, however, because psychology is also the science of cognitive processes. Psychologists must study intangible qualities such as motives, emotions, needs, perceptions, thoughts, and feelings. These facets of our inner life cannot be observed directly.

We cannot see motivation, for example. It is an internal driving force inaccessible to observation. Its effects, however, can be seen. An angry person may display that emotion in such behaviors as a flushed face, rapid breathing, and clenched fists. A person driven by a high need to achieve success exhibits that motivation in behaviors that differ from those of a person content merely to get along, whether on the job, at a party, or under observation in a psychology experiment.

We cannot see intelligence directly, but we can observe the overt behavioral manifestations of different levels of intelligence. Psychologists can objectively record that one person performs at a higher level than another person on a test of cognitive abilities and can then infer that the first person is more intelligent. Inference based on the objective observation of behavior enables us to draw conclusions regarding personal factors or conditions, even when we cannot see them directly.

This is how I-O psychologists conduct their work. They observe the behavior of employees on the job under well-controlled and systematic conditions. They record behavioral responses, such as the number of parts produced each hour on an assembly line, the number of keystrokes per minute made by a computer clerk, or the quality of telephone service provided to customers by airline reservations agents. They vary the conditions under which a job is performed and measure any resulting differences in performance. Using these and other techniques, I-O psychologists observe, seeking a better understanding of human behavior. They look, listen, measure, and record objectively and precisely, adhering to the principles of the scientific method.

How did I-O psychology become so necessary to modern organizational life? The field was formed and fashioned of necessity. An urgent practical problem needing a novel solution gave the initial impetus to the field, and the demands of crisis and need have continued to stimulate its growth and influence.

Pioneers in Personnel Selection

Industrial psychology had its formal beginning in the early years of the twentieth century. The honor for sparking the development of the field is usually given to Walter Dill Scott (1869–1955). A college football player at Northwestern University, Scott graduated from a theological seminary, intending to be a missionary in China. By the time he was prepared to undertake this calling, however, he learned that there were no vacancies for missionaries in China. And so he became a psychologist instead.

Scott was the first to apply psychology to advertising, employee selection, and management issues. At the turn of the last century he spoke out on the potential uses of psychology in advertising. Encouraged by the response of the business leaders, Scott wrote several articles and published a book entitled *The Theory and Practice of Advertising* (Scott, 1903), which is generally considered to be the first book about using psychology to help solve problems in the business world. In 1919 Scott formed the first consulting company in industrial psychology, providing services to more than 40 major American corporations, primarily in the area of personnel selection.

In 1913, Hugo Münsterberg (1863–1916), a German psychologist teaching at Harvard University, wrote *The Psychology of Industrial Efficiency*. He was an early advocate of the use of psychological tests to measure a prospective employee's skills and to match that person with the requirements of a particular job. He con- ducted considerable research in real-world work situations and workplaces, with the goal of improving on-the-job efficiency. His writing, research, and consulting activities helped spread the influence of industrial psychology, and he became a celebrity, America's most famous psychologist. Münsterberg befriended kings, presidents, and movie stars and was one of only two psychologists ever accused of being a spy.

World War I and the Testing Movement

The work of Scott and Münsterberg provided a beginning for the field, but it was a request by the U.S. Army during World War I (1917–1918) that marked the emergence of industrial psychology as an important and useful discipline. Faced with the task of screening and classifying millions of men recruited for military service, the army commissioned psychologists to devise a test to identify people of low intelligence so that they could be eliminated from consideration for train- ing programs. Two tests resulted from their efforts: The Army Alpha, designed for recruits who could read and write, and the Army Beta, which used mazes, pictures, and symbols for recruits who could not read. The Army Beta was also suitable for immigrants who were not fluent in the English language.

Additional tests were prepared for selecting candidates for officer and pilot training and for other military classifications that required special abilities. A per- sonality test, the Personal Data Sheet, which could be administered to large groups of people at one time, was developed to detect neurotic tendencies among the army recruits.

After the war, businesses, manufacturing concerns, school systems, and other organizations that needed to screen and classify large numbers of people demanded more and better testing techniques. The tests devised for the army were adapted for civilian use, and new ones were designed for a variety of situa- tions. Enthusiasm for psychological testing spread throughout the United States. Soon, millions of schoolchildren and job applicants routinely faced batteries of psychological tests. Thus, the initial contributions of industrial psychologists fo- cused on issues in personnel selection—evaluating individuals and placing them in the appropriate grades, jobs, or training programs.

The Hawthorne Studies and Motivational Issues

Hawthorne studies A long-term research program at the Hawthorne, Illinois, Western Electric Company plant. It documented the influence of a variety of managerial and organizational factors on employee behavior.

The scope of the field broadened considerably in 1924 with the commencement of a now-famous series of studies conducted on the job. Called the **Hawthorne studies** because they were conducted at the Hawthorne, Illinois, plant of the Western Electric Company, this long-term research program took industrial psy- chology beyond employee selection and placement to the more complex prob- lems of motivation, interpersonal relations, and organizational dynamics (Roeth- lisberger & Dickson, 1939).

The research began as a straightforward investigation of the effects of the physical work environment on employee efficiency. The researchers asked such questions as: What is the effect on productivity if we increase the lighting in the workroom? Do temperature and humidity levels affect production? What will happen if management provides rest periods for the workers?

The results of the Hawthorne studies surprised both the investigators and the plant managers. They found that social and psychological factors in the work environment were of potentially greater importance than physical factors. For example, changing the level of illumination in a workroom from very bright to dim did not diminish worker efficiency. More subtle factors were operating to induce these workers to maintain their original production level under nearly dark conditions.

With another group of workers, lighting was increased and production levels rose. The researchers made other changes—rest periods, free lunches, a shorter workday—and with the introduction of each change, production increased. However, when all the benefits were suddenly eliminated, production continued to increase. The researchers concluded that physical aspects of the work environment were not as important to employees as management had assumed.

The Hawthorne studies opened up new areas for I-O psychologists to explore, such as the nature of leadership, the formation of informal groups among workers, employee attitudes, communication patterns, and other managerial and organizational variables now recognized as influences on efficiency, motivation, and job satisfaction.

Although the Hawthorne studies have been criticized for a lack of scientific rigor, there is no denying their impact on the way psychologists view the nature of work and on the scope and direction of I-O psychology.

World War II and Engineering Psychology

World War II brought more than 2,000 psychologists directly into the war effort. Their major contribution was the testing, classifying, and training of millions of recruits in various branches of military service. New skills were required to operate sophisticated aircraft, tanks, and ships, and it was necessary to identify persons capable of learning to perform these tasks.

The increasingly complex weapons of war sparked the development of a new field: engineering psychology. Working closely with engineers, psychologists supplied information about human abilities and limitations for operating high-speed aircraft, submarines, and other equipment, and thus influenced their design.

I-O psychology achieved greater stature as a result of these contributions to the war effort. Government and industry leaders recognized that psychologists were equipped to solve many practical business problems. The experience also demonstrated to many psychologists, who before the war had worked in the relative isolation of their university laboratories, that there were vital and challenging problems in the real world that they could help solve.

The growth of I-O psychology since the end of World War II in 1945 has paralleled the growth of American business and technical enterprise. The size and complexity of modern organizations have placed additional demands on the skills of I-O psychologists. New technologies meant that employees needed enhanced and redesigned training programs. The advent of computers, for example, generated the need for programmers and technical support personnel and changed the way many jobs were performed. Psychologists had to determine the abilities required for these jobs, the kinds of people most likely to have these abilities, and the best ways to identify and train them.

The demands on engineering psychologists also increased. Inventions such as supersonic aircraft, missiles, and advanced weapons systems required additional training for safe and efficient operation. Engineering psychologists became involved in the design of industrial robots, high-tech office equipment, and the redesign of work spaces for today's automated operations.

Organizational issues have assumed greater importance (the "O" side of I-O psychology). Human relations skills are recognized by managers and executives as vital to maintaining the high job performance of their employees. The nature of leadership, the role of motivation and job satisfaction, the impact of the organizational structure and climate, and the processes of decision making are continuously being analyzed. In recognition of the significance of organizational variables, the Division of Industrial Psychology of the American Psychological Association (APA) became the Society for Industrial and Organizational Psychology (SIOP).

> **ONLINE!**
>
> Explore the Web sites for the American Psychological Association (*www.apa.org*) and the Society for Industrial and Organizational Psychology (*www.siop.org*).

CHALLENGES FOR I-O PSYCHOLOGY

The rapidly changing nature of work, together with technological advances and a more diverse population, mean new demands and responsibilities for I-O psychologists in the twenty-first century. One such change relates to the kinds of jobs available and the ways in which they will be performed.

The Virtual Workplace

A prominent organizational psychologist describes the nature of work as follows:

> Consider the new paradigm of work—anytime, anywhere, in real space or in cyberspace. For many employers the virtual workplace, in which employees operate remotely from each other and from managers, is a reality now, and all indications are that it will become even more prevalent in the future (Cascio, 1998, p. 32).

It is becoming commonplace for organizations to have large numbers of employees who work off-site, telecommuting from a home office, phoning from a car or airplane while traveling on business, or teleconferencing from a hotel room or vacation spot.

This dramatic shift in where and how we work is an effect of the information age. Many jobs can be performed anywhere within electronic reach of the home office or the actual workplace, thanks to e-mail, voicemail, pagers, cell phones, laptop computers, and personal data systems.

To function efficiently and productively, these virtual workplaces require three types of information access (Cascio, 1998):

- Online material that can be downloaded and printed
- Databases on customers and products, and automated central files, that can be accessed from remote locations
- A means of tracking employees and their work assignments at any time of day

The downside of electronically connected virtual workplaces is that employees are often expected to work, or to be available, beyond the normal working hours of the organization. Some companies require their employees to carry phones or beepers at all times, keeping them effectively tethered to the office, with no way to escape the demands of their jobs. As a writer for the *New York Times* noted, "The 24/7 culture of nearly round-the-clock work is endemic to the wired economy."

Virtual Employees

Not only are more people performing their work at locations away from the office, they are also less likely to be full-time employees who can expect to remain with the same employer for the duration of their career. Whereas previous generations of workers presumed a kind of unwritten psychological contract with their employer—"If I do my job well, my company will keep me on until I'm ready to retire"—today's workers have no such certainty of lifelong job security.

The notion of long-term loyalty and commitment to one organization faded in the closing decades of the twentieth century, during a frenzied period of corporate mergers and acquisitions, downsizing, and plant closures in which millions of workers and managers lost their jobs.

More of today's employees are likely to be contingent workers, freelancers, independent contractors, or part-time seasonal labor. The largest single private employer in the United States is Manpower, Inc., a temporary staffing agency. Millions of Americans work on a freelance basis. At the professional level, the Department of Labor estimates that more than 8 million people can be classified as independent contractors.

Many workers, especially younger ones, report that they prefer contingent work because it provides flexibility, independence, challenges, and the opportunity to continually upgrade their work experience and job skills. Many corporations also prefer this arrangement because they save on administrative expenses and taxes and do not have to provide such benefits as insurance or pension plans.

Worker Involvement

The ways in which organizations today conduct business are changing drastically, both in existing jobs and in the new jobs that are being created. In the twenty-first century, employees at blue-collar, supervisory, and upper management levels are facing revolutionary challenges.

The days when a worker could be taught how to perform a simple task and told to keep doing it that way without question, are disappearing. Today's workers want quality management. Their key words are "empowerment," "involvement," and "participation." Workers are expected to master not merely the tasks of a single job, but also to assemble a cluster of personal skills that they can transfer from one job to another. They must continually upgrade these skills and

Temporarily Yours

Ten years ago, I took a job stuffing envelopes. It was a necessity: I had just graduated from college and had no idea what I wanted to do with my life, but the lenders who had financed my college education weren't sympathetic to my existential crisis. The job came through a temporary-employment agency, which paid me $7.25 an hour to cram manila envelopes with a company's pap. I lasted one day. Since then, the temp world has changed dramatically. . . .

Temporary employment has grown in part because employers are more cautious about committing themselves. "They want to try people out before hiring them," said James Essey, president of the Tempositions Group of Companies in Manhattan [New York]. Many companies also prefer temps because they may not have to give them full benefits, or any benefits at all.

But it is not only employers who are fickle. Many young people engage in serial workplace monogamy, refusing to enter into serious relationships until they have sowed their corporate oats. "You test each other out, like a trial marriage," said Georgia Ellis, a vice president at Fifth Avenue Temporary Services in Manhattan. "And it doesn't look bad on your résumé, because it doesn't look like you've jumped from place to place. You have an excuse. You're a temp."

Kristin Robinson, 29, has morphed into what is known as a "permanent temp"—one with a long-term assignment. For the last 2 years, Ms. Robinson, who is also an actress, has had a continuing temporary position as a graphics artist, 3 days a week, at Andersen Consulting in Manhattan. She freelances the other 2 days from connections made at other temp jobs. The freedom, she said, is invaluable: "I try to be respectful and give notice, but if I need to leave I leave. And I don't take work home."

Most young corporate nomads, some of whom are actors, musicians, and writers, want to focus on their "real" careers without having to ask, "Do you want fries with that?" They thrive on the flexibility and often use their day jobs as floating office spaces for managing the rest of their lives.

In a full-employment economy, the competition among temp agencies has intensified. Many offer benefits to attract workers; employees staying 6 months may be eligible for vacation pay, child-care reimbursement, and the purchase of medical coverage at group rates.

But the life of a temp isn't all free Krispy Kremes. Stories abound of demeaning treatment from employers and permanent workers. For details, check *Tempslave*, a magazine, or the Temp24–7 Web site (*www.temp24–7. com*), where temps can vent. Temp24–7 includes "Temps vs. suits," a game in which temps can attack a virtual boss. . . .

Cyberwrath aside, most of today's temps have strong bonds with bosses and agencies. Some employers are so fond of their longer-term temps that, when they take time off, other temps are hired to stand in.

> Once displeased, temps can also request transfers. Or walk away. Suzanne Lynn, 27, said she left a Greenville, S.C., law firm for lunch and, angry about being yelled at, didn't come back. Her agency understood and handed her another assignment. With that kind of freedom and unconditional love, temporary work might be the wave of the future.
>
> ───────────
> *Source:* Abby Ellin, *New York Times*, April 18, 1999.

learn to participate in decision-making teams to determine how the work is best carried out. Today's workers are also assuming increasing responsibility for their part in the production or service process, even including the selecting and hiring of new workers.

This involvement of workers affects the ways managers perform their jobs. No longer can they rule by command, telling their employees what to do and when and how to do it. Now they function more as guides and mentors than traditional leaders. These changes require substantial adjustments for workers and managers, and are, in part, a response to technological change in the workplace.

Changing Technology and Skills

A radical change in the workplace stems from advances in microelectronics—in word processors, computers, and industrial robots. In a recent survey, 205 I-O psychologists were asked what workplace trend they believed would have the greatest impact on their field. An overwhelming 72% said, "developments in Internet technology" (Waclawski & Church, 2000).

Work environments large and small have become automated, with sophisticated equipment taking over functions once performed by humans. The majority of office workers today use word-processing or data-processing equipment that eliminates clerical jobs requiring lower-level skills. Workers must be technically proficient in systems and procedures unknown to previous generations of employees. Computers, faxes, modems, cell phones, electronic notebooks, e-mail, and the Internet have changed the functions of many jobs and created others that never existed before.

Some companies are using electronic equipment as job perks. For example, both Ford and Delta Airlines provide their employees—whether they work in offices, on the factory floor, or in the maintenance hangar—with computers and printers for home use, plus free Internet access.

With the reduction in the number of manufacturing jobs and the demands of modern technology, there are fewer job opportunities for computer-illiterate or poorly educated men and women. By the year 2006, traditional manufacturing jobs for unskilled laborers will constitute only 12% of the U.S. labor market, a drop of 5% over a 20-year period.

Consider the job of longshoreman, or stevedore, whose tasks were once described as requiring considerably more brawn than brain. In 1969, it took 500 men 3 months to unload a 900-foot cargo ship. Today, using automated equipment, 10 workers can unload a container ship in 24 hours. In 1969, the International Longshoremen Association had 27,000 members. By 2000, only 2,700 members remained, and their work requires skills not needed 30 years ago, such as the ability to run computerized inventory checks on a ship's cargo.

As many as 25 million Americans over the age of 17 are functionally illiterate, which means they do not have sufficient writing and reading comprehension skills to fill out an application blank for a job. Basic math skills are also lacking. One study showed that when a group of 21- to 25-year-olds were confronted with the task of calculating the change due from a two-item restaurant bill, no more than 34% of whites, 20% of Hispanics, and 8% of blacks could do so correctly.

From an employer's standpoint, it is increasingly difficult to recruit entry-level workers who possess the basic skills needed to learn to perform many jobs. A telecommunications company in the northeastern United States had to interview and test 90,000 job applicants to find 2,000 who could be trained for a job that did not even require a high school diploma. General Motors found that workers who lacked appropriate reading, writing, and math skills had difficulty completing the training programs provided every few years to update skills and acquaint employees with new manufacturing processes.

Diversity Issues

Another change in the workplace is demographic. It involves a shift in the ethnic composition of the work force. In these early years of the twenty-first century, persons of African, Asian, and Hispanic heritage constitute at least 35% of all new workers. Further, half of all new employees are women. White men workers are becoming a minority. Organizations large and small must be increasingly

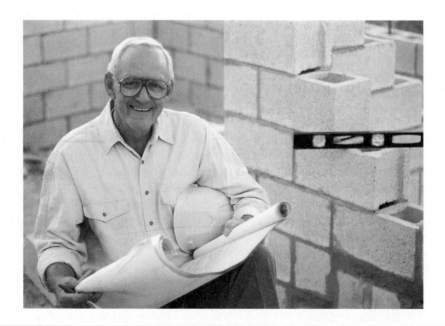

The U. S. work force today includes a growing number of older workers.

sensitive to the needs and concerns of a work force that comprises many cultures and backgrounds.

Up to 800,000 immigrants enter the United States every year. Most of them are eager to work, but they lack English-language training and other literacy skills. They may also be unfamiliar with corporate work habits. This presents an additional challenge to business and industry.

All these changes in the workplace and the composition of the work force pose opportunities for I-O psychologists in selecting and training workers, redesigning jobs and equipment, refining management practices, raising morale, and dealing with health and safety issues. These challenges suggest that this is an exciting time to consider a career as an I-O psychologist.

I-O PSYCHOLOGY AS A CAREER: TRAINING AND EMPLOYMENT

Although few people believe that they are qualified to be physicists, chemists, or biologists after taking one or two courses, many people consider themselves expert psychologists even when they have had no formal training. Some think that the practice of psychology requires nothing more than common sense and a lot of time interacting with other people. This will no more make you a psychologist, however, than years of taking medicines will make you a physician.

Modern I-O psychology is a complex and demanding profession that requires university training, practical experience, and continuing study to keep aware of new developments. The minimum requirement for working as an I-O psychologist is a master's degree, which usually requires 42 semester hours and 2 to 3 years to complete. Most master's degree students work full-time or part-time while in school. Of all the graduate degrees granted in I-O psychology each year, two thirds are at the master's level.

The majority of I-O master's degree graduates find professional jobs in their specialty areas at competitive salaries in industry, government, consulting firms, and research organizations. Their most marketable skills are in the areas of psychological test and survey construction and validation, human resources selection and placement, performance appraisal, fair employment practices, and employee training. College course work in motivation, job satisfaction, and organizational development are also useful on the job. Thus, a master's degree program in I-O psychology provides valuable preparation for a productive and rewarding career. However, the higher positions in businesses and universities typically require a doctoral degree, which requires from 3 to 5 years of graduate study.

The number of graduate students in I-O psychology continues to grow, with the bulk of the increase being among students at the master's level. These students have a sound practical reason for their choice. They are responding to the projected demand for psychologists. The U.S. Bureau of Labor Statistics expects an increase in job opportunities for psychologists in business and research, in nonprofit organizations, and in computer firms.

The training requirements for a career in I-O psychology are difficult, but the rewards can be great. I-O psychologists have higher salaries than any other group of psychologists. In 1997, the median annual income for I-O psychologists

NEWSBREAK

But What Can You Do with a B.A. in Psychology?

Fewer than half of all psychology graduates with bachelors' degrees from U.S. colleges and universities go on to attend graduate school. What happens to them? Where do they find work? What sort of career opportunities can they expect? Relax. If this is your situation, the future looks promising, even if you're not planning on studying for a master's or doctoral degree.

Psychology majors with 4-year degrees find employment in all sectors of the economy. Approximately 50% work for private corporations, 15% are employed by government agencies, 14% find jobs in education, 12% run their own businesses, and 9% work for charitable organizations.

Of those in the corporate sector, most are in managerial positions; the rest work in sales, human resources, training, and other staff functions.

Nearly half of the recent B.A. graduates in psychology report that their job duties are closely related to their course work. They also say that their jobs have high career potential. Managers and salespersons are particularly optimistic about their future with their organization, largely because analysts foresee a 10% to 20% growth in these types of jobs.

So, yes, even if you do not plan on graduate school, good jobs are out there for you.

Source: N. Fogg, P. Harrington & T. Harrington (1999). *The college majors handbook: The actual jobs, earnings, and trends for graduates of 60 college majors.* Indianapolis, IN: JIST. Also J. Kohout, A look at recent baccalaureates in psychology. *Monitor on Psychology,* January 2000, p. 13.

with doctoral degrees in the United States was $90,000. The top 10% reported annual incomes greater than $180,000. At the master's level, the median salary was $55,000, with the top 10% earning more than $150,000 (Burnfield & Medsker, 1999).

In addition, the rewards for I-O psychologists of stimulating work, challenging responsibilities, and intellectual growth are notable. As Ann Howard, a past president of the Society for Industrial and Organizational Psychology, commented, it is a field in which "you can make things happen. You put in a program, and you see some results. You might see better people selected, or job satisfaction go up, or turnover go down. But you've made something happen, and that's a very exciting kind of reward."

I-O psychologists work in business, industry, government agencies, service organizations, consulting firms, and universities. Many of the psychologists who teach courses in I-O psychology also undertake research and consulting activities. Percentages for the various employment settings of I-O psychologists are shown in Figure 1–1. Employment opportunities, as reflected in examples of job titles, responsibilities, and types of organizations, are shown in Table 1–1.

Smaller organizations that cannot afford a full-time I-O psychologist rely on the services of consulting psychologists who are employed on a contract basis to

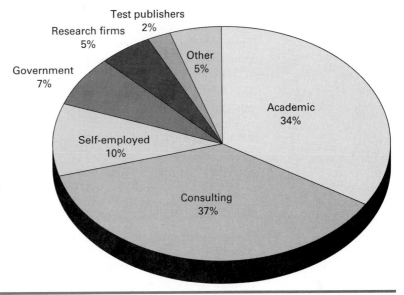

FIGURE 1–1. Employment settings of I/O psychologists. (Data from survey of SIOP members. W. C. Borman & G. L. Cox, "Who's doing what: Patterns in the practice of I/O psychology." *The Industrial-Organizational Psychologist*, 1996, 33(4), 21.)

fill a specific need or solve a particular problem. Consultants may evaluate candidates for employment, design a piece of equipment or an assembly line, establish a training program, conduct a survey on consumer acceptance of a new product, or try to determine why morale or productivity is declining. The value of consulting services lies not only in the technical skills the I-O psychologist offers, but also in the freshness of approach and objectivity that an outsider can bring to the company.

More than half of the I-O psychologists studying for PhDs today are women. There has been a higher rate of increase in the number of women earning doctoral degrees in I-O psychology than in any other specialty. But despite intensive efforts to recruit minority graduate students, African-Americans and Hispanics account for fewer than 5% of I-O psychologists. Most minority graduate students choose to specialize in clinical psychology.

I-O psychologists are affiliated primarily with four divisions of the American Psychological Association (APA): the Society for Industrial and Organizational Psychology (SIOP), the division of Military Psychology, the division of Applied Experimental and Engineering Psychologists, and the Society for Consumer Psychology. Many academic and research-oriented I-O psychologists are also affiliated with the American Psychological Society.

ONLINE!   Explore the Web sites recommended by psychology graduate students for information on how to survive graduate school and find a job. See *www.apa.org/apags* (American Psychological Association of Graduate Students), *www.users.erols.com/fezworth* (PsycHits: the graduate student's psychology reference site), *www.socialpsychology.org* (the Social Psychology Network), and *www.personal.umich .edu/~ danhorn/graduate.html* (Graduate Student Resources on the Web).

TABLE 1–1   Places of Employment and Job Responsibilities of Selected I-O Psychologists

Human Resources Consulting Firm
Test development and validation, interview training, assessment center design, performance appraisal system design, career development programs, attitude surveys.

Market Research, Consulting, and Promotional Services Firm, Marketing Research Project Director
Apply social science research skills to proposal development, analysis, writing, and presentation.

International Airline, Assessment Center Specialist for Overseas Development
Coordinate and supervise assessment center for evaluation of employees being considered for promotion: Develop assessment materials, make recommendations to improve effectiveness, select and train staff to become qualified assessors.

Management Consulting Firm, Senior Level Manager
Oversee projects involving the systems approach to training, training technologies, and management/career development training.

Human Resource Research and Consulting Associates, I/O Project Manager
Work with interdisciplinary staff (psychologists, sociologists, computer science specialists, and educators) on information systems, test development, survey design, and equal employment issues, including providing expert witness testimony in selected court cases.

Employee Decisions Consulting Firm, Director of Human Resources
Provide services in counseling, coaching executive candidates for job interviews, assessment and test interpretation, and career development.

Pharmaceutical Firm, Manager of Psychological Services
Design psychological strategies for employee testing and job analysis, assess legal considerations in hiring, research and recommend changes in corporate compensation procedures, develop and monitor performance appraisal practices.

Public Utility (Gas and Electric Company), Executive Consultant in Organization Planning and Development
Work with unions, line operations, human resource departments, and senior management groups to redesign human resource systems and implement major organizational changes.

Electronics Corporation, Team Leadership and Communication Trainer
Implement self-directed production work teams: Train workers in manufacturing team concepts, problem-solving techniques, leadership development, communications, and cooperative decision making. Monitor and evaluate programs and document results.

Telecommunications Company, Human Resource Research Intern
Predoctoral internship for person admitted to doctoral candidacy at accredited university to conduct research on human resource programs while working with licensed I-O psychologists and human resource professionals.

State College, Assistant Professor of Psychology
Teach courses in organizational behavior, group processes, tests and measurements; direct undergraduate research projects.

PROBLEMS FOR I-O PSYCHOLOGISTS

No field of study is free of internal and external problems. I-O psychologists face several difficulties, all aggravated by the very factor that has made the field so successful, namely, the demand for its services.

Fraudulent Practitioners

More than any other science, psychology has been victimized by quackery, that is, by the illicit and fraudulent practice of psychology by people who have little or no professional training. This problem is particularly apparent in clinical psychology, where untrained people set themselves up as "counselors" and often do great harm to emotionally disturbed persons who are seeking help.

Quackery also affects I-O psychology. Mary Tenopyr, a past president of SIOP, wrote:

> A major complication in the lives of psychologists in business is the ill-trained or unscrupulous person who offers psychological-type services to companies. . . . Some of the most difficult situations I have had to cope with in my career have resulted from the actions of pseudopsychologists who have captured the ears of high-level managers (Tenopyr, 1992, p. 175).

An uninformed business organization can be just as gullible as an individual. Unethical consulting firms have sold their so-called services to industry and made quick money—and a quicker getaway—before the company realized it had been duped. Not only is such unethical behavior dangerous and unfair to business (consider, for example, all the competent people who were not hired because they performed poorly on the quack's phony test), but it is also harmful to psychology as a science and profession. If a company is damaged by the charlatan's actions, the field as a whole receives the blame. The executives of an organization defrauded in the past will be reluctant to consider legitimate psychological services in the future.

Credentials and Certification

The problem of the phony practitioner is being reduced in clinical psychology because states now license or certify psychologists in the same way they license physicians. It is illegal for people to represent themselves to the public as psychologists or to use any of the tools of psychology unless they have met the licensing or certification requirements. These are usually a graduate degree and satisfactory performance on an exam covering knowledge of all areas of psychology.

These procedures were established specifically to protect the public from charlatans in the areas of clinical and counseling psychology. The question of licensing I-O psychologists is controversial within the profession. Many I-O psychologists practicing in states that offer licensing have chosen to apply for it.

Although some 40% of SIOP members are licensed, SIOP takes the position that they need not be (Pieper, 2000).

A business must exercise care when seeking the services of a psychologist. It is not enough to flip through the pages of the telephone directory or enter the words "I-O psychology" on a search engine. The educational and professional qualifications of anyone called a psychologist must be examined carefully.

Communication with Management

All sciences develop a specialized technical jargon that its members use to communicate with one another. This vocabulary is sometimes not understood by those outside the discipline. Because I-O psychologists must work closely with people who are not psychologists, that is, with managers and employees, they must make the effort to communicate clearly their ideas, activities, and research results. The recommendations of I-O psychologists will be of no value to an organization if they cannot be comprehended. The reports will be filed in the nearest wastebasket. Psychologists must be able to present their contributions in a way that can be understood by those who are using their services.

Resistance to New Ideas

This problem might be called, "I've always done it this way, and I'm not going to change now!" Psychologists who work in business and industry often meet this attitude—a resistance to change, an unwillingness to try something new or consider novel ideas. When an I-O psychologist recommends altering the usual way of performing a job, workers sometimes view the suggestion as a threat. Employees who are told to modify their work habits to conform to the potentially more efficient system proposed by the psychologist may actively resist because they believe that the company is trying to get them to work harder for the same pay. Insecure workers may also feel that management is criticizing their past job performance. This resistance to change is a serious problem at all levels, from the worker on the assembly line or the phone bank to the CEO at corporate headquarters.

If the findings of I-O psychologists are to have any impact, they must have the support of the managers and employees who will be affected by them. Psychologists need the cooperation of those employees whose jobs will be changed. They must show considerable human relations skills, patience, and persuasiveness in addition to their technical expertise.

Research versus Application?

The question of research versus application continues to concern I-O psychologists in their relations with management. Some managers complain that too little of the research published in I-O psychology journals is oriented toward the practical real-world problems with which they deal every day. Although it is true that much academic research may appear to have no immediate application, psychologists who work directly for organizations know that the two functions, research and application, are interdependent.

Without research, there would be no reliable information to apply to critical problems on the job. This point is often overlooked by managers who demand immediate solutions to specific problems and who cannot understand the hesitation of the psychologist who tells them that the answer can come only from research.

The conflict between research and application arises because organizations often need prompt answers. Production schedules and contract deadlines do not always wait for the design and execution of a research study. Managers facing time constraints may have unrealistic expectations and become impatient when the company psychologist—their so-called "expert" on human behavior—cannot provide a quick fix.

We are not suggesting that whenever I-O psychologists are asked a question, they run to the laboratory to begin a month-long experiment. The history of psychology already provides a wealth of empirical data about human behavior in a variety of situations, and well-trained psychologists know how to apply these findings to specific problems in the workplace. The value of these data, however, depends on the similarity between the situations in which they were obtained and the present situation.

For example, studies about how college sophomores learn complex material are not as relevant to the learning abilities of employees in a chemical company as is research conducted on the learning abilities of employees in a steel company. The steel company research, performed in an actual work setting, will probably provide the more useful results. But a learning study conducted in another chemical company will be even more applicable. And a study conducted on the very workers whose learning habits are in question will be the most useful of all.

Sometimes circumstances do not allow sufficient time or resources for research to be undertaken. SIOP offers the following advice:

> *You can't research every question.* While it is desirable to have a body of research to support your actions, it is not always possible. When you find yourself having to make a decision in the absence of research, you have to take what you know about similar situations and use your own judgment (Baker, 1996, p. 103).

Properly devised research can be of immense value to an organization's productive efficiency, but the needs of the workplace often call for compromise, patience, and understanding by both managers and psychologists. The fundamental issue is not research *versus* application but research *plus* application. The two functions are compatible and complementary.

AREAS OF I-O PSYCHOLOGY

We have noted how I-O psychology affects many aspects of the relationship between you and your work. We describe here the specific interests of I-O psychologists that are covered in the following chapters.

The Tools and Techniques of Science (Chapter 2).   Psychologists study human behavior through the tools and techniques of science. To understand their work, we must become acquainted with the ways in which they perform research, analyze data, and draw conclusions.

Recruiting and Selecting Employees (Chapters 3 and 4).   Despite the opinion of some executives and personnel managers that they can judge job applicants by a handshake, eye contact, or style of dress, selecting and evaluating employees are complex processes that continue long after the initial recruitment and hiring. Throughout your career, questions of promotion and salary increases will arise. Many of the selection devices, such as interviews and psychological tests, that were used in making your first hiring decision will also be applied to subsequent career decisions. Thus, it is important for you to understand the selection process. It is also to your advantage that your potential employer use the most valid techniques available. Improper matching of the person and the job can lead to inefficiency and dissatisfaction for employer and employee.

Evaluating Employee Performance (Chapter 5).   The periodic evaluation of the quality of your job performance will continue throughout your working career. Promotions, pay increases, transfers, and dismissals will be based on these appraisals. It is vital that these decisions be made as fairly and objectively as possible and not be subject to the personal likes and dislikes of your supervisor. I-O psychologists have devised appraisal methods for many types of jobs. Because your future satisfaction and security depend on these appraisals, it is important that your company have a fair and appropriate system for evaluating your job performance.

Employee Training and Development (Chapter 6).   Virtually every new employee receives some sort of job training. Inexperienced workers must be taught the specific operations they are expected to perform and may also need training in good work habits. Experienced workers who change jobs must be taught the policies and procedures of their new employer. Workers whose jobs are altered by changing technology require retraining. As the machinery of production and the dynamics of organizational life become more complex, the demands made on employees to learn and on employers to teach increase in scope and significance.

Organizational Leadership (Chapter 7).   One of industry's greatest challenges is selecting, training, and developing effective leaders. The problem is of concern to you for two reasons. First, as an employee you will work under a supervisor or manager, and your efficiency and satisfaction will be affected by his or her leadership style. Second, because most business leaders come from the ranks of college-educated persons, you will most likely serve at some level of management in the course of your career. Psychologists are also concerned with the abilities of leaders in various situations and the effects of different leadership styles on subordinates. It is necessary to the continuing growth of any organization that its most competent people be placed in positions of leadership and that they exercise their skills in the most effective manner.

Motivation, Job Satisfaction, and Job Involvement (Chapter 8). Vital to the efficiency of any organization are the motivations of its employees, the satisfactions they receive from their work, and the extent of their commitment to the company. Many aspects of the work environment affect motivation, satisfaction, and involvement. These include the quality of leadership, advancement opportunities, job security, and characteristics of the physical and psychological work climate. Negative aspects of a job can produce undesirable effects, such as absenteeism, turnover, low productivity, frequent accidents, and labor grievances. I-O psychologists work to identify and modify conditions that can impair the quality of working life before they have serious psychological and economic consequences for employees and employers.

Organizational Psychology (Chapter 9). Few people work in isolation. Whether our work is in a classroom, a department store, or a software company, it takes place within a particular organizational climate or culture. This culture includes the formal structure and policies of the organization, the nature of its leadership, and the informal groups that arise among workers. Informal groups may dictate norms and behaviors at variance with company policy.

Working Conditions (Chapter 10). The physical aspects of the work environment were the first to be studied by I-O psychologists. Much research was conducted on lighting, temperature, noise, workspace design, and working hours. Later, attention shifted to more complex social and psychological conditions of work. A job's psychological climate, including such factors as fatigue and boredom, may be more important than the physical climate because psychological effects are subject to greater individual variation.

Employee Safety, Violence, and Health (Chapter 11). In addition to the tragic physical and personal consequences of industrial accidents, economic losses cost organizations billions of dollars in lost work hours, employee compensation, and the expense of hiring and training new workers. Because the majority of accidents are caused by human error, the work of I-O psychologists is crucial in reducing the accident toll. Psychologists are also involved in efforts to deal with alcohol and drug use on the job, and with violence in the workplace.

Stress in the Workplace (Chapter 12). Job-induced stress has widespread effects on physical and mental health. It can interfere with job performance and lead to serious illness. Many organizations attempt to deal with the effects of stress through counseling programs and by redesigning jobs to be less stressful.

Engineering Psychology (Chapter 13). The design of the tools and equipment needed to perform a job is directly related to the physical work environment, to employee motivation and morale, and to job safety. As the machinery of the manufacturing, transportation, and service industries becomes more complex, so do the demands placed on the human operators of this equipment. It is the job of the engineering psychologist to ensure the best working relationship between person and machine by taking account of the strengths and weaknesses of both.

Consumer Psychology (Chapter 14).   The work of consumer psychologists is important to you if you are employed by a company that manufactures and sells consumer products and services, and if you hope to be a smart and informed buyer. Psychologists are involved in defining the markets for consumer goods, determining the effectiveness of advertising campaigns, and analyzing the motivations and needs of the buying public.

SUMMARY

Work provides a sense of personal identity, defines your social status, contributes to your self-esteem, and satisfies your need for belonging to a group. **Industrial-organizational (I-O) psychology** is defined as the application of the methods, facts, and principles of the science of behavior and mental processes to people at work. As a science, psychology relies on observation and experimentation and deals with overt human behavior—behavior that can be observed objectively.

Industrial psychology began in the early twentieth century and grew under the impetus of the two world wars. A major change in industrial psychology came with the recognition of the influence of social and psychological factors on worker behavior, as demonstrated by the **Hawthorne studies** of the 1920s and 1930s. The area of engineering psychology emerged out of the development of the sophisticated weaponry of World War II. Organizational psychology developed in the 1960s in response to a concern with the organizational climate in which work takes place.

Continuing challenges for I-O psychologists relate to virtual workplaces and virtual employees, the demands of new skills, the diversity of the work force, and the changing nature of work itself.

To work professionally as an I-O psychologist, you need a master's degree, but you will find a position of greater responsibility with a doctoral degree. I-O psychologists in organizations face several problems brought about, in part, by the demand for their services. These include the fraudulent practice of I-O psychology by persons who are not professionally trained, the difficulty of translating technical jargon so that ideas can be communicated to management, the unwillingness of managers and workers to try new ways of doing things, and the necessity of balancing research and timely solutions to problems.

Areas of I-O psychology discussed in the following chapters are employee selection, psychological testing, performance appraisal, training and development, leadership, motivation and job satisfaction, organizational psychology, working conditions, safety and health, stress, engineering psychology, and consumer psychology.

KEY TERMS[1]

hawthorne studies
industrial-organizational (I-O) psychology

ADDITIONAL READING

Graduate study in psychology: 2000 edition. (2000). Washington, DC: American Psychological Association. Describes more than 500 departments that offer graduate degrees in psychology. Includes current information about programs, admission requirements, financial aid, tuition, and housing. Also available at *www.apa.org/gradstudy/.*
The science and practice of industrial and organizational psychology. Survey of graduate programs in industrial-organizational psychology and organizational behavior.

[1]Key terms are defined in the margin of the page on which they are first mentioned. These definitions are cumulated in alphabetical order in the Glossary section at the back of the book.

These two brochures prepared by SIOP describe research and applied inter-ests of I-O psychologists and graduate school programs. Copies are available from the SIOP Administrative Office, PO Box 87, Bowling Green, OH 43402–0087.

Bowe, M., & Streeter, S. (2000). *Gig: Americans talk about their jobs at the turn of the millennium.* New York: Crown. More than 125 employees, ranging from a fa-mous film producer to a welfare-program street cleaner, describe their jobs and how they got them.

Fraser, J. A. *White-collar sweatshop: The deterioration of work and its rewards in corpo-rate America.* (2001). New York: Norton. A grim portrait of the American workforce as full of stressed-out people caught up in a race they cannot win. Blames the situation on lengthening workdays, fears of layoffs and replace-ment by temporary workers, dilution of employee benefits, and the perva-sive technology that allows the job to follow employees home.

Lookout Media & Westerdahl, J. (1999). *Nice job—The guide to cool, odd, risky, and gruesome ways to make a living.* Berkeley, CA: Ten Speed Press. Profiles a vari-ety of unusual jobs, including ice cream flavor developer, shopping mall Santa, and body part model. Describes job duties, compensation, prerequi-sites, perks, and risks.

Lowman, R. L. (Ed.). (1998). *The ethical practice of psychology in organizations.* Washington, DC: American Psychological Association. A casebook illustrat-ing a wide range of issues in the professional practice of I-O psychology.

Sternberg, R. J. (Ed.). (1997). *Career paths in psychology: Where your degree can take you.* Washington, DC: American Psychological Association. Eminent psychol-ogists pursuing a variety of careers discuss a typical work week and offer ad-vice on following their diverse career paths.

Tenopyr, M. L. (1992). Reflections of a pioneering woman in industrial psychol-ogy. *Professional Psychology: Research and Practice, 23,* 172–175. Mary Tenopyr has worked as selection and testing director of human resources for AT&T. A noted contributor to the development of I-O psychology, she describes her career and the role of women in business.

Techniques, Tools, and Tactics

WHY STUDY RESEARCH METHODS?

The importance of research in I-O psychology to the world of work is well established, but what is its value to you? Why do you need to know about how psychologists collect and analyze research data? Although you may not be interested in becoming an I-O psychologist, you will probably have to deal with the findings of I-O psychologists. As a potential manager, you will interact with psychologists to find solutions to management problems, and you will be responsible for making decisions based on the recommendations of the company psychologist or of the consulting psychologist your organization has hired.

Suppose, for example, that you are charged with implementing a new manufacturing process to produce color monitors for computers. A modern production facility must be designed and built, and part of your job will be to facilitate the changeover from the old process to the new.

You must consider several issues. How will the workers react to an abrupt change in the way they do their jobs? Will they be sufficiently motivated to operate the new equipment and maintain a high standard of production? Will they need retraining? If so, how and where should the training be undertaken? How will the new process affect the company's safety record? These are just a few of the questions you would be expected to answer. If you make a bad decision or a misjudgment, the cost to you and your company will be high.

Using information based on psychological research, I-O psychologists may be able to assist you. But if you are to evaluate their advice and recommendations, you must understand how they studied the problems and arrived at their conclusions. You may also be asked to decide whether a research program is worth the time and money. A knowledge of research methods will help you make this decision more wisely.

Our goal in this chapter is not to train you to conduct research but to acquaint you with the requirements, limitations, and methods of the scientific approach. By applying the **scientific method** to problems that are too often dealt with by intuition or guesswork, I-O psychology makes a distinctive contribution to improved management and work practices. If you understand these research tools, you will be able to ensure that they are used properly on the job.

Scientific method A controlled, objective, and systematic approach to research.

Requirements of Psychological Research

Three requirements of scientific research are objective observation, control, and verification.

Objective Observation.   A basic requirement and defining characteristic of scientific research in any discipline is objective observation. Ideally, researchers base their conclusions on objective evidence, which they view without preconceived ideas or biases. For example, when a psychologist chooses to use a particular test or training method or workspace design, that choice cannot be determined by private hunches, by the recommendation of some prestigious authority, or even by past research. The decision should be based on an objective evaluation of the facts of the present situation.

Control.   A second requirement of psychological research is that observations must be well controlled and systematic. The conditions under which objective observations are made should be predetermined so that every factor that could possibly influence the outcome is known to the researcher. For example, if we are studying the effects of background music on the efficiency of employees in data-entry jobs, we must control the experimental situation so that no factors other than the music can affect worker productivity.

Duplication and Verification.   The systematic control of objective observation allows for the fulfillment of a third research requirement, that of duplication and verifiability. With careful control of conditions, a scientist working at another time and place can duplicate the conditions under which the earlier experiment was conducted. We can have more confidence in research findings if they have been verified by other investigators. This verification is possible only under carefully controlled conditions. Thus, psychological research in any setting requires systematic planning, control of the experimental situation so that the findings can be duplicated and verified, and objective observation.

> **ONLINE!**   For everything you wanted to know, and more, about research methods in psychology, log on to *www.methods. fullerton.edu.*

Limitations of Psychological Research

Psychologists face many challenges in designing and executing a psychological research program within the confines of a university laboratory. But when a study is undertaken in the real-life setting of a factory or office, the problems are magnified.

Not All Behavior Can Be Studied.   One obvious limitation is that research methods cannot be applied to every problem. For example, social psychologists cannot conduct controlled observations of how people behave in riots. The situation is too complex and dangerous to arrange in advance. Similarly, in industry it is not feasible to conduct systematic research on some mechanical safety devices that might expose workers to possible injury. There is a limit to what people should be asked to risk in the interest of scientific research.

Observing Behavior Can Change It.   A second problem is that the act of observing people in an experiment can interfere with or change the behavior that the psychologist is trying to study. For example, if employees are asked to take a personality test as part of research on job satisfaction, they may deliberately distort their test responses because they do not want to answer personal questions or because they don't like their boss or the company psychologist. For another example, consider research to investigate the effects of jet engine noise on the efficiency of airline mechanics. If the mechanics are aware that they are part of a psychological research study, they may deliberately work faster or slower than they would on a normal workday when they were not being observed.

The Hawthorne Effect. Sometimes employee behavior changes just because something new has been introduced into the workplace. This phenomenon was first observed during the Hawthorne experiments and so has come to be called the Hawthorne effect. Recall from Chapter 1 that one of the Hawthorne studies involved increasing the level of lighting in a work area. Production rose with each increase in illumination and then remained high even when the lighting level was reduced. It didn't seem to matter whether the light was brighter or dimmer. It was the change, the fact that something new was happening in the workplace, that affected worker productivity. The I-O psychologist conducting the research must determine whether the differences observed in the behavior of the research participants result from the actual working conditions under study or arise from the novelty of the change itself, independent of working conditions.

Artificial Settings. Some studies must be conducted in artificial settings. Management may not allow the psychologist to disrupt production by experimenting with various work procedures on the assembly line or in the office. As a result, research may have to be conducted in a simulated job environment. In such cases, the research results will be based on performance in a situation that is not identical to the job environment in which the findings are to be applied. This artificiality may reduce the usefulness of the research findings.

College Students as Subjects. The problem of artificiality is complicated by the fact that much research in I-O psychology is conducted in universities and relies on college students as subjects. A review of five leading journals showed that 87% of the studies published used students as subjects. A majority of the studies comparing the characteristics and behaviors of student and non-student samples reveal important differences between the two groups. For example, experienced business managers and college students performing the same task—evaluating applicants for a management position—showed that the students rated the applicants much higher and deserving of higher starting salaries than did the business managers.

   Thus, college students may behave differently from employees and managers on the job, and these differences limit the generalizability of the research findings. Although some I-O psychologists argue that research conducted in university laboratories can be generalized to human resources and organizational issues, other psychologists maintain that the differences are so great that only the most cautious generalization is acceptable. To maximize the usefulness of the findings we discuss in this book, we rely primarily on research that studies employees and managers in actual work situations.

METHODS OF PSYCHOLOGICAL RESEARCH

Several methods are available to I-O psychologists who conduct research in the workplace. Selecting the most effective technique is one of the first issues to be resolved in any research program. In most cases, the technique will be determined by the nature of the problem to be investigated. We discuss the following techniques: experiments, naturalistic observations, surveys, and Web-based research.

THE EXPERIMENTAL METHOD

The **experimental method** is simple in its basic concept but can be difficult to implement. The purpose of an experiment is to determine the effect or influence of a variable on the performance or behavior of the people being studied (the "subjects" or "research participants").

Psychologists distinguish two variables in an experiment. One is the stimulus, or **independent variable,** the effects of which we are interested in determining. The other is the participants' resulting behavior, called the **dependent variable** because it depends on the independent variable. Both variables can be objectively observed, measured, and recorded.

Designing an Experiment

Consider the following experiment. Management is concerned about the poor productivity of a group of workers who assemble television sets. Company psychologists are asked to study how output could be increased. At first they suggest a number of factors that could be responsible for the low level of production, such as low pay, inadequate training, an unpopular supervisor, and obsolete equipment. After they inspect the workplace, however, the psychologists suspect that the problem is insufficient lighting. They design an experiment to test this hypothesis.

The two variables in the experiment are easy to identify and measure. The independent variable is the level of lighting. This is the stimulus variable, which the psychologists will increase during the experiment to determine the effects. The dependent variable is the workers' response rate—in this case, their measured rate of production with the changed lighting.

The psychologists arrange for the lighting level in the workroom to be increased, and they measure production before the experiment and after two weeks of the brighter lighting. Prior to changing the lighting, each worker assembled an average of three television sets an hour. Two weeks later, individual production averaged eight units an hour, a considerable increase.

Why Did Production Increase?   Can we conclude that the change in the independent variable (the brighter lighting) brought about the change in the dependent variable (the greater productivity)? No. We cannot draw this conclusion on the basis of the experiment as described.

How do we know that some factor other than lighting was not responsible for the higher production? Perhaps the boss was nicer to the workers during the 2-week experiment because he knew the company psychologists were hanging around. Maybe the workers purposely produced more because they thought their jobs were being threatened. Maybe sunny weather made the workers happier, or perhaps production increased because of the Hawthorne effect, the fact that some change had been introduced to break the usual monotony of the workday. Many other factors could account for the increase in production, but the psychologists must be certain that nothing operated to influence the subjects' behavior except the stimulus being manipulated.

The Element of Control.   An essential feature of the scientific method was omitted from our experiment: the element of control. Controlling the experimental conditions assures us that any change in the behavior or performance of the research participants is solely attributable to the independent variable.

Experimental method The scientific way to determine the effect or influence of a variable on the subjects' performance or behavior.

Independent variable In an experiment, this is the stimulus variable that is manipulated to determine its effect on the subjects' behavior.

Dependent variable In an experiment, this is the resulting behavior of the subjects, which *depends* on the manipulation of the independent variable.

Experimental group In an experiment, this is the group of research participants exposed to the independent variable.

Control group In an experiment, this is the group of research participants that is not exposed to the independent variable.

To produce this necessary control, psychologists use two groups of subjects in an experiment: the **experimental group,** which consists of the subjects exposed to the independent variable, and the **control group.** The experimental and control groups should be as similar as possible in every respect except that the control group is not exposed to the independent variable.

To conduct our experiment properly, then, we must divide the workers into these two groups. Their productivity is measured before and after the experimental period. The production level of the control group serves as a standard against which to compare the resulting performance of the experimental group.

If the groups of workers are similar and if the performance of the experimental group at the end of the experiment is significantly higher than that of the control group, then we can conclude that the improved lighting was responsible for the increased production. Extraneous factors, such as the weather, the supervisor's behavior, or the Hawthorne effect, could not have influenced the subjects' behavior. If any of these factors had been influential, then the performance of both groups would have changed similarly.

Selecting Research Participants

The control group and the experimental group must be as similar as possible. There are two methods experimenters can use to ensure this: the random group design and the matched group design.

Random group design A method for ensuring similarity between experimental and control groups that assigns subjects at random to each condition.

The **random group design** involves assigning the subjects at random to the experimental and control groups. In our experiment, if the company employed 100 television set assemblers, we would arbitrarily assign 50 to the experimental condition and 50 to the control condition. Because the basis for dividing the workers into experimental and control conditions is random, we may assume that the groups are essentially similar. Any possible influencing variables, such as age or length of job experience, should be evenly distributed over the two groups because these factors were not allowed to influence the assignment of the subjects.

Matched group design A method for ensuring similarity between experimental and control groups that matches subjects in both groups on characteristics, such as age, job experience, and intelligence, that could affect the dependent variable.

In the **matched group design,** to ensure similarity between experimental and control groups, subjects in one group are matched with subjects in the other group on the basis of characteristics that could affect their performance (the dependent variable). For our experiment we could find pairs of subjects who are matched on age, job experience, intelligence, and supervisor ratings, and then we could assign one member of each pair to each group. In this way, the experimental and control groups would be as alike as possible.

Although desirable, the matched group technique is costly and difficult to carry out. To find enough pairs of subjects, we would need an even larger pool of potential research participants from whom to choose. Also, it becomes extremely complicated to equate pairs of subjects on more than one factor. Matching people on length of job experience alone presents few problems, but matching them on several factors at the same time is cumbersome.

On the Job: Training Effects on Turnover and Productivity[1]

As a classic example of a typical experiment, let us consider the research conducted in a factory in which sewing machine operators produced women's lin-

[1]*Source:* J. Lefkowitz (1970). Effect of training on the productivity and tenure of sewing machine operators. *Journal of Applied Psychology, 54,* 81–86.

gerie. Management had asked a consulting psychologist to find out why 68% of the sewing machine operators quit within a year. After taking a survey of employee attitudes and interviewing the supervisors, the psychologist hypothesized that the reason for the high turnover was insufficient job training.

The psychologist devised a study to investigate the effects of several training conditions on the rate of turnover and the rate of productivity. Note that the initial problem leading to the research was the high number of people quitting. In the process of designing an experiment to focus on this problem, the psychologist realized that with little extra effort, data could also be secured on a second dependent variable: the level of production.

Subjects and Experimental Design. The research participants were 208 women employees hired in 1 year as trainees. The dependent variables were (1) job turnover, defined as the percentage of workers who quit in their first 40 days on the job, and (2) productivity, defined in terms of daily output figures in the first 40 days on the job. The psychologist chose the 40-day period because company records showed that most terminations occurred during that time. The dependent variables were easy to observe, measure, and record with precision.

The independent variable was the level of training. The psychologist specified four training periods. The company's standard practice was to provide 1 day of training for new employees, conducted in a special training facility. This 1-day training was designated as the control condition, against which other training periods would be compared.

Trainees assigned to Group I took the standard 1-day training course. Group II received 2 days of training in the training facility, and Group III received 3 days of training in the training facility. Group IV had 3 days of training, but part of it was conducted in the training room and part of it took place in the workroom.

The workers were assigned to each of the four conditions on the basis of the date of their initial employment with the company. Those hired during the first month of the study were placed in Group I, those hired during the second month in Group II, and so on, repeating the cycle throughout the year the study was in progress. Statistical comparisons of each group's initial performance demonstrated their similarity.

Results. The results of the turnover study revealed that the longer the training received in the training facility (Groups I, II, and III), the lower the rate of turnover (see Figure 2–1). The 3-day training period combining on-the-job expe-

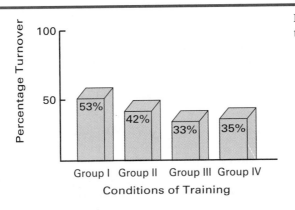

FIGURE 2–1. Turnover rates of four training conditions.

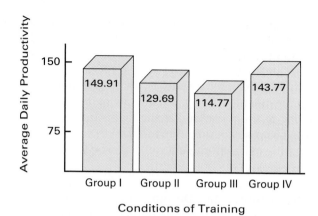

FIGURE 2–2.   Production levels of four training conditions.

rience with the training facility (Group IV) did not reduce the turnover rate when it was compared to the 3-day training period conducted wholly in the training facility (Group III). As you can see, however, comparing Groups I and III shows that the additional days of training reduced turnover from 53% to 33%.

The second part of the study (the effect of training on productivity) produced unexpected complications. The data showed that the longer the time spent in the training facility, the lower the average daily rate of production (see Figure 2–2). The 3 days of training in the facility and on the job (Group IV) led to greater productivity than did the 3 days of training in the facility alone (Group III).

Thus, the independent variable (the different training levels) produced conflicting results on the dependent variables. Greater time in the training room resulted in lower turnover, but it also yielded lower productivity. It is at this point—interpreting the research results—that the training and experience of the I-O psychologist are put to their most severe test. Experiments do not always turn out the way the researcher hopes. Hypotheses are not always confirmed. Results are not always clear and consistent, and considerable interpretive skill is necessary to relate the data to the job or the problem being studied and to explain the options to management.

The psychologist conducting this experiment evaluated the productivity and turnover data and concluded that the 3-day integrated training condition (Group IV) would be the most profitable for the company. It yielded a close second-highest level of production and a close second-lowest rate of turnover.

We must keep in mind that I-O research proceeds on two levels: (1) designing the experiment and (2) interpreting and implementing the results. At both levels, psychologists depend on the cooperation of managers and workers who understand the requirements of psychological research.

THE NATURALISTIC OBSERVATION METHOD

In the study of human behavior at work, it is not always possible to bring the relevant variables under the precise control required by the experimental method. Also, it may be more useful to study behavior as it occurs in real life. We mentioned that one of the limitations of the experimental method is artificiality. To avoid this, psychologists sometimes prefer to observe behavior in its natural setting without introducing any manipulation of the independent variable. This is the essence of the method of **naturalistic observation.** Although this method does not involve the manipulation of the independent variable, the psychologist is still able to maintain some control over the situation.

One advantage of naturalistic observation is that the behaviors being observed and the situations in which they are observed are typical of what occurs in everyday life. The findings of naturalistic observation can be more readily generalized and applied to real life because that is where they were obtained. After all, our ordinary daily activities occur in situations that are not under the stringent control necessary in the experimental method.

This advantage is also a major weakness. Because researchers do not manipulate the independent variable, it is sometimes difficult to conclude with assurance what brought about any resulting change in the subjects' behavior or performance. Another limitation is that the observation cannot be repeated. It is impossible to duplicate the exact conditions that prevailed during the initial observation.

The experimental method also has problems, as we noted. Nevertheless, when it can be used, it is a better choice than naturalistic observation because the experimenter can control and systematically manipulate the independent variable. However, both methods, when applied with precision and interpreted with care, are valuable in the study of human behavior in the workplace.

> **Naturalistic observation**
> The scientific observation of behavior in its natural setting, without any experimental manipulation of the independent variable.

On the Job: Friendly Behaviors of Store Clerks[2]

A nationwide chain of convenience stores instituted a training program to teach its clerks to be friendly toward customers. The company wanted to determine whether the friendly behaviors would lead to an increase in sales and thus justify the expense of the training. Arranging an experiment would have been difficult and might not have been informative. The company could have compared sales at two stores, one of which had clerks trained to be friendly whereas the other did not, but that might have meant a loss in sales at the control group store and the possible alienation of customers.

The company could have designed a laboratory experiment in which people would pose as courteous clerks and rude clerks. Persons playing the role of customer would be asked if they thought they would buy more from the courteous clerks than from the rude clerks, but that would have been too artificial a situation. Also, the results would not tell the company anything about the impact of friendly behavior on actual sales.

Research Design.   The psychologists decided to conduct a naturalistic observation in which the behavior of 1,319 clerks in 576 convenience stores was secretly watched by trained observers during 11,805 transactions with customers. The clerks had been informed that their level of courtesy would be monitored at some time, but they were not told when and how the observations would take place.

The observers, chosen to fit the profile of a typical customer, pretended to be making purchases. They spent from 4 to 12 minutes in each store, depending on

---

[2]*Source:* R. I. Sutton & A. Rafaeli (1988). Untangling the relationship between displayed emotions and organizational sales: The case of convenience stores. *Academy of Management Journal,* 31, 461–487.

how many real customers were present. The more crowded the store, the longer the observers could linger without causing the clerks to be suspicious. Observers reported that they thought clerks were suspicious of them in fewer than 3% of the observations; these data were excluded from consideration. The clerks' friendly behaviors, as recorded by the observers, included smiling at customers, greeting customers, thanking customers, and maintaining eye contact with customers. These behaviors, along with the sales figures for each store, were the dependent variables.

Although no independent variables were manipulated, factors that might have influenced behavior and sales were controlled. For example, the proportion of women clerks to men clerks was considered in order to control for variation in courteous behavior by sex; past research had suggested that women tend to be more courteous than men in any setting. The proportion of women to men customers was recorded to control for sex differences in purchasing behavior. Why? Because if some stores were patronized primarily by women, for example, and if women typically made more purchases than men did, then the sales figures for those stores would be higher, independent of the clerks' behavior.

The stores for the observations were selected at random, but all were in heavily populated urban districts. None was from a suburban or rural area where the sales pattern might differ from an urban area. Recognizing that people in various regions of the United States have different buying habits, independent of the company's training program, the data from four sectors—Northeast, South, Midwest, and West—were analyzed separately. Thus, taking the research out of the laboratory and conducting it in the real world still permitted the psychologists to control relevant variables and make objective observations.

Results. To the researchers' surprise, the findings showed that the higher the incidence of courteous behaviors, the lower the sales. Analysis of the data revealed that a store's level of sales influenced the clerks' behaviors, and the courteous behaviors taught in the training program did not lead to increases in sales. The busier the store (the higher the sales), the less time the clerks had to be courteous. In stores with lower sales, clerks had time to be friendlier. The results also confirmed that women clerks were more courteous than men clerks and that clerks in the West were more courteous than those in the Northeast.

The behavior being observed in this example was not as well controlled as it could have been under laboratory conditions, but the greater realism afforded by the use of the real-life situation offset this disadvantage. In many cases, the nature and complexity of the phenomena under investigation determine the most appropriate method of study. In other instances, the psychologist must decide whether to sacrifice some measure of control for greater applicability.

SURVEYS AND OPINION POLLS

Survey research method
Interviews, behavioral observations, and questionnaires designed to sample what people say about their feelings or opinions, or how they say they will behave in a given situation.

Surveys and opinion polls rely on the observation of behavior as it is revealed in the subjects' responses to personal interviews and questionnaires. The focus in the **survey research method** is not on what people do (as in experiments or naturalistic observations) but on what they *say* they will do.

Survey questionnaires and interviews have many applications in I-O psychology. Psychologists use surveys to ascertain factors that contribute to job satisfaction and morale. Some large organizations maintain a staff of poll-takers to conduct

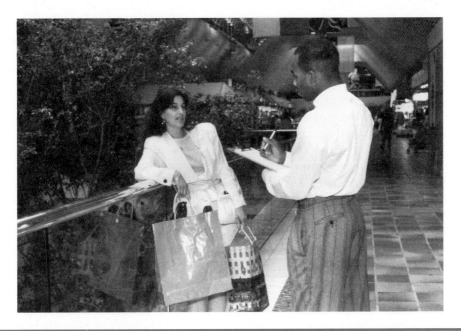

The focus of the survey method is on what people tell interviewers they will do rather than on what they actually do.

periodic employee surveys on a variety of work-related issues. This polling gives employees the chance to air gripes and complaints (a form of upward communication). It also assesses reactions to changes in work procedures and policies and provides the opportunity for employee participation in policy making.

As a result, surveys have the potential for raising employee morale, reducing turnover, and avoiding costly union grievance procedures. In some plants, maintaining an open channel of communication between employees and employers has prevented unionization. Workers who believe their opinions are heard and valued by management are less likely to feel the need for union representation.

Advertising and motivation research firms use survey techniques to uncover consumer preferences. For example, Campbell Soup questioned more than 100,000 consumers to determine their food likes and dislikes. On the basis of the survey results, the company changed the seasonings in its frozen food dinners and introduced a line of low-salt soups.

In addition, public opinion polls are routinely used in political campaigns to assess voter reaction to candidates and to the issues in their platforms.

Problems with Surveys.   Even the best polling organizations have difficulty, however, with the precise measurement of personal opinions and attitudes. One problem is that some people deliberately lie when they are asked questions in a survey. They may say they will do one thing and then do something else. Sometimes they change their minds, for example, telling an interviewer in October that they will vote Republican and then voting Democratic in the November elections.

People may say they prefer a particular brand of clothing or automobile because they believe this choice will make them appear sophisticated. They may claim to drink an expensive imported beer, for example, but if interviewers could look in the refrigerator, they might find cans of an inexpensive local brew instead.

Sometimes people express an opinion in response to a survey question even when they do not have one, because they do not want the interviewer to think they are uninformed. An analysis of 37 surveys found that 64% of the respondents claimed to have read the magazine article the poll-takers were questioning them about. In reality, no such article had ever been published. The results also showed that people were more likely to be honest in their responses when they completed a questionnaire in private than when they were asked the same questions in a face-to-face interview.

Another complication, particularly with telephone surveys, is the difficulty of finding people to respond. Many people are annoyed by junk telephone callers pretending to take a survey when the real purpose is to sell magazines or dance lessons. Also, some people are no longer willing to spend their time responding to surveys. Although it is relatively easy to poll retired people and full-time homemakers, it is more difficult to reach a representative sample of office workers, young adults, and high-income people. Surveying these groups adequately requires considerable time and effort.

These difficulties with the survey method can explain some lost elections, failed businesses, and bad management decisions. The fault lies not with the method itself but with the complex, subjective, and sometimes perverse nature of our attitudes, preferences, and behaviors. Keep in mind, however, that properly designed surveys can be highly accurate and that they succeed more often than they fail.

Personal Interviews

Three basic ways to collect survey data are personal interviews, questionnaires, and telephone surveys. The personal interview, the most expensive and time-consuming technique, requires a face-to-face meeting with the respondents.

Finding and training capable interviewers is vital because their appearance, manner, and behavior can influence the way people cooperate with them and answer their questions. Research has shown that people respond differently to interview questions, depending on the interviewer's age, race, and sex.

More subtle interviewer variables can also affect survey results. For example, if an interviewer asking questions about drug use shows by smiling or frowning apparent agreement or disagreement with what the respondent is saying, that person may change subsequent answers because of the perception of the interviewer's own opinion about drug use.

An effective interviewing technique that is growing in popularity is the computer-assisted personal interview. In one approach, questions are displayed on a computer screen and a voice-over reading is provided through headphones. The subject then enters his or her responses to the questions on a standard keyboard.

Questionnaires

Questionnaires offer a cheaper and more convenient way to obtain information from large numbers of people over a wide geographical area. In I-O psychology today, questionnaires are the most frequently used survey technique for collecting information from employees. Because employees can remain anonymous, they are more likely to respond freely and openly. Also, because they can take their time, they can formulate their answers more carefully and thus their reported views are often more reliable than those in a personal interview.

"Push Polls" Can Win Elections

NEWSBREAK

Public opinion polls not only collect information from voters but they can also provide information. And some of it may be false or distorted information about a political candidate that can ruin his or her chances of winning. These polls are called "push polls," because they are designed to see if certain negative information can push voters away from one candidate in favor of the candidate who is paying for the poll.

Here's how they work. A polling firm hired by Congressman Green, let us say, calls several thousand registered voters in the congressional district. The callers are asked if they intend to vote for Green or for the opponent, Candidate Brown. Those voters who say they plan to vote for Brown or who have not yet made up their minds are asked a question of this type: "If I told you that Brown was once arrested for fraud—for cheating senior citizens out of their life savings—would that make a difference in your vote?"

Note how the question is phrased. The pollster is not saying that Brown had actually been arrested on such charges—which, in truth, he had not—but merely by raising the issue, the implication is clearly that Brown had been arrested. In this way, thousands of people in the voting district can be fed false information about an opposition candidate in the otherwise innocent guise of taking a poll.

Push polls have been used by candidates of major political parties at all levels of government. And, as you might expect, their use has raised ethical questions. One poll-taker criticized this questionable practice in the trade journal *Campaign Elections,* writing that "The truth is that polls are being used in today's campaigns as much to shape public opinion as to simply report it. Some polling may be used to mislead the public by skewing questions or reporting results out of proper context."

In the world of public opinion polling, the results may not always be what they seem.

The major disadvantage of questionnaire surveys is that the response rate is typically only 40 to 45%. Follow-up procedures are sometimes used to try to secure additional returns. A reminder letter or postcard can be mailed to all questionnaire recipients explaining the importance of the survey and requesting cooperation. Letters sent by registered mail and follow-up telephone calls can also be used to encourage compliance. Some companies offer incentives for responding to a survey. A few hold contests with valuable prizes as inducements for returning the questionnaires. Most companies offer only a token payment, such as a dollar bill, which is often sufficient to make respondents feel guilty if they take the money and do not answer the questions.

Many organizations today use electronic methods to conduct polls of their employees. Questions are posted through e-mail, Intranet, or Internet services, and employees respond by using their keyboards to enter their answers. Electronic polls can be completed more quickly than face-to-face polls. Companies such as Allstate, Duke Power, IBM, and Xerox have conducted electronic surveys and posted the results online, accessible to all their employees.

I-O psychologists have conducted research to compare responses to paper questionnaires with responses to computer-administered questionnaires. They report no significant differences (Donovan, Drasgow, & Probst, 2000; Stanton, 1998). However, the rates of response vary greatly. A study conducted at Hewlett-Packard showed a response rate of less than 26% to a paper questionnaire mailed to a sample of employees. When the same survey was sent to employees by e-mail, the response rate exceeded 42%. The response rate to a Web-based survey was 60%. Also, employees responded faster to the electronic surveys than they did to the mail survey (Frame & Beaty, 2000).

Since electronic surveys are faster and less expensive than other types of surveys, the growing tendency is to solicit employees' opinions just because it can be done so easily. Sometimes management does not have a clear objective in mind about how it intends to use the survey results. Employees complain about being questioned so frequently when they fail to see any action taken or change initiated in response to their opinions and suggestions. When employees believe that their input is not being considered or appreciated, they are likely to disregard future surveys.

Telephone Surveys

Telephone surveys offer the advantage of a low cost per interview and the possibility that a single interviewer can contact several hundred people a day. With perseverance, it is possible to reach most of the people in the sample by continuing to phone until they answer. Telephone surveys have been aided by computerized phone systems that speed up the contact process. Telephone surveys cost approximately half as much as personal interviews and obtain comparable data.

For surveys of voters, television viewers, and shoppers, the telephone approach is the major data collection technique even though the refusal rate is higher than for personal interviews. As we noted, many people are annoyed by the persistence of telemarketing callers, some of whom claim to be taking a survey. As a result, these people are less likely to respond to a phone call from a

Telephone surveys offer a low cost per interview and the likelihood that an interviewer can contact hundreds of people in the course of a workday.

NEWSBREAK

Call Me Unresponsive

Blame me, if you wish, for the poor showing of conservatives in opinion polls. I refuse to respond to telephone polls. It's not that I'm unpatriotic, or that I don't want my opinion to count. I vote in every election, and it's partly because my name appears on voter lists that I get so many calls—about one or two a week. I used to respond to pollsters. Why did I swear off them?

- Polls take up my time. The calls interrupt me, whatever I'm doing. What right does Gallup or whoever have to something of mine that he intends to turn around and sell to political parties and publications?

- How do I know it's Gallup or Harris or Fox News or Time/CNN or whoever at the other end of the line? Back when I did answer polls, one pollster asked me what bank I went to and how often I visited it. Thus began my refusals.

- Some questions are too personal, or even dangerous, to answer—like the bank questions. I've also been asked the number of people in my household, whether I have a dog and a gun, and my total household income. These touchy questions get asked late in a poll, since it's harder to stop answering midway than never to begin answering at all.

- Many pollsters are nice, but some are rude. One waited until 10 minutes into our conversation before hitting me with the family income stuff. When I declined to answer, she blew up. She said I had to answer or the entire in-depth survey and her time would be wasted. So both of us had wasted our time.

- Some pollsters are salespeople. Under the pretense of polling, a caller might ask, for instance, if you belong to a church, then if you believe in God, and then if you would like to visit his group's new chapel or buy its religion book.

- Many pollsters try to influence opinion. They may ask if you are aware of the horrible things their political opponents have done lately. They don't really want a yes or no; they want to open a discussion in which they mold your views and maybe get a contribution from you for their cause.

- Poll responses often aren't private. They can be recorded and circulated, with respondents' names attached. One evening at a Republican Party caucus, I was treated to a computer printout of a poll taken in my neighborhood. Whom did we intend to vote for, Candidate A, Candidate B, No Opinion, or Refused to Answer? There it was—my entire block, house by house, with my address listed as Refused to Answer. But wasn't it fun gawking at the political leanings of all those people I knew? . . .

I do my part by taking opinion poll results with a grain of salt. Others might do likewise.

Source: Genie Dickerson. *New York Times,* July 13, 1999.

legitimate poll-taker. They often hang up without waiting to find out the purpose of the call.

Types of Questions

With any survey, regardless of the method used to collect the data, two basic problems must be resolved: (1) what questions will be asked, and (2) who will be questioned. In general, surveys use open-end questions or fixed-alternative questions.

With **open-end questions,** which are similar to the essay questions you have faced on college exams, respondents present their views in their own words without any restrictions. They are encouraged to answer as fully as they desire and to take as much time as they need. If the questionnaire contains many open-end questions, the process will be time-consuming. The usefulness of the replies depends on how skillfully the subjects can verbalize their thoughts and feelings. Open-end questions place considerable pressure on interviewers to be complete and accurate in recording the answers.

Fixed-alternative questions, like the multiple-choice exam questions you are familiar with, limit a person's answer to specific alternatives. A typical open-end question might be: How do you feel about raising taxes to provide money for schools? A fixed-alternative question on the same topic might be: With regard to raising taxes to provide more money for schools, are you in favor _____, opposed _____, or undecided _____? Thus, the person is faced with a finite number of choices and a restricted way in which to answer.

Fixed-alternative questions simplify the survey, allowing more questions to be asked in a given period of time. Also, answers to fixed-alternative questions can be recorded more easily and accurately than can answers to open-end questions.

One disadvantage is that the limited number of alternatives may not accurately reflect the respondent's opinion. A person could be in favor of higher school taxes under some circumstances and opposed to them under others. When their answers are restricted to yes, no, or undecided, people cannot make these feelings known to the interviewer. If enough people in the sample have such unexpressed reservations, the results will be misleading.

Usually it is a good idea to pretest the survey questions on a small sample of respondents to make sure that the questions are worded clearly. If subjects misinterpret a question or detect unintended meanings, the results may be biased. For example, the annual survey by the National Center for Health Statistics routinely questioned Americans about "abdominal pain" until poll-takers discovered that a number of people—enough to skew the survey results—did not understand the phrase or know where the "abdomen" was located. When respondents were shown a diagram of the body and the abdominal region was pointed out, their answers turned out to be quite different.

The wording of survey questions presents a challenge for I-O psychologists because approximately 25% of the American work force is functionally illiterate. People who cannot read and comprehend questionnaire items and instructions will not be motivated to complete the survey and may not have the ability to do so properly even if they wanted to.

Sampling Methods

Suppose a consulting psychologist is asked by the Texas state legislature to ascertain the opinions of automobile owners about a proposed increase in the driver license fee. To question every car owner would be tedious and difficult, even

Open-end questions Survey questions to which respondents state their views in their own words. They are similar to essay questions on college exams.

Fixed-alternative questions Survey questions to which respondents limit their answers to the choices or alternatives presented. They are similar to multiple-choice questions on college exams.

with sufficient time and money, and it would not be possible to locate and interview everyone. Nor is it necessary. With careful planning, surveying a representative sample of car owners will provide the desired information and predict the responses of the total population.

To select a sample of car owners in Texas, we could stop people at shopping centers, gas stations, or busy intersections. However, this would not guarantee that the people we talked to would be typical of all car owners in the state. The people found at an exclusive shopping mall in the suburbs of Dallas or Houston, for example, would be more likely to represent a higher income bracket than the state's large and diverse population. A better way needs to be found to identify a representative sample of the population for the survey.

Two ways to construct a representative sample of a population are probability sampling and quota sampling. In **probability sampling,** each person in the population has a known probability or chance of being included in the sample. By securing from the state department of motor vehicles a list of all automobile owners, we can select every 10th or 25th name, depending on how large a sample we need. In this way, every person in the population of registered car owners has the same chance (1 in 10, or 1 in 25) of being included in the sample. This method is satisfactory as long as there is a list of everyone in the population. If we wanted to study all eligible voters in the United States, this method would not be useful because only registered voters are listed.

In **quota sampling,** the researcher attempts to construct a duplicate in miniature of the larger population. If it is known from census data that in Texas 20% of all car owners are college graduates, 50% are men, 40% are of Hispanic origin, and so on, then the sample must reflect these proportions. Interviewers are given quotas for people to interview in the various categories and must find appropriate respondents. Because the persons questioned are chosen by the interviewers, however, their personal feelings and prejudices can affect the selection of the sample. One interviewer may prefer to talk only to people who appear well dressed; another might select only women respondents.

Probability sampling A method for constructing a representative sample of a population for surveys or polls. Each person in the population has a known probability or chance of being included in the sample.

Quota sampling A method for constructing a representative sample of a population for surveys or polls. Because the sample must reflect the proportions of the larger population, quotas are established for various categories such as age, gender, and ethnic origin.

Noncompliant Employees

Some employees decline to respond to surveys, regardless of how carefully the survey questions are phrased or how attractive the incentives offered for answering them may be. This refusal can bias the results. In some instances, employees may have failed to receive a questionnaire or may have misplaced and forgotten about it. But others adamantly refuse to participate in any survey by their employer about their attitudes, opinions, interests, and feelings.

The number of noncompliant employees has been rising, often because managers survey their employees too frequently, asking for information so often that employees become annoyed. When the response rate to organizational questionnaires is thus reduced, the resulting data can provide managers with misleading information.

A study of 194 employees found that people who said they would not fill out a company survey differed in important ways from those who agreed to answer the company's questions (Rogelberg, Luong, Sederburg, & Cristol, 2000). The noncompliant employees were found to have a greater stated intention of quitting their jobs. Compared to the employees who did complete the survey, the noncompliant employees were less committed to the company and less satisfied with their supervisors and their work. Further, these employees placed a low value on the response the company had made to previous surveys. In this instance, then, the replies that management received to its survey came primarily from employees who were highly satisfied with their jobs and supportive of the organization. Therefore, the company did not obtain a representative selection of their employees' views.

> For current survey results on a variety of issues, log on to *www.ropercenter.uconn.edu, www.gallop.com,* and *www.polling report.com.* The American Association for Public Opinion Research maintains a Web site at *www.aapor.org.* Opinion polls on political, social, and marketing issues in Russia may be viewed at *www.romir.ru/eng/default.htm.* Marketing surveys in Mexico are available in English and Spanish at *www.amai.org.*

VIRTUAL LABORATORIES: WEB-BASED RESEARCH

I-O psychologists today can use the Web to conduct research. In a virtual laboratory, they can run faster and less costly studies and draw upon a more diverse pool of subjects than in a university laboratory or an organizational setting. Web-based research has included questionnaires for job applicants, surveys of employee attitudes, and psychological tests, as well as interactive experiments in which employees respond to stimuli presented on their computer screens.

The linking, or networking, of individual laboratories into a so-called NetLab makes it possible to conduct large-scale studies that collect data from thousands of research participants from different companies and different countries. Net-Labs can operate virtual reality group experiments in which subjects respond to simulations of situations in their actual work environment.

Critics of Web-based research note that it is impossible to assess the honesty and accuracy of responses on criteria such as age, gender, and ethnic origin, or to know whether subjects are cheating by being coached on their responses. Also, people who are computer literate and comfortable interacting with Internet sources are likely to differ in their educational and socioeconomic characteristics from people who are not so familiar with computers. Thus, the respondents are, in a sense, self-selected and not representative of the population as a whole. However, proponents of Web-based research point out that college students—the typical subjects for psychological research studies—are also not representative of the general population.

> Explore these sources for information on Web-based surveys and experiments. A site maintained for the American Psychological Society organizes research by topic area: *psych.hanover.edu/APS/exponnet.html.* An "idiot's guide" to Web-based research, from the University of Nebraska, can be found at *http://129.93.53.69/guide/guide.asp.* Templates for creating Web-based surveys can be downloaded from "survey assistant" at *http://or.psychology.dal.ca/~wcs/hidden/home.html.*

METHODS OF DATA ANALYSIS

In psychological research, as in research in any science, collecting the data is only the first step in the scientific approach to solving problems. Let us assume that we have conducted an experiment to measure the productivity of 200 assembly-line workers, or have administered an aptitude test to 200 applicants for sales jobs. What have we learned? So far, we have simply amassed 200 numbers—the raw scores. Now it is necessary to analyze and interpret these data so that we may draw conclusions about their meaning and apply the results to current situations. To do so, we apply statistical methods to summarize and describe the data.

Descriptive Statistics

You are already familiar with the word *descriptive*. When you describe a person or an event in words, you try to convey a mental picture or image. Similarly, when psychologists use **descriptive statistics,** they are trying to describe or represent their data in a meaningful fashion. Let us examine some research data and see how statistics can describe them.

Descriptive statistics Ways of describing or representing research data in a concise, meaningful manner.

To evaluate a new test for job applicants that was designed to predict their success in selling life insurance, a corporate psychologist administered the test to 99 applicants. The test scores are shown in Table 2–1. Looking at this swarm of numbers should tell you why it is important to have a way to summarize and describe them. It is not possible to make sense of the data as they are. You cannot formulate a useful prediction or make a meaningful evaluation of the potential

TABLE 2–1 Raw Scores of 99 Job Applicants on Life Insurance Sales Test

141	91	92	88	95	113
124	119	108	146	120	123
122	118	98	97	94	89
144	84	110	127	81	120
151	76	89	125	108	90
102	120	112	89	101	118
129	125	142	87	103	147
128	94	94	114	134	114
102	143	134	138	110	128
117	121	141	99	104	127
107	114	67	110	124	122
112	117	144	102	126	121
127	79	105	133	128	118
87	114	110	107	119	133
156	79	112	117	83	114
99	98	156	108	143	99
96		145		120	

Frequency distribution A graphic representation of raw data that shows the number of times each score occurs.

job performance of these applicants as a whole by looking at a table of individual numbers.

One way to describe the data is to construct a **frequency distribution** or bar graph by plotting the number of times each score occurs (see Figure 2–3). For convenience in dealing with so many scores, we can group them in equal intervals. Grouping the data is not required, but it does make them easier to work with. The graph offers a clearer idea of the test performance of our group of job applicants than does the table of raw scores alone. Also, the graph provides useful information about group performance by showing that most of the subjects who took the test scored in the middle range.

Mean, Median, and Mode. Scientific analysis of the data requires that the raw scores also be summarized and described quantitatively. We must be able to represent the data with a single number, a measure of the central tendency of the distribution. To find the typical score in a distribution, we can calculate the mean, median, or mode.

Mean The arithmetic average; a way of describing the central tendency of a distribution of data.

The most common and useful measure of central tendency is the arithmetic average, or **mean,** which is calculated by adding the scores and dividing the resulting sum by the total number of scores. The mean for our group of 99 job applicants is 11,251 divided by 99, yielding 113.6 as the average score. Thus, averaging reduces our raw data to a single number. The mean provides the basis for many higher-level statistical analyses.

Median The score at the midpoint of a statistical distribution; half the scores fall below the median and half above.

The **median** is the score at the midpoint of the distribution. If we arrange the 99 scores in order from lowest to highest, the median is the score obtained by the 50th person. Half the job applicants scored higher than the median, and half scored lower. In our sample, the median is 114, which is close to the mean. The median is a useful measure when dealing with skewed distributions.

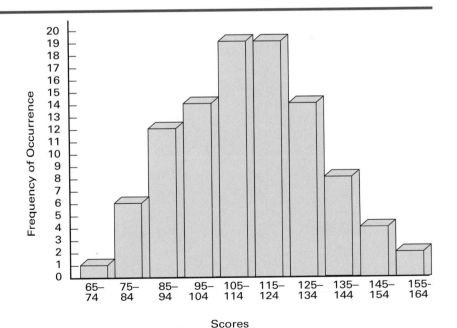

FIGURE 2–3. Distribution of life insurance sales test scores (grouped data).

The **mode** is the most frequently obtained score in the distribution; a distribution may have more than one mode. With our data, the mode is 114. The mode is seldom applied to describe data but is useful in certain work situations. For example, a store manager concerned with stocking an adequate inventory of stereo sets would want to know which components were being purchased more frequently than others.

Mode The most frequently obtained score in a distribution of data.

Normal Distributions and Skewed Distributions.   In Figure 2–3 you can see that most of the job applicants achieved test scores in the middle of the distribution and that only a few scored very high or very low. Many measurements approximate this bell-shaped distribution. In general, this normal curve of distribution occurs when a large number of measurements are taken of a physical or psychological characteristic. Whether we measure height, weight, or intelligence, for example, a sample of sufficient size will yield a distribution in which most scores fall near the middle and few fall at the extreme low and high ends.

The **normal distribution** is predicated on the random nature and size of the sample tested. If the sample is not representative of the population but is biased in one direction or another, the distribution will not approximate a normal curve.

Normal distribution A bell-shaped distribution of data in which most scores fall near the center and few fall at the extreme low and high ends.

Suppose we administered an IQ test to a group of high school dropouts, persons with little formal schooling and little experience in taking standardized tests. Such a group is not typical or representative of the general population, so the distribution of their test scores will not look like the normal curve. When measurements are taken from specially selected groups, the distribution will most likely be an asymmetrical or **skewed distribution** (see Figure 2–4).

In dealing with skewed distributions, the median is the most useful measure of central tendency. The mean is affected by a few extreme scores in either direction and thus may provide a misleading description of the data. The median is less affected by extreme scores.

Skewed distribution An asymmetrical distribution of data with most scores at either the high or the low end.

FIGURE 2–4.   A skewed distribution.

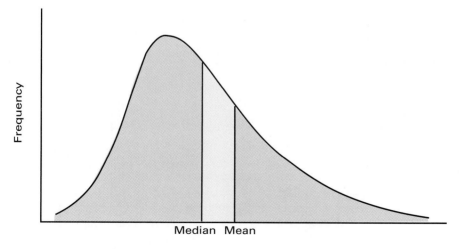

You have no doubt heard people say that statistics lie. Although statistics can be used to mislead people, the fault is usually in applying them inappropriately, and not with the statistical techniques themselves. Consider the data in Figure 2–5, for example, which represent median and mean monetary awards in corporate liability cases between 1960 and 1984. The mean or average awards increased from about $60,000 to $250,000 whereas the median awards decreased slightly.

The interpretation of these data sparked a controversy. Lawyers, who benefit from larger liability awards to their clients, argued that the liability judgments did not increase over the 24-year period. Insurance companies, who have to pay these liability awards, argued that there had been a fivefold increase.

The lawyers were using *median* liability awards; the insurance companies were citing *mean* liability awards. Both sides were technically correct, although the median is the better measure with a skewed distribution. As an employee, manager, voter, and consumer, you will find that it pays to be skeptical when you hear about "average" figures. Ask which average is being used. Is it the median or the mean?

Variability and the Standard Deviation. Having calculated and diagrammed the central tendency of a distribution, you may not be happy to learn that more analysis is needed to provide a comprehensive description of a distribution of scores. It is not sufficient to know the central tendency. We must also have a numerical indication of the spread of the scores around the center if we are to make good use of the data.

Consider the normal distributions in Figure 2–6. If we take the mean or median as the measure of central tendency of these distributions, we would conclude that the distributions are identical. The means and medians are the same for both curves. You can see, however, that the distributions are not identical. They differ in their spread, or variability.

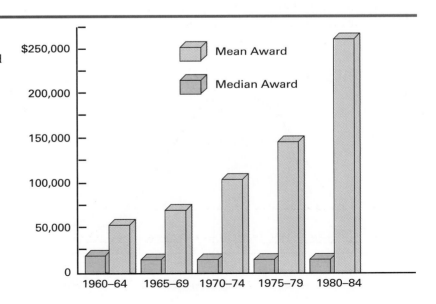

FIGURE 2–5. Median and mean liability awards, 1960–1984. (Data from Institute for Civil Justice, Rand Corporation; *New York Times*, April 13, 1986.)

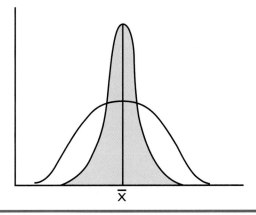

FIGURE 2–6. Normal curves with the same central tendency but different variability.

The basic measure of variability is the **standard deviation** (SD), a precise distance along the distribution's baseline. Once we determine this distance, we can learn a great deal about the data and describe them more meaningfully.

Let us examine the distribution of IQ scores presented in Figure 2–7. The data form a normal curve with a mean of 100 and a standard deviation of 15. Knowing that the SD is 15 tells us that an IQ score of 115 is +1 SD unit or distance above the mean of 100. An IQ score of 130 is +2 SD units above the mean, and so on. Similarly, an IQ score of 85 is 1 SD distance below the mean (–1 SD).

With the standard deviation, we can determine the percentage of scores in the distribution that fall above or below any particular raw score. Tables based on the mathematical formula for the normal distribution give us the percentage of cases, or frequency of scores, that fall between standard deviation units.

For example, as you can see in Figure 2–7, 99.5% of the population have IQ scores below 145, 97.5% below 130, and 84% below 115. These percentages hold for any measured variable as long as the distribution of the data follows the normal curve. If we know the standard deviation of a distribution, we can determine the meaning of any particular score. We can tell where it falls in terms of the performance of the group as a whole.

Standard deviation A measure of the variability of a distribution, the standard deviation is a precise distance along the distribution's baseline.

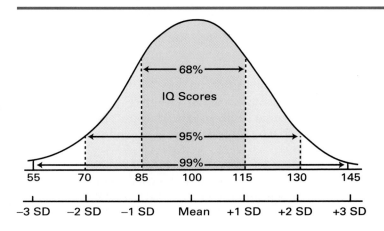

FIGURE 2–7. Normal distribution of IQ scores showing standard deviation units.

Suppose we develop an aptitude test for dental school students that we will use to measure the motor skills needed to manipulate the implements used in dental surgery. Your roommate takes the test and obtains a score of 60. This number by itself tells us nothing about that student's aptitude relative to that of all the other students. However, if we know that the distribution of test scores follows the normal curve, that the mean is 50, and that the standard deviation is 10, then a score of 60 (+1 SD from the mean) indicates that only 16% of the students scored higher and 84% scored lower. Your roommate might make a pretty good dentist after all.

There is a method by which raw scores can be converted to standard deviation scores, allowing us to interpret each raw score in the distribution. The standard deviation also permits us to compare the performance of individuals on two or more measures that use different scoring systems. By converting the distributions on all tests to standard deviation units, we can compare performance on one test with performance on another test because the scores will be expressed in the same terms.

Correlation. We have been discussing the statistical treatment of one variable at a time, such as a set of test scores from a group of job applicants. I-O psychologists more often are concerned with the relationships between two or more variables. Any situation in which a prediction must be made about whether a person is likely to succeed on the job involves matching two or more variables. For example, an employee's performance on a selection test must be compared with a later measure of actual job performance. That is the only way the psychologist can determine whether that selection technique is a valid means of choosing the best people for the job. (We discuss the concept of *validity* in more detail in Chapter 4.) Psychologists use the correlational method to investigate the relationships among variables.

Correlation The relationship between two variables. The strength and direction of the relationship is expressed by the correlation coefficient.

A **correlation** tells the researcher two things: (1) the direction of the relationship between the variables, and (2) the strength of that relationship. The direction of the relationship may be positive or negative, depending on whether high scores on one variable are accompanied by high scores or low scores on the other variable.

In a positive relationship, increasing scores on one variable are accompanied by increasing scores on the other variable. For example, a positive correlation between employees' test scores and supervisors' ratings of the employees' job performance tells us that the higher the test score, the higher the supervisory rating. As one variable increases, so does the other. We can predict that job applicants who do well on the aptitude test will likely perform well on the job. In other words, applicants who earn a high test score are apt to get a high rating from their supervisor.

In a negative correlation, increasing scores on one variable are accompanied by decreasing scores on the other variable. In our example, applicants who got high scores on the selection test would be likely to receive low ratings from their supervisors. In other words, those who do well on the test tend to do poorly on the job.

Through the application of the statistical formula for the correlation coefficient, we can calculate the direction and strength of the relationship between the variables. Positive correlations range from zero to +1.00. Negative correlations range from zero to −1.00.

A correlation coefficient of −1.00 indicates just as strong a relationship or correspondence as a coefficient of +1.00. Only the direction is different. In both cases, performance on one variable, such as job ratings, can be predicted from performance on the other variable, such as test scores. The closer the correlation coefficient is to +1.00 or −1.00, the more accurately we can predict performance on one variable from performance on the other. Correlation is a valuable and widely used tool in I-O psychology, and we shall see its use in many examples throughout this book.

> **ONLINE!**
>
> For more information on the use of statistics in I-O psychology, click on the statistics section of the *Internet Survival Guide of Industrial-Organizational Psychology* at *www.allserv. rugac.be/~flievens/guide.htm*.

Inferential Statistics

In the typical psychology experiment, researchers are interested in comparing the performance levels of two groups—the experimental group and the control group. In an experiment to test the value of a new training method, for example, the job performance of the experimental group, which has had the training, is compared with the control group, which has not been exposed to the new training. An important decision rests on this comparison. Should the new training method be implemented throughout the organization? The decision hinges on the size of the difference between the two groups on their job performance.

Levels of Significance.   How do I-O psychologists know when the difference between the two groups is large enough to justify the cost of establishing the training program throughout the company? They must determine the level of **statistical significance** of the difference between the means of the two groups. Their answer will be expressed in terms of probabilities rather than certainties. The problem is this: Is the difference between the means of the groups large enough so that it is unlikely it could have occurred by chance?

Statistical significance The level of confidence we can have in the results of an experiment. Significance is based on the calculation of probability values.

Probability.   Applying techniques of **inferential statistics** to the data from the experimental and control groups, we can calculate a **probability** value for the difference between the means. This number represents the probability that the difference could have occurred by chance.

Inferential statistics Methods for analyzing research data that express relationships in terms of probabilities.

Psychologists recognize two levels of statistical significance: a probability (p) of .05 and a p of .01. A probability value of .01 means that a difference as large as that obtained in the experiment would occur by chance only 1 time out of every 100. Thus, a difference at this level of significance could be attributed to the new training method used with the experimental group and not merely to chance. If the probability value was .05, we would have a little less confidence in the results, because this would tell us that there was a probability of 5 in 100 that the difference could have occurred by chance.

Probability The idea that the differences between the means of experimental and control groups could have occurred by chance.

Meta-analysis The large-scale reanalysis of the results of previous research studies.

Meta-Analysis.   In I-O psychology, **meta-analysis** is a level of analysis higher than significance testing. Meta-analysis involves the large-scale reanalysis of previous studies to determine overall trends. This technique has been adopted by many psychologists as a way of reaching more objective conclusions about issues on which a considerable body of research data exists. Meta-analysis has been used in fields as diverse as I-O psychology, economics, and medical research.

Regardless of the specific techniques used to analyze research data, statistical tools help the I-O psychologist reach informed decisions and recommendations about crucial problems in business and industry. The use of statistics does not eliminate the need for human decision making, but it does help guide the researcher, manager, or executive in that task. Statistical tools are means to an end, not an end in themselves.

SUMMARY

In psychological research, observations must be objective, well controlled and systematic, and capable of being duplicated and verified. Research has several limitations. For example, some problems are too complex to investigate by psychological research methods. The act of observing some behaviors may interfere with them. The novelty of change may alter behavior more than the actual change itself (the Hawthorne effect). Also, some research must be conducted in artificial settings, limiting the generalizability of the findings.

In the **experimental method,** psychologists investigate one influencing variable while holding all others constant. The variable being investigated is the **independent variable;** the behavior that results is the **dependent variable.** Two groups of subjects are used: the **experimental group** and the **control group.** The groups must be as similar as possible, a condition brought about by **random group design** (assigning subjects at random to the two groups) or by **matched group design** (matching the subjects in the groups on a number of personal characteristics).

Naturalistic observation involves observing behavior in its everyday setting. The experimenter can control the independent variables but cannot manipulate them with the precision permitted by the experimental method.

Survey research focuses on attitudes and opinions. Survey techniques include personal interviews (conducted face-to-face or by computer), telephone surveys, and questionnaires. E-mail questionnaires ask questions and obtain responses through an organization's in-house computer system. Survey questions can be **open-end,** allowing respondents to answer in their own words, or **fixed-alternative,** restricting respondents to a few choices. Representative samples of the people to be questioned in a survey can be selected through **probability sampling,** in which each person in the population has a known chance of being included in the sample, or through **quota sampling,** in which a replica in miniature of the larger population is constructed.

Employees who refuse to answer survey questions may be more dissatisfied with their jobs than are employees who are willing to answer questions.

Psychologists also conduct Web-based research in virtual laboratories, where large and diverse subject populations can be studied.

The raw data obtained in a research project can be summarized, described, and analyzed by **descriptive statistics.** Data can be presented in graphs or reduced to a few meaningful numbers. Three ways to measure the central tendency of a distribution of data are the **mean, median,** and **mode.** When sufficient data are collected from a representative sample of the population, they form a bell-shaped or **normal distribution,** in which most of the scores fall in the center or average range. To measure a distribution's variability, psychologists use the **standard deviation,** which is a distance along the distribution's baseline. The standard deviation provides information on the percentage of scores that fall above or below any particular raw score. The **correlation coefficient** denotes the direction and strength of the relationship between two variables and enables psychologists to predict performance on one variable from performance on another variable.

Inferential statistics are used to determine the level of **statistical significance** of the difference between the means of two groups by indicating whether the difference is so large that it is unlikely to have occurred by chance. **Meta-analysis** is a technique for averaging the results of a large number of studies.

KEY TERMS

control group
correlation
dependent variable
descriptive statistics
experimental group
experimental method
fixed-alternative survey questions
independent variable
inferential statistics
mean
median
meta-analysis

mode
naturalistic observation
normal distribution
open-end survey questions
probability
probability sampling
quota sampling
skewed distribution
standard deviation
statistical significance
survey research methods

ADDITIONAL READING

Allen, J. D., & Pittenger, D. J. (2000). *Statistics tutor: Tutorial and computational software for the behavioral sciences* (2nd ed.). New York: Wiley. A comprehensive software tutorial program and exercise manual for statistical concepts.

Birnbaum, M. H. (Ed.). (2000). *Psychological experiments on the Internet.* Orlando, FL: Academic Press. Discusses advantages and disadvantages of Web-based research and offers examples from cross-cultural studies.

Mitchell, M., & Jolley, J. (2001). *Research design explained* (4th ed.). Fort Worth, TX: Harcourt College Publishers. An undergraduate research methods textbook.

Pagano, R. R. (2001). *Understanding statistics in the behavioral sciences* (6th ed.). Belmont, CA: Wadsworth. An introductory statistics textbook.

The Development of Human Resources

The I-O psychology specialty referred to as "human resources" includes selecting, training, and evaluating new and current employees. When you apply for a job, you may undergo an extensive selection process. An organization may use techniques ranging from application blanks to sophisticated psychological tests. Once hired, you must be trained to perform the job efficiently. Selection and training techniques will also be used when you are being considered for promotion. The company will want to match your skills with the new job's requirements. When you are promoted to a more responsible job, you must be trained for this new role. Periodically, your supervisor will evaluate your performance. You will want this appraisal to be as fair and objective as possible, and to provide you with feedback about your progress on the job.

Employee selection, training, and appraisal methods determine the kind of job for which you will be hired and the way in which you will perform your duties. Chapters 3 and 4 deal with problems of selection. Chapter 3 discusses such selection techniques as application blanks, interviews, letters of recommendation, and assessment centers. Chapter 4 describes intelligence, interest, aptitude, personality, and integrity tests used for selection purposes. Performance appraisal methods are covered in Chapter 5, and training techniques in Chapter 6.

Employee Selection Principles and Techniques

■　　　■　　　■　　　■

Have you ever spent Spring Break in Panama City, Florida? Thousands of students do every year, which is the reason that so many job fairs are held there. Recruiters from a variety of organizations set up booths and try to entice college seniors to go to work for them. A survey of seniors was conducted at the job fair in March, 2000. One of the questions was: Do you think you will stay in your first job for more than two years? The results were unsettling to the recruiters, who rely on hiring new college graduates to help their companies grow. Of the seniors who took part in the survey, two-thirds said they did not expect to remain with their first employer for more than two years (Dunn, 2000).

How long do you think you will want to keep your first job after college? Considerable research suggests that at least half of the graduating seniors in your class will not find enough satisfaction in their work to stay very long with the first organization they join. They may find the job to be different from what they were told by the company recruiter or the interviewer in the human resources department. Or they may find that they did not know themselves so well, that their abilities and interests were not what they thought, or that they were socially or temperamentally unsuited to that particular kind of work.

Whatever the reasons for dissatisfaction with the job, it is an unfortunate situation in which the employee and the employer both stand to lose. This dilemma emphasizes the importance of employee selection principles and practices. Improper matching of the person and the job, of the person's skills and characteristics with the job's demands and requirements leads to unhappiness and poor performance in the work situation.

Before you enter the personnel office of a potential employer, or before you complete an application blank on a company's Web site, certain preselection factors will already have influenced your choice of job. Some of these are internal, such as your preferences about the kind of work you want to do and your expectations about the organization. Other factors are external, such as the nature of the recruiting effort that brought you in contact with the organization, and the amount of realistic information you are given about your possible place in it. I-O psychologists describe these preselection issues as problems of organizational entry.

ORGANIZATIONAL ENTRY

Your entry into an organization is of immense importance not only for the immediate satisfaction it may bring you, but also for your long-term contentment. Just as the nature of your first love affair will affect your subsequent emotional relationships, so your first job experience will affect your work performance and your expectations about your career.

Research has shown that people who demonstrate success early in their career are more likely to be promoted than those who are less successful early in their career. In other words, employees who start out well, who have positive experiences in the initial stages of their working life, continue to do well.

The amount of challenge your first job provides influences your commitment to your work, your level of achievement, and your motivation to do well for yourself and for your company. The positive impact of a challenging job stimulates a high level of performance and technical competence that can lead to continued success. Research in I-O psychology has documented this relationship between the level of initial job challenge and later success for employees in a variety of occupations in many different organizations.

Finding the right amount of challenge is of major importance in your organizational entry process. It is vital that the challenge offered by your first job be compatible with your expectations and preferences. Indeed, it is crucial to you and your employer that everything about your initial job comes close to satisfying your needs. That is why employers try to learn all they can about the expectations and interests of potential employees.

> ONLINE!
>
> To find out what people actually do in a variety of jobs, what education and training they need, what their working conditions are like, what their salaries and job prospects are, see the *Occupational Outlook Handbook* compiled by the U.S. Bureau of Labor Statistics. Check it out online at *www.stats.bls.gov/ocohome.htm.*

EMPLOYEE PREFERENCES

What are you looking for in a job? High salary? Stock options? A comprehensive health insurance plan? A reserved parking space? Although it may be easy to identify the single most important factor for you as an individual, there is no single answer for all employees. I-O psychologists have identified several job characteristics likely to be important to employees. Some of these are listed below. How would you rank them for yourself?

____*1*____ Challenging, interesting, and meaningful work
_____ High salary
_____ Opportunities for advancement
_____ Job security (no danger of being laid off or fired)

An online survey of 869 college students from more than 50 schools found that challenging work was the single most desirable factor mentioned in choosing a job. WebFeet.com, an online recruiting service, conducted the survey in the year 2000. Other factors important to the students were training for advancement, compatible colleagues and supervisors, appropriate salary, stock options, and being allowed to dress casually on the job.

A survey of 359 college seniors revealed significant preferences about the size of the organization. Nearly 75% of the students wanted to work for large companies—defined as those with more than 1000 employees—whereas only 25% would prefer to work for small companies employing fewer than 500 workers (Barber, Wesson, Roberson, & Taylor, 1999).

Another factor that affects employee preferences is level of education. College graduates have different expectations from those of high school graduates, who in turn have different preferences from those who did not complete high school. Not all college graduates have the same preferences. Engineering and computer science majors differ from liberal arts majors, and A students differ from C students. Younger workers' preferences differ from those of older workers, white-collar workers from blue-collar workers, and technical personnel from managerial personnel.

Employee preferences change as a function of economic conditions. In an economic downturn when jobs are scarce, new employees in the job market may be more interested in pay and job security. In a robust economic climate when jobs are plentiful, issues such as challenging work or the opportunity to develop new skills rank higher than security or salary.

Many people enter an organization with unrealistic or inflated expectations about the nature of the job and the company, which may explain why so many people leave their first job. The discrepancy between expectations and reality is too great. Expectations begin to clash with reality from the outset, when you have your first contact with a potential employer, typically at your initial meeting with the company recruiter. This marks the first opportunity for each to size up the other, and it is an important step in the preselection process of organizational entry.

THE RECRUITMENT PROCESS

I-O psychologists are concerned with several issues in the recruitment process: the sources employees use to find out about jobs, the characteristics of recruiters, college campus recruiting, and the kinds of information provided to job applicants.

Sources for Recruiting

The traditional recruiting sources available to organizations include online search services, help-wanted ads in newspapers, referrals from current employees, employment agencies and search services, placement services of professional associations, job fairs, and outplacement agencies. Another popular source for recruiting is the college campus. Almost half of all large corporations actively recruit managerial and professional employees through on-campus interviews.

Online recruiting is popular with a majority of medium-size and larger employers. Electronic bulletin boards post company advertisements for available positions, and job-seekers post their resumes. The use of online sources speeds up the entire recruitment and personnel selection process.

Surveys show that the typical user of online job search services is a white male under the age of 40 who is looking for a job in data processing and computer programming. The data in Table 3–1 indicate the importance of Web-based recruiting for these and other types of jobs (Stanton, 1999).

> **ONLINE!**
>
> Here are just a few of the thousands of Internet career sites. Most provide extensive databases of job openings, resumes of job seekers, and advice on applying for jobs: *www.monster.com*, *www.careerpath.com*, *www.careershop.com*, and *www.ipmaac.org* (a listing of organizations that recruit on the Web, maintained by the International Personnel Management Association Assessment Council).

TABLE 3–1   Web-based Job Listing Percentages[*]

Category	Percent of Jobs Listed
Data processing/programming	47.3
Engineering	17.2
Sales, marketing, and advertising	9.2
Technical (other than programming)	9.1
Clerical	4.1
Management	3.3
Accounting	2.6
Telecommunications	2.1
Financial	1.5
Medical	1.2

*Based on J. M. Stanton, Validity and related issues in Web-based hiring. *The Industrial-Organizational Psychologist*, 1999, 36 (3), p. 71.

THEY'LL BE PROUD TO BE HERE.

The Army offers young people great opportunities to learn self-discipline, confidence and teamwork, qualities they need throughout life.

WE'LL BE PROUD TO SEND THEM THERE.

And they can earn up to $40,000 to go to college if they qualify for the Montgomery GI Bill plus the Army College Fund.

CALL   1 - 800 - USA - ARMY   w w w . g o a r m y . c o m

Organizations of all types spend considerable time and money recruiting suitable employees. (Army materials courtesy of the U.S. Government, as represented by the Secretary of the Army.)

Recruiter Characteristics

The behavior and personal characteristics of company recruiters can have a significant impact on how college seniors choose their first job. Psychologists have found that characteristics likely to induce graduating seniors to accept a job offer include behaviors such as smiling, nodding, maintaining eye contact, demonstrating empathy and warmth, and showing thoughtfulness.

Other research on job applicants at on-campus placement centers showed that college seniors preferred recruiters to spend the interview period providing information about the company, soliciting information about the applicant, and answering the applicant's questions. When the college seniors thought that corporate recruiters were spending too much time talking about irrelevant topics, they were significantly less likely to accept a job offer.

A study of site visits questioned nearly 400 college seniors who had successfully completed the campus interview and then had been invited to visit the company offices. The purpose of the research was to determine the aspects of the visits that influenced the seniors' decision about accepting a job offer. The primary factor was the congeniality of the corporate host and how comfortable the applicant felt in his or her presence (Turban, Campion, & Eyring, 1995).

Campus Recruiting

College recruiting may not be living up to its potential, and companies may not be realizing full value from their recruitment programs. One explanation for this finding is that fewer than half of corporate recruiters receive training in the

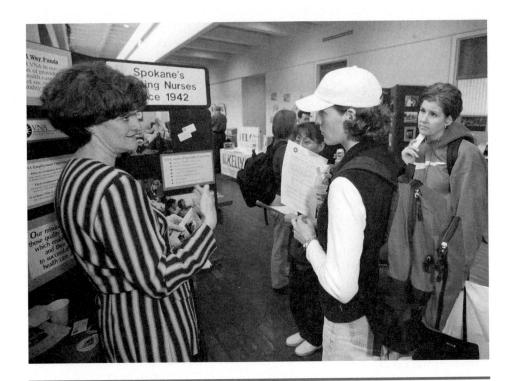

A recruiter for a health care service agency meets with nursing students at a job fair in Spokane, Washington.

proper techniques for interviewing job applicants. Recruiters tend to form a positive or negative impression about an applicant's qualifications in the first few minutes of an interview, hardly sufficient time to collect information on which to base a recruiting decision.

Recruiters also tend to spend more time talking with applicants they consider to be qualified and less time with applicants they dismiss on the basis of a superficial judgment. Often, recruiters do not agree on the topics to be covered in an interview and sometimes fail to discuss important issues with applicants. All these points reflect a lack of interviewing skills.

In an effort to reduce campus recruiting costs, many organizations have turned to computerized recruitment databases that compile student resumes. Subscribers who are searching for candidates with particular qualifications can prescreen and retrieve these documents.

Whether college recruiting is face-to-face or virtual, one major difficulty faced by corporate recruiters on campus is finding job candidates who have a realistic view of the business world. This is another reason why college recruiting often produces less than satisfactory results. During the campus recruitment interview, many students obtain a false picture of the job and the organization, sometimes because they have had no experience in corporate life and, therefore, do not know what questions to ask the recruiter. They want to make a good impression and may try to hide attitudes and characteristics they think the recruiter might not like. Another reason for the misleading image is the fault of the recruiters. Their goal is to find people with promise for their company, and to accomplish this, they may paint an idealized picture of their organization and of the new graduate's first job in it.

Thus, each side may be guilty of misleading the other. The result, when they turn out to be a less-than-perfect match, is likely to be dissatisfaction. The obvious solution is greater honesty, with each party being open about good and bad points. Some corporations deal with this problem by presenting a realistic preview of the job as part of their organizational entry procedures.

Realistic Job Previews

Realistic job previews A recruitment technique that acquaints prospective employees with positive and negative aspects of a job.

Realistic job previews provide information that is as accurate as possible about all aspects of a job. Such information can be supplied through a brochure or other written description of the job, through a film or videotape, or through an on-the-job sample of the work to see if the applicant can perform the required tasks. The purpose of a realistic job preview is to acquaint prospective employees with both positive and negative aspects of the job. The hope is that this practice will reduce overly optimistic or unrealistic expectations about what the job involves.

A meta-analysis of 40 studies on realistic job previews found them to have a significant positive correlation with subsequent job performance. In addition, applicants who participated in realistic job previews tended to have lower initial expectations about the nature of the job and a lower incidence of quitting (Phillips, 1998). One study of 82 nurses who were given brochures that provided realistic job previews found that they were only half as likely to quit as were the 72 nurses in the control group, who were not given the brochures (Hom, Griffeth, Palich, & Bracker, 1998).

Other research has supported the finding that realistic job previews correlate positively with job satisfaction, job performance, and reduced turnover. Realistic job previews have also been found to reduce the number of applicants initially accepting jobs, because potential employees can learn, even before starting a job, whether certain aspects of the work situation are unappealing or otherwise not appropriate for them.

A REVIEW OF THE SELECTION PROCESS

There is more to proper selection methodology than placing an ad in the newspaper or with an online search service, having people come to the office to fill out an application blank, and questioning them in a brief interview. A successful selection program involves several additional procedures. Let's suppose that the head of the human resources department is told that 200 new employees must be hired to operate the complex machinery that is being installed to produce fax machines. How will these workers be found?

Job and Worker Analyses

Ideally, the first step is for I-O psychologists to investigate the nature of the job. The organization will not know what abilities potential employees should have unless it can describe in detail what they are expected to do to perform the job effectively. A process called **job analysis** is undertaken to determine the specific skills necessary to the job. From the job analysis, a profile of worker qualifications can be developed.

> **Job analysis** The study of a job to describe in specific terms the nature of the component tasks performed by the workers.

Once these abilities have been specified, the human resources manager must determine the most effective means of identifying these characteristics in potential employees. Does the job require the ability to read complex diagrams? To manipulate small component parts? To demonstrate knowledge of electronics? And how will the company find out whether an applicant has these skills?

The necessary background characteristics and aptitudes, as revealed by the job and worker analyses, must be assessed or evaluated in each applicant, for example, by asking specific questions in an interview or by administering appropriate psychological tests. Cutoff test scores or levels for the various abilities will be established. A minimum score on a test or a fixed number of years of education or experience will be proposed, and no one who falls below that level will be hired. It may be necessary for the I-O psychologist to evaluate present workers in the same or similar jobs to determine where the cutoff scores should be set.

Recruitment Decisions

Recruitment decisions are next. Should the company recruit new employees through print or online ads? Through an employment agency? Through referrals from current employees? The number of potential employees attracted by these efforts affects the caliber of those ultimately offered jobs. If ads and referrals bring in only 250 applicants for the 200 jobs, the company must be less selective in hiring than if there were 400 applicants to choose from. I-O psychologists call this the **selection ratio,** the relationship between the number of people to be hired and the number who are available to be hired. Thus, the potential labor supply directly affects the strictness of the requirements established for the job. If there is a shortage of applicants and the jobs must be filled within a few weeks,

> **Selection ratio** The relationship between the number of people to be hired (the number of jobs) and the number available to be hired (the potential labor supply).

some requirements (perhaps the cutoff score on a test of cognitive abilities) will have to be lowered.

A shortage of job applicants may also force the company to expand its recruiting campaign and to offer higher wages, enhanced benefits, or improved working conditions to attract and retain new employees. Thus, the size of the labor supply can greatly influence not only recruitment and selection procedures but also features of the job itself.

Selection Techniques

Selecting the new employees and classifying them as suitable or unsuitable for the job are accomplished by a variety of techniques, including application blanks, interviews, letters of recommendation, assessment centers, and psychological tests. Hiring decisions typically are based not on a single technique but on a combination of methods. In addition, testing for drug use is now widespread for many types of jobs (see Chapter 12). Some jobs also have physical requirements and may require tests of strength and endurance. Some organizations are testing for HIV, chemical sensitivity, and genetic predisposition to certain diseases.

The next step in the selection process is to test the selection procedures to find out if they have succeeded in identifying the best workers for the jobs. In our example, after the initial 200 workers have been hired, the human resources department must track their progress to see how they perform on the job. This is the major test of the worth of a selection program.

Every new selection program must be investigated to determine its predictive accuracy or validity. This is done by evaluating the performance of the employees selected by the new procedures. For example, after 6 months on the job, the supervisors of the 200 new workers can be asked to rate their job performance. By comparing these ratings with performance on the selection techniques, we can determine how the two measures correlate. We want to know whether the selection techniques were able to predict which of the applicants turned out to be the better workers.

Suppose we learn that the employees who received high ratings from their supervisors had performed an average of 10 points above the cutoff score on a test of manual dexterity and had earned a high school diploma. Employees who received low ratings from their supervisors performed within 1 or 2 points of the cutoff score on the manual dexterity test and had not completed high school. These findings tell us that the two factors (manual dexterity and a high school diploma) were able to distinguish between potentially good and potentially poor workers. In the future, then, the human resources department can use these criteria with confidence to select the best people for these jobs.

Keep in mind that to evaluate employee selection procedures we must have some measure of job performance with which to compare performance on the selection techniques. Some ways to appraise and measure work performance are discussed in Chapter 5.

FAIR EMPLOYMENT PRACTICES

Successful employee selection programs must conform to the regulations of the Equal Employment Opportunity Commission (EEOC), established in 1972, and the provisions of the 1964 and 1991 Civil Rights Acts. All job applicants, regardless of race, religion, sex, or national origin, are guaranteed equal opportunities in seeking and maintaining employment. Discrimination in hiring is unethical, immoral, and illegal. (The impact of civil rights legislation on psychological testing in employee selection is noted in Chapter 4.)

Adverse Impact on Minority Groups

When any minority group of job candidates is treated markedly worse than the majority group, that minority group is said to be the target of **adverse impact** in the selection process. Any selection rate for a minority group that is less than 80% of the selection rate for the majority group is evidence of adverse impact.

Adverse impact When a minority group of job applicants or employees is treated markedly worse than the majority group in staffing decisions.

Let us say that a company had 200 job applicants (100 blacks and 100 whites) and hired 100 of them (20 blacks and 80 whites). In this instance, 80% of the white applicants were hired but only 20% of the black applicants. The selection rate for blacks was only one fourth, or 25%, of that for whites, much less than the 80% rule for showing adverse impact. This company could be challenged in court for maintaining vastly different rejection rates for minority and majority applicants.

We noted earlier that the typical user of online job search services is a white male. This complicates EEOC hiring guidelines. Women and ethnic minorities are underrepresented in access to jobs advertised in online sources.

Another source of discrimination that may lead to adverse impact is the consideration of an applicant's grade point average (GPA). Research on the GPAs of 7,500 college seniors found large ethnic disparities: GPAs for whites were higher than those for blacks. If a GPA cutoff score is set as the major criterion for employment, then black applicants could be unfairly screened out of consideration for jobs (Roth & Bobko, 2000).

> **ONLINE!** For current news on federal discrimination and affirmative action issues, go to *www.fullcoverage.yahoo.com/fc/us/affirmative_action*. For press releases on EEOC activities, fair employment practices, and relevant court decisions, see the Web site *www.eeoc.com*. EEOC statistics on job patterns by race, ethnic group, and gender can be found at *www.aflcio.org/articles/affirmativeaction/eeoc.htm*.

Discriminatory Questions

Interviews and application blanks have also been affected by civil rights legislation. Questions that discriminate against a particular group can lead to lawsuits. For example, it is illegal to ask questions that identify applicants' national origin, race, creed, or color. Applicants cannot be required to name their birthplace or that of their relatives, to identify their religious affiliation, if any, or to give the maiden names of female relatives. It is also unlawful to inquire about the clubs or societies to which applicants belong and to ask them to submit photographs with their employment applications. These questions can be considered discriminatory and have no relation to an applicant's fitness or potential for success on the job.

In addition, employers cannot ask applicants if they have ever been arrested for any crime, because members of some minority groups are much more likely to be arrested on suspicion of wrongdoing. It is lawful, however, to ask applicants if they have ever been *convicted* of any crime. Conviction could be considered relevant to job performance in certain instances, such as when a person convicted of embezzlement applies for a job as a bank teller.

Reverse Discrimination

The impetus to recruit, hire, and promote members of minority groups and to implement EEOC rulings has sometimes resulted in discrimination against members of the majority group. An organization may be so intent, for example, on increasing the number of women in its ranks to meet federal guidelines that it denies equal opportunities to men. In 1992, a white male medical school professor in Florida filed a discrimination lawsuit charging that the university had unfairly denied him a salary increase because the money available for pay raises was distributed only to women and minority faculty. This phenomenon, called **reverse discrimination,** has also occurred in graduate and professional schools, where some white applicants have been denied admission in favor of minority applicants whose grades and test scores were not as high as those of the white applicants.

Reverse discrimination The phenomenon that may occur when recruiting, hiring, promotion, and other human resources decisions in favor of members of a minority group result in discrimination against members of the majority group.

Reverse discrimination may operate in promotion decisions on the job when women and ethnic minorities are offered greater opportunities for advancement than are similarly qualified white men.

Equal opportunity programs can stigmatize those persons hired or promoted on an affirmative action basis. Majority group member employees may come to believe that preferential hiring practices for women and minorities have led to the hiring of unqualified people. As a result, some white men feel resentful. A backlash against affirmative action programs has been expressed by dissatisfied employees, employers and political leaders.

I-O psychology research has found that women, blacks, and Hispanics are more favorably disposed toward affirmative action than are white men. In one study, black engineers and black engineering students were more likely to apply to organizations with clearly stated affirmative action policies than to companies that did not use the phrase, "equal opportunity employer," in their job advertisements (Highhouse, Stierwalt, Bachiochi, Elder, & Fisher, 1999).

A telephone survey of 414 whites, 392 blacks, 162 U.S.-born Hispanics, and 177 immigrant Hispanics found that affirmative action programs were most strongly supported by blacks, and less so by Hispanics. The majority of the whites polled opposed such programs. In addition, blacks tended to believe that affirmative action was fair and rarely involved preferential treatment (Kravitz & Klineberg, 2000).

Overall, the effect of fair employment legislation may not have lived up to its promise or intent. Employment data for women and minorities show only a slight improvement in their situation as a direct result of civil rights laws. Affirmative action programs apparently have had only a minimal impact on organizational effectiveness (Hough & Oswald, 2000).

Other Forms of Discrimination

Discrimination against Older Workers.   The work force in the United States is aging. Most employers, however, still prefer to hire younger workers, despite consistent evidence from I-O psychology research that older workers are often

NEWSBREAK

It's No Longer the Back of the Bus

We are unable to get taxis to pick us up in front of office buildings. We are frisked and detained on suburban commuter trains. We are watched in department stores and mistaken for coat-check clerks and restroom attendants while lunching in the best restaurants. We are directed to freight elevators and delivery windows by receptionists who fail to recognize us in our own company offices. We are black professionals in corporate America.

Although I am at my desk each morning facing the same corporate challenges as my white co-workers, a great deal of my job-related stress comes from sources totally unrelated to my job. My father dreamed of the day when his son would work in a towering office with a city view. What he didn't know was that arriving there would not be the end of the struggle for black Americans.

Even though I have been the beneficiary of affirmative action, I can acknowledge some of its flaws—its tendency to create resentment among white men and its potential for generating a sense of "group entitlement" among minorities and women. But my experiences as a corporate lawyer, professor, and black professional in a mostly white environment have shown me that workplace bias in America, even today, is so intractable that it justifies establishing affirmative action as a permanent policy.

For those who believe I am overzealous in suggesting the permanent enforcement of affirmative action, I offer an incident that took place soon after I started a new job as a corporate lawyer in Manhattan.

A receptionist with a security guard in tow came running past my secretary's desk just as I was joining a conference call with a client in my office.

"Excuse me, Larry, but I've got security here," the receptionist said breathlessly, interrupting our call. "Did you see a delivery boy get past reception and come through here with a purple bag?"

I looked to the corner where a Bergdorf Goodman [an upscale department store] bag sat with a hat that I had bought for my wife.

"That's the boy!" shouted the security guard, pointing to me.

When the receptionist saw the shopping bag, recognition and relief washed over her face. "That's so funny," she laughed while closing the door. "We thought you were a delivery boy. Sorry to bother you."

The client looked at me with the slightest hint of skepticism.

Source: Lawrence Otis Graham. The case for affirmative action. *The New York Times,* May 21, 1995.

more productive than younger workers and have lower absenteeism and turnover rates. In general, older employees do not suffer from poorer health, diminished vigor, or declining mental abilities when compared with younger employees.

The stereotypes about older workers persist. Older workers tend to receive more negative performance evaluations than younger workers, appraisals that are likely based more on age than on actual work performance. A meta-analysis of studies of ratings of older employees found that workers 34 years old and younger tended to give less favorable ratings to workers age 55 and older than they did to younger workers. Younger workers were rated as having higher job qualifications and more potential for development and as being more qualified for physically demanding work (Finkelstein, Burke, & Raju, 1995).

Older workers are protected by law against age discrimination in hiring and promotion. The Age Discrimination in Employment Act of 1967 legislated against using age to deny employment opportunities to people in the 40- to 65-year-old age bracket. The act was amended in 1978 to raise the age at which employees could be forced to retire from 65 to 70.

Discrimination Against Workers with Disabilities.   Employees with physical and mental disabilities are protected by federal laws against job discrimination. The Vocational Rehabilitation Act of 1973 made it mandatory for organizations to recruit, hire, and promote qualified disabled persons. The 1990 Americans with Disabilities Act (ADA) prohibits employers, state and local governments, employment agencies, and labor unions from discriminating against qualified individuals with disabilities in job application procedures, hiring, firing, advancement, compensation, job training, and other conditions of employment. The act requires employers to make reasonable accommodations to the physical or

The Americans with Disabilities Act of 1990 prohibits employers from discriminating against qualified persons who have disabilities.

mental impairments of a qualified applicant or employee with a disability if it would not impose an undue hardship on normal business operations.

In one "reasonable accommodation" case, a supermarket employee who suffered from fatigue due to lupus (a tubercular disease) was provided with a stool so that she could perform her cashier's job without having to stand throughout her shift. Accommodations for other persons with disabilities include providing oral or braille instructions to visually impaired job applicants or employees, and constructing ramps and other structural modifications for people who use wheelchairs. Some employers still resist implementing workplace changes on behalf of disabled persons. A survey of 114 managers showed that the greater the adjustment required, the more resistant the managers were to making them (Florey & Harrison, 2000).

Thus, prejudice against hiring disabled workers can still be found, even though it is at variance with their actual job performance. Research by I-O psychologists shows that disabled employees perform as well as or better than nondisabled employees. Many large U.S. corporations, such as Du Pont, 3M, and McDonnell Douglas, routinely hire disabled workers because they have found that they make good employees. Companies such as McDonald's and Marriott routinely hire people with mild to moderate cognitive impairments and find them to be as productive as their other employees. However, fewer than 20% of the people of working age who can be classified as mentally disabled have found jobs, and half of these jobs are in federally subsidized programs (Johnson, 1999). Such jobs include janitor, gardener, grocery store clerk, office receptionist, toll collector, and fast-food restaurant cook.

Passage of the 1990 ADA has led to the filing of thousands of formal job discrimination complaints and lawsuits against employers. Unfortunately, the prospect of legal challenges has made many organizations wary of hiring disabled employees. This fear of litigation may explain why the number of disabled persons in the workforce has not increased over the past decade. Russell Redenbaugh, a member of the U.S. Civil Rights Commission who himself is disabled, has concluded that the effect of the Americans with Disabilities Act has been "a complete disappointment."

Discrimination Against Women Workers.   Women face discrimination in the workplace, particularly when they apply for what are still considered to be traditionally male jobs. Research shows that women receive lower wages than do men with similar skills and qualifications for performing the same or comparable jobs. Other studies fail to confirm a gender-based wage gap, noting that in some occupational categories, salaries for men and women are the same.

Discrimination Based on Sexual Orientation.   Gay men and lesbian women face discrimination in hiring in public agencies and private companies. To date, no federal civil rights legislation protects homosexuals from workplace discrimination. However, several states now include sexual orientation among the protected categories in their civil rights laws, and more than 80 cities have passed ordinances forbidding job discrimination against gay people.

An increasing number of U.S. corporations are developing antidiscrimination policies with regard to gay persons. Some companies, such as AT&T, Xerox, Lockheed, and Levi Strauss, sponsor support groups and networks for their gay employees. The major American automakers (Ford, General Motors, and

DaimlerChrysler), as well as IBM, Citigroup, and some local governments, offer standard fringe benefits to partners of employees in same-sex relationships.

Discrimination Based on Physical Attractiveness.   Some job applicants have a more pleasing appearance than others in terms of currently accepted cultural standards. This type of judgment, called *beautyism* by some, affects hiring and promotion decisions in the business world.

Many people believe that physically attractive persons also possess more desirable personal and social traits, an attitude summed up by some I-O psychologists as "what is beautiful is good." Physically attractive persons are perceived as more sociable, dominant, and mentally healthy than less physically attractive persons.

Some people also believe that attractive persons are better qualified and more successful in the workplace than less attractive persons. In one simulated hiring situation, 112 managers (46 men and 66 women) evaluated resumes, to which photographs were attached, for male and female job applicants. The photographs had been judged by human resources personnel as being either highly attractive or slightly below average in attractiveness. Not surprisingly, the managers preferred the more physically attractive candidates to the less attractive candidates. This bias was found to decrease with the managers' length of job experience. In other words, the more experienced the manager, the less his or her tendency to discriminate among potential workers on the basis of their physical appearance. However, even among the most experienced managers, the less attractive female job applicants received the lowest ratings on suitability for hiring (Marlowe, Schneider, & Nelson, 1996).

There is also considerable evidence of a pervasive cultural bias, particularly in Western countries, against hiring and promoting people who are seriously overweight. The cities of San Francisco and Santa Cruz, California, Washington, D.C., and the state of Michigan have made it illegal to discriminate against people on the basis of size. Other municipalities are expected to follow.

ONLINE!

An activist task force of the National Association to Advance Fat Acceptance successfully pressured Hallmark Cards to withdraw from sale greeting cards that ridiculed overweight people. The group's Web site is at *www.naafa.org*.

Discrimination Based on Genetic Factors.   Genetic testing today can identify people who have an increased risk of developing a variety of diseases, including breast and ovarian cancer, cystic fibrosis, and Alzheimer's disease. This presents a dilemma for employers. If a highly qualified applicant shows a genetic predisposition for a disease that is likely to result in high health insurance costs and lost time from work, that applicant might be dropped from consideration for a job.

A federal executive order was issued in February, 2000, prohibiting discrimination based on genetic factors in hiring, firing, and promotion decisions for U.S. government and civil service jobs. Legislation has been introduced in the U.S. Congress to extend the ban to private-sector jobs.

JOB ANALYSIS

The purpose of **job analysis** is to describe in specific terms the nature of the component tasks performed by workers on a particular job. A job analysis includes information about the tools or equipment used, the operations performed, the education and training required, the wages paid, and any unique aspects of the job such as safety hazards.

It is important to note that many I-O psychology practitioners prefer to use the term **work analysis** instead of *job analysis*. Work analysis focuses on certain tasks and skills that can be transferred from one job to another. In today's job market, employees must develop and continue to refine a diverse package of skills that they can apply to different jobs. Unlike workers in previous generations, employees in the twenty-first century do not expect to spend their working lives performing routine and repetitive tasks.

We mentioned earlier the value of job and work analyses in employee selection. Unless the company knows precisely what a job entails and what is required for successful performance of these tasks, it will have no way of knowing what qualities to seek in applicants for that job.

Job and work analyses have other important uses in organizational life. To establish a training program for a particular job, for example, the nature of the job and the skills it requires must be known. A company cannot expect to train a person to perform a job unless the tasks and operations required for job success can be described.

Job analysis can also aid in efforts to design a job or a workspace for more efficient performance. If a job analysis reveals that a lathe operator has to walk 50 yards from the machine to the storage shelves every time it is necessary to replenish the supply of raw materials, redesigning the work area can eliminate this wasted time and effort. Job analysis can also uncover safety hazards or dangerous operating procedures.

I-O psychologists have devised a number of techniques for conducting job and work analyses. One approach is to refer to previously compiled analyses. The U.S. Department of Labor has developed the Occupational Information Network (O*NET), a database that summarizes such information. It defines, classifies, and describes a variety of occupations. This online database is updated frequently to provide employers with examples and analyses of the knowledge, skills, and abilities employees need to perform these jobs. In general, the O*NET provides the following information for each job.

- Personal requirements: the skills and knowledge required to perform the work
- Personal characteristics: the abilities, interests, and values needed to perform the work
- Experience requirements: the training and level of licensing and experience needed for the work
- Job requirements: the work activities and context, including the physical, social, and organizational factors involved in the work
- Labor market: the occupational outlook and pay scales for the work

Table 3–2 shows examples from the O*NET of the knowledge required to perform different types of tasks. Table 3–3 presents descriptions of verbal, quantitative, and cognitive abilities needed for various tasks.

Job analysis The study of a job to describe in specific terms the nature of the component tasks performed by the workers.

Work analysis The study of certain tasks and skills that workers can transfer from one job to another.

TABLE 3–2   O*NET Job Descriptions and Levels of Knowledge

Category and Operational Definition	Level of Knowledge
Administration/Management—Knowledge of principles and processes involved in business and organizational planning, coordination, and execution. Includes strategic planning, re-source allocation, manpower modeling, leader-ship techniques, and production methods.	*High*—Managing a $10 million company. *Low*—Signing a pay voucher.
Clerical—Knowledge of administrative and cler-ical procedures and systems such as word pro-cessing, filing and records management, forms design, and other office procedures and terminology.	*High*—Organizing a storage system for company forms. *Low*—Filing letters alphabetically.
Sales/Marketing—Knowledge of principles and methods involved in showing, promoting, and selling products or services. Includes marketing strategies, product demonstration and sales techniques, and sales control systems.	*High*—Developing a marketing plan for a nationwide phone system. *Low*—Selling cakes at a bake sale.
Computers/Electronics—Knowledge of circuit boards, processors, chips, and computer hard-ware and software including applications and programming.	*High*—Creating a program to scan for computer viruses. *Low*—Operating a VCR to watch a pre-recorded tape.
Engineering/Technology—Knowledge of equipment, tools, and mechanical devices and their applications.	*High*—Designing a clean, efficient power plant. *Low*—Installing a door lock.

Other techniques for conducting job and work analyses for specific jobs in-clude interviews, questionnaires, observation, activity logs, and critical incidents.

Interviews.   The use of interviews for job and work analyses involves extensive meetings with the persons directly connected with the job (the so-called "subject matter experts"). These include the workers performing the job, their supervi-sors, and the instructors who trained the workers for the job. Job analysts may supplement interviews with questionnaires. The persons being interviewed should be told the purpose of the interview and why it is important to answer the questions fully and honestly. The questions should be carefully planned and clearly worded to elicit as much information as possible.

Questionnaires.   Two types of questionnaires are used in job analysis: the un-structured questionnaire and the structured questionnaire. In the unstructured or open-end approach, the subject matter experts (workers, supervisors, and trainers) describe in their own words the components of the job and the tasks performed.

When the structured questionnaire approach is used, the people being inter-viewed are provided with descriptions of tasks, operations, and working condi-tions and are asked to rate the items or to select those items that characterize the

TABLE 3–3   O*NET Examples of Specific Work Abilities

Abilities	Level
Verbal	
Oral comprehension—The ability to listen to and understand information and ideas presented through spoken words and sentences.	*High*—Understanding a lecture on advanced physics. *Low*—Understanding a television commercial.
Written comprehension—The ability to read and understand information and ideas presented in writing.	*High*—Understanding a book on repairing a missile guidance system. *Low*—Understanding signs on the highway.
Oral expression—The ability to communicate information and ideas in speaking so that other people will understand.	*High*—Explaining advanced principles of genetics to 1st-year college students. *Low*—Cancelling newspaper delivery by phone.
Written expression—The ability to communicate information and ideas in writing so that other people will understand.	*High*—Writing an advanced economics textbook. *Low*—Writing a note to remind your spouse to take something out of the freezer to thaw.
Quantitative	
Mathematical reasoning—The ability to understand and organize a problem and to select a mathematical method or formula to solve the problem.	*High*—Determining the math required to simulate a spacecraft moon landing. *Low*—Determining the cost of 10 oranges when priced at 2 for 29 cents.
Number facility—The ability to add, subtract, multiply, and divide quickly and correctly.	*High*—Manually calculating the flight path of an aircraft, considering speed, fuel, wind, and altitude. *Low*—Adding 2 and 7.

job. Research has shown, however, that people can be careless in providing ratings, which can lead to less-than-accurate job and work analyses.

A widely used questionnaire is the Position Analysis Questionnaire (PAQ), which consists of 194 job elements related to specific behaviors and activities. The job elements are organized into six categories of job behavior: information input, mental processes, work output, relationships with other persons, job context, and other job activities and conditions. Employees and supervisors rate each element for its importance to the job in question. Such quantifiable ratings have an obvious advantage over the kind of information yielded by the unstructured questionnaire. As with other types of surveys conducted today, job analysis questionnaires can be administered online as well as in printed versions.

Direct Observation.   A third approach to job and work analyses is the direct observation of workers as they perform their jobs. Because people may behave differently when they know they are being watched, it is necessary for the job analysts to remain as unobtrusive as possible. Also, they should observe a representative sample of workers and make observations at various times throughout the workday to take account of changes caused by factors such as fatigue.

Much of the direct observation conducted today is through electronic performance monitoring. (We discuss in Chapter 5 the use of this technique for employee performance evaluation.) For example, trucking companies use onboard computers to monitor running time, down time, and speed. Cable television companies monitor maintenance workers electronically to record the time spent per service call.

Systematic Activity Logs. With systematic activity logs, workers and supervisors maintain detailed written records of their activities during a given time period. If prepared with care, these logs can reveal details about a job that are not otherwise obtainable.

Critical-incidents technique A means of identifying specific activities or behaviors that lead to desirable or undesirable consequences on the job.

Critical Incidents. The **critical-incidents technique** is based on the identification of those incidents or behaviors that are necessary to successful job performance. The goal is to have subject matter experts indicate the behaviors that distinguish good from poor workers. The critical-incidents technique focuses on specific actions that lead to desirable or undesirable consequences on the job. A single critical incident is of little value, but hundreds of them can effectively describe the unique behaviors required to perform the job well. (We note in Chapter 6 that critical incidents can also be used to identify areas where employee retraining might be needed.)

Job analysis continues to be an important part of the employee selection process. Every employing organization must be able to justify each of its job requirements to show that whatever it asks of a job applicant is related directly to the abilities required to perform the job. The company must not set arbitrary qualifications that can be used to discriminate against groups of workers and to deny them equal opportunity for employment. Detailed job and work analyses provide justification for determining specific job requirements. For example, if a company is charged with sex discrimination because women employees are paid less than men employees for what appears to be the same job, the company would have to show that the men are performing different tasks that justify the greater pay. A job analysis can provide that information. Therefore, organizations take seriously the task of job analysis. Equal employment opportunity and successful selection programs are not possible without it.

Let us consider some specific employee selection techniques currently in use: biographical information forms, interviews, references, and assessment centers. Psychological tests for employee selection are discussed in Chapter 4.

BIOGRAPHICAL INFORMATION

The collection of biographical information, or *biodata,* on the backgrounds of job applicants is a common method of employee selection. The rationale for this technique is the belief that our past experiences or personal traits can be used to predict our work behavior and potential for success. Because many of our behaviors, values, and attitudes remain consistent throughout life, it is not unreasonable to assume that our behavior in the future will be based on our behavior in the past.

The initial determination about your suitability for employment is likely to be based on the information you supply on a company's application blank. You probably have already filled out application blanks to apply for college entrance, a part-time job, a car loan, or a checking account. Today, fewer organizations use the standard paper forms, relying instead on applications completed online. Some companies accept applications from your home computer. Others process applications from kiosks in the stores that are hiring, or from recruiting stations in shopping malls. Typically, some combination of touch-tone responses and interactive voice-recognition technology is used with artificial intelligence software. Here's how it works.

People who want to apply for jobs are advised to call a toll-free telephone number available at any time—24 hours a day, 7 days a week. Once they make the phone connection, they are told to press one key to indicate "yes" and another key to indicate "no" in response to a computer-generated voice that asks questions about their background. The entire process is automated, and the questions are essentially the same as those on a paper application form.

Applicants whose answers are considered satisfactory are usually asked a second set of questions that request more specific biographical information. The results are transmitted instantly to employer and employee. The company's human resources department does not have to commit personnel time to the process, and applicants can participate in this initial screening on their own time, at their own pace, without even dressing up.

Two major techniques for collecting biographical information are the standard application blank and the biographical inventory.

Application Blanks

The information routinely solicited on application blanks includes biographical data such as name, address, education, and work experience. It can also cover medical history, specific skills, and criminal convictions. For higher-level positions, applicants might be asked to describe their interests and hobbies, civic activities, reading habits, and career goals.

The crucial problem in the construction of employment applications is deciding what information to ask. What does the employer need to know to determine whether the applicant is suitable for the job? Beyond basic biographical data, the company must ascertain those facts about the candidate that correlate with successful performance on the job.

Research may show, for example, that most successful executives are college graduates who maintained grade point averages of 3.5 or better and who served in the student government association. Obviously, then, this is the kind of information the human resources department will want to elicit about an applicant early in the selection process. If the completed application blank indicates that the candidate does not possess these qualities, then the company will not want to pursue the process and undertake the expense of administering a battery of psychological tests or arranging for the candidate to visit the company headquarters.

The usefulness of the information obtained depends on the thoroughness of the research conducted to develop the items on the application blank. Each relevant item must be correlated with a later measure of job success. If a high positive correlation is found, then that item can be used with confidence to select new employees.

One problem with applications is the honesty of the applicant's responses. Is the information the applicant supplies complete and correct? Did the person actually graduate from the college indicated on the form? Did he or she really supervise 50 workers in the previous job? Is the reported annual salary correct or exaggerated? A sizable number of job applicants provide misleading or fraudulent information, especially about their previous job title, pay, and degree of responsibility.

A survey of human resources managers conducted by the Society for Human Resource Management found that 90% of the managers had encountered applicants who had lied about the length of time they had held their previous job. Some 78% of the managers later learned that some applicants had lied about having college degrees (Butler, 2000). Other surveys report similar results. Applicants often distort the truth about their background, but many employing organizations do not have the time or resources to confirm the information that applicants supply. Sometimes false information can be reduced by scheduling follow-up interviews and by warning applicants in advance that the company intends to verify the information provided on an application blank.

Many organizations do attempt to confirm the accuracy of biographical information by contacting former employers and the persons named as references. However, many companies are reluctant to release personal information for fear of lawsuits. A former employee may sue a company for providing unfavorable information, claiming libel or slander. Therefore, many employing organizations hesitate to supply more than limited factual data, such as job title and dates of employment. Few give evaluative information, such as performance ratings, or answer questions about why the employee left or whether the company would

---

NEWSBREAK

How Not to Get Hired: Part 1

It pays to proofread your resume and review your answers on an application blank to correct typographical errors, misspellings, and awkward phrasing, and to consider carefully the image it presents to a prospective employer. The following items are taken from actual resumes, application forms, and cover letters to employers. Do you think any of these people were hired?

- "I received a *plague* for Salesperson of the Year."
- "I'm a *rabid* typist."
- "I'll only accept a position within walking distance of the ocean."
- "I have the ability to meet deadlines while maintaining my *composer*."
- "I have an excellent eye for *derail*."
- "My typing speed is 756 words per minute."
- "I have formed a partnership with three business *collies*."

And to close a cover letter, one job seeker wrote, "Thank you for your consideration. I hope to hear from you *shorty*."

rehire the employee. Thus, it is difficult for an organization to verify certain kinds of information provided on an application blank.

Biographical Inventories

The **biographical inventory,** or biographical information blank, is a more systematized form of application blank. Typically, biographical inventories are longer than application blanks and seek greater detail about a person's background and experiences. The rationale for this extensive probing is that on-the-job behavior is related to attitudes, preferences, and values, as well as to past behavior in a variety of situations.

Biographical inventory An employee selection technique covering an applicant's past behavior, attitudes, preferences, and values. These questionnaires are longer and more extensive than standard application blanks.

Whereas a standard application blank might ask for the name of your college, your major field, and the dates you attended, a biographical inventory might ask the following questions about your college experience:

- How often did you have problems with other students because of different social groups or cliques?
- How often have other students come to you for advice?
- How often have you set a goal to do better than anyone else at something?
- How often did you feel you needed more self-discipline?

Considerable research is required to determine the background experiences that correlate with job success. The process of validating the items on a biographical inventory is similar to that for any selection technique. Each item must be correlated with a measure of job performance.

Research on biographical inventories confirms their a high predictive value. To evaluate one company's biographical inventory, psychologists tested it on a sample of more than 7,300 managers and staff professionals in 24 other organizations. The results showed that the biographical inventory was a valid predictor of promotional progress for positions throughout these organizations. It was found to be valid for both men and women employees, and for a broad range of ages, levels of education, and lengths of service. The researchers concluded that this inventory, developed for a particular organization, could successfully be used by other employers. Thus, the costly process of developing separate forms for each employer could be avoided (Carlson, Scullen, Schmidt, Rothstein, & Erwin, 1999).

In a study of nearly 400 clerical workers, their biographical data, combined with scores on tests of cognitive ability and personality, were found to be highly accurate predictors of their future job performance (Mount, Witt, & Barrick, 2000).

Research with 2,535 U.S. Army recruits revealed that many items on a biographical inventory could be grouped in one of four personality categories: rugged/outdoors, solid citizen, team sports/group orientation, and intellectual/achievement orientation. The individual responses or scores on these factors showed a strong positive correlation with the recruits' identification with military service and with their later decision to leave the army before their term of enlistment was up. Thus, the scores on these factors could be used prior to enlistment to predict who would succeed in the military and who would not (Mael & Ashforth, 1995).

As with standard application blanks, faking on biographical inventories can be a problem. Some applicants deliberately distort their answers to put a more positive spin on their work and life experiences. Advising applicants that their answers will be checked sometimes reduces this problem. Also, written notice that a scale to detect faking is built into the questionnaire, or that the scoring system will deduct points for dishonest answers, can be effective.

As we noted, biographical inventories have been found to be valid predictors of job success. Unfortunately, the technique is not used extensively in business and industry. Some managers claim to be unfamiliar with biographical inventories. Others say they do not have the time, money, or expertise to develop them. And still others are skeptical of research showing the utility of biographical inventories. It appears that the I-O psychologists working for these companies or conducting research on biographical inventories have not been effective in communicating the value of these techniques to the persons who are in a position to apply them.

This situation illustrates the gap that sometimes arises between research and application in I-O psychology. With biographical inventories, researchers have developed a highly successful employee selection tool, but it is seldom used in the workplace. Psychologists need to provide data that persuade human resources managers that this technique for selecting the best employees will save more money in the long run than the initial costs of developing and implementing the inventory.

INTERVIEWS

The personal interview is a widely used employee selection technique. Regardless of any other techniques that are part of an organization's selection program, almost every prospective employer wants the chance to meet an applicant in person before making the offer of a job. It is important to remember that the employment interview, like the college recruiting interview, is a two-way process. Its purpose is to allow a company to evaluate a candidate's suitability for employment. But it also offers the opportunity for candidates, if they ask the right questions, to determine whether the company and the job are right for them.

First Impressions

The impression you make during an interview will be a decisive factor in whether the organization offers you a job. I-O psychology research has shown that interviewers' assessments of job applicants are often influenced more by their subjective impressions of the applicants than by such specifics as work history, academic qualifications, or extracurricular activities. Personal qualities, such as perceived attractiveness, sociability, and skill at self-promotion, are often key factors in an interviewer's hiring recommendations.

A study of videotaped interviews with 60 managers from various utility companies found that visual and vocal cues influenced their judgments about the job applicants whom they were interviewing. Visual cues that managers approved included maintaining eye contact, smiling, leaning toward rather than

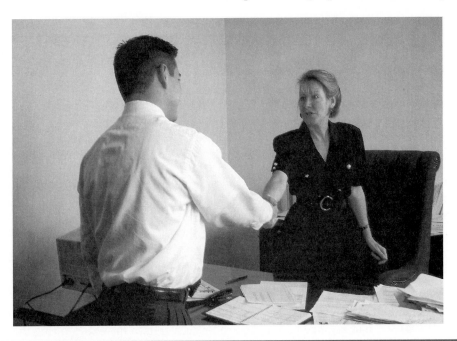

The personal interview is part of virtually every employee selection program.

away from the interviewer, and gesturing in a friendly way. Vocal cues that impressed the interviewers were a low-pitched rather than a high-pitched voice and expressive vocal inflections rather than a monotone. Interviewers were also more favorably disposed toward applicants who spoke faster rather than slower and who allowed few pauses in the conversation (DeGroot & Motowildo, 1999). You might keep these behaviors in mind the next time you participate in an interview, whether as a candidate or as an interviewer.

Of course, as you probably know from your own experience, it is possible to act deliberately so as to make the right impression; that is, to present yourself in the most favorable light. I-O psychologists call this skill **impression management,** and have noted two approaches job applicants can take: ingratiation and self-promotion.

Ingratiation refers to ways of behaving that attempt to persuade the interviewer to like you. For example, you may compliment the interviewer's style of dress, or appear to agree with his or her opinions and attitudes. *Self-promotion* tactics include praising your accomplishments, character traits, and goals. Self-promotion tactics are used more frequently than ingratiation behaviors. Research has shown that impression management techniques are effective in significantly influencing interviewers' judgments (Stevens & Kristof, 1995).

Impression management
Acting deliberately to make a good impression, to present oneself in the most favorable way.

Unstructured Interviews

Three kinds of interviews used in the business world are the standard or unstructured interview, the patterned or structured interview, and the situational interview.

How Not to Get Hired: Part 2

Would you show up for a job interview wearing a bathing suit? Would you tilt way back in your chair and prop your feet on the interviewer's desk? Yes, people have actually done those things. Here are descriptions of other not-too-bright interview behaviors taken from the files of corporate interviewers.

- The reason the applicant took so long to answer my question became apparent when he began to snore.
- When I gave the applicant my business card at the beginning of the interview, she immediately crumpled it and tossed it in the wastebasket.
- The interview was going well until the applicant told me that he and his friends always wore the clothing my company manufactured. At that point I told him that we made office products, not clothing.
- She had arranged for a pizza to be delivered to my office during the interview.
- Without asking if I objected, he casually lit a cigar and tossed the match onto the carpet. He did not seem to understand why his behavior annoyed me.
- The applicant was asked to bring a resume and two references to the interview. She arrived with resume in hand—and two friends!

Unstructured interviews
Interviews in which the format and questions asked are left to the discretion of the interviewer.

The **unstructured interview** can be described as an interview that lacks advance planning. Sometimes it is little more than a general conversation. The format and the questions asked are left to the discretion of the interviewer. It is possible, therefore, that five interviewers conducting separate unstructured interviews with the same applicant will receive five different impressions.

Thus, a basic weakness of the unstructured interview is its lack of consistency in assessing candidates. Interviewers may be interested in different aspects of an applicant's background, experience, or attitudes. The recommendations of the interviewer may then reflect more of the biases and prejudices of the interviewers than the objective qualifications of the applicants.

A now-classic study on this topic, published in 1929, asked 12 interviewers independently to rate 57 applicants on their suitability for a sales job (Hollingworth, 1929). Although the interviewers were experienced sales managers who had conducted many interviews with job applicants, there was a significant lack of agreement among them. Some applicants who were ranked first by one interviewer were ranked last by another. The results of the judgments made about a single applicant are shown in Figure 3–1. You can see that the ratings for this person range from a low of 1 to a high of 55. This information would be of little help to a manager trying to decide whether to hire this applicant because it offers no firm basis on which to judge the person's suitability.

In addition to a lack of consistency, or reliability, the predictive validity of the unstructured interview is low. This was demonstrated decades ago by Walter

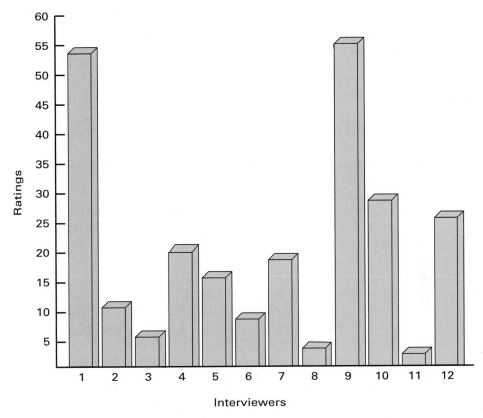

FIGURE 3–1.   Ratings of 1 applicant by 12 interviewers. (Data from H. L. Hollingworth, *Vocational psychology and character analysis.* New York: Appleton, 1929.)

Dill Scott, mentioned in Chapter 1 as a founder of the field of industrial psychology. Scott's conclusion has been supported by considerable empirical research.

Training interviewers in the kinds of questions to ask and how to ask them can improve the usefulness of the unstructured interview. A study of 364 interviewer evaluations showed that trained interviewers were far less likely to digress into conversation about non-job related issues than were untrained interviewers. In addition, trained interviewers elicited more pertinent information from the job applicants, information that could be used as the basis for deciding whether to offer the applicants jobs (Stevens, 1998).

Despite the recognized limitations of low reliability and validity, unstructured interviews are still used far too often by employing organizations.

Structured Interviews

The **structured interview** uses a predetermined list of questions that are asked of every applicant. Thus, the interview procedure is standardized so that the resulting assessment of the job candidates is less open to interviewer bias.

In conducting a structured interview, the interviewer follows a printed form that contains the questions to be asked. The applicant's responses are recorded

Structured interviews Interviews that use a predetermined list of questions that are asked of every person applying for a particular job.

on the same form. The interview session has been described as more like an elaborate application blank that the interviewer completes on the basis of what the applicant says.

The following structured interview questions are typical of those used by an organization selecting college graduates for management positions. Because the items deal with work experience, they are intended for graduates who have held at least one job since graduation:

1. What was your first job after completing college?
2. What were your major accomplishments on that job?
3. What were some of the things you did less well, things that point to the need for further training and development?
4. What did you learn about yourself on that job?
5. What aspects of the job did you find most challenging?
6. What sort of work would you like to be doing five years from now?

Because all applicants are asked the questions in the same sequence, there is a more reliable basis for comparison of the candidates than with the random questioning procedures of the unstructured interview.

Structured interviews are a considerable improvement over unstructured interviews and have the potential for higher predictive validity. Research has shown that structured interviews can be as valid predictors of job success as cognitive ability tests. Structured interviews are high in reliability as well. One study found that even when structured interviews were conducted over the telephone instead of face-to-face, they were as effective in predicting subsequent job performance as were traditional structured in-person interviews (Schmidt & Rader, 1999).

Therefore, the interview is a more useful selection technique if it is formalized and structured. If your career should take you into management and make you responsible for selecting employees to hire, you will want to choose techniques that you can count on to help you make the best prediction about who is likely to succeed on the job.

Situational Interviews

Situational interviews Interviews that focus not on personal characteristics or work experience but on the behaviors needed for successful job performance.

A **situational interview** is developed specifically to meet the requirements of a particular job. The interview questions are not designed to inquire about general work experience or personal characteristics and abilities but, rather, about the specific behaviors needed for successful performance of the job in question. These behaviors are determined by a job analysis conducted by the critical-incidents technique.

The first step in developing the situational interview is to prepare a list of critical incidents that differentiate between successful and unsuccessful employees currently on the job. These incidents are typically identified by supervisors who have a comprehensive knowledge of the job. The supervisors determine benchmarks for scoring the incidents, assigning a score of 5 to those behaviors displayed by successful employees, 3 to behaviors displayed by average employees, and 1 to behaviors displayed by poor employees. The incidents are rephrased as questions to be asked in the situational interview, and therefore they represent issues directly related to how an applicant would behave on the job. The numerical benchmarks make it possible to score the interview objectively.

Once constructed, situational interviews are easy to administer and interpret. Because the interview questions are clearly and directly related to job behaviors, this kind of situation can increase the motivation of job applicants to answer accurately and completely.

Situational interviews are used most often to select workers for skilled and semiskilled factory jobs, for sales jobs, and for first-line supervisory positions. Situational interview results correlate positively with measures of later job performance and, in some instances, are more valid than structured interviews.

Online Interviews

Online interviewing uses computer software to conduct the initial interview. Applicants answer a fixed sequence of multiple-choice questions. All applicants for a specific position are asked the same questions in the same order. Questions on sensitive issues, if appropriate, can be included in an online interview, whereas many interviewers are hesitant to ask about personal matters in the traditional face-to-face interview situation. Corporate users of online interviews report that most applicants are comfortable with this type of screening and are willing to respond with honesty and candor.

Online interviews are now conducted routinely by Target, Macy's, Home Depot, and other large retailing chains. Home Depot has placed computer kiosks in its stores where job applicants can complete an interview in less than an hour. The online presentation includes psychological tests, and a video provides a realistic preview of the job's demands. The company reported that turnover dropped by more than 11% during the first year of the online interview program. Also, managers saved time since they no longer had to interview applicants and score tests. Personal interviews are used only for those applicants who complete and pass the online screening (Richtel, 2000).

Influences on Interviewer Judgments

We discuss three factors that can bias an interviewer's judgment about a job applicant: (1) prior information, (2) the contrast effect, and (3) interviewers' prejudices. These influences can be reduced or minimized by training interviewers to recognize their effects.

Prior Information.   Interviewers generally have some prior information about job candidates, such as recruiter evaluations, application blanks, online screening results, or the results of psychological tests. The nature of that prior information can predispose an interviewer to have a favorable or unfavorable attitude toward an applicant before he or she even shows up for the interview.

In one study, 90 interviewers from 54 companies conducted on-campus interviews with 691 job candidates. Some of the applicants had been prescreened, and some had not. The prescreened applicants had been recommended for the interviews by the company recruiters. The unscreened applicants had been selected for the interview by means of a lottery. The interviewers judged applicants who had passed the preliminary recruitment screening much more favorably than the unknown applicants selected by lottery (Cable & Gilovich, 1998).

In another study, three interviewers for a large energy corporation received application blank and test score data on 79 applicants prior to their interviews. Toward applicants the interviewers were already impressed with because of favorable prior information, the interviewers behaved differently than they did toward those applicants they found not so impressive. Interviewers showed more approval for candidates whose prior information was favorable. The interviewers' behavior was more encouraging, understanding, and friendly. Interviewers also spent more time selling the company and providing job information to the more impressive applicants, as well as less time soliciting information from them, than they did to applicants who had less favorable prior information (Dougherty, Turban, & Callender, 1994).

The Contrast Effect. Interviewers see many job applicants, often one after another, and how they evaluate a particular applicant may depend on their standards of comparison; that is, the characteristics of the applicants they interviewed previously. For example, after having interviewed three undesirable candidates, an interviewer may rate the next candidate in line as more favorable than the candidate's qualifications merit. That same average candidate may be rated less favorably if the previous candidates have all been highly qualified.

Not only does this contrast tendency highlight the importance of your place in an interviewer's schedule, it also means, as we noted earlier, that interviewers do not always have objective standards for the type of person considered to be a suitable employee. Applicants are not evaluated on an absolute basis, or on their merits alone, but are judged relative to the other applicants interviewed during the same time period. Thus, the standard for the acceptable employee may frequently change.

Interviewers' Prejudices. Another characteristic of interviewers that affects their judgment is their personal likes and dislikes. For example, men sometimes think that women employees are incapable of performing certain jobs. Interviewers of both sexes are more likely to hire women for so-called traditional female jobs, such as schoolteacher or nurse, than for traditional male jobs, such as those in management or engineering. Conversely, some female interviewers are reluctant to consider men for teaching or counseling jobs.

Racial and ethnic prejudice can skew interviewers' evaluations of job candidates, although this bias is not quite as strong today as it was toward previous generations of employees. A meta-analysis of 31 studies involving interview data on 4,169 black job applicants, 1,200 Hispanic applicants, and 6,307 white applicants found that interviewer ratings were only about one-fourth of a standard deviation lower for the minority applicants. These differences varied, however, with the complexity of the job for which the applicant was interviewing. When jobs of low complexity, such as custodian or mill worker, were considered separately, the interview ratings for minority applicants were noticeably lower than those for white applicants. But in companies that used structured rather than unstructured interviews, racial differences were minimized. The structured interview limited the possible biasing effect of racial and ethnic stereotypes (Huffcutt & Roth, 1998).

A study of four-member panel interviews of 153 police officers applying for promotion showed a racial biasing effect. With racially balanced interview panels (two black raters and two white raters), individual interviewers gave significantly higher ratings to candidates of the same race. When the majority of the panel members were white, white candidates received significantly higher ratings from both black raters and white raters. When the majority of the panel members were black, black candidates received higher ratings from both black raters and white raters, although, in this instance, the differences were not statistically significant (Prewett-Livingston, Feild, Veres, & Lewis, 1996).

Thus, interviewers may prejudge applicants who display certain qualities or traits and refuse to consider their other abilities or characteristics. They may also recommend hiring some applicants merely because they display some quality the interviewers like, such as a shared interest in baseball, even though it may bear no relation to job performance.

The phenomenon of generalizing from one trait or characteristic to the entire person in a positive or a negative direction is called the **halo effect.** It influences the decision-making process whenever people have to make personal judgments about others.

Halo effect The tendency to judge all aspects of a person's behavior or character on the basis of a single attribute.

As difficult and error-prone as the interview can be, it remains part of virtually every selection program in business, industry, education, and government. The danger lies in placing too much emphasis on its results. If used wisely, however, and in conjunction with other valid selection measures, the interview can be of help to both organization and applicant. Its predictive accuracy can be greatly improved by the use of structured and situational techniques and by appropriate training of interviewers.

REFERENCES AND LETTERS OF RECOMMENDATION

At one time, employee selection programs routinely involved obtaining information about job applicants from persons who knew something about the applicants' background, skills, and work history, such as former teachers, employers, co-workers, and friends. The purpose was to examine other people's impressions of the applicants and to verify the information the applicants reported.

A major limitation of these references was that they often presented a false picture of the applicant. The person providing the reference—whether in a letter, in person, or in a telephone interview—sometimes deliberately responded in a misleading manner for several reasons. Past employers wanted to be kind and to say only favorable things about former employees. Current employers who hoped to get rid of undesirable employees wrote glowing letters of recommendation. Professors wrote positive letters because they knew that students would be able to read their files in the university placement center.

A more important limitation on the usefulness of references is that many organizations are no longer willing to supply evaluative information about former employees for fear of lawsuits. If a company makes a false statement about why a former employee was fired, for example, the employee can sue the company for defamation of character. Thousands of such lawsuits have been filed against U.S. corporations. The mere threat of legal action has prevented many companies from cooperating in even the most basic reference checking effort.

Companies are advised to refuse to reveal any information about former employees beyond dates of employment, job title, and final salary. If a company chooses to discuss the job performance of a fired employee, it should have for its own protection written evidence from objective performance appraisals citing specific instances documented by date, time, and place. In addition, managers

NEWSBREAK

A Deadly Recommendation

Around the Allstate Insurance Company office in Tampa, Florida, where he worked, Paul Calder had frequently seemed to be acting weird. He told people he was an alien. He wrote *blood* and other strange words on his computer screen and refused to let the boss see them. He threatened to kill a masseuse who refused to give him a refund. And then he brought a gun to work.

"I was reasonably sure I had a total lunatic on my hands," his boss said. "A nut case."

The boss was afraid to fire Calder because he believed the employee was capable of killing him and others in the office, but he knew somehow he had to get rid of Calder. So he made up a story about a corporate restructuring that would eliminate Calder's job and offered him severance pay if he would resign. When Calder chose to resign, the boss wrote him a letter of recommendation that was bland and innocuous, as most such letters are nowadays. It did not indicate that there was anything at all wrong with Paul Calder.

The letter said Calder resigned because of organizational restructuring and that his resignation "is in no way a reflection upon Paul's job performance."

To do otherwise—to put an employee's faults and failings on paper—is to open yourself and your organization to a lawsuit for libel or slander. It has become prudent in corporate life today to say nothing about an ex-employee but the bare facts: job title and dates of employment.

Paul Calder found a job with another Tampa insurance company, but his bizarre behavior continued and he was fired. Several months later, he returned to that office to see the people who had fired him. He carried a 9mm handgun. He killed three men and wounded two women, then drove to nearby Clearwater and killed himself.

The families of the murdered employees filed a multi-million dollar lawsuit against Allstate—Calder's original employer—for failing to disclose the problems with Calder's behavior. Allstate was sued for writing a misleading letter of recommendation, which, ironically, it wrote out of fear of being sued.

Source: L. Dougherty. Shooting victims' families can sue Allstate. *St. Petersburg (FL) Times*, August 8, 1995.

and supervisors should assume that anything they include in a letter of recommendation may one day be scrutinized by a judge and jury.

Even though the amount and kind of information obtained from references is minimal, many employers still make at least a cursory attempt to check references. Because of the legal complications, however, they are used less frequently today as a selection technique than in the past.

ASSESSMENT CENTERS

The **assessment center** is a widely used method of selection that places candidates who are being considered for hiring or for promotion in a simulated job situation so that their behavior under stress can be observed and evaluated. This approach, initially called **situational testing,** was developed by the German army in the 1920s to select officer candidates of high quality. It was first used extensively in the United States by psychologists during World War II when it was adopted as a selection technique by the Office of Strategic Services (OSS), the forerunner of today's Central Intelligence Agency (CIA).

Assessment centers usually involve 6 to 12 candidates at a time who are evaluated as they work through a series of exercises over several days. Candidates are interviewed extensively and may be given intelligence and personality tests, but most of their time is devoted to exercises designed to simulate the actual problems of high-level jobs. The major techniques for eliciting these work samples are the in-basket exercise and the leaderless group discussion.

Assessment center A method of selection and training that involves a simulated job situation in which candidates deal with actual job problems.

Situational testing An early term for the assessment-center technique for employee selection and performance appraisal. Employees are placed in a simulated job setting so that their behavior under stress can be observed and evaluated.

The In-Basket Technique

The **in-basket technique** presents each applicant with the sort of in-basket that is found on virtually every managerial desk, whether in the form of a work tray or in the files on a computer. The in-basket used in the assessment center exercise contains the typical problems, questions, and directives that managers would expect to find when they returned to the office from vacation. The applicants must process this material in a fixed period of time, demonstrating precisely how they would handle the questions and problems on the job. After the exercise, they may be required to justify their decisions during interviews with the assessors.

In-basket technique An assessment center exercise that requires job applicants to process memos, letters, and directives found in a typical manager's in-basket.

The program at AT&T relies heavily on the in-basket exercise. Each candidate, playing the role of a manager, must process 25 items (e-mail messages, executive orders, and correspondence) in 3 hours. Trained assessors observe the candidates to see if they are systematic, establish priorities, delegate authority to subordinates, or become enmeshed in trivialities.

Leaderless Group Discussions

In the **leaderless group discussion,** the applicants meet as a group to discuss an actual business problem. For example, they may be given information about a group of subordinates from among whom they must select one for promotion. As the meeting proceeds, the behavior of the candidates is observed to see how they interact and what leadership and communications skills each person displays.

Leaderless group discussion An assessment center exercise in which job applicants meet to discuss an actual business problem under the pressure of time. Usually, a leader emerges from the group to guide the discussion.

In the leaderless group discussion exercise at AT&T, a group of six candidates are told that they are managers of a corporation and are directed to increase profits in a fixed period. They are given information about the company and the market, but no one person is appointed leader and no rules are established about how to accomplish their goal. Usually, one candidate assumes the leader's role, and that person's capabilities can be evaluated. The other group members are assessed on their cooperation in performing the tasks assigned to them by the leader.

To induce additional pressure, participants are notified frequently of changes in costs or market conditions, sometimes immediately after the total problem has been solved. The new information must be processed and incorporated into the planning. All the while, the clock ticks, the assessors watch, and the stress mounts. Some participants become angry, disrupting the group's ability to function cohesively. The contrast between those who can operate well under stress and those who cannot becomes obvious.

Assessment centers also use oral presentations and role playing. In the oral presentation exercise, candidates are given a packet of information about some aspect of corporate operations, such as the development of a new product or a new sales campaign. They must organize this material and present it to the group, a task typical of executive responsibilities. In role playing, the candidate acts out the role of manager in a simulated job situation, showing, for example, how he or she would conduct a job interview, fire an incompetent worker, or deal with an irate boss.

Computers and video cameras can be used in assessment centers as a way of reducing costs. Information is provided to the candidates on computer terminals. The assessors videotape the candidates' behavior for later and more extensive evaluation.

In another variation of the assessment-center method, candidates are presented with a written description of a typical job problem and must select from among five alternatives offered the way in which they would most likely or least likely solve the problem. Research conducted in seven retail organizations with almost 4,000 employees found that their scores on a 40-item paper-and-pencil test assessing their probable behavior in a variety of problem-solving situations showed a significant positive correlation with their later job performance (Weekly & Jones, 1999).

Predictive Validity of Assessment Centers

Although researchers are not certain which attributes or dimensions of behavior are being evaluated by the assessment-center situation, they have found the techniques to be useful in predicting subsequent job success. For example, a 10-year follow-up study of 206 managers at a large insurance company found that their assessment-center ratings for career motivation predicted their actual career advancement more effectively than did ratings of their knowledge and skills (Jones & Whitmore, 1995).

Also, research has indicated that performance on assessment-center tasks tends to demonstrate fewer differences in leadership behaviors and skills between black applicants and white applicants than is shown on tests of cognitive ability. One study of more than 600 managers from seven organizations found no significant differences in the management skills of black managers and white managers (Goldstein, Yusko, Braverman, Smith, & Chung, 1998). I-O psychologists have concluded that assessment-center exercises may be a more equitable way to evaluate the management skills of candidates of different racial and ethnic backgrounds because they focus directly on a person's ability to perform the necessary job-related tasks.

Employee Attitudes toward Assessment Centers

Some job candidates, particularly those who perform poorly, resent assessment-center exercises. Many people believe that a poor evaluation in an assessment center marks the end of their career, no matter how excellent a record they have compiled in their years with the company. Some candidates believe that success in the assessment center depends more on being articulate and personable than on actual competence at managerial tasks. There may be some truth to these charges. Interpersonal skills do count strongly in these assessments, and active and forceful participation is rewarded. However, assessment-center ratings are also based on organizational and decision-making skills, as well as on motivation.

Participation in assessment centers can lead to changes in candidates' perceptions of their interpersonal and administrative skills. Those who perform well tend to believe they have the ability to develop and refine their skills. Those who do poorly tend to have lowered expectations for promotion. In this sense, assessment centers serve as a realistic job preview, demonstrating to applicants what life as a manager or executive would be like.

The assessment-center experience also serves as a training exercise. Candidates can develop and refine their managerial and interpersonal skills by using the feedback they receive from the assessors.

Assessment Centers

Performance on assessment-center exercises can be a highly valid predictor of job success, particularly for managers and executives. Candidates in assessment centers are observed by trained assessors (usually company managers) while they perform a variety of tasks that simulate on-the-job problems. They are interviewed extensively and usually given personality and cognitive ability tests.

The assessment-center technique is expensive and time-consuming. Managers must take time away from their regular duties to be trained in observation and assessment techniques and, later, to evaluate the candidates. These demands on managers led I-O psychologists to ask whether similarly valid results could be obtained if candidates assessed themselves and their peers instead of being assessed by company managers.

To answer this question, the psychologists monitored the progress of 394 men and women employees of a large oil company who had been nominated by their immediate supervisors to participate in an assessment center. The assessment-center exercises were designed to identify management potential early in an employee's career. The candidates were from different divisions of the company, and the majority of them did not know one another before attending the assessment center. Thus, they had few preconceived notions about the abilities of the other participants.

The candidates participated in both group and individual exercises and completed tests of reasoning, quantitative ability, reading speed and comprehension, and personality. Their performance on the assessment-center exercises was rated by three trained manager-assessors on a 5-point scale from 1 (low) to 5 (high). The candidates rated their peers (in groups of 6 or 12) on six dimensions, plus an overall evaluation, such as "best bet for top management responsibility." The candidates made self-rankings on the same dimensions, assigning themselves to the top, middle, or lower third of the group.

Assessors did not use peer ratings or self-ratings to determine a candidate's management potential. They used their own performance ratings and the test scores in deciding whether to recommend a candidate for promotion. The criterion used by the psychologists to measure job advancement was the job level attained 5 to 10 years after the assessment-center evaluation.

The results showed that the peer assessments were the best predictor of job advancement. These evaluations had been based almost solely on the candidates' contact with one another during the assessment-center experience. Further, the candidates had been given no training in assessment methods.

The psychologists suggested that one reason for the greater predictive validity of peer assessments was that the behavior of the candidates in the exercises directly influenced the behavior of their peers. In other words, the candidates, as members of the same work group, were in a position to see how effective or ineffective the others in their group were in handling management situations and how the actions of each group member affected the candidates personally.

The manager-assessors, on the other hand, were observing the candidates' behavior without being directly affected by it. Thus, the peer experience may have led to more useful insights into what it would be like to work with each person. The results raise the following question: If such peer ratings can effectively predict management potential and job advancement, are trained manager-assessors really necessary?

Think About It

1. If you were in charge of the assessment center for your company, would you eliminate, based on the results of this study, the use of managers as assessors and substitute peer evaluations? Why or why not?
2. Based on our discussion of the experimental method (Chapter 2), what criticisms would you make of this study? How would you de-

Source: T. H. Shore, L. M. Shore, & G. C. Thornton III. (1992). Construct validity of self- and peer evaluations of performance dimensions in an assessment center. *Journal of Applied Psychology, 77,* 42–54.

sign a study to investigate assessor, peer, and self-ratings in assessment centers?

3. What factors other than assessment-center performance could have influenced the peer evaluations? What factors can influence ratings made by manager-assessors?

4. What are the advantages of using managers as assessors?

5. If you were a candidate for promotion and knew that your career advancement depended on your performance in the assessment center, would you prefer to be evaluated by your peers or by trained assessors? What are the reasons for your choice?

6. What are the advantages and disadvantages of assessment centers for selecting employees?

SUMMARY

The proper selection of employees—matching the right person with the right job—is a complex process. Problems of organizational entry involve the applicant's preferences and expectations as well as the company's recruiting efforts. Because our first job experience influences the rest of our working life, it is important that our expectations match the realities of the job. This can be accomplished through a **realistic job preview.**

An employee selection program requires job and work analysis, establishing requirements and cutoff scores, recruiting, administering selection devices, and validating the selection devices by determining how they correlate with measures of subsequent job performance.

Equal employment opportunity legislation mandates fair employment practices in hiring. Selection techniques should be job-related and should minimize **adverse impact** on minority groups. Companies must also try to prevent **reverse discrimination** against qualified members of the majority group. Fair employment practices appear to have had a minimal impact on organizational effectiveness. Targets of discrimination include minorities, older workers, women, disabled persons, homosexuals, unattractive or overweight people, or those with genetic predispositions to certain diseases.

Job analysis involves a detailed description of the component tasks performed on a job. Job analysts can use already published work analyses available on O*NET, interview the people directly concerned with the job, observe workers performing the job, have workers keep a systematic activity log, or record critical incidents related to successful job performance. On the basis of the information collected, a job specification can be written that defines the characteristics to be sought in job applicants.

Application blanks on paper or online provide information about job candidates that can be directly related to their probability of success on the job. Weighted application blanks and **biographical inventories** are useful in predicting job success and are similar to psychological tests in objectivity and types of questions. Because many companies are reluctant to release information on former employees for fear of lawsuits, it can be difficult to confirm the accuracy of information provided on applications.

Although the face-to-face or online interview consistently receives unfavorable evaluations in research on employee selection, most companies continue to use it. The weakest type of interview is the **unstructured interview;** the **structured interview** is a more valid predictive device. Weaknesses of interviews are failure of interviewers to agree on the merits of a job candidate, failure of interviews to predict job success, subjectivity of interviewers' standards of comparison, and interviewers' personal prejudices. In the **situational interview,** questions relating to actual job behaviors are developed from a critical-incidents job analysis; this may be the most valid type of interview for predicting an applicant's potential for job success. The halo effect and the contrast effect can also bias interviewers' judgments.

Letters of recommendation are part of most employee selection programs, despite the recognized tendency of writers to be overly kind and the reluctance of employers to reveal more than basic, factual information in order to avoid lawsuits.

In **assessment centers**, used primarily for managerial and executive positions, job candidates perform exercises that realistically simulate problems found on the job. Using the **in-basket technique,** the **leaderless group discussion,** oral presentations, and **role playing,** applicants are assessed by trained managers on their interpersonal skills and their leadership and decision-making abilities.

KEY TERMS

adverse impact
assessment centers
biographical inventories
critical-incidents technique
halo effect
impression management
in-basket technique
job analysis
leaderless group discussion

realistic job previews
reverse discrimination
selection ratio
situational interviews
situational testing
structured interviews
unstructured interviews
work analysis

ADDITIONAL READING

Barber, A. E., Wesson, M. J., Roberson, Q. M., & Taylor, M. S. (1999). A tale of two job markets: Organizational size and its effects on hiring practices and job search behavior. *Personnel Psychology, 52,* 841–867. Investigates employee preferences for large versus small companies and discusses how this factor can influence organizational recruiting.

Hough, L. M., & Oswald, F. L. (2000). Personnel selection. *Annual Review of Psychology, 51,* 631–664. Reviews current research on personnel selection issues including job analysis, interviews, assessment centers, validity generalization, and adverse impact, and the use of personality predictors.

Huffcutt, A. I., & Roth, P. L. (1998). Racial group differences in employment interview evaluations. *Journal of Applied Psychology, 83,* 179–189. Assesses differences in interview ratings given to White, Black, and Hispanic job applicants.

Kraut, A. I., & Korman, A. K. (Eds.). (1999). *Evolving practices in human resource management: Responses to a changing world of work.* San Francisco: Jossey-Bass. Includes chapters on job and work analysis, recruitment programs, applicant assessment, and other employee selection issues for the 21st century.

Kravitz, D. A., & Klineberg, S. L. (2000). Reactions to two versions of affirmative action among Whites, Blacks, and Hispanics. *Journal of Applied Psychology, 85,* 597–611. Reviews responses of American-born White, Black, and Hispanic job applicants in the Houston, Texas, area to different types of affirmative-action recruitment plans.

Peterson, N. G., Mumford, M. D., Borman, W. C., Jeanneret, P. R., & Fleishman, E. A. (Eds). (1999). *An occupational information system for the 21st century: The development of O*NET*. Washington, D.C.: American Psychological Association. Describes the development and validation of this global data base of job descriptions, the successor to the *Dictionary of Occupational Titles* (DOT).

Psychological Testing

CHAPTER OUTLINE

If you think you'll be finished taking tests when you graduate from college, think again. You will be expected to take tests for many more years. How well you perform on them can determine the path of your career, and even your life. Do you plan to continue your education in graduate school to get a master's degree in psychology? Perhaps a law degree or an MBA? Graduate and professional schools all have admissions and certification tests.

Do you expect to find a full-time job right after graduation? Few organizations will be interested in hiring you until they see how you score on their tests for job applicants. Once you're hired, you'll be asked to test for training programs and possible promotions. Even NFL football teams administer psychological tests to prospective players. One uses personality tests to detect whether a player might tend to be overly aggressive and likely to cause trouble on or off the field.

Psychological testing is big business in today's workplaces. I-O psychologists are responsible for designing, standardizing, and scoring the tests that will play an important part in your future.

> **ONLINE!** For general information about tests, log on to the American Psychological Association's FAQ site at *www.apa.org/science/ test.html*. Just for fun, try *www.davideck.com* for online tests of personality, intelligence, health, and career interests. This site has some surprises, too.

PRINCIPLES OF PSYCHOLOGICAL TESTING

Carefully developed and researched psychological tests have several characteristics that set them apart from the tests published in the Sunday newspaper or on a self-help Web site, the ones that ask "Are You a Good Spouse?" or "What Is Your Sex Quotient?" A good test involves more than a list of questions that appear to be relevant to the variable being measured. A proper psychological test is standardized, objective, based on sound norms, reliable, and valid.

Standardization

Standardization refers to the consistency or uniformity of the conditions and procedures for administering a psychological test. If we expect to compare the performance of several job applicants on the same test, then they must all take that test under identical circumstances. This means that every student or job applicant taking the test reads or listens to the same set of instructions, is allowed the same amount of time in which to respond, and is situated in a similar physical environment.

Any change in testing procedure may produce a change in individual test performance. For example, if the air conditioning system in the testing room breaks down during a summer day, the people taking the test may not perform as well as people who took the test under more comfortable conditions. If an

Standardization The consistency or uniformity of the conditions and procedures for administering a psychological test.

inexperienced or careless tester fails to read the complete instructions to a group of job applicants, then those applicants are not taking the test under the same conditions as other applicants.

Appropriate testing procedures can be designed into a test by its developers, but maintaining standardized conditions is the responsibility of the persons administering the test. Therefore, the training of test administrators in proper procedures is vital. An excellent test can be rendered useless by an untrained or inattentive tester.

Computer technology is helping to maintain standardized conditions of test administration. Organizations are increasingly using computer-assisted testing to ensure that everyone taking the test receives the same instructions in the same format.

Objectivity

Objectivity refers primarily to the scoring of the test results. For a test to be scored objectively, it is necessary that everyone scoring the test obtain the same results. The scoring process must be free of subjective judgments or biases on the part of the scorer.

Objective tests Tests for which the scoring process is free of personal judgment or bias.

In your college career you have taken both objective and subjective examinations. With **objective tests** (such as those containing multiple-choice and true-false items) scoring is a mechanical process that requires no special training or knowledge. A clerk in a company's human resources department, an undergraduate grader in the psychology department, or a computer program can score an objective test accurately as long as a scoring key with the correct answers has been provided.

Subjective tests Tests that contain items such as essay questions. The scoring process can be influenced by the personal characteristics and attitudes of the scorer.

Scoring **subjective tests** (such as those containing essay questions) is more difficult, and the results can be influenced by the scorer's personal characteristics, including a like or dislike for the person who took the test. For a fair and equitable assessment of a job applicant, then, an objective test is more desirable.

Test Norms

To interpret the results of a psychological test, a frame of reference or point of comparison must be established so that the performance of one person can be compared with the performance of others. This is accomplished by means of the

Test norms The distribution of test scores of a large group of people similar in nature to the job applicants being tested.

Standardization sample The group of subjects used to establish test norms. The scores of the standardization sample serve as the point of comparison for determining the relative standing of the persons being tested.

test norms, the distribution of scores of a large group of people similar in nature to the job applicants being tested. The scores of this group, called the **standardization sample,** serve as the point of comparison in determining the relative standing of the applicants on the ability being tested.

Suppose a high school graduate applies for a job that requires mechanical skills and achieves a score of 82 on a test of mechanical ability. This score, alone, tells us nothing about the level of the applicant's skill, but if we compare that score of 82 with the test norms—the distribution of scores on the test from a large group of high school graduates—then we can ascribe some meaning to the individual score.

If the mean of the test norms is 80 and the standard deviation is 10, we know immediately that an applicant who scores 82 has only an average or moderate amount of mechanical ability. With this comparative information, we are in a better position to evaluate objectively the applicant's chances of succeeding on the job relative to the other applicants tested.

The most widely used psychological tests have sets of norms for men and women, for different age groups, for various racial and ethnic groups, and for levels of education. The adequacy of a test's norms can determine its usefulness in any employee selection program.

Reliability

Reliability refers to the consistency or stability of response on a test. If a group takes a cognitive ability test one week and achieves a mean score of 100, and repeats the test a week later and earns a mean score of 72, we would have to conclude that something is wrong. We would describe the test as unreliable because it yields inconsistent measurements. It is common to find a slight variation in test scores when a test is retaken at a later date, but if the fluctuation is great, something is amiss with the test or the scoring method.

> **Reliability** The consistency or stability of a response on a psychological test.

Three ways to determine reliability are the test-retest method, the equivalent-forms method, and the split-halves method. The **test-retest method** involves administering a test twice to the same group of people and correlating the two sets of scores. The closer the correlation coefficient (called, in this case, the reliability coefficient) approaches a perfect positive correlation of +1.00, the more reliable the test is considered to be. In choosing a test for employee selection, the reliability coefficient ideally should exceed +.80, although in practice a value of approximately +.70 is considered acceptable. This method has several limitations, however. It is uneconomical to ask employees to take time from their jobs to take the test twice. Also, the effects of learning (remembering the test questions) and the influence of other experiences between the two testing sessions may cause the group to score higher the second time.

> **Test-retest method** A way to determine test reliability that involves administering a new test twice to the same group of subjects and correlating the two sets of scores.

The **equivalent-forms method** for determining reliability also uses a test-retest approach, but instead of using the same test a second time, a similar form of the test is administered. The disadvantage of the equivalent-forms method is that it is difficult and costly to develop two separate and equivalent tests.

> **Equivalent-forms method** A way to determine test reliability that involves administering similar forms of a new test to the same group of subjects and correlating the two sets of scores.

In the **split-halves method,** the test is taken once, the items are divided in half, and the two sets of scores are correlated. This method is less time-consuming than the other methods because only one administration of the test is required. There is no opportunity for learning or recall to influence the second score.

> **Split-halves method** A way to determine test reliability that involves administering a new test to a group of subjects, dividing in half the total number of items, and correlating the two sets of scores.

Validity

Validity is the most important requirement for a psychological test or any other selection device; that is, the test or selection device must be shown to measure what it is intended to measure. I-O psychologists consider several different kinds of validity.

> **Validity** The determination of whether a psychological test or other selection device measures what it is intended to measure.

Criterion-Related Validity. Suppose that an I-O psychologist working for the U.S. Air Force develops a test to measure the proficiency of radar operators. The test will be considered valid if it measures those skills needed for competent performance on the job. One way to determine this is to correlate test scores with some measure, or criterion, of subsequent job performance. If persons who score high on the radar operator proficiency test also perform well on the job, and if those who score low on the test perform poorly on the job, then the validity coefficient between test scores and job performance will be high. We will know that the test truly measures the skills needed to be a good radar operator and is a valid predictor of job success. Validity coefficients of +.30 to +.40 are considered acceptable for employee selection tests.

This approach to defining and establishing validity is called **criterion-related validity.** It is not concerned with the nature or properties of the test itself but rather with the relationship between test scores and later measures of job performance.

Two approaches to establishing criterion-related validity are predictive validity and concurrent validity. **Predictive validity** involves administering the new test to all job applicants for a specified period and hiring them all, regardless of their test scores. At a later date, when some measure of job performance, such as production figures or supervisor ratings, can be obtained on each worker, the test scores and the job performance criteria are correlated to determine how well the test predicted job success. In most organizations, however, top management is unwilling to use this approach because obviously some of the people hired will turn out to be poor workers.

Concurrent validity is more popular with management than is predictive validity. It involves giving the test to employees already on the job and correlating the scores with job performance data. The disadvantage of this method is that by testing only current workers, the validation sample contains mostly the better employees. Poorer workers will probably already have quit or been fired, demoted, or transferred. Therefore, it is difficult to establish by the concurrent validity method whether the test is truly distinguishing between good and poor workers.

Another problem with concurrent validity is that applicants for a job and employees already on the job have different motivations and are likely to perform differently on psychological tests. Applicants may be more highly motivated to perform well on employment tests than current workers, who may feel more secure in their work situation.

The job performance criterion most often used in the establishment of criterion-related validity is ratings assigned by a supervisor to an employee's present level of job performance. Such ratings are made routinely as part of the employee performance appraisal process for all types of jobs. (We discuss performance appraisal in Chapter 5.)

Rational Validity.   I-O psychologists are also interested in **rational validity,** the kind of validity that relates to the nature, properties, and content of a test, independent of its relationship to measures of job performance. In some employment situations it is not feasible to establish criterion-related validity, perhaps because the company is too small to support the expensive and time-consuming validation process or because the job has no precedent. In the initial selection of the original U.S. astronauts, for example, before any space flights had taken place, there were no measures of job performance that could be correlated with test scores.

Two approaches to establishing the rational validity of a test are content validity and construct validity. In **content validity,** the test items are assessed to ensure that they adequately sample the knowledge or skills the test is designed to measure. This assessment can be accomplished by conducting a job analysis and determining if the test items are related to all those abilities needed to per-

Criterion-related validity A type of validity concerned with the relationship between test scores and subsequent job performance.

Predictive validity An approach to establishing criterion-related validity in which a new test is administered to all job applicants, and all applicants are hired, regardless of test scores. Later, when a measure of job performance can be obtained, test scores are correlated with job performance to see how well the test predicted job success.

Concurrent validity A way to establish criterion-related validity that involves administering a test to employees on the job and correlating their scores with job performance data.

Rational validity The type of validity that relates to the nature, properties, and content of a test, independent of its relationship to job performance measures.

Content validity A type of validity that assesses test items to ensure that they adequately sample the skills the test is designed to measure.

form the job. With a word-processing job, for example, test questions about word-processing computer software are job-related, whereas questions about musical abilities may not be. In the classroom, if your professor announces that you will be tested on the first three chapters of this book, then questions about information from other chapters would not be considered content valid.

Construct validity is an attempt to determine the psychological characteristics measured by a test. How do we know that a new test developed to measure intelligence or motivation or emotional stability really does so? One way to measure construct validity statistically is to correlate scores on the new test with scores on established tests that are known to measure these variables. If the correlation is high, then we can have some confidence that the new test is measuring the trait it claims to measure.

Construct validity A type of validity that attempts to determine the psychological characteristics measured by a test.

Face Validity. **Face validity** is not a statistical measure but a subjective impression of how well the test items seem to be related to the job in question. Airline pilots would not think it unusual to take tests about mechanics or navigation because these topics are directly related to the job they expect to perform, but they might balk at being asked if they loved their parents or slept with a light on in their room. Such questions might be related to emotional stability, but they do not appear to be related to flying an airplane. If a test lacks face validity, applicants may not take it seriously, and this may lower their test performance.

Face validity A subjective impression of how well test items seem to be related to the requirements of a job.

College students from the United States and from France (a total of 259 subjects) were asked to rate the effectiveness and fairness of several selection procedures, to assess the students' degree of favorability toward the measures. The selection procedures included personality, ability, honesty, and work-sample tests, as well as interviews, résumés, biographical data, references, personal contacts, and handwriting analysis (a selection technique popular in European countries). The single strongest correlate of favorable ratings of these techniques was the face validity of the measures (Steiner & Gilliland, 1996).

The best psychological tests include in their manuals the results of validation studies. Without this information, the human resources or personnel manager can have little confidence that the tests in the company's employee selection program are actually measuring the qualities and abilities being sought in new employees. Test validation is expensive, but proper validation procedures will more than pay for themselves.

Validity Generalization

Until the late 1970s, I-O psychologists followed a doctrine of "situational specificity," which recommended validating a test in every situation—that is, every job and every organization—for which it was chosen as a selection device. Tests were assumed to be differentially valid. A test appropriate for selecting laboratory technicians in one company was not automatically considered valid for selecting technicians in another company. Therefore, no test could be used with confidence for employee selection without first determining its validity in the given instance, no matter how valid the test had proven for other, similar jobs.

The idea of situational specificity or differential validity has been replaced by **validity generalization.** On the basis of meta-analyses of previous validation studies, I-O psychologists have concluded that tests valid in one situation may

Validity generalization The idea that tests valid in one situation may also be valid in another situation.

also be valid in another situation. In other words, once established, the validity of a test can be generalized (Schmidt et al., 1993).

The Society for Industrial and Organizational Psychology (SIOP) supports validity generalization. It has also been endorsed by the National Academy of Sciences and is included in the Standards for Educational and Psychological Testing of the APA. Validity generalization is widely accepted not only for tests but also for biographical data, assessment centers, interviews, integrity tests, and other selection devices. Many large corporations and government agencies apply the concept of validity generalization in their selection programs.

Validity generalization has important practical implications for psychological testing as an employee selection technique. Organizations have realized that if tests no longer require expensive validation procedures for every job at every level, then they can improve their selection programs by including tests, while saving time and money.

FAIR EMPLOYMENT PRACTICES

One result of fair employment legislation has been an increase in validity research to document whether a test is discriminatory. If studies show that applicants of all races who score below a certain level on a test perform poorly on the job, then the test is not discriminatory by race. I-O psychology research confirms that tests with high validity coefficients have relatively low levels of adverse impact. Criterion-related validation procedures (correlating test scores with job performance measures) are required, when feasible, by the guidelines of the Equal Employment Opportunity Commission (EEOC). Rational validation procedures may also be used to meet EEOC requirements.

A test that is found to be valid for one group is expected to be valid for another. Research has demonstrated that racial differences among average test scores are not the result of test bias but arise from educational, social, and cultural differences. A group of internationally known scientists issued the following statement, published in 1994 in the *Wall Street Journal*:

> Intelligence tests are not culturally biased against American blacks or other native-born, English-speaking peoples in the U.S. Rather, IQ scores predict equally accurately for all such Americans, regardless of race and social class.

A report prepared by the American Psychological Association's Board of Scientific Affairs in 1996 concluded that cognitive ability tests are not biased against African Americans. In other words, the tests do not discriminate against minority groups. Rather, they reflect in quantitative terms the discrimination that has been created by society over time.

However, the empirical demonstration of validity does not guarantee that a test will not be declared discriminatory and barred from further use. This occurred with the General Aptitude Test Battery (GATB) used by the U.S. Employment Service. The GATB is a test of cognitive functioning; it also assesses manual and finger dexterity. More than 750 validity studies have confirmed the high validity of the test as a screening instrument for employment. Test validities for whites and minorities were comparable, although minority job applicants showed lower average scores and hence were less likely to be hired.

To avoid the adverse impact that would result from continued use of the GATB, the U.S. Employment Service adopted the controversial practice of **race norming.** Scores for minority applicants were adjusted upward to equalize hiring rates. Thus, political, social, and legal imperatives were given precedence over scientific ones. The 1991 Civil Rights Act prohibits the practice of race norming, specifically banning any form of score adjustment based on race, color, religion, sex, or national origin.

Race norming A controversial practice, now outlawed, of boosting test scores for minority job applicants to equalize hiring rates.

With race norming outlawed, the technique of **banding** was suggested. This was another attempt to equalize hiring rates by race by compensating for the consistently lower scores obtained by minorities on cognitive ability tests. Let us consider a simplified example. A company's human resources director could examine the test scores of job applicants and decide to band or group together all applicant scores between, say, 91 and 100, calling this range of scores "Band 1." Band 2 would encompass all scores between 81 and 90, Band 3 the scores between 71 and 80, and so on. Of course, any bandwidth could be selected; that is, Band 1 might just as easily include all scores between 81 and 100.

Banding A controversial practice of grouping test scores for minority job applicants to equalize hiring rates.

To equalize hiring rates by race, then, all applicants included in Band 1 would be considered equal in terms of the ability being tested. No distinction would be drawn between the applicant with a score of 100 and the applicant with a score of 91 if both were in the same band. Further, the order of selection within a band would not necessarily be by test score, but, rather, could be by race. Thus, the person who scored 100 would not always be selected over the person who scored 91; within that band, hiring decisions could be made by racial or ethnic background.

A study of 85 candidates for the job of police officer found that black applicants and white applicants held different attitudes toward the idea of banding test scores. Blacks who believed that the purpose of banding was to achieve affirmative action goals rated banding as a fairer employee selection procedure than did applicants who did not agree with that stated purpose. White applicants perceived no difference in fairness in terms of their beliefs about the purpose of banding test scores. In other words, so the researchers concluded, applicants who stood to benefit from banding were more likely to believe it was an equitable technique (Truxillo & Bauer, 1999).

Discrimination against disabled job applicants and employees has been substantially reduced in recent years as a result of EEOC regulations and the Americans with Disabilities Act of 1990. Many psychological tests were modified for disabled persons and have been supported by empirical validation studies.

For visually handicapped persons, test questions can be presented orally, in large print, or in braille, and people can be allowed more time in which to complete the test. Test questions relating to color, shape, and texture cannot be used with persons who were born without sight and have never seen colors and objects. Applicants with hearing disabilities can be given written instead of oral test instructions.

AN OVERVIEW OF A TESTING PROGRAM

The basic steps in establishing a testing program are essentially those necessary for any kind of employee selection program. The first requirement is to investigate the nature of the job for which testing will be used. Once job and worker analyses have been conducted, the appropriate tests to measure the behaviors and abilities related to job success must be chosen or developed.

Where do I-O psychologists find appropriate tests? They can use tests already available or develop new tests specifically for the job and company in question. The best tests include information on reliability, validity, and test norms. Additional evaluative information is provided by the periodically revised *Mental Measurements Yearbook*, the 13th edition of which was published in 1998. This 1,300-page resource offers reviews of nearly 700 tests.

There are several issues to consider in deciding whether to use a published test or develop a new one. Cost is always important. It is less expensive to purchase a test than to construct one, especially if only a small number of employees are to be selected. Time is also important. If the organization needs qualified workers as soon as possible, management may be unwilling to wait for a test to be developed.

If an organization decides to develop its own test for a particular job, the I-O psychologist overseeing the project will prepare a list of suitable test items. Then the test must be validated to determine whether it measures what it is supposed to measure. An item analysis will show how effectively each test item discriminates between those who score high on the total test and those who score low. This evaluation involves correlating a person's response on each item with the response on the test as a whole. A perfectly valid test question is one that was answered correctly by everyone who scored high on the complete test and was answered incorrectly by everyone who scored low. Only items with a high correlation coefficient will be retained for the final version of the test.

The level of difficulty of each item must be determined. If the majority of the test questions are too easy, then most people will obtain high scores. The resulting range of scores will be too narrow to distinguish those who are high on the trait or skill being measured from those who are only moderately high. A test on which most items are too difficult presents the opposite problem. It will be difficult to distinguish between those who possess extremely low ability and those who possess moderately low ability.

Much of this validity research requires the determination of some measure of job performance, a criterion with which the test scores can be correlated. Ideally, the test will be administered to a large group of applicants and all will be hired regardless of the test scores. At this point, the value of the test is unknown, so it makes little sense to base hiring decisions on its results. Later, after workers have been on the job long enough to develop some competence, their job performance will be assessed, and these ratings will be compared with the test scores. Economic and time constraints usually preclude this approach to establishing predictive validity. The more common method is to test workers already on the job.

Once the validity and reliability of a new test have been found to be satisfactory, a cutoff score must be set. No one scoring below this level will be hired. The cutoff score depends partly on the available labor supply. The greater the number of applicants, the more selective a company can be. The higher the cutoff score, the higher the quality of the applicants hired. However, by being increasingly selective, the organization must spend more money to recruit and evaluate more applicants to find sufficient numbers who meet or exceed the cutoff score. There is a point of diminishing returns at which the increase in the quality of new hires is less than the cost of recruitment and selection.

Most of the procedures for establishing cutoff scores involve job analyses and criterion-related validity studies to determine the minimum acceptable level of job performance. One frequently used technique asks employees and supervisors to assess the probability that a minimally competent person would answer each test item correctly.

NEWSBREAK

Testing for Common Sense

If you are planning to go to graduate school to earn an M.B.A., you will probably be required to take the Graduate Management Admission Test, the standard test used by business school admissions departments since 1954. This 4-hour test assesses verbal, math, and analytical writing skills. It includes 41 verbal questions, 2 essays, and 37 quantitative questions.

The test is reliable and valid; it is known to predict success in M.B.A. programs. But it is less successful in indicating which of those thousands of M.B.A. students will go on to pursue successful business careers. The test cannot identify the seemingly lazy student who will become, at age 27, CEO of a start-up company worth millions. Nor does the test distinguish the all-A student who will never rise above a paper-pushing job in middle management.

The business school at the University of Michigan tried to change that situation by adopting a new kind of selection test, one that focuses on "practical intelligence," otherwise known as common sense. The test was developed by Dr. Robert Sternberg, a Yale psychologist, who argues that traditional admissions tests do not pinpoint the ability to advance practical ideas and develop the analytical and creative skills that lead to success in the corporate world.

The practical intelligence test for business school admissions presents applicants with a set of realistic business scenarios, including financial statements, press releases, news articles, and other market information. The applicants are then given a problem to solve by answering a series of questions. The goal of the test is to evaluate an applicant's ability to handle changing situations, learn from misjudgments, and cope with less-than-adequate information—the same everyday challenges that managers confront on the job.

Beginning with the academic year 2000, the test was administered to all entering M.B.A. students. The school will track those students' grades, their extracurricular leadership activities, and their job offers. When sufficient data have been accumulated, they can be correlated with the test scores to determine the test's validity. Do you think such a test of common sense—of the ability to perform well on the job (not only in the classroom)—will prove useful in selecting business school students?

Source: D. Leonhardt. On testing for common sense. *New York Times*, May 24, 2000.

ADMINISTERING PSYCHOLOGICAL TESTS

Psychological tests can be categorized in two ways: (1) how they are constructed and administered and (2) the skills and abilities they are designed to measure.

Individual and Group Tests

Group tests Psychological tests designed to be administered to a large number of people at the same time.

Some tests are designed so that they can be administered to a large number of people at the same time. These **group tests** can be given to 20, 200, or 2,000 applicants simultaneously. The only limitation is the size of the testing room or the number of computerized testing stations available.

Individual tests Psychological tests designed to be administered to one person at a time.

Individual tests are administered to one person at a time. Because this makes them more costly than group tests, they are used less frequently by employing organizations. Usually they are reserved for selecting senior management personnel. Individual tests are more popular for vocational guidance and counseling and for diagnostic work with patients.

Computerized Adaptive Tests

Computerized adaptive tests A means of administering psychological tests in which an applicant's response to an item determines the level of difficulty of succeeding items.

Designed for large-scale group testing, **computerized adaptive tests** provide an individual testing situation in which the applicant takes the test at a computer terminal. This approach is sometimes referred to as tailored testing because the test is tailored, or adapted, to the person taking it.

If you were given a standard cognitive ability test in paper-and-pencil format, you would have to answer questions designed to sample the full range of

Because individual tests are costly and time-consuming to administer, they are used mostly for vocational counseling and for selecting management personnel.

your intelligence. Some questions would be easy because your level of intelligence is higher than the level at which the questions are targeted, whereas other questions would be more difficult because they are at or above your level of intelligence. To complete the test, you must spend time answering all the questions, even the simple ones.

In computerized adaptive testing, you do not have to waste time answering questions below your level of ability. The computer program begins with a question of average difficulty. If you answer correctly, it proceeds to questions of greater difficulty. Had you answered incorrectly, it would have given you a less difficult question.

Another advantage of computerized adaptive testing is that the testing can be done at any time during the selection process. It is not dependent on finding a qualified test administrator and scheduling a testing session. Because a range of abilities can be measured in a relatively short time, there is less opportunity for the applicant's interest and motivation to diminish. Also, immediate results are available to the human resources department.

Computers also allow for the use of different types of test items. For example, computerized adaptive tests of spatial ability allow the use of three-dimensional objects moving in space instead of two-dimensional stationary images. Questions can be presented with full-motion video and stereo sound. Test-takers can use either a standard keyboard response or a joystick, mouse, or trackball to respond to test questions.

Computerized adaptive testing requires a larger initial investment than does a paper-and-pencil test, but it is more economical in the long run. Consultants estimate that the U.S. Department of Defense could save $5 million annually by computerizing the basic enlistment test given to military recruits.

Comparisons of the same tests given in paper-and-pencil format and computerized adaptive versions show little difference in the resulting scores. In one study, 874 college students took four work-related noncognitive tests. Half of the subjects received the computerized version and half the paper-and-pencil version. No significant differences were found in test performance (King & Miles, 1995). Also, other studies have shown no significant differences between computerized and print versions of the same test in terms of the tendency to fake responses (Richman, Kiesler, Weisband, & Drasgow, 1999). Tests on which there is a time limit have shown less valid responses for computerized formats. However, psychologists have found that using an electronic stylus or light pen to respond to test items, instead of making keyboard entries, tends to equalize these differences (Overton, Taylor, Zickar, & Harms, 1996).

One growing problem with computerized tests is that many tests are available on Internet sites and can be accessed from any computer terminal. Since they are not administered in a controlled environment, such as a company's human resources office or testing room, ample opportunity exists for cheating. For example, for an intelligence test, an applicant could consult source books or have someone else present to help with the answers.

Speed and Power Tests

The difference between speed tests and power tests is the time allotted for completion of the tests. A **speed test** has a fixed time limit, at which point everyone taking the test must stop. A **power test** has no time limit. Applicants are

Speed tests Tests that have a fixed time limit, at which point everyone taking the test must stop.

Power tests Tests that have no time limit. Applicants are allowed as much time as they need to complete the test.

allowed as much time as they need to complete the test. A power test often contains more difficult items than does a speed test. Large-scale testing programs often include speed tests because all test forms can be collected at the same time.

For some tasks, working speed is an important component of successful job performance. A test for a computer keyboarding job would contain relatively easy questions. Given enough time, most people would be able to respond correctly. The important predictive factor for keyboarding or word processing is the quality of the work that can be performed in a given period: in this case, data entry accuracy and speed. A power test would not be able to evaluate this skill properly.

TYPES OF PSYCHOLOGICAL TESTS

A more familiar distinction among psychological tests for employee selection is in terms of the characteristics or behaviors they are designed to measure. The basic categories are tests of cognitive abilities, interests, aptitudes, motor skills, and personality.

Cognitive Abilities

Cognitive ability tests (intelligence tests) are widely used for employee selection. Group intelligence tests, the kind given most often, are a rough screening device. They are brief, take little time to complete, and can be easily scored by hand or machine. Research studies involving thousands of people in the military services and in a variety of civilian jobs have shown consistently that cognitive ability tests are highly valid for predicting success in job training programs and in actual job performance (Behlong, 1998; Hough & Oswald, 2000).

A meta-analysis of thousands of studies conducted over a period of 85 years compared the predictive validities of 19 selection techniques. The results showed that cognitive ability tests had the highest validity for predicting success in job training and performance (Schmidt & Hunter, 1998). An additional meta-analysis of studies of more than 40,000 people also supported the predictive value of cognitive ability tests for job performance (Bobko, Roth, & Potosky, 1999).

The Otis Self-Administering Tests of Mental Ability has been found useful for screening applicants for jobs such as office clerk, assembly-line worker, and first-line supervisor. The test is group administered and takes little time to complete. It is less useful for professional or high-level managerial positions because it does not discriminate well at the upper range of intelligence.

The Wonderlic Personnel Test, a reliable 50-item measure of general mental ability, is a popular individual or group test for selection, placement, promotion, and reassignment. It is applicable to more than 140 jobs in business and industry, such as flight attendant, bank teller, store manager, and industrial engineer. Because the test has a 12-minute time limit, it is an economical screening device. Test items measure the ability to understand instructions, to solve job-related problems, and to propose ideas that can be applied to new work situations. Test norms are based on more than 450,000 working adults. Computer and hand scoring versions are available.

Wonderlic scores show a high positive correlation with scores on the Wechsler Adult Intelligence Scale, a longer and more complex individual test. A hiring kit to facilitate employer compliance with the Americans with Disabilities Act of 1990 offers large-print, braille, and audiotape versions of the test. Since its introduction in 1937, the Wonderlic has been administered to more than 125 million people. A study of college-age applicants to a computer applications training center found no significant differences between mean scores of persons who took the computerized version and scores of those who took the print version (Dembowski & Callans, 2000).

ONLINE!

The latest developments and applications for the Wonderlic test can be found at *www.wonderlic.com.*

A nonverbal measure of cognitive ability, the Revised Beta Examination, Second Edition (Beta-II), a 15-minute group or individual test, is designed for use with people who read poorly or who cannot read at all. Instructions are provided for English-speaking and Spanish-speaking job applicants. The test has been used extensively for occupational rehabilitation programs in correctional facilities and for unskilled workers in large-scale manufacturing job retraining programs. The six timed subtests include mazes, coding, paper form boards, picture completion, clerical checking, and picture absurdities (see Figure 4–1). The

Mazes ask examinees to mark the shortest distance through a maze without crossing any lines *(1.5 minutes)*

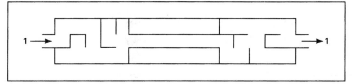

FIGURE 4–1.   Sample items from Revised Beta Examination, Second Edition (Beta-II). (Reproduced by permission. Copyright 1978 by The Psychological Corporation, San Antonio, TX. All rights reserved.)

Coding requires labeling figures with their corresponding numbers *(2 minutes)*

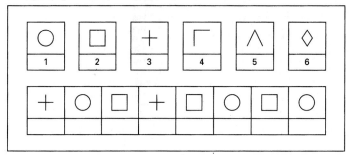

Beta-II can be scored for professional, managerial, technical, clerical, sales, crafts, and service occupations.

The Wechsler Adult Intelligence Scale-Revised (WAIS-R) is a lengthy (approximately 75 minutes), individually administered test used primarily for jobs requiring a comprehensive psychological assessment, such as senior management personnel. Its administration, scoring, and interpretation require a well-trained and experienced clinical examiner. The WAIS-R includes 11 subtests, as follows: the verbal subtests are information, digit span, vocabulary, arithmetic, comprehension, and similarities; the performance subtests are picture completion, picture arrangement, block design, object assembly, and digit

NEWSBREAK

Too Bright for the Job?

Bob Jordan wanted to be a cop in New London, Connecticut, the town where he lived. He applied for the job, took the Wonderlic Personnel Test, and waited to be called for an interview. No call came. He was sure he had passed the test—the questions seemed so easy—and when he heard that other people who had applied at the same time had been hired, he went to the police station to find out what had happened to his application.

He was advised that he did not "fit the profile" of a successful police officer. Had he performed poorly on the test? Had he scored so low that he was considered unfit for training or too dumb to ever learn how to do the job? No. Bob's problem was that he scored too high.

Too high? He was too smart? Yes. The test norms for the Wonderlic provide an optimum range of scores for a variety of jobs. If your score is too low, the norms suggest that you lack the ability to succeed on the job. And if you score too high, the test makers say that you are too intelligent, that you will be bored by the job and will probably quit before long. According to the test manual, "Simply hiring the highest scoring employee can be self-defeating." Bob Jordan scored six points too high to be considered a good candidate for the job.

An interview with the deputy police chief revealed more information. "Bob Jordan is exactly the type of guy we would want to screen out. Police work is kind of mundane. We don't deal in gunfights every night."

Jordan was so angry that he did what any good American does when he feels he is being treated unfairly. That's right. He sued, claiming he was discriminated against because of his level of intelligence. But a judge ruled that since the police department treated all highly intelligent job applicants the same, it had not discriminated against him. The judge noted that the decision to disqualify Jordan might have been unwise, but he had not been denied equal protection. Jordan now works as a prison guard.

Source: M. Allen. Help wanted: The not-too-high-Q standard. *New York Times,* September 9, 1999.

symbol. Separate verbal and performance measures of cognitive ability can be obtained as well as an overall IQ score. Computer scoring and interpretation are available.

Interests

Interest tests include items about daily activities from among which applicants select their preferences. The rationale is that if a person exhibits the same pattern of interests and preferences as people who are successful in a given occupation, then the chances are high that the person taking the test will find satisfaction in that occupation.

It is important to remember, however, that just because a person shows a high degree of interest in a particular job, it is no guarantee that he or she has the ability to be successful in that job. What interest test scores show is that the person's interests are compatible with the interests of successful people in that career. If a test shows that a person has no interest in a field, then the chances of succeeding in it are limited.

Cross-cultural research on nearly 50,000 people showed no significant differences in vocational interests. African Americans, Mexican Americans, Asian Americans, Native Americans, and Caucasians expressed highly similar patterns of likes and dislikes for various types of work (Day & Rounds, 1998).

Two frequently used interest tests are the Strong Interest Inventory and the Kuder Occupational Interest Survey.

The Strong is a 317-item, computer-scored group test that covers occupations, school subjects, leisure activities, types of people, and work preferences. Items are rated as "like," "dislike," or "indifferent." Scales for more than 100 vocational, technical, and professional occupations are grouped around six themes on which test-takers are ranked from low interest to high interest. These themes are: artistic, conventional, social, realistic, investigative, and enterprising. In addition, many of the test's occupational scales are gender-differentiated; that is, they have separate male and female norms. Research on the Strong has shown that people's interests tend to remain stable over time.

The Kuder items are arranged in 100 groups of three alternative activities. Within each forced-choice trio, applicants select the most preferred and least preferred activities. The test can be scored for more than 100 occupations. Typical groups of items are as follows:

Visit an art gallery.   Collect autographs.
Browse in a library.   Collect coins.
Visit a museum.   Collect butterflies.

Both of these interest inventories are used primarily for career counseling, where the focus is on trying to select the right kind of occupation for an individual. One problem with using them for personnel selection is the possibility of applicants' faking their responses to make themselves appear more suitable for a particular job. Presumably, when a person is taking an interest test for the purpose of career counseling, he or she will answer more honestly because the results will be used to select a broad area of training and employment rather than a particular job.

Interest tests Psychological tests to assess a person's interests and preferences. These tests are used primarily for career counseling.

Aptitudes

Aptitude tests Psychological tests to measure specific abilities, such as mechanical or clerical skills.

For many jobs, **aptitude tests** are administered to applicants to measure specific skills. Sometimes these tests must be specially designed for a particular job, but there are also tests available that measure general clerical and mechanical aptitudes.

The Minnesota Clerical Test is a 15-minute individual or group test in two parts: number comparison (matching 200 pairs of numbers) and name comparison (see Figure 4–2). Applicants are instructed to work as fast as possible without making errors. The test measures the perceptual speed and accuracy required to perform various clerical duties. It is useful for any job that requires attention to detail in industries such as utility companies, financial institutions, and manufacturing.

The Revised Minnesota Paper Form Board Test measures those aspects of mechanical ability that require the capacity to visualize and manipulate objects in space, necessary skills for occupations with mechanical or artistic orientation, such as industrial designer or electrician. Applicants are presented with 64 two-dimensional diagrams of geometric shapes cut into two or more pieces and are given 20 minutes to picture how the figures would look as whole geometric shapes (see Figure 4–3). Research shows that the test successfully predicts performance in production jobs, electrical maintenance work, engineering shopwork, power sewing machine operation, and various other industrial tasks.

The Bennett Mechanical Comprehension Test uses 68 pictures with questions about the application of physical laws or principles of mechanical operation (see Figure 4–4). Tape-recorded instructions are provided for applicants with limited reading skills. The Bennett is designed for individual or group administration. It takes 30 minutes to complete. The test is used for jobs in aviation, construction, chemical plants, oil refineries, utilities, glass manufacturing, steel, paper and plywood manufacturing, and mining.

The Computer Competence Tests include five individual or group subtests containing multiple-choice items to assess an applicant's level of knowledge of basic computer terminology and ability to operate computers in the workplace. A

FIGURE 4–2.   Sample items from Minnesota Clerical Test. (Reproduced by permission. Copyright 1933, renewed 1961, 1979 by The Psychological Corporation, San Antonio, TX. All rights reserved.)

When the two numbers or names in a pair are exactly the same, make a check mark on the line between them.

66273894 _____ 66273984
527384578 _____ 527384578
New York World _____ New York World
Cargill Grain Co. _____ Cargil Grain Co.

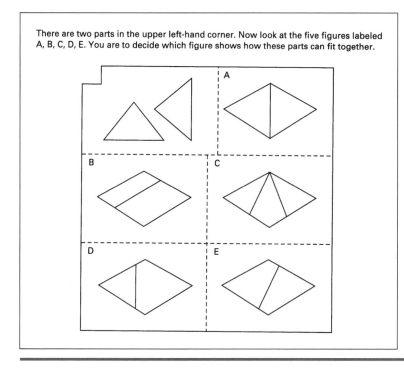

There are two parts in the upper left-hand corner. Now look at the five figures labeled A, B, C, D, E. You are to decide which figure shows how these parts can fit together.

FIGURE 4–3. Sample item from Revised Minnesota Paper Form Board Test. (Reproduced by permission. Copyright 1941, renewed 1969, 1970 by The Psychological Corporation, San Antonio, TX. All rights reserved.)

typical question is: Which component of a computer system is used to perform arithmetic operations? (a) Input device; (b) Output device; (c) Storage unit; (d) Processing unit. The test is useful for any job that requires computer expertise.

Motor Skills

Many jobs in industry and the military require abilities involving muscle coordination, finger dexterity, and eye-hand coordination.

FIGURE 4–4. Sample items from Bennett Mechanical Comprehension Test. (Reproduced by permission. Copyright 1940, renewed 1967; 1941, renewed 1969; 1942, renewed 1969; 1967, 1968, 1980 by The Psychological Corporation, San Antonio, TX. All rights reserved.)

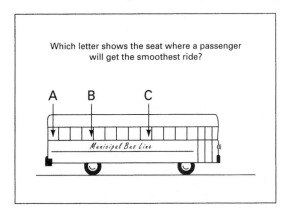

Which letter shows the seat where a passenger will get the smoothest ride?

Which would be the better shears for cutting metal?

The Purdue Pegboard is a performance test that simulates assembly-line conditions and measures fingertip dexterity and eye-hand coordination necessary for assembly tasks, general factory work, and vocational rehabilitation. The task is to place 50 pegs in a series of holes in a pegboard as rapidly as possible, first with one hand, then the other, then both. Each task is limited to 30 seconds. The test also includes a 1-minute task involving the simultaneous use of both hands to assemble pins, collars, and washers.

The O'Connor Finger Dexterity Test and the O'Connor Tweezer Dexterity Test measure how fast an applicant can insert pins into small holes by hand and by the use of tweezers. These tests are standard measures of finger dexterity and have proven to be useful in predicting job success for occupations that require precise manipulative skills.

Personality

Personality tests Psychological tests that assess personal traits and feelings.

Certain personality characteristics can contribute to job satisfaction and job performance. For example, empathy and nurturance are important traits for counselors to have; autonomy and persistence are vital to investigative reporters; and orderliness and precision are needed by accountants. **Personality test** scores have been found to correlate with job success in virtually all occupations. The predictive validities of personality test scores can be as high as those for assessment centers and biodata questionnaires.

Self-report personality inventories Personality assessment tests that include questions dealing with situations, symptoms, and feelings. Test-takers are asked to indicate how well each item describes themselves or how much they agree with each item.

Two approaches to personality assessment are self-report inventories and projective techniques. **Self-report personality inventories** include items dealing with specific situations, symptoms, or feelings. Applicants are asked to indicate how well each item describes themselves or how much they agree with each item.

Honesty of responses may be the major problem with self-report personality tests. Test questions are often transparent, and people can usually figure out how to respond to make themselves appear to possess whatever qualities they think the organization wants.

Projective techniques A personality assessment technique in which test-takers project their feelings onto an ambiguous stimulus such as an inkblot.

Projective techniques for personality testing present applicants with an ambiguous stimulus such as an inkblot. The task is to tell what is seen in the figure or picture. The rationale is that people will project their thoughts, wishes, and feelings onto the stimulus in an effort to give it meaning. These tests cannot be faked because there are no right and wrong answers.

The best known projective technique is the Rorschach Inkblot Test, in which subjects are shown 10 standardized inkblots and asked to describe what they see in the figures. In the Thematic Apperception Test (TAT), subjects are asked to respond to 30 ambiguous pictures of people and situations.

ONLINE!

The *www.rorschach.org* site provides technical information on the Rorschach Inkblot Test and links to related sites. The search engine Yahoo! lists more than 500 Web sites dealing with the Rorschach. Not all of them are serious.

Projective tests are time-consuming and must be administered individually. Examiners must be thoroughly trained and experienced. Because few of the tests have objective scoring keys, there is ample opportunity for subjective bias to affect the scoring and interpretation of the results. Although projective techniques are used for employee selection at the executive level, research shows that they have low validity.

Self-Report Inventories.   The Guilford-Zimmerman Temperament Survey is a widely used paper-and-pencil personality test. The items are statements rather than questions, and the applicant responds by checking "yes," "?," or "no." Three sample items are the following:

> You start work on a new project with a great deal of enthusiasm.
> You are often in low spirits.
> Most people use politeness to cover up what is really cutthroat competition.

The test yields separate scores for 10 independent personality traits. As a check against faking or carelessness in responding, there are three falsification scales based on answers to selected items.

The Minnesota Multiphasic Personality Inventory (MMPI-2), first published in 1943 and revised in 1989, is the most frequently used personality test for employee selection and for clinical diagnostic work. The test is widely used in screening for jobs that require a high level of psychological adjustment, such as police officer, firefighter, air traffic controller, and airline flight crew member.

The 1989 revision of the MMPI, the MMPI-2, consists of 567 statements answered by "true," "false," or "cannot say." The items cover physical and psychological health; political and social attitudes; educational, occupational, family, and marital factors; and neurotic and psychotic behavioral tendencies. A number of items can be scored to determine whether the person taking the test was faking, careless, or misunderstood the instructions.

One problem with any test as popular as the MMPI-2 is that some people will take it more than once, should they apply to different organizations that use it. Among a sample of 1997 workers in the nuclear power industry, more than 200 were found to have taken the MMPI four times, 102 had taken it five times, 26 had taken it six times, and 3 had responded to all 567 items seven times.

The scores of these examinees showed that repeated administrations of the test resulted in less extreme scores. One reason for this finding is that the job applicants became more "test-wise" with each additional exposure to the test. The psychologists who conducted this survey concluded that

> the usefulness of the Inventory appears to decrease with an increasing number of administrations. [Therefore] it becomes increasingly difficult to identify unfit employees with the [MMPI] (Kelley, Jacobs, & Farr, 1994, p. 575).

This problem is not unique to the MMPI; it applies to any psychological test used by a large number of employers.

The California Psychological Inventory, developed in 1957 and revised in 1987, consists of 462 items calling for "true" or "false" responses. It provides scores on 17 personality dimensions and has been shown to be useful for predicting success in teaching and in health care occupations (physicians, dentists, and nurses). The test has scales to identify leadership and management potential, creative potential, and social maturity.

The Big Five Personality Factors.   Predictive validities for self-report personality tests are generally in the low to moderate range. However, research using self-report inventories to assess the so-called Big Five personality factors has shown higher validities. These are the basic personality factors:

1. Extraversion
2. Agreeableness
3. Conscientiousness (or the will to achieve)
4. Neuroticism
5. Openness to experience

Two of these factors, conscientiousness and extraversion, have been found to be particularly effective in predicting job performance. Conscientiousness includes such characteristics as being responsible and dependable, able to plan, organized, and achievement-oriented. Conscientiousness has been found to be a valid predictor for many occupations, including managerial, sales, professional, law enforcement, and skilled and semiskilled jobs.

Extraversion, which includes the characteristics of sociability, talkativeness, ambition, assertiveness, and high activity level, correlates highly with success for salespersons and managers. Extraversion also shows a high positive correlation with success in obtaining a job. A study of 83 job-seeking college seniors found that their level of extraversion was the best single predictor of whether they received a job offer (Caldwell & Burger, 1998). A study conducted in Europe of 401 college graduates found that their test scores on extraversion and conscientiousness distinguished between those who had found jobs and those who had not, when surveyed a year after graduation. The people who had scored high in extraversion and conscientiousness were the ones most likely to be employed (DeFruyt & Mervielde, 1999).

In a study involving 146 civilian managers employed by the U.S. Army, extraversion and conscientiousness were found to be more valid predictors of job performance for managers whose jobs offered a high degree of autonomy than for managers whose jobs offered low autonomy. In other words, managers who were highly conscientious and extraverted were more successful when their jobs offered them the opportunity to be independent and to take responsibility (Barrick & Mount, 1993).

The traits of agreeableness and conscientiousness were found to be highly valid predictors of successful performance when the job involved participation as a member of a work team. A study of 79 four-person human resources work teams showed that high scores on agreeableness and conscientiousness were closely related to task achievement, getting along well with other group members, and dealing effectively with conflicts (Neuman & Wright, 1999).

Much additional research has been conducted on the role of conscientiousness as it relates to work behavior. A study of 91 sales representatives employed by a large appliance manufacturer found that salespersons who were high in conscientiousness were more likely to set goals and to be committed to them. This, in turn, was related to higher sales volume and higher supervisor ratings of their job performance (Barrick, Mount, & Strauss, 1993). A study of 130 resort hotel employees found that conscientiousness correlated significantly with self-direction—that is, the performance of desirable on-the-job behaviors undertaken at the worker's own initiative (Stewart, Carson, & Cardy, 1996). A meta-analysis of 36 studies of workers conducted in several countries in Europe showed conscientiousness to be a valid predictor of job performance in professional, police, managerial, sales, and skilled labor jobs (Salgado, 1997).

Other studies have found that conscientiousness is a highly valid predictor of successful performance for U.S. employees working for multinational corporations in other countries, whether they are newly hired or long-term employees (Caligiuri, 2000; Stewart, 1999). In research showing a negative correlation, low scores on conscientiousness were found to be a valid predictor of dysfunctional behaviors such as alcoholism, substance abuse, and reckless driving. People scoring high in conscientiousness were much less likely to exhibit these behaviors than were people scoring low (Sarchione, Cuttler, Muchinsky, & Nelson-Gray, 1998). In view of these and many other similar studies, it is clear that conscientiousness is a desirable characteristic for employees to show and for employers to seek in job applicants.

Studies of managers who make hiring decisions confirm that conscientiousness (along with general mental ability) is the most important attribute related to suitability for hiring (Dunn, Mount, Barrick, & Ones, 1995). Other research found that ratings of conscientiousness and extraversion made by supervisors, co-workers, and customers of 105 salespeople were valid predictors of job performance (Mount, Barrick, & Strauss, 1994). Thus, whether conscientiousness and extraversion are assessed by self-report inventory or by ratings given by others, both correlate positively with high job performance.

Inventories have been developed to measure other specific personality characteristics, such as introversion, self-esteem, sociability, emotional maturity, and proactivity. Proactivity refers to a tendency to take action to try to influence or change one's environment. The Proactive Personality Scale consists of 17 items to which respondents indicate the extent of their agreement or disagreement. A sample item is: "No matter what the odds, if I believe in something I will make it happen." People who express a high degree of agreement with a statement such as that should perform well in certain jobs, particularly those in sales.

A study of real-estate agents found a high positive correlation between high scores on the Proactive Personality Scale and objective measures of job performance such as commission income, number of homes sold, and number of new listings obtained (Crant, 1995). Research on nearly 500 people employed in a variety of jobs found that proactivity correlated positively with salary, promotions, and job satisfaction (Seibert, Crant, & Kraimer, 1999).

ONLINE!

If you need a break, check out the lighthearted view of personality tests at *www.goofiness.com/personality/test.*

Integrity Tests

American companies lose billions of dollars every year to theft, embezzlement, and other forms of employee dishonesty. The polygraph (the so-called lie detector) has been discredited as an effective means of detecting employee theft. A more valid way to predict and detect employee dishonesty is with integrity tests, a paper-and-pencil approach developed as an alternative to the polygraph. I-O psychologists estimate that every year more than 15 million employees and job applicants take integrity tests. Currently, some four dozen such tests are in use.

There are two types of integrity tests: (1) overt integrity tests, which directly assess attitudes toward theft and other dishonest behaviors, and (2) personality-oriented integrity tests which measure general delinquency, impulse control, and conscientiousness. Both types of test appear to be valid predictors of theft and of such counterproductive behaviors as absenteeism, drug abuse, and malingering. They have also been found predictive of general job performance as assessed by supervisor ratings. A comparison of overt integrity test results from 725,000 job applicants found that women scored higher than men did. No significant differences were found between applicants below and above the age of 40, or between groups of Blacks, Whites, Hispanics, Asians, and Native Americans (Ones & Viswesvaran, 1998).

Research evidence suggests that most integrity tests are probably measuring the Big Five factor of conscientiousness, which would explain why the tests are such valid predictors of job performance.

LIMITATIONS OF PSYCHOLOGICAL TESTING

Uncritical Use.   A continual danger with psychological tests is their uncritical or inappropriate use by trusting human resources managers who may be taken in by slick brochures and promises of instant success in solving problems of employee selection and equal employment opportunity. A manager may choose a test because it is new, without investigating the test's norms, reliability, or validity. A test may continue to be used despite negative information about its dependability because the employment office is unaware of the research. Often, there are no data to support a test because no research has ever been conducted on it. The harm generated by an improper testing program affects not only the organization but also applicants who may be unfairly disqualified from a job by an ineffective test.

Rejection of Qualified Applicants.   Even the best psychological tests are not perfectly valid. No validity coefficients for tests reach a perfect positive correlation of +1.00. There is always some margin for error in the prediction of job success. Sometimes unqualified persons will be hired, and sometimes otherwise qualified applicants will be incorrectly identified as unqualified or ineligible on the basis of their test performance. (This type of error also applies to other selection techniques.) These false-positive errors can be reduced when tests with the highest predictive validities are chosen for the selection program.

To minimize these errors, an employee selection program should not be based on a single technique. The use of several techniques allows for the compilation and evaluation of much more information about an applicant.

Faking. We mentioned earlier that organizations using tests for employee selection must be sensitive to the possibility of faking. Suppose you are in desperate need of a job and apply for a sales position. You are given a test that includes the following questions:

I enjoy meeting new people.	Yes_____ No_____
I get along well with most people.	Yes_____ No_____
I find it easy to talk to people.	Yes_____ No_____

You can easily anticipate the way the company expects salespersons to answer. Unless these characteristics apply to you, however, your answers will provide the company with a false impression. You may be hired, but you probably will not be successful or satisfied with the job because it requires abilities that you do not possess. In the long run, then, faking test responses works to your disadvantage, but it is hard to convince some avid job seekers of this in advance.

Ethical Issues. The American Psychological Association is concerned about the ethical practices of all psychologists, whether engaged in clinical practice, in academic laboratory research and teaching, or in employee selection. Principles for proper conduct state that psychologists must protect the dignity, worth, and welfare of the persons with whom they deal. Unfortunately, this ideal is sometimes violated in applying psychological tests to employee selection. The APA ethics code describes safeguards for the distribution and use of psychological tests.

1. *Test users.* Persons who administer and interpret psychological tests should be aware of the principles of psychological measurement and validation and the limitations of test interpretation. They must avoid bias and should consider more than one means of assessment. They must adhere to standardized test administration procedures and make every effort to achieve accuracy in recording and scoring test results.
2. *Test security.* Actual test questions should never be reprinted in a public medium such as a newspaper or magazine. It is permissible to publish sample questions (similar to real questions) but not items used in the actual scoring of a test. [The examples in this chapter are sample questions.] Tests should be sold only to professionals who will safeguard their use.
3. *Test interpretation.* Test scores should be given only to those qualified to interpret them. They should not be given to anyone outside the human resources department, such as the applicant's potential supervisor, unless the supervisor has been trained to interpret the scores. The person being tested has the right to know the test score and what it means.
4. *Test publication.* Tests should not be released for use without adequate background research to support the test developers' claims. Informative and current test manuals containing reliability, validity, and normative data should be made available. Advertisements should describe tests accurately, without emotional or persuasive appeals.

Privacy Issues. One aspect of psychological testing that has come under attack is the use of questions about personal or intimate issues. Critics charge that such personal probing is an unnecessary invasion of privacy. Individual freedom is violated when organizations request or require information that cannot be shown

Store Sued Over Personality Test

NEWSBREAK

When Sibi Soroka applied for a job as a security guard at Target Stores in California, he didn't know he would be asked about his religious beliefs or his sex life. And he didn't like it when he was. As part of the employment screening process, he had to take Psychscreen, a personality test used by Target, which contains items from two well-known psychological tests, the Minnesota Multiphasic Personality Inventory and the California Psychological Inventory.

Soroka felt that his privacy had been invaded when he was asked if he believed there was a devil and a hell in an afterlife. He was also asked whether he was strongly attracted to members of his own sex, or if he dreamed a lot about sex. Questions like these were entirely too personal, he said, and besides, what did his religious beliefs or sexual behavior have to do with being a security guard? Soroka sued Target for violating his right to privacy.

The trial judge denied Soroka's motion for an injunction to prohibit further use of the personality test by Target Stores and ruled that Psychscreen was not an unreasonable device for screening job applicants. Soroka appealed his case to the California Court of Appeals, which ruled in his favor. Psychscreen's questions about religion and sex, wrote the judges in a 39-page decision, violated a job applicant's right to privacy, unless the company could prove that such information was directly related to job performance.

The appeals court ruling did not object to the psychological screening of the store's security guards; it acknowledged that Target had a legitimate and justifiable interest in hiring emotionally stable applicants. Nor did the court find fault with the idea of using personality tests to select guards. What it did criticize was the asking of questions about sex and religion when the company could not provide any empirical demonstration of a compelling interest in that kind of personal information about an applicant.

Although Target Stores appealed to the California Supreme Court, it made an out-of-court settlement with Soroka before a decision could be rendered. Between the legal fees and the undisclosed amount of the settlement, plus the public notoriety, the use of Psychscreen turned out to be an expensive selection technique for this company.

Source: D. C. Brown (1993). Target Stores settle out of court in *Soroka v. Dayton Hudson. The Industrial-Organizational Psychologist, 31*(2), 88–89. Also D. N. Jackson & J. D. Kovacheff (1993). Personality questionnaires in selection: Privacy issues in the Soroka case. *The Industrial-Organizational Psychologist, 30*(4), 45–50.

to be related to performance of the job for which the person is applying. Few people question the right of an organization to investigate the background, training, abilities, and personality of job applicants. But personal questions about sex, religion, political beliefs, and health have been successfully challenged in court as unwarranted invasions of privacy. Even if such questions were related to job performance, there remains the issue of how much of ourselves we should be required to reveal to a potential employer.

Are Personality Tests Color-Blind?

The Big Five personality factors, particularly extraversion and conscientiousness, have been shown to be highly valid predictors of success in obtaining jobs, in training programs, in job satisfaction, and in job performance. Research has documented the presence of these five components of personality in both Eastern and Western cultures, suggesting that they may characterize all job applicants, regardless of ethnic affiliation.

However, some Black psychologists have questioned whether the five-factor model is appropriate for African Americans. Is there truly a universal personality in which the same factors will predict job success for everyone? Proposing a different view, these psychologists suggest that the five-factor structure of personality does not describe Blacks because their personality has been shaped by the adverse cultural influences of generations of racial prejudice.

If the so-called Black personality is unique, as these psychologists suggest, then measures of personality factors from self-report inventories are unfair to Blacks and should not be used for employee selection. This basic question—whether the five-factor model of personality can be related to job success for Blacks—was tested with two groups of applicants (281 Blacks and 183 Whites) for the job of prison guard. All applicants took the same highly valid personality test, the 80 Bipolar Adjective Checklist.

The results, as measured by scores on this inventory, failed to support the idea of a distinct

Source: J. M. Collins & D. H. Gleaves (1998). Race, job applicants, and the five-factor model of personality. *Journal of Applied Psychology, 83,* 531–544.

Black personality. The five factors were shown to be equivalent for both groups; there were no significant racial differences in personality structure or mean scores between the two groups.

In interpreting the results, the researchers cited two reasons for the similarity in test scores. First, they observed that Black applicants left significantly more items unanswered than Whites did, suggesting to the researchers an important personality difference. They said that Blacks are more reluctant to reveal aspects of their personality because of a general distrust and cultural paranoia resulting from racism and oppression.

Second, the scores may have been similar for the two groups because past experience with discrimination motivated Blacks to distort their responses. The belief that racial discrimination would keep them from obtaining a job may have driven them to fake their responses so that they would appear to be more like the ideal employee.

Think About It

1. Do you think it is possible that every minority group possesses a unique personality and that different personality tests should be developed for each group? Defend your answer.
2. Do you think a cultural or racial bias results from the use of cognitive ability tests as predictors of job success? Do these tests discriminate against minority groups?
3. Describe how job applicants of different ages, genders, and ethnic identities might try to present themselves in the most favorable way on psychological tests. Do you think such behavior is permissible?
4. If you were designing a program to select applicants for the position of prison guard, what selection measures would you use?

SUMMARY

Psychological tests must meet the following criteria: standardization, objectivity, norms, reliability, and validity. **Standardization** refers to the consistency of procedures and conditions under which people take tests. **Objectivity** involves accurate and consistent test scoring that is unbiased by the scorer's personal characteristics and beliefs. **Test norms** are the scores of a group of people who are similar to persons taking the test; norms serve as a point of comparison for individual test scores. **Reliability** refers to the consistency of responses; it can be determined by the test-retest, equivalent-forms, or split-halves methods. **Validity** is concerned with how well a test measures what it is intended to measure. **Criterion-related validity** is determined by the methods of predictive or concurrent validity. **Rational validity** is established by content or construct validity. The concept of face validity refers to how relevant the test appears to the person taking it. **Validity generalization** indicates that a test valid for one job may be valid for other jobs, and a test valid for one ethnic group may be valid for others.

Fair employment legislation prohibits the use of tests to discriminate against job applicants because of race, color, religion, sex, or national origin. A valid test may be declared discriminatory if adverse impact on minority groups can be demonstrated.

To establish a testing program, I-O psychologists conduct job and worker analyses, develop suitable tests, conduct an item analysis of each test question, determine the level of difficulty of each question, establish the test's reliability and validity, and set cutoff scores.

Psychological tests differ in terms of how they are constructed and administered and in terms of the type of behavior they measure. Categories include **individual** and **group tests,** and **speed** and **power tests. Computerized adaptive tests,** designed for large groups, involve individual interaction with a computer. Psychological tests can measure **cognitive ability, interests, aptitudes, motor skills,** and **personality.** Personality characteristics are assessed by **self-report inventories** or **projective techniques. Integrity tests** are designed to predict and detect employee dishonesty.

Psychological tests can be of great value in employee selection because of their objectivity and validity. Limitations of tests include uncritical use, unfair rejection of applicants, and faking of responses. Ethical issues include invasion of privacy and confidentiality of test questions and answers.

KEY TERMS

aptitude tests
banding
computerized adaptive tests
criterion-related validity
group tests
individual tests
interest tests
objective tests
personality tests
power tests

projective techniques
race norming
rational validity
reliability
self-report personality inventories
speed tests
standardization
subjective tests
validity
validity generalization

ADDITIONAL READING

Hornaday, J. A., & Gibson, L. A. (1998). *The Kuder book of people who like their work.* Atlanta: Motivation Research Corp. A collection of nearly 1500 job descriptions provided by people who are satisfied with their work. Employees describe their job duties, a typical day, and the abilities and personality characteristics required for job success.

Kaplan, R. M., & Saccuzzo, D. P. (2000). *Psychological testing: Principles, applications, and issues,* 5th ed. Belmont, CA: Wadsworth. A popular textbook reviewing all types of psychological tests.

Wainer, H. (2000). *Computerized adaptive testing: A primer,* 2nd ed. Hillsdale, NJ: Erlbaum. An accessible state-of-the-art guide to the elements of computerized adaptive testing including computer technology, test development, statistics, and test theory.

Performance Appraisal

CHAPTER OUTLINE

There's no getting away from it. Someone somewhere will always be monitoring or evaluating your performance at something. Maybe it's your roommate, a classmate or team member, a friend, lover, spouse, or boss. Someone is assessing your behavior and appraising your abilities, whether informally or formally.

Throughout your career, your performance will be monitored and appraised, and your level of salary, rank, and responsibility will depend on how well you satisfy the established criteria for job performance. Of course, the **performance appraisal** of your work is nothing new to you. It has been going on since you started school. Your performance has been appraised continuously through classroom examinations, term papers, standardized tests, and oral presentations—all techniques designed to gauge or assess the quality of your work. In principle, they are similar to the techniques used on the job, and the results of these evaluations obviously have an important bearing on your future.

> **Performance appraisal** The periodic, formal evaluation of employee performance for the purpose of making career decisions.

Although you may not take formal examinations during your years with an organization, performance appraisals at work are just as important as those in college. Your pay raises, promotions, and job duties affect not only your income and standard of living but also your self-esteem, emotional security, and general satisfaction with life. Performance appraisals can also determine whether you keep your job. In a sense, then, you are never finished passing tests; once you have been evaluated and hired by a company, your performance will continue to be assessed.

Keep in mind that performance appraisal can be as beneficial to you as to your company. Just as classroom tests show where you stand and where you need improvement, so the effective performance appraisal program can help you assess your competence and personal development on the job. Performance appraisal will reveal your strengths and weaknesses, enhancing your self-confidence in some areas and motivating you to improve your performance in others.

FAIR EMPLOYMENT PRACTICES

The Equal Employment Opportunity Commission (EEOC) guidelines apply to any selection procedure that is used for making employment decisions, not only for hiring, but also for promotion, demotion, transfer, layoff, discharge, or early retirement. Therefore, performance appraisal procedures must be validated like tests or any other selection device. Employers who base their personnel decisions on the results of a well-designed performance review program that includes formal appraisal interviews are much more likely to be successful in defending themselves against claims of discrimination.

Racial Bias. Most performance evaluation programs are based on supervisor ratings, which are subjective human judgments that can be influenced by personal factors and prejudices. Race discrimination is known to persist in job assignment, pay, promotion, and other personnel decisions. For example, an analysis of ratings made by 20,000 supervisors showed that both black supervisors and white supervisors gave higher ratings to subordinates of their own race (Mount, Sytsma, Kazucha, & Holt, 1997). Another study, however, involving 23,316 white employees and black employees, found that it made no difference whether a supervisor of the same or of a different race rated an employee. Thus, no evidence was found of bias against black employees (Rotundo & Sackett, 1999).

Age Bias.   The evidence with regard to age bias shows that older workers tend to receive significantly lower ratings than do younger workers on measures of self-development, interpersonal skills, and overall job performance. We have noted that job proficiency does not necessarily decline with age. In some cases, then, raters may be basing their assessments on their expectations of an older worker's skills rather than on his or her actual job performance.

Criteria for Compliance.   Performance appraisal systems, which depend on having one person evaluate another, provide opportunities for unfair treatment in terms of pay, promotion, and other job outcomes. For organizations to ensure compliance with fair employment practices, performance appraisals should be based on job analyses to document specific critical incidents and behaviors that are related to successful job performance. The appraisers should focus on these actual job behaviors rather than on personality characteristics. They should review the ratings with the employees who are being evaluated and offer training and counseling to employees who are not performing well.

In addition, appraisers should be trained in their duties, have detailed written instructions about how to conduct the evaluation, and observe the workers on the job. It is vital that all relevant notes, records, and supporting documentation be well organized and maintained to ensure the accuracy and objectivity of the appraisals and to support the company's position in any future challenges from workers who claim they were treated unfairly.

PERFORMANCE APPRAISAL: WHY DO IT?

The overall purpose of performance appraisal is to provide an accurate and objective measure of how well a person is performing the job. On the basis of this information, decisions will be made about the employee's future with the organization. In addition, performance evaluations are often used to validate specific selection techniques. Thus, there are two broad purposes for conducting performance appraisals: (1) administrative, for use with personnel decisions such as pay increases and promotions, and (2) research, usually for validating selection instruments.

Can the purpose of an appraisal affect the results? In other words, do supervisors give different appraisals to their employees when they know that their evaluations and judgments will directly affect their subordinates' careers, rather than when the appraisals are to be used solely for research purposes? The answer is yes.

In a study of 223 first-line supervisors in a Fortune 500 company, the results showed that the supervisors gave significantly more lenient ratings when they knew those ratings would be used for administrative or personnel decisions affecting their subordinates' careers (Harris, Smith, & Champagne, 1995).

Let us consider the purposes of performance appraisal in more detail.

Validation of Selection Criteria.   We noted in Chapters 3 and 4, on employee selection, that to establish the validity of selection devices, they must be correlated with some measure of job performance. Whether we are concerned with psychological tests, interviews, application blanks, or some other technique, we cannot determine their usefulness until we examine the subsequent performance of the workers who were selected and hired on the basis of those techniques. Therefore, a major purpose of performance appraisal is to provide information for validating employee selection techniques.

Training Requirements.   A careful evaluation of employee performance can uncover weaknesses or deficiencies in knowledge, skills, and abilities. Once these are identified, they can be corrected through additional training. Occasionally, an entire work crew or section is found to be deficient on some aspect of the work routine. Information of this sort can lead to the redesign of the training program for new workers and the retraining of current workers to correct the shortcomings. Performance appraisal can also be used to assess the worth of a training program by determining whether job performance improved after the training period.

Employee Improvement.   Performance appraisal programs should provide feedback to employees about their job competence and their progress within the organization. I-O psychologists have found that this kind of information is crucial to maintaining employee morale. Appraisals can also suggest how employees might change certain behaviors or attitudes to improve their work efficiency. This purpose of performance appraisal is similar to that of improving training. In this instance, however, a worker's shortcomings can be altered through self-improvement rather than through formal retraining. Workers have a right to know what is expected of them—what they are doing well, and how they might improve.

Pay, Promotion, and Other Personnel Decisions.   Most people believe they should be rewarded for above average or excellent performance. For example, in your college work, fairness dictates that if your performance on an exam or term paper is superior to that of others taking the course, you should receive a higher grade. If everyone received the same grade regardless of academic performance, there would be little incentive for continued hard work.

In employing organizations, rewards are in the form of salary increases, bonuses, promotions, and transfers to positions providing greater opportunity for advancement. To maintain employee initiative and morale, these changes in status cannot depend on a supervisor's whim or personal bias but must be based on a systematic evaluation of employee worth. Performance appraisals provide the foundation for these career decisions and also help to identify those employees with the potential and talent for contributing to the company's growth.

Opposition to Performance Appraisal

Not everyone is in favor of formal performance appraisal systems. Many employees—especially those affected most directly by such ratings—are less than enthusiastic about them. The list of critics also includes labor unions and managers.

Labor Unions.   Labor unions, which represent nearly 14% of the U.S. work force, require that seniority (length of service) rather than assessment of employee merit be taken as the basis for promotion. However, length of job experience alone is no indication of the ability to perform a higher-level job. For

Tough Graders Get Low Scores

NEWSBREAK

Paul Trout is unhappy about his performance appraisals. Not the ones he gives to his students as a professor at Montana State University, but the ones they give him. At the end of every semester, at colleges throughout the United States, students have the opportunity to evaluate how well their teachers are doing their job.

Do the instructors show concern for the students? How thoroughly do they know the subject matter? Can they communicate the material clearly and with enthusiasm? Do they grade assignments and tests promptly and fairly? Are they available to discuss students' problems? These are just some of the questions students use to rate their professors. The evaluations are factored into the college's decisions about contract renewals, promotions, salary increases, and tenure.

At Montana State, faculty members need to maintain an average score of 3.6, on a 4-point scale, to qualify for a pay raise. "To get scores this high," Professor Trout said, "I have to make a lot of students happy." And to make them happy, he cannot be too demanding. He has to be careful about the amount of work he requires, about his expectations for student performance, and about the standards he sets for grading. A reputation as a tough grader can be costly.

Research on student evaluations shows that students consistently assign low ratings to teachers who set high standards and strict course requirements. Teachers known to offer easy courses receive higher ratings. Have these performance appraisals become nothing more than popularity contests?

According to Trout, "To get high scores, most instructors have to please [their students] or at least not upset them. Even a few students, angry about a demanding workload or a C grade, can have a devastating effect on evaluation scores simply by giving an instructor a zero on every item, as some disgruntled students do."

Is this how you would like your work performance to be evaluated? And what kind of ratings will you give your professor when this semester ends?

Source: P. Trout. Students give top teachers low marks. *St. Petersburg (FL) Times*, March 24, 2000.

---

example, a worker with 10 years of experience in an auto body plant may know everything about the assembly line. But unless the company has a formal, objective evaluation of that worker's competence in other areas—such as the ability to get along with people or the verbal skills to write reports for management—there is no basis for concluding that the worker will make a good supervisor.

Senior people should be given the first opportunity for promotion, but they must qualify for that promotion because of their abilities, not solely because of length of service. Performance evaluations can provide a reliable basis for these decisions.

Employees.   Few of us like being tested or evaluated, particularly if we believe we may receive an unfavorable rating. Not many people are so confident of their skills that they expect consistently to receive praise from their superiors. And few of us welcome criticism, no matter how objective it is or how tactfully it is offered. Because many of us would rather not be assessed and told of our weaknesses or deficiencies, we may react with suspicion or hostility to the idea of performance appraisals.

Managers.   Managers who have had unsatisfactory experiences with inadequate or poorly designed appraisal programs may be skeptical about their usefulness. Some managers dislike playing the role of judge and are unwilling to accept responsibility for making decisions about the future of their subordinates. This tendency can lead them to inflate their assessments of the workers' job performance, giving higher ratings than deserved. Also, managers may be uncomfortable providing negative feedback to employees and may lack the skills to conduct the postappraisal interview properly.

Despite these sources of opposition to performance appraisal, it remains a necessary activity in organizational life. Its critics overlook the point that some form of appraisal is inevitable. Some basis must be established for employee selection and training and other personnel decisions. These determinations should not be based on personal likes and dislikes. Job competence must be measured in a way that reflects, as objectively as possible, the qualities and abilities required to do the job.

Techniques of Performance Appraisal

I-O psychologists have developed a number of techniques to measure job performance. The specific technique used depends on the type of work being evaluated. The abilities needed to work satisfactorily on an assembly line differ from those required on a sales job or a high-level administrative position. The performance measures chosen must reflect the nature and complexity of the job duties. For example, repetitive assembly-line work can be assessed more objectively than the daily activities of a bank executive.

Performance measures may be described as either objective or judgmental. Proficiency on production jobs is more readily appraised by objective performance and output measures. Assessing competence on nonproduction, professional, and managerial jobs, however, requires more judgmental and qualitative measures.

OBJECTIVE PERFORMANCE APPRAISAL METHODS

The measurement of performance on production jobs is relatively easy in principle. It typically involves recording the number of units produced in a given time period. Such measures of quantity are widely used in industry in part because production records are readily available. In practice, performance appraisal of production jobs is not so simple, particularly for nonrepetitive jobs. Quality of output must also be assessed.

Output Measures

Consider the productivity of two employees doing word processing. One enters 70 words a minute, and the other enters 55 words a minute. If we use quantity as the sole measure of job performance, we must give the first worker the higher rating. However, if we examine the quality of the their work, we find that the first worker averages 20 errors a minute and the second makes none. We must now adjust the performance evaluations to reflect the quality of output, and the second worker should receive the higher rating.

Even though we have corrected the output data to compensate for the different quality of performance, we must consider the possibility that other factors can influence or distort the performance measure. Perhaps the employee who made so many keyboard errors works in a vast, open room surrounded by many other employees and a lot of noisy office equipment. The other employee being evaluated may have a private office and few distractions. Or perhaps one is responsible only for short, routine business letters and the other transcribes technical reports from the engineering department. It would be unfair to assign performance ratings without correcting for differences in office environment and level of difficulty of the job tasks.

Another possible contaminating factor is length of job experience. In general, the longer employees are on a job, the greater is their productivity. The performance appraisals of two otherwise identical workers doing the same job may be expected to differ if one has 2 years of experience and the other 20 years.

Therefore, many factors have to be recognized in evaluating performance on production jobs. The more of these influences that must be taken into account, the less objective is the final appraisal. The impact of these extraneous factors

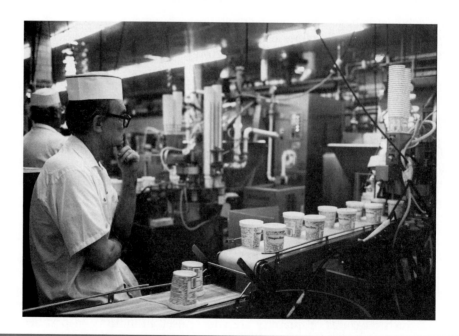

Some routine production jobs can be evaluated in terms of the number of units produced in a given period.

requires raters to make personal judgments. Thus, even with production jobs in which a tangible product can be counted, performance appraisal may not always be completely objective. In repetitive jobs, such as assembly-line work, subjective judgments may have less impact on the final appraisal. In these instances, a straightforward record of quantity and quality of output will suffice as a measure of job performance.

Computerized Performance Monitoring

Work performed at video display terminals can be thought of as a kind of virtual assembly line. Computers are part of the work environment for more than 30 million people in the United States, largely in word-processing, data-entry, insurance, and customer-service jobs. Many organizations have programmed their computers to monitor employees' on-the-job activities. Every time a worker produces a unit of work, such as a keystroke, it is automatically counted and stored, providing an objective measure of job performance. Computers can record the number of keystrokes per unit of time, the incidence of errors, the pace of work over the course of a shift, and the number and length of work breaks or rest pauses. More than half of all workers who use computer terminals are subject to this continuous monitoring and evaluating of their job performance by the "electronic supervisor," the machine that is always watching. It detects and remembers everything.

Computers are also being used to assess workers in telecommunications jobs, such as airline and hotel reservations agents and telephone operators. An airline based in San Diego, California, monitors its reservations agents throughout the work period, timing their calls and comparing their performance with company standards for the number of seconds spent on each inquiry and the

In computerized performance appraisal, data entries made by employees are monitored and evaluated automatically.

number of minutes allotted for rest breaks. Employees who exceed the standards receive demerits and unfavorable ratings.

Attitudes Toward Computerized Monitoring.   Think about it for a minute. How would you like to have your behavior throughout the workday monitored and recorded? Would it bother you? It may surprise you to learn that a lot of employees, perhaps the majority, are not bothered by electronic performance monitoring. Some of them like it and prefer it to other forms of performance appraisal. Psychologists have found that a person's reaction to electronic monitoring depends on how the data compiled on their job performance are ultimately applied. When the information is used to help employees develop and refine job skills (instead of reprimanding them for taking long rest breaks, for example), most workers report a favorable attitude toward computerized monitoring.

Many employees like this high-tech performance appraisal technique because it ensures that their work will be evaluated objectively, not on the basis of how much their supervisor may like or dislike them. Also, employees believe that such objective measures can provide support for their requests for pay raises or promotions.

Stress and Computerized Monitoring.   Having noted that many employees like computerized performance monitoring, it may seem contradictory to report that they also find it stressful, or so they claim in surveys asking whether the technique causes stress. Keep in mind, as we try to reconcile these disparate findings, that the research results may not be contradictory after all. It is quite conceivable that many employees like computerized monitoring and prefer it over other, more subjective, forms of appraisal, yet still find it stressful. Indeed, it would be surprising if some workers did not claim that *all* forms of appraisal are stressful to some degree. (If you were asked on a questionnaire whether you find college exams to be stressful, you would probably answer yes.)

The monitoring of an individual's job performance is far more stressful for that employee than when the performance of the work group as a whole is monitored. In the latter case, each worker's performance is combined with that of other group members.

Also, both field studies and laboratory studies show that people who work alone experience greater stress from computerized monitoring than people who work as part of a cohesive group, even when they are monitored individually. The social support provided by the other members of a close-knit work group helps to reduce the stress.

The knowledge of continuous monitoring, of knowing that every action one takes or fails to take is being recorded, can lead workers to focus more on the quantity of their output than the quality. Thus, the stress of computerized monitoring may result in a reduction of work quality, which has a negative effect on overall job performance and satisfaction.

As with many innovations in the workplace, computerized performance monitoring has both advantages and disadvantages. As advantages, the technique provides immediate and objective feedback, reduces rater bias in performance evaluations, helps identify training needs, facilitates goal setting, and may contribute to increases in productivity. However, it also invades workers' privacy, may increase stress and reduce job satisfaction, and may lead workers to focus on quantity of output at the expense of quality.

Big Brother in a Black Box

The reach of computerized performance monitoring in the twenty-first century is being widened as more and more jobs come online. The see-all, know-all electronic supervisor is now watching assembly-line workers, fast-food workers, machine operators, retail clerks, salespeople, accountants, personnel managers, and health care professionals.

Consider how the typical United Parcel Service (UPS) delivery-man performs his job. Not so long ago, he picked up the packages for his route from the dispatcher in the morning and then was on his own, unobserved and unreachable, until he returned at the end of his shift. Not anymore.

Now he carries a personal computer in a box, all day long. The screen shows his tasks, each one timed to the minute. When he completes a delivery, he enters the details into the computer and the information is instantly transmitted to his supervisor. Thus, the supervisor knows at any time where each delivery person is and whether he is on schedule.

There is no hiding. UPS drivers and millions of other workers are being watched over by what one writer called "the boss that never blinks." The boss that is always observing, recording, and measuring.

Long-distance truckers are another group being monitored electronically. They used to enjoy considerable freedom. You know the image—alone in their 18-wheel rigs, barreling down the highway, exchanging greetings in their own language on their CB radios, with no one to tell them what to do. Those days are gone. Those trucks now carry computers that are on all the time. Using satellite links and on-board recorders, employers can monitor a driver's speed, rate of braking, and time spent off the road at a stop. Some systems will beep when a driver exceeds the prescribed speed or shifts improperly.

A trucker who hauls mattresses from Indiana to Florida told a reporter that the on-board computer saves time by keeping his daily logbook up-to-date and making it easier for him to get help when his truck has a breakdown, since the company is always aware of his location. Still, there is a downside. "You know they are always watching."

Source: In a nonstop economy, truckers keep rolling. *New York Times*, November 24, 1999; Truckers face monitoring to make sure they rest. *St. Petersburg (FL) Times*, February 26, 2000; Big brother in a black box. *Civilization*, August/September 1999, pp. 53–55.

Job-Related Personal Data

Another objective approach to performance appraisal involves the use of personal data, such as absenteeism, earnings history, accidents, and advancement rate. It is usually easier to compile job-related personal information from the files in the human resources office than it is to measure and assess production on the

How would you evaluate the job performance of a documentary filmmaker?

job. I-O psychologists have found that personal data may provide little information about an individual worker's ability on the job, but these data can be used to distinguish good from poor employees. The emphasis here is on a semantic distinction between *workers* and *employees*.

Highly skilled and experienced machine operators who are prone to excessive absenteeism and tardiness may be outstanding workers when they are actually on the job. They may be considered poor employees, however, because the company cannot rely on them to show up regularly and contribute to the efficiency of the organization. Job-related personal data have a use in assessing the relative worth of employees to an organization, but they are not a substitute for measures of job performance.

JUDGMENTAL PERFORMANCE APPRAISAL METHODS

Jobs on which employees do not produce a countable product—or one that makes sense to count—are more difficult to assess. How would you evaluate the performance of firefighters? Should we count the number of fires they put out in a day? How would you appraise brain surgeons? By the number of brains they operate on each week? For business executives, do we tally the number of decisions they make each month?

In each of these instances, I-O psychologists must find some way to assess the merit of the person's work, not by counting or keeping a precise record of output but by observing work behavior over a period of time and rendering a judgment about its quality. To determine how effective or ineffective an employee is, we must ask people who are familiar with the person and the work, usually a supervisor, but sometimes colleagues, subordinates, and even the employee being evaluated.

Written Narratives

Although some organizations use written narratives, which are brief essays describing employee performance, to appraise performance, most also apply numerical rating procedures. Although both narrative and rating approaches are subjective, the narrative technique is more prone to personal bias. An essay written by a supervisor can be ambiguous or misleading when describing an employee's job performance. Sometimes these misstatements are inadvertent, and sometimes they are deliberate, to avoid giving a negative appraisal. An article published in the *Harvard Business Review* listed some common expressions used in written performance appraisals—and suggested what the rater really meant.

- "exceptionally well qualified" (has committed no major blunders to date)
- "tactful in dealing with superiors" (knows when to keep quiet)
- "quick thinking" (instantly offers plausible-sounding excuses for errors)
- "meticulous attention to detail" (a fussy nitpicker)
- "slightly below average" (stupid)
- "unusually loyal to the company" (no one else wants them!)

In an attempt to reduce ambiguity and personal bias, various merit rating techniques have been developed to provide greater objectivity for judgmental performance appraisals.

Merit Rating Techniques

In many everyday situations we make judgments about the people with whom we come in contact. We assess them in terms of their appearance, intelligence, personality, sense of humor, or athletic skills. On the basis of these informal judgments, we may decide whether to like or dislike them, hire them, become friends with them, or marry them. Our judgments are sometimes faulty; a friend can become an enemy, or a spouse an adversary in divorce court. The reason for errors in judgment lies in the fact that the process is subjective and unstandardized. We do not always judge people on the basis of meaningful or relevant criteria.

The process of judgment in **merit rating** is considerably more formalized and specific because job-related criteria are established to serve as standards for comparison. There is still opportunity for raters to impose personal prejudices on the process, but that is not the fault of the method. Merit rating is designed to yield an objective evaluation of work performance compared with established standards.

Merit rating Objective rating methods designed to provide an objective evaluation of work performance.

Rating Technique.   Performance **rating scales** are the most frequently used merit rating technique. The supervisor's task is to specify how or to what degree the worker possesses each of the relevant job characteristics. To rate work quality based on observations of the worker's performance, the supervisor expresses a judgment on a rating scale such as the following. The worker in this example has been judged to exhibit a slightly above average level of task proficiency.

Rating scales A performance appraisal technique in which supervisors indicate how or to what degree a worker possesses each relevant job characteristic.

1	2	3	4	5
Poor		Average		Excellent

Some companies rate employees on specific job duties and on broader factors such as cooperation, supervisory skills, time management, communications skills, judgment and initiative, and attendance. In addition, many organizations compare current employee performance with past evaluations, asking supervisors to indicate whether employees have improved, worsened, or shown no change since the last appraisal.

Supervisors may also be asked to note any particular strengths and to explain extenuating circumstances that might have affected a worker's performance. Some companies allow employees to add their own written comments to the evaluation form. A portion of a typical performance rating form is shown in Figure 5–l.

Ratings are a popular way of evaluating performance for two reasons: (1) they are relatively easy to construct, and (2) they attempt to reduce personal bias.

Ranking technique A performance appraisal technique in which supervisors list the workers in their group in order from highest to lowest or best to worst.

Ranking Technique.   In the **ranking technique,** supervisors list their workers in order from highest to lowest or best to worst on specific characteristics and abilities and on overall job proficiency. You can see that there is a major conceptual difference between rating and ranking. In ranking, each employee is compared with all others in the work group or department. In rating, each employee is compared with his or her past performance or with a company standard. Thus, ranking is not as direct a measure of job performance as is rating.

An advantage of the ranking technique is its simplicity. No elaborate forms or complicated instructions are required. It can be accomplished quickly and is usually accepted by supervisors as a routine task. Supervisors are not being asked to judge workers on factors such as initiative or cooperation, qualities they may not be competent to assess.

However, ranking has its limitations when there are a large number of employees to appraise. Supervisors would have to know all the workers on their shifts quite well in order to make comparative judgments of their efficiency. With a work group of 50 or 100 subordinates, it becomes difficult and tedious to rank them in order of ability or merit.

Another limitation is that because of its simplicity, ranking supplies less evaluative data than does rating. Worker strengths and weaknesses cannot be readily determined by ranking, and there is little feedback or information to provide to workers about how well they are doing or how they might improve their task performance.

The ranking technique for performance appraisal also makes it difficult for supervisors to indicate similarities among workers. For example, in ranking 10 workers, a supervisor may believe that three are equally outstanding and two are equally poor, but there is no way to indicate this. The supervisor is forced to rank the workers from highest to lowest. Thus, only one of the three outstanding workers can be at the top of the list even though all three deserve it.

These limitations make the ranking technique a crude measure of performance appraisal. It is usually applied only when a small number of workers are involved and when little information is desired beyond an indication of their relative standing.

Paired-comparison technique A performance appraisal technique that compares the performance of each worker with that of every other worker in the group.

Paired-Comparison Technique.   The **paired-comparison technique** requires that each worker be compared with every other worker in the work group or section. It is similar to ranking, and the result is a rank ordering of workers, but

Name _____ Position _____ Time in Position _____ Date _____

Department _____ Location _____ Evaluator (Name/Title) _____

Type of Evaluation: Initial 6 Months ☐ Annual ☐ Other _____ Evaluation Period Dates _____

INSTRUCTIONS: Place a check mark (✓) in the box corresponding to the appropriate performance level. Possible elements to consider in evaluation are suggested.

PERFORMANCE RATING LEVELS ————————————————————————————————————

Commendable (C) Performance exceeded expectations for the position in most areas and results were fully accomplished in all other areas. Assignments always produce results above "good" performance standards established for this position.

Good (G) Performance met most of the expectations for the position. Overall performance was satisfactory. Assignments and major job duties are accomplished with minimal supervision and direction.

Needs Improvement (NI) Performance is below expectations. Work may lack consistency or require more frequent and closer supervision than normally expected. Attitude or attendance may affect performance.

Unsatisfactory (U) Performance does not meet minimum expectations. This may include below standard performance, lack of ability, lack of application, or disruptions in the workplace. After a final warning and if performance does not improve, the employee will be terminated.

PERFORMANCE RATING FACTORS (Use additional paper if necessary) ————————————————————

Specific Responsibilities and Duties _____	(C)	(G)	(NI)	(U)
1.				
2.				
3.				

PERFORMANCE RATING FACTORS (Continued) — (NA) Does Not Apply (S) Satisfactory (NI) Needs Improvement (U) Unsatisfactory

General Responsibilities and Requirements _____	(NA)	(S)	(NI)	(U)
1. Cooperation. Ability to demonstrate a spirit of willingness and interest when working with superior(s) and co-workers.				
2. Supervision. Ability to direct, control and train subordinates. Also consider degree to which assistants are helped to establish work objectives.				
3. Time Management. Ability to organize time effectively. Also consider ability to set priorities, anticipate problems, estimate time requirements, and meet deadlines.				
4. Communication. Ability to explain, convince and be understood in oral and written communications with employees at all levels. Also consider evidence of an understanding of people's views and of the effect of own actions on others.				
5. Judgment and Initiative. Ability to identify and appropriately solve or refer problems. Willingness to expand responsibilities.				
6. Attendance. Attendance and timeliness meet acceptable standards. Days Absent _____ Days Late _____				

FIGURE 5–1. Performance appraisal form. (*continued on page 142*)

COMPLETE THIS SECTION

Principal Strengths _____

Areas for Development _____

Comments: _____

_____

Overall Performance Rating: ☐ Commendable   ☐ Good   ☐ Needs Improvement   ☐ Unsatisfactory

Last Performance Review: ☐ Exceptional   ☐ Commendable   ☐ Good   ☐ Needs Improvement   ☐ Unsatisfactory

Date _____

Evaluated by (Name/Title): _____   _____   _____
                              Please print   Signature   Date

   Signature of Reviewer: _____   _____
                                                              Date

   Signature of Employee: _____   _____
                                                              Date

Note: Employee's comments, if any, should be attached to this form.

FIGURE 5–1.   Performance appraisal form. (*continued*)

the comparative judgments are more systematic and controlled. Comparisons are made between two people at a time, and a judgment is made about which of the pair is superior.

If specific characteristics are to be rated, the comparisons are repeated for each item. When all possible comparisons have been made, an objective ranked list is obtained that is based on the worker's score in each comparison. If a supervisor evaluates six workers by this technique, comparing each worker with every other worker, 15 paired comparisons must be made because there are 15 possible pairs. The following formula is used (N represents the number of persons to be evaluated):

$$\frac{N\ (N-1)}{2}$$

An advantage of the paired-comparison approach over the ranking technique is that the judgmental process is simpler. The supervisor has to consider only one pair of workers at a time. Another advantage is that it is possible to give the same rank to those of equal ability.

A disadvantage lies in the large number of comparisons required when dealing with many employees. A supervisor with 60 employees would be required to make 1,770 comparisons. If the performance evaluation calls for the appraisal of, say, five separate traits or factors, each of the 1,770 comparisons would have to be made five times. The use of the technique is necessarily restricted to small groups or to a single ranking of overall job effectiveness.

Forced-Distribution Technique.   The **forced-distribution technique** is useful with somewhat larger groups. Supervisors rate their employees in fixed proportions, according to a predetermined distribution of ratings. The standard distribution is as follows:

Superior	10%
Better than average	20%
Average	40%
Below average	20%
Poor	10%

If your college instructors grade on a curve, then you are already familiar with forced distribution. The top 10% of the class receives a grade of A, regardless of their specific test scores. The next 20% receive Bs, and so on, until all grades are forced into the categories of the distribution resembling the normal curve.

A disadvantage of the forced-distribution technique is that it compels a supervisor to use predetermined rating categories that might not fairly represent that particular group of workers. All workers in a group may be better than average or superior in job performance, and all deserve good ratings. However, the forced distribution technique dictates that only 30% can be rated as above average.

Forced-Choice Technique.   One difficulty with the merit rating techniques we have discussed is that raters are aware of whether they are assigning good or poor ratings to employees. This knowledge may permit their personal biases, animosities, or favoritism to affect the ratings. The **forced-choice technique** prevents raters from knowing how favorable or unfavorable are the ratings they are giving their employees.

In the forced-choice technique, raters are presented with groups of descriptive statements and are asked to select the phrase in each group that best describes an employee or is least applicable to that employee. The phrases within each group are designed to appear equally positive or equally negative. For example, raters may be asked to choose one statement in each of the following pairs that best describes a subordinate.

Is reliable
Is agreeable

Is careful
Is diligent

Next, raters may be asked to select one statement in each of these pairs that least describes the subordinate.

Is arrogant
Is not interested in working well

Is uncooperative
Is sloppy in his/her work habits

Forced-distribution technique A performance appraisal technique in which supervisors rate employees according to a prescribed distribution of ratings, similar to grading on a curve.

Forced-choice technique A performance appraisal technique in which raters are presented with groups of descriptive statements and are asked to select the phrase in each group that is most descriptive or least descriptive of the worker being evaluated.

When given a number of sets of statements, it is difficult for supervisors to distinguish the items that represent desirable or undesirable characteristics. Therefore, they are less likely to deliberately assign favorable or unfavorable ratings.

When I-O psychologists develop statements for forced-choice rating scales, they correlate each item with a measure of job success. Although the statements in each pair may appear to be equally favorable or unfavorable, they have been found to discriminate between more efficient and less efficient workers.

Although the forced-choice technique limits the effect of personal bias and controls for deliberate distortion, it has several disadvantages and is unpopular with raters. Considerable research is necessary to determine the predictive validity for each item. Thus, the technique is more costly to develop than other merit-rating methods. The instructions can be difficult to understand, and the task of choosing between similar alternatives in a large number of pairs is tedious.

Behaviorally anchored rating scales (BARS) A performance appraisal technique in which appraisers rate critical employee behaviors.

Behaviorally Anchored Rating Scales (BARS). **Behaviorally anchored rating scales** (BARS) attempt to evaluate job performance in terms of specific behaviors that are important to success or failure on the job rather than in terms of general attitudes or factors such as communications skills, cooperation, or common sense. The usual way to develop behavioral criteria is through the critical-incidents technique described in Chapter 3 as a method of job analysis.

Supervisors familiar with the job observe the performance of their workers and note those behaviors necessary for effective job performance. A series of critical-incident behaviors are established, some associated with superior performance and others with unsatisfactory performance. These behaviors, based on actual job behaviors, are used as standards for appraising worker effectiveness.

The BARS items can be scored objectively by indicating whether the employee displays that behavior or by selecting on a scale the degree to which the employee displays that behavior. Figure 5–2 shows a BARS scale for the position of Superman or Wonder Woman, though there are not many applicants for those jobs.

FIGURE 5–2. Behaviorally anchored rating scale (BARS). (Adapted by Hurd Hutchins from *The Industrial-Organizational Psychologist*, 1980, 17(4), 22.)

Area of Performance	Degree of Performance				
	Far Excels Job Requirements	Exceeds Job Requirements	Meets Job Requirements	Needs Improvement	Does Not Meet Minimum Requirements
Quality of work	Leaps tall buildings in a single bound	Leaps tall buildings with running start	Can leap over houses, if prodded	Often stumbles into buildings	Is often knocked down by buildings
Promptness	Is faster than a speeding bullet	Is as fast as a speeding bullet	Would you believe a slow bullet?	Misfires frequently	Wounds self when handling a gun
Initiative	Is stronger than a locomotive	Is as strong as a bull elephant	Almost as strong as a bull	Shoots the bull	Smells like a bull
Adaptability	Walks on water	Strong swimmer	A good water treader	Favorite haunt is the water cooler	Passes water in emergencies
Communication	Talks with God	Talks with the angels	Talks to self	Argues with self	Loses most of these arguments

Much of the success of the BARS approach depends on the observational skill of the supervisors in identifying behaviors that are truly critical to successful or unsuccessful performance on the job. If the list of critical incidents is inadequate, any performance appraisal based on these behaviors may be misleading. In some applications of the BARS technique, behaviors are listed in terms of expectations; in this instance, the instrument is called a behavioral expectation scale (BES). One advantage of BARS and BES approaches to performance appraisal is that they meet federal fair employment guidelines. The criteria on which workers are assessed are job related because they derive from actual job behaviors.

Behavioral Observation Scales (BOS).   In the **behavioral observation scale (BOS)** approach to performance appraisal, employees are also evaluated in terms of critical incidents. In that respect, it is similar to BARS. However, the BOS appraisers rate subordinates on the *frequency* of the critical incidents as they are observed to occur over a given period. The ratings are assigned on a 5-point scale. The evaluation yields a total score for each employee, obtained by adding the ratings for each critical incident.

The behavioral incidents for the rating scale are developed in the same way as for BARS, through identification by supervisors or other subject matter experts. Similarly, BOS meet equal employment opportunity guidelines because they are related to actual behaviors required for successful job performance.

I-O psychology research comparing BARS and BOS techniques has been inconclusive. Some studies demonstrate the superiority of one technique over the other; other studies fail to confirm these findings.

Management by Objectives (MBO)

Management by objectives (MBO) involves a mutual agreement between employees and managers on goals to be achieved in a given time period. Instead of focusing on abilities or traits as in merit rating, or on job behaviors as in BARS and BOS, management by objectives focuses on results—on how well employees accomplish specified goals. The emphasis is on what employees *do* rather than on what their supervisors think of them or perceive their behaviors to be. Further, MBO actively involves employees in their own evaluations. They are not simply graded or rated by others.

MBO consists of two phases: goal setting and performance review. In goal setting, employees meet individually with supervisors to determine the goals for which they will strive in the time before the next appraisal, usually 1 year, and to discuss ways of reaching those goals. The goals must be realistic, specific, and as objective as possible. For example, it is not enough for salespersons to say that they will try to sell more products. A fixed number of items or a dollar volume must be established as the goal.

In performance review, employees and supervisors discuss the extent to which the goals were met. Again, this is a mutual process involving both parties. The performance appraisal is based on job results, not on characteristics such as initiative or general skills.

Employees in MBO programs may feel pressured to set higher goals with each appraisal to show evidence of improvement. A supervisor may not accept

Behavioral observation scales (BOS) A performance appraisal technique in which appraisers rate the frequency of critical employee behaviors.

Management by objectives (MBO) A performance appraisal technique that involves a mutual agreement between employee and manager on goals to be achieved in a given period.

last year's quota as a sufficient goal for this year's job performance. Thus, the goals may become increasingly unrealistic. Also, MBO is not useful for jobs that cannot be quantified. It would be silly to expect research chemists to agree to make five more scientific breakthroughs this year than last.

The MBO technique satisfies fair employment guidelines and has been found to be effective in increasing employee motivation and productivity.

PERFORMANCE APPRAISAL FOR MANAGERS

The performance appraisal of managerial personnel presents problems not faced in the assessment of other employees. Merit rating techniques are often used to evaluate low- and middle-level managerial personnel, but additional appraisal methods are required. Paradoxically, senior executives are rarely evaluated. They seldom receive feedback or judgments about the quality of their job performance unless the company faces a crisis. Indeed, high-level management failure is sometimes rewarded with generous severance packages. Interviews with top executives have shown that at higher levels of management, performance reviews are less systematic and informative.

Evaluation Techniques

Assessment Centers.   Assessment centers (discussed in Chapter 3 as an employee selection technique) are a popular method of performance appraisal. Managers participate in simulated job tasks such as management games, group problem solving, leaderless group discussions, in-basket tests, and interviews. Recall that assessment centers do not assess actual job behavior but, rather, a variety of activities that are like those encountered on the job. Assessment-center evaluations appear to have high validity when used for performance appraisal purposes.

Evaluation by Superiors.   The most frequently used technique for the performance appraisal of managers is assessment by their superiors in the organization. Standard rating sheets are rarely used. Typically, the rater writes a brief descriptive essay about the person's job performance. An evaluation by an immediate superior is often supplemented by the judgments of executives at higher levels.

Peer rating A performance appraisal technique in which managers or executives at the same level assess one another's abilities and job behaviors.

Evaluation by Colleagues: Peer Rating.   **Peer rating** (also called "buddy rating") was developed during World War II. It is a technique for having managers or executives at the same level assess one another in terms of their general ability to perform the job and their specific traits and behaviors. Although ratings given by peers and colleagues tend to be higher than ratings assigned by superiors, research shows a positive correlation between high peer ratings and subsequent promotion. Peer ratings also show high reliability and a focus on job-related skills.

Attitudes toward peer rating among managers are generally positive. However, managers are far more favorable toward peer rating when the evaluations are used for career development or improving job skills than when they are used for promotion or other career decisions.

Self-Evaluation.   Another approach to managerial performance appraisal is to ask people to assess their own abilities and job performance. One technique is similar to management by objectives (MBO), discussed earlier in this chapter. Managers and their superiors meet to establish goals for managerial performance—not specific production targets but personal skills to be developed or deficiencies to be corrected. After a time, the managers meet again with their superiors to discuss their progress.

Self-ratings tend to be higher than evaluations by superiors and to show greater leniency. Self-ratings also focus more on interpersonal skills, whereas ratings by superiors emphasize initiative and specific job skills. Leniency can be reduced if raters are told that their self-evaluations will be validated against more objective criteria.

Self-ratings A performance appraisal technique in which managers assess their own abilities and job performance.

A study of 1,888 managers at a large accounting firm compared self-ratings and subordinate ratings collected twice during a 1-year period. Those managers who rated themselves much higher than their subordinates did tended to show improvement in their own job performance over time. Those managers who rated themselves lower than their subordinates did tended to show a decline in job performance. These results suggested to the researchers that self-ratings can have a motivating effect for people who tend to overestimate their job performance (Johnson & Ferstl, 1999).

In another study, each of 110 supervisors in a state law-enforcement agency was rated on leadership ability by at least two subordinates. The supervisors who received feedback on these ratings later lowered their self-ratings. Supervisors who received no feedback did not change their self-ratings. The researchers concluded that the feedback from subordinates influenced the supervisors' view of their leadership ability (Atwater, Waldman, Atwater, & Cartier, 2000).

Evaluation by Subordinates.   Another approach to the performance appraisal of managers involves evaluation by subordinates, as used in the studies just described. The technique, sometimes described as upward feedback, is similar to having students evaluate their classroom instructors.

Upward feedback is effective in developing and improving leadership abilities. In one global corporation, more than 1,500 employees completed two behavioral observation scales 6 months apart to rate 238 managers. Managers who received top scores in the first rating did not show improvement at the second rating; they were already seen to be performing well. Managers who received moderate to low ratings initially did show improved leadership effectiveness by the second rating. Thus, the managers who needed to improve did so, most likely in response to the upward feedback from subordinates (Reilly, Smither, & Vasilopoulos, 1996).

Another study showing that subordinates' ratings lead to improved job performance involved 252 bank managers. In research conducted over a 5-year period, psychologists found that managers who received poor to moderate ratings from subordinates at the beginning of the period showed far more improvement in subsequent ratings than managers who received higher initial ratings. Managers who met with subordinates to discuss their ratings improved more than managers who did not meet with subordinates (Walker & Smither, 1999).

At the U.S. Naval Academy in Annapolis, Maryland, where students and cadet officers live and work together, 978 leaders were rated by 1,232 followers 8 weeks and 14 weeks after the beginning of the academic year. Overall, the behavior of the cadet officers improved following the evaluations by their subordinates. When the leaders then rated themselves, however, the self-ratings of those who had received negative feedback from their subordinates declined, whereas the self-ratings of those who had received positive feedback increased. Apparently, the cadet officers placed great importance on the ratings their subordinates had given them (Atwater, Roush, & Fischthal, 1995).

A study of nearly 250 managers who were rated on team-building skills by two peers and two subordinates concluded that peer ratings and subordinate ratings were equivalent (Maurer, Raju, & Collins, 1998).

Rating Your Boss: No Names, Please!

NEWSBREAK

You know the drill. About every 6 months, your boss calls you in for a chat about how you're doing at your job. It's called a performance appraisal. You sit there, perhaps seething inside, while the boss tells you what you're doing wrong and how you could improve. And you're thinking how you'd like to tell the boss a thing or two about how he or she is doing.

Nowadays, some employees *can* talk back. Growing numbers of companies are asking workers to participate in an upward feedback appraisal process—that is, to appraise the performance of their supervisors and managers. These appraisals or ratings are then used to help determine promotions and pay raises for the boss. Does this sound great? A chance to get back at the supervisor? Maybe get that obnoxious guy fired? But suppose you had to sign your name to the appraisal? Would that affect your comments? Most likely it would, unless, of course, you had already lined up another job.

To test this hypothesis, a management professor at the University of Wisconsin asked 183 employees at an insurance company to rate 38 managers. The employees were all volunteers for the task and were told that the managers would take no reprisals, regardless of what the employees reported. To further reassure the employees, they were given the phone number of a contact in the human resources department whom they could call in the event of any backlash.

Half the employees in the study appraised their bosses anonymously. The other half signed their names to the evaluation form. Did the act of identifying themselves make a difference in the ratings? You bet it did! Employees who signed their names to the appraisal forms gave higher ratings to their managers than did the employees who were doing the ratings anonymously. All employees reported that they would feel much more comfortable rating their bosses if they could remain anonymous.

Upward feedback can be an effective tool for improving manager effectiveness. Just don't sign your name to the form.

Source: D. Antonioni (1994). The effects of feedback accountability on upward appraisal ratings. *Personnel Psychology, 47,* 349–356.

360-Degree Feedback

Another approach to performance appraisal involves combining evaluations from several sources into an overall appraisal. Any number of individual ratings sources can be so combined, but the ultimate multisource approach is called 360-degree feedback. It combines the full circle of ratings from all sources—superiors, subordinates, peers, and self, and even evaluations by the organization's customers or clients who have dealings with the person being rated.

Multisource feedback can provide information that would not otherwise be available about the ratees because it provides data from unique perspectives. For example, subordinates and peers have different experiences and relationships with their managers than do the managers' bosses. Evaluations from clients or customers provide yet another view of how well managers are performing their jobs. One study of ratings of 153 managers found that peers provided the most reliable ratings, followed by subordinates, then by supervisors (Greguras & Robie, 1998).

Multisource feedback may also reduce many forms of bias. If all parties are told that their ratings will be compared with those assigned by others, they are likely to be more objective in their assessments. When combined ratings are consistent, decisions about a manager's future with the organization can be made with greater confidence. Also, if ratings show a high level of agreement, a manager may be more willing to accept criticism because it comes from sources other than the immediate supervisor. When ratings disagree, however, the manager may be reluctant to accept and act on criticism.

The use of 360-degree feedback is more costly than appraisals from a single source, but the approach is growing in popularity. Surveys show that 360-degree feedback is already in use in up to 10% of U.S. corporations, including nearly all of the Fortune 500 companies. Despite its popularity, there is little research evidence showing that it is effective. Although studies show that both managers and employees like this type of appraisal, sufficient data to support its use are not yet available.

BIAS IN PERFORMANCE APPRAISAL

Regardless of the sophistication of the techniques used, performance appraisal still involves one person judging, assessing, or estimating the characteristics and performance of another. This inevitably means that human biases and prejudices affect the judgments. Some common sources of error that can distort performance appraisals include the halo effect, constant or systematic bias, most-recent-performance error, inadequate information error, average rating or leniency error, the rater's cognitive processes, and role conflict.

The Halo Effect

The **halo effect** involves the familiar tendency to judge all aspects of a person's behavior or character on the basis of a single attribute. For example, if we find a person to be physically attractive, we may tend to think of that person also as friendly, likeable, and easy to get along with, generalizing from one attribute to personality characteristics and other abilities. A supervisor who scores an

Halo effect The tendency to judge all aspects of a person's behavior or character on the basis of a single attribute.

employee high on one factor of a merit rating scale may tend to grade that person high on all other factors. This distortion is particularly likely to occur when a high rating is given on one or two traits and the other traits to be rated are difficult to observe, unfamiliar, or not clearly defined.

One way to control for the halo effect is to have more than one person rate a worker, on the assumption that any personal biases will tend to cancel each other out. Another way is to have supervisors rate all subordinates on one trait or characteristic at a time instead of rating each person on all items at once. When workers are judged on a single characteristic, there is a smaller chance for one rating to carry over to other traits.

Recent I-O psychology research suggests that the halo error may be less a problem than previously thought. The halo effect does not appear to diminish the overall quality of ratings, often cannot be detected, and may, in many cases, be illusory. Halo has been attributed to factors such as deficiencies in measurement and common errors of memory or observation, rather than to the direct influence of personal bias.

Other Sources of Error

Constant bias A source of error in performance appraisal based on the different standards used by raters.

Constant or Systematic Bias.   Constant bias as a source of performance appraisal error has its basis in the standards or criteria used by raters. Some raters or supervisors expect more than others from their employees. Similarly, in college some professors are known as easy graders and expect less from their students than those known as hard graders. The constant biasing error means that a top rating given by one supervisor may not be equivalent to a top rating given by another supervisor, just as an A from one professor may not mean the same as an A from another professor as an evaluation of merit or ability.

Constant bias can be corrected by requiring supervisors to distribute ratings in accordance with the normal curve. However, as we noted with the forced distribution technique, this means that some workers will receive ratings that are undeserved.

Most-Recent-Performance Error. Performance appraisals are usually made every 6 or 12 months. There is an understandable tendency to base ratings on the workers' most recent behavior, without considering their performance throughout the entire rating period since the last appraisal. It is natural for memory to be clearer about events that have occurred more recently, but recent behavior may be atypical or distorted by extraneous factors.

For example, if a worker performs poorly in the weeks just before an evaluation because of illness or marital problems, the result may be a distortion of a previous record of exemplary job performance. If a worker is aware that a performance evaluation is due, he or she may strive to work more efficiently just before the rating. In both cases, performance is not typical of the workers' overall job behavior, and a falsely low or high rating will result.

One way to reduce this **most-recent-performance error** is to require more frequent appraisals. By shortening the time between performance reviews, there is less tendency for supervisors to forget a worker's usual behavior. Making supervisors aware of the possibility that this type of error can occur can also be effective in reducing it.

Most-recent-performance error A source of error in performance appraisal in which a rater tends to evaluate a worker's most recent job behavior rather than behavior throughout the period since the last appraisal.

Inadequate Information Error. Supervisors are required to rate employees at specified intervals whether or not they know enough about the employees to do so fairly and accurately. To admit to superiors that they lack adequate knowledge of their subordinates can be construed as a personal failing. The resulting appraisals will be worth little to the organization or to the employees because they will not be based on a comprehensive knowledge of worker behavior.

A way to deal with this **inadequate information error** is to educate raters about the value of performance appraisals and the harm done by ratings based on incomplete information. Supervisors should be given the opportunity to decline to rate employees about whom they have little knowledge and the assurance that they will not be penalized for such refusal.

Inadequate information error A source of error in performance appraisal in which supervisors rate their subordinates even though they may not know enough about them to do so fairly and accurately.

Average Rating or Leniency Error. Some raters are reluctant to assign extreme scores in either direction. The tendency is to be lenient and to assign average ratings to all workers. Particularly when dealing with a small number of employees, it is not unusual to find their ratings clustered around the middle of the scale, separated by no more than one or two points. Thus, the range of abilities indicated is restricted, and the ratings are so close that it is difficult to distinguish between good and poor workers. This **average rating error** does not reflect the range of differences that exist among workers, and the ratings provide no useful information to the company or to employees.

Research involving three real-world appraisal situations dealt with the following groups of employees: 38 police sergeants rating 328 patrol officers, 31 head nurses rating 243 nurses, and 44 supervisors rating 376 social workers.

Average rating error A source of error in performance appraisal in which a rater is unwilling to assign very good or very poor ratings. Consequently, most ratings fall in the middle of the rating scale.

The results showed that the leniency error is a stable rater characteristic, independent of rating format or situational and personal variables (Kane, Bernadin, Villanova, & Peyrefitte, 1995). Some supervisors, then, will always tend to give more lenient evaluations than others. The challenge for employers is to identify the raters who show this tendency and to take it into consideration when making personnel decisions based on their appraisals of subordinates.

Cognitive Processes.   The cognitive or thought processes of raters underlie their judgments of worker effectiveness. We discuss four cognitive variables that can influence evaluations of employee performance: category structures, beliefs, interpersonal affect, and attribution.

1. *Category structures.* The category structures that managers use in evaluating their employees can affect their assessments. When an appraiser thinks about a worker as belonging to a particular category, the information he or she recalls about that worker will be biased toward that category. For example, if an employee is perceived to be a team player, then this becomes a category in the rater's mental picture. The employee's job performance will likely be observed, interpreted, and remembered in terms of how a typical team player is expected to behave rather than in terms of how that employee actually behaves.

2. *Beliefs.* A related cognitive variable that can influence performance appraisals involves raters' beliefs about human nature. These ideas can lead raters to make evaluations in terms of how they view people in general rather than in terms of a specific worker's characteristics and behaviors. For example, supervisors who believe that people are basically good and trustworthy give more generous ratings than those who think that people are spiteful and narrow-minded. Managers who accept the idea of individual differences among people and who are tolerant of those differences may give different ratings from managers who believe most people are alike.

3. *Interpersonal affect.* The cognitive variable of **interpersonal affect** refers to one person's feelings or emotions toward another person. Common sense suggests that, except for those raters who can maintain impartiality and objectivity toward their subordinates, ratings will be influenced by the personal relationship between rater and ratee. In general, raters who have positive emotions or affect toward the persons they are rating give higher marks than do raters who have negative affect.

   It is possible to manipulate interpersonal affect through impression management techniques. A study of 111 pairs of subordinates and supervisors found that impression management strategies such as flattery, doing favors, or agreeing with one's supervisor's opinions significantly affected how much the supervisor liked the worker. This, in turn, led to higher performance ratings. The impression management strategy designed by the employee to enhance his or her own situation—assertive behaviors such as boasting about one's accomplishments—did not affect the level of the supervisor's liking for the subordinate (Wayne & Liden, 1995).

   These findings probably coincide with our everyday experiences. We tend to be more lenient, forgiving, and generous toward people we like.

Interpersonal affect Our feelings or emotions toward another person. In performance appraisal, the emotional tone of the relationship between manager and employee, whether positive or negative, can influence the assigned ratings.

However, interpersonal affect may not influence ratings in all situations. An analysis of the ratings of 631 soldiers by their supervisors found that dependability was a more powerful influence on ratings than friendliness and likability. It was more important for an officer to believe that a soldier could be trusted or counted on to perform under fire than to believe that the soldier was pleasant or sociable (Borman, White, & Dorsey, 1995).

4. *Attribution.* The concept of **attribution** derives from social psychology research on the way we form impressions of other people. In performance appraisal, one person forms an impression of the abilities and characteristics of another. The rater mentally attributes or assigns reasons to the worker's behavior. These beliefs about why an employee behaves in a particular way can affect the rater's evaluation. For example, a supervisor may observe that two employees frequently seem tired. That supervisor may be lenient and understanding toward the tired employee who has young children but less forgiving of the tired employee who is known to enjoy late-night partying.

Attribution can also be influenced by interpersonal affect. Managers may attribute poor job performance to internal factors, such as lack of motivation or inadequate skills, when they dislike (have negative affect toward) the person being rated. In other words, the managers appear to believe that the poor performance of the workers they do not like is the fault of the workers themselves. On the other hand, the poor performance of workers they do like may be attributed to external factors such as bad luck, a heavy work load, or equipment failure.

The attribution error can be reduced by having supervisors spend time performing the job they are evaluating. This experience exposes them to the kinds of external factors that can influence job performance. Raters should also be made aware of how their perceptions of a worker's behavior on the job can differ from the worker's own point of view.

> **Attribution** A source of error in performance appraisal in which raters attribute or assign positive or negative explanations to an employee's behavior.

Role Conflict.   A final source of error in the performance appraisal process is the amount of role conflict experienced by the supervisor. **Role conflict** refers to the disparity or contradiction between the job's demands and the supervisor's standards of right and wrong. Sometimes the nature of a job requires supervisors to compromise those standards (we shall see in Chapter 12 that role conflict is a source of job stress).

Self-report measures of role conflict, and of the tendency to deliberately inflate performance ratings, were obtained from two groups totaling 177 supervisors. Those who scored high in role conflict tended to deliberately inflate the ratings they gave to their subordinates. The researchers suggested that supervisors who experienced role conflict may have given inflated ratings for several reasons (Fried & Tiegs, 1995):

> **Role conflict** A situation that arises when there is a disparity between job demands and the employee's personal standards.

- as a way of establishing control over the work situation
- as a way of avoiding the confrontation with subordinates that might result from giving them lower ratings
- as a way of obtaining subordinates' gratitude and goodwill

Whatever the reasons, it is clear from this and similar research that role conflict, and the stress associated with it, may lead supervisors to give higher-than-justified performance ratings. Managers may inflate performance appraisals as a way of satisfying personal needs and dealing with organizational pressures.

HOW TO IMPROVE PERFORMANCE APPRAISALS

The fact that performance appraisals can be so easily biased is no reason to abandon hope of achieving more objective evaluations. We have noted various steps that can be taken to reduce some sources of error. Providing training and feedback to raters, and allowing subordinates to participate, can also decrease errors, increase accuracy, and promote satisfaction with the evaluation process.

Training.   Training the persons who conduct performance appraisals involves (1) creating an awareness that abilities and skills are usually distributed in accordance with the normal curve, so that it is acceptable to find broad differences within a group of workers, and (2) developing the ability to define objective criteria for worker behaviors—the standards or average performance levels against which workers can be compared. I-O psychology research supports the idea that rater training can reduce errors in performance appraisal, particularly leniency and halo. Further, the more actively the raters are involved in the training process, the greater the positive effects. Having raters participate in group discussions and in practice sessions to provide feedback to subordinates generally produces better results than having raters attend lectures about the rating process.

Providing Feedback to Raters.   Providing feedback to raters can also improve performance appraisal. In a now-classic study, marketing managers in a large high-tech company received feedback from trained raters about the evaluations those managers had given their subordinates. The feedback included information about how each manager's ratings differed from the ratings given by other managers. When these marketing managers evaluated their subordinates a year later, they assigned lower ratings than did a control group of marketing managers who had received no feedback about their earlier ratings. More than 90% of the managers in the experimental group said that the feedback had influenced their second set of ratings. The researchers concluded that the feedback had reduced the leniency error (Davis & Mount, 1984).

Subordinate Participation.   Allowing employees to participate in the evaluation of their own job performance has been shown to lead to improvements in the appraisal process. In a study of 529 production workers and their supervisors, employees were asked to complete self-appraisal forms and to meet with their supervisors to reconcile discrepancies between self-ratings and supervisor ratings. The researchers found that employee participation led to a significant improvement in employee trust in management and to an enhanced perception of the accuracy of the performance evaluation system (Mayer & Davis, 1999).

In other research, a meta-analysis of 27 studies confirmed that allowing employees to have a say in how their job performance is assessed significantly increases satisfaction with and acceptance of the organization's performance appraisal system. Employee participation also led to a heightened belief in the fairness and usefulness of the appraisal process and to an increased motivation to improve job performance (Cawley, Keeping, & Levy, 1998).

THE POSTAPPRAISAL INTERVIEW

We have noted that two goals of performance appraisal programs are to supply information to management for personnel decisions and to diagnose strengths and weaknesses of employees and provide them with the means for self-improvement. To fulfill the second goal, the job performance ratings and the recommendations of the appraisers must be communicated to the employees.

Offering Feedback.   Offering feedback to employees is usually accomplished during a postappraisal interview between worker and supervisor, a situation that can easily become antagonistic, even hostile, especially when a performance evaluation contains criticism. Negative feedback during a postappraisal interview can make employees angry and lead them to reject any criticism or suggestions. Employees may attempt to shift the blame for alleged deficiencies in job performance by dismissing the usefulness of the appraisal, downgrading the importance of the job, or criticizing the supervisor.

In the postappraisal interview, the supervisor should be positive and supportive and should focus on specific job behaviors rather than on the worker's personal qualities.

A review of more than 600 research studies dealing with postappraisal feedback found that only one-third of the studies reported improvements in employee job performance following feedback. Another one-third of the studies reported deterioration in job performance following feedback. And one-third found no performance changes in either direction (Kluger & DeNisi, 1996).

A meta-analysis of 131 studies showed that postappraisal information provided by computer instead of in a personal interview with a supervisor was considered more desirable by the employee and was more effective in improving job performance. Apparently, eliminating the face-to-face interview situation reduced any personal antagonism between worker and supervisor that might otherwise have interfered with the employee's acceptance of criticism (DeNisi & Kluger, 2000).

Reaction to Criticism.   The primary purpose of the postappraisal interview is to stimulate employees to improve their job performance. This expectation may be wishful thinking. Some workers, when criticized, will act to exaggerate their faults—coming to work late or showing sloppy work habits—as an imagined means of revenge. If workers are told that they request assistance too frequently, they may stop doing so and, as a result, make more mistakes. In such cases, criticism can lead to reduced motivation and job performance.

It may also be unrealistic to expect that a brief meeting every 6 or 12 months will provide sufficient impetus for employees to change. In addition, it may be unwise to believe that supervisors, unless they are specially trained, possess the insight and skill to diagnose the reasons for a worker's unsatisfactory job performance and to prescribe a program for improvement.

If feedback on employee performance were provided more frequently and competently and not restricted to the formal postappraisal interview, then employee motivation to change job behavior and to persist in that behavior could be enhanced.

Improving Postappraisal Interviews.   Despite the limitations and problems of postappraisal interviews, they can be structured to fulfill the purposes for which they are intended. I-O psychology research has identified several factors related to successful postappraisal interviews. Employees are more likely to be satisfied with postappraisal interviews and to follow their supervisors' suggestions about improving job performance under the following conditions:

1. Employees should be allowed to participate actively in the appraisal process.
2. The postappraisal interviewer should adopt a positive, constructive, and supportive attitude.
3. The interviewer should focus on specific job problems rather than on the employee's personal characteristics.
4. The employee and the supervisor should establish jointly specific goals to be achieved in the period before the next appraisal.
5. The employee should be given the opportunity to question, challenge, and rebut the evaluation without fear of retribution.
6. Discussions of changes in salary and rank should be linked directly to the performance appraisal criteria.

PERFORMANCE APPRAISAL: A POOR RATING?

Performance appraisal may be one of the least popular features of modern organizational life. Two British psychologists offered this judgment: "The general attitude to performance appraisal is 'Oh my God, it's appraisal time again. I suppose we had better do it.' But what the hell are we doing it for?" (Redman & Snape, 1992, p. 36).

Why do performance appraisal programs get such a poor rating? We have already discussed the opportunities for personal bias and other errors to enter into the evaluations. Here are some additional reasons.

A Poor Rating from Managers.   Consider the person who must make the ratings or conduct the observations and appraisals. Despite a great deal of impressive research supporting the benefits of performance appraisals made by subordinates or peers, the fact remains that on the job, most performance ratings are made by managers or supervisors. Performance appraisal requires their considerable time and effort in addition to their other job duties. They must spend many hours observing subordinates to develop sufficient knowledge on which to base their assessments. They spend additional hours on paperwork, completing the appraisal forms, and yet more time in rater training programs.

In practice, some managers and supervisors resist appraisal programs and fill out the forms only when pressured by their superiors. Thus, the evaluations are often not thorough and systematic but are compiled in haste. Many supervisors loathe the idea of judging employees and taking responsibility for their progress in the organization, and therefore they are reluctant to give low ratings, even for poor performance.

Further, supervisors may deliberately delay providing feedback, particularly when the evaluation is negative. Or they may inflate the ratings or suppress unfavorable information. By pretending that the employee is performing at a higher level than actual job performance justifies, the supervisor eliminates the potential for confrontation and reduces the negative impact of an unfavorable appraisal.

A Poor Rating from Employees.   Employees do not like performance appraisals, although most recognize that some means of evaluating job performance is necessary. They express concern about the effect of performance assessments on their career, apprehensive that a supervisor will use the appraisal to exaggerate misunderstandings or highlight personality clashes that have nothing to do with job competence. Employees are often not sufficiently informed about the criteria by which they are being judged or even precisely what is expected of them on the job. In addition, employees may be given low ratings for faults that lie within the organization or in the way jobs are structured. These are matters over which employees have no control but for which they may be blamed.

In many organizations, the results of performance appraisal programs are never used to help make decisions about promotions or to help employees improve their skills, the major purposes for which such programs were developed. Performance appraisal as conducted in organizations today is largely unsatisfactory, which may help explain why correlations between ratings and results-oriented job performance criteria (such as sales and output data) are relatively low. However, assessments of employee ability at all levels of employment are necessary. The question is not whether to use an employee appraisal system but, rather, which is the most effective approach to use.

Stress and Electronic Performance Monitoring

Electronic monitoring of the job performance of employees who work at computer terminals and in telecommunications can provide comprehensive and accurate measures of output and competence. This type of monitoring is widespread in business and industry, not only for employee surveillance and control but also for performance appraisal. Some employees like the computer-aided approach because it yields an objective evaluation of job performance. Others find it to be stressful and object to the continuous monitoring of their work.

To investigate the relationship between stress and electronic performance monitoring, a study was conducted at the Work Stress Laboratory of the National Institute for Occupational Safety and Health (NIOSH). The subjects were 47 women data-entry operators with a mean age of 24 recruited from a temporary employment agency. They were paid $7.55 an hour for the 3-day study. Each workday consisted of six 40-minute work periods. To ensure the work would be demanding, no subject was selected who was able to exceed the performance standards of 200 keystrokes per minute and no more than six errors per minute.

The subjects were required to enter numbers from bogus federal tax forms using the numeric keypad of an IBM M3163 VDT. On the first workday, the subjects performed the data-entry task at their usual work pace; there was no monitoring of their performance. On the second and third days, the subjects were randomly assigned to one of two conditions: half had their work monitored electronically, and the other half continued to work as they had on the first day, with no monitoring of their performance.

The electronic performance monitoring (EPM) group received feedback on their video screens following each 40-minute work period. Those subjects who did not meet the speed and accuracy standards of 200 keystrokes a minute and no more than six errors a minute received a negative-feedback message informing them that they had not met the performance criteria and that their work was unsatisfactory. Those who met the standards received a positive message, indicating that their performance was satisfactory. The no-EPM group received no feedback. At the end of each work period, subjects in both groups completed questionnaires assessing their level of irritation, perceived time pressure, tension, workload dissatisfaction, boredom, and fatigue.

In the group whose performance was monitored electronically, the workers reported significant increases in irritation, tension, perceived time pressure, and workload dissatisfaction from the beginning to the end of the 3-day study period. The researchers also found among the EPM group a significant increase in reported discomfort in the right hand (the hand used for data-entry by all subjects). They concluded that electronic performance monitoring was highly stressful.

Think About It

1. Do you think this study is a realistic simulation of actual working conditions for employees? In what ways might the simulation differ from the conditions of a real job?

2. Based on our discussion of survey research in Chapter 2, how would you devise a survey on computer-aided performance monitoring? Would you use interviews or mailed questionnaires? Open-end or fixed-alternative questions? Probability sampling or quota sampling?

3. In what ways, other than computerized monitoring, can the job performance of tax agency employees be appraised objectively?

4. Even with objective measures such as those provided by computerized monitoring, can rater bias affect performance appraisals? Explain your answer for each potential source of error.

Source: L. M. Schliefer, T. L. Galinski, & C. S. Pan (1995). Mood disturbance and musculoskeletal discomfort effects of electronic performance monitoring a VDT data-entry task. In S. L. Sauter & L. R. Murphy (Eds.), *Organizational risk factors for job stress* (pp. 195–203). Washington, DC: American Psychological Association.

5. If you were a company manager, what would you do about employees who opposed electronic monitoring on the grounds of invasion of privacy? Would you refuse to promote them? Transfer them to another department? Evaluate their performance by some other means? Why?

SUMMARY

Performance appraisal programs are used to validate selection criteria, determine the need for and success of training programs, improve employee behavior, determine promotions and pay raises, and identify employees with promotion potential. To ensure compliance with EEOC guidelines, performance appraisals must be based on job analyses, must focus on job behaviors rather than personal traits, and must be reviewed with the person being evaluated. Labor unions oppose performance appraisal because of their commitment to seniority as the basis for personnel decisions. Employees dislike performance appraisal because few of us like to be judged or criticized. Managers dislike making appraisals that will affect their subordinates' careers.

Performance appraisals may be objective or judgmental. Objective measures include quantity and quality of output, computer-aided appraisal, and data on accidents, salary, advancement, and absenteeism. Judgmental methods involve having supervisors assess their workers' ability to perform the job. These assessments are made by **merit rating** techniques, including **rating, ranking, paired comparisons, forced distribution,** and **forced choice,** techniques that involve one person judging the abilities or characteristics of another. The **BARS** and **BOS** approaches to merit rating attempt to evaluate performance in terms of specific behaviors critical to success or failure on the job. BARS and BOS meet EEOC guidelines and can reduce rating errors. **Management by objectives** (MBO) involves mutual agreement between supervisors and subordinates about setting and achieving specific goals.

Evaluating managerial performance may be accomplished through assessment centers or evaluation by supervisors, colleagues (peers), subordinates, or self-ratings. Combining ratings into an overall appraisal (360-degree feedback) is of particular value.

Sources of rater error include the **halo effect, most-recent-performance error, inadequate information error, average rating error,** the rater's **cognitive processes,** and **role conflict.** Three ways to improve performance appraisals are better training for raters, providing feedback to raters, and allowing subordinates to participate in their own ratings.

Performance appraisal results must be communicated to employees to provide them with information about their strengths and weaknesses. Feedback should be given with tact and sensitivity, particularly when criticism is involved, because it can lead to defensiveness and a decline in job performance. Feedback sessions should be informal and frequent and focus on specific goals. Workers should be allowed to participate freely in the discussions.

KEY TERMS

attribution
average rating (leniency) error
behavioral observation scales (BOS)
behaviorally anchored rating scales (BARS)

constant (systematic) bias
forced-choice technique
forced-distribution technique
halo effect

inadequate information error
interpersonal affect
management by objectives (MBO)
merit rating
most-recent-performance error
paired-comparison technique

peer rating
performance appraisal
ranking technique
rating scales
role conflict
self-ratings

ADDITIONAL READING

Arvey, R. D., & Murphy, K. R. (1998). Performance evaluation in work settings. *Annual Review of Psychology, 49,* 141–168. Reviews recent research on performance appraisal, including rating techniques, sources of bias, and rater training.

Cawley, B. D., Keeling, L. M., & Levy, P. E. (1998). Participation in the performance appraisal process and employee reactions. *Journal of Applied Psychology, 83,* 615–633. Reviews the results of 27 studies on the importance of employee participation in evaluations—that is, giving employees the opportunity to make their opinions known to management.

Ghorpade, J. (2000). Managing five paradoxes of 360-degree feedback. *Academy of Management Executive, 14*(1), 140–150. Notes the popularity of the 360-degree performance appraisal method in the Fortune 500 companies and discusses several problems relating to privacy, validity, and effectiveness. See also in the same issue, A. S. DeNisi and A. N. Kluger, "Feedback effectiveness: Can 360-degree appraisals be improved?"

Tornow, W. W., & London, M. (1998). *Maximizing the value of 360-degree feedback.* San Francisco: Jossey-Bass. Discusses performance ratings from multiple sources including supervisors, peers, subordinates, and customers or clients. Describes the use of these 360-degree ratings for individual employee improvement as well as organizational development.

Walker, A. G., & Smither, J. W. (1999). A five-year study of upward feedback. *Personnel Psychology, 52,* 393–423. Tracks the improvement of managers and administrators as part of a performance appraisal program that included feedback from subordinates.

Training and Development

CHAPTER 6

THE SCOPE OF ORGANIZATIONAL TRAINING PROGRAMS

"When I look at the money we spend on education and training," said a chemical company executive, "I wonder whether we're running a chemical business or a college." From the high school dropout to the college graduate, from the long-time unemployed to the high-level executive, millions of people today are participating in some form of organizational training in their workplace. Employers spend some $55 billion annually on formal training programs and another $180 billion on informal on-the-job instruction.

Training is big business, and it begins at an elementary level, often teaching basic literacy and mathematics skills before offering instruction in specific job skills. When Motorola geared up to meet global competition by converting a plant to cellular technology, the company found that 60% of its work force had difficulty doing simple arithmetic and reading and understanding English. Without remedial training in these skills, the employees could not be taught to perform their new jobs. Polaroid spent $700,000 to offer basic language and math instruction to 1,000 employees. Domino's Pizza teaches reading and math so that employees can follow instructions for making pizza dough.

A 1999 survey of U.S. companies, conducted by the American Management Association, found that more than 38% of job applicants did not possess sufficient basic reading, writing, and math skills to perform the jobs for which they were applying. In 1997, the figure was 22%. In practical terms, this growing illiteracy rate means that more than one of every three job applicants today cannot read instructions, write reports, or do arithmetic well enough to perform common workplace tasks such as making change from a cash register. According to the American Management Association survey, remedial training in basic skills costs an average of $289 per person, a heavy price to pay for companies that are hiring thousands of new workers annually.

Training for skilled high-tech jobs is a priority in industry, government, and the military. Aerospace, telecommunications, and Web-based industries rely heavily on reprogrammable robots, multifunctional machinery, and computer-assisted design and manufacturing equipment. The companies need a highly trained work force to design, operate, and maintain this sophisticated equipment.

As we described in Chapter 1, the nature of work in the twenty-first century has changed. We can no longer count on learning one job and keeping it until retirement. We must learn to think not of a single chosen career over a lifetime but of several careers during which we will master a cluster of skills that must be continually upgraded. Our careers require lifelong learning, which means that appropriate training has become even more vital today than it was for previous generations.

A Sample Training Program.   Let us describe a classic example of a high-level organizational training program. Western Electric Company established a company college, the Corporate Education Center, to provide instruction in engineering and management. The facility contained state-of-the-art equipment and offered more than 300 courses on a 190-acre campus, complete with dormitories.

Newly hired engineers participated in 6-week orientation programs, one during the first 6 months of employment and a second during the next 6 months.

Employees Who Can't Read Directions

Cindy Marano forgot her glasses when she left her office to go to lunch, otherwise she would never have noticed it. Marano, who directs a job training program in Washington, DC, could not read the menu posted on the wall of her local sandwich shop without her glasses. She asked the middle-aged woman behind the counter to read it to her. At first, the woman pretended not to hear, then she became flustered and rude before finally asking another waitress to read the menu aloud. "Suddenly, the light went on for me," Marano said. The woman was unable to read. And Marano knew, from her work with the job training program, that many of the 40 million Americans who have trouble reading and writing are able to fake it on the job and conceal their handicap, as the waitress had done.

Marano also knew how expensive employee illiteracy is, costing the American economy some $225 billion a year in lost productivity. Someone else very much aware of that cost is Peter Coors, CEO of Colorado's Coors Brewing Company. He calls employee illiteracy a crisis for American industry, and he has taken the lead in promoting corporate awareness and creating industry-based training programs to teach employees how to read.

How do workers who can't read get jobs in the first place? How do they fill out an application blank? By indulging in the same kinds of tricks they use to keep the jobs once they are hired. They tell the personnel director they forgot their glasses, or they're in hurry and will complete the application form at home. Then they can ask a friend or family member to do it online and so can be hired without the employer knowing of their inability to read.

But with today's increasingly high-tech jobs, it is becoming harder to apply these ruses, to pretend you can read when you can't. Coors found that out when the company instituted a computerized inventory control system. The new system required forklift operators to punch information into a computer, and it soon became obvious that many of them could not do the job. Why? Because they could not recognize the letters on the computer keyboard or read the product codes on the items to be inventoried.

Even low-tech companies lose money to illiteracy. The Outback Steakhouse chain found that some of their cooks were mistakenly preparing more expensive instead of less expensive steaks because they could not read the waiters' orders. Outback started a training program to teach all employees a list of abbreviations, so that even workers for whom English was a new language could do their jobs without making costly mistakes. Other restaurant and fast-food chains use symbols instead of words on their computer screens.

Every company would operate more efficiently if all their employees could read. It would be better for the employees, too. Sharon Thomas, a

(continued)

34-year-old high school dropout living in Washington was on welfare for 15 years, until she learned to read and was hired for a well-paid job in construction. "I had a lot of hurdles to get over," she said, "but once I was in the work force, I was so happy. I feel good about myself."

Source: K. D. Grimsley. Battling against workplace illiteracy. *Washington Post*, September 29, 1995.

Engineers were able to choose among various courses in their specialty areas, classes designed to keep them up-to-date. Supervisors could select courses to upgrade their technical knowledge and managerial skills. The center provided management training at several levels to persons with promotion potential, with courses ranging from planning and interdepartmental relations to urban affairs and I-O psychology.

This ambitious venture is not unusual in American business. Training centers have been established by such organizations as IBM, Xerox, General Electric, and Avis Rent A Car. So, do not be surprised if, during your first month on the job and periodically throughout your career, you find yourself back in the classroom.

Training for Disabled Employees. Many organizations provide specialized training for disabled employees. At McDonald's, more than 9,000 workers with visual, hearing, orthopedic, or learning disabilities, or mental retardation, have

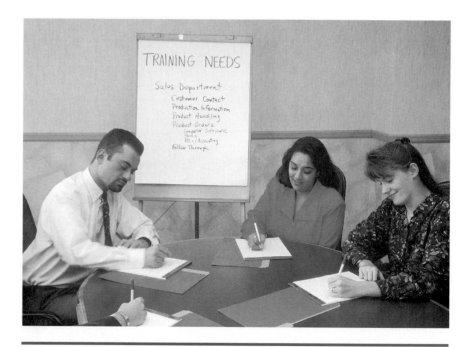

New employees find themselves back in the classroom to learn about company policies and objectives.

been trained for various jobs at the company's fast-food restaurants. In an attempt to dispel stereotypes and to make all employees sensitive to the problems of being disabled, training is provided not only for the disabled employees but also for the other employees who will be working with them. Over a 10-year period, more than 90% of the disabled persons who began training in a "McJobs" program completed it and became productive employees. The company believes that people with disabilities constitute a large pool of under-used labor and is determined to train them to do whatever they are capable of doing.

Training and Fair Employment Practices.   Organizational training programs may have an adverse impact on minority employees because performance in a training program is often used as a basis for career decisions about promotion, transfer, or dismissal. Any technique that results in personnel decisions has the potential for discriminating against ethnic minority, women, older, or disabled employees. Therefore, training programs must meet equal employment opportunity guidelines and must be clearly related to job performance before their results can be applied to career decisions.

ONLINE!

For up-to-date articles on workplace training and development check out the Web site of the American Society for Training and Development at *www.astd.org.*

GOALS OF ORGANIZATIONAL TRAINING PROGRAMS

The first step in establishing a formal training program is the precise formulation of objectives. These objectives must be stated in terms of specific behavioral criteria, the acts or operations employees must perform on the job and the way they should perform them to maximize job efficiency. It is impossible to determine what the training program should include unless the organization knows what the program is supposed to accomplish. In other words, what knowledge, skills, and abilities are critical to learning to perform the job successfully?

Needs Assessment.   The goals of the training program should be derived from the needs of the organization and the employees. A **needs assessment** should be conducted to determine corporate and individual goals and how a training program would help to achieve them. Such assessments, more ideal than real in organizational life, are used to determine specific job components and the skills required to perform them.

Needs assessment An analysis of corporate and individual goals undertaken before designing a training program.

Situations do arise in which the need for a training program is obvious. For example, a company that automates a manufacturing process, eliminating a number of jobs, may choose to retrain its employees for other work. Rapid expansion that creates new jobs requires a program to train workers to fill the positions. A high accident rate may call for additional safety training. Frequent complaints from dissatisfied customers may lead to employee training in human relations skills. In the absence of a clear indication that training is needed, however, it is management's responsibility to analyze its operations periodically to determine if any aspect could benefit from additional training.

Organizational Analysis. A general organizational analysis can suggest broad training needs that can then be translated into specific needs of employees or work groups. The next step is a task analysis to identify the specific tasks performed on a job and the knowledge, skills, and abilities needed for those tasks. A person analysis is undertaken to determine which workers need retraining and what kind of training is necessary. These evaluations can be accomplished by job analysis methods, critical incidents, performance appraisal techniques, and self-assessments.

Job analysis is the most frequently used technique for determining training needs and objectives. It yields a detailed list of the characteristics needed to perform a job successfully and the sequence of operations required. From a job analysis, the company can determine how new training procedures can improve job performance.

The critical-incidents technique, which focuses on specific desirable or undesirable job behaviors, provides information on how employees are equipped to cope with significant workday events. For example, how do assembly-line workers deal with jammed machinery? How do supervisors handle disputes among subordinates? How do managers deal with charges of sexual harassment? An analysis of critical incidents can alert the training director to areas in which additional training or instruction is needed.

Performance appraisals are an obvious source of information on training needs. They can document employee weaknesses and lead to recommendations for retraining to correct specific deficiencies. Self-assessment is based on the assumption that the person who is performing a job well is a good source of information about the skills needed to do that job and the areas in which training may be desirable.

STAFFING FOR ORGANIZATIONAL TRAINING PROGRAMS

The quality of an instructor can have a tremendous impact on your performance as a student. Some teachers are able to bring the subject matter to life, to organize and present the material with enthusiasm, and to inspire interest among the class members. Other instructors teaching the same material can make the classroom experience frustrating, tiring, and boring. The most important factor in teaching anything at any level seems not to be competence or expertise in the subject matter. Although competence is necessary, the instructor must also have the ability to teach, to impart information in a clear and compelling manner.

The same principle holds for organizational training. Too often, corporate training is conducted by people who have vast experience on the job but no ability to communicate their skills effectively to others. The solution is to use professional instructors, persons trained in teaching methods and in job skills. Larger organizations maintain full-time training staffs equipped to teach a number of subjects and job skills.

THE PRETRAINING ENVIRONMENT

The pretraining environment established by an organization includes those decisions and cues, communicated directly or indirectly to employees by supervisors and peers, that indicate the value management places on training programs. These factors may include organizational policies, supervisor attitudes toward training, resources available for training, and employee participation in needs assessments. These cues influence the effectiveness of training programs because they tell employees how supportive the company is of training efforts.

The more training opportunities a company offers, the more likely its employees are to believe that training is an important and relevant activity for their careers. Trainees are also more likely to regard training as worthwhile and to be more motivated to achieve in training programs when they know their supervisors support training, know their post-training skills will be assessed, and are given a realistic picture of what the training involves. When these conditions are not met—when the organization's pretraining attitude or climate is perceived as unsupportive—a training program is likely to be rendered ineffective before it even begins.

Pretraining Attributes of Employees

A number of psychological characteristics can influence our desire to learn from a training program as well as the amount and kind of material we are capable of learning. These attributes include individual differences in ability, pretraining expectations, motivation, job involvement, locus of control, and self-efficacy.

Individual Differences in Ability. Individual differences in training ability can be predicted through cognitive ability tests, biographical data, and performance in an initial training experience, such as a work sample. Trainability tests, such as work samples or minicourses, are also valid predictors of performance in a full course of training. Work samples, when used as measures of trainability, offer a short period of formal job skill instruction followed by a test of job performance in a training facility.

Pretraining Expectations. Employees' expectations about the outcome of training can influence the program's effectiveness. When a training program fails to live up to the trainees' expectations, they are less likely to complete the program. Trainees whose expectations are not met but who do complete the program are likely to be dissatisfied on the job, to have a low sense of commitment to the organization, and to have a high rate of job turnover. Trainees whose pretraining expectations are met by the training program develop strong organizational commitment, a high sense of self-efficacy, and enhanced motivation to succeed.

Motivation. The motivation or desire to learn is vital to employees' success in a training program. Learning will not occur unless trainees truly want to learn, regardless of their ability. In every occupation we can find examples of people who have achieved success with less than an optimal level of ability but with a great drive or motivation to succeed.

Research has shown that trainees with higher motivation learn more in training programs than do trainees with lower motivation. Trainees who are highly motivated are more likely to complete the program and to apply their training on the job. When 106 junior-level managers in a British company were studied over a 4-month training program, their pretraining level of motivation (as measured by questionnaires) was found to be significantly related to the amount of material they learned. The direction of the relationship was clear: the higher the pretraining motivation, the higher the level of learning (Warr & Bunce, 1995).

Management can increase trainees' motivation by involving them in decisions about the training program, allowing them to participate in the needs-assessment process, and giving them a choice of training courses. Research has shown that previous negative events or experiences can increase motivation to learn. For example, trainees in an assertiveness training course who had experienced undesirable incidents (when being more assertive might have helped them) were more motivated to learn the training material (Smith-Jentsch, Jentsch, Payne, & Salas, 1996).

Job Involvement.   Trainees who show greater job involvement—whose sense of self-identity is closely linked with their work—show higher motivation to learn than do trainees who are less involved. Long-term career plans are also a factor. Training opportunities may be wasted on employees who display low job involvement and a lack of career interest because their motivation to learn is likely to be low. Further, employees with low job involvement have low potential for showing improvement in their job performance as a result of their training. Thus, pretraining programs to increase job and career involvement may be desirable for some employees.

Locus of Control.   Another variable that affects trainee motivation is locus of control. People identified as having an internal locus of control believe that job performance and such work-related rewards as pay and promotion are under their personal control, dependent on their own behaviors, abilities, and efforts. People with an external locus of control believe that life events in and out of the workplace are beyond their control. They are dependent on such outside forces as luck, chance, or whether their boss likes them.

Employees who have an internal locus of control are likely to be highly motivated to succeed in a training program because they believe that mastering the job skills is under their control and within their capabilities. They are more likely to accept feedback during training and to take action to correct deficiencies. They also show higher levels of job and career involvement than do employees with an external locus of control.

Self-Efficacy.   Another factor that influences employee motivation to succeed in training programs is self-efficacy, the belief in one's capacity to perform a task. It may be described as our sense of adequacy, efficiency, and competence in coping with life's demands.

The relationship between self-efficacy and motivation to learn, and between self-efficacy and actual success in training programs, has been amply demonstrated. One study, using a highly realistic computer-based Naval Air Defense simulation training task, found a significant positive relationship between pretraining level of self-efficacy and the subjects' expressed motivation to learn

(Quiñones, 1995). The study also showed that experimentally enhanced self-efficacy resulted in higher learning.

A meta-analysis of 114 studies involving more than 21,000 employees found that people higher in perceived learning efficacy (their belief in their ability to acquire new skills) were able to learn complex skills more readily than were people low in perceived learning efficacy. This analysis also demonstrated a high positive correlation between self-efficacy and job performance (Stajkovic & Luthans, 1998). Thus, self-efficacy can affect performance in the training program and, later, on the job.

In turn, self-efficacy can be affected by training. Certain types of training, such as behavior modeling, can be used to increase self-efficacy. Even simply telling trainees that the skill they are trying to learn can be mastered through practice may increase self-efficacy, as was demonstrated with a group of university employees taking a computer training course. Trainees who were told that computer skills could be easily acquired through practice showed a significant increase in their efficacy beliefs compared to trainees who were told that computer skills were difficult to acquire (Martocchio, 1994).

Training-enhanced self-efficacy can have long-term effects beyond the duration of the training program. An analysis of 112 newly-hired accountants at 10 accounting firms found that the increase in self-efficacy that resulted from training had beneficial effects on socialization and adjustment to the new job during the first year of employment. Those accountants with higher post-training self-efficacy scored higher on such measures as ability to cope, job satisfaction, and job commitment than those lower in self-efficacy (Saks, 1995).

HOW PEOPLE LEARN: PSYCHOLOGICAL FACTORS

Psychologists have devoted considerable effort to the study of learning. The published literature in the field contains thousands of research reports on human and animal learning under various conditions. Although psychologists do not pretend to have all the answers about this complex activity, they have observed and described several factors that can facilitate or hinder learning and performance in training programs. In this section we deal with several factors that relate to teaching methods and to the nature of the material to be learned.

Active Practice.   Practice may not always make perfect, as the saying goes, but it does help. For learning to be most effective, trainees must be actively involved in the learning process, not merely passive recipients of information. For example, it is not sufficient to read about the operation of a construction crane or to watch a video of someone operating it. The training program should provide the opportunity for the trainee to sit in the operator's cab and have hands-on practice of the skills required to perform the job.

Imagine learning to drive a car only by listening to a lecture and memorizing traffic regulations. This can make you a better driver, but you will not actually learn how to drive until you sit in the driver's seat and start practicing. The same principle holds for academic material. Actively taking notes during lectures, highlighting and outlining the textbook, and discussing questions with classmates facilitate learning much more than sitting passively in the lecture hall soaking up the professor's words like a sponge.

Mental practice, the cognitive rehearsing of a task prior to performing it, can have a significant positive effect on the actual performance of the task. This was demonstrated by a meta-analysis of 100 studies conducted between 1934 and 1991. The results confirmed that mental practice is effective for both physical and cognitive tasks, though it is less effective than overt physical practice. Thus, mentally rehearsing a task can help to learn it, but actively performing it helps more (Driskell, Copper, & Moran, 1994).

Massed and Distributed (Spaced) Practice. Some tasks are learned more readily when the training program schedules one or a few relatively long practice sessions (massed practice). Other tasks require a large number of relatively short practice sessions (distributed, or spaced, practice). In general, spaced practice results in better learning, particularly for motor skills.

A meta-analysis of 63 studies showed that subjects trained under spaced practice conditions performed significantly better than subjects trained under massed practice conditions. For jobs requiring relatively simple tasks, spaced practice interspersed with short rest periods held the advantage. For more complex tasks, longer rest periods between the spaced practice sessions resulted in more effective learning (Donovan & Radosevich, 1999).

The research evidence is less clear for the learning of verbal skills. Massed practice may be more useful, but much depends on the complexity of the task to be mastered and the type of material to be learned. Short, simple material can be learned well by massed practice because the sessions do not have to be too long for the trainees to absorb the content. More difficult material must be divided into shorter units and learned by distributed practice.

Whole and Part Learning. The concept of whole or part learning refers to the relative size of the unit of material to be learned. The training course content can be divided into small parts, each of which is studied individually, or the material can be learned as a whole. The decision depends on the nature and complexity of the material and the ability of the trainees. More intelligent trainees are capable of rapidly learning larger units of material than are less intelligent trainees. However, when slower learners are offered the chance to learn the same material in smaller units, they may be able to master it better than when forced to apprehend it as a whole.

Some skills are obviously better suited to the whole learning method. For example, when learning to drive a car, it serves no useful purpose to divide driving behavior into component skills. You do not practice separately and repeatedly movements such as fastening the seat belt, turning on the ignition, releasing the emergency brake, adjusting the rearview mirror, and moving the gearshift lever from park to drive. Driving is an interdependent flow of movements and actions that can be learned more effectively as a whole.

When a task requires the initial learning of several subskills, the part method is more efficient. For example, piano students confronting a new piece of music may choose at first to practice the right-hand and the left-hand parts separately. Trainees can practice these various subskills until a particular level of efficiency has been achieved before integrating them into the total behavior or operation.

Transfer of Training. Organizational training often takes place in an artificial setting, a training facility that may differ in several ways from the actual job environment. This discrepancy between training and job situations must be bridged. The training program must ensure that there will be a transfer of training—a carryover of the skills mastered during the training program—to the job itself.

The issue is one of relevance: Is the information provided during the training program relevant and meaningful to actual job performance? Is there a correspondence between the behaviors and attitudes taught in the training sessions and the behaviors and attitudes needed to perform the job successfully? Can all the information mastered in the training facility be applied in the production facility or the office? In many instances, the answer to these questions is no.

If there is close correspondence between training requirements and job requirements, positive transfer will develop. The material learned during training will aid or improve job performance. The greater the similarity between the training and work situations, the greater will be the transfer. This question of similarity is increasingly important in view of the growing use of virtual work environments for training purposes.

Does training on a computer simulator transfer to the real-world job? For 58 aviation cadets in the air force of Israel, the answer was yes. Some of the cadets received 10 hours of training in a computer game, Space Fortress, before beginning flight training. The game simulated the kinds of activities a pilot would be called on to perform in the cockpit of an actual fighter aircraft. The results showed that cadets who trained first on the computer game performed significantly better in flight training than did cadets who did not have the computer game pretraining (Gopher, Weil, and Baraket, 1994).

If there is little similarity between training situations and work situations, negative transfer will result. In that case, the skills learned in the training program will hamper or interfere with job performance. In negative transfer, these skills or behaviors must be unlearned or modified before employees can perform the job.

Several conditions in the post-training environment can facilitate positive transfer. The most important is supervisor support for and reinforcement of the behaviors and skills taught in the training program. Also influential are the opportunity to apply on the job the skills learned in the training program and a follow-up discussion or assessment shortly after completing the training program. Another important factor is the overall organizational climate. The more supportive it is of training, the greater the opportunities for transfer of the training experience to the actual work situation.

Feedback. People learn more readily when they are given a clear idea of how well they are doing. Feedback (sometimes called "knowledge of results") indicates to the trainees their level of progress. Feedback is also important in maintaining motivation. If trainees are not provided with feedback during a training program, they might persist in learning and practicing inappropriate behaviors and incorrect techniques of job performance.

To be maximally effective, feedback must be offered as soon as possible after the inappropriate behavior occurs. If a sequence of operations is being practiced incorrectly, the desired change is more likely to be brought about if the trainees are told immediately. Overall training progress is greater when the program allows for frequent feedback. The more specific and detailed the correction, the more useful it will be.

Reinforcement.   The greater the reward that follows a behavior, the more easily and rapidly that behavior will be learned. The reward, or reinforcement, can take many forms—a good test grade, a gold star on a chart, a pat on the back from a supervisor, or a promotion for successful completion of a training program. By establishing a program of reinforcement, management can maintain employee motivation and effectively shape behavior by rewarding only those actions that the trainees are supposed to learn and display.

Reinforcement should be provided immediately after the desired behavior has occurred. The longer the delay between behavior and reinforcement, the less effective the reinforcement will be because the trainee may fail to perceive the connection between the correct behavior and the reward for having behaved in that way.

In the early stages of training, reinforcement should be given every time the desired behavior is displayed. Once some learning has taken place, continuous reinforcement is no longer necessary. Then, partial reinforcement will be sufficient, for example, rewarding trainees every third or every tenth time they perform the appropriate behavior.

TRAINING METHODS

Now that we have described the pretraining attributes of trainees and the psychological factors that affect learning, let us consider specific organizational training techniques. Each technique offers advantages and disadvantages, depending on the goals of the training program, the abilities of the employees, and the nature of the information to be learned.

> ONLINE!   For a history of job training, from early on-the-job training situations to more modern techniques, see *www.msu.edu/ sleightd/trainhst.html*. Information about internships for college students that provide pay or college credit for on-the-job experience is at *www.internsnet.com*.

On-the-Job Training

One of the oldest and most widely used training methods takes place directly on the job for which the worker is being trained. Under the guidance of an experienced operator, supervisor, or trained instructor, trainees learn while working. They operate the equipment in the production facility or assist customers out on the sales floor and have the opportunity to develop proficiency while they work.

In an on-the-job training program at a window screen factory, new employees practice job skills under the supervision of an experienced worker.

The major advantage of **on-the-job training** is economy; the organization does not have to establish, equip, and maintain a separate training facility. If current workers and supervisors serve as trainers, even the cost of a professional instructor is saved.

A more obvious advantage is positive transfer of training. There is no concern about whether job performance in a training situation will carry over to the actual work situation because training and job situations are the same. In terms of other psychological factors, active practice is provided from the outset. Motivation to learn should be high because the training situation is clearly relevant to the job situation. Feedback is immediate and visible. Good performance will elicit praise, and poor performance will show in a faulty product or dissatisfied customer.

On-the-job training can be expensive in the long run, however. Workers and supervisors must take time from their regular jobs to train new employees. This can lead to an overall reduction in productivity. Additional costs come with the slower work pace of the trainees and any damage they cause to equipment or product because of their inexperience. On certain jobs, permitting untrained workers to operate machinery may be hazardous not only to the trainees but also to other employees. Accident rates for trainees on the job are typically higher than for experienced workers.

Using current workers or supervisors as trainers does not ensure adequate training for new employees. Just because a person performs a job competently or has been on the job for a considerable time does not mean that person has the ability to teach the job to someone else. On-the-job training is often haphazard and inadequate, amounting to no more than the supervisor's saying to the trainees, "Go ahead and start. If you have any questions, come see me."

On-the-job training Training that takes place directly on the job for which the person has been hired.

On-the-job training is also used at the management level. Much managerial and executive training and development occurs through informal and unstructured on-the-job experiences. Indeed, on-the-job experiences can contribute more significantly to the development of managerial ability than any formal classroom instruction.

Vestibule Training

Vestibule training Training that takes place in a simulated workspace.

Because on-the-job training has the potential for disrupting the production process, many companies prefer **vestibule training.** They establish a simulated workspace in a separate training facility. (A vestibule is a hallway or entrance foyer between the outer door of a building and its main rooms. In the early days of American industry, vestibule schools were organized just inside the doors of industrial plants to introduce new workers to their jobs with a few weeks of specialized training. The word *vestibule* is used in this context to denote that the training program is like an entryway or passageway the employee must cross before getting to the job itself.)

Using the same kind of equipment and operating procedures as the actual work situation, a vestibule training program relies on skilled instructors, rather than experienced workers and supervisors, to teach new workers how to perform their jobs.

Because the sole purpose of vestibule training is training, there is no pressure to maintain a given level of productivity. Trainees do not have to be concerned about making costly or embarrassing errors or about damaging actual production equipment. They can concentrate on learning the skills necessary to be successful on the job.

The greatest disadvantage of vestibule training is the cost. The organization must equip the facility and maintain a teaching staff. This expense is particularly burdensome when there are not enough new workers to make full-time use of the training facility. Further, if the training situation does not correspond closely to the work situation, negative transfer of training will occur, and the trainees may need informal, on-the-job instruction once they start to work. This problem can be aggravated by the common business practice of using obsolete equipment, retired from the production floor, in the training facility. However, if a vestibule training program is properly designed, staffed, and equipped, it can be an effective training technique.

Apprenticeship

Apprenticeship A training method for skilled crafts and trades involving classroom instruction and on-the-job experience.

Perhaps the earliest recorded training method still in use today is the **apprenticeship** program for skilled crafts and trades in private-sector industries such as construction and manufacturing. Programs are available for plumbers, carpenters, electronics technicians, painters, and auto mechanics, among others. Conducted in the classroom and on the job, apprenticeship involves extensive background preparation in the craft as well as actual work experience under the guidance of experts.

Apprenticeships average 4 to 6 years. The standard procedure is for the trainees to agree to work for a company for a fixed period in return for a specified program of training and a salary, usually half that earned by skilled and licensed craftspersons. Trainees must complete their apprenticeship before they are allowed to join a union. Membership in a labor union is necessary to securing employment. Thus, apprentice programs constitute a joint effort by industry and organized labor to maintain an adequate supply of skilled workers.

In recent years, apprenticeships in the public sector have grown in popularity. A number of federal, state, and local government agencies have adopted them for skilled blue-collar jobs in civilian and military programs, such as building maintenance worker, highway maintenance worker, prison correctional officer, and firefighter. The Smithsonian Institution in Washington, DC, operates an apprenticeship program for carpenters, electricians, and plaster masons to build displays for their museums.

Computer-Assisted Instruction

Computer-assisted instruction (CAI), sometimes called computer-based training (CBT), is widely used by private- and public-sector organizations. In CAI, the program of instruction, usually on CD-ROM, serves as the teacher. Trainees interact with the material on computer terminals. Their responses are recorded and analyzed automatically, and the difficulty of each item presented is based on the correctness of the response to the previous item.

Computer-assisted instruction (CAI) A computer-based training method in which trainees learn material at their own pace and receive immediate feedback on their progress.

One of the most widespread uses of computer-based training is to teach computer literacy skills. With millions of workers now using computers daily on the job, the development of computer operating skills is critical. Another popular use is in training airline flight crews. The software used by airlines presents displays and touch-panel graphics to simulate the buttons, switches, dials, and signal lights in the cockpit. This type of instruction reduces the number of hours pilots and copilots would otherwise have to spend in a more expensive flight simulator.

With computer-assisted instruction, trainees are actively involved in the learning process and work through the material at their own pace. They receive immediate feedback on their progress and reinforcement for displaying mastery of a skill. The technique offers more individualized instruction than does a traditional lecture-based training course. It is not unlike private tutoring by an excellent teacher who has a comprehensive knowledge of the subject, never becomes impatient or annoyed with the student, and displays no prejudice or error. Because CAI keeps accurate records and maintains a current performance analysis on each trainee, the training staff is free to devote time to any unusual learning problems that arise.

Computer-assisted instruction can be used with even a small number of trainees so that the company does not have to make them wait until there are enough to fill a classroom and schedule a course. It can also be provided to a large number of trainees simultaneously in different locations. Studies have shown that the technique significantly decreases training time and provides positive transfer of training.

Net-Based Training

Net-based training is now being used by companies such as Xerox, Texaco, Unisys, and Crate & Barrel. It involves the Internet and the Intranet (the within-company site). The technique is a type of distance learning, and it is transforming traditional training programs by delivering up-to-the-minute programs on demand.

Through net-based training, a company can provide training courses for any number of workers to access from their desks at work or at home, or from laptops and hand-held computers while traveling. Instruction is being prepared for nearly every type of training, from certification in information technology to advanced accounting practices and coursework for an MBA degree.

Net-based training offers the same advantages as computer-assisted instruction: active involvement of the trainees, the opportunity to proceed at their own pace, immediate feedback and reinforcement, plus flexibility as to the time and place of training.

The cost of net-based training has been estimated to be 20% to 35% lower than the cost of traditional classroom instruction, where trainers and trainees must assemble on a prescribed schedule. The technique has been described as a cheaper, better, and faster way of reaching a wider range of employees.

Behavior Modification

The use of positive reinforcement to change behavior has many applications to organizational training. An assessment called a performance audit is conducted first, to determine the problems or behaviors that can be modified for more efficient job performance. A program of positive reinforcement is then introduced to reward employees for displaying the desired behaviors, such as reducing errors or production time per unit. Punishment or reprimands are not used. Although they may temporarily eliminate an undesirable behavior, they may leave in its place anxiety, hostility, and anger. Providing positive reinforcement is much more effective in improving employee productivity and behavior.

Behavior modification A training program of positive reinforcement to reward employees for displaying desirable job behaviors.

A classic program of **behavior modification** was developed at Emery Air Freight, where the behavioral changes induced were directly connected to job performance. A performance audit revealed two problem areas: (1) despite the employees' belief that they were responding within 90 minutes to 90% of customer telephone inquiries, they were actually responding to only 30% of the inquiries within that time, and (2) employees were combining packages into containers for shipment only 45% of the time, whereas management expected containers to be used 90% of the time. The goals of the behavior modification training program were to have employees respond faster to customer inquiries and to use containers for shipment whenever possible.

Managers were taught a number of recognitions and rewards to bestow on employees as reinforcers, ranging from a smile and a nod to specific praise for a job well done. Financial incentives to improve performance were not used. Praise and recognition were found to be sufficient reinforcers for improving job performance and for bringing about positive changes in behavior. Managers were told to reinforce desirable behaviors as soon as they occurred and gradually to shift from constant reinforcement to occasional, or intermittent, reinforcement.

Employees were required to keep a detailed record of their accomplishments so that they could compare their performance with the company standards. This record keeping provided daily feedback on their progress.

The company estimated that the improved productivity and response time saved $3 million in 3 years, considerably more than the cost of instituting the behavior modification program initially.

Job Rotation

Job rotation is a popular management training technique. It exposes trainees to different jobs and departments to acquaint them with all facets of their organization. It is frequently used with new college graduates who are just beginning their working careers. Through job rotation, trainees gain perspective on various aspects of organizational life. They have the opportunity to see and be seen by higher management in different departments, and to learn through direct experience where they might best apply their knowledge, abilities, and interests.

The rotation phase of a management career may last several years, taking employees from one department to another or from one plant or office in the United States to others throughout the world. Such changes can promote the development of the management trainees' flexibility, adaptability, and self-efficacy as employees learn to deal successfully with new challenges. Job rotation programs are also used for skilled and semiskilled jobs. They allow workers to increase their skill levels in diverse occupations, and they serve to alleviate the boredom that can result from years of performing the same tasks.

Disadvantages of the job rotation technique include frequent moves, which can disrupt family life and interrupt a spouse's career. If the rotation period is too brief, there may not be sufficient time to become fully acquainted with a particular job. If top management is more interested in using management trainees as temporary office help, instead of the rising group of managers in need of mentors, the trainees will not have the opportunity to acquire the necessary skills to transfer to upper-management positions. This can defeat the purpose of the program.

> **Job rotation** A management training technique that assigns trainees to various jobs and departments over a period of a few years.

Case Studies

The use of **case studies,** a method developed by the Harvard University School of Business, is popular in executive training programs. A complex problem, or case, of the kind faced daily by managers and executives, is presented to the trainees prior to a general meeting. The trainees are expected to familiarize themselves with the information and to find additional relevant material. When they meet as a group, each member must be prepared to interpret the problem and offer a solution. Through the presentation of diverse viewpoints, the trainees come to appreciate different perspectives on a problem and, consequently, different approaches to solving it. Usually the cases have no one correct solution. The group leader does not suggest an answer. The group as a whole must reach consensus and resolve the problem.

A limitation of the case study method is that the solution may not be relevant to the requirements of the job. There may be a discrepancy between the theoretical solution to the case problem and the solution that is practical for the organization. Therefore, actions taken on the basis of the case study solution proposed in the training program may not transfer positively to actions that are appropriate on the job.

> **Case studies** A method of executive training in which trainees analyze a business problem and offer solutions.

Business Games

Business games attempt to simulate a complex organizational situation. They are intended to develop problem-solving and decision-making skills and to provide practice in using those skills in a situation in which a management trainee's mistake will not prove costly or embarrassing to the organization.

> **Business games** A training method that simulates a complex organizational situation to encourage the development of problem-solving and decision-making skills.

In a typical business game, management trainees operate an imaginary company and make decisions about personnel, production goals, marketing, and finances.

Trainees compete in teams, each team representing a separate, hypothetical business organization. The team companies are given detailed information about the operation of their organization, including data on finances, sales, advertising, production, personnel, and inventories. Each group must organize itself and assign various tasks and responsibilities to each member. As the teams deal with corporate problems, an instructor evaluates their reasoning processes and decisions. They may be required to consider additional problems based on the outcomes of their initial decisions.

Because the business problems presented to the trainees are so realistic, many trainees form an emotional commitment to their virtual company. They gain experience in making decisions on real-life problems under the pressures of time and the actions taken by rival organizations. For new employees, business games may provide their first exposure to actual job tasks and stresses managers face. This type of realistic job preview persuades some trainees that they would be happier in another line of work.

In-Basket Training

The in-basket technique was discussed in Chapter 3 as a method of employee selection. The same technique is used to train prospective managers. Each trainee is given a stack of letters, memos, customer complaints, employee requests, and other items that present various problems typical of those dealt with by managers on the job. The trainees must take action on each item within a specified period. After completing the tasks, the trainees meet with a trainer to discuss their decisions and receive feedback on the outcomes.

Role Playing

In role playing, management trainees pretend to act out a particular role, displaying whatever behaviors they believe are appropriate in a given situation. For example, they may be asked to imagine themselves to be a supervisor discussing a poor performance appraisal with a subordinate. They act out these situations in front of a group of trainees and instructors, who offer comments on their performance. A trainee may play the role of supervisor at first, then the situation will be reversed and the same trainee will play the employee. Sessions can be videotaped for later analysis. Many people feel foolish or awkward acting out in front of a group, but once they begin, most people develop a sensitivity for the part and project their feelings onto it.

Role playing can be a valuable learning device. It enables trainees to understand the views of subordinates and acquaints them with the roles they will be expected to play as managers. It provides practical experience as well as feedback from other trainees and instructors. Trainees have the opportunity to practice job-related behaviors in a situation in which mistakes or inappropriate behaviors will not jeopardize interpersonal relations on the job.

Self-Management Training

Self-management training (SMT) teaches people to exert control over their own behavior. Employees learn to assess their own actions, set specific goals for themselves, monitor their progress toward those goals, administer rewards for achieving goals (and punishments for not achieving goals), and maintain the behaviors that lead to the attainment of their goals. In a study of 60 life insurance salespersons who had failed to reach their company's performance standards, SMT instruction was offered in four weekly 2-hour training sessions. The results showed that SMT resulted in significant increases in job performance and in self-efficacy. These positive benefits lasted throughout the 12-month period of the research (Frayne & Geringer, 2000).

Behavior Modeling

The behavior modeling approach to management training involves having trainees attempt to imitate or model their behavior on examples of exceptional job performance. It is a popular technique for teaching interpersonal and leadership skills. Behavior modeling is usually conducted with groups of 6 to 12 supervisors or managers. Sessions may last 2 to 4 hours a week for up to 4 weeks. In the intervals between training sessions, the trainees are on the job, applying what they have learned, which provides them with feedback from their subordinates.

The usual procedure is for a trainer, using a prepared script, to provide a general introduction. Then the trainees watch a videotape of a manager who is acting out appropriate procedures and behaviors for handling a job situation with a subordinate—for example, discussing poor job performance, excessive absenteeism, or low morale.

Virtual Training

You've seen it in the movies. A jet fighter eases its way upward, below and behind a mammoth flying tanker loaded with aviation fuel. A long thin tube with a funnel extends from the rear of the tanker aircraft. The fighter pilot maneuvers the jet so that its fuel tank port connects with the tiny funnel, while traveling at more than 500 miles an hour. It's called in-flight refueling, a tricky, delicate, and dangerous operation every fighter pilot has to learn.

Lt. Charlie Howard, a newly graduated 26-year-old pilot, is trying to perform the maneuver for the first time. He has listened to the lectures, read the operating manual, and paid close attention to the video showing a pilot's-eye view of the connection, but now he feels his fear mount as he closes in on the monster plane overhead.

He never takes his eyes off the funnel. It's only 20 feet away. He draws closer. Suddenly, his plane is buffeted by high wind gusts and his body is slammed into the seat as the fighter bounces on an updraft. Frantically, Charlie forces the control stick forward, but it is too late. The wind whips faster than he can react, and his tiny plane smashes into the side of the tanker.

"Boom," rings a voice in his ear. "You're dead, Charlie. And so is everybody in the tanker. OK, let's try it again."

Charlie Howard is flying in a virtual aircraft, a flight simulator, wearing a head-mounted virtual reality apparatus that provides lifelike computer-generated images. The only damage he suffered from the "crash" was to his ego, and now he can try the maneuver again and again until he perfects it. Only then will he be permitted to try it in a real airplane.

The U.S. military has invested millions of dollars in virtual training for pilots, air-traffic controllers, and tank commanders, so they can learn their jobs without inflicting harm on themselves and others or damaging expensive equipment.

Virtual reality allows researchers to shape the training to the specific needs of the various branches of the armed forces. U.S. Air Force psychologist Wesley Regian said, "people can practice one part of a more complicated task. Or simulations can start out easy—as with removing the wind in the refueling simulation—and increase in difficulty as a student grasps the basics."

One day Lieutenant Howard will practice refueling in a real plane under genuine wind conditions, but thanks to the I-O psychology research on virtual reality simulation devices, he will be well trained by then. He will have performed the required maneuvers many times already, and survived.

Source: B. Azar. Training is enhanced by virtual reality, *APA Monitor*, March 1996.

Next, the trainees engage in behavior rehearsal, practicing the behaviors they saw the model perform. Trainees are not being asked to play a role; instead, they are imitating the actual behaviors they will use on the job, the behaviors the model has displayed. The trainer and the other trainees provide feedback by telling each trainee how closely he or she imitated the model's behavior and where their behavior diverged. This social reinforcement helps trainees gain confidence in their ability to display the appropriate behavior.

The interpersonal and leadership behaviors learned by behavior modeling will transfer directly to the job. Because the modeled situations between manager and subordinate are actual job situations, the behaviors should carry over to job performance. Thus, there is a high degree of relevance between behavior modeling as a training technique and the job requirements, a condition that increases trainees' motivation to accept and apply the training.

Reports from organizations using behavior modeling show that the technique is effective in raising employee morale, improving communication with customers, increasing sales, decreasing absenteeism, enhancing supervisory skills, improving production quantity and quality, and reducing employee resistance to change.

Executive Coaching

A new approach to management training involves one-to-one training sessions in which a coach works with a manager to improve a particular aspect of the manager's job performance. Can the manager give a good speech? Can the executive use the Internet? Do performance appraisals show that colleagues and subordinates think the boss has lousy human relations skills? Get a coach!

Executive coaching is designed to solve individual problems as they arise. The most frequent use of executive coaching has been as a follow-up to poor ratings on 360-degree feedback appraisals. Recognizing that feedback alone is often not sufficient motivation for a manager to alter his or her behavior, a coach will be brought in to help interpret the feedback and work with the manager to devise strategies for eliciting the desired behavioral changes. Several sessions of coaching may be required to deal with perceived deficiencies. Most executives who have received coaching tend to agree with their coaches' recommendations and to rate the process as valuable to their career development (Hollenbeck & McCall, 1999).

> **ONLINE!**
>
> On the Web site of the International Coaching Federation, *www.coachfederation.org*, see the links to corporate coaching, small business coaching, and career coaching.

Diversity Training

We described in Chapter 1 how the nature of the work force is changing to include more women and ethnic minority workers. To aid their employees in coping with an increasingly diverse work force, many organizations have instituted diversity training programs to teach people to confront personal prejudices that could lead to discriminatory behaviors. Through lectures, videos, role playing, and confrontational exercises, employees are learning, in a way, how it might feel to be a female worker being sexually harassed by a male boss, or a Hispanic worker receiving an unsatisfactory performance appraisal from a Black supervisor. Trainees are forced to deal with their own sexist and racist attitudes, and to learn to be more sensitive to the concerns and viewpoints of others.

U.S. companies are spending up to $10 billion annually for diversity training. One consultant is said to charge up to $35,000 to conduct a "cultural audit" of a company to analyze the employees' discriminatory attitudes and practices.

The success of diversity training depends on several factors: support from management, mandatory attendance, and the size of the organization. Large organizations with strong support from top executives, a staff of diversity specialists, and required attendance for all employees are the most likely to have successful diversity training programs. However, posttraining interviews with participants suggest that for some people these programs foster negative reactions as well as charges that the programs are offered only because it appears to be the "politically correct" thing to do.

CAREER DEVELOPMENT AND PLANNING

We have discussed specific training methods designed to improve employees' knowledge, job skills, and interpersonal relations. Most training programs are mandatory and oriented toward a specific job or specific career stage, such as the entry-level worker, the employee who needs retraining, or the midcareer manager. Some organizations also offer personal development opportunities throughout an employee's career. These career development and planning efforts, which are strictly voluntary, involve a lifelong learning approach.

Organizations as diverse as General Electric, AT&T, Merrill Lynch, TRW, and Xerox operate career development centers. They provide information on company career paths and opportunities and offer counseling and self-analysis programs so that employees can determine how their personal goals coincide with organizational goals. Many companies sponsor workshops to assist employees in career planning and in the development of human relations skills. Employees are encouraged to set career objectives—for example, specifying where they hope to be within the corporate hierarchy in 5 years' time—and to review these goals periodically. Some companies offer tuition refund plans that enable employees to return to college or graduate school to upgrade job skills or to learn new skills. Employees are also encouraged to participate in in-house training courses.

We have noted that one of the forces of change in the workplace today is the decline of the idea of a lifetime career with a single employer. Increasingly, we may choose to or be forced to change careers several times during the course of our working lives and to continually enhance and upgrade our personal package of skills. This necessity for lifelong learning increases the importance of career development and planning efforts.

Career Development and Life Stages

Psychologists have long recognized individual differences in terms of people's values, goals, and needs at different ages and stages of life. The job or lifestyle that is appropriate in our twenties may be inappropriate for our thirties or fifties. Three distinct career stages have been proposed (Hall, 1986):

- *Establishment*. During this stage, approximately ages 20 to 40, people are becoming established in their careers and adjusting to work routines. Toward the middle of this period, they learn whether they are going to be successful or not, through promotions and a sense of personal satisfaction, or through an unwanted transfer or dismissal. If they are successful, they develop feelings of self-efficacy and organizational commitment. If they are unsuccessful, they may need self-analysis, counseling, and a revision of their career plans.
- *Maintenance*. This stage lasts from approximately ages 40 to 55, the time of the so-called midlife crisis. People become aware that they are aging. They have either approached or achieved their goals or they know they will never reach them. It is a time of self-examination, which may lead to a change in interests, values, and lifestyles. Some people seek challenge and satisfaction in new jobs, hobbies, or relationships. Some organizations offer counseling to their managerial personnel to help them cope with this period.
- *Decline*. From age 50 or 55 through retirement, employees confront the end of the career to which they devoted their adult life. They must consider the prospect of living on a reduced income and of diminished physical capacity. Retirement brings not only the loss of work and a sense of identity, but also the loss of colleagues with whom to socialize. Additional counseling may be required to assist employees in planning for retirement.

Career development and planning efforts at each stage of working life involve responsibilities shared by employers and employees. Organizations should offer opportunities for personal growth and development. Employees must make effective use of these programs. They should be willing periodically to reanalyze their skills and job performance and to formulate realistic career development plans.

Career Self-Management

As a result of years of corporate mergers, restructuring, and downsizing, many companies today are less able or less willing to provide opportunities for the career development and growth of their employees. They are urging employees to take more responsibility on their own for actively planning and managing their careers. The term "career self-management" refers to the degree to which a person regularly and routinely gathers information and formulates or revises plans for his or her own career, solving problems and making decisions.

Organizations are offering training to help employees assume this responsibility to upgrade their skills and learn new ones. More than half of the U.S. corporations with a workforce of more than 100 employees are offering career self-management training. A typical program consists of three stages or programs presented on successive days:

1. Assessing career attitudes, values, plans and goals
2. Analyzing how these goals have or have not been met by the current job
3. Discussing career strategies to create opportunities to meet one's plans and goals, whether on or off the job (This stage includes upgrading skills, soliciting feedback from colleagues and supervisors, networking, and being mobile in seeking new job opportunities.)

To date, there has been little research on the effectiveness of career self-management training. However, one study of more than 300 managers reported an unexpected conclusion. When interviewed several months after the training, the managers who had participated in the program were significantly less likely

---

NEWSBREAK

It's Your Job: Make the Most of It!

Gary Herman is a 55-year-old systems analyst with the data services division of GTE in Tampa, Florida. He's concerned about his future because he's working in a field where the technology changes so fast and so radically that a person's skills can become obsolete in the space of only a year or two. He spends considerable time reeducating himself to stay marketable.

"People need to be retooled," said James Harris, Herman's boss. "If they don't choose to do that, they could lose their jobs. Either you retrain or you don't move along in your career. It's that simple."

Internet-based technological advancements pose continual challenges for people like Gary Herman. When his employer offered a 2-month course on state-of-the-art developments, he added those 8 hours per day of study time to his full-time work schedule. His boss had not told him to take the course. Herman knew it was up to him to take advantage of the opportunity to improve his skills. But he also knew that if his next performance appraisal, which included a critical skill reevaluation, did not show that he was making an effort to manage the direction of his career, he would not remain on his chosen career path with GTE and would no longer be marketable elsewhere.

"You have to adopt a pattern of lifelong learning in this field," said John Bonanno, executive director of Boston University's corporate education center. "A lot of what you learn today will, in 2 or 3 years, be obsolete."

But not everyone is capable of being retrained. GTE's training director, Rene Lutthans, found that 25% of the employees who participate in such training are unable to master the new skills. "The company tries to find a place for such people, but as projects are phased out, there are no guarantees of employment."

If you can't keep up, you're out. If you don't manage your own career, no one else will.

Source: Lifelong learning. *St. Petersburg (FL) Times*, July 21, 1999.

to be undertaking career self-management behaviors than were the managers in a control group who had received no career self-management training (Kossek, Roberts, Fisher, & Demarr, 1998).

EVALUATING ORGANIZATIONAL TRAINING PROGRAMS

Regardless of how impressive and sophisticated a training program or facility may appear, or how much employees seem to like it, it is necessary that the outcomes or results be evaluated in systematic and quantitative terms. One way to measure the worth of a training program is to assess the following results:

1. Changes in cognitive outcomes, such as the amount of information learned
2. Changes in skill-based outcomes, such as improvements in quantity and quality of production
3. Changes in affective outcomes, such as positive attitudes and higher motivation

Unless such evaluative research is conducted, the organization will not know how effective is its investment of time and money.

Are employees learning the skills they need for their jobs? Are productivity, safety, and efficiency rising? Have communications and leadership skills improved? Have the attitudes of majority-group employees toward minority-group employees changed? To answer these questions, comparisons must be made of trained and untrained workers performing the same jobs. Or the same workers before and after training can be compared with a control group of workers who were not exposed to the training. Only through such research can the organization determine whether its training program should be modified, extended, or eliminated.

Even with such a substantial investment at stake, most organizations do not make a systematic effort to evaluate their training programs. Or, they may accept subjective or intuitive evidence that the trainees are actually learning something. As a result, many organizations do not have a clear idea whether the millions of dollars they spend on training is worthwhile. One psychologist summed up the attitude this way: "With corporate training, it's often, 'Let's spend the money and hope for the best'" (Ellin, 2000). This failure to examine the effectiveness of training programs is increasingly expensive as more and more training is dependent on computer technology.

In addition to cost, other factors help explain the lack of assessment of the effectiveness of training programs. Many training directors do not have the skills to conduct such research. Also, they may overestimate the usefulness of programs they have initiated and designed. Some companies offer training not because management believes in it or expects it to meet specific corporate goals but merely because their competitors do it.

Some training programs are established because some new technique or management style has produced a flood of anecdotal reports in the popular media attesting to its value. One example is "time management," supposedly a method for learning to use one's time in the most efficient manner. Supporters claimed time management increased employee productivity and satisfaction and reduced stress. With the growing number of magazine articles and television reports about the success of time management, companies hired time-management consultants to train employees in this latest miracle cure for the ills of the workplace. The only problem was, time management did not work.

This was demonstrated convincingly when an I-O psychologist conducted research with 353 state civil service employees and 341 college students. The documented conclusion was that time-management training was ineffective (Macan, 1994). No one knows how many companies initiated expensive time-management training programs and maintained them in the absence of data to support their effectiveness.

Assessing the behavioral changes that may occur following training can be difficult. If a worker operates a simple machine or assembles a part, the goal of the training program and the measurement of the outcome are relatively straightforward. The number of items produced per unit time by trained and untrained workers or by workers trained by different techniques can be determined objectively and compared. At this work level, training programs have been shown to be effective. When dealing with human relations, problem solving, or other management behaviors, it is far more difficult to assess the usefulness of the training.

One 4-year investigation of 18 training programs in a large pharmaceutical company found that management training was less effective in changing behavior (as measured by performance ratings) than were the more goal-oriented sales and technical training (Morrow, Jarrett, & Rupinski, 1997). Yet the face validity of management training is high. The programs are popular, everyone says they are necessary, and management looks good for providing them. However, the question remains: Are they truly worthwhile?

Training directors defend their programs by pointing out that management trainees are subsequently promoted to higher levels of responsibility. This is not a valid or sufficient measure of a training program's success because it is usually only the most capable and promising candidates who are chosen to participate in management training initially. These trainees are the ones most likely to be promoted anyway, even without the training programs. Training directors also like to boast that employees like the programs. That's nice, but feelings and other subjective reactions are no substitute for research to investigate whether training results in better job performance. Organizations must be willing to expend the resources necessary to evaluate their elaborate training and development programs. It makes little sense to continue to support such activities without empirical evidence of their worth.

We can see, then, that problems with organizational training provide many challenges for I-O psychologists:

- to identify the abilities required to perform increasingly complex jobs
- to provide job opportunities for unskilled workers
- to assist supervisors in the management of an ethnically diverse work force
- to retrain workers displaced by changing economic, technological, and political forces
- to help organizations remain competitive in the international marketplace

Transfer of Training: The Importance of the Work Environment

Regardless of how well designed and rigorous a training program is, if employees cannot carry over or transfer their newly learned skills to actual job duties, the training efforts will have been less than maximally effective. The degree of similarity between the training situation and the work situation affects transfer of training. Transfer is aided when supervisors show support for employees who use new skills and when employees are given the opportunity to apply those skills on the job. Therefore, transfer of training depends on more than the quality of the training program itself. It also depends on the overall organizational climate.

This was demonstrated in a study of 505 supermarket managers from 52 stores who participated in a 3-day training program on basic supervisory behaviors and skills. The mean age of the supervisors was 32; 57% of them were women. Training focused on *interpersonal skills* (such as customer and employee relations) and *administrative skills* (such as purchasing and the scheduling of work hours).

Three weeks prior to the training program, the managers and their superiors completed questionnaires assessing the managers' level of knowledge of supervisory skills and behaviors. (The specific skills and behaviors covered were taken from the curriculum content of the training program.) The same questionnaires were retaken by the managers and supervisors 6 to 8 weeks after the training program. The difference in scores for the managers between this posttraining test and the pretraining test would constitute a measure of how well they had learned the new skills. The difference between the pretraining and posttraining scores given by the supervisors would provide a measure of how well the managers were actually applying their newly acquired skills on the job.

Source: J. S. Tracey, S. I. Tannenbaum, & M. J. Kavanagh (1995). Applying trained skills on the job: The importance of the work environment. *Journal of Applied Psychology, 80,* 239–252.

After the training period, the managers completed two additional questionnaires dealing with their work environment. One questionnaire assessed the organization's transfer of training climate. It dealt with such issues as the following:

- The extent to which supervisors and co-workers encouraged and set goals for trainee-managers to use new skills and behaviors acquired in training
- The extent to which trainees were openly discouraged from using new skills and behaviors acquired in training
- The extent to which trainees received extrinsic and intrinsic rewards for using newly learned skills and behaviors

The second questionnaire assessed organizational support for continuous learning, such as social support from supervisors and co-workers and company-wide efforts to be innovative.

The results showed that the trainees demonstrated significantly more knowledge of supervisory skills and behaviors and that they used these skills on the job to a greater extent after the training than before. Also, the findings from the transfer-of-training questionnaire and the organizational-support questionnaire were significantly related to posttraining behavior. The extent of support provided by the work environment directly influenced the application of the managers' newly acquired skills and knowledge. The work environment facilitated the transfer of training from the training situation to the job.

Think About It

1. What factors other than those studied can affect transfer of training?
2. If employees do not have the opportunity to perform on the job the tasks for which they have been trained, how would this affect their job satisfaction, turnover intentions, self-efficacy, and job performance?

3. What weaknesses or omissions do you find in the study as described? How would you redesign the experiment to improve it? Would you include a control group? Why or why not?

4. If you were the training director of a large corporation, what steps would you take to maximize transfer of training among your employees?

SUMMARY

Training and development take place at all levels of employment, from unskilled teenagers who need remedial work in basic math and language skills to seasoned corporate vice presidents, from the first day on a job to the final months before retirement. Fair employment legislation affects training programs because decisions on placement, promotion, retention, and transfer are often based on performance during training. Therefore, training has the potential to be discriminatory.

The first step in establishing a training program is to specify the training objectives. A **needs assessment** based on organizational, task, and worker analyses is conducted using job analysis, critical incidents, performance appraisal, and self-assessment techniques. The training staff should be knowledgeable about the subject matter, be able to communicate effectively, and have the requisite interpersonal skills.

Pretraining characteristics of the trainees can influence how much they will benefit from a training program. These attributes include individual differences in ability, pretraining expectations, motivation, job involvement, locus of control, and self-efficacy. Psychological factors in learning include active practice of the material, massed or spaced practice, whole or part learning, transfer of training, feedback, and reinforcement.

In **on-the-job training,** trainees learn while actually working at the job. **Vestibule training** takes place in a simulated work area. In **apprenticeship,** trainees undergo classroom instruction and work experience under the guidance of skilled craftspersons. In **computer-assisted instruction,** trainees interact with computer software that presents the material to be learned. Net-based training offers instruction over the Internet or the company's in-house Intranet network. This makes training available both on and off the job, whenever and wherever the employees choose to log on. In **behavior modification,** trainees are reinforced, or rewarded, for displaying the desired behaviors.

Job rotation exposes trainees to various jobs at their level of employment. In **case studies,** management trainees analyze, interpret, and discuss a complex business problem. **Business games** require groups of trainees to interact in a simulated business situation. The in-basket technique, also a simulation, asks trainees to respond individually to letters, memos, and other office tasks. In role playing, trainees act out the problems of workers and managers. Behavior modeling has trainees pattern their behavior on that of successful managers. Executive coaching offers one-to-one training to improve a particular aspect of a manager's job performance. It is frequently a follow-up to poor ratings on a 360-degree performance appraisal. In diversity training, employees learn to confront and deal with racist and sexist attitudes.

Career development is a lifelong learning approach to enhancing job skills and abilities and fostering personal development. Through self-analysis and company counseling and training programs, employees are assisted through various career stages. Career self-management refers to lifelong learning and skill enhancement initiated by the employee rather than by the company.

Organizations rarely undertake systematic or quantitative evaluation of their training programs. Many training programs are continued because of subjective beliefs about their effectiveness rather than empirical evidence of actual behavior changes that result from training.

KEY TERMS

apprenticeship

behavior modification

business games

case studies

computer-assisted instruction

job rotation

needs assessment

on-the-job training

vestibule training

ADDITIONAL READING

Kilburg, R. R. (2000). *Executive coaching: Developing managerial wisdom in a world of chaos*. Washington, DC: American Psychological Association. A guide to the psychodymanics of executive behavior and job performance designed to help managers learn from mistakes and gain mastery over their organizational roles.

Robinson, P., & Schiff, N. (2001). *If I don't do it now: Career makeovers for the working woman*. New York: Pocket Books. Practical advice for retraining women who want a new career.

Salas, E., & Cannon-Bowers, J. A. (2001). The science of training: A decade of progress. *Annual Review of Psychology, 52*, 471–499. Reviews training theory, needs analysis, training and post-training conditions, and strategies for motivating trainees. Methods and instructional strategies discussed include distance learning, simulations, games, and team training.

Organizational Psychology

Organizational psychology is concerned with the social and psychological climate at work. Few people work alone. Most of us work in groups, such as a crew on an assembly line or the staff of a department in a corporate office. We develop informal cliques that generate and reinforce standards, values, and attitudes that may differ from those of the organization. We are also influenced by the formal structure of the company that employs us. Like informal groups, these formal groups generate a psychological climate or culture of ideals and ideas that affect our feelings about our job. Thus, our attitudes and behaviors in the workplace are influenced by the social climate of the organization and the psychological characteristics of its members. Organizational psychologists study the relationships between these two sets of factors.

Leadership (Chapter 7) is a major influence on work attitudes and behaviors. Organizational psychologists study the impact of various leadership styles and the characteristics and responsibilities of leaders.

Motivation, job satisfaction, and job involvement (Chapter 8) relate to employee needs and the ways organizations can satisfy them. We discuss the nature of employee identification with a job and with organizational goals and how this identification affects job performance and satisfaction.

The chapter on the organization of the organization (Chapter 9) discusses formal and informal groups and their psychological climate. We describe participatory democracy, adaptation to social and technological change, the socialization of new employees, and efforts to improve the quality of our working life.

Organizational psychology affects your working career directly. It influences your motivations, the style of leadership under which you function best, the leadership qualities you may display, and the structure of the organization for which you work. These factors determine the quality of your work experience, which, in turn, influences your general satisfaction with life.

Leadership

CHAPTER 7 *(vertical, right margin)*

CHAPTER OUTLINE

Did you know that half of all new business ventures and start-up companies fail within their first 2 years? Did you know that only one-third survive as long as 5 years? In most cases, these costly business failures can be traced to one source: poor leadership.

Did you know that up to half of all corporate decisions may be wrong? An I-O psychologist examined 356 decisions made by managers in companies of medium to large size in the United States and Canada and showed that these actions were directly related to the managers' personal style of leadership (Nutt, 1999). Leaders who imposed solutions arbitrarily, limited the search for alternative solutions, and operated dictatorially were the ones most likely to make disastrous decisions. Leaders who were less dictatorial and who allowed subordinates to participate in the decision-making process were far more likely to reach successful conclusions and make correct decisions.

More than half of all managers and executives may display, at times, some degree of incompetence. Thus, many employees—perhaps including you—probably work for someone who is an inept leader. Working for such a person can have a negative effect on how you perform your job and how you relate to the people and situations in your life off the job. Poor leadership hurts the company, too, by contributing to work slowdowns, poor customer service, sloppy work habits, and high absenteeism and turnover. The subordinates of a bad boss feel no commitment to their organization, report reduced job and life satisfaction, and experience high levels of stress.

An opinion poll of several hundred workers found that only 11% of those who rated their supervisor's performance as excellent said they would be seeking to change jobs in the coming year. In contrast, 40% of those who rated their supervisor's performance as poor said they would be looking for another job (Zipkin, 2000).

Obviously, the quality of leadership is a critical factor in the workplace. It is not surprising that organizations are greatly concerned with selecting, developing, and supporting their managers and executives and in making the best use of their leadership abilities on the job.

In addition to selection and training efforts, I-O psychologists have conducted considerable research on leadership techniques. They have explored the qualities and behaviors of successful and unsuccessful leaders, the effects of different leadership styles on subordinates, and the ways of maximizing leadership abilities.

ONLINE!

Want to complain about your boss or read about other people's experiences? Try one of these sites: *www.myboss.com, www.donsbosspage.com,* or *www.dilbert.com.*

A Bad Boss Can Ruin Your Day

NEWSBREAK

We've all worked for someone like Ellen Brower at some time in our lives, or we've known someone who did. She's arrogant, abrasive, and abusive. She gets angry at the slightest provocation and chews out her employees in front of their colleagues, berating them as incompetent and stupid—and a lot worse. No matter how hard you work, no matter how good a job you do, it's never good enough. She's never satisfied.

You dread going to work, and maybe you have a headache or an upset stomach by the time you reach the office. You have trouble sleeping because of the stress at work, thanks to her. You plan to quit as soon as you can, but until then, you're likely to remain an unhappy employee, getting little from your job but a paycheck. And no amount of money, you tell yourself every day, is worth having to put up with a boss like her.

If you do work for someone like Ellen Brower, you're not alone. Psychologist Robert Hogan of the University of Tulsa says that as many as 7 out of every 10 managers may be incompetent, exploiting, domineering, irritable, and untrustworthy. They refuse to delegate authority and have poor decision-making skills. In short, they are lousy bosses.

There are thousands of "bad boss" stories, like the one about the manager who would not let his employees phone for an ambulance when an elderly co-worker collapsed at his desk with a heart attack. The boss insisted that they wait until quitting time so that they didn't disrupt the work routine. Besides, as the boss said, "the guy was dead anyway." Or the insensitive department head who refused to believe a female employee who said she had missed work because she had suffered a miscarriage. He insisted that she obtain a written explanation from her physician. When she later requested bereavement leave to deal with her loss, he demanded to see the death certificate.

Some 75% of American workers believe that the worst thing about their jobs, and the greatest single cause of stress, is their boss. The most common complaints from workers are that supervisors are unwilling to exercise authority, tyrannize subordinates, and treat employees as if they were stupid.

How did such incompetent people get to be in charge? Hogan says it's because many companies select their best workers and promote them to supervisory positions. The catch is that being the best worker may have nothing to do with having the skills and abilities needed for good leadership. "What these bad guys are good at," Hogan claims, "is sucking up to *their* boss. These people have good social skills. That's how they got their job." Clearly it takes a lot more than social skills to make a good boss.

Source: A real piece of work: "Worst boss" contest lets employees vent. *Washington Post*, October 16, 1997; R. Hogan, G. J. Curphy, & J. Hogan (1994). What we know about leadership. *American Psychologist, 49,* 493–504.

APPROACHES TO LEADERSHIP

The ways in which leaders behave—the specific actions by which they play out their leadership roles—are based on certain assumptions about human nature. Consciously or unconsciously, leaders operate on the basis of some personal theory of human behavior, a view of what their subordinates are like as people. For example, managers who exercise close supervision on the job—who watch to make sure their employees are doing the work exactly as they have been instructed—hold a different view of human nature from that of managers who give their subordinates the freedom to work independently, in whatever way they think best.

Scientific Management

In the early years of the twentieth century, foremen (the first supervisory level over production workers) were promoted from the ranks of the workers and received little formal training for their leadership role. They had complete control over their subordinates' working lives. Foremen hired and fired, determined production levels, and set pay rates. There were few reins on their authority—no labor union, no industrial relations department, no human resources or personnel manager, no one to whom a worker could complain. Foremen usually gave hiring preference to their relatives and friends, and applied a combination of autocratic behavior, aggression, and physical intimidation to force workers to meet production goals.

Scientific management A management philosophy concerned with increasing productivity that regarded workers as extensions of the machines they operated.

The management philosophy during that period was called **scientific management,** an approach promoted by Frederick W. Taylor, an engineer. Taylor's concern was finding ways to increase productivity by getting the workers and the machines they operated to run faster and more efficiently.

Scientific management regarded workers simply as extensions of the machinery they operated. No consideration was given to the employees as human beings, as people with different needs, abilities, and interests. Workers were considered to be lazy and dishonest and likely to have a low level of intelligence. This view was reinforced by research that psychologists were then conducting on the general level of intelligence in the U.S. population. The psychologist H. H. Goddard argued that people with low intelligence required supervision by people with greater intelligence. "Laborers," Goddard said, "are but little above the child [and] must be told what to do and shown how to do it" (Goddard quoted in Broad & Wade, 1982, p. 198). Therefore, the only way for an organization to increase productivity and efficiency was to compel workers to submit to the dictates of their supervisors and the requirements of the manufacturing process.

The Human Relations Approach

It is difficult to imagine people working under the scientific management approach. Most modern organizations regard the satisfaction of employee needs as a legitimate corporate responsibility. This changed view, called the human relations approach, arose in the 1920s and 1930s under the impact of the Hawthorne studies (discussed in Chapter 1), which focused attention on workers instead of on the needs of the production equipment.

One change introduced into the work situation in the Hawthorne studies was the style of leadership. At the Hawthorne plant, workers were routinely treated harshly by supervisors who berated them for dropping parts, talking on the job, and taking breaks. As we noted, workers were treated like children who needed to be watched, shouted at, and punished. In the Hawthorne experiments, supervisors were trained to act differently, allowing workers to set their own production pace and to form social groups. They were permitted to talk to one another on the job, and their views about the work were solicited. The new supervisors treated them like human beings, not interchangeable cogs in some giant production machine.

Theory X and Theory Y

The scientific management and human relations approaches to leadership behavior were given formal expression by Douglas McGregor as Theory X and Theory Y (McGregor, 1960). The **Theory X** approach to management assumes that most people are innately lazy and dislike work, avoiding it whenever they can. They must be coerced, watched, and scolded on the job to make them work hard enough to meet the organization's goals. Theory X assumes that most people have no ambition, avoid responsibility, and prefer to be led and directed. Indeed, they would not work at all without a dictatorial leader. Theory X is compatible with scientific management and with the classic organizational style known as **bureaucracy.**

Theory Y proposes that most people seek inner satisfaction and fulfillment from their work. Control and punishment are not necessary to bring about good job performance. According to Theory Y, then, people are industrious and creative and seek challenge and responsibility on the job. They function best under a leader who allows them to participate in setting and working toward personal and organizational goals.

The Theory Y viewpoint is compatible with the human relations movement in management and with the participative, democratic style of organization. An example of the application of Theory Y is the management by objectives (MBO) approach to performance appraisal. We noted that MBO involves a high degree of employee participation in setting goals for job performance and personal growth.

> **Theory X/Theory Y** The Theory X approach to management assumes that people are lazy and dislike work and therefore must be led and directed. Theory Y assumes that people find satisfaction in their work and function best under a leader who allows them to participate in working toward both personal and organizational goals.
>
> **Bureaucracy** A formal, orderly, and rational approach to organizing business enterprises.

THEORIES OF LEADERSHIP

I-O psychologists recognize that effective leadership depends on the interaction of three factors:

1. the traits and behaviors of the leaders
2. the characteristics of the followers
3. the nature of the situation in which leadership occurs

We describe several theoretical explanations of leadership: contingency theory, cognitive resource theory, path-goal theory, normative decision theory, and the leader-member exchange.

Contingency Theory

In **contingency theory,** developed by Fred Fiedler (Fiedler, 1978), leadership effectiveness is determined by the interaction between the leader's personal characteristics and aspects of the situation. Leaders are classified as primarily

> **Contingency theory** A leadership theory in which a leader's effectiveness is determined by the interaction between the leader's personal characteristics and the characteristics of the leadership situation.

person-oriented or task-oriented. The type of leader who will be the more effective depends on the leader's degree of control over the situation.

Control is contingent on three factors: the relationship between the leader and followers, the degree of task structure, and the leader's authority or position power. If leaders are popular, are directing a highly structured or routine task, and have the authority or power to enforce discipline, then they have a high degree of control over the situation. We may describe this condition as favorable. For example, army sergeants who get along well with the soldiers in their squad are high-control and effective leaders. On the other hand, an unpopular president of a social club that has no formal goals and who has no authority to require attendance or collect dues is a low-control leader in an unfavorable situation.

According to contingency theory, the task-oriented leader will be more effective in extremely favorable or extremely unfavorable situations. When the situation is moderately favorable, the person-oriented leader will be more effective.

Contingency theory has stimulated a great deal of research, some of which is supportive and encouraging. However, most of that research was conducted in laboratory settings, not on the job. The validity of contingency theory remains in question, and it has not been determined whether the laboratory findings can be generalized to the workplace. In response to these criticisms, Fiedler revised his contingency theory. The cognitive resource theory of leadership is an outgrowth of his earlier work.

Cognitive Resource Theory

Cognitive resource theory
A leadership theory that focuses on the interaction among the following factors: a leader's cognitive resources (intelligence, technical competence, and job-related knowledge), job performance, and level of stress.

The **cognitive resource theory** of leadership focuses on leaders' cognitive resources—their intelligence, technical competence, and job-related knowledge. The leader's level of cognitive ability is related to the nature of the plans, decisions, and strategies that will guide the actions of a work group. The better the leader's abilities, the more effective the plans, decisions, and strategies. If the group supports the leader's goals and if the leader is not under unusual stress, then the leader's programs are likely to be implemented.

The cognitive resource theory is based on the following hypotheses (Fiedler & Garcia, 1987):

1. When leaders are under stress, their cognitive abilities are diverted from the task and they focus instead on problems and activities that are less relevant. As a result, group performance will suffer.
2. The cognitive abilities of directive leaders show a higher positive correlation with group performance than will the cognitive abilities of nondirective leaders.
3. Plans and decisions cannot be implemented unless the group complies with the leader's directives. Therefore, the correlation between a leader's cognitive resources and group performance will be higher when the group supports the leader than when it does not.
4. The leader's cognitive abilities will enhance group performance only to the degree to which the task requires those abilities; that is, the degree to which the task is intellectually demanding.

5. The leader's directive behavior will be partly determined by the nature of the relationship between leader and followers, the degree of task structure, and the leader's control over the situation (elements of the contingency theory described earlier).

Cognitive resource theory describes the interaction between cognitive resources, job performance, and stress. The emphasis on stress has practical implications because it is partially under the leader's control. Through stress-management techniques, a leader's cognitive resources can be developed and applied more effectively. A major source of stress for leaders arises from their own superiors in the organization. When managers have a stressful relationship with their boss, they tend to rely on responses or behaviors that worked for them in the past rather than on their cognitive resources. When leaders are free of stress, they rely on their intelligence instead of being constrained by past experiences.

Fiedler has presented impressive research support for the cognitive resource theory, although most of his work was conducted in the laboratory, not in the workplace. The generalizability of the theory remains in question. Other research has been less supportive, resulting in a spirited exchange of views, charges, and countercharges in the pages of the *Journal of Applied Psychology*. This debate demonstrates that scientists are not devoid of passion, particularly when their own work is under attack (Fiedler, Murphy, & Gibson, 1992; Vecchio, 1990, 1992).

Path-Goal Theory

The **path-goal theory** of leadership focuses on the kinds of behaviors a leader exercises to allow subordinates to achieve their goals. The theory states that leaders can increase their subordinates' motivation, satisfaction, and job performance by administering rewards that depend on the achievement of particular goals. In other words, effective leaders will help employees reach personal and organizational goals by pointing out the paths they should follow and by providing them with the means to do so.

Four styles that leaders can adopt to facilitate employee attainment of goals are as follows (House, 1971; House & Mitchell, 1974):

Path-goal theory A leadership theory that focuses on the kinds of behaviors leaders should exercise to allow their subordinates to achieve personal and organizational goals.

- Directive leadership—the leader tells subordinates what they should do and how they should do it.
- Supportive leadership—the leader shows concern and support for subordinates.
- Participative leadership—the leader allows subordinates to participate in decisions that affect their work.
- Achievement-oriented leadership—the leader sets challenging goals for subordinates and emphasizes high levels of job performance.

The leadership style that will be most effective depends on characteristics of the situation and the attributes of the subordinates. Leaders must be flexible and should choose whichever style is called for. For example, employees who have a low level of the skills required to perform a task will function better under directive leadership. Employees who have high skills need less direction and function better under supportive leadership. Leaders must be able to perceive accurately the nature of the situation and the abilities of their subordinates and respond with the most appropriate approach.

Research findings on the path-goal theory are contradictory, but in general the support is weak. It is a difficult theory to test experimentally because basic concepts, such as "path" and "goal," are hard to define in operational terms.

Normative Decision Theory

Normative decision theory
A leadership theory that focuses on the correct norms or standards of behavior for leaders to follow.

Normative decision theory focuses on a single aspect of leadership—decision making—and attempts to prescribe specific behaviors for leaders to follow. The word *normative* refers to those norms or standards of behavior considered to be correct. The theory is concerned with the extent to which leaders allow their subordinates to participate in making decisions (Vroom & Jago, 1988).

Normative decision theory proposes five styles on a continuum of leader behavior ranging from autocratic—in which all decisions are made by the leader—to fully participatory—in which decisions are reached through consensus. The most effective style of leadership depends on the importance of the decision, the degree to which it is accepted by subordinates, and the time required to make the decision.

A decision reached through participation might be better accepted by subordinates than a decision made by their leader, but sometimes the demands of the job require a faster response than can be provided by the participatory decision-making process. Leaders must be flexible in selecting the decision-making approach that yields maximum benefits in terms of quality, acceptance, and time constraints.

Normative decision theory has empirical support to show that some decisions reached through prescribed procedures for a given situation were more effective than decisions reached in other ways. However, other research questions the applicability of those decision-making procedures in the workplace.

The Leader-Member Exchange

Leader-member exchange
A leadership theory that focuses on how the leader-follower relationship affects the leadership process.

The **leader-member exchange** model deals with the ways in which the leader-follower relationship (the leader-member exchange, or LMX) affects the leadership process (Graen & Schliemann, 1978). The proponents of this model criticized other leadership theories for focusing on average leadership styles or behaviors and for ignoring individual differences among subordinates. The relationship between each leader-subordinate pair (or dyad) must be considered separately because leaders behave differently with each subordinate.

Subordinates are of two types: the in-group employees, whom the supervisor views as competent, trustworthy, and highly motivated, and the out-group employees, whom the supervisor views as incompetent, untrustworthy, and poorly motivated.

The LMX model also distinguishes two leadership styles: supervision, in which leadership is based on formal authority, and leadership, in which influence is exerted through persuasion. With out-group subordinates, leaders use supervision and assign tasks requiring low levels of ability and responsibility. There is little personal relationship between leaders and out-group members.

With in-group subordinates, leaders practice leadership rather than supervision and assign members important and responsible tasks that require high levels of ability. Leaders and in-group members establish personal relationships in which in-group subordinates provide support and understanding.

On-the-job research has generally supported the leader-member exchange model for various levels of management and has shown that the quality of the leader-subordinate relationship can be improved through training, resulting in the display of more leadership than supervision. Significant improvements in job satisfaction and productivity and decreases in errors have been found among subordinates as a result of training to improve the quality of the LMX.

A study of 125 salespersons in a large retail organization found that employees who had a strong relationship with their supervisor (a high LMX) were more committed to achieving assigned goals than were employees with a low LMX (Klein & Kim, 1998). Research involving 106 employees and their supervisors in an importing firm found that a high LMX between employee and supervisor was significantly related to delegation of authority. In other words, supervisors in high LMX relationships with their subordinates were far more likely to delegate authority to them. As a result, the employees felt empowered and showed improvements in job performance and job satisfaction (Schriesheim, Neider, & Scandura, 1998).

An analysis of the performance of 317 bank employees confirmed the positive relationship between a high employee-supervisor LMX and high job performance. This study also showed that the relationship was maintained even when the employees and the supervisor were geographically remote from one another; that is, when the employees worked in a different office or a different city from their direct supervisor. The researchers concluded that the mutual trust and respect of a high-quality LMX relationship overcame physical distance so that employees and supervisors worked jointly to accomplish organizational goals (Howell & Hall-Merenda, 1999).

Questionnaire data was obtained from 102 hospital employees and 26 supervisors. The more the leader-member exchanges were based on positive interpersonal interactions such as mutual trust, loyalty, and respect, the more the subordinates were likely to engage in behaviors to help co-workers and the organization (behaviors in addition to their job duties) (Settoon, Bennett, & Liden, 1996).

Finally, a study of 191 employees of the research and development department of a chemical company found that LMX affected creativity, at least for those employees characterized by a particular cognitive style. The researchers used psychological test results and supervisor ratings to identify employees as cognitive innovators (able to generate ideas that deviated from the norm) or cognitive adapters (able to generate ideas consistent with accepted conventions). Innovators were found to be highly creative on the job, regardless of the nature of their relationship with their supervisor. Adapters were consistently more creative when they had a high LMX relationship with their supervisor than when they had a low LMX relationship (Tierney, Farmer, & Graen, 1999). These on-the-job research findings have given the leader-member exchange model a practical advantage over most other leadership theories.

The Deputy Assistant to the Assistant Deputy . . .

Suppose you were offered the following choice. Either a $2,000 pay raise or a new job title with the word *manager* in it—not a new job, just a new title. Which would you choose? When the president of On-Line Systems offered his sales force that choice, the $2,000 or the title "sales manager" instead of "salesman," almost everyone opted for the new label.

"The thing that makes people stay," he said, "is not necessarily money. Why do they stay, day after day, coming back to you? It's because they're happy. A showy title makes them feel appreciated."

Employees especially like ego-boosting titles that include "manager" or "director." Managers get their phone calls returned. Clients respond faster to their emails and faxes than they do to those from someone with a lower-level title. Being a manager means never being put on hold. All those advantages will make them more productive.

Companies that recruit on college campuses are aware of this phenomenon and have been upgrading the job titles for their starting positions. Instead of seeking a "sales representative," they want a candidate for their "management leadership development program." Same job, but different label. The result? Many more job applicants.

Nowhere is title inflation more blatant than in the government bureaucracy. At the federal level in Washington, D.C., there are, at last count:

- 484 deputy assistant secretaries
- 148 associate assistant secretaries
- 220 assistant assistant secretaries
- 82 deputy assistant assistant secretaries

Paul Light, a Senior Fellow at the Brookings Institution, who studies what he calls "job title creep," joked about his own job. He says that he needs to have a Chief of Staff, "but I won't really be somebody until I have a *Deputy* Chief of Staff."

Source: Please hold for the Deputy Deputy, *New York Times,* March 14, 1999; Title search: What's in a name? *St. Petersburg (FL) Times,* July 26, 1998.

STYLES OF LEADERSHIP

Much I-O psychology research focuses on leadership styles and the behaviors by which they are manifested on the job. We discuss the differences between authoritarian and democratic leaders, and between transactional and transformational leaders.

For police officers, who hold stressful jobs that require rapid decision-making skills and efficient job performance, authoritarian leadership is desirable. Often, law-enforcement situations do not allow time for a more democratic approach.

Authoritarian and Democratic Leaders

Leadership in the workplace involves various styles along a continuum. The continuum ranges from a highly **authoritarian leadership** style, in which the leader makes all decisions and tells followers what to do, to a highly **democratic leadership** style, in which leader and followers discuss problems and jointly make all decisions that affect their work. The style that is most effective depends on the nature of the situation and the needs and characteristics of the followers.

Authoritarian leadership A leadership style in which a leader makes all decisions and tells followers what to do.

Democratic leadership A leadership style in which a leader and followers discuss problems and make decisions jointly.

In stressful work situations that require unusually rapid and highly efficient job performance, productivity and satisfaction are more likely to be maintained under authoritarian leadership. I-O psychologists suggest that these employees recognize that the nature of their work does not allow time for a participative approach. For example, firefighters must respond to a fire alarm immediately and follow the directions of their chief. They do not have time to hold a committee meeting to determine the best way to deal with the fire.

Transactional and Transformational Leaders

Transactional leaders focus on the social transactions or exchanges between leaders and followers. The leaders' freedom to act is constrained by their followers' perceptions of them. The key to this interaction is the followers' perceptions of and expectations about the leaders' abilities, competence, and source of authority. In other words, the behavior of transactional leaders depends on what

Transactional leadership A leadership style that focuses on the social interactions between leaders and followers, based on followers' perceptions of and expectations about the leader's abilities.

their followers think of them. Transactional leaders conduct their business by identifying the needs of their followers and bestowing rewards to satisfy those needs in exchange for a certain level of performance.

Transformational leaders have more latitude in their behavior. They are not limited by their followers' perceptions. Rather than believing that they must act in accordance with what their followers expect of them, transformational leaders work to change or transform their followers' needs and redirect their thinking.

Transformational leaders challenge and inspire subordinates with a sense of purpose and excitement about what can be accomplished. These leaders create a vision of what the corporate culture can be and communicate it to their employees, stimulating them to develop their abilities while accepting feedback and suggestions. A study of nearly 200 managers (from supervisors to CEOs) in a wide variety of industries found that transformational leaders scored higher on the personality factors of extraversion and agreeableness than did nontransformational leaders (Judge & Bono, 2000).

Three components of transformational leadership have been identified (Bycio, Hackett, & Allen, 1995):

1. Charismatic leadership—the level of confidence and inspiration engendered by the leader
2. Individualized consideration—the amount of attention and support the leader supplies to the followers
3. Intellectual stimulation—the extent to which leaders persuade followers to think differently about how they perform their jobs

Studies of business executives, high-ranking military officers, and high-level administrators in government and universities have found that those described by their subordinates as transformational leaders were more effective on the job. They also had better relations with superiors, and made greater contributions to organizational goals than did those described as transactional leaders. Employees reported that they worked harder for transformational leaders than for transactional leaders. The greater effectiveness of transformational leaders has been demonstrated in a wide range of employing organizations and in several countries including the United States, India, Spain, Japan, China, and Austria.

Often, transformational leaders display **charismatic leadership,** mentioned above as one of three components of this type of leadership. Charismatic leaders have a broad knowledge of their field, a self-promoting personality, a high energy level, and a willingness to take risks and use unconventional strategies. They use their power effectively to serve others and inspire their trust. Charismatic leaders stimulate their followers to think independently and to ask questions. They maintain open communication with subordinates and freely share recognition with them. They tend to generate high job performance and positive work attitudes among their followers.

Charismatic leaders also communicate a vision to their followers. They act to implement that vision, and they display a powerful communications style, such as a captivating tone of voice, animated facial expressions, and a dynamic way of interacting with other people. Charismatic leaders are the ones who launch new enterprises, direct organizational change, and stimulate impressive gains in employee productivity. But charismatic leaders can also misuse their power over

Transformational leadership A leadership style in which leaders are not constrained by their followers' perceptions but are free to act to change or transform their followers' views.

Charismatic leadership A leadership style characterized by a self-promoting personality, a high energy level, and a willingness to take risks. Charismatic leaders stimulate their followers to think independently.

others. They can be insensitive to the needs of their followers and act only for personal gain.

THE ROLE OF POWER IN LEADERSHIP

Among the issues relating to power in leadership behavior are (1) the power that leaders have over their subordinates and (2) the ways in which leaders are motivated by power. Leaders may exert different kinds of power, depending on the situation, the nature of their followers, and their personal characteristics.

Types of Power

Psychologists have proposed five types of leadership power (Yukl & Taber, 1983). These are the first three:

1. *Reward power.* Organizational leaders have the ability to reward subordinates with pay raises and promotions. This power gives leaders a means of control over employees and can affect employee behavior.
2. *Coercive power.* Organizational leaders have an equally strong source of power in their ability to punish subordinates by firing them, by withholding promotions and raises, and by keeping them in undesirable jobs.
3. *Legitimate power.* Legitimate power derives from the organization's formal power structure. The hierarchy of control legitimizes the right of the leader to direct and supervise the activities of followers and the duty of followers to accept that supervision.

These three sources of power are derived from and defined by the formal organization to which leaders and subordinates belong. They are types of power dictated or prescribed by the organization. The next two types of power derive from the leaders themselves and are earned or merited by the leaders' personal characteristics as these are perceived by followers. We might call these attributes "respect" as well as power.

4. *Referent power.* Referent power refers to the degree to which employees identify with their leaders and the leaders' goals, accept those goals as their own, and work with their leaders to achieve the goals.
5. *Expert power.* Expert power refers to the extent to which leaders are believed to have the skills necessary to attain the group's goals. If employees acknowledge their leader's expertise, then they are more likely to become willing and supportive subordinates.

Effects and Uses of Power

As you may know from your own experience, coercive power can be counterproductive. Leaders who rely primarily on coercive power in dealing with subordinates are less likely to be effective than are leaders who exercise the other types of power. People who work for coercive leaders tend to rank low in job satisfaction, productivity, and commitment to the organization. In order, the types of leadership power that research has shown to be most effective are expert power, legitimate power, and referent power.

How does power motivate organizational leaders? High-level executives and middle-level managers often show a great personal need for power. Effective managers tend to demonstrate a higher need for power than do less effective managers. However, the most effective managers do not seek power for personal gain. Their power need is directed toward the organization and is used to achieve organizational goals. As a result, they are usually successful in establishing and maintaining a good work climate, high morale, and high team spirit among their subordinates.

Managers motivated by the need for personal power serve themselves rather than their organization. They are capable of creating loyalty among subordinates, but it is a loyalty toward themselves, not toward the organization. These managers are more effective than those who show no need for power, but they are not as effective as those whose power is oriented toward the organization.

THE ROLE OF EXPECTATIONS: THE PYGMALION EFFECT

Leaders' expectations about their employees' job performance can influence that performance. For example, managers who expect high performance tend to get high performance, and those who expect poor performance tend to get poor performance.

This instance of a self-fulfilling prophecy was first observed in the classroom. In a now-classic demonstration, teachers were told that some of their students had a high level of potential and others had a low level of potential. In reality, there were no such differences between the two groups; the students were equal in their abilities. The differences existed only in the teachers' expectations, as created by the experimental situation. Yet, the group of students with the allegedly high potential later scored significantly higher on IQ tests than did the other group. The teachers had subtly communicated their expectations to their students, thereby affecting the students' academic performance (Rosenthal & Jacobson, 1968).

Pygmalion effect A self-fulfilling prophecy in which managers' expectations about the level of their employees' job performance can influence that performance.

This expectancy effect was labeled the **Pygmalion effect,** named after Pygmalion, a king of Cyprus who fell in love with an ivory statue of a beautiful woman named Galatea. In answer to Pygmalion's prayers, the statue came alive, turning his fantasy into reality.

The self-fulfilling prophecy has been widely demonstrated in the workplace. A meta-analysis of 17 studies involving nearly 3000 employees in a variety of jobs showed that the phenomenon was particularly strong in the military. It was more prevalent among men than women, and it was also found extensively among disadvantaged employees—those employees considered by management, and by themselves, to have low expectations (McNatt, 2000). Their job performance usually matched their expectations. Other research, involving 30 squads of soldiers in the Israel Defense Force (the Israeli army), confirmed these findings. Women recruits who were held in low esteem by their female superior officers tended to perform poorly (Davidson & Eden, 2000).

Additional studies in the Israeli army involved squad leaders who were told that some of their male paratrooper trainees who had received low scores on a physical fitness test were expected to perform just as well as trainees who had tested higher in fitness. Leaders in the control group squads were told nothing about the physical potential of the low scorers under their command. Thus, expectancies were established about some of the low scorers but not about others. The results showed that low-scoring trainees in the experimental groups improved significantly more than did low-scoring trainees in the control group. The researchers concluded that the squad leaders' higher expectations led them to expect more and demand more from the trainees. The result was higher performance from those trainees. The leaders of the low-scoring trainees in the control group, however, had no great expectations about the performance of their trainees, who made significantly smaller gains (Oz & Eden, 1994).

THE FUNCTIONS OF LEADERSHIP

A comprehensive research program to identify the functions of leaders on the job began in the late 1940s at Ohio State University. A variety of leadership tasks and behaviors were grouped into two categories of functions called **consideration** and **initiating structure** (Fleishman & Harris, 1962).

Consideration leadership functions Leadership behaviors that involve awareness of and sensitivity to the feelings of subordinates.

The Consideration Dimension

The functions in the consideration dimension involve awareness of and sensitivity to the feelings of subordinates. These functions are allied with the human relations approach to management. Leaders high in consideration understand and accept subordinates as individuals with unique motivations and needs. Successful leaders must relate to each employee by being considerate of that person's feelings. This necessarily places an additional burden on managers. They must be

Initiating structure leadership functions Leadership behaviors concerned with organizing, defining, and directing the work activities of subordinates.

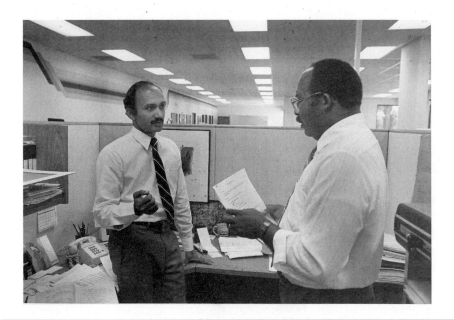

Effective managers balance consideration behaviors (sensitivity to subordinates' needs) with initiating structure behaviors (providing a framework within which to meet the company's goals).

sympathetic, warm, and understanding of their employees while maintaining production levels and other organizational goals.

You can see the similarity between the consideration leadership function and the leadership styles proposed by some of the theories we discussed earlier. High consideration relates to the person-oriented leader in contingency theory, to participative leadership in path-goal theory, to full participation in normative decision theory, and to the leadership condition in the leader-member exchange model.

NEWSBREAK

Management Always Wins: The Canoe Race

A Japanese company and an American company decided to have a canoe race on the Missouri River. Both teams practiced long and hard to reach their peak performance before the race. On the day of the race, the Japanese won by a mile.

The American team was crushed. They felt very discouraged and morally depressed. Management prepared a mission statement and made it their goal to uncover the reason for the defeat. A Measurement Team of senior management personnel was formed. They would investigate and recommend appropriate action.

Their finding was that the Japanese team had eight people rowing and one person steering, whereas the American team had one person rowing and eight people steering. So American management hired a consulting firm for an enormous amount of money to advise them. The consulting company concluded that too many people were steering the boat and not enough people were rowing.

To prevent another humiliating loss to the Japanese team the following year, the American rowing team's management was reorganized. The new management structure included four steering managers, three area steering superintendents, and one assistant area steering superintendent liaison. The group then implemented a new performance system intended to give the one person rowing the boat greater incentives to work harder. The system was called the Rowing Team Quality-First Program, designed to give the rower empowerment and job enrichment. It was kicked off with meetings, dinners, and free pens and tee-shirts for the rower.

The next year, the Japanese won the boat race by two miles. American management fired the rower for poor performance, halted funds for the development of a new canoe, sold the paddles, and cancelled capital investment for new equipment. They gave awards for high performance to the steering managers and distributed the money saved as bonuses to the senior executives.

An Internet story of unknown source, provided by Marty Salo.

The Initiating Structure Dimension

The functions in the initiating structure dimension include tasks traditionally associated with a leadership role—organizing, defining, and directing the work activities of subordinates. Sometimes this aspect of a manager's job conflicts with the demands of the consideration dimension. To accomplish a job (to initiate structure), managers must assign specific tasks to employees, direct the way in which the tasks should be performed, and monitor the work to ensure that it is being done properly.

These work activities may call for some authoritarian behavior and decision making, and there may not be time or opportunity for leaders to consider their subordinates' needs or feelings. A certain amount of work must be accomplished at a specified level of quality in a fixed period of time. The organization's success and the manager's job depend on meeting these standards consistently. Thus, it is not always easy for managers to balance the behaviors of consideration and initiating structure.

The leadership functions in the initiating structure dimension are similar to those of the task-oriented leader in contingency theory, directive leadership in path-goal theory, autocracy in normative decision theory, and supervision in the leader-member exchange model.

CHARACTERISTICS OF SUCCESSFUL LEADERS

The characteristics required for successful leadership vary with a manager's level in the organizational hierarchy. The CEO of an automobile manufacturing company performs different functions and thus needs different abilities from those of a supervisor on the auto painting assembly line. In general, the higher the position on the corporate ladder, the fewer consideration activities and the more initiating structure activities are required. A high-level executive needs fewer human relations skills than a supervisor, because the executive typically controls and interacts directly with fewer subordinates. The corporate vice president may deal only with a half-dozen department heads, whereas the first-line supervisor may have 100 or more workers to manage. Therefore, leaders at different levels have different functions, characteristics, and problems on the job.

First-Line Supervisors

I-O psychology research on first-line supervisors suggests that supervisors with the most productive work groups have the following qualities:

1. Effective supervisors are person-centered. They rate higher in the consideration function than do unsuccessful supervisors.
2. Effective supervisors are supportive. They are more helpful to employees and more willing to defend them against criticism from higher management.
3. Effective supervisors are democratic. They hold frequent meetings with employees to solicit their views and encourage participation. Less effective supervisors are more autocratic.

A first-line supervisor at an automobile plant meets with subordinates to discuss problems and hear grievances.

4. Effective supervisors are flexible. They allow employees to accomplish their goals in their own way whenever possible, consistent with the goals of the organization. Less effective supervisors dictate how a job is to be performed and permit no deviation.
5. Effective supervisors describe themselves as coaches rather than directors. They emphasize quality, provide clear directions, and give timely feedback to their workers.

Managers and Executives

At higher levels of an organization, managers and executives engage in fewer consideration behaviors and more initiating structure behaviors. In other words, they are less people-oriented and more work-oriented. Successful executives share other characteristics. We discuss the impact of college attendance, the role of power, and the importance of self-promotion. We also note the characteristics of unsuccessful executives.

The College Experience.   Research has shown that college attendance correlates positively with later job success at the executive level. Employees with a college background rise faster and higher through the management ranks than do those who did not attend college. College grades correlate positively with assessment-center ratings of management potential and later advancement on the job. People who earn higher grades in college show greater potential for promotion, obtain their first promotion early in their career, and rise higher in management than those who earn lower grades. The quality of the college attended is a less useful predictor of later job performance, although assessment-center ratings are higher for managers who attended better-quality colleges.

A more valid predictor of potential and actual promotion is college major. Those who major in humanities and social sciences receive superior ratings in assessment-center exercises and job performance and move faster and farther up the corporate ladder. Those who major in business administration rank second. Mathematics, science, and engineering majors are third. Humanities and social science majors excel in decision making, creativity in solving business problems, intellectual ability, written communications skills, and motivation for advancement. They, and the business majors, rank higher in interpersonal skills, leadership ability, oral communications skills, and flexibility than the math, science, and engineering majors.

Some collegiate activities, such as student government, student newspaper, and debating society, correlate positively with measures of management potential, although they do not seem to be related directly to actual job advancement. Participation in sports shows no relationship to management potential.

The Role of Power. We noted that power was an important motivating force for successful executives. Decades ago, psychologist David McClelland proposed a leadership motive pattern (LMP) that is informally described as "empire building." Executives with a high LMP are believed to be effective managers. They have a high need for power, a lower need for affiliation with other people, and considerable self-control. They have a greater need to influence people than to be liked (McClelland, 1975).

Research on this personality pattern has found it to be highly predictive of success for managers in nontechnical jobs. The managers' need for achievement (the need to perform well) also predicted success in nontechnical positions. In addition, managers high in the LMP prefer jobs that are high in prestige and status.

Self-Promotion. People who are good at promoting themselves, so that they acquire the support or sponsorship of mentors within the company, are often the ones more likely to advance within the corporate hierarchy. A mentor is a coach or counselor who provides support and advice to a younger protégé. Those managers fortunate enough to have had good mentors are far more likely to receive pay increases and promotions, compared to those who do not have mentors.

Survey data collected from 147 college graduates during their early years of employment showed that employees themselves can influence the amount of mentoring they receive. Specifically, people high in internal control, emotional stability, and self-monitoring (the ability to be sensitive to social cues and to alter one's behaviors to fit various situations) were much more likely to initiate a mentoring relationship with a senior manager. The data also confirmed the positive relationship between mentoring and career achievement (Turban & Dougherty, 1994).

The factor of self-monitoring was investigated in a study of the first 5 years on the job for 139 MBA graduates. Those who scored high on a questionnaire to measure self-monitoring answered yes to such items as "I would change my behavior to become the kind of person this situation requires." High-scorers were found to be flexible, adapting themselves to any work environment. Low-scorers maintained more consistent and stable attitudes, values, and behaviors, often refusing to change to fit the demands of changing situations or different supervisors. High self-monitors advanced further in the company than low self-monitors (Kilduff & Day, 1994).

Unsuccessful Executives. It is just as important for organizations to know what characteristics lead some managers to fail as it is to understand what makes others succeed. Such failure is usually referred to as "derailment," such as when a train unexpectedly leaves the track.

Executives who once showed management potential but who are later dismissed or retired early typically fail because of personality factors rather than job performance. Derailed executives are judged by their superiors to lack consideration behaviors. Insensitive, arrogant, and aloof, they display an abrasive and domineering leadership style and are overly ambitious to attain personal rather than organizational goals.

These findings have been supported by considerable research: Executive failure is related to personality factors. Interviews with 20 senior executives from U.S. companies and 42 senior executives from European companies revealed that the major reason for executive derailment was poor interpersonal relations—that is, an inability to get along with other people (Van Velsor & Leslie, 1995).

A meta-analysis of derailment research described the failed executive in the following terms:

> Many managers who are bright, hardworking, ambitious, and technically competent fail (or are in danger of failing) because they are perceived as arrogant, vindictive, untrustworthy, selfish, emotional, compulsive, overcontrolling, insensitive, abrasive, aloof, too ambitious, or unable to delegate or make decisions (Hogan, Curphy, & Hogan, 1994, p. 499).

MANAGEMENT TEAMS

In large organizations, management functions are increasingly being performed by groups of managers rather than by a single manager. I-O psychologists have been studying the composition and effectiveness of these management teams under different corporate conditions. They have found that the most responsive teams are receptive to change, willing to take risks, and creative in their decision making. As a result, their companies operate more efficiently and are more successful.

One problem for management teams relates to self-limiting behaviors in decision making; that is, people on management teams tend to deliberately limit their involvement. Individual self-limiting behaviors reduce the decision-making capability of the team as a whole because not all members will be committed to participation in the process.

A survey of 569 managers revealed that they limited their input in 56% of the teams in which they participated (Mulvey, Veiga, & Elsass, 1996). Their reasons for limiting their behavior are given in Table 7–1. In addition, self-limiting

TABLE 7–1 Reasons for Self-Limiting Behavior

	Frequency (percent)
The presence of someone with expertise	73%
The presentation of a compelling argument	62
Lack of confidence in one's ability	61
An unimportant or meaningless decision	52
Pressure from others to conform to the team's decision	46

Adapted from "When Teammates Raise a White Flag" by P. W. Mulvey, J. F. Veiga, & P. M. Elsass, 1966, *Academy of Management Executive, 10*(1), p. 44.

behaviors were found to increase with group size. It should be disturbing to top executives to realize how often their managers fail to participate in decision making, thus reducing their ability to offer dynamic leadership.

PROBLEMS OF LEADERSHIP

Just as leader characteristics vary with a manager's level in the organizational hierarchy, so do the pressures and problems.

First-Line Supervisors

In some ways, supervisors have more difficult jobs than executives, yet they receive less formal training in how to manage other people. In fact, supervisors may receive no training at all, and they are not selected as carefully as people who begin their careers at higher-level management positions. Often, the most competent workers are chosen to be supervisors, without any assessment of their leadership potential.

Supervisors promoted from the ranks face conflicting demands and loyalties. Before promotion, they were accepted by those who worked with them and shared their attitudes and values. They may have socialized with co-workers off the job. Their work group gave them a sense of identity and belonging that provided a measure of emotional security.

After they become supervisors, they can no longer enjoy the same relationship with co-workers and friends. Even if they try to remain part of the group, their former co-workers do not respond to them in the same way because of the changed relationship. This costs newly promoted supervisors the emotional security that comes from group affiliation and identification.

Supervisors are the point of contact between management and workers, trying to weigh the conflicting needs of both sides. If supervisors expect to establish and retain the loyalty and cooperation of their workers, they must present management's needs and decisions to the workers and must present the workers' needs to management, serving as a buffer and an open channel of communication. In practice, it is often necessary for supervisors to be more responsive to the demands of their superiors if they hope to keep their jobs.

The trend toward increased worker participation complicates the job of first-line supervisors. They stand to lose what little autonomy they have by being forced to share leadership and decision-making power with subordinates. **Self-managing work groups** are another threat to supervisory power and autonomy. In these programs, instead of sharing power, supervisors must abandon their traditional responsibilities and act as resource persons rather than leaders. If the work groups are less effective than expected, the supervisor will be blamed. If the work groups are effective, top management usually attributes the favorable results to the workers, not to the supervisor.

Self-managing work groups Employee groups that allow the members of a work team to manage, control, and monitor all facets of their work, from recruiting, hiring, and training new employees to deciding when to take rest breaks.

Computer technology in the workplace has also made supervision more difficult. First-line supervisors are responsible for hardware they often are not trained to understand. Computers can control and monitor quantity and quality of production and provide top management with data on employee performance, output, and other aspects of office or manufacturing processes, thus bypassing any input from the first-line supervisor.

Managers and Executives

A department or section head faces stresses that are different from those of the CEO. Middle-level managers, despite comfortable salaries and fringe benefits, typically express considerable discontent. A frequent complaint is the lack of influence in formulating company policy, policy they are expected to implement without question. Middle managers also complain about having insufficient authority and resources to carry out company policy. They must fight for recognition from superiors and compete for support for their ideas and projects. As a result, middle managers often experience considerable frustration as they vie for the few top management slots in the hierarchy.

Another source of dissatisfaction is the feeling of obsolescence that comes to middle-level managers in their late thirties and early forties. Most of them have reached a plateau and will receive no additional promotions. That realization often becomes part of a general midlife crisis, a period of self-examination for middle managers who feel threatened by younger subordinates, by changing cultural values, and by redefined organizational goals. Their productivity, creativity, and motivation may decline, and they may in effect retire on the job, making little contribution to the organization.

Employee participation in decision making is another source of stress for middle managers. Although they have no influence in decisions affecting their own jobs, they see that assembly-line, production, and office workers have gained the right to participate in decision making and job design. Participatory democracy leads to drastic changes in the ways managers can exert control over their employees. Shared leadership results in a loss of managerial authority, status, and power. Democratization may also eliminate traditional management perquisites such as reserved parking spaces, corporate dining rooms, and private offices.

Because of corporate mergers, acquisitions, and buyouts, as well as the competitiveness of the world economy and the changes in the nature of work, several million middle-management jobs have been lost over the last few decades. Massive layoffs create a motivational crisis among middle-level managers. Seeing that their companies are less loyal and supportive of fired co-workers than they expected, middle managers tend to feel less organizational commitment in return. Mergers and layoffs also mean fewer opportunities for promotion and more competition for the available positions.

A source of stress more common among high-level managers is the intense commitment of time and energy to the organization. It is not uncommon for executives to work 60- or 80-hour weeks and to bring work home for evenings and weekends. With portable electronic equipment such as cell phones, beepers, laptop computers, and fax machines, executives can work at home and while traveling, rarely escaping the demands of the office. This leads to an imbalance in their personal lives, leaving little time for family demands.[1]

NEWSBREAK

Teaching the Boss

When General Electric's top management launched a major drive to encourage their high-level executives to embrace information-age technology and use it in their daily work, they made a startling discovery: Many of the veteran managers were computer illiterate. They had never used the Internet, never gone on-line to search the Web (not even for shopping), never even sent an e-mail, unless they asked a secretary to do it. They claimed they were too busy to use a computer. The real reason was that they did not know how.

Jack Welch, GE's chairman and CEO, was irate when he found out that his key executives didn't have a clue about using this basic tool of modern organizational life. But then, neither did he. He still used handwritten notes to communicate.

Welch also liked to get things done quickly, so he issued an edict: The top executives would have to find mentors who would teach them to become computer literate. That posed a problem. These managers ranged in age from the late thirties into the sixties. Where would they find mentors—who, by tradition, are older and wiser? Welch had an answer: reverse mentoring. Search the company's younger employees for techies and Internet junkies to teach the older bosses new tricks.

The 63-year-old Welch set the example by asking for help from the 37-year-old director of the company's Web site. The other executives quickly followed, meeting regularly with the computer-literate subordinates who became their mentors. Both sides benefited from the reverse mentoring. One employee in her twenties talked about the 54-year-old executive she was mentoring. "I can actually teach him things," she said. "I know things he doesn't know." Executives learned how to use computers in their work, and subordinate-mentors learned to be more at ease with the top leaders, observing first-hand the abilities needed to be successful at that level.

As for Welch, he was pleased with the outcome of his reverse mentoring program and with his own skills. "I can go to chat rooms and see what people are saying about GE."

Source: Web-savvy employees mentor their GE bosses. *St. Petersburg (FL) Times,* February 28, 2000.

---

[1]See Chapter 12 for a more detailed discussion of work-family conflicts.

The potential rewards of an executive position—power, money, status, challenge, and fulfillment—are great, but so are the demands. Still, there are more positive aspects to life at the top of the organizational hierarchy. Although middle managers are not a particularly happy group, top executives report high job satisfaction. Surveys show that most upper-level executives would remain on the job even if they were financially independent. Their work provides much more than financial satisfaction.

WOMEN IN MANAGEMENT

After decades of being underrepresented in management positions, women employees are finally making progress in the upper ranks of corporate life. According to the latest data, women hold 12% of the top corporate officer jobs in the Fortune 500 companies. In 1995, they held only 8% of those jobs. Greater numbers of women are being appointed to corporate boards of directors. Approximately 85% of the Fortune 500 companies have at least one woman board member.

Despite these positive signs, however, most women in leadership roles hold low- or middle-level management jobs. Those who have attained higher levels typically worked harder than men in management positions did to earn their promotions. In a survey of 786 women vice presidents and CEOs of major corporations, the women executives agreed that three factors had been essential to their advancement (Ragins, Townsend, & Mattis, 1998):

1. They had consistently exceeded performance expectations.
2. They had developed a leadership style that men were comfortable with.
3. They had sought and successfully accomplished difficult and highly visible assignments.

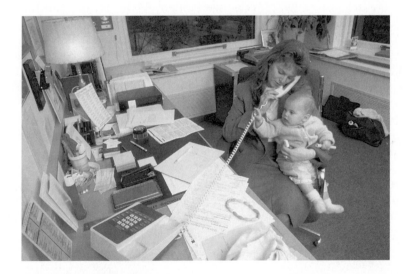

Most women managers hold low- or middle-level jobs. Often, these managers must balance the demands of work and family life.

The women executives also identified several major obstacles to successful management careers for women:

- The persistence of male stereotypes and preconceptions about women
- The exclusion of women from informal networks such as after-hours socializing
- The lack of general management or line experience
- An inhospitable corporate culture

Women managers are often stopped in their career progress by the so-called glass ceiling, an impenetrable barrier that allows them to view the rewards and responsibilities of upper management but prevents them from reaching it. One of the few organizations to shatter this glass ceiling has been the U.S. government, where women have an advantage over private industry because of the federal commitment to the doctrine of equal employment opportunity.

The commitment to hiring women for senior positions is less common in the private sector. There, many women managers are restricted to staff jobs in departments that are low in status, such as human resources, public relations, and consumer affairs, instead of line jobs in more powerful departments such as engineering, manufacturing, and marketing.

A comparison of 69 women middle- and upper-level managers with 69 men managers at the same levels showed that women reported more barriers to advancement than men did. Women experienced a lack of fit with the corporate culture and felt that they were deliberately excluded from informal networks. They noted difficulty in getting good assignments and were rarely considered for job opportunities that required geographical relocation.

Like the women executives in the survey cited previously, these women managers believed that they had to work much harder and meet higher standards than men managers did. In addition, the women found it harder than men to develop mentoring relationships with higher-level executives and to have their achievements recognized by the company's top decision-makers (Lyness & Thompson, 2000).

A common sex stereotype is being applied here: discrimination against women managers by keeping them in jobs that require so-called feminine attributes such as empathy and sensitivity. So-called masculine attributes, such as aggressiveness, ambition, and self-reliance, are seen as more suited to line jobs in manufacturing and sales. As we noted, it is the line departments that are the stepping-stones to top management. When women do succeed on the job, their superiors (usually men) are likely to attribute that success to luck or other external conditions, not to personal ability. When men succeed, it is usually attributed to personal ability.

Women managers are assessed differently from men managers in terms of their leadership behaviors. When men and women managers display assertiveness, women are typically judged as pushy. These judgments are made by women as well as by men. A woman lawyer wrote:

> There's nothing men hate more—especially men in power—than a woman who is [too much] like a man. It's a very negative thing. There was a very well-qualified woman who interviewed at our firm for a position. She had years of experience in the exact practice area that we were recruiting

for, but when she showed up, people hated her. Men and women alike said, "She's too mannish." She didn't get the job (Ely, 1995, p. 617).

Men managers expect women managers to be assertive but will tolerate that assertiveness only up to a point. They expect women managers to take risks but always be outstanding, to be tough and ambitious but not "masculine," and to take responsibility but follow the advice of others. In other words, women managers are expected to perform better than men managers, but they should not expect better, or even equal, treatment. The higher the management position in the corporate hierarchy, the more traditionally masculine characteristics managers of both sexes are expected to display.

With regard to job performance, a meta-analysis of 96 studies of leader effectiveness found that men and women were rated equally effective in laboratory studies and in research conducted on the job. However, these ratings differed by gender when the jobs were judged to require different abilities. For example, women were rated as more effective leaders in situations that required the ability to cooperate and get along with other people. Men were rated more effective in situations requiring the ability to direct and control subordinates. Despite these differences, in general men and women leaders were rated equally effective (Eagly, Karau, & Makhijani, 1995).

Men and women subordinates tend to rate men and women managers as equally effective leaders. Subordinate ratings of men and women managers revealed no gender differences in their task-oriented and people-oriented behaviors, or in their levels of consideration or initiating structure behaviors (the leadership functions we discussed earlier). Research also shows that women managers often display a higher drive to succeed than men managers.

Some evidence suggests that women managers are less effective at maintaining discipline with their subordinates. Interviews with 68 women and 95 men who had been reprimanded by their supervisors revealed that only 40% of the employees believed that women bosses had handled the disciplinary procedure appropriately and effectively, whereas 57% thought that men bosses had done so (Meece, 2000).

Job satisfaction is higher for women executives than for women in middle- and lower-level management positions. Overall, women managers report greater job satisfaction than do women employees in nonmanagerial positions. Job satisfaction among women managers is not diminished by the fact that most of them believe they have been discriminated against and must work harder than men to achieve the same level of success.

Contrary to expectations, studies of women managers have also found that they experienced the same frequency of mentoring from higher-level managers as did men managers. This equal access to mentors is vital in assisting upward mobility in an organization. In the survey of women vice presidents and CEOs cited above, 91% of those highly successful executives reported having had a mentor at some point in their career. Of these, some 80% believed that their mentor was crucial to their advancement.

The researchers quoted a vice president of a major utility company:

I think [mentoring] is critical to women advancing careerwise. In my experience, you need somebody to help guide you and go to bat for you. I'm not saying to take care of you because you're a woman. I'm saying, because you're a woman, you need somebody to fight some of your battles in the male environment (Ragins, Townsend, & Mattis, 1998, p. 32).

Does it make a difference if a woman employee's mentor is male or female? Yes, according to a study of more than 350 women and 250 men in engineering, social work, and journalism jobs. The women who had male mentors earned significantly higher salaries than did the women who had female mentors. Men who had female mentors reported being less satisfied with their mentors than did men who had male mentors. Men with female mentors also felt less accepted by their mentors and believed they were given fewer challenging assignments and less time with their superiors than did men with male mentors (Ragins & Cotton, 1999). It is interesting to speculate on possible explanations for these findings.

Other developmental activities are less open to women managers. Comparisons of men and women managers consistently show that both formal training programs and on-the-job growth experiences (such as high-profile, challenging

---

NEWSBREAK

Tips for Hiring Women: 1943 Version

During World War II (1941–1945), many organizations in the United States found that they needed to hire, for the first time, large numbers of women to perform "men's jobs" because the men had gone off to war. The advice that follows was offered seriously at the time. It was believed to be absolutely necessary to help "the girls" (as they were called then) adjust to working outside the home. Needless to say, the bosses were all men.

■ General experience indicates that "husky" girls (those who are just a little on the heavy side) are more even-tempered and efficient than their underweight sisters.

■ Give the female employee a definite day-long schedule of duties so that she will keep busy without bothering management for instructions every few minutes. Women make excellent workers when they have their job cut out for them, but they lack initiative in finding work themselves.

■ Give every girl an adequate number of rest periods during the day. You have to make allowances for feminine psychology. A girl has more confidence and is more efficient if she can keep her hair tidied, apply fresh lipstick, and wash her hands several times a day.

■ Be tactful when issuing instructions or in making criticisms. Women are sensitive. They can't shrug off harsh words the way men do. Never ridicule a girl. It breaks her spirit and cuts off her efficiency.

■ Get enough size variety in the workers' uniforms so that each girl can have a proper fit. This point cannot be stressed too much in keeping women happy.

Fortunately, we've come a long way since these tips were published.

assignments that increase one's visibility to senior management) are less available to women. Also, women managers appear to receive considerably less encouragement from superiors than men managers at the same level.

Some women managers become discouraged by their lack of progress and opportunity relative to that of men managers and decide to leave the corporate world to start their own companies. In the last years of the 20th century, five times as many women as men left organizational life to start their own businesses. A comparison of the reasons given by men and women managers for quitting their corporate jobs found that women were far more likely than men to leave because they believed that their career expectations had not been met (Rosin & Kobarik, 1995). However, even working for themselves, women face discrimination. Women-owned businesses tend to operate in certain occupational categories, notably retail sales, education, and personal services. Nevertheless, women entrepreneurs tend to be as successful as men entrepreneurs.

Many women managers and executives have been leaving the traditional business world for positions with dot.com Internet companies. The job opportunities in these start-up companies are varied, and the need for talented people is great. The average age of the employees is younger than in standard businesses, and their organizational climate is more open to men and women of diverse backgrounds and interests. By the year 2000, women held top management jobs in 45% of new Internet ventures. Gayle Crowell, president of www.e.piphany. net, said, "The Internet is a new game. The old rules don't apply."

> **ONLINE!** For information about the problems and progress of women employees at all levels, log on to *www.feminist. com, www.fairpay.htm, www.aflcio.org/women, www.now.org* (National Organization for Women), *www.dol.gov/dol/wbi* (Women's Bureau of the U.S. Department of Labor), and *www.nafe.com* (National Association for Female Executives).

MINORITY EMPLOYEES IN MANAGEMENT

Although minority employees have access to management positions in increasing numbers, they continue to face stereotypes, prejudice, and unique problems and challenges. Like women managers, black and other minority managers meet a glass ceiling that effectively bars them from attaining many top management jobs. That ceiling may be lower for minorities than for women. Most minority employees in management are black; few are Hispanic or Asian-American. Most of the research on minority personnel in management jobs has studied black subjects.

Blacks must usually work harder than whites to prove themselves, and their job performance may be evaluated more stringently. They may find that white employees resent their presence, believing they were hired or promoted with fewer qualifications simply to meet equal employment opportunity requirements. Racist attitudes openly expressed can make everyday interactions with superiors, co-workers, and subordinates unpleasant. Some minority managers quit in frustration. Corning Glass found that black managers were leaving the company at three times the rate of white managers. Monsanto Chemical reported that the major reasons black managers gave for quitting were problems with superiors, a sense of not belonging, and a lack of challenge.

Data from the Bureau of Labor Statistics show that minority women have fewer opportunities than white women or minority men in terms of the type of job and salary they are able to obtain (Abelson, 1999). In a survey of 1,735 black, Asian, and Hispanic women from 30 different companies, more than half of these women employees reported that they had been victims of discrimination. Although the majority of U.S. companies have formulated policies to encourage and promote diversity, the women surveyed said that the policies failed to prevent the subtle racism and sexism they had experienced on the job. They believed that the formal diversity programs were ineffective and that their job opportunities had not improved over the previous 5 years.

Nearly 35% of the women questioned did believe that diversity programs had created a more supportive environment, but only 25% felt that the programs had opened a broader career development path for them. When minority women employees were asked to note the greatest hindrance to their career advancement, the most popular answers were the lack of a mentor and the difficulty of networking informally with colleagues.

Other research has confirmed this finding on racial differences in mentoring. A survey of 1,018 managers who received MBA degrees in the early 1980s found that black managers and Hispanic managers were significantly less likely to have mentoring relationships with their white managers than were their white colleagues. Those who did not have white mentors earned significantly less money than those who did have such mentors (Dreher & Cox, 1996).

> **ONLINE!**
>
> For more on these issues, check out an online magazine for African-American executives and entrepreneurs at *www. blackenterprise.com.*

Conflict may arise when a black manager is promoted over an equally qualified white manager. Research has shown that the common reaction of those passed over for promotion is that the black person was given the job on the basis of race. This attitude can create hostility on both sides. Black managers may also have difficulties dealing with other minority employees. Hispanic-Americans and Asian-Americans often believe that blacks receive preferential treatment. This perception presents problems when black managers must conduct performance appraisals of subordinates. Minority employees of all races expect black managers to be more lenient than white managers. Black managers may be pressured by black subordinates to give them special consideration or overlook poor job performance. Any perceived display of favoritism on the part of a manager can create animosity, which, in turn, can affect the work group's performance.

Workplace diversity training programs can be successful in reducing bias and discrimination on the job and teaching employees of all races to behave with greater sensitivity toward the needs, values, and concerns of all groups.

Leader Expectations for Women Workers

Leaders who expect more from their subordinates tend to be rewarded with better performance, whereas leaders who expect less tend to get less. This example of a self-fulfilling prophecy, called the Pygmalion effect, has been demonstrated in classroom situations and in the workplace. When teachers or managers are told that some of their students or employees are exceptionally talented or qualified, they develop higher expectations for the performance of these subordinates and communicate their expectations, often unconsciously, in subtle ways. They may give the "better" students more opportunities to speak out in class or allow the "better" employees to assume greater responsibility. The results are often just what the leaders expected—superior performance from subordinates believed to be superior.

However, the Pygmalion effect does not seem to apply to adult women in training programs, as suggested by two studies conducted with Israeli army trainees. In one study, a group of women officer-cadet trainees were led by female squad leaders. In the three conditions in the other study, men trainees were led by men, women trainees were led by men, and women trainees were led by women. There were no groups in which men were led by women.

The experimental procedure was the same for all groups. Squads were randomly assigned to the Pygmalion condition or the control condition. All trainees were 18- to 20-year-old high school graduates selected because they had shown in previous training and on psychological tests a high aptitude for leadership. Thus, trainees were assumed to be equally qualified.

To confirm that the leaders' expectations in the Pygmalion groups were raised, squad leaders rated the command potential (CP) of each cadet in their squad on a 9-point scale. These ratings were made during the 1st, 4th, and 6th weeks of the 7-week officer training course. The trainees' level of performance in the training program was assessed by multiple-choice tests.

Before the squad leaders in the Pygmalion condition met their trainees, they were told that on the basis of aptitude and ability tests, as well as ratings by previous commanders, their trainees had a much higher-than-normal command potential. As a result, so the leaders were informed, they could expect a better-than-average level of achievement from their cadets.

The results showed that the Pygmalion manipulation was effective. Squad leaders in the Pygmalion condition rated the CP of their trainees significantly higher than did squad leaders in the control condition. Results also showed that when the squad leader was a man, a significant Pygmalion effect was produced in every case, whether the trainee was male or female. When the squad leader was a woman, however, no Pygmalion effect occurred. The expectations of the women leaders had been raised by the Pygmalion instructions, but those expectations did not translate into increased performance on the part of their trainees. Thus, the Pygmalion effect was produced in women trainees, but it could not be brought about by women leaders.

Think About It

1. Why do you think the Pygmalion effect was not produced by women leaders in this study? Can you suggest additional instructions or other forms of manipulation that might result in the Pygmalion effect being produced by women leaders?
2. What factors other than those described in this study might account for the Pygmalion effect?
3. What ethical and moral considerations are involved in applying the Pygmalion effect in the workplace? What are the practical objections to its use?
4. How might leader expectations of the performance of ethnic minority employees affect productivity and job satisfaction?
5. If research has shown that the Pygmalion effect is effective in increasing job performance, then why has it not been applied more widely?

Source: T. Dvir, D. Eden, & M. L. Banjo (1995). Self-fulfilling prophecy and gender: Can women be Pygmalion and Galatea? *Journal of Applied Psychology, 80,* 253–270.

SUMMARY

Half of all new companies fail within two years because of poor leadership, which also accounts for the finding that half of all corporate decisions are incorrect. Incompetent leadership results in poor employee performance, low job commitment, low job satisfaction, and high stress.

The **scientific management** philosophy, concerned solely with production, was replaced in the 1920s and 1930s by the human relations approach, concerned with satisfying the personal growth needs of employees and maintaining production. McGregor's **Theory X** holds that people dislike work and need strong, directive, and punitive leadership. **Theory Y** holds that people are creative, industrious, responsible, and function best under leaders who allow them to participate in decisions that affect their work.

Contingency theory suggests that leader effectiveness is determined by the interaction between the leader's personal characteristics and aspects of the situation. **Cognitive resource theory** focuses on leaders' cognitive abilities (intelligence, technical competence, and job-related knowledge). **Path-goal theory** emphasizes the leadership behaviors that allow subordinates to achieve their goals. **Normative decision theory** deals with the extent to which leaders allow subordinates to participate in making decisions. **Leader-member exchange** (LMX) is concerned with ways in which leaders behave toward subordinates.

Authoritarian and **democratic leaders** differ in the degree of participation they extend to subordinates. **Transactional leaders** are constrained by their followers' expectations. **Transformational leaders** inspire subordinates and redirect their behavior through personal **charisma,** intellectual stimulation, and consideration.

Leaders may display reward, coercive, legitimate, referent, or expert power. Through the **Pygmalion effect,** leaders' expectations can affect subordinates' behavior in a self-fulfilling prophecy. Leadership functions are grouped in two categories: **consideration** and **initiating structure.** Consideration behaviors are concerned with subordinates' feelings. Initiating structure behaviors are concerned with achieving organizational productivity goals.

Leadership characteristics vary with the level of leadership; the higher the level, the fewer consideration functions and the more initiating structure functions are required. Successful first-line supervisors are person-centered, supportive, and loyal to the company and to subordinates. They exercise a democratic supervisory style. Effective executives need decision-making and technical skills more than they need human relations skills. Self-promotion behaviors influence the amount of mentoring managers receive from their superiors. Self-monitoring behaviors result in higher promotion rates. Derailment (executive failure) is related more to personality factors than to job performance.

Management teams have problems with turnover and self-limiting behavior in decision making. Other leadership problems also vary with level. First-line supervisors may be poorly trained in supervisory skills and face conflicts between organizational demands and demands of subordinates. Participative management, **self-managing work groups,** and computer technology are stressful for supervisors. Middle managers have lost authority because of participative management and may find themselves obsolete at midcareer. Executives face long working hours yet show greater job satisfaction than do persons at lower levels of leadership.

Women managers are often restricted to staff jobs and low-status departments because of sexist stereotypes; the glass ceiling is often a barrier to promotion. Black managers face similar problems of stereotyping and discrimination and may have difficulties dealing with white and other minority subordinates.

KEY TERMS

authoritarian leadership
bureaucracy
charismatic leadership
cognitive resource theory
consideration leadership functions
contingency theory
democratic leadership
initiating structure leadership functions
leader-member exchange

normative decision theory
path-goal theory
Pygmalion effect
scientific management
self-managing work groups
Theory X/Theory Y
transactional leadership
transformational leadership

ADDITIONAL READING

Avolio, B. J. (1999). *Full leadership development: Building the vital forces in organizations.* Thousand Oaks, CA: Sage Publications. A dynamic presentation of the advantages of the transformational style of leadership.

Book, E. W. (2000). *Why the best man for the job is a woman.* New York: Harper Business. Profiles of women chief executives of Fortune 500 companies. Describes what they have learned from their climb up the organizational ladder and how they balance work and family demands.

Cappelli, P. (1999). *The new deal at work: Managing the market-driven workforce.* Boston: Harvard Business School Press. Analyzes the nature of leadership in an environment that includes downsizing, volatile economic conditions, and the weakening of employees' commitment to the organization.

Conger, J. A., & Benjamin, B. (1999). *Building leaders: How successful companies develop the next generation.* San Francisco: Jossey-Bass. Describes effective in-house training programs tailored to specific organizational needs.

Heil, G., Bennis, W., & Stephens, D. C. (2000). *Douglas McGregor, Revisited: Managing the human side of the enterprise.* New York: Wiley. Reviews McGregor's classic work on the Theory X/Theory Y approaches to management and argues that they are still relevant today.

Kanigel, R. (1997). *The one best way: Frederick Winslow Taylor and the enigma of efficiency.* New York: Viking. A biography of Taylor (1856–1915), who promoted the philosophy of "scientific management," which depicted workers as extensions of the industrial machinery they were hired to operate.

Powell, G. N. (Ed.). (1999). *Handbook of gender and work.* Thousand Oaks, CA: Sage Publications. A reference book on gender issues for the 21st century, including the changing nature of work, so-called corporate masculinity, pay equity, sex segregation in occupations, gender influence on performance evaluation, barriers to leadership, and work-family issues.

Renshaw, J. R. (1999). *Kimono in the boardroom: The invisible evolution of Japanese women managers.* New York: Oxford University Press. An interesting cross-national study of successful Japanese businesswomen, comparing them with their American counterparts. Considers cultural and historical influences as well as the contemporary context.

Motivation, Job Satisfaction, and Job Involvement

CHAPTER OUTLINE

■   ■   ■   ■

Among the problems facing organizations today is how to motivate employees to work more productively and to increase their feelings of satisfaction, involvement, and commitment. Every day we see examples of shoddy work in products such as automobiles with faulty parts, or in careless mistakes made in offices. Manufacturers, retail stores, and service industries echo the complaint. Too many employees don't seem to care about doing a good job.

Organizations have made tremendous strides in applying the findings of I-O psychology to recruit, select, and train their workers and to provide effective leadership. But none of these functions can improve the quality of the work being performed if employees are not motivated to do the best job possible.

The study of motivation is important to you for two reasons. First, as a consumer you are often the victim of dissatisfied workers who produce faulty products or who process your requests improperly. Second, you will likely spend one-third to one-half of your waking hours at work for 40 to 45 years. That is a long time to feel frustrated, dissatisfied, and unhappy, especially since these feelings will carry over to your family and social life and affect your physical and emotional health.

Psychologists have studied motivation, job satisfaction, job involvement, and organizational commitment. They have proposed various theories to explain employee motivation—why people behave as they do on the job. Some of these theories emphasize the impact of factors in the workplace. Other theories focus on personal characteristics. The theories have stimulated a great deal of research and have spawned a number of techniques to modify work behavior. Thus, they may provide options for making your work life more satisfying and fulfilling.

We discuss here two types of motivation theories: content theories and process theories. Content theories focus on the importance of the work itself and the challenges, growth opportunities, and responsibilities work provides for employees. These theories deal with the content of motivation; that is, with the specific needs that motivate and direct human behavior. Process theories do not focus directly on work but rather deal with the cognitive processes we use in making decisions and choices about our work.

CONTENT THEORIES OF MOTIVATION

We describe five content models: achievement motivation theory, needs hierarchy theory, ERG theory, motivator-hygiene (two-factor) theory, and job-characteristics theory.

Achievement Motivation Theory

We mentioned the need for achievement, or **achievement motivation,** as a characteristic of successful executives. This desire to accomplish something, to do a good job, and to be the best typifies many people, not only business leaders. People who have a high degree of the need for achievement derive great satisfaction from working to accomplish some goal, and they are motivated to excel in whatever task they undertake.

Achievement motivation
The theory of motivation that emphasizes the need to accomplish something, to do a good job, and to be the best.

Since the early 1950s, achievement motivation has been studied intensively by David McClelland and his colleagues (Atkinson & Feather, 1966; McClelland, Atkinson, Clark, & Lowell, 1953). Their research, conducted in several countries, shows that successful business managers consistently display a high need to achieve, regardless of the culture. For example, in Poland, which was then a Communist country, the level of concern for achievement was almost as high as in the United States. McClelland concluded that the economic growth of organizations and societies can be related to the level of the achievement need among employees and citizens (McClelland, 1961).

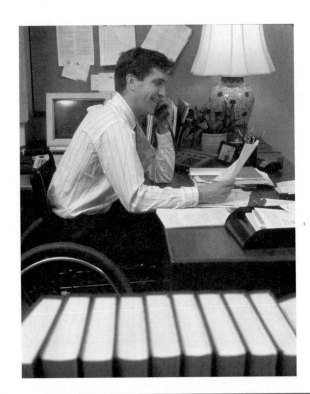

People high in the need for achievement are motivated to excel. They derive satisfaction from working hard to accomplish their goals.

McClelland's research identified three major characteristics of people who have a high need to achieve:

1. They favor a work environment in which they are able to assume responsibility for solving problems.
2. They tend to take calculated risks and to set moderate, attainable goals.
3. They need continuing recognition and feedback about their progress so that they know how well they are doing.

Studies have shown a high positive correlation between the achievement motivation scores of executives and the financial success of their companies. Research also shows that managers high in the need to achieve display more respect for their subordinates. These managers are more receptive to new ideas and are more accepting of participative management programs than are managers low in the need to achieve. Need achievement is positively related to subsequent promotions among middle- and upper-level managers. Also, both men and women entrepreneurs have been found to score significantly higher in the need to achieve than men and women employees who are not entrepreneurs.

Although not all research supports the achievement motivation theory, the idea provides a plausible explanation for the motivation of some employees. It is considered to have widespread application in the workplace.

Needs Hierarchy Theory

Needs hierarchy theory The theory of motivation that encompasses physiological, safety, belonging, esteem, and self-actualization needs.

Abraham Maslow, a founder of humanistic psychology, developed the **needs hierarchy theory** of motivation in which human needs are arranged in a hierarchy of importance (Maslow, 1970). According to Maslow, we always want what we do not yet have. Consequently, the needs that we have already satisfied no longer provide any motivation for our behavior and new needs must rise to prominence. Once we have satisfied our lower-level needs, we can pay attention to higher-level needs. The needs, from lowest to highest, are as follows:

- *Physiological needs:* The basic human needs, including food, air, water, and sleep, and the drives for sex and activity
- *Safety needs:* The needs for physical shelter and for psychological security and stability
- *Belonging and love needs:* The social needs for love, affection, friendship, and affiliation that involve interaction with and acceptance by other people
- *Esteem needs:* The needs for self-esteem and for esteem, admiration, and respect from other people
- *Self-actualization need:* The need for self-fulfillment, for achieving our full potential and realizing our capabilities

These needs should be satisfied in the order presented. People who are hungry or who fear for their physical safety are too busy attempting to satisfy these needs to be concerned about self-esteem or self-fulfillment. In times of economic hardship, when jobs are scarce, most people are so intent on survival that they cannot attend to higher needs such as self-actualization. However, once we reach a sufficient level of physical and economic security, we can move on; that is, we will be motivated to satisfy the next level of needs.

The belonging needs can be important motivating forces on the job. Workers can develop a social support network and a sense of belonging through interactions with co-workers. Esteem needs can be satisfied by buying a bigger house or car, which contributes to the feeling that we are successful, and through on-the-job rewards such as praise from the boss, an office with a window, or a reserved parking space. To satisfy the self-actualization need, employees should be provided with opportunities for growth and responsibility so that they can exercise their abilities to the utmost. A routine and boring job will not satisfy the self-actualization need, no matter how high the salary.

Maslow's theory has received little research support and is judged to have low scientific validity and applicability. Its complexity makes it difficult to test empirically. However, the self-actualization concept became popular with managers and executives who accepted this high-level need as a potent motivating force.

ERG Theory

Related to Maslow's needs hierarchy theory is the **ERG theory** of work motivation developed by Clayton Alderfer. He proposed three basic needs: Existence needs, Relatedness needs, and Growth needs. These needs encompass the needs proposed by Maslow and they can be satisfied within the work environment (Alderfer, 1972).

ERG theory The theory of motivation based on three types of needs: existence needs, relatedness needs, and growth needs.

Existence needs, at the lowest level, are concerned with physical survival and include the needs for food, water, shelter, and physical safety. Organizations can satisfy these needs through pay, fringe benefits, a safe working environment, and job security. *Relatedness needs* involve interaction with other people and the satisfaction these social relationships bring in terms of emotional support, respect, recognition, and belonging. The relatedness needs can be satisfied on the job by interactions with co-workers and mentors and off the job by family and friends. *Growth needs* focus on the self, such as our need for personal growth and development. These needs can be satisfied by using our skills and abilities to the fullest. Growth needs include Maslow's self-esteem and self-actualization needs. A job can satisfy growth needs if it involves challenge, autonomy, and creativity.

The ERG needs are not arranged in a hierarchy; all the needs can influence us at the same time. Therefore, satisfaction of one set of needs does not automatically lead to the emergence of higher needs. However, frustration of the relatedness or growth needs can lead us to revert to the existence needs. Whereas Maslow believed that a person will persevere to satisfy a need, Alderfer suggested that a person will give up on that need and refocus attention on a more basic need. For example, if employees cannot find emotional support or recognition on the job (relatedness needs), they may demand higher pay or better health care coverage (existence needs) as compensation for failing to satisfy the other needs.

Maslow suggested that once a need is satisfied, it no longer motivates us. By contrast, Alderfer said that satisfying a need may increase its strength. For example, if a job provides a great deal of challenge and creativity, our growth needs might become stronger, leading us to seek greater challenges at work.

The ERG theory has considerable empirical research support as well as an intuitive appeal. It is more directly applicable to employee motivation than is Maslow's needs hierarchy theory.

Motivator-Hygiene (Two-Factor) Theory

Motivator-hygiene (two-factor) theory The theory of motivation that explains work motivation and job satisfaction in terms of job tasks and workplace features.

The **motivator-hygiene (two-factor) theory,** which deals with both motivation and job satisfaction, was proposed by Frederick Herzberg. The theory has inspired a great deal of research, although the results have not been consistently supportive. The scientific validity of the theory is low, yet it has led many organizations to redesign jobs in order to increase employee motivation (Herzberg, 1966, 1974).

According to Herzberg, there are two sets of needs: the motivator needs, which produce job satisfaction, and the hygiene needs, which produce job dissatisfaction. The *motivator needs* (the higher needs) motivate employees to high job performance. Motivator needs are internal to the work itself. They include the nature of the individual job tasks and the worker's level of responsibility, achievement, recognition, advancement, and career development and growth. The motivator needs are similar to Maslow's self-actualization need and Alderfer's growth needs. They can be satisfied by stimulating, challenging, and absorbing work. When these conditions are met, job satisfaction will result. However, when these conditions are not met—when work is not challenging—the result is not necessarily job dissatisfaction.

Job dissatisfaction is produced by the *hygiene needs* (the lower needs). The word *hygiene* relates to the promotion and maintenance of health. Hygiene needs are external to the tasks of a particular job and involve features of the work environment, such as company policy, supervision, interpersonal relations, working conditions, and salary and benefits. When the hygiene needs are not satisfied, the result is job dissatisfaction. However, when the hygiene needs are satisfied, the result is not necessarily job satisfaction, merely an absence of dissatisfaction. The hygiene needs are similar to Maslow's physiological, safety, and belonging needs. Both Maslow and Herzberg insisted that these lower needs be satisfied before a person can be motivated by higher needs.

Herzberg's theory focused attention on the importance of internal job factors as motivating forces for employees. If the motivator needs stimulate employees to perform at their best and to develop a positive attitude toward the job, then why not redesign the job to maximize opportunities to satisfy motivator needs? This effort, called **job enrichment,** expands jobs to give employees a greater role in planning, performing, and evaluating their work, thus providing the chance to satisfy their motivator needs. Herzberg suggested the following ways of enriching a job:

Job enrichment An effort to expand the scope of a job to give employees a greater role in planning, performing, and evaluating their work.

1. Remove some management controls over employees and increase their accountability and responsibility for their work, thus increasing employee autonomy, authority, and freedom.
2. Create complete or natural work units where possible—for example, allow employees to produce a whole unit instead of one component of that unit. This policy increases the likelihood that employees will regard their work as meaningful within the total organizational process.
3. Provide regular and continuous feedback on productivity and job performance directly to employees instead of through their supervisors.
4. Encourage employees to take on new, challenging tasks and to become experts in a particular task or operation.

All these proposals have the same goals of increasing personal growth, fulfilling the needs for achievement and responsibility, and providing recognition. Proper job enrichment, therefore, involves more than simply giving the workers extra tasks to perform. It means expanding the level of knowledge and skills needed to perform the job.

This was demonstrated in a study involving 1,039 employees of a glass manufacturing plant. The research showed that job enrichment programs significantly increased their sense of self-efficacy—their belief in their ability to do their jobs (Parker, 1998). The program, which offered opportunities for greater accountability, responsibility, and autonomy, enhanced the employees' feelings of adequacy, efficiency, and confidence that they were performing their jobs well.

> ONLINE!
>
> Information on job enrichment programs, including a discussion of advantages and disadvantages for employers and employees, can be found at *www.unm.edu/~hraup/cardev/job.htm.*

Job-Characteristics Theory

The job enrichment movement led two psychologists to ask which specific job characteristics could be enriched. J. Richard Hackman and G. R. Oldham developed the **job-characteristics theory** of motivation based on their research on objective measures of job factors that correlated with employee satisfaction and attendance (Hackman & Oldham, 1976, 1980). Evidence suggested that certain characteristics influence behavior and attitudes at work, but these characteristics do not influence all employees in the same way. For example, the research documented individual differences in the need for growth. People with a high growth need were found to be more affected by changes in job characteristics than were people with a low growth need. Also, changes in these job characteristics did not seem to influence employee attitudes and behavior directly but were filtered by the employees' cognitive processes—that is, their perceptions of the changes.

Job-characteristics theory The theory of motivation that states that specific job characteristics lead to psychological conditions that can increase motivation, performance, and satisfaction in employees who have a high growth need.

The presence of certain job characteristics causes employees to experience a positive emotional state when they perform their job well. This condition motivates them to continue to perform well, on the expectation that good performance will lead to good feelings. The strength of an employee's motivation to perform well depends on the strength of the need to grow and develop. The stronger the need, the more one will value the positive emotional feelings that result from good job performance. Thus, the job-characteristics theory states that specific job characteristics lead to psychological conditions that lead, in turn, to higher motivation, performance, and satisfaction—if employees have a high growth need to begin with.

The core job characteristics identified by Hackman and Oldham are as follows:

1. *Skill variety:* the extent to which workers use various skills and abilities on the job. The more challenging a job, the more meaningful it will be.

2. *Task identity:* the unity of a job—that is, whether it involves doing a whole unit of work or completing a product instead of making only part of a product on an assembly line.
3. *Task significance:* the importance of a job to the lives and well-being of co-workers or consumers. For example, the job of aircraft mechanic affects the lives of more people in a more significant way than does the job of postal clerk.
4. *Autonomy:* the amount of independence employees have in scheduling and organizing their work.
5. *Feedback:* the amount of information employees receive about the effectiveness and quality of their job performance.

Jobs can be redesigned to maximize these characteristics in a manner similar to that proposed earlier by Herzberg:

- Combine small, specialized tasks to form larger work units; this enhances skill variety and task identity.
- Arrange tasks in natural, meaningful work units to make the worker responsible for an identifiable unit; this enhances task identity and task significance.
- Give workers responsibility for direct contact with clients or end users; this enhances skill variety, autonomy, and feedback.
- Give workers authority, responsibility, and control over the job tasks; this increases skill variety, task identity, task significance, and autonomy.
- Arrange for workers to learn regularly how well they are performing the job; this increases feedback.

Hackman and Oldham developed the Job Diagnostic Survey (JDS) to measure three aspects of the theory: (1) employees' perceptions of the job characteristics, (2) employees' level of the growth need, and (3) employees' job satisfaction. The JDS is a self-report inventory consisting of short descriptive phrases about the various job characteristics. Respondents rate how accurately each statement describes their job. A revised version, using positively worded items only, has been found to be more valid than the original version.

Research suggests that the JDS provides useful information about perceptions of job characteristics but that other objective measures are needed for complete assessment of the nature of a job. Additional job characteristics that should be considered include, for example, cognitive demand and production responsibility in dealing with such developing technologies as computer-controlled machine tools.

The job-characteristics theory continues to stimulate research. Studies on job enrichment programs based on this theory have been more supportive and have shown that adding challenge, complexity, and responsibility to some jobs results in greater employee satisfaction and self-efficacy.

PROCESS THEORIES OF MOTIVATION

We describe four process models: valence-instrumentality-expectancy (VIE) theory, equity theory, goal-setting theory, and the high performance cycle.

Driven by the Work Ethic

On September 8, 1995, a baseball player made history. He did it by showing up for work. Cal Ripken, Jr., showed up for work 2,131 times, every time his team, the Baltimore Orioles, played a major league baseball game.

The 42,000 fans in Oriole Park at Camden Yards stadium went wild the night Ripken broke the previous record, held by Lou Gehrig, for the longest streak of consecutive games played. The President of the United States witnessed the historic moment and praised Ripken's discipline, determination, and constancy. A television reporter summed up the excitement that gripped the nation when he described Ripken as "a paragon of the work ethic."

The *work ethic* is a term we hear a lot, and it has been a guiding rule and way of life for generations of American workers. It drives, pushes, goads, and motivates people to work hard like Cal Ripken, to do the best job they can, to be on time, and to show up for work every day. If you are curious about the great driving force of the 19th and 20th centuries that led to unimagined heights of industrial, agricultural, and commercial productivity and economic success, then the work ethic is where you should begin. In most progressive economies, work is not a four-letter word.

It wasn't always that way. There was a time when people were not motivated to perform a job well, or even to do it at all. To the ancient Greeks and Romans, there was nothing noble about work. It was a curse of the gods that brutalized the mind and ruined an otherwise good day. The early Hebrews agreed. Work was a punishment from God, although it was also a necessary evil, a way of improving society and atoning for sin.

The early Christians put a more positive spin on work, viewing it as a way to serve God by sharing the proceeds of one's work with people who were less fortunate. Wealth was a means to charity. Work became holy, and idleness sinful.

But it was John Calvin, the 16th-century French Protestant leader, who gave us the ultimate work ethic. Work alone pleases God, he declared, but to achieve that end, work must be methodical and disciplined. "Not leisure and enjoyment but only activity serves to increase the glory of God."

To Calvin, and others who refined what came to be called the Protestant work ethic, work was an emblem of faith. And so was wealth. It was OK to make a lot of money and not feel guilty about it, as long as you did not enjoy it. Old-fashioned, puritanical, nose-to-the-grindstone toil for its own sake became the motivation that drove millions of people to work hard all their lives and to feel virtuous for doing so. And it still drives many of us each and every day to do the best job we can. And to show up for every game.

Source: R. Todd. All work, no ethic. *Worth Magazine*, January 1996, pp. 78–84; J. Bair & S. J. Sherer. What happened to the work ethic? *College Park Magazine*, Fall 1995, pp. 18–22.

Valence-Instrumentality-Expectancy (VIE) Theory

Valence-instrumentality-expectancy (VIE) theory The theory of motivation that states that people make choices that are based on their perceived expectations that certain rewards will follow if they behave in a particular way.

The **VIE theory,** originated by Victor Vroom, asserts that people make choices that are based on their perceived expectancy that certain rewards will follow if they behave in a certain way (Vroom, 1964). In the workplace, employees will choose to perform at the level that results in the greatest payoff or benefit. They will be motivated to work hard if they expect this effort to lead to positive outcomes such as a promotion or pay raise and if those outcomes will be instrumental in leading to other desired results.

The psychological value, or valence, of the reward varies with the individual. In other words, our personal perception of the importance of the outcome determines its strength to us as a motivator. A high salary and increased responsibility have a positive valence for many people. Dangerous working conditions have a negative valence for most people. The outcome may not be as satisfying as we expected, but it is the level of expectancy that determines whether we will work hard to obtain that outcome.

The three facets of the VIE theory are related as follows:

1. Employees must decide whether they expect certain job behaviors—such as coming to work on time, following safe procedures, or improving productivity—to have a high probability of leading to a particular outcome (expectancy)
2. Employees must determine whether that outcome will lead to other outcomes—for example, whether a good attendance record leads to a bonus (instrumentality)
3. Employees must decide whether those outcomes have sufficient value to motivate them to behave a certain way (valence)

The VIE theory has received a great deal of research support. It appears to agree with personal experience and common sense. The greater our expectation of receiving a reward, assuming it is of sufficient value to us, the harder we will work for it.

Equity Theory

Equity theory The theory of motivation that states that our motivation on the job is influenced by our perception of how fairly we are treated.

J. Stacy Adams advanced the **equity theory,** the notion that motivation is influenced by our perception of how equitably or fairly we are treated at work (Adams, 1965). He proposed that in any work environment—whether office, shop, factory, or classroom—we assess our inputs (how much effort we put into the work) and our outcomes (how much reward we receive for the work). We calculate, perhaps unconsciously, the ratio of outcome to input and mentally compare it with what we believe are the ratios for our co-workers. If we think we are getting less than other people, the feeling of tension or inequity that results motivates us to act, to do something to bring about a state of equity. If we perceive that we are receiving the same ratio of reward-to-effort that others are receiving, then a state of equity exists.

Other psychologists have extended the equity theory, suggesting three behavioral response patterns to situations of perceived equity or inequity (Huseman, Hatfield, & Miles, 1987). These three types are benevolent, equity sensitive, and entitled. The level of reward received by each type affects motivation, job satisfaction, and job performance.

Benevolent persons, described as altruistic, are satisfied when they are underrewarded compared with co-workers and feel guilty when they are equitably rewarded or overrewarded. *Equity sensitive* persons (the type described by the equity theory), believe that everyone should be rewarded fairly. They feel distressed when underrewarded and guilty when overrewarded. *Entitled* persons believe that everything they receive is their due. They are satisfied only when they are overrewarded and are distressed when underrewarded or equitably rewarded.

It seems intuitively correct to state that if we believe we are being treated fairly in comparison to others, in accordance with our expectations, then we will be motivated to maintain our level of job performance. In contrast, if we think we are being treated unfairly, then we will try to reduce that inequity by reducing our level of performance. Consider the example of major league baseball players (infielders and outfielders). If they have their salaries cut or lose at arbitration during their first year as free agents, they are likely to perform at lower levels during the following season. They may reduce their inputs (batting averages and runs batted in) if they believe that their outcomes (salaries) are too low.

Goal-Setting Theory

Developed by Edwin Locke, **goal-setting theory** has a commonsense appeal and is clearly relevant to the workplace. Locke argued that our primary motivation in a work situation is defined in terms of our desire to achieve a particular goal (Locke, 1968; Locke & Latham, 1990). The goal represents what we intend to do at a given time in the future. For example, we may set the goal of graduating from college with honors, or achieving the highest sales record in the company, or getting a pay raise within a year so we can buy a new house.

Setting specific and challenging performance goals can motivate and guide our behavior, spurring us to perform in more effective ways. Research has shown that having goals leads to better performance than not having goals. Specific goals are more powerful motivating forces than general goals. Goals that are difficult to attain are greater motivators than goals that are easy to attain. However, difficult goals may spur greater motivation toward attaining the goals at the expense of other behaviors, such as helping co-workers. This type of behavior has the potential for reducing overall organizational effectiveness. In addition, goals that are too difficult, perhaps beyond our capabilities, are worse than having no goals in terms of their impact on motivation and job performance.

An important aspect of the goal-setting theory is individual goal commitment, which is defined in terms of the strength of our determination to reach our goal. A meta-analysis of 83 research studies confirmed that goal commitment has a strong positive effect on the level of our task performance (Klein, Wesson, Hollenback, & Alge, 1999). Goal commitment is influenced by three types of factors: external, interactive, and internal. The external factors that affect goal commitment are authority, peer influence, and external rewards. Complying with the dictates of an authority figure such as a boss has been shown to be an inducement to high goal commitment. Goal commitment increases when the authority figure is physically present, supportive, and trusted. Peer group

Goal-setting theory The theory of motivation based on the idea that our primary motivation on the job is defined in terms of our desire to achieve a particular goal.

pressure and external rewards such as pay increases also strengthen goal commitment.

The interactive factors that influence our commitment to reaching our goals are competition and the opportunity to participate in setting goals. These factors have been shown to be an inducement to setting higher goals and to working harder to reach them. Internal cognitive factors that facilitate goal commitment are self-administered rewards and our expectation of success. Commitment to the goal is reduced when our expectation of achieving it declines.

Other personal and situational factors have been related to high goal commitment. These include the need for achievement, endurance, aggressiveness, and competitiveness (so-called Type A behavior), success in achieving difficult goals, high self-esteem, and an internal locus of control.

The goal-setting theory has generated considerable supportive research. Setting goals has been found to produce substantial increases in employee output. In general, the motivating effects of setting goals are strongest for easy tasks and weakest for more complex tasks. These effects generalize across a variety of organizations, jobs, and tasks. Also, goal-setting theory is high in scientific validity and in applicability on the job.

The High Performance Cycle

High performance cycle
The theory of motivation and job satisfaction that suggests that goals affect job performance, depending on the kind of task and the abilities of the worker.

Research on the goal-setting theory led to the formulation of a more comprehensive theory to account for motivation and job satisfaction. This refinement and extension of the goal-setting theory expands the role of cognitive factors and describes the relationship between motivation and satisfaction (Locke & Latham, 1990). Called the **high performance cycle,** this model is conceptually more complex than goal-setting theory.

The cycle begins with the demands, goals, or challenges provided by the job. This is the goal-setting theory, which asserts that goals motivate employees to improve job performance. In addition to the goals we set for ourselves, challenges can come from authority figures (supervisors or managers), from participation (joint decisions between subordinates and superiors), from peer pressure to produce, or from role models. Whatever the source, these specific, attainable, and difficult goals do not automatically produce high performance. Rather, they lead to an increase in work motivation. Having challenging goals does not guarantee high performance, but they will lead to high performance if other factors, called moderators, are present.

Moderators affect the strength of the relationship between goals and job performance. A specific and challenging goal will enhance motivation and lead to high job performance when the employee has the following:

- High level of ability to perform the task
- Commitment to the goal
- Feedback demonstrating progress toward the goal
- High self-efficacy or expectation of performing well
- A task that is not too difficult

Assuming, then, the existence of challenging goals and demands and the moderators just listed, the next step in the cycle is how goals actually affect performance. This occurs through mediating mechanisms called universal task strategies, which are necessary to the accomplishment of a task. The strategies are the direction of our attention, the effort we choose to exert, and whether we persist at the task over time.

Given challenging demands, the moderators that facilitate job performance, and the mediating strategies that translate goals into action, then employee performance will be high. The rewards that follow can serve as an incentive to maintain job performance. Rewards can be external, such as pay raises, promotions, or other organizational recognition, or internal and self-administered, such as feelings of achievement, self-efficacy, and pride in one's accomplishments. There are also noncontingent rewards that are based simply on having a job, such as fringe benefits, job security, and socializing with co-workers. Noncontingent rewards do not motivate performance directly as moderators do, but they can encourage people to remain on the job.

If the internal and external rewards, which are contingent on high job performance, satisfy employee needs and values, employees will have high job satisfaction. If the rewards do not satisfy these needs, the result is dissatisfaction. High satisfaction leads to greater organizational commitment and a willingness to accept new goals and challenges; this illustrates the cyclical nature of the high performance model. High satisfaction results from high performance rather than causes it. In other words, high performance comes first. Once satisfaction is experienced, it is related indirectly to future performance by the strength of the employee's organizational commitment and willingness to work toward new goals.

The high performance cycle has a commonsense feel and is applicable to many work situations. Research supports the importance of moderators and mediators in job performance and the impact of rewards on job satisfaction. The influence of cognitive factors such as self-efficacy as mechanisms by which goals affect performance has also been demonstrated. The high performance cycle suggests that motivation and job satisfaction can be affected by the same factors.

JOB SATISFACTION: THE QUALITY OF LIFE AT WORK

Job satisfaction refers to the positive and negative feelings and attitudes we hold about our job. It depends on many work-related factors, ranging from our assigned parking space to the sense of fulfillment we get from our daily tasks. Personal factors can also influence job satisfaction. These factors include age, health, length of job experience, emotional stability, social status, leisure activities, and family and other social relationships. Our motivations and aspirations, and how well these are satisfied by our work, also affect our attitudes toward our jobs.

Job satisfaction Our positive and negative feelings and attitudes about our jobs.

For some employees, job satisfaction is a stable, enduring characteristic, independent of the features of the job. Changes in job status, pay, working conditions, and goals have little effect on the job satisfaction of these people. Their personal tendency toward happiness (satisfaction) or unhappiness (dissatisfaction) varies little over time and circumstances.

I-O psychologists have suggested, based on research conducted with twins, that attitudes toward work and the satisfactions we expect from it may have a hereditary component. In other words, these feelings may be influenced more by our genetic endowment than by features of the work environment. Neverthe-

How Does Your Job Rate?

Let's face it. Some jobs are better than others. Some satisfy your desires to achieve and to grow, to expand your knowledge and skills. Others offer better pay, more perks and prestige, stock options, reserved parking, and an espresso machine in the employee lounge. And then there are all those other jobs out there that offer none of the above, that are routine and boring, that have lousy fringe benefits and no job security—the jobs that won't motivate you or make you happy or stimulate you to care about the company you work for.

To learn how American employees rate their jobs, author Les Kranz analyzed 250 jobs and ranked them from best to worst—from most desirable to least desirable—in terms of six criteria: income, level of stress, physical demands, potential for growth, job security, and work environment. He published the results in a book called the *Jobs Rated Almanac* (1999).

Would it surprise you to learn that 9 of the top 10 jobs are in computer- or math-related fields? That the absolutely top-rated job is Web site manager? Kranz's own job, that of author, ranks well down the list at 117, just below college professor. Psychologists rank 58th but the president of the United States is way down the list at 229. Why? Kranz said it's because the job has high stress, a low salary compared to that of a sports celebrity or a CEO, and no room for personal growth. "Where do you go from there?"

Are you wondering what career to choose? Here's the list of the top 100 jobs.

1.	Web site manager	13.	meteorologist
2.	actuary	14.	technical writer
3.	computer systems analyst	15.	medical secretary
4.	software engineer	16.	medical technologist
5.	mathematician	17.	financial planner
6.	computer programmer	18.	medical lab technician
7.	accountant	19.	astronomer
8.	industrial designer	20.	historian
9.	hospital administrator	21.	postal inspector
10.	Web site developer	22.	dental hygienist
11.	paralegal assistant	23.	biologist
12.	parole officer	24.	insurance underwriter

less, it is clear that some people are generally more satisfied with life and, thus, with their work. People who have positive attitudes toward their work are likely to have positive feelings about their personal and family life.

So it is generally accepted that job satisfaction and life satisfaction are positively related, but which one causes the other? Or are both influenced by some third factor? To explore this relationship, a sample of 804 employees, selected to

25. sociologist
26. urban planner
27. physiologist
28. bank officer
29. broadcast technician
30. agency director
31. dental lab technician
32. statistician
33. motion picture editor
34. audiologist
35. industrial engineer
36. nuclear engineer
37. vocational counselor
38. computer service technician
39. optometrist
40. medical records technician
41. dietitian
42. physicist
43. political scientist
44. federal judge
45. mechanical engineer
46. speech pathologist
47. pharmacist
48. occupational therapist
49. publications editor
50. economist
51. Protestant minister
52. aerospace engineer
53. philosopher
54. electrical engineer
55. purchasing agent
56. chiropractor
57. geologist
58. psychologist
59. podiatrist
60. attorney
61. electrical technician
62. oceanographer
63. TV/radio newswriter
64. chemist
65. physical therapist
66. petroleum engineer
67. executive headhunter
68. anthropologist
69. tax examiner
70. civil engineer
71. market research analyst
72. personnel recruiter
73. newscaster
74. military officer
75. advertising executive
76. optician
77. architectural drafter
78. musical instrument repairer
79. engineering technician
80. flight attendant
81. computer consultant
82. family practice physician
83. jeweler
84. school principal
85. agricultural scientist
86. dentist
87. cashier
88. symphony conductor
89. computer operator
90. public relations executive
91. zoologist
92. bookbinder
93. archeologist
94. court reporter
95. senior corporate executive
96. antiques dealer
97. warrant officer
98. respiratory therapist
99. word processor
100. airplane pilot

be representative of the U.S. workforce, was interviewed and given questionnaires to assess job and life satisfaction. The results showed a positive and reciprocal relationship between job and life satisfaction in the short term; that is, each one influenced the other. Over time, however, the impact of life satisfaction on job satisfaction was significantly stronger, indicating that general life satisfaction may be the more influential of the two factors. This conclusion was supported in

Assembly-line workers tend to have low job satisfaction. Routine, repetitive work offers little opportunity for personal growth and development.

a study of 479 police officers. For them, life satisfaction was influenced more by nonwork factors than by satisfaction with their jobs (Hart, 1999). However, it does not follow that attempts to improve job satisfaction are useless. Remember that the two are interrelated. Job satisfaction still has an effect on life satisfaction.

Measuring Job Satisfaction

The approach used most often to measure employee attitudes is the anonymous questionnaire, typically distributed to employees through the company's e-mail network. Because participation is voluntary, not all workers will complete a questionnaire. There is no way of knowing which employees responded and which did not, or how those who failed to respond differ from those who did respond. It might make a difference if more good workers than poor workers completed the questionnaires.

Two popular attitude surveys are the Job Descriptive Index (JDI) and the Minnesota Satisfaction Questionnaire (MSQ). The JDI contains scales to measure five job factors: pay, promotion, supervision, the nature of the work, and the characteristics of one's co-workers. It can be completed in 15 minutes and has been published in several languages. The MSQ is a rating scale for various levels of satisfaction and dissatisfaction, ranging from very satisfied to very dissatisfied. It covers 20 job facets including advancement, independence, recognition, social status, and working conditions. The MSQ takes 30 minutes to complete; a 10-minute form is also available. These questionnaires have high construct validity.

Personal interviews are sometimes used in conjunction with the questionnaires. In these interviews, employees discuss aspects of their jobs with supervisors or interviewers from the organization's human resources department.

Another method of measuring job attitudes is the sentence completion test. Employees are presented with a list of phrases to complete. For example, "My job is _____." or "My job should be _____." In the critical-incidents technique for evaluating job satisfaction, employees are asked to describe job incidents that occurred at times when they felt very good or very bad about their jobs.

Job Facet Satisfaction

Many I-O psychologists suggest that data on overall job satisfaction may not be an adequate measure of the full range of employees' positive and negative attitudes toward all aspects of the work situation. Employees may be satisfied with certain conditions and dissatisfied with others. For example, you may like your work and be comfortable in your office, but you may dislike your boss or your company's health insurance program. A single measure of overall job satisfaction fails to make these distinctions. For this reason, psychologists are focusing on measuring more specific facets or aspects of job satisfaction. Some facets appear to apply to all types of jobs and organizations, whereas others are present in only certain job categories.

Job Satisfaction Data

Every year the Gallup Poll organization asks a representative sample of U.S. workers the following question: On the whole, would you say you are satisfied or dissatisfied with the work you do?

The results show consistently that only 10 to 13% of the workers questioned each year say that they are dissatisfied with their jobs. Thus, the majority of people are assumed to be satisfied with their jobs. However, when more specific questions are asked about job satisfaction, the results are different. For example, when factory workers are asked if they would like to change jobs, many say yes, even though they say they are satisfied with their present jobs. When people say they are satisfied, they often mean that they are not dissatisfied. Therefore, when we consider the data on job satisfaction, we must examine the kinds of questions that are asked.

Some job satisfaction studies survey a representative national sample of workers. Others deal with targeted populations, such as the workers in a particular industry, or with specific facets of job satisfaction. Job satisfaction varies with type of occupation. For example, assembly-line workers are significantly less satisfied with their jobs than are office workers. Managers in government agencies are significantly less satisfied than are managers in private industry and business.

In Britain, a comparison of 557 senior civil service managers and 1,056 senior managers in private industry found job dissatisfaction to be significantly higher among the government managers. Also, their mental and physical health was reported to be poorer than for managers in the private sector (Bogg & Cooper, 1995). The consistency of results over time and over different cultures suggest serious organizational and morale problems in government employment.

Involuntary temporary workers (those in temp jobs because they cannot find full-time employment) rate significantly lower in job satisfaction than workers who voluntarily choose temporary assignments. A study of 174 temp employees found, as expected, that involuntary workers scored low in satisfaction with their growth opportunities, pay, supervision, and socialization with co-workers (Ellingson, Gruys, & Sackett, 1998).

Impact of Personal Characteristics

Many characteristics of the job and the workplace affect job satisfaction. By re-designing job and work environments, it is possible for management to increase job satisfaction and productivity. Jobs can be redesigned to maximize opportunities to satisfy the needs for achievement, self-actualization, and personal growth. Jobs can be enriched to enhance the motivator needs and the core job characteristics.

Personal characteristics linked with job satisfaction include, among others, age, gender, race, cognitive ability, job experience, use of skills, job congruence, organizational justice, personality, and occupational level. Some of these factors can be used to predict satisfaction among various groups of workers.

Age. In general, job satisfaction increases with age; the lowest job satisfaction is reported by the youngest workers. This relationship holds for blue-collar and white-collar employees and for men and women employees. Many young people are disappointed with their first jobs because they fail to find sufficient challenge and responsibility. Why does job satisfaction tend to increase with age when the typical reaction to our first job is often disappointment? Three possible explanations have been suggested:

1. The most strongly dissatisfied young workers may drop out of the work force or change jobs so frequently in their search for satisfaction that they are no longer counted in surveys. This means that the older the sample of employees studied, the fewer dissatisfied people are likely to be included.
2. A sense of resignation may develop as workers grow older. Older employees may give up looking for fulfillment and challenge in their work and seek these satisfactions elsewhere. Therefore, they tend to report less dissatisfaction with their jobs.
3. Many older workers have greater opportunities to find fulfillment and self-actualization on the job. Age and experience usually bring increased confidence, competence, esteem, and responsibility. In turn, these feelings lead to a greater sense of accomplishment. In other words, older workers are more likely to have better jobs than are younger workers.

Gender. The research evidence about possible differences in job satisfaction between men and women employees is inconsistent and contradictory. Psychologists have found no clear pattern of differences in job satisfaction. It may not be gender, as such, that relates to job satisfaction as much as the group of factors that vary with gender. For example, women are typically paid less than men for the same work, and their opportunities for promotion are fewer. Most women employees believe that they have to work harder and be more outstanding on the job than men employees before they receive comparable rewards. Obviously, these factors influence a person's satisfaction.

Race. In general, more white than nonwhite employees report satisfaction with their jobs. However, before a person can be concerned with job satisfaction, he or she must have a job. Although there is a large, thriving middle class among black and ethnic minority employees, large numbers of people who want to work are unemployed, are employed irregularly, or are too discouraged to seek employment. Many who have full-time work are confined to low-level jobs that offer marginal pay and little opportunity for advancement or fulfillment. Thus, the primary concern for many workers is not satisfaction but finding a job that pays a decent wage.

Cognitive Ability.   Cognitive ability does not appear to be a significant determinant of job satisfaction, but it may be important when related to the type of work a person chooses. For many jobs, there is a range of intelligence associated with high performance and satisfaction. People who are too intelligent for their work may find insufficient challenge, which leads to boredom and dissatisfaction. A survey of 12,686 U.S. workers, a majority of whom were African American or Hispanic, showed that the more intelligent people held jobs with high interest and challenge. People whose jobs were not sufficiently challenging for their level of intelligence reported great dissatisfaction with their work (Ganzach, 1998).

A factor sometimes related to intelligence is level of education. Some studies have shown that education has a slight negative relationship to job satisfaction. The higher the level of formal education, the more likely a person is to be dissatisfied with the job. One explanation is that better-educated persons have higher expectations and believe that their work should provide greater responsibility and fulfillment. Many jobs do not satisfy these expectations. Employees with college degrees are somewhat more satisfied with their jobs than employees who attended college but did not graduate. This finding may be related to the fact that many higher-level positions are open only to college graduates.

Job Experience.   During the initial stage of employment, new workers tend to be satisfied with their jobs. This period involves the stimulation and challenge of developing skills and abilities, and the work may seem attractive just because it is new. This early satisfaction wanes unless employees receive feedback on their progress and tangible evidence of their achievements. After a few years on the job, discouragement is common, often being brought on by the feeling that advancement in the company is too slow.

Job satisfaction appears to increase after a number of years of experience and to improve steadily thereafter. The relationship between job satisfaction and length of work experience parallels the relationship with age. They may be the same phenomenon under different labels.

Use of Skills.   A common complaint, particularly among college graduates in engineering and science, is that their jobs do not allow them to exercise their skills or apply the knowledge acquired during their college training. Surveys of engineers show high dissatisfaction with job facets such as pay, working conditions, supervisors, and opportunities for promotion. Other studies show that people are happier at work if they have the chance to use their abilities. Interviews with workers on an automobile assembly line in Sweden revealed that a major factor in their job satisfaction was the opportunity to perform their work at a high level of quality (Eklund, 1995). When working conditions or the actions of co-workers interfered with work quality, job satisfaction declined.

Job Congruence.   **Job congruence** refers to the match between the demands of a job and the abilities of the employee. The higher the congruence—the closer the fit between a person's skills and attributes and the job's requirements—the

Job congruence The match between our abilities and the requirements of our jobs.

greater the job satisfaction. Conversely, a poor fit between job demands and personal skills reduces the potential for job satisfaction.

Organizational Justice.   Organizational justice refers to how fairly employees perceive themselves to be treated by their company. When workers believe they are being treated unfairly (a perceived lack of organizational justice), their job performance, job satisfaction, and organizational commitment are likely to decline. Under these circumstances, employees also report higher levels of stress, and they are more likely to file grievances or seek other jobs. Employees who work for large organizations or for companies with an authoritarian culture are likely to have a low opinion of the level of organizational justice in their workplace. Participation in decision making can contribute to an increase in organizational justice (Schminke, Ambrose, & Cropanzano, 2000).

Personality.   Research suggests that employees who are more satisfied in their work are better adjusted and more emotionally stable. Although the relationship seems clear, the cause-and-effect sequence is not. Which comes first, emotional stability or job satisfaction? Emotional instability or job dissatisfaction? Emotional instability can cause discontent in every sphere of life, and prolonged job dissatisfaction can lead to poor emotional adjustment.

Two personality factors related to job satisfaction are alienation and locus of control. Employees who feel less alienated and who have an internal locus of control are more likely to be high in job satisfaction, job involvement, and organizational commitment. Two dimensions of the Type A personality are also related to job satisfaction. *Achievement striving* (the extent to which people work hard and take the work seriously) is positively related to job satisfaction and job performance. *Impatience/irritability* (intolerance, anger, hostility, and a sense of time urgency) is negatively related to job satisfaction. The higher the impatience score, the lower the job satisfaction.

Job satisfaction appears to be highest among employees with a high degree of social and institutional trust; that is, those who believe that people and organizations are basically fair and helpful and can be trusted.

An unusual research program studied the self-evaluations of 384 employed adults, including psychological measures of self-esteem, self-efficacy, locus of control, and neuroticism. This long-term study assessed these factors in childhood and again in adulthood. People who scored high in esteem and efficacy and low in neuroticism, and showed an internal locus of control, showed significantly higher job satisfaction in their middle adult years than did people who scored in the opposite direction. Thus, personality factors measured in childhood showed a direct relationship to job satisfaction measured some 30 years later (Judge, Bono, & Locke, 2000).

Occupational Level.   The higher the occupational or status level of a job, the higher the job satisfaction. Executives express more positive job attitudes and feelings than do first-line supervisors, who, in turn, are usually more satisfied than their subordinates are. The higher the job level, the greater is the opportunity for satisfying motivator needs. Also, high-level jobs offer greater autonomy, challenge, and responsibility. Satisfaction of Maslow's esteem and self-actualization needs also increases with each level in the organizational hierarchy.

Job satisfaction varies with job category. High job satisfaction is more likely to be reported by entrepreneurs (self-employed persons) and by people in technical, professional, and managerial jobs. The least satisfied employees are in manufacturing and service industries and in wholesale and retail businesses.

Losing Your Job

There can be no job satisfaction without a job. I-O psychology research confirms the obvious. Losing one's job or being laid off is stressful for employees and their families. In Japan, layoffs are considered so traumatic that they are called *kubi kiri*, which means "beheading." Specific consequences of layoffs can include feelings of guilt, resentment, depression, and anxiety about the future, as well as physical complaints, alcohol abuse, drug abuse, divorce, spouse and child abuse, and thoughts of suicide.

Employees with higher-level jobs appear to suffer more greatly from unemployment. Employees with lower-level jobs seem to be more adaptable. Executives, managers, and professionals tend to become defensive and self-critical. Losing a job typically leads to significant changes in lifestyle, expectations, goals, and values. The psychological contract these employees believed they had with their employer has been breached. The unwritten agreement stating that if they worked hard and showed loyalty to the company, then the company would respond with job security, pay raises, and promotions, can no longer be relied upon. Many people who have lost their jobs feel a sense of betrayal.

Negative reactions to layoffs can be minimized if management is honest with employees about the reasons for the dismissals. A study of several hundred laid-off employees found that those who had received full explanations about why

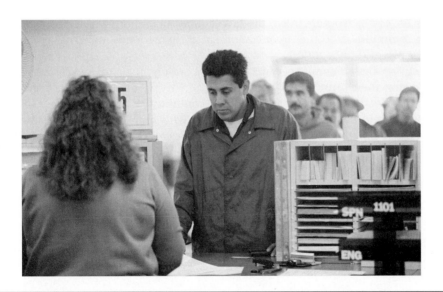

Unemployment can lead to anxiety that may persist even after a new job has been found.

the terminations were being made and how the employees were selected reacted far less negatively than did those who had received inadequate information (Wanberg, Bunce, & Gavin, 1999). The well-informed employees were more likely to view the layoffs as fair, to continue to speak positively about the company, and to express no intention of suing for wrongful termination.

Finding a new position typically reverses the negative effects of losing one's job. However, the nature of the new job relative to the old one can make a difference. A study of 100 workers found that those who were dissatisfied with their new job continued to experience most of the negative effects associated with being dismissed from their previous job (Kinicki, Prussia, & McKee-Ryan, 2000). In research on a group of nearly 300 unemployed adults, the results showed that the people who exerted the most effort to find a new job rated higher in educational level, financial hardship, goal setting, and persistence (Wanberg, Kanfer, & Rotundo, 1999).

A survey of 202 adults who had lost their jobs showed that those who began job-hunting immediately did not improve their chances of finding a new job. Those who waited to begin their job search until they had dealt with such negative emotions as depression and low self-esteem appeared more secure and confident and less nervous during their subsequent job interviews. The people who waited also reported higher job satisfaction with their new jobs than did those who began their job search right away (Gowan, Riordan, & Gatewood, 1999).

Surveys 13 months apart of 207 assembly-line workers who had survived layoffs showed that the extended period of job insecurity was related to significant decreases in job satisfaction and increases in levels of stress (Heaney, Israel, & House, 1994). A report for the U.S. Department of Labor noted that half of the layoff survivors questioned reported increased job stress, lower morale, and reduced job commitment. Also, 60% reported greatly increased workloads because workers remaining on the job still had to meet production goals even though there were fewer workers. Also, the layoff survivors reported a decrease in feelings of commitment to the organization since their friends and co-workers had been dismissed (Shah, 2000).

A survey of 283 employees in a company undergoing a major reorganization showed that their sense of job insecurity, from worry about being laid off, was related to a decrease in their organizational commitment and an increase in their stress levels and health problems. Employees who reported a high sense of job involvement experienced health problems and greater stress than did employees who were less involved with their jobs (Probst, 2000).

ONLINE!

For current coverage of layoffs from a variety of organizations, and for related Web sites on downsizing, retraining, and job-seeking, see *www.fullcoverage.yahoo.com/fc/business/downsizing_and_layoffs*.

NEWSBREAK

Grades Slipping?
Maybe It's Not Your Fault

How good are you at assessing your parents' moods? Can you sense when they seem worried or upset about something, like maybe losing a job?

Psychologists have learned that children from ages 10 to 17 are keenly aware when their parents experience feelings of insecurity about their work. For example, when children believe that their fathers are uneasy about their work situation, the children's attitudes toward their schoolwork will change and their grades are likely to drop. However, this effect was found only with fathers' jobs. When mothers experienced job insecurity, the children did not seem to be affected.

At Queen's University in Canada, psychologists investigated this situation in college students, even though they were no longer living with their parents at home. Would college students pick up on their parents' job anxiety and insecurity even though they didn't see or talk to them every day? And if so, would their own work, their academic performance, be altered?

The subjects in this experiment were 120 undergraduates under the age of 21. A questionnaire surveyed their perception of their parents' level of job security. A sample question was the following: *My mother/father can be sure of his/her present job as long as he/she does good work.* Two other questionnaires were administered. One measured cognitive functioning, and the other measured the student's level of identification with his or her parents.

Parents were asked to complete a questionnaire about their perceived level of job security. It included such items as this: *I am not really sure how long my present job will last.*

The results showed that college students were sensitive to their parents' feelings about their work, even though they no longer had daily contact with them. Like the younger children studied, the college students' grades fell with a decline in their parents' job security. Again, the effect was greater with fathers than with mothers. However, students who indicated a greater level of identification with their mothers were more likely to show a decline in grades than were students who identified more closely with their fathers.

So if you're a parent, remember that being laid off, or even fearing a layoff, can have consequences for your children. And if you're a college student, maybe you should think twice before calling home and asking Mom or Dad how they're doing at work.

Source: J. Barling, A. Zacharatos, & C. G. Hepburn (1999). Parents' job insecurity affects children's academic performance through cognitive difficulties. *Journal of Applied Psychology, 84,* 437–444.

JOB SATISFACTION AND ON-THE-JOB BEHAVIOR

We have described several factors that influence job satisfaction. Now let us consider those aspects of our behavior at work that can be affected by our level of satisfaction.

Productivity.   Research suggests a positive, though weak, relationship between satisfaction and productivity. However, it has not been demonstrated consistently in the laboratory or in studies conducted on the job. Part of the problem is that some jobs lend themselves more readily than others to objective assessments of performance. In other words, different measures of productivity are appropriate for different jobs.

Also, the direction of the relationship is an issue. Instead of assuming that job satisfaction leads to improved performance, the converse may be true. Improved performance may cause job satisfaction. (Recall that this idea was formalized as the high performance cycle.) Satisfaction derives from the fulfillment of our needs. If our work meets those needs, then we can, in effect, administer our own rewards by improving our job performance.

This notion may be more applicable to managers than to lower-level employees. Managers have more opportunities on the job to express and fulfill their needs for self-actualization, achievement, and personal growth. Workers in clerical or assembly-line jobs have little control or opportunity to fulfill these higher-order needs. However, in the study of 174 clerical temporary employees we mentioned earlier, the researchers found a significant positive correlation between job satisfaction and job performance (Ellingson, Gruys, & Sackett, 1998).

But research suggests that job satisfaction test scores may not be the most appropriate measure of job performance. In two studies of human service workers and juvenile probation officers, psychological well-being (broadly defined as "happiness") showed a significant positive relationship to job performance. Well-being was more predictive of the level of job performance than was job satisfaction (Wright & Cropanzano, 2000).

Prosocial and Counterproductive Behavior.   High job satisfaction has been related to **prosocial behavior;** that is, to helpful behavior directed at customers, co-workers, and supervisors to the benefit of employees and their organization. Does it follow that low job satisfaction is related to antisocial actions or to counterproductive behavior that may thwart organizational goals? Negative employee behavior can interfere with production and lead to faulty products, poor service, destructive rumors, theft, and sabotaged equipment. Employees may view these behaviors as a way of striking back at an organization because of real or imagined grievances.

Studies have shown a positive relationship between job dissatisfaction and counterproductive behavior for workers over the age of 30. This does not mean that older workers engage in more negative behaviors than do younger workers; the *frequency* of negative behaviors is higher for employees under 30. What the research indicates is that only in older workers has counterproductive behavior been related to job dissatisfaction (McNeely & Meglino, 1994; Organ & Ryan, 1995). A study of 181 firefighters and police officers with an average age of 40 found that job satisfaction showed a significant negative relationship to counterproductive behavior on the job. In other words, the higher the job satisfaction,

Prosocial behavior
Behaviors directed toward supervisors, co-workers, and clients that are helpful to an organization.

the less likely the employees were to engage in antisocial behaviors, and the less likely they were to look for another job (Duffy, Ganster, & Shaw, 1998).

Absenteeism.   Absenteeism is widespread and costly for organizations. On any given workday in the United States, up to 20% of employees do not show up for work. Absenteeism accounts for more time lost from work than do strikes and lockouts, and it costs businesses more than $30 billion a year.

Absenteeism has plagued industry since the invention of machines. In textile mills in Wales in the 1840s, the absenteeism rate was approximately 20%. During the 2-week period following each monthly payday, absenteeism often reached 35%. Throughout the 19th century in England, workers typically took off Mondays—"Saint Monday," they called it—to recover from weekend drinking bouts. Factory owners levied stiff fines and dismissed many workers, but that had no impact on attendance.

Much of industry's absenteeism data come from self-reports. Suppose you were filling out a questionnaire dealing with your job performance. One of the questions asked how many days of work you missed over the last year. Would you answer accurately? Or would you underreport the number of times you were absent? Would you be tempted to say that you missed only 2 days when the actual number was nearer to 10? Studies with diverse groups of workers consistently demonstrate the underreporting of absences by as much as 4 days a year. Managers also tend to underreport the extent of absenteeism in their work groups. About 90% of employees claim to have above-average attendance records. Clearly, many of us are less than honest about admitting the amount of time we lose from work.

If self-report absenteeism data are sometimes inaccurate, then why not use a company's personnel records to get a true indication of the absenteeism situation? That's a good idea in theory, but it does not work well in practice. Many companies do not compile attendance data in any systematic fashion. For managers and professional employees, such as engineers and scientists, such data are rarely collected at all. So when you read a study about absenteeism and learn that the data come from self-reports, you know that the actual number of absences is likely to be higher.

Not surprisingly, the more liberal an organization's sick-leave policy, the higher its absenteeism rate. Absenteeism is also high in companies that do not require proof of illness, such as a physician's note. High-paying manufacturing industries have higher absenteeism rates than do low-paying industries. The more money employees earn, the more likely they are to feel entitled to take time off. Workers in routine jobs often have a higher absence rate than workers in more interesting, challenging jobs.

Societal values may foster absenteeism, as is evident in variations in absentee rates for different countries. In Japan and Switzerland, where job attendance is considered to be a duty, absenteeism rates are low. In Italy, where societal attitudes toward work are more permissive, companies routinely hire 15% more workers than needed to make sure that enough people report to work each day to maintain operations.

A cross-cultural survey of more than 1,200 managers and employees in Canada and in China found that while Canadian employees considerably underreported their absenteeism rates, Chinese employees did not. When questioned about the reasons for missing work, the Chinese were more likely to cite domestic concerns, such as house maintenance or personal business, as legitimate reasons for missing work, whereas the Canadians were more likely to consider medical causes as legitimate reasons for missing work (Johns & Xie, 1998).

Management often contributes to an organizational climate that appears to condone absenteeism by failing to enforce company policy. If management is believed to be lenient and unconcerned about absences, some employees will take advantage of the situation. A study of 800 clothing factory workers and their 41 supervisors revealed a significant negative relationship between supervisory standards of acceptable absenteeism and actual absenteeism rates. Supervisors with high standards (who tolerated few absences in their work group) had lower absenteeism rates than did supervisors who had low standards. In other words, supervisors who were more tolerant of absences, and so created a climate that seemed to condone absenteeism, had—as you would expect—more absences among their workers (Markham & McKee, 1995). It is interesting to note that in this study the company kept accurate records so that self-reported absences could be verified.

Economic conditions can influence absenteeism rates. In general, when a company is in the process of laying off workers, absenteeism rates decline. Absenteeism increases when the overall employment rate is high, a time when workers feel more secure about their jobs. Also, younger workers are far more likely to take unauthorized time from work than are older workers.

A 70-month study of 419 U.S. government civil service employees found that job satisfaction was a valid predictor of absenteeism. The higher the job satisfaction, the lower the number of absences. Extent of job involvement was also a valid predictor of absenteeism (Steel & Rentsch, 1995).

Turnover.   Turnover is also costly for organizations. Every time someone quits, a replacement must be recruited, selected, and trained, and permitted time on the job to gain experience. Evidence relating high turnover to high job dissatisfaction is strong. Studies have shown that both intended and actual turnover can be attributed to dissatisfaction with various aspects of the job.

A study of trucking companies found that the turnover rates for its drivers correlated with pay and with electronic monitoring. Drivers whose pay was low and who were monitored by their company office showed the highest rate of quitting (Shaw, Delery, Jenkins, & Gupta, 1998). Organizational commitment is strongly related to turnover. The greater a person's commitment to the job and the company, the less likely he or she is to quit. Age, however, does not seem to be a factor that affects turnover. A meta-analysis of 46 samples involving 46,625 employees found virtually no relationship between age and turnover (Healy, Lehman, & McDaniel, 1995).

Turnover is higher in times of low unemployment and expanding job opportunities than it is in times of high unemployment and limited opportunities. When people perceive that the economic climate is good and the economy is growing, they find it easier to consider changing jobs in the hope of increasing their job satisfaction.

A study of what has been called "organizational citizenship behavior" was shown to be related to turnover in a study of 205 pairs of subordinates and supervisors in 11 companies in China. Organizational citizenship behavior was defined as any discretionary or voluntary behavior not required by the job, such as helping co-workers with work-related problems. Employees rated low by their supervisors on organizational citizenship behavior were far more likely to quit their jobs than were employees rated high on that behavior (Chen, Hui, & Sego, 1998).

Jobs that require a high level of creativity tend to be high in challenge, complexity, and autonomy and low on organizational control and supervision. A survey of 2,200 employees showed that people in highly creative and challenging jobs reported higher job satisfaction and lower turnover intentions than did people whose jobs did not offer these characteristics (Shalley, Gilson, & Blum, 2000).

There is a crucial difference between absenteeism and turnover. Whereas absenteeism is almost always harmful to the organization, turnover is not necessarily so. Sometimes it is the unsatisfactory employees who leave the company. I-O psychologists distinguish between **functional turnover,** when poor performers quit, and **dysfunctional turnover,** when good performers quit.

Functional turnover The situation that arises when poor employees quit their jobs. This type of turnover is not necessarily detrimental to the organization.

Dysfunctional turnover The situation that arises when good employees quit their jobs. This type of turnover can be harmful to the organization.

NEWSBREAK

Keep Good Employees from Quitting: Give Them BMWs!

Al Galdi, CEO of a wireless communications company in New Jersey, had a big problem. His most valuable employees were defecting to other Internet companies. He offered sizable signing bonuses and such fringe benefits as flexible hours, telecommuting assistance, even on-site dry-cleaning pickup, but the good ones kept quitting.

Then Galdi figured out a way to solve his turnover problem. Every employee who remained on the job for at least one year got a leased BMW 3-Series sedan or a Z3 roadster. As long as they stayed, they could keep the car. If they quit, they had to give it back. Nowadays, his company doesn't lose many people, and it's been a lot easier to hire new ones.

You're probably thinking: Sure, it works. Who wouldn't want to keep a job that came with a Bimmer, though it must be costing the company a bundle. That's true, but leasing the cars is a lot less expensive than recruiting, hiring, and training new employees only to lose them to the competition. Here's how it went in the first year: The lease on each car, plus insurance, cost the company $9,000 a year; total cost for the first batch of cars was $270,000. But Galdi had spent more than three times that amount (approximately $900,000) on recruiting and training staff over the previous 18 months. So, he concluded, by spending less, he has built a company of eager, goal-oriented employees who have no desire to leave. He has increased employee motivation and licked the turnover problem. Would the promise of an upscale car keep you on the job?

Source: The new key to employee loyalty may unlock a leased BMW. *New York Times,* June 18, 1999.

MOTIVATION, JOB SATISFACTION, AND PAY

Considerable research has demonstrated a positive relationship between pay and job satisfaction.

Perceived Pay Equity

The perceived equity or fairness of one's pay can be more important than the actual amount. Survey respondents who believed that people with similar qualifications earned more than they did reported dissatisfaction with their pay. They thought they were being paid less than they deserved. It is not surprising, then, that people who think their salaries are higher than those of their colleagues are likely to be more satisfied with their pay.

Most of us develop personal standards of comparison that are based on the minimum salary we consider acceptable, the pay we believe our job deserves, and the amount we think our co-workers are being paid. Thus, satisfaction with pay is determined by the discrepancy between our standards and our actual salary.

Of course, as we have seen, for some groups in American society there is little pay equity, either actual or perceived. In general, women are paid less than men for the same or similar work, and many ethnic minority employees are paid less than whites. When pay rates of 197 Hispanic, black, and white men and women workers were compared, the results showed that women and minorities earned significantly less than white men. Further, the older the workers, the greater the income gap (Barnum, Liden, & Ditomaso, 1995).

Merit Pay

Merit pay A wage system in which pay is based on level of performance.

Merit pay, or pay for performance, means that the better performing workers in an organization are paid more than the less productive workers. This wage system is fine in theory but does not translate well to the realities of the workplace. I-O psychologists have studied various influences on the size of the pay raises given under merit pay plans. They have found widespread disagreement among managers about the behaviors that they consider important in making decisions about a worker's pay increase. A worker in one department might receive a sizable raise for job behaviors that bring no recognition in another department. Supervisors who receive substantial pay raises tend to recommend larger raises for their subordinates than do supervisors who receive smaller pay raises.

Pay raises are also related to the degree to which managers rely on their subordinates' expertise and support and whether managers consider such dependence a threat. For example, a manager who is low in self-esteem may want subordinates to provide praise or positive feedback and therefore may be reluctant to give them low pay increases. The manager may fear that if subordinates do not receive a sufficient salary, they will withhold their support or reduce their productivity to make the manager look bad.

Wage-Incentive Pay Systems

Wage-incentive system The primary pay system for production workers, in which the more units produced, the higher the wage.

There are also problems with **wage-incentive systems,** the primary pay scheme for production workers. Through a time-and-motion analysis of a production job, an average or standard number of units produced in a given time can be determined. The wage-incentive system is based on this rate. In theory, the system provides an incentive for high job performance—the more units produced, the higher the wage—but it seldom works in practice. Many work groups establish their own standard for a good shift's production. Regardless of the incentive offered they will not produce more but will spread out the work to comfortably fill the hours. Surveys show that most workers prefer a straight hourly payment system.

JOB INVOLVEMENT AND ORGANIZATIONAL COMMITMENT

Closely related to motivation and job satisfaction is job involvement; that is, the intensity of a person's psychological identification with the job. Usually, the higher one's identification or involvement with a job, the greater the job satisfaction. Job involvement is related to several personal and organizational variables.

Personal Factors

Personal characteristics important in job involvement are age, growth needs, and belief in the traditional work ethic. Older workers are usually more involved with their jobs, perhaps because they have more responsibility and challenge and more opportunity to satisfy their growth needs. Older workers are also more likely to believe in the value of hard work. Younger workers, typically in entry-level positions, hold less stimulating and challenging jobs.

Because growth needs are important in job involvement, it follows that the job characteristics most relevant to job involvement are stimulation, autonomy, variety, task identity, feedback, and participation, the characteristics that allow for the satisfaction of the growth needs.

Social factors on the job can also influence job involvement. Employees who work in groups or teams report stronger job involvement than employees who work alone. Participation in decision making is related to job involvement, as is the extent to which employees support organizational goals. Feelings of success and achievement on the job enhance one's level of job involvement.

The relationship between job involvement and job performance is unclear. Employees with high job involvement are more satisfied with, and more successful at, their jobs. Their rates of turnover and absenteeism are lower than those of employees with low job involvement. However, we cannot state with certainty that high job involvement correlates with high performance.

Another variable allied with motivation and job satisfaction is organizational commitment—that is, the degree of psychological identification with or attachment to the company for which we work. Organizational commitment has the following components:

- Acceptance of the organization's values and goals
- Willingness to exert effort for the organization
- Having a strong desire to remain affiliated with the organization

Organizational commitment is related to both personal and organizational factors. Older employees who have been with a company more than 2 years and who have a high need to achieve are more likely to rate high in organizational commitment. Scientists and engineers appear to have less organizational commitment than do employees in other occupational groups. Employees who have reached a career plateau, have held the same position for 5 years, and believe they are less marketable, usually show a decline in organizational commitment. In addition, government employees have lower organizational commitment than employees in the private sector. Government employees, as we have seen, are also likely to be lower in job satisfaction.

Organizational Factors

Organizational factors associated with high organizational commitment include job enrichment, autonomy, opportunity to use skills, and positive attitudes toward the work group. Organizational commitment is influenced by employees' perception of how committed the organization is to them. The greater the perceived commitment to employees, the higher the employees' expectations that if they work to meet organizational goals, they will be equitably rewarded.

There is also a positive relationship between perceived organizational support and organizational commitment, diligence, innovative management, job performance, and attendance. Organizational commitment is positively related to the amount of support received from supervisors and co-workers and to the degree of satisfaction with supervisors (Bishop & Scott, 2000; Liden, Wayne, & Sparrowe, 2000).

Studies have confirmed a positive relationship between organizational justice and organizational commitment. People who believe their employer treats them fairly are more likely to feel a commitment to the company than are people who believe they are being treated unfairly (Dessler, 1999).

Another organizational factor involves the increasing diversity of the workforce. A study of 1705 supervisory and nonsupervisory personnel at a state government agency and two large private firms found that the greater the diversity of the work group, the lower the level of organizational commitment of the majority white male employees. Racial differences had the greatest impact. The more ethnic minority employees in the work group studied, the less committed were its white male workers. The reverse did not hold true. Organizational commitment for minority employees was not affected by the number of white male employees in their work group. However, an extensive research review concluded that, in general, minority employees in work groups tend to exhibit lower organizational commitment than majority employees (Milliken & Martins, 1996).

Gender seems to be related to organizational commitment. The more women employees in a work group, the lower the commitment of the men. With women, however, the reaction is the opposite. The more men there are in a work group, the higher the level of organizational commitment among the women.

Job Satisfaction

Although organizational commitment correlates positively with job satisfaction and attendance and negatively with turnover, it has little direct influence on job performance. This finding was supported by a study of 469 recent college graduates. The researchers found no significant relationship between job performance and commitment to the organization, but a relationship was noted between job performance and commitment to one's immediate supervisor. These results suggest that commitment may be directed in different ways, one of which would be loyalty to one's boss (Becker, Billings, Eveleth, & Gilvert, 1996).

Employee commitment to top management is a better predictor of job satisfaction than is employee commitment to the organization as a whole. This finding highlights again the need to determine the specific aspects of the organization to which employees feel committed.

A study of 977 employees in The Netherlands found that commitment to a work team is different from commitment to the organization. Team-oriented commitment correlates positively with work satisfaction and is rated as being of greater importance to employees than is organizational commitment (Ellemers, deGilder, & van den Heuvel, 1998).

Types of Commitment

I-O psychologists have identified three kinds of organizational commitment: affective or attitudinal commitment, behavioral or continuance commitment, and normative commitment (Meyer & Allen, 1991). In *affective commitment*, the type we have been discussing, the employee identifies with the organization, internalizes its values and attitudes, and complies with its demands. Affective commitment correlates highly with perceived organizational support. Managers perceive those employees who are high in affective commitment as having greater management potential than those high in behavioral commitment.

In *behavioral commitment*, the employee is bound to the organization only by peripheral factors such as pension plans and seniority, which would not continue if the employee quit. There is no personal identification with organizational goals and values. Research suggests that affective commitment is positively related to job performance, but behavioral commitment is negatively related to job performance.

Normative commitment involves a sense of obligation to remain with the employer, a feeling that develops when the employees receive benefits such as tuition reimbursement or specific skills training.

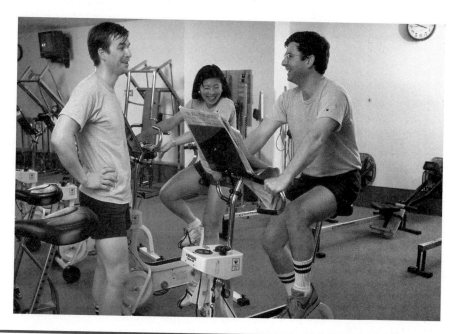

Job satisfaction is related to workplace conditions. For some employees, an exercise facility at the workplace fosters a positive attitude toward the job.

Employee Commitment and Job Performance

We saw that employees who are high in organizational commitment are also high in job satisfaction and attendance, and low in turnover. In other words, these people like their jobs, are seldom late or absent, and don't want to quit. In view of these highly positive findings about organizational commitment, you may find it surprising that little research has been done on the relationship between organizational commitment and employee performance.

One group of researchers suggested that an employee's commitment to an organization may have several components rather than being a global or single tendency. One of these factors might be the employee's supervisor, because it is the immediate supervisor, rather than the organization as a whole, who sets the standards for job performance and rewards employees for reaching or exceeding them.

To determine the effect on job performance of commitment to one's supervisor, questionnaires were mailed to 1,803 members of the 1993 graduating class of a large university. Usable data were obtained from 469 respondents. The mean age was 24. Of the 469 subjects, 55.1% were women, 85.5% white, 2% Hispanic, and 4.2% Asian. Fewer than 2% were African-American or Native American. All graduates had been working for approximately 11 months at the time they were surveyed. The subjects were asked for permission to contact their supervisors. A survey was then sent to the 355 supervisors identified, asking them to rate the job performance of the graduate. Usable data were received from 315 supervisors, an impressive 88.7% return.

The researchers wanted to assess the employees' degree of identification with their supervisor and with the organization, as well as the extent to which the employees internalized the values and goals of both supervisor and organization. To measure identification and internalization, employees were asked questions such as the following. They checked which of the two items in brackets applied to them:

- When I talk about [my supervisor, this organization] I usually say "we" rather than "they."
- When someone criticizes [my supervisor, this organization] it feels like a personal insult.

To assess internalization of values and goals, items such as the following were asked:

- If the values of [my supervisor, this organization] were different, I would not be as attracted to [my supervisor, this organization].
- Since starting this job, my personal values and those of [my supervisor, this organization] have become more similar.

The results showed that commitment to the supervisors was significantly and positively related to job performance. There was no significant correlation between commitment to the organization and job performance. No significant differences were found between performance and commitment based on identification with supervisor or organization and commitment based on internalization of organizational values. Employee commitment to their supervisors was clearly related to job performance; commitment to the organization was not.

Think About It

1. Define organizational commitment and distinguish it from job involvement.
2. What personal and organizational factors are related to high organizational commitment?
3. What weaknesses or limitations can you find in this study? How would you design an experiment to study organizational commitment and its components?

Source: T. E. Becker, R. S. Billings, D. M. Eveleth, & N. L. Gilbert (1996). Foci and bases of employee commitment: Implications for job performance. *Academy of Management Journal, 39,* 464–482.

4. In what ways might the results have been different if older employees who had been with an organization for many years had been studied?

5. If you were the CEO of an organization, how would you attempt to switch your employees' commitment from their immediate supervisors to the organization as a whole?

SUMMARY

Content theories of motivation deal with internal needs that influence behavior. Process theories focus on cognitive processes involved in making decisions. **Achievement motivation** theory posits the need to accomplish something and to be the best in whatever one undertakes. **Needs hierarchy theory** proposes five needs (physiological, safety, belonging, esteem, and self-actualization), each of which must be satisfied before the next becomes prominent. **ERG theory** posits three needs (existence, relatedness, and growth). Growth needs include self-actualization. **Motivator-hygiene theory** proposes motivator needs (the nature of the work and its level of achievement and responsibility) and hygiene needs (aspects of the work environment such as pay and supervision). An outgrowth of motivator-hygiene theory is **job enrichment,** the redesign of jobs to maximize motivator factors. **Job-characteristics theory** proposes individual differences in growth needs and suggests that employee perceptions of job characteristics influence motivation.

The **valence-instrumentality-expectancy (VIE) theory** describes a person's perceived expectation of the rewards that will follow certain behaviors. **Equity theory** deals with the ratio of outcome to input and how equitably that ratio compares with those of co-workers. **Goal-setting theory** suggests that motivation is defined by one's intention to achieve a particular goal. The **high performance cycle** suggests that goals affect performance through moderators and mediators.

Job satisfaction can be measured through questionnaires and interviews. It may be partly an inherited characteristic reciprocally related to overall life satisfaction. Job facet satisfaction refers to individual aspects of the job that can influence employee attitudes. Job satisfaction increases with age, length of job experience, and occupational level. Sex differences in reported job satisfaction are inconsistent. Job satisfaction appears unaffected by cognitive ability, assuming one's job is sufficiently challenging. Other factors affecting job satisfaction include **job congruence,** organizational justice, use of skills, and personality. Losing one's job can be damaging to self-esteem and health. Large-scale layoffs also affect those workers remaining on the job.

The relationship between job satisfaction and productivity is inconsistent. High performance may lead to job satisfaction, or job satisfaction may lead to high performance. Job satisfaction can result in **prosocial behavior;** job dissatisfaction can lead to counterproductive behavior that interferes with organizational goals. Absenteeism is higher among younger workers and in companies with liberal sick-leave policies. Absenteeism is high in low-status jobs and in high-paying jobs. Turnover is allied with low job involvement, low organizational commitment, poor promotion opportunities, and dissatisfaction with pay and supervision. In **functional turnover,** low performers quit; in **dysfunctional turnover,** high performers quit.

There appears to be a positive relationship between pay and job satisfaction. An important factor in pay satisfaction is its perceived equity and relationship to job performance. Blue-collar workers on **wage-incentive systems** and managers on **merit pay** systems report pay dissatisfaction. Merit pay can lower work motivation because of perceived unfairness; one's true abilities may not be sufficiently rewarded.

Job involvement (intensity of psychological identification with work) is related to job satisfaction. Involvement is affected by personal characteristics such as age, growth needs, and belief in the work ethic, and by job characteristics such as level of challenge and opportunity for employee participation.

Organizational commitment is related to motivation and satisfaction and is greater among older employees and those high in achievement motivation. Also contributing to organizational commitment are job enrichment, autonomy, perceived organizational support, organizational justice, and a positive attitude toward the work group. Three types of commitment are affective commitment, behavioral commitment, and normative commitment.

KEY TERMS

achievement motivation
dysfunctional turnover
equity theory
ERG theory
functional turnover
goal-setting theory
high performance cycle
job-characteristics theory
job congruence

job enrichment
job satisfaction
merit pay
motivator-hygiene theory
needs hierarchy theory
prosocial behavior
valence-instrumentality-expectancy
 theory
wage-incentive systems

ADDITIONAL READING

Dessler, G. (1999). How to earn your employees' commitment. *Academy of Management Executive, 13*(2), 58–67. Describes how modern organizations must clearly communicate the organization's mission, guarantee organizational justice, and support employee development.

Ellingson, J. E., Gruys, M. L., & Sackett, P. R. (1998). Factors related to the satisfaction and performance of temporary employees. *Journal of Applied Psychology, 83,* 913–921. Discusses job satisfaction among temp employees (a large but rarely studied subject group) and relates it to whether the decision to undertake temporary work is voluntary or involuntary.

Ganzach, Y. (1998). Intelligence and job satisfaction. *Academy of Management Journal, 41*(5), 526–539. Reviews research on the relationship between cognitive variables, level of education, and job satisfaction as affected by the complexity of the job.

Hart, P. M. (1999). Predicting employee life satisfaction. *Journal of Applied Psychology, 84,* 564–584. Reports on personality correlates (such as neuroticism, extraversion, and job satisfaction) that relate to overall life satisfaction in a group of police officers.

Wright, T. A., & Cropanzano, R. (2000). Psychological well-being and job satisfaction as predictors of job performance. *Journal of Occupational Health Psychology, 5*(1), 84–94. Analyzes the idea that the so-called happy worker is a more productive worker. Relates happiness (psychological well-being) and job satisfaction to job performance.

The Organization of the Organization

CHAPTER 9

All of us live and work within the framework of some kind of organization, a context that provides written and unwritten, formal and informal rules about how its members conduct themselves. You grew up in an organization called a family. Your parents established a culture that defined the guidelines by which the family functioned—the acceptable attitudes, values, and behaviors that made your family a unique organization, different from the families of your friends and acquaintances.

Perhaps a family in the house across the street had a culture based on orthodox religious beliefs and unusually strict standards of behavior, whereas a family next door was more moderate in its beliefs or reared its children more permissively. These families operated within different organizational styles. They established a structure based on a specific set of expectations, needs, and values that were expected to hold for all family members.

Various organizational styles are also evident in your college classes. One professor may be stern, even dictatorial, allowing no student discussion. Another may operate in a more democratic fashion, asking students to participate in decision making about course content and requirements.

Differences in organizational style in the workplace range from the rigid, hierarchical bureaucracy of the military and the civil service to the open, participatory approach that fosters high employee involvement. Bureaucracies regulate and prescribe what workers do and how they do it; little deviation is tolerated.

The modern organizational style attempts to humanize the workplace and has led to a modification of many traditional bureaucratic practices. Increasing numbers of organizations are treating their employees as integral members of the company and requesting their input in long-range planning and decision making. This shift in organizational style has brought about radical changes in the way work is organized and performed and has led to an improvement in the quality of work life for many employees.

Organizational psychologists study these changing trends in organizational life to determine their impact on employee satisfaction and behavior. We have described how the nature of leadership and the motivation of workers can affect job satisfaction, job performance, and organizational efficiency. In this chapter we describe the impact of organizational factors.

BUREAUCRACY: THE CLASSIC ORGANIZATIONAL STYLE

Bureaucracy A formal, orderly, and rational approach to organizing business enterprises.

The bureaucratic approach and the participatory approach represent two extremes in organizational style. We tend to think of **bureaucracies** in negative terms, as bloated, inefficient structures, top-heavy with layers of management and wrapped in miles of red tape that frustrates creativity.

As we know from our everyday experiences trying to deal with organizations of this type, there is much truth to this view. Yet the bureaucratic organizational style was once as revolutionary as the modern participative style, and it was considered just as humanistic in its intentions. Bureaucracies were devised to improve the quality of work life, and for a while they did.

As a movement of social protest, bureaucracy was designed to correct the inequities, favoritism, and cruelty that characterized organizations at the beginning of the Industrial Revolution. Companies were owned and managed by their founders, who had absolute control over the terms and conditions of employment. Employees were at the mercy of the owners' whims, prejudices, and decrees.

To correct these abuses, Max Weber, a German sociologist, proposed a new organizational style that would eliminate social and personal injustice (Weber, 1947). Bureaucracy was to be a rational, formal structure organized along impersonal and objective lines—an orderly, predictable system that would function like an efficient machine, unaffected by the prejudices of the factory owners. Workers would have the opportunity to rise from one organizational level to the next on the basis of their ability, not because of their social class or whether the boss liked them. Bureaucracy was a socially responsible improvement over the earlier system and served in its day to humanize the workplace.

The first practical application of the bureaucratic organizational style appeared in the United States even before Weber published his ideas on bureaucracy. The organization chart, which may be the most famous symbol of the bureaucratic approach, came into being in the 1850s. A general superintendent for the New York & Erie Railroad, Daniel McCallum, prepared a chart for his company and insisted that all workers abide by it (Chandler, 1988). McCallum's idea—formalizing the position and status of all employees in a hierarchical

The few executives at the top of the organization chart have little contact with lower-level employees and may have little awareness of their working conditions and personal concerns.

structure—quickly became popular and was soon adopted by most American companies. Thus, when Weber formally promoted the rules by which bureaucracies should operate, he was describing an organizational style already widely accepted in the United States.

Weber's ideas about bureaucracy, as depicted on the organization chart, involved breaking down or decentralizing the organization into component parts and operations. Each operation would be linked to others in a fixed rank order of control. The concept of division of labor, fostered by the scientific management approach, simplified jobs and made them more specialized. Responsibility or authority for each operation was delegated downward through the hierarchy, and communication flowed upward through the same channels. This arrangement effectively cut employees off from contact with other levels and sectors of the organization (see Figure 9–1).

Although organization charts look nice and give managers the feeling that employees are in their proper places and that the organization is running smoothly, these neat lines and boxes on paper do not always reflect daily operations on the job. There is, as we shall see, an organization within the organization—an uncharted complex of informal social groupings of workers—that can interfere with the most rigid rules of the most dictatorial structure. And it is often through these informal groups and networks that the work of an organization is (or is not) accomplished.

There are problems with bureaucracies, however. A bureaucratic management tends to ignore human needs and values. They treat employees as inanimate, impersonal boxes on the chart, as interchangeable as the machines they operate. Bureaucracies do not recognize human motivations, such as the needs for personal growth, self-actualization, and participation in decision making.

Employees within a bureaucracy have no individual identity and no control over their work or over the organizational policies that influence the quality of their working life. The ideal employees for a bureaucracy are docile, passive, dependent, and childlike. Decisions are made for them, for their own good, because they are considered incapable of deciding for themselves.

By being forced to channel all communication through their immediate supervisor, workers are isolated from higher management and prevented from

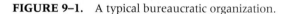

FIGURE 9–1.   A typical bureaucratic organization.

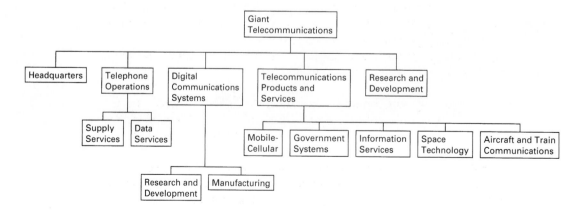

making suggestions about company practices that affect their jobs and their well-being. Workers in these situations score low on measures of job satisfaction and organizational commitment.

Bureaucracies can be criticized not only for their smothering effects on workers but also for their harmful effects on themselves. Just as they prevent personal growth for employees, bureaucracies minimize opportunities for organizational growth, in part because of the barriers to upward communication. Bureaucracies foster rigidity and permanence and do not adapt quickly or well to the kinds of changing social conditions and technological innovations characteristic of today's workplace. The orderly bureaucratic structure was designed to preserve existing conditions. New developments are viewed as threats. For all its initial revolutionary fervor and humanistic intentions, then, the bureaucracy has not been successful in meeting human needs and changing times.

PARTICIPATORY DEMOCRACY: THE MODERN ORGANIZATIONAL STYLE

We noted that a major criticism of bureaucracy is its tendency to treat workers as docile, passive, and dependent. The modern participative organizational style takes a different view of human nature, summarized by the Theory Y position of McGregor's Theory X/Theory Y formulation we described in Chapter 7.

Theory X describes a view of human nature compatible with the rigid requirements of a bureaucracy, which stifles individual motivation and the potential for growth. Workers need strict supervision because they are incapable of acting on their own initiative. This traditional, low-involvement organizational approach has the employees doing the work, middle managers controlling them, and only top management involved in strategy, planning, and long-range leadership.

In contrast, Theory Y assumes that employees are motivated to seek and accept responsibility for their work. In this view, people have a high level of creativity, commitment, and need for personal growth. Theory Y and other motivational conceptions supporting a participative approach suggest that organizations must decrease workers' dependency and subordination in order to take better advantage of their potential. Jobs and organizations must become less rigid in design and structure, allowing employees to help determine how best to perform their tasks. Jobs can be enriched to increase challenge and responsibility. Leaders should become less autocratic and more responsive to employee input. Decision making should involve participation at all levels. And organizations must become more flexible, capable of changing in response to employee needs and to social, technological, and economic conditions.

This high-involvement management style rests on three assumptions about people, participation, and performance (Lawler, 1986):

1. *Human relations.* People should be treated fairly and with respect. People want to participate, and when they are allowed to do so, they will accept change and become more satisfied with and committed to the organization.
2. *Human resources.* People are a valuable resource because they have knowledge and ideas. When they participate in decision making, the result is better solutions to organizational problems. Organizations must promote

The Workers Are Taking Over!

It's happening everywhere you look. Employees are taking on more responsibility and making decisions only their bosses used to make. Jobs have been enlarged, expanded, and enriched, and workers have been empowered, given the freedom to take charge and do their work in their own way.

Take the case of a major department store. A salesperson overheard a customer tell a companion that the suit she had bought three weeks ago was now on sale. She wished she had waited for the sale so she could have bought it for less. The alert salesperson asked for the customer's name and credited her account with the difference between the sale price and the original price. The salesperson acted on his own initiative, without asking his supervisor for an OK. Without even telling his supervisor! He was empowered to make these decisions for himself.

Nordstrom, the department store that prides itself on both customer and employee satisfaction, posts the following rules for its new employees:

Rule #1: Use your good judgment in all situations.
There will be no additional rules.

The rule says to use *your* good judgment. This means that decisions and the responsibility for them are in the hands of the employees, not the supervisors. This is nothing short of a revolution in the way we work.

A commercial printing company in Wisconsin encourages its printing press operators to make their own decisions. A corporate spokesperson explained:

Just as each lawyer is a partner and runs his own part of the business, I said each pressman is going to run his own press. I'd rather have 50 people out there thinking independently than for me to sit up here from the top and say, "This is the way we're going to do it."

At Compaq Computers, three-person teams assemble and test new computers. Each worker is capable of performing different tasks and coping with challenges. Previously, the computers were built on an assembly line, with each worker performing one small task repeatedly. Under the new system, the number of completed units per worker increased 50%. Profits improved, and the employees reported greater satisfaction with their jobs. They feel important—and they are. The workers are taking over!

Sources: D. P. Levin. Compaq storms the PC heights from the factory floor. *New York Times*, November 13, 1994; J. Pfeffer (1995). Producing sustainable competitive advantages through the effective management of people. *Academy of Management Executive, 9*(1), 55–70.

the personal development of their employees because it makes them more valuable to the company.

3. *High involvement.* People can be trusted to develop the knowledge and skills to make important decisions about the management of their work. When people are allowed to make such decisions, the result is an improvement in organizational performance.

The kind of work behavior stimulated by high-involvement management has been labeled, simply, "taking charge." Taking charge in this context involves employees in making decisions about how their work should be performed and then implementing those decisions by actively restructuring the way they do their job. In research on this idea, a study of 275 white-collar workers found that they were far more likely to exhibit take-charge behaviors when they perceived that top management was open to their suggestions. Employees who were more likely to take charge were found to be high in self-efficacy and in responsibility for bringing about change. Both of these factors can be enhanced by a supportive management climate (Morrison & Phelps, 1999).

High-involvement management calls for active employee participation in decision and policy making at all levels and can lead to greater opportunities for personal growth and fulfillment and increased organizational effectiveness. These changes in organizational style have been expressed in various quality-of-work-life (QWL) programs.

QUALITY-OF-WORK-LIFE PROGRAMS

An ambitious **quality-of-work-life program** was undertaken by General Motors with the support of top management and the United Auto Workers union. The program began when company and union officials agreed to form a labor-management committee to assess QWL projects. All projects had to consider extrinsic factors (physical working conditions) as well as intrinsic factors (employee involvement and satisfaction). Teams of I-O psychologists, managers, and employees were empowered to enlarge jobs, redesign production facilities, and revise the old low-involvement bureaucratic organizational structure.

Quality-of-work-life (QWL) programs Organizational programs based on active employee participation in decision and policy making.

Consider the GM assembly plant in Fremont, California. The company closed the plant in 1982 because the quality of the cars assembled there was exceptionally poor. Absenteeism stood at 20%, on-the-job use of alcohol and illicit drugs was widespread, and more than 800 grievances had been filed against the company. The plant reopened three years later as New United Motors Manufacturing Incorporated (NUMMI), a joint venture of GM and Toyota that was committed to participative management.

NUMMI employees work in teams of four to six members and perform a variety of tasks throughout the workweek. Cars are built on the traditional assembly line, but employees rotate from one job to another, mastering new skills in the process. They solve production problems and devise ways to increase productivity on their own, without being told what to do by their supervisors.

Artificial status barriers have been eliminated. Workers and managers eat in the same cafeteria, and all begin the workday with a group exercise period. The majority of the employees who worked in the old GM plant like the high-involvement participative organizational style, and the quality of the cars

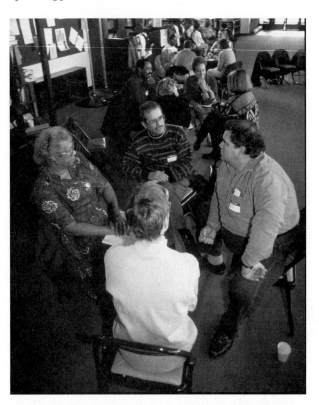

Under a quality-of-work-life program, small teams of workers meet periodically to discuss problems of productivity and employee involvement.

produced has improved markedly. Labor productivity is reported to be at least 50% higher than at other GM plants and nearly as high as at Toyota plants.

Encouraged by NUMMI's success, General Motors adopted the participatory approach for its Saturn Motors plant in Spring Hill, Tennessee, which opened in 1990. Workers are organized into teams of about a dozen members, and they make all major decisions about their work, including the hiring of new employees. Management perks, such as reserved parking places, were eliminated, and communication is encouraged across all levels without employees having to obtain permission from supervisors or union shop stewards. Absenteeism is reported to be less than 1%, a rate similar to that of Japanese auto plants, and less than a tenth of other U.S. auto plants.

Productivity increased markedly in all GM plants that instituted QWL programs. Ford and DaimlerChrysler (then Chrysler) started similar programs and reported increases in worker productivity. One result was that the entire U.S. auto industry finally began to catch up with the success of Japanese auto makers. In 1999, a Ford plant in Atlanta, Georgia, building the Taurus, became the first American plant to surpass Japanese-owned factories in worker productivity.

The major factor driving these advances in the auto industry and other sectors of the economy is increased worker involvement and participation. Management has seen that taking an interest in what workers have to say really does pay off.

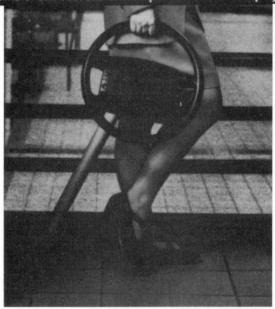

Modern organizations invite employee participation in decision making. (Courtesy of Ford Motor Company.)

Why Programs Fail

There are many reports of successful QWL programs, but it should be noted that some have failed. Consider Volvo, which has been building cars by the team approach for decades. Although productivity is lower than at standard assembly plants, the participative approach has resulted in substantial improvements in quality and reductions in turnover and absenteeism. Volvo expanded the concept of worker participation at a new car assembly factory in Sweden in 1988. Instead of having employee teams build a portion of each car, which then moves on to the next team, the teams at the new plant were expected to build an entire car. The results were dismal. It took 50 hours to assemble a car at the new plant, compared to 37 hours using the team approach. At a Volvo plant in Belgium that uses a traditional assembly line, it takes 25 hours to assemble a car. Absenteeism at the plant in Sweden is high because many employees did not realize the demands the redesigned job would entail. In addition, the training period to provide workers with the skills required to assemble an entire car turned out to be longer than anticipated.

Other QWL programs have failed because some employees have no desire to participate in decision making or to assume responsibility for determining the best way to perform their jobs. Some workers prefer, or need, more rather than less direct supervision. Also, QWL efforts can be doomed when managers continue to try to control their subordinates instead of working with them to share power and authority. QWL programs have a high probability of failure when they do not have the forceful advocacy and commitment of senior executives and when supervisors and union shop stewards view such programs as a threat to their power. Managers and supervisors must give up some of the power and authority by which they once directed and controlled their subordinates. They must also learn to share power and to function willingly as coaches, guides, mentors, and resource persons. Many managers find this a difficult adjustment to make.

Two characteristics of today's workplace may tend to dampen the positive effects of QWL programs. These are diversity and the growing number of contingent workers. While the workforce as a whole is becoming increasingly diverse, there are still organizations dominated by a majority of white males. Women and ethnic minority employees are often left out of the informal social network through which majority employees share job-related information and social support. Thus, minority employees have fewer opportunities to participate in decision making and in efforts to restructure and redesign their jobs. In addition, an organization's permanent, full-time staff may actively exclude contingent employees (like temporary or contract employees, or virtual workers) from participative programs.

Quality Control Circles

Quality control circles Employee groups organized to deal with specific production problems.

Quality control circles, based on the work of Maslow, McClelland, and Herzberg (described in Chapter 8), are concerned not so much with the overall quality of work life but with specific ways to improve the finished product and the level of production. Quality circle programs also have the potential to raise employee satisfaction and morale and contribute to personal growth and development, although these are by-products of the process. The overall goal is enhanced quantity and quality of production.

Quality control circles require that workers be given greater responsibility for their work and be allowed to participate in decisions affecting the nature of the work and the way in which it is performed. A quality circle typically consists of 7 to 10 employees from the same section or department. Membership is voluntary, and meetings are usually held once a week. Members are trained in human relations skills and problem-solving techniques before they are permitted to deal with specific problems relating to productivity.

Although quality control circles afford workers the opportunity to advise management and to participate in the decision-making process, they do not affect long-range organizational decisions. They typically have an impact only on their organizational unit; the hierarchical structure of the organization remains untouched. Managers do not share power with quality control circles as they do with QWL programs.

Companies using quality control circles have reported savings in money and time, increases in production and satisfaction, and decreases in absenteeism and turnover. Quality control circle members often receive significantly higher job performance ratings and more frequent promotions than do nonmembers. One explanation for the greater job success of quality control circle members is the visibility provided by weekly interactions with supervisors and higher-level managers.

I-O psychologists have found that the longer a quality control circle operates, the more likely it is to yield benefits for the organization. Management-initiated quality circles appear to solve more problems, and solve them faster, than do worker-initiated programs.

One problem with quality control circles is that not all eligible workers volunteer to participate in the programs. Another difficulty is that some circles disband after a relatively brief period of time. Reasons for these terminations include a lack of support from management or resistance from midlevel managers who have difficulty accepting suggestions from their subordinates. Failure to implement workers' suggestions can lower employees' expectations and willingness to continue to participate. Other quality control circles have become victims of their own success. Having solved major problems and maximized productivity, there is no longer any reason for them to continue.

Self-Managing Work Groups

Self-managing work groups allow the members of a work team to manage, control, and monitor all facets of their work, from recruiting, hiring, and training new employees to deciding when to take rest breaks. These autonomous work groups have become highly popular in business and industry today.

An early analysis of the first self-managing work groups yielded the following behavioral characteristics (Hackman, 1986):

Self-managing work groups Employee groups that allow the members of a work team to manage, control, and monitor all facets of their work, from recruiting, hiring, and training new employees to deciding when to take rest breaks.

1. Employees assume personal responsibility and accountability for the outcomes of their work.
2. Employees monitor their own performance and seek feedback on how well they are accomplishing their tasks and meeting organizational goals.

3. Employees manage their performance and take corrective action when necessary to improve their performance and the performance of other group members.
4. Employees seek guidance, assistance, and resources from the organization when they do not have what they need to do the job.
5. Employees help members of their work group and employees in other groups to improve job performance and raise productivity for the organization as a whole.

Self-managing work groups require a level of employee maturity and responsibility not called for in supervisor-managed groups. Self-managing work groups also need clear direction from the organization about production goals, a support staff to provide technical expertise, and adequate material resources. In some cases, engineers and accountants are added to the self-management teams so that they can deal with a full range of problems, operating, in effect, like minibusinesses within the larger organization.

Self-managing work groups also depend on the maturity and responsibility of managers, who must be willing to surrender authority to their subordinates. Indeed, management support is the most critical variable in determining the effectiveness of self-managing work groups. The extent of managerial support is also highly predictive of employee satisfaction.

An analysis of 111 work teams in several businesses (an insurance company, a high-tech manufacturing firm, and two textile mills) confirmed the importance of management support for ensuring the success of self-managing work groups. The study also showed that more empowered teams, as measured by questionnaire responses, were more productive, more proactive, and more attentive to customer needs than less empowered teams. The more empowered teams also reported higher levels of job satisfaction and commitment to their work groups (Kirkman & Rosen, 1999).

We noted that self-managing work groups get involved in all aspects of their job, including recruiting, hiring, and training of team members. In addition, they are responsible for maintaining standards and discipline, and they are empowered to dismiss members who perform poorly. To test the willingness of team members to discipline one another, as well as to gauge the leniency or severity of their actions compared to those of managers, a study was conducted of 41 work teams in four organizations. The subjects included 231 employees and their managers. The results showed that disciplinary decisions made by managers were more severe than were the judgments made by individual team members. However, when the group consensus was measured, the work teams were more likely to impose harsher measures than were the managers (Liden, et al., 1999).

Many other studies of self-managing work groups confirm the positive effects on productivity, quality of work, turnover, and job satisfaction. But self-managing work groups also have their problems. Converting from traditional bureaucratic management to self-management is difficult, expensive, and time-consuming, and many organizations underestimate the extent of the investment required. In particular, they underestimate the amount of training and meeting time involved and have unrealistic expectations about how soon self-managing groups can become productive. The need to monitor and review the progress of self-managing work groups can also dampen the initial enthusiasm for this approach.

Virtual Self-Managing Work Groups

A new type of self-managing work group is the virtual team. Members may work in geographically separate offices (or home offices) for different units of the same company or even in different companies but linked by the same project. They meet by electronic means to perform a specific task, though they may rarely assemble in person. Their efforts are wired through such information systems as the Desktop Videoconferencing System (DVCS).

NEWSBREAK

Everybody Wanted to Go Home Early

Did you know that Harman Automotive, Inc., is the most famous automobile rearview mirror factory in the history of I-O psychology? The plant, located in Bolivar, Tennessee, was the first real-life experiment in employee empowerment—giving workers control over their own jobs. When this bold venture began, a quarter of a century ago, it was so phenomenally successful that the Big Three auto makers used it as a model when they planned and implemented similar changes in their workplaces.

So many corporate presidents, foundation executives, and university scholars descended on the plant to see the miracle firsthand that the workers soon felt overwhelmed. They were so busy conducting tours that they had little time left for making rearview mirrors. They decided to limit the visitors to one group a week.

And then it all went wrong. Workers decided that they wanted to go home as soon as they met their daily production quota. Managers agreed. They called it "earned idle time." Well, this was fine for the assemblers and polishers, who, by working in teams, could finish their mirrors in half a day. But it caused friction with the workers who ran the huge metal-casting machines. They had to remain on the job for the full shift, to tend to their equipment.

So before long, everybody was demanding a shortened workday. Some managers bent the rules to allow their workers to leave early. Other managers refused. Many employees began to cut corners on quality so they could finish work in the morning and take most of the day off. Some workers devised shipping cartons with raised false bottoms so they would appear to be completely filled with mirrors when they were not. The temptation of paid time off was too great.

One worker said, "It turned us into thieves." A Harvard professor who had helped design the system lamented, "We were too idealistic."

Morale plummeted. Quality and quantity of product dropped. Absenteeism and turnover soared. Applicants for the jobs were easily attracted, however. Everybody had heard about the plant where you could get a full day's pay for a half day's work. The first question new hires asked was, "When can I go home?"

And one day in 1996, everybody went home early. Harman Automotive was forced to close.

Using e-mail and other means of telecommunication, DVCS re-creates the face-to-face interactions and dynamics of actual group meetings. Cameras mounted on computer monitors bring team members into visual contact, allowing their verbal contributions to be supplemented and enlivened by facial expressions and gestures that can be viewed by all team members. An important element of context is thus added to the team members' words and opinions.

Although research on virtual work groups is sparse to date, they offer challenges for team members and appear to have the potential to increase productivity, job satisfaction, job involvement, and organizational or team commitment (Cascio, 2000). Group members must manage their own projects and evaluate their own performance. Managers must master the means of communication and keep team members "in the loop." Attendance must be mandatory so that all team members have an opportunity to participate.

INTRODUCING ORGANIZATIONAL CHANGE

The employee participation programs we have discussed call for radical changes in organizational style. We have noted, however, that bureaucratic organizations by definition are resistant to change. When a structural change is to be introduced into an organization, it often meets with hostility, production slowdowns, strikes, or increased absenteeism and turnover. Whether the change involves new equipment, work schedules, procedures, office layout, or reassignment of personnel, it will usually be resisted at first.

Some organizations are able to change with the cooperation and support of employees and managers. The factor most responsible for determining whether change will be received positively or negatively is the way in which change is proposed and implemented. If change is imposed on employees in an autocratic manner and they are given no explanation or opportunity to participate, then they are likely to react negatively. However, when managers make an effort to explain the nature of the forthcoming change, the reasons for implementing it, and the benefits workers and management can expect from it, then workers are likely to respond positively and accept the change.

This effect was demonstrated, for example, in a study of 173 salaried employees whose wages had been frozen for a year and whose morale and job satisfaction had declined. In a series of workshops, half the employees were informed of the reasons for the pay freeze, namely, that the alternative would have been widespread layoffs. They were assured that the action had been structured to affect all employees equally. The other half of the employees (the control group) were given no such explanation. The employees who had received the explanation from management showed significant increases in job satisfaction and organizational commitment, and a decrease in expressed intentions to quit. Thus in this instance, providing detailed information about the organizational policy change had beneficial effects, even when the reasons were given long after the change had been implemented (Schaubroeck, May, & Brown, 1994).

A study of 130 public housing employees showed that their openness to change was positively affected by the amount of information they received from management and by the degree of their participation in the planning process. Employees who were the least receptive to change also showed lower job satisfaction, were more likely to quit, and displayed greater irritation with aspects of their jobs (Wanberg & Banas, 2000).

An analysis of 501 nurses in a hospital that introduced a job empowerment program measured organizational commitment and trust in management. Nurses who scored high in these variables were significantly more likely to believe management's reasons for the change than were those who were not committed to the organization or trusting of management (Rousseau & Tijoriwala, 1999).

Not all workers' acceptance of change depends solely on external factors such as management explanations. Receptivity to change is also influenced by personality. Some of us are more predisposed than others to try new ways of performing our jobs. We can see this in a cross-cultural study of 514 employees in six companies in the United States, Europe, Asia, and Australia. Workers were tested for positive self-concept, which includes the factors of locus of control, positive affectivity (defined as well-being, confidence, and energy), self-esteem, and self-efficacy. Test scores were also obtained for risk tolerance, which includes openness to experience, low aversion to taking risks, and tolerance for ambiguity. Workers who scored high in positive self-concept and risk tolerance coped with change significantly better than did those who scored low in these characteristics. In addition, high scorers rated high in job satisfaction, organizational commitment, and job performance (Judge, Thoresen, Pucik, & Welbourne, 1999).

Are the positive effects of worker participation in planning and implementing change permanent, or do they disappear once the researchers leave the office or factory? To study this question, two I-O psychologists visited a plant more than four years after it had undergone a radical change from a centralized bureaucracy to a flexible, innovative, participatory democracy. The change had been guided by the company president (a psychologist), with full worker participation, and was considered successful in terms of increased corporate profits, productive efficiency, and employee satisfaction.

The consulting psychologists in this now-classic study found that the benefits were evident four years later and that some of the effects were even greater than during the period immediately following the change. The increase in job satisfaction was accompanied by a higher concern with maintaining production levels (Seashore & Bowers, 1970). When properly introduced, then, a change in work procedures or in the entire organizational climate can have long-lasting positive effects.

Organizational Development (OD)

I-O psychologists have focused considerable attention on the problems of total organizational change and on systematic ways to bring about planned change. This effort, called **organizational development (OD),** involves techniques such as sensitivity training, role playing, group discussion, and job enrichment as well as survey feedback and team building.

Organizational development (OD) The study and implementation of planned organizational changes.

In the survey feedback technique, surveys are conducted periodically to assess employee feelings and attitudes. The results are communicated to employees, managers, and work teams throughout the organization. Their task is to provide feedback to higher management by suggesting explanations for the questionnaire findings and by recommending ways to correct the problems identified by employees in the surveys.

The team building technique is based on the fact that many organizational tasks are performed by small work groups or teams. To enhance a team's morale

Change agents Organizational development facilitators who work with business groups to implement change and develop group confidence and effectiveness.

and problem-solving abilities, OD consultants (called **change agents**) work with the groups to develop self-confidence, group cohesiveness, and working effectiveness.

Outside consultants or change agents are usually able to view an organization's structure, functions, and culture with greater objectivity than in-house managers. Change agents' first task is diagnosis, using questionnaires and interviews to determine the organization's problems and needs. They evaluate strengths and weaknesses and develop strategies for solving problems and for coping with future changes. However, they must be cautious about introducing change without allowing employees to participate in the process.

The implementation of the recommended strategies, a process called intervention, begins with top management. Unless organizational change has management support, the chance of success is small. The specific intervention techniques depend on the nature of the problem and on the organizational climate. The OD process is flexible and can be adapted to the needs of the situation. In general, regardless of the specific techniques applied, the OD process helps to free the typical bureaucratic organization from its rigidity and formality, allowing more responsiveness and open participation.

OD techniques have been applied by many public and private organizations. Although research results are mixed, some significant increases in productivity have been documented. Job satisfaction seems to be negatively related to OD, however, perhaps because the emphasis is on improvements in productivity rather than on employee considerations.

SOCIALIZATION OF NEW EMPLOYEES

Organizations are constantly undergoing change through the addition of new employees at all levels of the work force. New workers come with different levels of ability, motivation, and desire to perform their job well. They bring various needs and values that affect the organizations for which they work. At the same time, the culture of the organization makes its impact on the new employees. They have much to learn beyond the necessary job skills. They must learn their role in the hierarchy, the company's values, and the behaviors considered acceptable by their work group.

Socialization The adjustment process by which new employees learn their role in the organizational hierarchy, their company's values, and the behaviors considered acceptable by their work group.

This learning and adjustment process is called **socialization,** and it is not unlike a rite of passage in which members of a society enter a new stage of life. Those who cope successfully with this adjustment process are generally happier and more productive employees.

Poor socialization to an organization—that is, a negligent or haphazard introduction to company policies and practices—can undermine the accomplishments of the most sophisticated employee selection system. An organization can recruit and hire qualified people and then lose them in the early stages of employment because of an inadequate reception. Improper socialization can foster frustration, anxiety, and dissatisfaction for new employees, which can lead to low job involvement and organizational commitment, low motivation and productivity, and to dismissal or quitting.

Socialization involves several organizational strategies. Ideally, the company should provide new employees with challenging jobs that offer opportunities for growth and development, the mastery of skills, self-confidence, success experi-

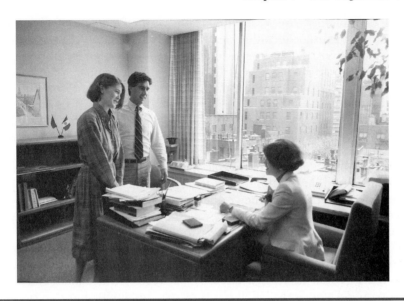

Positive interactions between current and new employees should be part of a company's socialization program.

ences, positive interactions with superiors, feedback, and co-workers who have high morale and a positive attitude toward the organization. A study of 295 business school graduates surveyed after 4 months and 10 months on a new job confirmed that formal socialization programs induced the newcomers to accept and conform to organizational goals, methods, and values (Ashforth & Saks, 1996).

Although institutionalized socialization strategies are effective in teaching new hires about the organization, most new employees are not passive learners in this rite-of-passage process. Many are highly proactive, taking an enthusiastic role in seeking the information they believe they need to adapt to their work environment. A study of 118 newly hired workers during their first 3 months on the job found that those high in extraversion and openness to new experiences demonstrated significantly higher proactive socialization behaviors than did those lower in these personality attributes. The extraverted employees were more likely to take steps to build relationships and to obtain feedback from co-workers and managers (Wanberg & Kammeyer-Mueller, 2000).

A group of 103 managers with a mean age of 27 years were studied during their first 6 months on the job. Researchers found that those with a high desire for control actively sought more information, socialized more, networked more with colleagues in other departments, and negotiated more job enrichment changes than those with a low desire for control (Ashford & Black, 1996).

It is important that newcomers' expectations about their jobs be met. A study of 128 MBA graduates over their first 2 years of employment found that the obligations they felt toward their employers declined when they believed that their organizations were not fulfilling their commitments in terms of expected advancement, training, and pay (Robinson, Kraatz, & Rousseau, 1994).

Other research on employee expectations found that establishing positive, high-quality relationships with co-workers and supervisors could reduce the potential detrimental effects of unmet expectations. Expectations were also found to affect turnover. Providing realistic job previews, which served to define and clarify employee expectations, resulted in higher turnover during the first month on the job for 61 low-level workers at a hospital and at a fast-food chain (Waung, 1995). Presumably, the employees knew what to expect from the job and found it not to their liking.

Socialization will occur more quickly when there is greater interaction between new and established employees. Interactions can include asking questions, having informal conversations, and taking coffee breaks together as well as formal activities such as mentoring and performance appraisals. However, some evidence indicates that socialization programs should not rely on the employees who are being replaced by the newcomers. There is the possibility that departing employees will teach their successors established and perhaps inefficient job performance techniques and thus discourage innovation.

Role ambiguity A situation that arises when job responsibilities are unstructured or poorly defined.

Role conflict A situation that arises when there is a disparity between job demands and the employee's personal standards.

I-O psychologists have identified two factors that relate to socialization: **role ambiguity** (when the employee's work role is poorly structured or defined) and **role conflict** (when there is a disparity between job demands and the employee's personal standards). High levels of role ambiguity and role conflict are associated with low levels of job satisfaction, satisfaction with supervisor, and organizational commitment, and with a high rate of turnover. To resolve role ambiguity and role conflict, many new employees act on their own to obtain information about the job and organization from their co-workers and supervisors.

Resocialization

Most of the research we have cited here has dealt with new college graduates entering their first full-time job. But nowadays, most people can expect to change jobs several times during their working life. This means that, throughout your career, you are likely to experience new rites of passage, new socialization experiences (or resocialization) every time you join a different organization.

Common sense suggests that having had one or more prior jobs should make socialization to the next job easier. Also, it is expected that performance, job satisfaction, and organizational commitment will be higher among workers who have had previous jobs because of their experience in adjusting to different organizations. However, that expectation was *not* confirmed in a study of 171 mental health specialists starting new jobs. There were no significant differences in performance, job satisfaction, and commitment between those with prior work experience and those for whom this was their first job (Adkins, 1995). This study shows the importance of careful I-O research. Sometimes our common-sense expectations and intuitive beliefs are not supported by scientific study.

What about employees who stay with the same company but are transferred from one location to another? Do they also need resocialization? Yes, because each unit of the organization will have different values, expectations, and acceptable behaviors. Although there is usually not a formal socialization process for transferees, there is an informal one in which they seek feedback from peers and supervisors to test the adequacy of their job behaviors in their new situation.

A study of 69 transferees in 15 organizations assessed feedback-seeking behaviors. It was found that seeking feedback from peers declined significantly over the first year in the new location, whereas seeking feedback from supervisors remained stable. These results indicate that feedback from supervisors is seen as more important in the resocialization process (Callister, Kramer, & Turban, 1999).

ORGANIZATIONAL CULTURE

A major organizational factor to which new employees must be socialized is the culture of the group they are joining. Just as nations have cultural characteristics—beliefs, customs, and behaviors that distinguish them from other nations—so do organizations. **Organizational culture** may be defined as a general pattern of beliefs, expectations, and values, some conscious and some unconscious, that are expected to guide the behavior of all members of an organization.

Organizational culture The organization's pattern of beliefs, expectations, and values as manifested in company and industry practices.

An organization's culture is influenced by the type of industry of which it is part; different companies within the same industry can be expected to have a common organizational culture. For example, steel manufacturers share cultural characteristics that are distinct from those of publishers, insurance companies, hospitals, Internet companies, or movie studios because of different market conditions, competitive environments, and customer expectations. Also, society expects different services from, say, an electric power company and a furniture manufacturer. There is a greater societal need for continuous and uninterrupted service from the former than from the latter. Different departments within a company, such as research, engineering, and marketing, can develop their own subcultures that may differ from the dominant organizational culture.

Some I-O psychologists use the terms *organizational culture* and *organizational climate* interchangeably, arguing that the concepts share a fundamental similarity. Others note that climate is the surface manifestation of culture. Organizational climate is what we perceive when we observe the way a company functions, whereas organizational culture relates to deeper issues, the causes of an organization's operating style.

From our descriptions of participatory management programs, you have seen that organizational culture can influence a company's effectiveness. For example, companies with a culture of high involvement and high participation consistently outperform companies that do not favor employee participation and involvement.

Person-Organization Fit

The concept of **person-organization fit** can be defined as the degree of congruence between an employee's values and the organization's values. That agreement can be maximized through recruitment, selection, and socialization procedures.

Person-organization fit The congruence between an employee's values and the organization's values.

Person-organization fit may be enhanced when the values of newcomers closely agree with those of their supervisors. This was demonstrated in a study of 154 new employees and 101 supervisors from 68 European companies based in The Netherlands. High congruence correlated with low turnover intentions. At the same time, a high level of incongruence or disparity between employee and supervisor values was associated with a low level of organizational commitment from that employee (Van Vianen, 2000).

A related variable is personality. A person-organization fit should encompass not only similar values but also similar personalities. Most organizations are relatively homogeneous in terms of instilling a modal personality among its managers. A self-selection factor is involved here: job applicants tend to be attracted to companies whose structure, mission, and attitudes they seem comfortable with.

Think about a dot-com start-up company staffed by people in their 20s who dress casually, put in long hours hunched over their computers, and bring their dogs to work. Now imagine a major investment banking firm with people in suits who arrive in limousines and conduct their business in hushed voices. The differences in personality are obvious.

Organizational personality was studied in a group of 13,000 managers in 142 U.S. companies and government agencies. The results supported the idea that organizations are homogeneous in terms of the personality characteristics of their managers. In addition, these modal personality profiles were found to differ significantly from one organization to another (Schneider, Smith, Taylor, & Fleenor, 1998).

Gimme an Order of Fries—Sir!

NEWSBREAK

When Tom White was hired by Foodmaker, the parent company of the Jack-in-the-Box fast-food chain, he did no work for 2 months. Although his job title was vice president, he spent this introductory period learning about the company's culture, starting from the bottom up. This meant cooking fries, flipping burgers, and mastering the socialization program called "on boarding."

In addition, he was assigned a mentor and coach who showed him the Foodmaker way of doing things and who closely monitored his progress to make sure he would fit in. Finally, after 8 weeks of experiencing in person more of the company's operations than most executives see in 8 years, Tom was permitted to start his new job.

"It was probably the first time," he said, "that I've taken a new position and from Day One knew my duties and how to get things done in the organization. Without the on-boarding program, I would probably be 6 months to a year behind where I am now."

Corporate consultants report that few companies give their executives this type of opportunity to acquaint themselves with the organizational culture before undertaking their new job duties. The result is a high washout rate. Up to half of all new high-level executives quit or are dismissed within 3 years.

A survey of 46 executives who recently changed jobs revealed that one third said they would need as long as a year to adjust to their new company. They agreed that the toughest part was adapting to the corporate culture. One human resources director described organizational culture as the "framework in which you get your job done—or not!"

Source: P. Sweeney. Teaching new hires to feel at home, *New York Times*, February 14, 1999.

Some organizational psychologists advocate revising the typical approach to employee selection, suggesting that companies should evaluate not only whether the applicants' knowledge, skills, and abilities are suitable for a particular job but also whether those applicants' personalities are compatible with the organization's culture and personality.

LABOR UNIONS

One aspect of organizational life that helps define a company's culture is the presence or absence of labor unions, in which workers act collectively to protect and promote their interests. Union members form a subculture within the larger organizational culture. Membership in a union can contribute to job satisfaction and productivity and have a powerful influence on employees' attitudes toward their jobs and their employers.

The socialization of new union members is similar to the process of becoming acclimated to any new organization. Unions offer formal institutionalized socialization as well as informal individual socialization. The formal procedures include orientation lectures and training programs. Informal procedures involve attending union meetings with co-workers, being introduced to the shop steward, or having a work problem solved by the union. A study of 305 new members of the letter carriers' union, in which they were surveyed twice over a 1-year period to obtain presocialization and postsocialization attitudes, found that individual socialization practices produced a higher level of commitment to the union. More formal socialization procedures had little effect on commitment and had a negative impact on participation in union activities (Fullagar, Gallagher, Gordon, & Clark, 1995). At least for that union, then, a formal socialization program was found to be counterproductive.

Almost one third of union members in the United States are women, yet they hold less than 10% of the elected offices and are less likely to serve on committees or participate in union activities. Research shows that women are more likely to get involved in local union activities under the following conditions (Mellor, 1995; Mellor, Mathieu, & Swim, 1994):

- When more rather than fewer women hold office in the union
- When the local union is more formalized in its rules and procedures
- When the local union is receptive to participatory democracy in decision making

Despite the claim of union leadership to represent all its members, a study of employees in two high-tech companies in Israel (one unionized and the other not) found that union membership did not protect women members from facing discrimination in pay and promotion. Women who worked at the unionized company experienced as much gender bias as did women who worked at the nonunion company (Bamberger, Admati-Dvir, & Harel, 1995). If unions expect to recruit and retain the ever-growing number of women in the work force, they will have to pay more attention to the issues facing *all* of their members.

A review of pay scales in the United States shows that unionized employees are paid wages up to 33% greater than nonunion employees. In addition to higher pay, membership in a labor union can result in better and safer working conditions, job security, and fringe benefits, thus contributing to satisfaction of what Maslow called the lower-order needs. Union membership can also satisfy higher-order needs for status, belonging, and esteem and can provide a sense of power through the knowledge that unionized employees have an important bargaining tool: the threat of a strike. Some union members report a greater loyalty to their union than to their company.

Unions initially resisted quality-of-work-life programs because they feared such efforts would erode union loyalty. This resistance has been declining as more union members participate in and support QWL programs and other forms of worker participation.

Organized labor currently faces a crisis of declining membership. At the end of World War II, in 1945, more than 35% of the U.S. workforce belonged to unions. By 2000, that figure had fallen to less than 14%. In the private sector, only 11% of U.S. workers are union members. Economic conditions play a part in the stability of union membership. The greater the threat of job loss, the greater the union commitment because the union is seen as the only organization from which the workers can expect help.

Union Grievances

One aspect of union activity that affects employee attitudes and behaviors is the grievance process. Specified in union contracts, the grievance process establishes a formal mechanism for airing and resolving worker complaints. The number and focus of worker grievances serves as an indication of job dissatisfaction and can pinpoint the causes of problems in the workplace. Grievance procedures provide employees with a means of upward communication to management and an approved way of venting frustrations that might otherwise be expressed in work slowdowns, stoppages, or sabotage. Thus, the grievance process can be useful for both workers and managers.

The number of grievances varies with the nature of the job. Monotonous and repetitive assembly-line jobs performed under uncomfortable conditions by unskilled workers are associated with a high grievance rate. Social factors are also important. Highly cohesive work groups tend to file more grievances than do groups that lack a sense of unity. First-line supervisors who are low in consideration behaviors are the targets of more grievances than are supervisors who are high in consideration. In general, when a complaint is resolved in favor of the worker, job satisfaction rises along with the perception that the grievance system is fair and unbiased. When a grievance is settled in favor of management, labor-management relations often deteriorate.

ONLINE!

For a detailed look at today's important work issues from the standpoint of labor unions, check out the Web site of the AFL-CIO at *www.aflcio.org*.

INFORMAL GROUPS: THE ORGANIZATION WITHIN THE ORGANIZATION

Informal work groups develop within every organization. These groups have tremendous power to shape employee attitudes, behavior, and productivity. Workers come together informally to establish and promote a set of norms and values, a subculture within the larger organizational culture. These informal groups do not appear on the organization chart and are beyond the control of management. Often, management is not aware of their existence.

Informal groups determine for new employees how they will come to perceive management and other aspects of organizational culture. These groups can work for or against the organization by encouraging cooperation with company policies and procedures or by thwarting productivity and management goals.

The Hawthorne Studies

The classic Hawthorne studies provided empirical evidence of informal work groups. A team of 14 workers in the telephone bank wiring room of the Western Electric plant was observed for 6 months. The observer noticed that the group had developed its own standards of behavior and productivity. The workers shared many interests, engaged in rough but friendly teasing, and stood ready to help one another on the job. They valued one another's friendship and acceptance and displayed many of the characteristics of a family. They avoided doing anything that might bring disapproval from the group.

In terms of productivity, the group determined what it considered to be a fair and safe day's output. Management had set one standard, with an incentive to be paid for meeting or exceeding the daily level (an employee could make more money by working faster). But the group had set its own standard, which was below the company's level. The workers believed that if they met or exceeded management's demands, the company would then raise the standard and force them to work harder. Therefore, the informal work group set a leisurely, easily attainable production goal, willing to forgo the opportunity to earn extra money. The workers admitted to the observer that they were capable of producing more but to do so would have defied the group's norms. The group had assumed such prominence in the workers' lives that they considered group acceptance more important than extra pay.

> **ONLINE!**
>
> For more about the Hawthorne studies log on to *www.accel-team.com/motivation/hawthorne_02.html*.

Social Loafing

Another effect of informal work groups is the phenomenon known as **social loafing,** the idea that people do not work as hard in a group as they do when

Social loafing The idea that people do not work as hard in a group as they do when working alone.

Members of informal work groups usually have similar backgrounds and interests and may determine for themselves an acceptable standard of productivity, which may differ from the one set by management.

working alone. One explanation for social loafing is that people believe they can get lost in the crowd and that their slower work pace will not be noticed. Also, people tend to expect, on the basis of past experience, that others in the group will goof off, so they might as well do so too.

Social loafing is less likely to occur when workers believe that their supervisors are aware of how hard they work as individuals. Social loafing is more likely to occur when workers believe that their personal efforts are not recognized by their supervisors. Men are more likely to engage in social loafing than are women. Further, workers in Eastern cultures (which are more collectivist or group-oriented) are less likely to practice social loafing than are employees from Western, more individualistic, cultures.

One analysis suggests that workers are likely to engage in social loafing under the following conditions:

1. When their individual outputs cannot be evaluated
2. When working on tasks that are not meaningful or personally involving
3. When working with strangers
4. When they expect their co-workers to perform well on the task

In addition, the researchers found that more cohesive work groups showed less social loafing than did groups that were less cohesive (Karau & Hart, 1998).

Group Cohesiveness

Informal groups exist in virtually every type of organization. They are characterized by personal interactions that occur over an extended period because frequent interactions are necessary to the development of closeness and a commonality of interests. Groups must also have a focus, such as workers in the same department who share a physical workspace. The groups cannot be too large, or the sense of personal and direct contact will be lost.

Most of us have a need for affiliation and companionship, and this need can be satisfied by an informal work group. The group also serves as a source of information about work procedures and about what constitutes an acceptable day's output. Group closeness was also found to influence employee perceptions of organizational issues. For example, employees who form personal relationships in a work group tend to interpret organizational events in a similar way. Employees in less cohesive informal groups tend to interpret the same events in a different way.

Group norms and standards are pervasive throughout organizational and personal life. The group can influence political and racial attitudes, style of dress, even where to eat or go on vacation. Because group membership satisfies so many needs, employees strive to be accepted by group members. Deviant behavior is rarely encountered, except from new workers who need time to absorb the group's ways.

Informal groups tend to attract and retain people with similar personality characteristics and to take on a consistent affective or emotional tone. As a result, group members tend to have similar moods and feelings about their work. A group's affective tone influences the group's work performance. A negative affective tone is related to a low level of helping behaviors, manifested in rude and uncooperative behavior. Positive affective tone is related to a low level of absenteeism.

Positive affective tone is also positively related to organizational spontaneity, which includes such behaviors as helping co-workers, protecting the organization, making constructive suggestions, developing one's personal skills, and spreading good will. Positive affect in a group is likely to be stronger when the group is small and the members work in physical proximity.

The degree of closeness within a group is called group cohesiveness. The greater the cohesiveness, the greater is the group's power over its members and the greater the pressure on group members to conform. Several factors influence cohesiveness. As the group gets larger and there is less opportunity for frequent contact among group members, cohesiveness declines. Larger groups generally splinter into subgroups or competing groups. Diversity of background, interests, and lifestyles reduces group cohesiveness.

Working conditions are also important. Workers under a wage-incentive system that rewards on an individual rather than a team basis find that the resulting personal competition reduces feelings of closeness. Team rewards enhance group cohesiveness by encouraging cooperation; everyone works for a common goal.

Outside pressures and threats affect group cohesiveness. Just as citizens of a nation under attack usually cooperate to submerge personal or regional differences, so will a work group faced with an unfair supervisor or an unpopular policy.

TECHNOLOGICAL CHANGE AND ORGANIZATIONAL STRUCTURE

The widespread use of computer-aided manufacturing and office equipment has changed the ways in which daily work is performed and has also affected the formal and informal structure of organizations. Computer technology creates the need for greater coordination and integration of an organization's basic units, which requires the development of new reporting hierarchies. For example, at one plant in which operations were computerized, the engineering staff had to be reorganized so that it reported to the marketing department, a unit with which it previously had had no direct contact. The change was necessary to co-ordinate customers' needs (marketing) and the development of new products (engineering).

Computer technology requires greater formalization of work procedures. Rules for entering data into computer files must be precise. They permit no employee discretion or deviation. These formal procedures reduce opportunities for individuality in structuring and organizing work. Computers also change the source of decision-making authority, although the direction of the change is not always clear. In practice, automating an office or manufacturing plant sometimes results in greater centralization of decision making, restricting it to fewer levels on the organization chart. In other cases it results in decentralization, giving greater decision-making authority to the worker at the video display terminal. For some jobs, computer operators may be more knowledgeable than their supervisors about the equipment's capabilities. This shift in power from supervisors to employees can disrupt traditional working relationships and leave managers with a reduced understanding of the work they are supposed to be managing.

Computers are also changing the procedures for the meetings that result in corporate decisions. Instead of asking a group of employees to sit around a table and discuss a problem, some organizations hold "virtual" meetings in which the interaction takes place through computers. Participants express their ideas simultaneously and anonymously and comment on one another's work. Anecdotal evidence from organizations as diverse as hotels, banks, plastics companies, and aircraft manufacturers indicates that virtual meetings are shorter and less stressful. Leaders are able to stick to an agenda because employees do not digress or waste time at the computer to the extent they do in person. Electronic brainstorming—the generation of ideas by the group during a virtual meeting—has been found to be more productive than traditional face-to-face brainstorming.

Laboratory research with undergraduate and MBA student subjects in the United States and Canada supports the usefulness and productivity of electronic brainstorming for groups of up to 12 participants. These groups were found to generate more unique and better ideas than did traditional face-to-face groups or nominal groups (the same number of people working alone whose ideas are then pooled) (Gallupe, Cooper, Grisé, & Bastianutti, 1994; Valacich, Dennis, & Connolly, 1994). With very small groups (up to three members), a significantly greater number of ideas was produced by face-to-face meetings. However, there was no significant difference in the *quality* of the ideas generated by computer-mediated or face-to-face groups.

Communication by computer may lower the social inhibitions and status barriers present in face-to-face groups. High-level managers tend to dominate group meetings as well as informal conversations. However, one series of studies showed that high-status group members continued to dominate group discussions whether conducted via computer or face-to-face (Weisband, Schneider, & Connolly, 1995).

Computers can force changes in the organization's informal structure by disrupting traditional lines of communication and power. For example, in companies where workers have side-by-side work stations, they communicate freely and easily about both work-related and personal matters. Where such jobs are automated, workers are often separated by partitions that inhibit talking and socializing.

Reducing the chances for personal interaction reduces the group's cohesiveness. Even though workers have found ways to use their computers for informal communication, this approach lacks the closeness and the privacy afforded by face-to-face contact. Also, many companies routinely monitor the messages on their internal e-mail system, an action that discourages its use for promoting the personal and social interactions necessary to maintain group cohesiveness.

Along with the loss of group cohesiveness, increased computer use on the job has led to employees' growing sense of isolation, both on and off the job. Instead of being able to walk into the neighboring office or down the hall to consult with a colleague in person, you can ask your question without leaving your cubicle—and thus without any meaningful personal contact. Instead of gossiping around the water cooler, employees are chatting online.

Even lunch breaks are at risk as growing numbers of employees rush back to their computer terminals rather than visit with co-workers or run errands. A survey of 1000 employees found that 14% ate by themselves at their desks so they could log on during their free time (Fickenscher, 2000).

The ideas once shared during informal gatherings of employees or generated and exchanged during spontaneous meetings are being lost, along with the opportunities to network and build social support. This situation is especially true for the millions of employees who work at home. Many of these telecommuters spend their entire workday connecting with other people only by electronic means.

A study of 169 people in 73 households during their first 2 years online found that as Internet use at home increased, communication with family members declined. The size of the users' social network also declined. Frequent Internet users rated themselves as more lonely and depressed than did people who spent less time online (Kraut et al., 1998).

Psychologists have suggested that excessive Internet use can lead to a form of addiction. The Center for Internet Studies surveyed 18,000 users and found that nearly 6% met the criteria for compulsive Internet use, characteristics similar to those that define compulsive gambling (DeAngelis, 2000). These people were especially hooked on chat rooms, pornography sites, online shopping, and e-mail. One third of them said they logged on regularly as a form of escape or to alter their mood.

How does employer monitoring of computer use affect employees' feelings about their organization? As you might guess, it has a disruptive effect on the employee-employer relationship. Workers may come to view their bosses as

ONLINE!

Are you spending too many of your waking hours interacting with your computer instead of with people? Are you neglecting your studies or your job because you feel the need to play just one more computer game? Here are a couple of sites for you to check out: The Center for Internet Studies at *www.virtual-addiction.com* and the Center for Online Addiction at *www.netaddiction.com.*

Beware of Big Brother

It pays to be careful when you log on at work these days. What you say could get you fired. That was the painful lesson was learned by Michael Smyth, who used to be a sales manager at The Pillsbury Company until he messaged his boss one day and referred to the boss's superior as a "back-stabbing bastard."

Smyth thought his e-mail was private and personal, just like sending a letter through the regular mail. But it wasn't. A co-worker found a printout of the message and brought it to the attention of the "back-stabbing bastard." Smyth was fired right away. He sued for wrongful discharge, arguing that his communication was private, but a judge turned down his claim.

The judge ruled that Smyth forfeited any and all reasonable expectations of privacy when he used the company network, even though his message was clearly intended for only one person. A lawyer for the company pointed out that a warning appears on the screen every time employees log on, reminding them that their mail might be intercepted and read by anyone else on the network.

So be careful what you say on line. You don't know who might be monitoring your mail. And be careful where you surf. That can get you in trouble, too.

Andrew Quinn, systems manager in charge of monitoring for a Canadian company, checks every e-mail employees send and receive as well as every Web site with which they connect. "Look at this guy," he told a visiting reporter. "He's sending out jokes on e-mail. That's all he's been doing for the last hour!" What does that tell you about his job productivity?

The *New York Times* fired 23 workers at their Virginia office for sending and receiving obscene messages. Xerox fired 40 workers when records showed that they had spent up to 8 hours a day on porn sites. Other workers misuse their work time conducting personal business, day-trading, planning trips, shopping, and playing computer games. This so-called cyber-slacking has caused meltdowns of company networks, costing many hours of down time and hundreds or thousands of dollars for repair. Sometimes the situation gets so bad that business has to be conducted over that ancient device known as the telephone!

Sources: L. Gvernsey. The Web: New ticket to a pink slip. *New York Times*, December 16, 1999; You've got inappropriate mail. *New York Times*, April 5, 2000. J. L. Seglin. You've got mail; you're being watched. *New York Times*, July 18, 1999.

watchdogs, always spying on their behavior. To examine the pervasiveness of electronic snooping in the workplace, the American Management Association surveyed nearly 1,000 major U.S. companies. They found that electronic surveillance of employees grew rapidly during the last several years. Almost 75% of the companies questioned reported that they routinely monitor their employees' behavior on the job, including checking telephone calls, e-mail, Internet connections, and computer files. More than half of the firms used blocking software to prevent connections to unauthorized telephone numbers and about a third blocked Internet access to so-called inappropriate Web sites.

A survey of 224 mid-size companies conducted by the Center for Internet Studies found that 60% had disciplined employees for online abuse and 30% had fired workers for such behavior. The two most frequently reported abuses were using the Internet for personal e-mail on company time and for connecting to pornography sites (DeAngelis, 2000). Another survey questioned 1,000 Internet users and reported that 10% believed that their work had suffered as a result of the excessive amount of time they spent surfing Web sites. Another 13% blamed easy access to the Internet as being responsible for their inability to stay focused on their jobs (Fickenscher, 2000).

Employees who are monitored for Internet use report higher levels of depression, tension, and anxiety, and lower levels of productivity than do employees who are not monitored by their employers (Rosen, 2000). Employees who are being watched complain that their privacy and dignity are being violated. Employers argue that they need to ensure that their employees are not goofing off. Which side do you agree with?

An Orientation Training Program

Socialization is the process of introducing new employees to the unique culture of their organization. New hires learn about their role in the corporate hierarchy, the values and customs management thinks are important, and the behaviors co-workers consider acceptable. Learning these lessons well can instill in new employees a sense of organizational commitment as well as feelings of job satisfaction and involvement.

To determine how new employees at a large university who chose to take an orientation training program might differ from employees who did not, psychologists studied a group of people recently hired for nonfaculty positions. The jobs ranged from accountants, architects, and clerical personnel to technical, service, and maintenance workers. More than 83% of the employees were white, 70% were female, and their average length of time on the job was 87 days.

Questionnaires were mailed to 243 employees hired during the previous 3 months. The survey assessed the extent to which employees felt they had become socialized to the organization. Responses were received from 142 employees, a 58% response rate.

A voluntary 3-hour orientation program was scheduled several times during the 2 to 6 weeks following the mailing of the initial questionnaire. Employees who completed the first questionnaire received a second questionnaire to assess posttraining socialization and organizational commitment. Replies were received from 116 of the 142 employees. Of these 116, 55 had attended the orientation and 61 had not.

Source: H. J. Klein & N. A. Weaver (2000). The effectiveness of an organizational-level orientation training program in the socialization of new hires. *Personnel Psychology, 53,* 47–66.

The program included the following:

- A videotaped welcome message from the university president
- An exercise designed to familiarize new employees with the organization's traditions and language (technical vocabulary, acronyms, slang, and jargon)
- A videotape and a live discussion about the mission, history, and structure of the university
- A lecture and a discussion about basic workplace principles

The results showed that employees who had attended the orientation session were significantly better socialized to the university's goals, values, and people (though not language) than were employees who did not attend the session. The training also led to a significantly higher level of organizational commitment.

Think About It

1. The researchers admit that the study's major weakness is that new employees were not randomly assigned to the two conditions. How might this have affected the results?
2. The employees studied had already been on the job for three months. Is this another weakness of the research? How might this condition have affected the results?
3. What is your opinion of this orientation training program? What type of training would you advise for new employees at your university?
4. What factors have been found to influence the socialization of new employees?
5. Is socialization necessary for employees with prior work experience or who are transferring to new jobs within the same company? Why or why not?

SUMMARY

Organizational psychologists study organizational climates and styles and the ways they affect employees. The classic organizational style is **bureaucracy,** intended to be a rational structure in which rules of conduct and lines of authority were fixed and in which subjectivity and personal bias had no place. Bureaucracies ignored human needs and could not adapt easily to social and technological change.

The modern organizational style, a high-involvement participatory approach, is more concerned with employees' intellectual, emotional, and motivational characteristics. Workers participate in decision making at all levels. **Quality-of-work-life (QWL) programs** restructure job and management requirements to enhance worker participation. In **quality control circles,** small groups of workers meet periodically to solve problems relating to quality and quantity of production. In **self-managing work groups,** a work team controls all aspects of the job. Virtual self-managing work groups are linked electronically. Its members may never meet face-to-face.

Employees and managers may resist changes in work methods, equipment, or policies. If workers are allowed to participate in decisions about the change, they are more likely to support it. **Organizational development (OD)** involves techniques for introducing large-scale changes. The process is carried out by **change agents** who diagnose problems, devise appropriate strategies, and implement the interventions.

New employees undergo an adjustment period called **socialization.** A socialization program should involve a challenging job, appropriate training and feedback, a considerate supervisor, co-workers with high morale and organizational commitment, and a suitable orientation program.

Organizational culture is the pattern of beliefs, values, and expectations that guide the behavior of the organization's members. **Person-organization fit** refers to the congruence between an employee's personality and values and the organization's culture and values.

Membership in a labor union can affect job satisfaction and productivity and can satisfy lower-level needs through pay, job security, and fringe benefits. Membership can also satisfy belonging, esteem, status, and power needs.

Informal work groups, which influence employee attitudes and behavior, exist beyond management control. They operate by their own standards with regard to productivity and worker-management relations. **Social loafing** is the idea that people do not work as hard in a group as they do when working alone. Group cohesiveness refers to the degree of closeness of a group.

Computer usage has produced changes in organizational structure by causing a power shift from supervisors to employees. Meetings can now be held online (virtual meetings), reducing group cohesiveness and increasing social isolation. Electronic surveillance can reduce employees' trust in their organization.

KEY TERMS

bureaucracy

change agents

organizational culture

organizational development (OD)

person-organization fit

quality control circles

quality-of-work-life (QWL) programs

role ambiguity

role conflict

self-managing work groups

social loafing

socialization

ADDITIONAL READING

Ashkanasy, N. M., Wilderom, C. P. M., & Peterson, M. F. (Eds). (2000). *Handbook of organizational culture and climate.* Thousand Oaks, CA: Sage Publications. Reviews international research, theory, and practice. Includes basic concepts, measurement, assessment, and applications of organizational culture/climate theory to everyday management and human resources problems such as organizational commitment and socialization.

Boyett, J. H., & Boyett, J. T. (2000). *The Guru guide to entrepreneurship.* New York: Wiley. Profiles 70 highly successful entrepreneurs including the founders of Microsoft, Amazon.com, McDonalds, and Wal-Mart. Describes their organizational styles, including sharing information and perks with employees, and offers self-tests to assess your potential to start and run a business.

Schein, E. H. (1999). *The corporate culture survival guide.* San Francisco: Jossey-Bass. A readable, practical guide to the creation and evolution of organizational cultures, showing how to guide the inevitable changes. Emphasizes the importance of appropriate leadership in understanding values and shared assumptions in new, midlife, and mature companies.

Sundstrom, E. (Ed.). (1999). *Supporting work team effectiveness: Best management practices for fostering high performance.* San Francisco: Jossey-Bass. Discusses the leadership, staffing, training, feedback, and communication systems needed for effective work teams. Notes that different types of teams (whether for production, service, management, or a specific project) will require different support systems.

Characteristics of the Workplace

We have discussed some of the effects of the social and psychological climate in which work takes place. The structure of the organization, its style of leadership, and the motivations of employees all influence productivity and job satisfaction. We turn now to more tangible aspects of the workplace—physical features, working hours, safety issues, and concerns about physical and emotional health.

Chapter 10 deals with physical conditions of work, including lighting, noise, temperature, color, and music. Work hours and work schedules are discussed, along with factors such as fatigue, monotony, and sexual harassment.

Accidents, violence, alcoholism, and drug abuse are covered in Chapter 11. Psychologists help to determine the causes of workplace accidents and violence, and ways to prevent them. Dependence on alcohol or illicit drugs is both a personal tragedy and a personnel problem. Psychologists design employee assistance programs for troubled workers at all occupational levels.

Chapter 12 considers the stresses that result from various physical and psychological conditions of work. Psychologists have developed ways of preventing stress and of treating it on and off the job.

Working Conditions

CHAPTER 10

PHYSICAL WORKING CONDITIONS

Look around. Are you in the dorm? The library? An office? What is it like? Comfortable and quiet? Noisy and distracting? Bright and attractive? Cold and drab? These are just some of the physical characteristics of a work environment that can determine how well we are able to do our jobs. Whatever our task—whether we are trying to study, repair an engine, or sell a computer—our surroundings will affect our skill, motivation, and satisfaction.

An organization can recruit and select the best employees, train them thoroughly, provide outstanding leaders and an optimal organizational climate to maximize job performance, but if the physical working conditions are uncomfortable, productivity will suffer. Uncongenial work settings are related to decreased productivity, lower job satisfaction, greater errors and accidents, and more absenteeism and turnover.

When a workplace is made more comfortable, or working hours more flexible, productivity usually increases, at least temporarily. But the I-O psychologist must be careful in interpreting such changes in performance. What, precisely, has caused the greater productivity? Was it physical changes such as a new climate-control system, brighter lighting, or better soundproofing? Or was it more subtle psychological factors such as employees' more positive attitude toward management for instituting the changes?

Although the results may be beneficial for the company, whatever the cause, management needs to be able to explain the reasons for any improvement in productivity or satisfaction. Suppose they stem from the fact that employees are pleased that their company sees them as human beings rather than cogs in a machine. If so, the company will want to know whether there are other human-relations ways to improve satisfaction and productivity that do not involve expensive alterations to the physical workplace.

In many industries, people work at peak efficiency under what appear to be intolerable conditions. And there are many other instances of poor performance and low morale in well-equipped, lavishly decorated surroundings. The effects of changes in physical working conditions may be influenced or modified by how employees perceive, accept, and adapt to these changes. Therefore, the physical features of the workplace must be considered in light of complex psychological factors.

Questionnaire research with 641 blue-collar and white-collar employees in Australia suggested the importance of the following dimensions of the physical work environment (Carlopio, 1996):[1]

1. *Environmental design,* including lighting, air quality, and general atmosphere of the work area
2. *Facilities,* including restrooms, eating areas, and recreational facilities
3. *Work organization,* including work schedule and pace, and amount of time and information provided to do the job
4. *Equipment and tools,* including the design and efficiency of the tools and machines provided to do the job

---

[1]The first three dimensions are discussed in this chapter. Equipment and tools are covered in Chapter 13. Health and safety issues are dealt with in Chapter 11.

5. *Health and safety,* including organizational procedures to deal with physical safety issues, hazards, and other factors that may affect employee health

Work Sites

The physical work environment includes many factors, from the size of the parking lot and location of the building to the amount of natural light and noise in the work area. Inadequate parking spaces or a parking lot too far from the building can so irritate employees that their attitude toward the organization is negative before they even reach their work station.

The location of the work site, whether in the downtown of a large city or a more remote suburban area, can also affect employees' satisfaction with their jobs. For example, suburban office parks are often isolated from the shops, restaurants, and other services found in cities. Surveys show that young, single employees typically prefer living and working in cities, whereas married people tend to prefer the quieter suburbs as better places to work and rear children.

Many organizations offer various amenities to attract and retain dedicated employees. Some companies have turned themselves into vacation resorts with on-site spas, gyms, nurseries, shops, banks, and medical clinics. Why would organizations spend money on what used to be considered frills? At the luxury-laden Citicorp office complex in Tampa, Florida, an employee said, "You spend so much of your life at work, it's nice that you can have things like a fitness center or child-care facility. For me, it builds loyalty." And loyal employees are less likely to quit, take time off, or be sloppy about their work.

Child-Care and Dependent-Care Facilities

A growing number of companies have established day-care centers or on-site schools for the young children of their employees. Such facilities are increasingly seen as a significant, even expected, fringe benefit. A study of 155 hospital employees who used on-site day-care facilities concluded that child-care programs helped in recruiting and retaining new employees but had no measurable impact on job performance (Kossek & Nichol, 1992). A survey of 745 employees from several organizations found that those whose employers provided assistance with child care were significantly higher in organizational commitment and lower in intention to quit than employees whose companies did not provide help with child care (Grover & Crooker, 1995).

However, more recent research with employees of a large urban insurance company and a small-town textile plant showed only a weak connection between the use of on-site child-care facilities and employee attitudes (Rothausen, Gonzalez, Clarke, & O'Dell, 1998). Nevertheless, recognition of child-care needs usually gives companies a competitive edge in recruiting new employees.

A problem faced by middle-aged workers involves caring for elderly parents. A survey at Travelers Insurance found that 20% of employees over the age of 30 provided some sort of assistance for an aging parent. Other surveys put the figure as high as 40%. These employees experience considerable financial and emotional strain in trying to balance the needs of work and family. As the general population ages, growing numbers of workers are confronting this dilemma. The situation is having an impact on productivity, absenteeism, and stress.

Some employers have responded to this need by offering in-house counseling programs, long-term care insurance, generous paid leave policies, and on-site care for dependents of all ages. A problem with eldercare services to date, however, is that few people are using them. According to the National Council on Aging, employees are reluctant to give the impression that family matters are diverting their attention from the performance of their job.

Office and Workplace Design

Once inside our place of employment, we may find other physical features that create dissatisfaction or frustration. One source of complaints is the ventilating, heating, and air-conditioning systems in glass-wall, fixed-window buildings. Temperatures are often uncomfortably hot on the sunny side of the building and too cool on the shady side. Other irritants are slow elevators in high-rise buildings, the quality of the food in the company cafeteria, and inconvenient or poorly maintained rest rooms.

Office size and design can be related to employee satisfaction and productivity. The layout of a set of offices will affect the behavior of managers who rely on spontaneous encounters as a way of obtaining and exchanging information. The closer their offices, the more likely they are to meet throughout the workday. Physical separation, such as placing suites of management offices on different floors of a building, decreases the amount of contact.

The size of an office building can influence working relationships. The smaller the building, the closer the relationships among employees tend to be. In very large buildings, where employees have fewer interactions, relationships

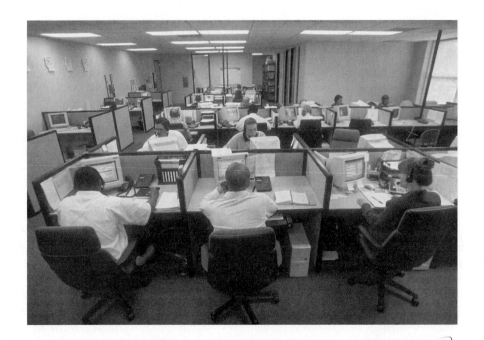

Landscaped offices have no floor-to-ceiling dividers. These settings may enhance employee communication and social interaction, but they are also noisy and distracting.

tend to be more formal and impersonal. All these factors, none of which involves actual job tasks, can impair productive efficiency. An unpopular location, poor design, or inconvenient layout can reduce morale and foster negative attitudes.

Workplace design and location are especially critical for disabled employees who may be barred from certain jobs not because of lack of ability, but because they do not have access to the work area. Steep flights of stairs, narrow doorways, and inadequate rest rooms may prevent them from being employed. The 1973 Rehabilitation Act and the 1990 Americans with Disabilities Act require the removal of architectural barriers. All parts of a building must be accessible to persons in wheelchairs. Compliance with the laws has meant modifications to the physical plant, such as automatic doors, ramps and elevators, handholds, wider doorways and corridors, and lower wall telephones and speakerphones. Surveys show that 60% of these required changes cost less than $100 and 90% cost less than $1000. Many disabled employees do not need any physical modifications of an office workspace. IBM, which has hired disabled workers for more than 40 years, took the lead in redesigning work stations to provide job opportunities for these employees.

ONLINE!

You can find a list of sites about workspace design for offices, classrooms, stores, and factories at *www.workspace-resources.com.*

Environmental Psychology and Landscaped Offices

In the 1960s, the field of **environmental psychology,** concerned with the relationships between people and their physical environment, sparked a revolution in workspace design. Combining architecture and psychology, environmental psychologists are concerned with natural and built environments and their impact on behavior. For example, research on office design and layout has focused on communications between and within departments, flow of job tasks among groups, relationships between managers and subordinates, and work group cohesiveness.

Environmental psychology
The study of the effect of workplace design on behavior and attitudes.

One result of environmental psychology research is the landscaped office. In contrast to private, separated offices, the landscaped office consists of a huge open space with no floor-to-ceiling walls to divide the area into separate rooms. All employees, from clerks to corporate officers, are grouped into cubicles, functional work units that are set off from others only by planters, screens or partitions, or cabinets and bookcases.

Inexpensive to construct and maintain, landscaped offices are believed to facilitate communication and work flow. The openness is supposed to enhance group cohesiveness and cooperation and reduce psychological barriers between employees and managers. Research on employee reactions has revealed both advantages and disadvantages. Employees report that landscaped offices are pleasant and are conducive to socializing. Managers report improved communication.

Complaints relate to lack of privacy, noise, and difficulty in concentrating. Because cubicles are typically separated only by low dividers, work areas tend to lack the personal touches—such as photos, plants, posters, or souvenirs—that contribute to feelings of individuality and comfort.

Despite these problems with landscaped offices, many organizations have invested considerable money in them and are reluctant to bear the additional expense of reconverting to more private offices. For companies with large numbers of employees at computerized work stations, the landscaped office has become standard.

As real estate costs escalate, organizations are trying to squeeze more employees into smaller facilities. The size of the typical office cubicle or individual work station is steadily shrinking. Some employees who travel frequently no longer have a permanently assigned work area but only a temporary space. For example,

---

NEWSBREAK

Clothes Encounters

You see it everywhere these days, in banks and law firms, in county offices, shops, and schools—employees breaking the formal dress code and showing up for work in casual clothing. It used to occur only on Friday, but now "business casual" is happening every day, and it represents a radical transformation in the look of many workplaces. A survey by the Society for Human Resource Management found that 42% of the 750 companies questioned allow casual dress every day. For large companies with more than 5,000 employees, more than half have relaxed the dress code.

This situation has created confusion for many people. What exactly is acceptable as business-casual clothing? Can you wear jeans? Tanktops? What about shorts and sandals? Fashion consultants have sprung into action to advise management and develop appropriate standards. A major New York law firm enlisted designer Ralph Lauren and *Esquire* magazine to conduct a casual wardrobe seminar for its employees. Here's what they proposed.

Men will wear shirts with collars and buttons (no T-shirts). Socks are definitely required. No halters or tanktops for women. Jeans and sneakers are out for everybody. Attorneys should keep a suit in the office in case they have to go to court on short notice or meet a client who does not dress casually. When a meeting is scheduled with someone from another firm, phone ahead to find out that firm's dress code.

The day may come when we all dress casually for work all the time, regardless of the nature of our job. But how far will the trend go? Would you have confidence in a lawyer or a banker or an insurance salesperson who showed up for a meeting in a jogging suit? Would you want to see your physician or your dentist in shorts? Or is a uniform still necessary to command respect and authority in some jobs? One attorney rebelled against the relaxation of standards. "For $350 an hour," he said, "clients want lawyers who look like, well, lawyers."

Source: C. Stracher. The law firm's new clothes. *New York Times,* March 24, 2000.

consultants who spend much of their time on-site at a client's workplace will phone ahead to reserve a cubicle for their next visit to the home office. Because the practice is not unlike booking a hotel room, it has come to be known as "hoteling."

Illumination

In addition to studying general issues of workspace design, I-O psychologists have conducted extensive research on specific environmental factors such as lighting, noise, and temperature. These aspects of the work environment are analogous to the hygiene needs proposed by Herzberg. All of these environmental factors have been found to affect job satisfaction.

Continued exposure to inadequate illumination while reading or performing detailed operations can be harmful to one's eyesight. Research confirms that inadequate lighting is a source of distress. High glare, dim bulbs, and a lack of natural light have negative effects on job performance.

Intensity.   Intensity, or level of brightness, is the most common factor associated with illumination. The optimal level of intensity varies with the nature of the task and the age of the worker. Older workers generally need brighter light than do younger workers for satisfactory performance of the same task. A job involving the precise manipulation of small component parts, as in electronics assembly, requires brighter light than an assembly line in a bottling plant. Lighting engineers have recommended minimum intensity levels for a variety of work areas (see Table 10–1).

TABLE 10–1   Recommended Lighting Levels for Selected Workplaces

Job	Minimum Footcandles[a]
Aircraft manufacturing (welding)	2000
Assembly, extra fine (computer chips)	1000
Clothing industry (cutting, cleaning, inspecting)	500
Dairy products (bottle washing)	200
Tobacco grading and sorting	200
Bank teller stations	150
Candy making and decorating	100
Barber shops, beauty salons	100
Photo engraving	50
Hotel lobbies	50
Retail store interiors	30
Laundries	30
Iron and steel manufacturing plants	20
Corridors and stairways	20
Airplane passenger compartments	5

[a] A footcandle of light (a standard candle at a distance of one foot) is approximately the brightness produced by a 100-watt bulb held ten feet above your head on a dark night.
Note: Adapted from *Footcandles in Modern Lighting*, 1971, Cleveland, OH: General Electric.

298 Part Four   Characteristics of the Workplace

Distribution of Light.   Another important factor in illumination is the distribution of light over the work area. Ideally, lighting will be distributed uniformly throughout the visual field. Illuminating a work station at a much higher intensity than its surroundings leads to eyestrain because of the natural tendency of the eyes to move. When a person looks from a brightly lit area to a dimly lit area, the pupils of the eyes dilate. Returning the gaze to the brighter area causes the pupils to contract. This constant reaction of the pupils leads to eyestrain. When you are sitting at your desk, you should have overhead lighting as well as a desk lamp focused on your work. This arrangement will give a uniform distribution of light throughout the room. Similarly, it is less fatiguing to the eyes to have additional lighting in the room where you are watching television or staring at your computer screen.

Uniform illumination throughout a work area can be provided by indirect lighting in which all light is reflected. Thus, no light will strike the eyes directly. In contrast, direct lighting, with bulbs located at various points in the ceiling, tends to focus or concentrate the light on specific areas, causing bright spots and glare.

Glare.   Glare reduces visual efficiency and contributes to eyestrain. Glare is caused by light of a brighter intensity than that to which the eye is accustomed. This brightness may come from the light source or from reflective surfaces. Glare can lead to an increase in errors in detailed work in as short a time as 20 minutes. It can obscure vision, something you may have experienced when driving at night and confronting an oncoming car that has its high-beam headlights on. Glare is also a problem with the video display terminals for computers.

There are several ways to reduce or eliminate glare. Extremely bright light sources can be shielded or kept out of the visual field. Workers can be supplied with visors or eyeshades. Reflective or glossy surfaces can be painted with a dull, matte finish.

Natural Light.   There is a definite psychological component with regard to natural (full-spectrum) light versus artificial light. Research has shown that people who work in windowless offices and receive no natural light express a strong desire for windows, regardless of the adequacy of the artificial illumination in their work area. Most workers like to be able to see outside, and they also believe that natural light is better for the eyes than is artificial light. People may have a physiological need for a certain amount of full-spectrum or natural light. Several European countries have laws requiring employers to ensure that all employees can see natural light from their work areas.

Noise

Noise is a common complaint in modern life. Noise makes us irritable and nervous, interferes with sleep, and produces physiological effects such as hearing loss. Noise is a documented occupational hazard for industrial employees such as riveters, boilermakers, aircraft mechanics, and foundry and textile workers. Businesses have been faced with employee claims of hearing damage that total millions of dollars each year.

The basic unit for measuring noise is the *decibel* (db), which is a measure of the subjective or perceived intensity of a sound. Zero db is the threshold of hear-

Miners are subjected to noise levels that can cause hearing loss.

ing, the faintest sound most of us can hear. Table 10–2 shows decibel levels in familiar situations. Some loudness levels are threats to hearing. A worker exposed regularly over a long period to decibel levels above 85 can expect to suffer some hearing loss. Exposure to levels over 120 db can cause temporary deafness. Brief exposure to levels in excess of 130 can cause permanent deafness. The U.S. government has established maximum permissible sound levels for industrial workers: exposure to 90 db for an 8-hour day, 100 db for a 2-hour period, and 110 db for a 30-minute period.

When people are exposed to sounds in the 95 to 110 db range, blood vessels constrict, heart rate changes, and the pupils of the eyes dilate. The constriction of the blood vessels continues for some time after the noise ceases, a condition that

TABLE 10–2   Decibel Levels for Familiar Sounds

Source of Noise	Decibel Level
Breathing	10
Whisper from 5 feet away	30
Quiet office	40
Conversation 3 feet away	70
City traffic	80
Kitchen appliances	95
Average factory	100
Power lawnmowers	110
Crying babies	110
Pneumatic hammers 3 feet away	120
Electronically amplified rock band	140
Jet aircraft at takeoff	150

alters the blood supply throughout the body. Continuous exposure to loud noise is associated with high blood pressure and muscle tension. High noise levels also impair emotional well being and induce stress. In a study of 40 women clerical workers, three hours' exposure to the noise of a typical open-office arrangement produced measurable physiological signs of stress. The noise also reduced the employees' motivation to work (Evans & Johnson, 2000).

Noise interferes with communication. If the background noise in an office is low (between 50 and 60 db), then two people can conduct a conversation without raising their voices at a distance of up to 5 feet. As the background noise level rises, workers must talk louder or must leave their work stations and come closer together to be heard. The decibel level of the average factory forces workers and supervisors to shout. It is likely that important information is lost in transmission.

Color

Exaggerated claims have been made about the benefits of color for homes, offices, and factories. It has been suggested that certain colors increase productivity, reduce accidents, and raise employee morale. These claims are not supported by empirical evidence, and there is no validity to any purported relationship between a specific color and productivity, fatigue, or job satisfaction.

However, there is a role for color in the workplace. Color can provide a more pleasant working environment and can be an aid in safety practices. Color is used in many manufacturing plants as a coding device. Fire equipment is red, danger areas yellow, and first-aid stations green. Color-coding allows these areas to be identified quickly. Color can prevent eyestrain because colors differ in their reflective properties. A white wall reflects more light than a dark one. Thus, the appropriate use of color can make a workroom or office seem brighter or darker. Colors also create different illusions of size. A room painted a darker color seems smaller than it actually is. Light-colored walls give the feeling of space and openness.

On U.S. Navy submarines, the 24 Trident missile tubes, which run through all four decks, are painted reddish-orange. The color is darker for tubes at one end of the ship than the other to create the illusion of depth. This makes the cramped quarters appear more spacious than they are. The captain of the *USS Tennessee* told an interviewer, "That's the psychologists looking out for us."

Interior decorators claim that blues and greens are cool colors and that reds and oranges are warm colors. Anecdotal evidence suggests that these colors influence our perception of temperature. In one example, an office was repainted from a drab brown to a bright blue. When winter approached, the employees complained that they were cold even though the indoor office temperature was the same as it had been during previous winters. The temperature was raised 5 degrees, but the complaints persisted. The office was repainted in warm colors, and the employees said they were too hot. The temperature was lowered 5 degrees to where it had been before, and complaints ceased.

If a work area is dingy, then repainting it may improve employee morale. A fresh coat of paint in any color can make workers feel better about their environment. But there is little I-O psychologists can conclude with assurance about the effects of color on employee behavior.

Music

The use of music at work is as old as work itself. Workers traditionally sang on the job, even in noisy factories at the time of the Industrial Revolution. During the late 1800s and early 1900s, quieter industries, such as cigar-making, encouraged singing on the job. Some companies hired musicians to play for the workers, and by the 1930s many organizations supported their own bands and singing groups.

Many claims have been made about the effects of music on productivity and morale. Employees are supposed to be happier and more efficient when they listen to music at work. Studies conducted by firms that supply recorded music support these claims, but such research often lacks scientific rigor and control. Early research on music showed that most employees liked the idea of having music during working hours and believed it would make them more productive. This finding depended partly on the kind of work involved. Music has been found to increase production slightly for assembly-line jobs that are reasonably simple and repetitive. Workers regard this type of job as monotonous and not sufficiently demanding to fully engage their attention. Thus, music can provide a focus for these workers, something to occupy the mind and to help the workday pass more quickly and enjoyably. For more demanding work, there is no evidence that music increases productivity because the complexity of the work requires more concentrated attention.

Most of the music piped into factories, offices, corridors, elevators, and waiting rooms is supplied by Muzak, which has been in business since 1934. The company estimates that its background music is played to 100 million people in more than 250,000 companies in a dozen countries. It has more than a million tunes in its database. Muzak-style music is intended to humanize the work environment by giving people an emotional lift. A different program is created for each type of business and each workday. The tempo corresponds to changes in mood and energy levels and is designed to be more stimulating at midmorning and midafternoon. Critics consider such music to be bland, or even a form of noise pollution.

Temperature and Humidity

We have all experienced the effects of temperature and humidity on our morale, efficiency, and physical well-being. Some of us are happier and have more vitality in cold weather, whereas others prefer hot weather. Some people are depressed by rainy days, and others barely notice them. Most of us work in facilities where temperature and humidity are controlled. But workers in construction, shipbuilding, and other industries are frequently exposed to temperature extremes.

Surveys conducted over a 10-year period by the Center for Building Performance and Design found that the primary complaint of office workers was that their workplace was kept too cold (Napoli, 1998). And what do you think was the second most frequent complaint? Yes, you guessed it—the workplace was too hot.

Climate conditions can influence the quantity and quality of physical production. A research review showed that temperatures around 90°F had no significant effect on mental or cognitive tasks but did correlate with lower perfor-

Wear Your Walkman to Work

NEWSBREAK

You see them on subways, city streets, jogging paths, the beach, and in the college library. Young and old wear the headsets all hours of the day and night. Personal stereos, best known by the trademark of the company that first developed them—the Sony Walkman—bring us music any time and place we want to listen to it.

What about in the workplace? Some employers permit workers to play personal stereos on the job. They claim it contributes to job satisfaction and morale. One large Illinois company wanted to test this idea, to find out what would happen if their office workers were allowed to tune in on the job. Because management wanted scientific proof, they called on a group of psychologists from the University of Illinois at Urbana-Champagne to do what psychologists do best: conduct a study.

For 4 weeks, 75 employees chosen at random brought their personal stereos to work and listened to their favorite music while on the job. A control group of 181 other employees did not. The psychologists administered questionnaires to measure moods, specifically, how nervous, relaxed, enthusiastic, and fatigued the workers felt. They were also questioned about their attitudes toward their jobs and their employer. From supervisors, the psychologists obtained hourly performance data for the workers as well as ratings of job complexity.

At the end of 4 weeks, the results were clear. Those employees permitted to listen to music at work showed statistically significant improvements in job performance and satisfaction. Those who worked without music showed no change in performance or satisfaction. However, there was one confounding variable: Although the use of personal stereos improved job performance for all employees, it was most effective for workers in simpler, less demanding jobs. The psychologists reasoned that for more complex and demanding tasks, there was greater potential for distraction. So, what's the moral of this story? If you have a simple, repetitive job, it's OK to crank up the volume. You'll probably be happier, and so will your boss.

Source: G. R. Oldham, A. Cummings, L. J. Mischel, J. M. Schmidke, & J. Zhou (1995). Listen while you work? Quasi-experimental relations between personal-stereo headset use and employee work responses. *Journal of Applied Psychology, 80,* 547–564.

mance levels on perceptual-motor tasks such as tracking or operating machinery (Ramsey, 1995). The negative effects of high temperatures were also demonstrated in a study comparing a strenuous motor task (lifting) with a sedentary motor task (typing). Subjects in both groups experienced a similar degree of heat stress, showing that even less physically demanding work can be affected by temperature (Chad & Brown, 1995).

Even if production levels hold steady, workers must expend more energy under difficult climate conditions in order to maintain the same output. Usually, they will need more frequent rest breaks. Motivation is also a factor. Highly motivated workers are better able to maintain production under temperature extremes than are poorly motivated workers.

Automated office equipment has been found to interfere with climate-control systems. A single computer terminal does not generate much heat, but when dozens of terminals, printers, and fax machines are operated in the same area, heat and static electricity levels increase. The drier air also leads to complaints about eye irritation from employees who wear contact lenses.

WORK SCHEDULES

A vital part of the overall work environment is the amount of time we spend on the job. There is no standard universal work schedule. The 40-hour workweek common in the United States is not the norm in every country. Americans spend more hours on the job than do workers in other industrialized nations. Employees in the United States work almost 2 weeks longer each year than employees in Japan, and 14 weeks longer each year than workers in Norway. Figure 10–1 shows the annual number of hours worked by each person for a dozen countries, based on data published in 1999 by the International Labor Organization.

A number of alternative work schedules have replaced the traditional 5-day, 40-hour week in which all employees of an organization arrived and left at the same time. We discuss the standard workweek, shift work, and alternative schedules such as permanent part-time employment, the 4-day workweek, and flexible hours (flextime).

Working Hours

At one time in the United States, people routinely worked 10 hours a day, 6 days a week. The 5-day, 40-hour week became the norm in 1938 with the passage of

Country	Hours
United States	1966
Japan	1889
Australia	1867
New Zealand	1838
Canada	1732
Britain	1731
France	1656
Ireland	1656
Switzerland	1643
Germany	1560
Sweden	1552
Norway	1399

FIGURE 10–1. Annual per capita working hours by country.

the Fair Labor Standards Act. The United States became the first country to formally establish a 5-day, 40-hour workweek, but this is not necessarily the most efficient work schedule. Workers have accepted it as normal, but in the past they accepted 60 hours and then 48 hours as normal.

Nominal working hours
The prescribed number of hours employees are supposed to spend on the job; not all of these hours are actually spent performing job tasks.

There is a difference between **nominal working hours** (the prescribed number of hours employees are supposed to spend on the job) and actual working hours (the amount of time employees devote to job duties). The two rarely coincide. Some research shows that employees spend no more than half the workweek actually performing required job tasks. Some of the lost time is scheduled by the company as rest pauses, but most of it is unauthorized and beyond the control of the organization. When employees arrive at the workplace, it may take them a long time to begin work. They may shuffle papers, sharpen pencils, or oil machines (whether needed or not). Throughout the workday employees may visit with co-workers, exceed the length of the lunch break, or linger at the coffee machine. Managers lose time waiting for meetings to begin or for telephone calls to be completed, or they may spend time using their e-mail for personal messages.

An interesting relationship has been documented between nominal and actual working hours. When nominal (prescribed) working hours are increased, actual working hours decrease. In other words, the longer the workday or workweek, the lower the worker productivity. This finding holds even for highly motivated workers. In the early days of World War II in England, patriotic fervor reached a peak. Dangerously low in supplies and equipment, the nation was fighting for survival. The government extended the workweek in defense plants from 56 to 69 1/2 hours. At first, productivity increased 10%, but it soon fell 12% below

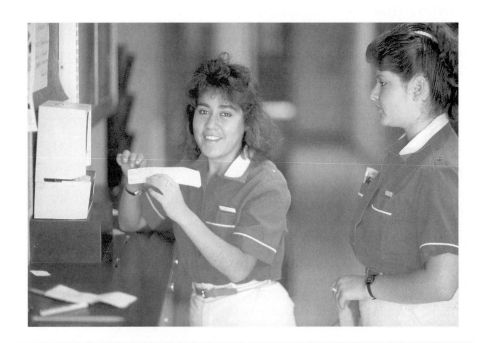

Some jobs require workers to punch a time clock at the beginning and end of each work shift.

the previous level. Other consequences of increasing nominal working hours included greater absenteeism and more frequent accidents. In the 69 1/2-hour workweek, actual working hours were only 51. With the shorter 56-hour workweek, actual working hours had been 53. A study conducted by the U.S. Bureau of Labor Statistics during World War II showed that the 7-day workweek that was adopted by many American companies during the war resulted in no greater production than the 6-day week. One day of the 7 days was lost time.

This relationship between nominal and actual working hours also applies to overtime when employees are asked to work beyond the normal workday for a markedly higher rate of pay. Much of the extra time is unproductive because people tend to adjust to the longer workday by performing at a slower pace. If productivity drops when the number of required working hours is increased, will productivity rise if the workday is shortened? Some research indicates that it will, but other studies show that a decrease in nominal working hours has no effect on actual working hours. In a case of historical interest, during the Great Depression of the 1930s a manufacturing plant reduced nominal working hours by more than 9 hours a week, yet actual working hours fell only 5 hours a week. Another plant reduced the workweek by 10 1/2 hours, and hourly production rose 21%!

Permanent Part-Time Employment

Part-time or half-time employment is the most widespread form of alternative work schedule. More than 25% of the U.S. workforce holds part-time jobs. Part-time employment has grown faster than full-time employment, particularly in service and retail trades. By shifting to part-time employment, organizations reduce the costs of keeping full-time staffs (which require higher salary and benefit packages) and increase their scheduling flexibility.

We noted that full-time employment does not mean that the organization is actually getting a full day's work from each employee. Further, management has recognized that much work, such as writing and independent research, can be performed satisfactorily part time. A lower-level assembly line or clerical job can be performed by two persons, each working half time.

The U.S. Department of Health and Human Services found that supervisors of part-time employees were strongly in favor of part-time employment. A study of welfare caseworkers in Massachusetts who worked 20 hours a week showed that they had a lower turnover rate and a higher caseload contact than did full-time employees. State government agencies in Wisconsin found that actual working hours among permanent part-time social workers, attorneys, and research analysts equaled or exceeded the actual working hours of full-time employees.

Part-time employment is attractive to people with pressing family responsibilities and to disabled persons who have mobility problems. Most part-time employees are women and they tend to be concentrated in lower-level jobs and receive lower rates of pay than do full-time employees. However, increasing numbers of professionals and managers are opting for part-time employment because it gives them the chance to return to school or to explore other career opportunities.

The Four-Day Workweek

Another way to alter the workweek significantly is to reduce it to 4 days. This usually involves 4 days at 10 hours a day (a 40-hour week) or 4 days at 9 hours a day (a 36-hour week with no reduction in pay). Union leaders, management consultants, and many companies that have tried the 4-day workweek are enthusiastic about it. Typically, the initiative to shorten the workweek came not from employees but from management for several reasons. These include the possibility of increasing worker productivity and efficiency, the idea of using the shorter workweek as an incentive to recruit workers, and the hope of reducing absenteeism, which in many organizations is unusually high on Mondays and Fridays.

Comments from managers and employees on the 4-day workweek have been positive. They cite improved job satisfaction and productivity, reduced absenteeism, and easier work scheduling. A nationwide Gallup Poll supported the appeal of the 4-day week. Some 45% of the men surveyed indicated that they would like a 4-day schedule. Women who did not work outside the home opposed the 4-day workweek by a ratio of two to one. Women who did work outside the home were far more favorable to the idea of a 4-day workweek.

A meta-analysis of 39 research studies found that compressed work schedules, such as the 4-day workweek, had a positive effect on job satisfaction in general and on satisfaction with the work schedule in particular. The 4-day workweek did not appear to have an impact on absenteeism rates or production rates. However, supervisors of employees on a 4-day workweek believed that productivity had increased (Baltes, Briggs, Huff, Wright, & Neuman, 1999).

Flexible Work Schedules

Flextime A system of flexible working hours combining core mandatory work periods with elective work periods at the beginning and end of the workday.

Another type of alternative work schedule permits employees to decide for themselves when to begin and end the workday. In the 1960s, several companies in Germany tried a flexible working hours (**flextime**) schedule to deal with traffic congestion at rush hours. Under this plan, the workday is divided into four segments, two of which are mandatory and two optional (see Figure 10–2).

In this example, employees can report to work any time between 7:30 a.m. and 9:00 a.m. and leave any time between 4:00 p.m. and 5:30 p.m. The mandatory work periods are the morning hours from 9:00 a.m. until the lunch break and the afternoon hours from lunch to 4:00 p.m. Thus, employees work a minimum 6 1/2-hour workday. The optional daily maximum is 9 1/2 hours. How long each employee will work is established individually as a function of the company's needs.

Flextime offers several advantages. Rush-hour traffic congestion around plants and offices is reduced. Because employees spend less time and energy commuting, they are often more relaxed at work, more satisfied with their jobs, and more likely to begin work promptly. Many workers make only minor changes in their work habits under a flextime schedule. The inflexible demands of car pools, commuter timetables, and family life hold them to schedules much

FIGURE 10–2.   A typical flextime work schedule.

like those they had before flextime. However, employees believe that having the choice of when to arrive and leave work enhances their personal freedom. The meta-analysis of 39 research studies noted in the previous section also found that flextime schedules decreased absenteeism and improved workers' productivity and their satisfaction with the job and the work schedule.

Flexible working hours appear to be most appropriate for jobs such as research and development, clerical and data-entry, and light and heavy manufacturing. For some assembly-line and shift-work operations, flextime is difficult to implement because of the interdependence of the work teams. Overall, flextime is a fair, sensible, and low-cost alternative work schedule that is popular with employers and employees.

ONLINE!

To see examples of flexible working hours programs used by U.S. government agencies, check out *www.hrsjobs.com/html/flextime/htm.*

Rest Pauses

Ever since the Hawthorne studies, management has recognized the importance of authorized rest breaks. Their beneficial effects have been amply demonstrated, but there is a more insistent reason for granting them. Why? Because employees

Many jobs are repetitive and physically demanding. These workers should be given formal rest periods to reduce boredom and fatigue.

will take breaks whether or not the company sanctions them. If the time is going to be taken anyway, the organization might as well appear benevolent and offer the rest pauses as a fringe benefit.

When authorized rest pauses are introduced, unauthorized breaks decline, though they do not disappear. Other benefits of rest periods include increased morale and productivity and reduced fatigue and boredom. This is another instance of how a decrease in nominal working hours can result in an increase in efficiency.

Workers who engage in heavy physical labor need rest pauses because muscles in continuous use will tire and become less effective. Rest pauses also reduce repetitive motion injuries to hands and wrists. For sedentary and intellectual work, a rest break provides a change of stimulation. It allows boredom to dissipate and provides the opportunity to think about something else or to socialize with co-workers. Rest pauses may also result in more positive attitudes toward management. When a rest program is implemented, workers tend to believe that it is an expression of management's concern for them as individuals.

> **ONLINE!**
>
> Take a break. Look up research on rest pauses at *www.possibility.com/powerpause/studies.html.*

Shift Work

Many industries operate around the clock. Workers in electric and natural gas utilities, transportation, steel, automotive assembly, hospital services, and telecommunications typically work one of three shifts, usually 7:00 a.m. to 3:00 p.m., 3:00 p.m. to 11:00 p.m., or 11:00 p.m. to 7:00 a.m. Some companies assign workers to one shift permanently, whereas others rotate assignments, switching workers each week or month to a different shift. Employees working evening or all-night shifts usually receive extra pay to compensate for the inconvenience of the working hours. Some 25% of the blue-collar and white-collar work forces perform shift work.

How does shift work affect job performance? Research shows that workers are less productive on the all-night shift than on the day shift. They are also more prone to make errors and to have more serious accidents. Nuclear power plant accidents in the United States and in Russia occurred during the night shift. A nuclear power plant in Pennsylvania was closed by the Nuclear Regulatory Commission when night-shift control room personnel were found to be asleep on the job.

The disruption of the normal sleep-wake cycle has physiological and psychological consequences. Humans develop a diurnal rhythm, a regular daily cycle of bodily activities that is consistent from one 24-hour period to the next. When this rhythm is disrupted, the body undergoes dramatic changes and sleep be-

NEWSBREAK

Asleep on the Job? Good for You!

There was a time when you could be fired for falling asleep on the job. But now a growing number of companies are urging their employees to do just that. They're even providing nap lounges and encouraging workers to "power nap" when they feel sleepy. Nike gives its employees access to so-called relaxation rooms and provides pillows, blankets, and alarm clocks. One California computer firm has converted a loft into a cozy room for naps. What's going on here? Why are companies encouraging employees to go to sleep during working hours? The answer is that they will be more alert and efficient when they wake up.

Sleep researchers have demonstrated that no matter how soundly we sleep at night, most of us become drowsy in early afternoon, whether we've eaten heavily at lunchtime or not. A sleepy worker is not efficient or productive and is likely to make mistakes or cause accidents.

Worse, many of us don't get enough sleep at night, so we begin the workday feeling sluggish. A study by the National Sleep Foundation reported that 64% of U.S. workers fail to sleep the recommended 8 hours a night. Some 32% of the people report sleeping fewer than 6 hours per night. As you might expect, this widespread lack of sleep affects how well we perform our jobs.

The same study found that 61% of the population said that a bad night's sleep impairs their decision-making ability, and 37% felt that it prevented them from doing their best work. The obvious antidote is to make up the sleep at work, to take brief power naps during the day to restore alertness and efficiency.

The work of the National Sleep Foundation is changing many corporate cultures. It has a slogan: *"Be productive. Take a nap!"* Why not do your part today!

Sources: J. Brody. New respect for the nap, a pause that refreshes. *New York Times,* January 4, 2000; Naps, all in a day's work. *St. Petersburg (FL) Times,* March 25, 1999.

comes difficult. The effect on sleep is the major complaint of employees on night-shift work; that is, they are unable to sleep during the day because of daylight and household routines. Family life suffers, and everyday activities such as shopping become difficult to schedule. Night-shift workers and those on a rotating-shift schedule report a high incidence of stomach disorders, sleep disorders, cardiovascular complaints, marital problems, and irritability.

A study of 61 nurses in England and Wales found significantly lower moods, alertness, and performance on cognitive tasks on rest days following a night shift as compared to a day shift. Recovery from the negative effects of the night-shift schedule required longer than the 1 day off they received (Totterdell, Spelten, Smith, Barton, & Folkard, 1995).

Fewer problems are encountered with the fixed-shift system than with the rotating-shift system, even when the fixed shift occurs at night. Workers permanently assigned to one shift are more likely to adjust to a new diurnal rhythm. With the rotating-shift system, workers must readjust every week or so, whenever the shift schedule is changed, and this system does not give the body time to adjust to one schedule before being forced to begin another.

There are other ways to alleviate some of the problems associated with shift work. When the rotating-shift system must be used, the changes from one shift to another should be made as seldom as possible—for example, every month instead of every week. Another way to ease the change from one shift to another is to lengthen the time off between shift changes. A longer interim period makes the change less abrupt and allows employees to rest before starting a new schedule. Because the night shift is the most difficult for employees and the least productive for employers, it could be shortened to make it less stressful.

A potentially harmful form of shift work that affects many of us is the erratic work schedule of commercial airline pilots, who often change from night flights to day flights and back, sleeping at irregular intervals and disrupting their bodily rhythms. Studies of civilian and military pilots and flight crews working unusually long and erratic hours (such as 10 to 24 hours continuously) confirm the harmful effects of severe disturbances of diurnal rhythms. The airline personnel reported considerable fatigue, slept poorly following their work periods, and took unauthorized naps in the cockpit for up to 2 hours. Examinations of aircraft flight recorders (so-called black boxes) revealed that deviations in pilot performance correlated positively with subjective feelings of fatigue.

Research conducted by psychologists for NASA's Fatigue Countermeasures Program found that allowing pilots 40-minute rest periods during low workload portions of long flights resulted in significantly increased alertness. Flight crews that were not supposed to nap during the study period did so anyway, although most of the personnel who took unauthorized naps were not aware of having done so (Wald, 1998). Several international airlines now permit cockpit rest breaks.

ONLINE!

For information on all aspects of sleep, including the effects of sleep deprivation, effects of shift work on sleep, and how to get better sleep yourself, log on to the National Sleep Foundation at *www.sleepfoundation.org*.

PSYCHOLOGICAL AND SOCIAL ISSUES

Other important factors in the work environment relate to the nature of the job and its impact on employees. Does your job provide you with a sense of satisfaction and achievement, or does it make you tired, bored, and ill? We have noted that the design of your job can affect your motivation and satisfaction. Some quality-of-work-life programs have been successful in improving morale and motivation, but jobs designed to be so simple that they make no demands on our intelligence, need for achievement, or attention will lead to boredom, fatigue, and inefficiency.

Job Simplification

Simplified, fragmented, and repetitive work affects mental and physical health. For example, assembly-line workers complain more about their physical health and visit company medical facilities more often than workers who do less repetitive work. Psychologists suggest that people who hold such jobs on a rigid work schedule are more anxious, depressed, and irritable than workers doing the same kinds of jobs on a more flexible schedule. Simplified and repetitive work can lead to the deterioration in cognitive functioning usually associated with old age. These workers are prone to absentmindedness and disorientation.

The history of **job simplification** dates from the beginnings of mass production systems in the early twentieth century. If relatively expensive consumer goods such as automobiles were to be produced cost-effectively in sufficient quantities to meet consumer demand, then old-style production methods, such as building each unit by hand, would have to change. Mass production called for product consistency and standardization so that parts would be interchangeable. It also required fractionation of job tasks. It was no longer economically or technically feasible for one person to make an entire product. The work had to be meticulously divided so that each worker produced only a small part of the finished product. The ideal was to reduce every manufacturing process to the simplest elements that could be mastered by an unskilled or semiskilled employee.

Job simplification The reduction of manufacturing jobs to the simplest components that can be mastered by unskilled or semiskilled workers.

Job simplification offered tremendous economic advantages to industry and to consumers, permitting the lowest possible cost per unit produced. When Henry Ford established his automobile assembly line, he was able to sell cars at a price within reach of people who previously could not afford them. The same was true for other consumer goods. The factory-produced chair in which you are sitting costs considerably less than a chair handmade by a skilled furniture craftsperson. This was an additional advantage of job simplification: Industry no longer had to rely on the skilled trades, the workers who required years of apprenticeship, expected high wages, and were apt to be independent of mind. The typical assembly line could be staffed by workers who had little skill and could be quickly trained to perform the job. The process made workers more docile and easier to manage. Because they had few marketable skills, they knew they could easily be replaced. Workers were as interchangeable as the parts they produced.

There is no denying that job simplification had a stimulating impact on the American economy. More jobs became available, and people had more money to buy the plentiful consumer goods. The more people bought, the more factories had to be built, which, in turn, meant even more jobs. New products required additional businesses to advertise, sell, and service them. Such economic growth could not have occurred if production methods had remained limited to the handcrafted approach.

Assembly-line workers have paid a price for their role in this industrial development. The farther removed workers are from the finished product, the less meaning and value they attach to their jobs. The carpenter who shaped a table from a piece of lumber knew the pride and fulfillment of achievement and the challenge of using skill and imagination. There is little challenge and satisfaction in operating a machine that attaches bumpers to automobiles day after day, year after year. The worker is an adjunct to the machine, pressing a button or pushing a lever or watching in case something goes wrong. The work has little meaning and quickly becomes frustrating and monotonous. Workers soon grow apathetic, morale declines, and the quantity and quality of production deteriorate.

Job simplification also affects white-collar and managerial jobs because computers have turned many offices into electronic assembly lines. In white-collar jobs, work is increasingly fragmented and simplified. As a result, office workers are becoming cheaper to train and easier to replace.

We noted in Chapter 9 how jobs can be enlarged, enriched, and expanded to provide employees with greater responsibility and challenge. The quality-of-work-life programs we discussed are real-world examples of making jobs more complex rather than simpler. Expanding the job has clear benefits for both employees and employers.

Boredom and Monotony

Two inevitable consequences of job fractionation and simplification—boredom and monotony—are important components of the psychological work environment. Boredom results from the continuous performance of a repetitive and uninteresting activity and can lead to restlessness, discontent, and a draining of interest and energy. However, what is boring for one person may be exciting for another. Although most people find assembly-line work to be monotonous, for example, others do not. And some workers in jobs that appear to be challenging also report feelings of boredom. The relevant factor is motivation. The data-entry clerk who is highly motivated to process entries without making errors will be less bored than the worker who lacks this motivation.

One obvious way to alleviate boredom is to enlarge the scope of the job, to make it more complex, stimulating, and challenging. Management can also alter work schedules and the physical and social conditions of the workplace to reduce boredom. Attention to noise reduction, lighting, and pleasant surroundings can help combat the negative effects of repetitive and monotonous work. A congenial informal work group helps, as do rest pauses to provide a change of activity. The greater the change in activity during rest pauses or lunch breaks, the less disruptive will be the effects of boredom.

Fatigue

Psychologists describe two types of fatigue: psychological fatigue, which is similar to boredom, and physiological fatigue, which is caused by excessive use of the muscles. Both types of fatigue can cause poor job performance and lead to errors, accidents, and absenteeism. Prolonged or heavy physical labor produces measurable physiological changes. People whose jobs require heavy lifting and hauling consistently show cardiovascular, metabolic, and muscle fatigue as well as a decline in the ability to maintain their initial productivity level.

Psychological or subjective fatigue is more difficult to assess but is no less disturbing to employees. We are all aware of experiencing strain, irritability, and weakness when we are excessively tired, and we may find it difficult to concentrate, think coherently, and work effectively.

On-the-job research has shown that productivity parallels reported feelings of fatigue. High reported fatigue is a reliable indicator that production will shortly decline. With most physically demanding work, employees say that they are most tired at the beginning of the work period, just before the lunch break, and again at the end of the workday. Thus, fatigue does not build up over the course of the work period but appears and disappears throughout the working hours. This suggests that factors other than physical labor (motivation, for example) can influence feelings of fatigue. It often happens that a person leaves the job at the end of the shift feeling exhausted but finds that the fatigue disappears on arriving home and anticipating some pleasurable activity.

Research on physiological fatigue shows that workers can undertake greater amounts of physical labor when the work pace is more gradual. Too rapid a rate of heavy work dissipates the body's energy too quickly so that the worker must then function at a slower pace for the remainder of the work period. An analogy can be made with long-distance runners who pace themselves so that they do not consume all their energy before covering the desired distance.

Rest periods are necessary for jobs that involve heavy physical labor and should be taken before fatigue is complete. The greater the amount of fatigue at the time of the rest break, the longer the recovery period must be. For some jobs, more frequent rest breaks are needed. Rest periods must provide total relaxation, not merely a stoppage of work. It is the manual laborer, more than the office worker, who will benefit from pleasant cafeterias and comfortable lounges in which to relax.

Ethnic Harassment

Another social-psychological condition of the workplace that affects productivity, job satisfaction, and emotional and physical health is on-the-job harassment, whether based on race, ethnicity, gender, or other personal characteristics. Harassment may come from co-workers or supervisors, or it may be part of the corporate culture.

The population of a typical workplace, like the population of many a nation, has become increasingly diverse. As organizations employ more people of various racial and ethnic groups, harassment is on the rise. Ethnic harassment is an obvious source of stress. It may be manifested at work as slurs or derogatory comments about a person's racial or ethnic group and may result in the exclusion of the person from work groups or social activities.

A study of 575 Hispanic men and women provided evidence of harassment on the job. Verbal slurs, derogatory comments, and offensive ethnic jokes were found to be more common than behaviors intended to exclude a person on ethnic grounds. People who were targets of verbal harassment reported a lowering of their sense of psychological well-being (Schneider, Hitlan, & Radhakrishnan, 2000).

ONLINE!

See how a major U.S. university deals with racial and ethnic harassment at *www.princeton.edu/ombuds/racialh.html*.

Gender Harassment

Women employees at all levels in an organization face harassment on the job ranging from suggestive remarks and obscene jokes to threats of job loss and physical assaults. A distinction can be made between sexual harassment and gender harassment. *Sexual harassment* involves unwanted sexual attention and coercion. *Gender harassment* refers to behavior that reflects an insulting, hostile, and degrading attitude toward women. Thus, gender harassment does not necessarily involve sexual harassment. Gender harassment is directed toward all women, whereas sexual harassment is targeted toward a specific woman.

> **HOTLINE!**
>
> To report incidents of sexual harassment and to receive advice on dealing with it, call the toll-free Job Survival Hotline maintained by Nine to Five, a working women's advocacy group. The number is 800-522-0925.

Gender and sexual harassment have been found in many workplaces and have resulted in costly and embarrassing lawsuits for a number of prominent organizations. Chevron paid $2.2 million to four women employees who were further harassed following their initial filing of sexual harassment charges. Mitsubishi was ordered to pay $34 million to several hundred women employees who charged that the company's Illinois plant failed to respond to their sexual harassment complaints.

A review of harassment claims filed with the Equal Employment Opportunity Commission (EEOC) showed that several types of companies were likely to be the target of lawsuits because they ignored reports of harassment. These include family-owned businesses, firms too small to maintain human resources or personnel departments, factories located in rural areas, and so-called male-dominated industries such as construction (Peirce, Smolinski, & Rosen, 1998). Younger women in low-level jobs, single or divorced women, and women in predominantly male environments report more harassment than do middle-age or older married women whose jobs are not in male-dominated organizations.

Like ethnic harassment, gender harassment can lead to physical ailments (gastrointestinal disorders, headaches, and weight loss) as well as psychological problems (fear, depression, anxiety, and loss of self-esteem). It also has a negative effect on job satisfaction and productivity. A study of 217 women employees at a large midwestern university showed that those who were victims of sexual harassment reported decreased levels of job satisfaction and general life satisfaction as well as increased levels of job withdrawal and stress (Glomb, Munson, Hulin, Bergman, & Drasgow, 1999). Multigroup research with 459 women at a large utility, 300 women employed by a university, and 419 women working for an agribusiness organization confirmed the harmful physical, psychological, and work consequences of sexual and gender harassment (Magley, Hulin, Fitzgerald, & DeNardo, 1999). Many other studies link harassment to low job satisfaction and high stress. A survey of office workers found that 70% reported harassment on the job, but it showed no differences in the frequency or consequences of that harassment for white women and nonwhite women (Munson, Hulin, & Drasgow, 2000).

ONLINE!

For current news about sexual harassment and links to related Web sites, visit *www.fullcoverage.yahoo.com/fc/us/sexual_harassment.* Remember the U.S. Navy's infamous Tailhook sexual harassment scandal? For a detailed review, try these sites: *www.inform.umd.edu/edres/topic,* *www.womens studies/gender/issues,* or *www.sexualharassment/tailhook-9.*

Telecommuting: The Virtual Workplace at Home

We have noted the growing flexibility in work scheduling in recent years. Now a similar flexibility has come to characterize the workplace itself. Many employees work at home, thanks to advances in personal computers, telecommunications, and fax machines. This move toward telecommuting—the decentralizing of

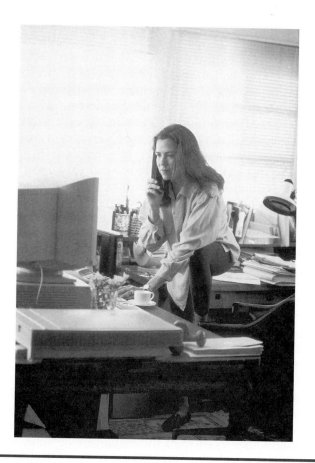

A typical telecommuter, operating a business from her home.

work—has affected hundreds of U.S. companies in life insurance, data processing, financial services, airline and hotel reservations, and mail-order merchandising. The Bureau of National Affairs estimates that more than 15 million people are performing such jobs at home using company-supplied equipment.

The opportunity to work at home is so widespread that some modern houses and apartment buildings are being constructed with built-in high-speed computer connections as a selling feature. As broadband Internet access becomes more widely available, home computers will become as fast as those in any office. Telecommuting is particularly attractive to employees with day-care or dependent-care problems and to disabled workers. Approximately half of all home-based employees are men and half are women.

Companies that provide for telecommuting cite gains in productivity, reduced costs for office overhead, and, obviously, a decline in absenteeism. People working at home may have fewer interruptions than people working in offices and may be able to concentrate better. They can perform their job in bad weather or when feeling poorly, whereas office-based employees in those situations might hesitate to come to work. Research at IBM comparing 157 virtual-office telecommuters with 89 in-house office employees found that telecommuting was associated with high productivity. Women employees in virtual offices were more productive than men employees in virtual offices, but both groups were pleased that they didn't have to spend time commuting. They enjoyed being able to schedule their work outside traditional office hours, and they reported fewer distractions and a more comfortable working environment (Hill, Miller, Weiner, & Colihan, 1998).

Los Angeles County administrators estimated that their telecommuting program involving 2,600 workers saved $11 million a year in increased productivity, reduced absenteeism, decreased overtime pay, and reduced office space. They also claimed that the program cut commuting time by 1.4 million hours, thus eliminating 7,500 tons of carbon monoxide from car exhausts. An AT&T poll of 1,005 home-based workers found that 80% believed they were more productive than when working in the company offices. In addition, 61% said they got sick less often, and 79% appreciated the chance to wear casual clothes while working. Surveys at other companies found increases up to 30% in productivity as well as a significant reduction in the nonproductive work time spent socializing. Telecommuting does not appear to be related to any decrease in an employee's opportunity for promotion.

Not everyone likes the idea of working at home, however. Some people miss the social interaction. Others are not sufficiently disciplined to work steadily without supervision. Some spouses object to having a partner work at home. Children may provide an additional distraction. Some managers believe they will lose their authority over subordinates if the subordinates are not physically present. And labor unions are concerned about the declining loyalty of members who do not work together on the job.

Some telecommuters feel pressured to work harder than they did in their traditional offices. Others say that by working at home, they are never free of the job. When the phone or fax or e-mail summons them after working hours, they feel compelled to respond. Nearly 20% of telecommuting programs fail for these reasons. Another reason for unsuccessful programs is that some teleworkers do not get the technical support they need from the employers. Despite these difficulties, many employees prefer working at home. Human resources managers already view telecommuting as the most important workplace trend of the twenty-first century.

Working the Night Shift by Choice

Shift work can have harmful effects because it tends to disrupt the body's normal diurnal rhythm. People who work on rotating shifts are usually less productive and more prone to make errors on the night shift. They have trouble sleeping during the day and report a high incidence of physical, emotional, marital, and family problems.

Research has shown that employees who work on a permanent shift arrangement report fewer difficulties, even when that shift is at night. A British psychologist decided to investigate whether employees who volunteered to work at night experienced fewer problems than did those who worked at night as part of a rotating shift arrangement.

To secure subjects, the psychologist contacted hospitals in England and Wales, inviting nurses and midwives to participate in the study. A total of 587 volunteered (530 females, 55 males, 2 unspecified). Of these, 240 employees served permanently on night-shift duty, and 347 worked on a rotating shift basis. The permanent night-shift subjects were significantly older than were those on the rotating shift, with a mean age of 38 years versus 30 years. Also, 75% of the permanent night-shift subjects were married; only 59% of the rotating-shift workers were married.

The subjects were given the Standard Shift-work Index survey, which contained items designed to assess the severity of health, sleep, and social disruptions experienced as a result of shift work. Six months later, the subjects completed additional questionnaires to assess several factors, including psychological and physical health, chronic fatigue, anxiety, neuroticism, sleep quality, job satisfaction, "morningness" (a preference for morning rather than evening activities), and their reasons for working their particular shift arrangement.

The results showed that nurses on the rotating shift reported significantly more social disruptions and sleep problems than did nurses on permanent night shifts. There were no significant differences between the two groups on measures of psychological or physical health. Nurses on the permanent night shift did report significantly greater job satisfaction than those on the rotating shift.

Overall, subjects on permanent night-shift duty had fewer health, sleep, social, and domestic problems. Also, those who had chosen that shift had fewer problems than did those who had been assigned to the shift. Thus, the psychologist suggested that employees who choose to work at night are better able to tolerate the effects of this arrangement than are those whose night-shift job is not their own choice.

Think About It

1. Describe the effects of shift work on job performance and on physical and psychological well-being, as reported by the research described in this chapter.
2. How might the differences in age and marital status between the two groups in this study have influenced the findings?
3. If you were in charge of a factory that had to operate 24/7, what steps would you take to alleviate the problems related to shift work?
4. What characteristics of a job or work environment might be altered to minimize the harmful effects of shift work?
5. Describe the consequences of the long and erratic hours often worked by airline flight crews. What steps can be taken to relieve these problems?

Source: J. Barton (1994). Choosing to work at night. *Journal of Applied Psychology, 79,* 449–454.

SUMMARY

Physical working conditions include factors such as the location of the factory or office building, parking facilities, heating and air-conditioning systems, elevators, child-care facilities, cafeterias, and rest rooms. **Environmental psychology** is concerned with the impact of these workplace features on employee behaviors and attitudes. In the landscaped office employees are grouped in functional units with no floor-to-ceiling barriers.

Light distribution and glare must be considered in designing illumination for work spaces. Noise in the work area can lead to deafness and to physiological effects such as increased muscle tension and blood pressure. Color is a useful coding device and can create differing illusions of size and temperature and improve the aesthetic appearance of the workplace. Some employees like music on the job, but research shows that it does not influence productivity. Optimal temperature and humidity ranges have been established for different kinds of workplaces. The comfort level of a workspace also depends on humidity level and air circulation.

Temporal working conditions include the number of hours worked and how those hours are arranged. Much scheduled work time is lost to unauthorized breaks. When **nominal working hours** are reduced, production tends to increase. Part-time employment offers opportunities to combine career, family, educational, leisure, and other pursuits, and may result in greater productivity. The 4-day workweek seems to result in lower absenteeism and higher morale but has little effect on productivity. **Flextime** is popular with employees but has little effect on productivity or job satisfaction. Rest pauses will be taken whether or not they are officially sanctioned. They are necessary in manual labor to rest the muscles. For sedentary workers, rest pauses provide a change of pace and help alleviate boredom. Shift work disrupts the body's diurnal rhythm and can lead to social and psychological difficulties. In general, productivity is lower on the night shift; serious accidents and errors are higher.

Social-psychological working conditions relate to the design of the job and its effects on employees. **Job simplification** has made many jobs so unchallenging that they are boring and lead to psychological and physiological fatigue that reduces productivity. Repetitive, boring work is also tiring. Boredom can be relieved by enlarging the job scope, improving working conditions, and scheduling rest pauses. Ethnic and gender harassment occur frequently in the workplace and have harmful physical and emotional effects on their victims. They reduce job satisfaction and productivity.

Computers and telecommunications advances make working at home possible for many types of employees. Telecommuting is associated with higher productivity, lower absenteeism, and corporate savings on office space.

KEY TERMS

environmental psychology	job simplification
flextime	nominal working hours

ADDITIONAL READING

Bell, P., Green, T., Fisher, J., & Baum, A. (2001). *Environmental psychology*, 5th ed. Ft. Worth, TX: Harcourt College Publishers. A standard textbook on environmental psychology; covers the influence of physical workplace features on employee behaviors and attitudes.

Hill, E. J., Miller, B. C., Weiner, S. P., & Colihan, S. P. (1998). Influence of the virtual office on aspects of work and work/life balance. *Personnel Psychology, 51*, 667–683. Studies issues of working hours, productivity, and morale among IBM employees in virtual office settings.

Hochschild, A. R. (1997). *The time bind: When work becomes home and home becomes work.* New York: Metropolitan/Holt. Describes an organization in which employees routinely put in 10-hour workdays and identify more with colleagues and subordinates than with family members, deriving greater social support from office relationships than from relationships outside the workplace.

Peirce, E., Smolinski, C. A., & Rosen, B. (1998). Why sexual harassment complaints fall on deaf ears. *Academy of Management Executive, 12*(3), 41–54. Discusses reasons why many organizations are slow to respond to employees' complaints of sexual harassment, forcing victims to seek help through the court system.

Rothausen, T. J., Gonzalez, J. A., Clarke, N. E., & O'Dell, L. L. (1998). Family-friendly backlash. *Personnel Psychology, 51*, 685–706. Discusses the positive and negative effects on employees of employer-provided on-site child care facilities.

Safety, Violence, and Health in the Workplace

The shops, offices, and factories in which we work can be dangerous places. Every year some 5,000 accidental deaths occur on the job. The number of disabling injuries, although not fully documented, is thought to be around 4 million each year. Research by the Bureau of Labor Statistics indicates that for every disabling work injury reported, 10 are not reported by companies attempting to hide a poor safety record. The monetary cost of these injuries is staggering, not only to employees and their organizations, but also to the nation as a whole. Billions of dollars are forfeited through lost time and wages and paid out in medical benefits and workers' compensation claims.

The health of workers in some types of jobs can be undermined by their exposure to toxic chemicals in the workplace. Disabling illnesses caused or aggravated by these on-the-job conditions generally do not kill or maim as suddenly or dramatically as accidents, but they impose emotional and economic costs, shortening the lives of thousands of workers.

Although accidents are the primary cause of death on the job, murder is the second; for women employees it is the leading factor, accounting for 42% of women's on-the-job fatalities. Injuries from deliberate acts of violence are becoming more widespread.

In this chapter we examine these and other aspects of workplace health and safety, discussing what I-O psychologists have learned about accidents and violence on the job and what organizations can do about the problem. We deal with alcohol and drug abuse, both of which have adverse effects on employee health, safety, and job performance. We also discuss health problems related to the use of computers in the workplace.

WORK-RELATED HEALTH PROBLEMS

The toll from work-related diseases is as shocking as the accident rate. These illnesses are more insidious than a sudden, traumatic accident because they develop slowly over years before the worker experiences physical symptoms. For example, coal miners develop a unique respiratory condition called black lung disease, a progressively crippling disorder caused by prolonged inhalation of coal dust. Chemical industries pose health perils to their workers, dangers that are not fully known. Up to 10 million workers are exposed daily to chemicals for which safe thresholds have not been established. The Environmental Protection Agency (EPA) has designated as toxic more than 16,000 chemical substances regularly used in the workplace. Some 150 of these are neurotoxins; that is, they cause damage to the human brain and nervous system.

Miners, mill workers, and shipyard workers are exposed to asbestos on the job, facing the danger of lung cancer at seven times the national rate. Textile workers are at risk for brown lung disease, caused by inhaling cotton dust. Medical technicians face dangers from radiation exposure. Office workers face the potentially harmful effects of indoor pollutants.

Astronauts working in the International Space Station report a variety of symptoms, including nausea and headaches, which have been traced to chemical fumes and an accumulation of deadly carbon dioxide. Chemists employed by the BP-Amoco research center near Chicago, Illinois, were developing a rare form of brain cancer at eight times the national average. It was traced to two chemical agents used routinely in their work. The American Academy of Asthma estimates that approximately 15% of the asthma sufferers in the United States

The Sick Building Syndrome

Many of us spend our working days sealed off from fresh air, trapped in closed environments. We can't open the windows—in many buildings they're not designed to open—and we breathe only filtered cooled or heated air. The cooling and heating systems in modern office buildings may be cost-efficient to operate, but the results can be dangerous. What we inhale can make us sick.

According to the World Health Organization, the physical complaints brought on by these artificial environments include eye, ear, and throat irritations, dry nasal membranes, skin inflammations, fatigue, headaches, nausea, and dizziness. Consider a few examples. In a sealed office building in San Francisco, California, most of the 250 employees complained of headaches, sinus problems, allergic skin reactions, and general discomfort shortly after the building opened. The symptoms disappeared when the air-filtration system was modified to allow more fresh air to circulate. In another new building, workers became dazed and stuporous most afternoons, especially on hot days. The problem was traced to the roof, where melting tar released fumes that were drawn into the air-conditioning system and dispersed throughout the building. Bacterial infections have also been transmitted through ventilation and air-conditioning systems.

When hundreds of employees in a $37-million, 10-story county office complex in Florida developed symptoms of asthma, the building had to be abandoned. Experts concluded that construction flaws, a faulty air-conditioning system, a leaky roof, and vinyl wallpaper had combined to make the building a breeding ground for mildew and other contaminants.

Sealed buildings contain an alarming number of chemicals that are not dissipated or diluted by fresh air. Solvents, adhesives, cleaning fluids, fire-retardant materials, paint additives, formaldehyde in insulation, and chemicals in carpeting, wall coverings, and draperies can all be toxic. Copy machines produce ozone, which has been linked to headaches and upper respiratory tract infections. Solvents in carbonless paper are dangerous. Long-term exposure to electronic equipment has been related to headaches, eye problems, and neurological disorders. Harmful levels of microwaves and other sources of radiation have been linked to eye damage, memory loss, thyroid dysfunction, and leukemia. Perhaps some buildings should be labeled: *Caution: Working here may be hazardous to your health!*

For information on the sick building syndrome, visit *www.epa.gov/iaq/pubs/sbs.html.*

acquired their disease from chemicals on the job such as latex, nickel, chrome, and mercury. Occupational asthma has now become the single most common work-related respiratory disorder.

An alarming increase in the incidence of job-related cancers among women has been documented among textile workers and workers at dry-cleaning plants. Breast cancer is on the increase among nurses and medical technicians who deal with X-rays and chemotherapy agents. A higher than normal rate of spontaneous abortion (miscarriage) has been found among oncology nurses and among women working in the chemical industry. Table 11–1 lists some frequently used substances, their health effects, and the types of workers who are regularly endangered.

TABLE 11–1   Hazardous Substances and On-the-Job Diseases

Potential Dangers	Potential Diseases	Workers Exposed
Arsenic	Lung cancer, lymphoma	Smelter, chemical, oil-refinery workers; insecticide makers and sprayers—estimated 660,000 exposed
Asbestos	White-lung disease (asbestosis); cancer of lungs and lining of lungs; cancer of other organs	Miners; millers; textile, insulation and shipyard workers—estimated 1.6 million exposed
Benzene	Leukemia; aplastic anemia	Petrochemical and oil-refinery workers; dye users; distillers; painters; shoemakers—estimated 600,000 exposed
Bischloromethylether (BCME)	Lung cancer	Industrial chemical workers
Coal dust	Black-lung disease	Coal miners—estimated 208,000 exposed
Coke-oven emissions	Cancer of lungs, kidneys	Coke-oven workers—estimated 30,000 exposed
Cotton dust	Brown-lung disease (byssinosis); chronic bronchitis; emphysema	Textile workers—estimated 600,000 exposed
Lead	Kidney disease; anemia; central-nervous-system damage; sterility; birth defects	Metal grinders; lead-smelter workers; lead storage-battery workers—estimated 835,000 exposed
Radiation	Cancer of thyroid, lungs and bone; leukemia; reproductive effects (spontaneous abortion, genetic damage)	Medical technicians; uranium miners; nuclear-power and atomic workers
Vinyl chloride	Cancer of liver, brain	Plastic-industry workers—estimated 10,000 directly exposed

Note. Adapted from *Healthy People in Unhealthy Places: Stress and Fitness at Work* (p. 90) by K. R. Pelletier, 1984, New York: Delacorte.

We noted earlier that more than 5,000 workers are killed by accidents on the job every year and that many millions more are injured. These figures do not include those killed or injured commuting to and from the workplace. More than 90% of the employees killed on the job are men, though they constitute little more than half of the workforce. There is an obvious reason for this occurrence: more men than women work in construction and heavy industry, where an accident can have the most severe consequences. More men than women work as long-distance truck drivers, an occupation that contributes to 20% of all on-the-job fatalities every year.

Obviously, some jobs are more dangerous than others, which means that some workers are subject to greater risk of injury or death at work. Not surprisingly, exposure to a hazardous work environment can be stressful. This was demonstrated in a questionnaire study of 207 EMT (emergency medical technician) firefighters. The perceived risk of their work was significantly and positively related to physical and psychological symptoms of stress. Firefighters who were most familiar with the risks of their job were also the least satisfied with their work (McLain, 1995).

In 1970, the U.S. Congress passed the Occupational Safety and Health Act establishing the Occupational Safety and Health Administration (OSHA) in the Department of Labor. OSHA's purpose is to assure safe working conditions by developing and enforcing federal safety standards and by sponsoring research on the causes and prevention of accidents and diseases in the workplace.

Although progress has been made, OSHA has been so poorly funded that it has not been able to carry out its mandate to make our workplaces safer. More than 30 years after OSHA was established, it still has so few safety inspectors that on average a company can expect to be visited only once every 84 years.

ACCIDENT STATISTICS

We noted in Chapter 2 that statistics do not lie but that sometimes the people who use statistics distort ideas in their own interests, backing up the distortions with data. This is the situation with accident statistics. The problem is finding a precise, acceptable definition of an accident, which is not as ridiculous as it sounds.

How severe must an accident be for it to be included in an organization's accident statistics? Suppose a bakery worker drops a 100-pound sack of sugar. Is this an accident? Technically, yes. However, whether the company lists it as an accident depends on the consequences, not on the act itself. If the sack does not split and spill sugar all over the equipment and if no one is hurt, the episode will not be recorded as an accident. But what if the sack falls on the worker's foot and breaks a few bones? Is this considered an accident? Not necessarily. Many companies would not list this as an accident, even though the worker is injured and requires medical treatment. The worker may not be able to walk for a while, but if the company provides a desk job until the injury heals, then the employee will not have lost time from work. So here we have an accident that results in an injury, yet it will not be included in the accident statistics, and the company's safety record will remain intact. The definition of an accident in this case depends on whether the injured worker must miss time from work.

A few years ago, a large U.S. meat-packing firm was fined nearly $3 million for failing to report more than 1,000 job-related injuries among its workers.

Statistics on railroad accidents investigated by a Washington-based journalist contradicted official government reports. Where Amtrak cited 494 injuries in 25 train wrecks, the independent journalist found 1,338. It is this failure to record all job-related injuries, not just those that keep workers off the job, that led the Bureau of Labor Statistics to conclude that accidents are significantly underreported.

Incomplete reporting makes research on the causes and prevention of accidents more difficult. The statistics provided by business and industry show the results of only a small proportion of accidents and provide little information on their causes. By concentrating on lost-time accidents, the data provide an inaccurate picture of overall safety patterns.

An organization likes to boast about a good safety record. It shows that the company is a caring employer, doing all it can to promote a safe working environment for its employees. To preserve a good safety record and a favorable public image, a company may resort to extreme measures such as closed-door investigations, incomplete reporting, and outright distortion of facts. However, sometimes it is the employees who distort the facts. Some fail to report minor accidents for fear of acquiring a reputation as careless or accident-prone. Others fear disciplinary action if the accident was their fault because they failed to follow prescribed operating procedures or to activate safety devices.

Much research confirms the tendency to cite the employee as the cause of the accident rather than extenuating circumstances or defects in the working environment. Blaming the worker also reduces the company's potential legal liability. A study of 2,012 employees and 243 supervisors in a utility company found that supervisors were far more likely to attribute the cause of an accident to the worker than were the workers themselves. Workers were more likely to blame the working conditions (Hoffman & Stetzer, 1998). However, we shall see later in this chapter that most accidents do result from human error.

The underreporting and cover-up of accidents has been documented in many countries. In Japan, workers tend to conceal evidence of job-related injuries because of personal shame. To avoid losing face, Japanese workers attempt to hide even major injuries such as broken bones or to insist that they occurred at home. Managers conspire to conceal workplace injuries because they may represent negligence on their part as well.

CAUSES OF ACCIDENTS

Human error is the factor responsible for most accidents, whether they occur in the workplace, on the highway, or in the home. For example, an analysis of accidents that occurred on the flight decks of U.S. Navy aircraft carriers (an unusually dangerous workplace) showed that 90% of them were caused by human error (Shappell, 1995). However, conditions of the work environment and the nature of the job tasks can also contribute to accidents.

Workplace Factors

Workplace conditions that affect employee safety include type of industry, hours of work, lighting, temperature, equipment design, safety devices, and social pressure.

Type of Industry.   The frequency and severity of accidents vary as a function of type of industry. A steel mill provides more opportunities for accidents than does a bank. The greater the physical demands made on the worker, the higher the accident rate. Also, stressful and tiring work seems to result in more accidents.

Industries such as construction, highway transportation, timber, and mining are high in frequency and severity of accidents. Industries such as warehousing, aircraft and automobile manufacturing, and communications have a low frequency and severity of accidents. Cement and steel companies report a low frequency of accidents, but when accidents do occur, they are usually severe. Electric utilities also record few accidents, but these tend to be severe because of the high voltages involved. Wholesale and retail businesses have high accident rates, but lost-time injuries are rare. Data for high-risk industries are shown in Table 11–2.

Hours of Work.   We might assume that the higher the number of hours worked, the higher the accident rate, but research does not provide clear support for this idea. However, shift work seems to be related to accident rates. In general, fewer accidents occur during the night shift than during the day shift, although night shift accidents, when they do occur, are usually more serious. This situation may be related to level of illumination. The artificial lighting provided at night can be better for work than the natural lighting conditions during the day.

Research conducted on the U.S. nuclear power industry found that the more hours of overtime worked, the higher the frequency of safety problems and procedure violations. These errors can easily lead to serious accidents if not caught in time (Baker, Olson, & Morisseau, 1994).

Lighting.   Good lighting can lead to a reduction in accidents. The insurance industry estimates that poor lighting is a causal factor in one fourth of all industrial

TABLE 11–2   High-Risk Industries

Industry	Injury Rate per 100 Full-time Workers
Meat packing plants	33.4
Mobile home manufacturing plants	29.8
Vending machine manufacturing plants	28.1
Wooden roof supports manufacturing plants	27.1
Sugarcane processing plants	26.2
Wood buildings prefabricators	26.0
Scrap rubber reclamation plants	25.7
Sawmills	25.4
Boat builders and repairers	24.2
Plumbing fixture manufacturers	23.5

Note. Data from Bureau of Labor Statistics.

accidents. Accidents are higher in plants that continue production through dusk before the nighttime lighting is turned on. Dusk is also a time of frequent automobile accidents. The relationship between level of illumination and accident rates in industry has been firmly established. An alert management can easily correct the problem of a poorly lit work area.

Temperature.   Studies of factory workers show that accident rates are lowest when the workplace temperature is maintained at 68° to 70°F. Accidents increase when the temperature varies significantly, either warmer or cooler. Studies of coal miners show that minor accidents are three times more frequent under high temperatures (approaching 85°F) than under low temperatures (approaching 62°F). Workers seem to become more careless under the discomfort of higher temperatures. Older workers are more affected than younger workers by climatic extremes and are more likely to have accidents at higher temperatures.

Equipment Design.   Another physical factor related to accidents is the design of the tools, equipment, and machines used on the job. For example, if an engineer locates a stop button where it is difficult to reach, this can have deadly consequences for the worker who needs to shut down the machine immediately. Poor placement of switches and controls, inadequate warning lights for system malfunctions, and dials that are difficult to read have all been blamed for accidents.

Engineering psychologists strive to match equipment requirements with the capabilities of the human operators (see Chapter 13). Their work on safe workplaces and equipment has been highly effective, particularly with regard to cumulative trauma disorders and repetitive motion injuries such as carpal tunnel syndrome. These injuries are caused by continuous and repeated motions of hands and wrists and can affect shoulders and back as well. Repetitive motion injuries are prevalent among office workers using computer terminals and among certain types of factory workers. Redesigning keyboards, providing posture chairs and armrests, and allowing rest pauses are all effective in reducing repetitive motion injuries.

As an example of how equipment and tool redesign can reduce accidents, consider the case of a large meat-packing plant. These plants have high injury rates primarily because the work involves the constant use of knives. Joint management-worker teams were organized to investigate the jobs of all 800 workers in the plant, with the goal of reducing the number of accidents. The teams altered the shape and sharpness of the knives and redesigned the handles to change the wrist position. They adjusted the height of the workstations to reduce bending, designed conveyer systems to eliminate lifting and carrying, and provided floor mats to reduce the fatigue caused by standing throughout the work period. These changes resulted in significant reductions in the number and severity of cumulative trauma disorders and in lost production time attributable to accidents (May & Schwoerer, 1994).

Part of the reason for the success of this program in the meat-packing plant was the participation of the workers. They were actively involved in redesigning their work environment to make their jobs safer, less fatiguing, and easier to perform. Here we see another instance where change in the workplace is much better accepted when the workers have a say in decisions regarding that change.

Cumulative trauma disorders are also seen in grocery store checkout clerks who are required to make frequent repetitive wrist movements using electronic scanners. Every product must be moved over or in front of the scanner so that the price of the item will be registered. A comparison of 19 combinations of scanners and checkout stands, using both experienced and inexperienced cashiers, showed that a checkout station that allows the cashier to sit while working causes severe pressure on the back and shoulders.

The optimum workstation design for checkout clerks was found to be one in which the cashier stands and is able to use both hands interchangeably to distribute the workload between both wrists. This reduces the type of injury likely to occur if only one hand is used (Marras, Marklin, Greenspan, & Lehman, 1995). The next time you are in a checkout line, notice whether the cashier uses one hand or two when passing items by the scanner.

Safety Devices.   Also important in the design of safe machinery is the development of built-in safety devices and other aids to prevent accidents. Safety devices must function to keep a worker's hand away from sharp moving parts or to

A hazardous work environment such as a natural gas drilling plant must be designed so that emergency controls are within easy reach.

automatically disconnect the power supply in an emergency, but they must not interfere with the operation of the machine.

Personal protective equipment—such as respirators, safety glasses with shatterproof lenses, steel-tipped shoes, ear protectors, and padded gloves—can be provided to protect workers in dangerous jobs, but too often they are not used. Sometimes the reasons are practical; for example, workers object to using a safety device that interferes with job performance. A respirator can hinder communication among workers. Thick gloves make it hard to press buttons on a control panel.

Another reason safety equipment is often not used is that it can be uncomfortable. Workers using respirators for jobs performed under high-temperature conditions may find that the device when clamped to their face causes skin irritation. A survey of 208 employees in an automobile glass factory showed that 62% rated the safety devices uncomfortable. Only 30% considered them tolerable enough to wear (Akbar-Khanzadeh, Bisesi, & Rivas, 1995). These attitudes obviously influence workers' decisions about whether to use equipment that may protect them from harm but that causes considerable discomfort.

A study conducted in The Netherlands of workers at a lead smelter found that differences in the levels of lead in the workers' blood were directly related to their use of protective devices such as respirators. The more frequently the workers used the devices, the lower the level of lead detected in the bloodstream (Meijman, Ulenbelt, Lumens, & Herber, 1996).

Social Pressure.   Accidents can be caused by the pressure to maintain a production schedule or adhere to a timetable. Workers often perceive the threat of disciplinary action or dismissal if they fail to keep to a schedule. Shutting down a production line or power plant because they think conditions are unsafe costs the company huge sums of money. The employee or manager who assumes the responsibility for such an action may be punished.

Airline pilots who refuse to fly in bad weather or because ice is forming on the aircraft's wings cause passengers to miss connecting flights. Also, they are held responsible for reducing the company's on-time performance record. When pilots see their colleagues reprimanded for similar behavior, they feel considerable pressure to take off on time despite the weather.

Personal Factors

Proper attention to equipment design and to the physical and social conditions of the work environment can help reduce the frequency and severity of accidents. Overall, however, the human element is the more important cause. Some of the personal factors studied by I-O psychologists are alcohol and drug use, cognitive ability, health, fatigue, work experience, job insecurity, age, and personality characteristics.

Alcohol and Drug Use.   Large numbers of employees use alcohol or illegal drugs on the job. An employee with a drinking or drug problem is much more likely to be involved in an accident than is an employee without such a problem.

Cognitive Ability.   It seems reasonable to assume that workers with a lower measured level of intelligence would have more accidents than workers with a

NEWSBREAK

Look Out! The Driver Behind You May Be Asleep

That's a chilling thought to remember the next time you travel on an interstate highway. Take a look at those 40-ton 18-wheelers barreling along all around you and then think of this statistic: 78% of all truck drivers have a sleep disorder. It's called obstructive sleep apnea, and it causes a sleeping person to stop breathing momentarily and to awaken briefly. Someone with this disorder can wake up literally hundreds of times each night and not know it. The next day, however, the person will be sleepy.

"If someone wakes up every 2 or 3 minutes throughout the night," said psychologist William Dement, director of the Sleep Research Center at Stanford University, "it's as though they had very little sleep or no sleep at all." And then that person climbs into the cab of a tractor-trailer and drives at speeds up to 80 miles an hour, trying to keep awake for the duration of a 10- or 12-hour workday. No wonder fatigue is a major factor in truck accidents, when three out of four drivers have such disturbed sleep.

Drivers who fall asleep at the wheel of their rig account for up to 1,500 highway deaths a year. This figure means that while trucks represent only 3% of the traffic on the nation's highways, they are involved in 13% of all fatalities.

In case you're wondering whether you might be suffering from obstructive sleep apnea, don't worry. The disorder is three times higher among truck drivers than in the general population. One cause may be irregular work and sleep patterns. Long-distance drivers may work half the night, sleep for 2 hours, then continue driving. Other factors are lack of regular exercise and a tendency to be overweight.

There are cures for sleep apnea, but first you have to know you have it. Most truckers don't know. They may wonder why they feel so tired during the day, but there is a natural tendency to shrug it off, gulp another cup of coffee, and keep on trucking. That's their job.

Sources: T. Hilchey. Sleeping disorder may affect many truckers. *New York Times*, May 14, 1995; B. Gavzer. Is the long haul too long? *Parade Magazine*, May 16, 1999.

higher measured level of intelligence. However, research does not fully support this idea. Some studies have found that cognitive ability is related to accident-free behavior only in certain jobs, such as those requiring judgment and decision making as opposed to those involving repetitive manual labor.

Health.   I-O psychologists have documented a relationship between health and accidents. Employees who are in poor health or who are frequently ill tend to be highly susceptible to accidents. Workers with physical disabilities, assuming that their overall health is good and that they have jobs commensurate with their abilities, do not have a disproportionate share of accidents. Those disabled employees are usually highly motivated to work well and safely. One physical characteristic related to accidents is vision. In general, people who have good eyesight have fewer accidents than do people who have poor eyesight.

Fatigue.   Fatigue causes a decrease in productivity and an increase in accidents. During a typical 8-hour workday, periods of increased productivity are accompanied by decreased accidents. In the 10-hour workday in many heavy industries, a sharp rise in the accident rate during the last 2 hours of the shift has been reported, presumably because of fatigue.

Fatigue is a factor in highway accidents, a subject of study by I-O psychologists because highways are the workplace for bus and truck drivers. Fatigued bus and truck drivers who fall asleep at the wheel are involved in at least 10% of the collisions involving other vehicles. Fatigue contributes to one fourth of all single-car accidents.

Work Experience.   A shorter time on the job tends to mean a higher accident rate. After some months on the job, the accident rate usually drops and continues to decline as work experience increases. However, the relationship between accidents and time on the job is not always clear. Although studies have reported fewer accidents among employees with greater experience, these findings may be biased by self-selection. Workers who have had numerous job-related accidents are likely to have been fired or transferred or have quit to look for safer employment. Therefore, we cannot conclude with certainty that longer work experience, by itself, leads to a reduction in the accident rate. In some cases, the decrease in accidents among experienced workers can be explained by the fact that those who had more accidents have dropped out.

Job Insecurity.   Research was conducted on 237 food-processing plant employees in an organization that had already laid off some of its workers. The results showed that the workers who reported feeling insecure about their jobs and their future with the company had less motivation to adhere to safe working practices and to comply with safety policies. This lack of diligence, in turn, contributed to an increase in workplace accidents and injuries among these insecure employees (Probst & Brubaker, 2000).

Age.   The link between age and accidents is similar to the relationship between experience and accidents because there is an obvious relationship between age and length of work experience. Other factors that interact with age are physical health and attitudes toward the job. Overall health, as well as specific abilities such as vision and hearing, deteriorate with age. However, older workers have greater job knowledge and more highly developed skills. Reaction time and eye-hand coordination may no longer be as good, but older workers usually have a more complete grasp of the job's demands. Their attitudes toward safety tend to be more serious. However, when older workers do have accidents, they are likely to be more costly in terms of physical consequences and time lost from work.

That finding was confirmed in a study of 209 nuclear power plant workers. Researchers found that employees over the age of 50 took longer to recover from injuries than did younger employees. Also, these older workers took safety more seriously than did younger workers and reported engaging in safe work practices far more often (Ringenbach & Jacobs, 1995).

Personality Characteristics.   A popular belief is that people who have a great many accidents have some unique set of personality traits that distinguish them from people who rarely have accidents. Research does not support this contention, although some studies have found that people who have a high number of accidents manifest such characteristics as neuroticism, hostility, anxiety, social maladjustment, and a sense of fatalism. However, any relationship between personality variables and accident frequency is not strong. There is no basis for concluding that people who have frequent accidents have a personality pattern that is clearly different from that of accident-free individuals.

Temporary emotional states can contribute to accidents. The person who is angry with a spouse or boss or is preoccupied with money problems is likely to be less attentive on the job and hence more susceptible to accidents.

Accident proneness The idea that some people have personality traits that predispose them to have accidents, and that most accidents are caused by or involve these same few people. This theory is not supported by research.

Accident Proneness.   The theory of **accident proneness** holds that certain people are more likely than others to have accidents and that most accidents are caused by or involve the same few people. The theory also assumes that accident-prone persons are likely to have accidents regardless of the type of situation. An effective way to test this theory is to compare accident records for the same people for two different periods to determine if the people who had accidents in one period also had accidents in the other. Correlations from studies of this type are low, indicating that a person's past accident record is not a valid predictor of future accidents.

In a classic study, one psychologist reexamined accident statistics that had originally been interpreted as supporting the accident-proneness theory (DeReamer, 1980). In analyzing driving records of 30,000 people, it was found that fewer than 4% of them accounted for 36% of the accidents over a 6-year period. These data suggested that a small group of drivers were involved in a large number of accidents. If they could be prevented from driving, then the accident rate could be cut by more than one third. The data were reanalyzed by comparing accident records for the first 3 years of the period with accident records for the second 3 years of the period. It was found that the accidents during the two different periods did not involve the same drivers. Those identified as safe drivers during the first period accounted for more than 96% of the accidents in the second period, a finding that is highly damaging to the accident-proneness theory.

The theory no longer enjoys the credibility it once had, although evidence suggests that some workers may be predisposed to have more accidents in a particular type of work. Accident proneness may be specific to the work situation and not a general tendency over all situations, which limits the theory's predictive value.

ACCIDENT PREVENTION

An organization can take several steps to safeguard its employees and reduce accidents in the workplace. These include proper reporting of accidents, attention to workplace design, safety training, management support, and safety publicity campaigns.

Accidents and Adolescents

NEWSBREAK

Do you hold a job while you are attending school? The chances are good that you do, and you probably had an outside job during your high school years too. Some 75% of high school seniors in the United States are employed, and nearly half of them work more than 20 hours a week. Research shows that 16- to 19-year-olds are the group at the highest risk for on-the-job accidents.

Michael Frone, a psychologist at the Research Institute on Addiction, in Buffalo, New York, wanted to know why. What characteristics of high-school and college-age men and women could be related to these accidents and injuries? He started his research by investigating substance abuse (no surprise, given his own place of employment). He surveyed 319 adolescents and found that the use of marijuana and alcoholic beverages on the job showed a positive correlation with accidents and injuries.

But he also found other causes. One was simply being a guy. That's right. Male teenagers suffered more work-related injuries than female teenagers did. A high accident rate was also associated with heavy workloads, boring jobs, poor physical health, and a negative emotional outlook. It's hard enough being 18 or 19, but now it appears to be extra hazardous on the job.

Source: M. Frone (1998). Predictors of work injuries among employed adolescents. *Journal of Applied Psychology, 83,* 565–576.

Accident Reports

An accident prevention program is no better than the quality of its accident reports. All accidents, regardless of the consequences, should be investigated and described in detail. A comprehensive accident report will include the following:

- precise time and location of the accident
- type of job and number of employees performing it
- personal characteristics of the accident victim
- nature of the accident and known or suspected causes
- results of the accident—such as personal injuries and damage to plant, equipment, and supplies

Workplace Design

Although most accidents are caused by human error, conditions in the physical work environment are potential sources of accidents. Lighting in the workplace must be adequate for the job tasks, and temperature must be maintained at a comfortable level. Work areas should be clean and orderly. Many accidents have been traced to poor housekeeping. Oil or grease spots on the floor, electrical cables underfoot, and equipment stored in hallways or stairwells can cause serious accidents that can easily be prevented. First-aid kits, fire extinguishers, and other safety equipment should be located conveniently throughout a work area and painted in vivid and easily identified colors.

Controls that are hard to reach or that require excessive force to operate and displays that are excessively complicated and so easily misread are design mistakes that are ready sources of accidents. Emergency controls must be made accessible and easy to operate.

Engineering psychologists suggest two general principles for the design of safety devices: (1) The machine should not function unless the safety device is engaged (for example, a power saw that will not operate unless the hand guard is in place); and (2) the safety device must not interfere with production or cause the employee to work harder to maintain the same output.

Safety Training

Most organizational training programs devote time to accident prevention. Workplace dangers and hazards are pointed out and information is presented on the causes and results of past accidents. Rules for safe operating procedures are taught, along with the location of emergency and first-aid equipment. Periodic drills may be held to maintain awareness of safe working habits. When a company has an increase in accidents, it may mean that retraining of the work force is necessary. Experienced workers can become careless and need refresher courses to update their work habits. In general, companies that systematically continue safety training efforts are rewarded with substantial reductions in accidents and in hours lost from work. The money saved easily pays the cost of the training programs.

ONLINE!

For more general information on work-related health and safety issues, try these Web sites: *www.behavioral-safety.com*, *www.osha.gov* (the Occupational Safety and Health Administration), and *www.cdc.gov/niosh/homepage.html* (the National Institute for Occupational Safety and Health).

Management Support

Supervisors play a key role in any successful program for safety training and awareness. Because of their close association with workers, they must be alert to unsafe working conditions and practices. Supervisors are in the best position to remind employees of safe working habits and to arrange proper maintenance of equipment and the work environment. They are also able to recommend when retraining is advisable. If supervisors do not insist on adherence to safe working procedures, then any safety training program will be less than maximally effective. By example as well as instruction, supervisors can maintain employee motivation to work safely and to prevent accidents.

Safety devices such as face shields should be easy to use and should not interfere with production.

However, supervisors cannot be expected to practice safety awareness unless their superiors reinforce that concern. If management tolerates sloppy accident reporting or expresses even a neutral attitude toward safety, this does not encourage attention to safe practices. Active high-level management support of safety is a key dimension of an appropriate organizational climate. All levels of supervision must demonstrate to subordinates that safety is everyone's responsibility.

A study of 300 blue-collar employees at the U.S. plant of a multinational company confirmed that management support for safety programs significantly increased the employees' perception of the level of safe work practices at their plant (Janssens, Brett, & Smith, 1995). In the chemical industry, an investigation of safe and unsafe working practices among 222 workers found that the company's perceived safety climate, as measured by a questionnaire, was significantly related to the accident rate. Employees who perceived stronger organizational support for safety engaged in fewer unsafe behaviors on the job (Hofmann & Stetzer, 1996).

Research involving 49 supervisors and their work groups focused on the communication of safety-related concerns. The study found that employees who believed that their company supported safe working practices and who had a high-quality relationship with their supervisors were more likely to feel free to raise safety concerns with their supervisors than did employees who lacked these characteristics. The ability of employees to communicate freely with supervisors about safety problems led to a high degree of employee commitment to safe practices and to a lower accident rate (Hofmann & Morgeson, 1999).

In a study of 1,590 employees in 10 manufacturing and mining companies in Australia, the attitude toward safety promoted by management was shown to be significantly related to safe job performance (Griffin & Neal, 2000). And research on 534 production workers in 53 work groups found that the group safety climate created by the immediate supervisor significantly affected the rate of on-the-job injuries. The higher the group perceived its safety climate, the lower its accident rate (Zohar, 2000).

Safety Publicity Campaigns

To motivate employees to follow the safe work habits they have been taught, many organizations conduct publicity and promotional campaigns with posters and booklets, charts showing the number of accident-free days, and contests with appealing prizes.

Posters and Booklets.   Posters are a frequently used device, but their effectiveness depends on the kind of message depicted. Negative themes coupled with gruesome pictures of mangled bodies ("Don't do this—or this is what will happen!") are particularly ineffective. These fear-oriented appeals create resentment and anger toward the company and the message. The most effective safety posters stress positive themes (for example, "Wear hard hat in this area" or "Hold on to railing").

Posters should be attention-getting with bright colors, sharply defined lettering, and visible placement. I-O psychologists recommend the following criteria for posters and warning signs:

- *Signal word.* Warnings should have signal or key words that are appropriate to the level of danger—for example, DANGER, WARNING, or CAUTION.
- *Hazard statement.* Warnings should tell clearly what the dangers are.
- *Consequences.* Warnings should tell clearly the results of failing to comply.
- *Instructions.* Warnings should tell workers what to do or what not to do to avoid the danger. The example in Figure 11–1 meets these criteria.

Booklets of safety instructions and rules are relatively ineffective in encouraging safe working practices no matter how widely they are distributed. It is easy to ensure that all workers receive a booklet, but it is far more difficult to make them read it.

Safety Contests.   Safety contests can be effective in maintaining interest in accident prevention. Some contests reward workers on an individual basis for accident-free work over a given period. Other contests operate on a group basis, rewarding a work crew or department. Contests can be competitive, pitting one

FIGURE 11–1.   An effective warning poster.

WARNING	(Signal word)
UNDERGROUND GAS LINE	(Hazard statement)
EXPLOSION AND FIRE POSSIBLE	(Consequences)
NO DIGGING	(Instructions)

work unit against another to see which has fewer accidents. Such contests may make workers more conscious of safe operating procedures and thus reduce accident rates, but the effects may not last much longer than the life of the contest. One solution is to hold continuous contests, changing the awards frequently enough to maintain employee interest. An obvious disadvantage of safety contests is that they encourage workers, supervisors, and managers to suppress the accurate reporting of accidents.

Safety in Home Offices.   With an increasing number of employees now telecommuting, the problem of safety in home offices has become a national concern. Home-based workers report computer-related discomfort and injury to necks, backs, shoulders, and arms from poorly designed chairs and awkwardly positioned keyboards and monitors. Other dangers include overloaded power outlets, poor lighting, and hazards from children's toys underfoot or outstretched power cords.

Safety experts suggest that many accidents in these offices go unreported because employees do not want to risk losing the opportunity to work at home. OSHA has raised the issue of safety for home work environments. Should employers be held liable when employees are injured while working at home?

VIOLENCE IN THE WORKPLACE

Murder is the second leading cause of death on the job and the primary cause of death for women in the workplace. In addition, every year more than 2 million employees are physically assaulted at work or threatened with assault. The office, shop, and factory have become very dangerous places.

You have seen the stories on the TV news. A disgruntled ex-employee who has been fired returns to the office or store or factory with a gun and starts shooting, usually killing or wounding former co-workers and the supervisor who fired the employee. Because of the publicity given such incidents that have occurred in post offices, the phrase "going postal" has become a generic shorthand description of the phenomenon. In fact, postal workers are less likely to be harmed on the job than many other types of workers.

It is important to put such events in perspective. You need not fear that the person at the next desk is looking at you suspiciously. Although disturbed workers have, indeed, gone on murderous rampages, three fourths of workplace fatalities involve deliberate robberies rather than random, vengeful acts.

Victims of violence are typically taxicab drivers, convenience store clerks, pizza delivery drivers, and owners of small inner-city grocery and liquor stores. Ex-employees or co-workers commit approximately one third of workplace homicides. Women are especially vulnerable to workplace violence. Many are murdered by boyfriends or husbands who choose the women's workplaces as the sites of their actions. Some companies provide security for women employees who are being stalked by abusive partners.

A telephone survey of 598 employed men and women revealed that in the previous 12 months, nearly 15% had been threatened, and 21% said they had been attacked on the job. In this study, those most likely to have experienced threats or actual violence on the job included men and women under the age of 25, supervisors, employees who dealt with the public, and people who work primarily at night. The victims reported significantly lower job satisfaction and greater job stress than other workers and were more likely to consider changing jobs and carrying a weapon to work (Budd, Arvey, & Lawless, 1996).

A researcher questioned 1,400 workers about rude behavior on the job (Studies, 1999). Men were found to be responsible for 70% of the instances reported. Rudeness and incivility involve verbal rather than physical aggression, but these behaviors are still costly to employees and employers. In this survey, 12% of the workers who were targets of rude behavior quit their jobs to get away from their tormentors. More than half said they lost work time because of the hostile environment created by their co-workers.

ONLINE!

For a detailed examination of risk factors and prevention strategies associated with workplace violence, see the following government sites: *www.cdc.gov/niosh/violcont.html*; *www.opm.gov/workplac*; and *www.cdc.gov/niosh/homicide.html*

I-O psychology research has suggested ways to identify a tendency toward deviance in work behavior that may lead to violence. Supervisor ratings of specific job behaviors of 18,146 employees in 42 entry-level jobs (in retail sales, warehouses, nursing homes, courier services, and amusement parks) suggested eight dimensions or components of work behavior (Hunt, 1996):

1. Industriousness
2. Thoroughness
3. Attendance
4. Adherence to rules
5. Theft and drug misuse
6. Unruliness
7. Schedule flexibility
8. Off-task behavior

Of relevance to our discussion of violence in the workplace is the dimension labeled *unruliness,* which includes the following aggressive and violent behaviors:

■ Threatening or bullying other employees
■ Punching, kicking, throwing, or damaging something in anger
■ The loud and harsh use of profanity
■ Exhibiting emotional and irrational behavior when thwarted
■ Defacing or destroying company property

As you can see, none of these behaviors involves homicide or physical assault, yet the tendency toward unruliness may contribute to an atmosphere of violence and may even be found to become a significant precursor to violence.

Additional research describes a profile of characteristics of persons believed to be most likely to commit destructive acts. These are shown in Table 11–3. A telephone survey of 300 employed adults found that alcohol abuse correlated positively with committing acts of violence. Interestingly, heavy drinking also correlated positively with becoming a victim of violence (McFarlin, Fals-Stewart, Major, & Justice, 2000).

A broad-scale research program studied 187 employees from 35 work groups in 20 companies. The results showed that a worker's level of antisocial behavior was influenced by the antisocial behavior of co-workers. As we know, the groups to which we belong—such as peer groups, social groups, or work groups—can effectively dictate the kinds of behavior they find acceptable. It appears to be the same in the case of antisocial behavior. In this study, a group with a strong antisocial culture affected the behavior of all its members. The longer workers remained in such a work group, the more antisocial they became (Robinson & O'Leary-Kelly, 1998).

Protecting Employees from Violence

Ideally, companies would not hire anyone who is prone to violence, but employee selection techniques are not yet sufficiently accurate to accomplish that goal. In an effort to address this problem, two psychologists developed a seven-item scale to measure what they call "interpersonal deviance," that is, behaviors that are harmful to other people in the organization (Bennett & Robinson, 2000). The scale is useful for research purposes, but its value as an employee selection device is not yet established. Further, it seems doubtful that seriously antisocial job applicants would answer the questions honestly. Consider the following items. Would you hire someone who answered "yes" to any of them?

1. Have you made fun of someone at work?
2. Have you said something hurtful to someone at work?
3. Have you made ethnic, religious, or racial remarks at work?
4. Have you cursed at someone at work?
5. Have you played a mean prank on someone at work?
6. Have you acted rudely toward someone at work?
7. Have you publicly embarrassed someone at work?

Even if human resources directors or personnel managers had the selection techniques to identify applicants with violence-prone personality profiles, not all

TABLE 11–3 Characteristics of Violent Employees

- Male between the ages of 30 and 50
- Alcohol or drug abuser
- Past history of violent behavior, serious psychiatric disorder, and impulsive behavior
- History of trauma, abuse, and neglect
- A loner with few social outlets
- Intentifies strongly with the job
- Expresses feelings of shame or humiliation

such people would commit acts of violence on the job. Indeed, unless they were faced with sudden adverse situations, such as receiving a poor performance evaluation or a harsh reprimand, or being fired, they might never exhibit even minor unpleasant behaviors.

I-O psychologists recommend several positive steps to deal with workplace violence. Managers can be trained to recognize potentially violent workers. Difficult employees can be offered counseling. Supervisors can be taught tactful ways of communicating bad news such as disciplinary actions or terminations. OSHA has developed more tangible suggestions for reducing workplace violence, including installing metal detectors, alarm systems, extra lighting, video surveillance cameras, and bulletproof barriers. The agency also recommends hiring more security guards.

ALCOHOLISM IN THE WORKPLACE

More than 10 million people in the United States are known to be alcoholics, although the actual figure may be higher. The U.S. Public Health Service considers alcoholism to be a major health threat, along with heart disease and cancer. Alcoholism is defined as an illness characterized by an inability to control the consumption of alcohol to the extent that intoxication is inevitable, once drinking has begun. Medically, alcoholism is an addiction, a pathological drug dependence that is harmful to health and that interferes with normal functioning.

Up to 10% of the American work force is estimated to be alcoholic at a cost to employers in excess of $100 billion a year. This cost is attributable to absenteeism, tardiness, errors and accidents, low productivity, inefficiency, and, often, the dismissal of valuable employees in whom money and training time was invested. Although there is no dispute that alcoholism is a serious problem for American business, not everyone agrees on the extent of alcoholism in the work force. It is possible that the problem is overstated by therapists, consultants, and directors of rehabilitation programs, the people whose livelihood depends on the idea that alcoholism is rampant and that their programs can cure it.

Alcoholic employees can be found at all levels of organizational life. According to the National Institute on Alcohol Abuse and Alcoholism (NIAAA), more than 70% of known alcoholics are professional, semiprofessional, or managerial employees. More than half of all alcoholics have attended college. The greatest incidence of alcoholism is in the 35-to-55 age group.

The Drug Free Workplace Act of 1988 makes employers who hold $25,000 or more in federal government contracts responsible for the prevention of substance abuse on the job. The law requires these employers to notify employees that the possession, sale, or use of alcohol or illegal drugs on the job is prohibited. If employees are convicted of alcohol or drug offenses, employers are required to impose disciplinary action such as mandatory treatment programs, suspension without pay, or discharge.

Effects on Job Performance

Alcoholics tend to believe that drinking will not affect their behavior at work and that no one will detect a difference in the way they perform their jobs. This is untrue. The debilitating effects of excessive drinking are evident almost immediately. However, in the beginning stages only a trained observer will notice them.

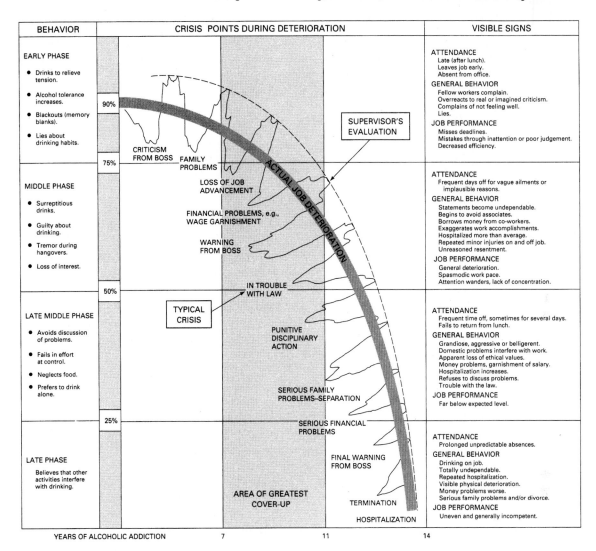

BEHAVIOR	CRISIS POINTS DURING DETERIORATION	VISIBLE SIGNS

EARLY PHASE

- Drinks to relieve tension.
- Alcohol tolerance increases.
- Blackouts (memory blanks).
- Lies about drinking habits.

MIDDLE PHASE

- Surreptitious drinks.
- Guilty about drinking.
- Tremor during hangovers.
- Loss of interest.

LATE MIDDLE PHASE

- Avoids discussion of problems.
- Fails in effort at control.
- Neglects food.
- Prefers to drink alone.

LATE PHASE

Believes that other activities interfere with drinking.

90%
75%
50%
25%

CRITICISM FROM BOSS   FAMILY PROBLEMS

LOSS OF JOB ADVANCEMENT

FINANCIAL PROBLEMS, e.g., WAGE GARNISHMENT

WARNING FROM BOSS

IN TROUBLE WITH LAW

TYPICAL CRISIS

PUNITIVE DISCIPLINARY ACTION

SERIOUS FAMILY PROBLEMS–SEPARATION

SERIOUS FINANCIAL PROBLEMS

FINAL WARNING FROM BOSS

AREA OF GREATEST COVER-UP

TERMINATION

HOSPITALIZATION

SUPERVISOR'S EVALUATION

ACTUAL JOB DETERIORATION

YEARS OF ALCOHOLIC ADDICTION   7   11   14

ATTENDANCE
Late (after lunch).
Leaves job early.
Absent from office.
GENERAL BEHAVIOR
Fellow workers complain.
Overreacts to real or imagined criticism.
Complains of not feeling well.
Lies.
JOB PERFORMANCE
Misses deadlines.
Mistakes through inattention or poor judgement.
Decreased efficiency.

ATTENDANCE
Frequent days off for vague ailments or implausible reasons.
GENERAL BEHAVIOR
Statements become undependable.
Begins to avoid associates.
Borrows money from co-workers.
Exaggerates work accomplishments.
Hospitalized more than average.
Repeated minor injuries on and off job.
Unreasoned resentment.
JOB PERFORMANCE
General deterioration.
Spasmodic work pace.
Attention wanders, lack of concentration.

ATTENDANCE
Frequent time off, sometimes for several days.
Fails to return from lunch.
GENERAL BEHAVIOR
Grandiose, aggressive or belligerent.
Domestic problems interfere with work.
Apparent loss of ethical values.
Money problems, garnishment of salary.
Hospitalization increases.
Refuses to discuss problems.
Trouble with the law.
JOB PERFORMANCE
Far below expected level.

ATTENDANCE
Prolonged unpredictable absences.
GENERAL BEHAVIOR
Drinking on job.
Totally undependable.
Repeated hospitalization.
Visible physical deterioration.
Money problems worse.
Serious family problems and/or divorce.
JOB PERFORMANCE
Uneven and generally incompetent.

FIGURE 11–2.   Deterioration in behavior and job performance of an alcoholic as a function of time. (From A. Carding, "Booze and business." *Administrative Management,* 1967, *30,* 21. © Doyle Lindley, Bechtel Corporation. Reproduced by permission.)

Although behavioral changes occur gradually, after a few years of steady drinking an employee's job performance and efficiency will have deteriorated so greatly that the changes will be obvious to supervisors and co-workers. The downward path of an alcoholic's behavior is depicted in Figure 11–2. The signs of altered job performance include excessive absenteeism, long lunch breaks, lies, errors, and low productivity. In the middle phase, gross changes are apparent that can no longer be overlooked. By this time, the alcoholic has usually received a warning from supervisors and is no longer being considered for promotion.

As the performance curve shows, everything goes downhill—career, family life, reputation, and financial stability. Ironically, each crisis precipitated by excessive drinking provides yet another reason to continue drinking. Unless the person recognizes the problem and accepts help, this cycle can lead to career failure, imprisonment, hospitalization, or an early death. When a worker's superiors continue to ignore excessive drinking, mistakenly believing that they are being kind or helpful, they are only prolonging the problem. Intervention at an early stage is vital to an alcoholic's recovery.

The Alcoholic Executive

The plight of any alcoholic employee is tragic, but when the alcoholic is an executive, the cost to the company is greater. When an organization loses an executive because of a drinking problem, it is deprived of someone in whom it has invested considerable training, a high salary and fringe benefits, and significant responsibilities, a person whose judgment and decision-making abilities have been considered important to the organization's success.

Alcoholic executives, more than lower-level employees, are adept at concealing their problem for a longer period. They may be aided by their subordinates, who are often willing to cover up for their bosses' indispositions. Thus, alcoholic executives can escape detection longer than people in the accounting office, the warehouse, or on the assembly line.

There is another comfort for alcoholic executives. They are not as apt to be fired as are lower-level employees. The executive is more likely to be retained and given a make-work job until retirement. Although management recognizes the problem of alcoholism on the factory floor, it is more reluctant to admit that it exists in the office next door.

Laboratory studies of the process of negotiation, a skill widely practiced by high-level managers and executives, showed that people who negotiate deals while under the influence of alcohol make costly mistakes for their organization. Subjects who conducted negotiations while intoxicated (having a blood alcohol level of 0.05) were significantly more aggressive in their dealings with others than were negotiators who were sober. Those who had been drinking were far more likely to insult, mislead, and threaten the people with whom they were bargaining. In addition, they were found to be cognitively impaired, which led them to make errors of judgment, focus on irrelevant information, and misinterpret or ignore key points of the problem under consideration (Schweitzer & Kerr, 2000).

Rehabilitation Programs

Many federal government agencies and more than half the largest U.S. corporations sponsor formal alcoholic rehabilitation programs. These efforts, called **employee assistance programs (EAPs),** return as much as 20 dollars for every dollar invested in them in terms of reduced absenteeism, reduced health care costs, and higher productivity. Most EAPs offer counseling services for various employee problems, but their major concerns are alcohol and drug abuse.

Employers can offer a greater motivation for alcoholic employees to seek treatment than can families or friends. Why? Because employers offer the hope of retaining a job. Psychologists and physicians who work with alcoholics agree that fear of losing one's job carries more weight than threats from spouses or the possibility of an early death. To alcoholics, keeping their jobs may be their last defense against admitting that they have a drinking problem. When that defense is jeopardized, the desire to seek and accept help is usually great.

Employee assistance programs (EAPs) Counseling and rehabilitative services for various employee problems, notably alcohol and drug abuse.

Most programs to combat alcohol abuse follow a three-step process suggested by the National Council on Alcoholism:

1. *Education of managers and supervisors.* The purpose is to persuade management that alcoholism is not a moral or ethical issue but a medical problem, a treatable illness.
2. *Early detection of alcoholic employees.* Managers should be trained to detect the symptoms of alcoholism and the resulting behavioral and performance changes. Early detection improves the alcoholic worker's chances for recovery.
3. *Referral of alcoholic employees for help.* Some companies rely on in-house physicians and psychologists to supervise rehabilitation programs for alcoholic employees. Other companies refer employees to outside clinics. Most organizations provide for treatment on company time and continue the workers' salaries while they are in treatment programs.

An especially effective treatment approach involves co-workers who are members of Alcoholics Anonymous. That organization has a high success rate in dealing with alcoholism because its members know the effects firsthand. There is some evidence, albeit weak, to suggest that recovering alcoholics become better workers. Their performance no longer suffers from their drinking, and they may expend extra effort, realizing that this is their last chance. However, even if the job performance of recovering alcoholics does not improve, at least the company has reclaimed experienced workers who would otherwise have been lost.

ONLINE!

Databases, research programs, and other resources on alcoholism are online at *www.niaaa.nih.gov* and *www. alcoholismhelp.com*

DRUG USE IN THE WORKPLACE

The use of illegal drugs on the job is a serious problem. Marijuana is the principal substance used; amphetamines, opiates, cocaine, PCP, and ecstasy have also been found in the workplace. In addition, prescription drugs such as tranquilizers, painkillers, and stimulants can be overused. Data show that 1 out of every 10 current and prospective employees has used or will use drugs. The National Institute of Drug Abuse reports that the use of illegal drugs is more widespread among younger employees, ages 18 to 25.

Although drug abuse has been detected at all corporate levels, it is highest among skilled and semiskilled laborers and lowest among managerial and professional personnel. The overuse of prescription drugs is highest among middle-aged and older workers. Drug users are found in all types of jobs. One nuclear power plant caught security guards using drugs. The U.S. Navy discovered that the majority of one aircraft carrier's crew regularly smoked mari-juana. And an oil company learned that offshore drilling rig crews in the Gulf of Mexico were often under the influence of illegal drugs.

The drug-dependent worker may present a more serious problem than the alcoholic worker in terms of the disruptive effects on production and efficiency. Drug users are potentially more dangerous because they may attempt to sell drugs to other workers to finance their own habit.

Effects on Job Performance

Behavioral effects of drug use on the job will vary with the type of drug taken. In general, however, the new user shows marked changes in behavior. There is a negligence about appearance, personal hygiene, and dress. Some take to wearing dark glasses. Emotional outbursts are common, along with a tendency to borrow money. There is also likely to be impairment in judgment and reflexes, sluggish-ness of movement, dilation or contraction of the pupils of the eyes, bloodshot eyes, and, in extreme cases, needle marks on the arms or elsewhere on the body. These behavioral changes affect job performance.

In addition, drug abusers have been found to have up to four times the number of accidents, three times the number of absences, three times the num-ber of health benefit claims, and five times the number of workers' compensa-tion claims. They are far more likely to be late for work and they rate low in job satisfaction.

Depending on what there is to steal from an organization, drug use can lead to an increase in employee theft. Thus, drug users are likely to become marginal employees who are a burden to management and a threat to the morale and safety of co-workers. In hazardous occupations, such as construction and trans-portation, drug users, like alcoholics, can be a menace to the public. Proponents of on-the-job drug screening argue that public safety is the best reason for mandatory drug testing. The public has a right to expect that operators of buses, trains, and airplanes will not have their judgment or reaction time impaired by drugs.

Drug Testing Programs

The chances are high that you will be tested for drug use when you next apply for a job. More than 80% of large U.S. corporations routinely screen job appli-cants for drug use, and the number is expected to rise. Most of the companies that test for drug use refuse to hire applicants who test positive. Drug testing is now part of the employee selection process, and the results of your drug test can override your performance on other selection measures.

Psychologists have suggested the following guidelines to make drug testing programs as equitable as possible:

- The organization should issue a statement to employees describing its pol-icy on drug abuse and testing.
- If employees belong to a union, the company's drug policies and testing procedures should be submitted to collective bargaining before being put into effect. Employers who refuse to bargain with the union are subject to charges of unfair labor practices.

- Drug testing procedures should apply to all employees. No specific group should be singled out for testing.
- Current employees should be tested only in documented cases of job impairment or because of other valid indications of probable cause.
- Employees should be informed in advance of drug testing procedures, including the drugs being screened for, the types of tests, and the consequences of refusing to be tested.
- Positive test results should be confirmed by a second test.
- Results of drug tests should be kept confidential.

Drug testing is controversial. It can be argued that testing infringes on employees' rights to privacy and confidentiality and security from unreasonable search and seizure. Primarily for these reasons, some governments have been reluctant to institute widespread drug testing programs for employees and instead require organizations to reassign workers in dangerous jobs to alternative tasks if they are known to be drug users.

The validity of drug testing is also an issue. The Centers for Disease Control report that mass drug screening, particularly with inexpensive and unsophisticated tests, can incorrectly indicate the presence of drugs in up to two thirds of the cases. This high rate of false positives means that a disturbingly large number of job applicants and employees are mistakenly labeled as drug users.

The lack of accuracy of the tests can be attributed to false readings, laboratory errors, and cheating by employees. Other substances in urine or blood samples can mimic the presence of drugs. Poppy seeds can falsely indicate the use of opiates. Marijuana can be inaccurately indicated by over-the-counter cough and cold products such as Contac or by painkillers such as Advil and Nuprin. An herbal tea that is a normal part of the diet in certain South American countries can lead to a positive test for cocaine. Laboratory technicians can inadvertently mix up samples. Some years ago, the U.S. Army found that half the urine samples of a group of 60,000 soldiers had been so carelessly handled in the laboratory that none of the test results could be considered reliable.

People being tested for drug use may try to cheat the system by substituting someone else's drug-free urine or by adding an adulterant such as laundry bleach to mask traces of drugs. For this reason, most employers insist that employees urinate in the presence of an observer, a practice most people find offensive.

A newer and more accurate test for drugs, using 1½-inch-long strands of hair, eliminates some of those problems. Fewer people object to having hair snipped from the back of their heads than to urinating in the presence of a company observer. Also, it is more difficult to substitute another person's hair or to add something to it to mask the presence of drugs.

The hair test, known as radioimmunoassay, is more accurate than urinalysis. When a group of 800 job applicants submitted to both tests, the urine samples showed that 3% of the applicants tested positive for drugs. The hair test found that 18% of the same applicants tested positive. The presence of drugs can be detected in hair for up to 90 days after the last drug use, whereas drug traces in urine disappear after 3 or 4 days. This means that applicants or employees cannot simply abstain from using illicit drugs for a few days and expect to pass the radioimmunoassay test, as they can with urinalysis.

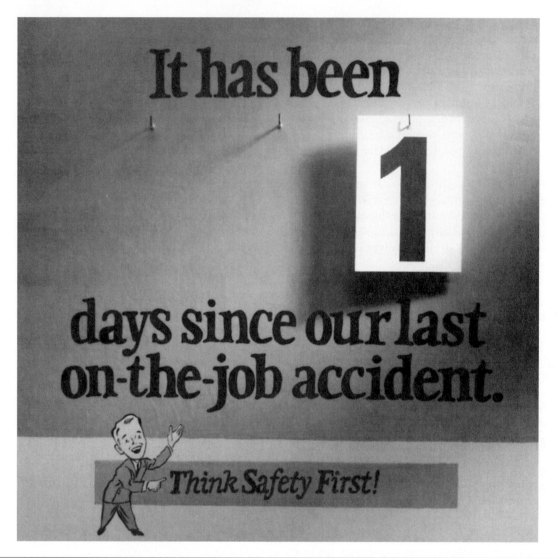

Drug users are highly likely to have accidents on the job. (Reproduced by permission of Partnership for a Drug-Free America.)

The first step taken by many organizations to deal with drug use on the job is a clear and direct statement to employees and job applicants about the policy concerning drug use, drug testing, and the consequences of violating that policy.

The second step is screening all job applicants, not only with drug testing but also by paying attention to gaps in employment history, criminal conviction records, dishonorable military discharges, and physical signs of addiction.

The third and most difficult step is to detect employees who are using or selling drugs on the job. One company hired an ex-addict to work at various jobs throughout the plant and identify drug users. Another company hired private detectives to pose as employees. Some employers have used drug-sniffing dogs to detect the presence of drugs in the workplace and in employees' cars in the company parking lot.

Most organizations differentiate between occasional users of soft drugs and addicts or pushers of hard drugs. If occasional users have a good performance record and agree to accept help, companies will usually arrange for a treatment program. If users refuse help, they will likely be fired. Drug pushers are subject to arrest.

Workers who are treated successfully for drug problems and return to their jobs show reduced absenteeism, accidents, sick leave, and claims for health benefits. In general, EAPs report success rates of up to 80%, with success defined as remaining drug-free and maintaining satisfactory job performance for 1 year after treatment. Once drug users have lost their jobs, the recovery rate drops to about 5%, a clear indication of the importance of detecting and treating a worker's substance abuse problem while he or she is still employed.

> **ONLINE!**
>
> A comprehensive source about drug use in the workplace is *www.pace.bc.ca/workplace.htm.* For a guide for employees and employers interested in creating a drug-free workplace, check out *www.health.org/wpkit/index.htm.*

COMPUTERS AND PHYSICAL HEALTH ISSUES

Some employees who work with computers report a high incidence of back pain, physical fatigue, and visual disturbances. These problems can often be eased by altering the design of the work area and correcting poor lighting conditions. The city government of San Francisco, California, passed legislation to regulate the use of video display terminals in the workplace in order to reduce eyestrain, muscle fatigue, and repetitive motion injuries. The law follows guidelines recommended by engineering psychologists and requires that workers be provided with adjustable chairs and adequate lighting and that computer terminals be equipped with detachable keyboards and adjustable screens. In addition, employees whose jobs do not include regular rest breaks must be given 15 minutes of alternative work every 2 hours.

Carpal tunnel syndrome, a repetitive motion disorder of the wrist, has plagued workers in many occupations for decades. Any job that requires repeated identical or similar motions can lead to this painful, crippling nerve injury. Once reported mainly by blue-collar workers such as meat cutters, carpenters, jackhammer operators, and assembly-line workers, it received little recognition or publicity.

Carpal tunnel syndrome A repetitive motion disorder that may involve numbness, tingling, or pain in fingers, hands, and forearms.

With the advent of computers, white-collar workers, such as newspaper reporters and editors, started feeling those characteristic shooting pains in hands and forearms accompanied by tingling and numbness in the fingers. That was when carpal tunnel syndrome became famous. And when media people started hurting, they wrote articles about this new-found condition. Psychologists and medical researchers began to study it, and OSHA became alarmed.

Repetitive motion injuries are said to afflict more than 2 million people in the American workforce, many suffering damage to the point of needing surgery to relieve the pressure on the affected nerve. The condition can often be pre-vented by proper attention to engineering psychology guidelines of the kind leg-islated by the city of San Francisco.

> **ONLINE!**
> For everything you've always wanted to know about car-pal tunnel syndrome, tense the muscles of your forearm and enter *www.health.yahoo.com/health/diseases_and_conditions/ disease_feed_data/carpal_tunnel_syndrome*.

There are additional health concerns for people who manufacture computer chips. This work is potentially dangerous because it exposes employees to ar-senic, cyanide, acids, and noxious solvents. Some workers claim that the job causes headaches and loss of concentration, and they are concerned about long-term health effects. Research to date neither confirms nor refutes these charges. Nevertheless, companies such as AT&T have taken the precaution of transferring pregnant women from computer chip manufacturing areas to other workstations. Other companies inform employees of the hazards and offer the opportunity for a transfer.

Studies have shown a higher rate of miscarriages among pregnant women who work with computers more than 20 hours a week, compared to pregnant women who do other kinds of office work. Research on animals has related the low-frequency, pulsed, electromagnetic radiation emitted by video display termi-nals to miscarriages and birth defects. However, the evidence with human sub-jects is less certain.

Psychologists suggest that the source of the problem is the stressful assembly-line atmosphere in which many computer operators function rather than the radiation emitted by the display screens. In an investigation of pregnant women in several occupations, clerical employees had a higher miscarriage rate than did managerial and professional employees who spent a comparable amount of time at a computer terminal. The jobs of the managerial and profes-sional women employees may have been less stressful and more satisfying. Re-search on pregnant women workers in several countries found no significant evidence of increased risk of miscarriages or birth defects from working with computers.

The issue raises a problem of discrimination. Some companies practice what is called **protective exclusion,** barring women of childbearing age from certain jobs, such as computer chip production, out of fear of eventual lawsuits should it be shown that computer work is related to miscarriages, birth defects, or other health problems. In some companies, women job applicants have been asked to supply urine samples that were tested, without the applicants' knowledge or consent, for evidence of pregnancy. In instances where women were not hired on the basis of such a policy, it constitutes sex discrimination.

In 1991, the U.S. Supreme Court struck down this practice of protective ex-clusion as a form of sex discrimination and ruled that employers could not

Protective exclusion The practice of barring certain groups of employees, such as women of childbearing age, from potentially hazardous jobs because of fear of lawsuits.

exclude women from jobs in which exposure to toxic substances might harm a developing fetus. The case before the court involved the Johnson Controls battery plant, which had excluded women of childbearing age (except those who could prove they were sterile) from high-paying assembly-line jobs that exposed them to potentially harmful lead fumes. Some women had undergone surgery to be rendered sterile rather than transfer to lower-paying jobs. It is interesting that the company's fetal-protection policy had never been applied to men even though the men's sperm was at risk of becoming malformed, a condition that could lead to birth defects.

Computers emit other forms of radiation, including X-rays and infrared, magnetic, and electrostatic fields. The long-term effects of these emissions have not been determined.

Victims of Workplace Violence

Considerable research has been conducted on the characteristics of workers considered most likely to commit violent acts at their place of employment. However, relatively little is known about the people who become victims of that violence. Are there certain shared personality characteristics that make them likely targets?

To answer this question, psychologists asked the employees of a public utility to participate in a survey. All responses would be anonymous. Some 371 of the company's employees agreed, a high response rate of 76%. Most were men; three fourths were Black. In terms of position in the company hierarchy, the participants held a variety of jobs. Approximately 58% worked in line, clerical, or technical support jobs; 18% were supervisors; 11% were managers; and the remaining 13% held other positions.

The questionnaire listed examples of hostility and aggression on the job and asked if the employees believed any of these behaviors had been directed toward them during the previous year. For example, had they been cursed, pushed, punched, threatened with physical harm, or been the target of an obscene gesture or ethnic slur?

The researchers hypothesized that two personality factors were related to victimization on the job: negative affectivity and self-determination. Negative affectivity involves high levels of negative emotions such as anger, hostility, fear, and anxiety. People high in negative affectivity focus on the negative aspects of themselves and others. They are often hostile, demanding, distant, and difficult to like. They tend to interpret the actions of other people as threatening. And when they react aggressively, this often provokes others to respond similarly.

Self-determination refers to an internal locus of control. Those high in self-determination actively exercise control over their lives. They decide when and how to interact with co-workers and are usually able to avoid encounters with unpleasant or overly assertive people. They are confident about defending themselves against the potentially harmful actions of others. People low in self-determination feel helpless and powerless in relation to others.

The researchers had expected that the people most likely to be victimized at work would be high in negative affectivity and low in self-determination. And that is precisely what the results showed. In addition, they had hypothesized that people lower in status in the organization's hierarchy would suffer from violent or antisocial acts more frequently than those in higher status jobs. The results, however, did not support this conjecture. Status was not shown to be related to victimization.

Source: K. Aquino, S. L. Grover, M. Bradfield, & D. G. Allen (1999). The effects of negative affectivity, hierarchical status, and self-determination on workplace victimization. *Academy of Management Journal, 42,* 260–272.

Think About It

1. How would you design a survey to study the problem of violence on the job? Could the phenomenon be studied in a laboratory experiment? Why or why not?
2. What other personality variables can affect victimization?
3. What aspects of the work environment contribute to a culture of violence?
4. If you were a manager, how would you deal with victims of workplace violence? With perpetrators of workplace violence?
5. Describe some of the characteristics of violent employees.

SUMMARY

OSHA's goal is to enforce federal industrial safety standards to protect workers from accidents and health problems on the job. One problem with research on accidents is that many organizations distort accident data through incomplete reporting in an effort to maintain good safety records. Workplace factors that affect accidents are type of industry, work schedules, lighting, temperature, and equipment design. Personal factors contributing to accidents include alcohol and drug use, health, fatigue, work experience, job insecurity, age, and certain personality variables. The theory of **accident proneness** has little research support.

To prevent accidents, organizations should practice complete reporting and analysis of accidents, consider the design of the job and work environments, provide managerial support for safe work practices, provide safety training, and sponsor safety publicity campaigns.

Workplace violence is increasing. Behaviors expressing incivility, anger, and hostility threaten workers at all levels. Those most likely to commit acts of violence are men between ages 30 and 50 with a history of substance abuse and psychiatric disorders.

Alcoholism on the job has been linked to tardiness, absenteeism, low productivity, and emotional problems. Organizations try to assist alcoholic employees through **employee assistance programs (EAPs)** and by training managers to detect signs of alcoholism in their workers. Drug use on the job has been found at all occupational levels. In general, organizations treat drug users more severely than they do alcoholics. The use of drug testing in employee selection is widespread, though the tests may not be accurate and may violate privacy rights. Effects on employee health of prolonged computer use, such as **carpal tunnel syndrome,** are being investigated.

KEY TERMS

accident proneness
carpal tunnel syndrome

employee assistance programs (EAPs)
protective exclusion

ADDITIONAL READING

Lewis, G. W., & Zare, N. C. (1999). *Workplace hostility: Myth and reality.* Philadelphia: Taylor & Francis. Offers a profile of the at-risk employee, including behavioral warning signs for the potential for violence (such as attendance records, job performance problems, and verbal and nonverbal cues). Suggests courses of action for the organization including referral for psychological evaluation, legal action, and the development and implementation of corporate anti-violence policies.

Schwenk, C. R., & Rhodes, S. L. (Eds.). (1999). *Marijuana and the workplace.* Westport, CO: Quorum. Reviews research on the effects of marijuana use on job performance and behavior in the workplace. Covers issues such as motivation, attention, learning and memory, and psychomotor skills as well as violent behavior, socially deviant behavior, and criminal conduct.

Sonnenstuhl, W. J. (1996). *Worker sober: The transformation of an occupational drinking culture.* Ithaca, NY: ILR Press/Cornell. Relates the incidence of alcoholism on the job to specific occupations and organizational cultures.

VandenBos, G. R., & Bulatao, E. Q. (Eds.). (1996). *Violence on the job.* Washington, DC: American Psychological Association. Describes approaches to managing workplace violence in high-risk settings and relates employee hostility and perceived injustice to the potential for violence. Covers the impact of domestic violence on the workplace and reviews the role of employee assistance programs in preventing violence.

CHAPTER 12

Stress in the Workplace

CHAPTER OUTLINE

We have described several ways in which work can be harmful to your health. Accidents and violence on the job and exposure to noxious chemicals in factories and sealed office buildings account for substantial numbers of injuries and deaths every year. Another danger—**stress**—affects millions of employees, but it operates in more silent and subtle ways. Whereas poorly designed chairs or toxic fumes are physical agents that affect health, productivity, and morale, stress is a psychological agent that influences physical and emotional well-being and our ability to perform our jobs.

Stress Physiological and psychological responses to excessive and usually unpleasant stimulation and to threatening events in the environment.

Stress-related diseases are widespread among employees in the United States. A national survey conducted by a life insurance company found that nearly half of all employed adults considered their jobs to be extremely stressful. One of every three Americans has seriously considered quitting their jobs because of stress.

As many as half of all visits to physicians are precipitated by stress. Further, a major share of physical complaints may be psychosomatic—that is, actual physical disorders caused by or related to emotional factors such as stress on the job. Physical problems associated with stress include high blood pressure (hypertension), ulcers, colitis, heart disease, arthritis, skin diseases, allergies, headaches, neck and lower back pain, and cancer. Stress has been linked to an increase in infectious diseases and may be implicated in disorders that involve suppression of the immune system.

Stress in the workplace is also costly to employers, as reflected in lower productivity, reduced motivation, and increased errors and accidents. High stress is related to increases in turnover intentions and counterproductive behavior, such

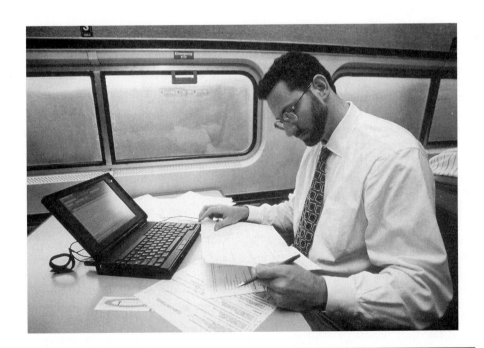

With portable office equipment such as laptop computers, employees can be connected to their office even while traveling. This constant job-induced stress can reduce efficiency and lead to physical complaints.

as theft and drug and alcohol abuse. Job stress contributes to spiraling health care costs. The estimated expenditures for only two stress-related conditions—heart disease and ulcers—is approximately $45 billion a year, which makes stress more costly for organizations than accidents. For every worker killed in a job-related accident, at least 50 suffer some form of heart disease. Research on more than 960,000 workers in the United States and in Sweden reported that employees in high-stress jobs had a rate of heart disease four times greater than did employees in low-stress jobs.

A survey of more than one million workers in Britain found that more than half of them reported physical health problems that resulted from the stress of unusually long working hours. British psychologists report that job stress accounts for 60% of all workplace accidents in that country (Cartwright, 2000).

Another investigation, involving 260 employees of a chemical company and a life insurance company in the United States, found that stressful job events, as measured by a self-report inventory, correlated positively with health care claims and costs. This relationship held for both 1-year and 2-year periods of study. In other words, employees who reported the greatest amount of job stress cost their employers significantly more in health care benefits than employees who reported experiencing little stress on the job (Manning, Jackson, & Fusilier, 1996a, 1996b).

Stress affects employees at all levels and types of jobs. It is unlikely that you can avoid the consequences of stress during your career, any more than you can avoid them in college. Some level of stress will probably affect the quality of your working life and, in turn, other aspects of your daily living.

OCCUPATIONAL HEALTH PSYCHOLOGY

Occupational health psychology The field of study dealing with the health effects of job stress and other aspects of employee well-being.

The problem of workplace stress has led to a new field of study—**occupational health psychology.** This concern for occupational health and employee well-being can be traced to the early years of industrial psychology practice. The German psychologist, Hugo Muensterberg, who taught at Harvard University, helped found the field of industrial psychology. Among the issues he considered were accidents and worker safety. During World War I (1914–1918), the British government established the Industrial Fatigue Research Board to study problems of inefficiency and fatigue in manual laborers. Since then, a great deal of research has been conducted on all aspects of employee health.

In 1990, psychologist Jonathan Raymond proposed the term *occupational health psychology* for this field. The Academy of Management formed the Health and Well-being Focus Group in its Organizational Behavior division. Similarly, the American Psychological Association and the National Institute for Occupational Safety and Health (NIOSH) launched programs to support the formal development of the field of occupational health psychology. International conferences were convened, graduate school programs established at major universities, and publication of the *Journal of Occupational Health Psychology* was begun.

The goal of occupational health psychology is to understand and combat the harmful effects of stress on employee health and safety. Much of the research discussed in this chapter is an outgrowth of this effort.

PHYSIOLOGICAL EFFECTS OF STRESS

Some of us feel stress every time we take an exam. People undergo stress when a car runs a stop sign and almost hits them or when a shadowy figure chases them down a dark street. When something like that happens, we become anxious, tense, and fearful. Stress involves physiological and psychological responses to excessive and usually unpleasant stimulation and to threatening events in the environment.

Dramatic physiological changes occur during stress. Adrenaline, released from the adrenal glands, speeds up all bodily functions. Blood pressure rises, heart rate increases, and extra sugar is released into the bloodstream. The increased blood circulation brings additional energy to the brain and muscles, making the person stronger and more alert to cope with the threat. A stressful situation mobilizes and directs one's energy, boosting it beyond its normal level. With the excess energy of this so-called "fight-or-flight" response, an organism (human or other animal) will either fight the source of the stress (perhaps an attacker or a predator) or flee from it.

Most of the research conducted on the fight-or-flight phenomenon has been conducted on male subjects. Only recently have enough data been compiled on female subjects to note that they respond differently to stress. Researchers characterize women's response to stress as "tend-and-befriend." *Tending* involves nurturing activities designed to protect themselves and their offspring from the stress; *befriending* refers to the development of social groups or networks that also help defend against stress (Taylor, et al., 2000). And although behavioral responses to stress may vary by gender, the physiological changes induced by stress (noted in the previous paragraph) are experienced by both men and women.

Most of us will not encounter extreme emergency situations, and few jobs expose people to threatening events such as those faced by police and firefighters. For the majority of us, the stresses we face on the job are psychological or emotional in nature, such as an argument with the boss, the belief that we have been treated unfairly, or concern about a promotion. These constitute what we commonly refer to as hassles or insults of everyday life. Individually, they are low-level sources of stress, but they are hard on the body because they accumulate. Each stress adds to the previous one and can tax the body's energy reserves because of the physiological changes it produces. If stressors are frequently found in the workplace, the body remains in a state of high physiological arousal and alertness for long periods, a condition that can lead to physiological damage as well as psychosomatic illnesses.

Psychosomatic disorders are not imaginary; they involve specific tissue and organ damage. Although their origin lies in psychological and emotional factors, they have a definite physical impact on the body. Further, the illnesses brought about by stress can serve as new sources of stress. When physical health has declined, resistance has been lowered, and bodily energy has been reduced. As a result, motivation and job performance are bound to suffer.

Not all employees are affected by stress in the same way. Consider air traffic controllers, who have one of industry's most stressful jobs. Hour after hour they must exercise constant vigilance, tracking aircraft at various speeds and altitudes converging on or departing from the same point. Their work is hectic, difficult, and demanding, with the additional burden of being responsible for hundreds of lives throughout each workday. Research on the physiological functioning of air traffic controllers shows that their bodies reflect the pressures of the job. As the number of aircraft in their sector increases, coronary arteries become more constricted and blood pressure rises. The incidence of hypertension among air traffic controllers is three times higher than normal for their age group.

This would appear to be a classic example of the deadly effects of stress. We would guess that the rate of heart attacks, strokes, and other stress-related disabilities is many times higher among air traffic controllers than among the rest of the population. But research indicates that this is not so. On some measures, air traffic controllers are healthier than the general population. Although some air traffic controllers show a pattern of disease and early death, others are apparently unaffected.

Job Satisfaction and Feelings of Control

What makes the difference? Why don't the job pressures affect them all in the same way? The difference seems to lie in the level of job satisfaction controllers get from their work. Those who report being very satisfied with their jobs suffer fewer harmful effects of stress. Those who are very dissatisfied with their jobs show many more stress-related effects.

A study of 1,886 business managers in the United States identified the following kinds of daily work stress (Cavanaugh, Boswell, Roehling, & Boudreau, 2000):

1. *Challenge-related stress,* which includes time pressure and a high level of responsibility that lead to feelings of fulfillment and achievement
2. *Hindrance-related stress,* which includes excessive job demands and constraints (such as red tape, poor support from higher management, and job insecurity) that interfere with achieving goals

Thus, not all stress is considered harmful. Challenge-related stress is motivating and positively related to job satisfaction. Hindrance-related stress is associated with frustration and low job satisfaction.

High job satisfaction contributes to health and longevity. Although both types of stress noted above cause similar physiological changes, only hindrance-related stress was shown to lead to detrimental health effects. This accounts for the fact that some people in high-stress jobs, such as air traffic controllers, maintain generally good health.

Consider another high-stress occupation—that of corporate executive. It is widely assumed that executives experience enormous job stress and consequently have a higher rate of heart attacks than does the general population. Research does not support this position. High-level executives have 40% fewer heart attacks than do middle-level managers, who are popularly assumed to work under less stressful conditions.

The primary reason top executives are relatively less affected by job stress is that they have more autonomy and control over their work than do middle-level managers. Research has shown that being able to control workplace events can significantly reduce perceived job stress. A comparison of more than 10,000 men and women civil servants in Britain focused on the issue of job control. The results showed that people with low levels of job control were one-and-a-half to two times more likely to develop heart disease than were those with greater control over the demands and responsibilities of their job (Bosma, Stansfeld, & Marmot, 1998).

A longitudinal study conducted in Sweden followed the working careers of more than 25,000 men. The findings confirmed that the employees most likely to die of heart attacks held jobs that involved routine work over which they had little control. Subjects who had held such jobs throughout their working lives were twice as likely to die of heart disease than subjects in jobs with a high degree of control. Also, men who had held high-control jobs but who had to change to low-control jobs during their careers were three times as likely to die from heart disease. Losing control was apparently more harmful than never having it in the first place (Hancock, 1996).

In addition to greater physical health, high-control jobs offer certain psychological benefits. A study of women employees in Canada compared 214 clerical workers (the low-control group) with 249 managers (the high-control group). People with low job control were described as more distressed and less satisfied than people with high-control jobs. The managers reported fewer hassles on the job and less depression, anxiety, and health complaints. The high-control employees also noted greater satisfaction with their jobs and with life in general (Long, 1998).

INDIVIDUAL DIFFERENCES IN STRESS RESPONSES

If we are to examine thoroughly the causes of stress on the job, then we must take account of personal factors that can render employees vulnerable to stress. Not all stressors at work affect people the same way. A source of stress that can ruin the health of one worker may have no noticeable effect on that of a colleague.

We have mentioned two factors that may reduce a person's susceptibility to stress: high job satisfaction and control over the conditions of one's work. Several other variables have been related to our vulnerability to the effects of stress. One factor involved in coping with stress is social support, our network of family and social ties. The person who lives alone or is emotionally alienated from others is more likely to be sensitive to stress than is someone who has strong ties to family, friends, and colleagues. Family support can help compensate for negative feelings about one's job and can enhance self-esteem, acceptance, and worth. Social support on the job, such as a cohesive work group or a good relationship with one's boss, can also reduce the effects of stress.

Research involving 543 workers in Germany found that social support offered by supervisors reduced the symptoms of depression that resulted from social stressors on the job (Dormann & Zapf, 1999). Another study of 90 German workers showed that social support given by supervisors, co-workers, friends, and family members significantly reduced physical and psychological effects of stress both on and off the job (Frese, 1999).

ONLINE!

Find more information on stress—how you get it and how you can cope with it—at *www.teachhealth.com, www. psychwww.com/mtsite/smpage.html, www.unl.edu/stress/mgmt/,* and *www.cdc.gov/niosh/stresswk.html.*

Perils of the Road Warrior

NEWSBREAK

Have you been in an airport lately? Then you probably know how stressful air travel has become. Long lines at the check-in counter, flight delays, cancelled departures, cramped aisles and seats. Not to mention the so-called "food" served on airplanes.

And if you think it's stressful taking a flight every now and then for vacation or to go home for the holidays, what must it be like for employees whose jobs require that they travel frequently? Some employees make more than 100 business trips a year, often covering several cities in a week's time: a meeting in New York on Monday, a Denver conference on Tuesday, a presentation in Germany on Wednesday. Sound glamorous? Maybe if you have your own corporate jet, but for most business travelers who don't have that perk, travel is a drudge.

A survey of frequent business travelers conducted by Hyatt Hotels found that one of every three employees said they would like to stop traveling, but they were sure it would hurt their careers. More than half said that in the future they would turn down a job that required so much travel. Those with families were particularly inconvenienced. They carried the additional burden of guilt for being away from home and missing so many of their children's activities.

Other surveys show that flight delays are a source of stress for up to 50% of all business travelers. Long waits for baggage are an annoyance for 30%. Questionnaires completed by Hilton Hotels customers indicated that more than half did not sleep well, despite the luxurious and well-equipped accommodations.

An additional problem for business travelers is becoming ill while away from home. A study of international business travelers conducted by Coca-Cola reported that diarrhea is the most common health complaint. Half of all business travelers admitted to overeating while on the road, and one fourth said they drank more than usual. The World Bank noted that their employees who travel frequently account for 80% more of the organization's medical claims than their employees who do not travel.

Clearly, it's not easy being a road warrior. The excitement may not be all you imagined.

Sources: R. S. DeFrank, R. Konopaske, & J. M. Ivancevich (2000). Executive travel stress: Perils of the road warrior. *Academy of Management Executive, 14*(2), 58–71; J. Sharkey, Business travel. *New York Times*, January 12, 2000.

Lack of social support can increase the risk of heart disease. In general, the lower the level of available social support, the greater the health risk. Variations in social support over the course of the workday have been found to affect blood pressure. Studies of men and women in various occupations showed that blood pressure rose when social support was low and dropped when social support was high.

General physical health is related to susceptibility to stress. People in better physical condition suffer fewer harmful effects from a stressful work environment than do people in poorer physical condition. Physical exercise is a good way to improve general well-being. Many companies provide exercise facilities to help employees alleviate stress.

Our level of ability to perform our jobs can make us more or less resistant to stress. Employees with high skill levels usually find their work less stressful than do employees with lower skill levels. You may have noticed this effect in your college classmates. Students who are barely able to keep up with the coursework are usually more anxious about exams than are students who have less difficulty mastering the required material.

The Type A Personality

Personality factors have been related to our tolerance of stress. This relationship is particularly apparent with **Type A** and **Type B personalities** and their differential susceptibility to heart disease, which, as we noted, is a major consequence of stress (Friedman & Rosenman, 1974). Although specific physical factors such as smoking, obesity, and lack of exercise are implicated in heart disease, they may account for no more than 25% of the cases. The rest may be linked to aspects of the Type A personality pattern. In contrast, Type Bs rarely have heart attacks before the age of 70, regardless of the nature of their jobs or their personal habits.

Type A/Type B personalities Personality patterns related to one's ability to tolerate stress; Type A persons have been associated with heart disease, anger, hostility, time urgency, and depression; Type B persons may work as hard as Type As but show fewer stress effects.

Two primary characteristics of the Type A personality are a high competitive drive and a constant sense of time urgency. Type As are described as intensely ambitious and aggressive, always striving to achieve, racing against the clock, rushing from one self-imposed deadline to another. They are attracted to high-stress, fast-paced, competitive, and demanding jobs. Type A personalities can be hostile, though they are successful in hiding that quality from others. They express their aggression through competitiveness, especially on the job. They are impatient and quick to get angry if they believe subordinates or colleagues are working too slowly.

Type As are thought to be in a continual state of tension, perpetually under stress. Even when their work environment is relatively free of stressors, they carry their own stress as a fundamental part of their personality. Type As also tend to be extraverted and high in self-esteem. They show a high level of job involvement and score high in the needs for achievement and power. Table 12–1 shows some typical Type A behaviors.

Type B personalities may be just as ambitious as Type As, but they have few of the other characteristics. Type Bs experience less stress at work and at leisure. They may work as hard and in equally stressful environments but they suffer fewer harmful effects. These two personality types respond differently to prolonged stress over which they have little control. For example, Type As will struggle to master a difficult situation, but if they are not successful, they will become frustrated and give up. Type Bs in a similar situation will try to function as effectively as possible and will not give up.

The early research on the Type A and Type B personality dimensions, conducted in the 1960s and 1970s, described a clear link between Type A behavior and coronary heart disease. More recent research has failed to confirm that relationship consistently, although few psychologists are willing to state that there is

TABLE 12–1   Are You a Type A Person?

Do you

_____   always do everything very rapidly? *Type A people eat, move, walk, and talk at a brisk pace. They speak with emphasis on certain words, and the ends of their sentences are spoken much faster than the beginnings.*

_____   become extremely impatient with the speed at which things are accomplished? *Type A people continually say "yes, yes" or "uh-huh" to whomever is talking to them, and even finish other persons' sentences for them. They become outraged by a slow car ahead of them or a slow-moving line in a restaurant or theater. When they read, they skim the material quickly and prefer summaries or condensations of books.*

_____   always think about or try to do two or more things at the same time? *For example, Type A people may think about one thing while talking to someone about something else, or they may try to eat and drive at the same time, in an effort to get more accomplished in a given period of time.*

_____   feel guilty when you are on vacation or trying to relax for a few hours?

_____   fail to be aware of interesting or beautiful things? *Type A people do not notice a lovely sunset or the new flowers of spring. If asked, they cannot recall the furnishings or details of an office or home they just visited.*

_____   always try to schedule more events and activities than you can properly attend to? *This is another manifestation of the sense of time urgency Type A people feel.*

_____   have nervous gestures or tics such as clenching your fists or banging on a desk to emphasize a point you are making? *These gestures point to the continuing tension at the root of the Type A personality.*

_____   consistently evaluate your worth in quantitative terms? *For Type A persons, numbers alone define their sense of accomplishment and importance. Type A executives boast about their salary or their company's profits. Type A surgeons tell how many operations they have performed, and Type A students report how many A's they have received in school. These people focus on the quantitative rather than the qualitative aspects of life.*

no relationship at all. For example, a meta-analysis of 87 studies reported a modest relationship between Type A behavior and heart disease but a stronger relationship between heart disease and the emotions of anger, hostility, and depression. These researchers concluded that the coronary-prone personality is not necessarily the typical workaholic but rather someone ridden by negative emotions such as anger and anxiety (Booth-Kewley & Friedman, 1987).

Other studies discount the importance of depression and anxiety as contributors to heart disease but support the role of hostility and impatience. We noted that Type A personalities are high in hostility, which they are adept at concealing from others. Thus, the relationship between heart disease and personality factors remains intact, but it may include psychological attributes other than those originally associated with Type A behaviors.

The Hardiness Factor

Another personality variable that may account for individual differences in vulnerability to stress is **hardiness.** People characterized as being high in hardiness have attitudes that may make them more resistant to stress. Hardy people believe they can control or influence the events in their lives. They are deeply committed to their work and to other activities of interest, and they view change as exciting and challenging rather than threatening.

Hardiness can be assessed by a 20-item scale designed to measure three components: control, commitment, and challenge (Kobasa, 1979, 1982). Research has shown that hardy persons develop fewer physical complaints under highly stressful conditions than do persons who are not hardy. Thus, hardiness may moderate the effects of stress through the way people evaluate and interpret the experiences and events in their lives.

Hardiness A personality variable that may explain individual differences in vulnerability to stress. So-called hardy persons believe they can control the events in their lives and thus may be more resistant to stress.

Self-Efficacy

Self-efficacy refers to the belief in one's ability to accomplish a task. It is the sense of how adequate, efficient, and competent we feel about coping with life's demands. People who are high in self-efficacy are less bothered by stress than are people who are low in self-efficacy. For example, a study of 2,273 U.S. Army soldiers subjected them to both psychological and physical stress associated with overly long workdays and unusual physical demands. Two levels of efficacy were measured, as follows (Jex & Bliese, 1999):

1. *Traditional self-efficacy:* the person's level of confidence about being able to perform the job
2. *Collective efficacy:* the person's level of confidence that the group to which the person belongs is able to perform the job

Both types of efficacy were found to be related to stress tolerance in the same way. Soldiers who scored high in both self-efficacy and collective efficacy reacted more positively to work stressors than did soldiers who scored low.

A study of 226 U.S. bank tellers showed that employees high in self-efficacy who believed that they had a high level of control over their jobs were more resistant to psychological stress than were employees with low self-efficacy (Schaubroeck, Lam, & Kie, 2000). Even when tellers who scored low in self-efficacy had high perceived control over their jobs, they still experienced the effects of stress. Thus, the researchers concluded that the determining factor in stress tolerance was self-efficacy.

ONLINE!

For more research on self-efficacy, visit *www.cc.emory. edu/education/mfp/effpage.html.*

Locus of Control

Locus of control One's belief about the source of one's rewards. People with an internal locus of control believe that job performance, pay, and promotion are under their control and dependent on their own behavior. People with an external locus of control believe such events depend on outside forces such as luck.

The personality variable of internal versus external **locus of control** influences a person's reaction to stress. People who rate high on internal control believe that they can influence the forces and events that shape their lives. People who rate high on external control believe that life is determined by other people and by outside events and forces such as luck or chance.

Managers high in internal control were shown to experience less stress than did managers in similar jobs who were high in external control. In other research, a study of 244 accountants conducted over a 1-month period confirmed that those with an internal locus of control and high social support were significantly less affected by stress than those with an external locus of control (Daniels & Guppy, 1994).

Self-Esteem

Organization-based self-esteem A personality dimension relating to our assessment of our adequacy and worth with regard to our place in the employing organization.

Self-esteem, which is similar to self-efficacy, refers to how we feel about ourselves. In the workplace this concept is referred to as **organization-based self-esteem** (OBSE). People high in OBSE have a high sense of personal adequacy and see themselves as important, effective, and worthwhile members of their organizations.

Research shows that people low in OBSE are more affected by job stress than people high in OBSE. Workers low in OBSE are likely to be more susceptible to the effects of role conflict (a major workplace stressor) and to poor support from their supervisors. Low OBSE workers also tend to be more passive in coping with stress.

Negative Affectivity

Negative affectivity A personality dimension characterized by a generalized life and job dissatisfaction and by a focus on negative aspects of life events.

Another personality characteristic that may influence our vulnerability to stress is **negative affectivity,** which is closely related to neuroticism, one of the so-called Big Five personality dimensions. People who measure high in negative affectivity are likely to experience distress and dissatisfaction in all areas of life, not just on the job. They focus on the negative aspects of their experiences and dwell on their failures, weaknesses, and shortcomings.

Although some research has found that people high in negative affectivity are likely to show high levels of stress, as measured by self-report inventories, other studies have failed to confirm any such effect (Spector, Chen, & O'Connell, 2000). Clearly, more research is needed.

Type of Occupation

Stress levels differ as a function of occupation. The National Institute for Occupational Safety and Health (NIOSH) ranked 130 jobs in terms of the level of stress they engender. The jobs with the highest stress levels include laborer, secretary, clinical laboratory technician, nurse, first-line supervisor, restaurant server, machine operator, farm worker, and miner.

Other stressful occupations are police officer, firefighter, computer programmer, dental technician, electrician, plumber, social worker, telephone operator, and city bus driver. One of the least stressful jobs is college professor. In general, clerical and blue-collar workers suffer more stress than do managerial and pro-

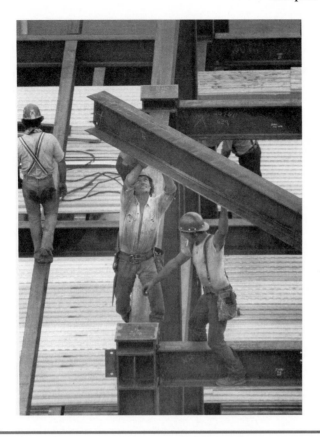

Construction work can be stressful not only because of physical hazards but also because of external factors such as completion deadlines.

fessional employees, largely because they have less opportunity to make decisions about their work and less control over working conditions.

Sex Differences

Women consistently report higher levels of job stress than men do. A study of 211 women laborers in the construction industry (traditionally a type of employment restricted to men) found that the stressors of sexual harassment and gender discrimination correlated positively with psychological and physical symptoms of poor health (Goldenhar, Swanson, Hurrell, Roder, & Deddens, 1998).

Other research has shown that women employees report headaches, anxiety, depression, sleep disturbances, and eating disorders more frequently than men employees do. Women also report more smoking and alcohol and drug use in response to workplace stress. Women in highly stressful jobs are more likely to experience spontaneous abortion and shorter menstrual cycles than are women in less stressful jobs. On the positive side, women are far more likely than men are to take advantage of social support networks to help them cope with stress (Nelson & Burke, 2000).

NEWSBREAK

At Wendy's, Every Second Counts

"Hi! May I take your order, please?" Try again. "HimayItake-yourorderplease." Talk about stress! Say it fast, as fast as you can, over and over, several hundred times a day. Your boss is holding a stopwatch to make sure you're not speaking too slowly. That's what's happening at Wendy's, the fast-food chain striving to become the fastest in the world.

"Every second is business lost," explained a Wendy's manager, eyeing the clock. He was pleased. His store had knocked 8 seconds off the average takeout delivery time. A survey of 25 fast-food restaurants found that customers' cars idled an average of 203.6 seconds from the instant they arrived at the menu board until they left the pickup window with their food. At Wendy's they cut that average down to 150.3 seconds, which put them 16.7 seconds ahead of McDonald's and 21 seconds ahead of Burger King.

But that's still not fast enough. For every 6 seconds saved at the drive-through, sales rise by 1%. A store that can increase its drive-through efficiency by 10% stands to grow its sales more than $50,000 a year.

If the timer beeps before you've finished your task, you know you're falling behind. If you can't take an order, make change, and deliver the food in less than a minute, you're too damn slow. If you can't cook 300 burgers in less than 7 seconds each, you should get out of the kitchen. Every second counts, and the boss is counting.

_____

Source: Faster food. *St. Petersburg (FL) Times*, May 19, 2000.

Minority women employees frequently experience the stress of discrimination in the workplace. A survey of 1,301 black women employed in a variety of jobs ranging from day laborer to upper-level manager found that perceived race-based discrimination was a major source of job stress. This stressor rated even higher among younger (ages 24 to 29) and better-educated black women (Mays, Coleman, & Jackson, 1996).

Women homemakers were also found to experience high levels of stress. The demands of family and the roles of wife and mother can lead to overwork, to dissatisfaction and a sense of loss of control, and to conflict with the need to seek employment outside the home. Many women homemakers report feeling depressed, believing that more demands are placed on them than on women with paying jobs.

WORK-FAMILY CONFLICTS

Both men and women report conflicts between the demands of family and the demands of the job, but the difficulties are usually greater for women. Work-family conflict has been documented among workers in many countries (see, for example, Yang, Chen, Choi, & Zou, 2000). A meta-analysis of 50 research studies showed a consistent negative relationship between work-family conflict and both job and life satisfaction. The higher the perceived amount of work-family conflict, the lower the level of satisfaction. The effects were far stronger in women than in men (Kossek & Ozeki, 1998).

The stressors associated with work-family conflict are apparently independent of type of job and working conditions, and they affect managerial as well as non-managerial employees. Today, more than 60% of all women with children 6 years of age or younger are employed outside the home. These working women are essentially holding two full-time jobs: one in the office, shop, or factory and the other at home. Spouses may help out, but the primary responsibility for family life remains with women. It is typically the woman worker who is called when a child becomes ill or who must adjust her work schedule when an elderly parent needs care.

Research conducted in Sweden on 1,800 employed men and women confirmed that a greater proportion of women than men bore the primary responsibility for child care. Therefore, employed women with children have a total workload (defined as hours spent working on the job plus hours spent working at home) that is far greater than that of employed men. In this study, the total weekly workload for women with 3 or more children was 90 hours, compared with 70 hours for men (Lundberg, 1996).

Another study in Sweden focused on 42 men and women managers. Both groups reported that their jobs were challenging and stimulating, but women showed greater physiological stress responses than did men. Women managers with children living at home continued to experience high levels of stress after the workday because of greater responsibilities connected with home and family life (Lundberg & Frankenhaueser, 1999).

In contrast, surveys of two large samples of employed parents in the United States (more than 1,100 workers combined) found no gender differences in reported work-family conflict. For both men and women, conflict was significantly and positively related to depression, poor physical health, and alcohol abuse (Frone, Russell, & Barnes, 1996). These findings were supported by a questionnaire survey of 94 mothers and 48 fathers in dual-earner families with at least one young child living at home. The results showed similar effects of work-family conflict; no significant differences were found between men and women on measures of work and family stress (Schwartzberg & Dytell, 1996).

Although women may be affected by conflicts between family and job demands, in general, women with paying jobs outside the home enjoy better health than full-time homemakers. Employed women score higher on measures of psychological well-being and have a lower risk of cardiovascular illness. The psychological and physical health advantages for employed women are greatest for women in high-status careers (Nelson & Burke, 2000).

Organizational Solutions for Work-Family Conflicts

As research continues on work-family conflicts, and as the data showing potentially harmful effects accumulate, organizations have begun to institute measures to deal with these effects. For example, providing day-care facilities at the workplace can relieve some of the concerns of employees with young children. Other approaches include flexible work scheduling, telecommuting, and opportunities for part-time work.

A survey of 1,239 organizations identified several factors among those companies most likely to provide help with work-family problems. These companies tend to be larger, to have more women employees, and to follow the lead of other companies in their industry or geographical area (Goodstein, 1994). Questionnaire results from 175 human resources executives showed that companies adopted policies on work-family conflict issues only when their personnel directors believed that failure to do so would adversely affect productivity (Milliken, Martins, & Morgan, 1998). In a study of 727 organizations, psychologists confirmed the importance of a company's size and of its emulation of the practices of competitors and neighboring companies in helping employees cope with work-family stressors. However, this survey found that it was a high percentage of women *managers,* not just of women employees in the work force as a whole, that increased a company's responsiveness (Ingram & Simons, 1995).

How effective are organizational efforts in reducing work-family conflicts? A study of 398 parents working as healthcare professionals found that flexible scheduling and supportive supervisors significantly increased employee perceptions of their degree of personal control over their work and family concerns. In turn, those perceptions of high control were significantly associated with lower levels of work-family conflict, job dissatisfaction, health complaints, and cholesterol levels. Thus, in this study, factors related to stress were found to be significantly reduced by two management practices—flexible scheduling and supportive supervisors—that are much easier and less expensive to implement than the establishment of child-care facilities (Thomas & Ganster, 1995).

Another way for organizations to help reduce work-family conflict is to provide a short period of maternity or paternity leave following the birth of a child. In 1993, the U.S. Congress passed the Family and Medical Leave Act, providing up to 12 weeks of parental leave. To investigate the effect of parental leave on job stress, 570 women (82% of whom were employed outside the home) were interviewed and asked to complete questionnaires during their pregnancy about their emotional health. The same questionnaires were administered again 1 month and 4 months after the women gave birth. The majority of the women (60%) took formal maternity leave from their jobs.

The results showed no correlation between the length of the leave taken and symptoms of stress. A longer period away from the job was not necessarily more effective than a shorter leave in alleviating the stress of balancing the demands of a new baby with the demands of the job. The researchers did find that women with full-time jobs showed higher levels of anxiety, indicating greater work-family conflict, 4 months after giving birth than did women with part-time jobs, independent of length of leave (Hyde, Klein, Essex, & Clark, 1995).

In addition, maternity leave may be harmful to a woman manager's career. An investigation involving nearly 12,000 women managers showed that taking leave for any reason was associated with significantly fewer subsequent promotions, smaller salary increases, and lower performance evaluations (Judiesch & Lyness, 1999).

> **ONLINE!**
>
> For more research on work-family conflicts, log on to *www.ilir.uiuc.edu/profs/chadwick/workfamilyfinal.htm.* To read questions from people experiencing work-family problems and to learn how they deal with them, go to *www.work family.com/wfcforum/asp/contents.asp.* For advice on balancing work and family demands, check out *www.montana. edu.wwwpb/pubs/mt9506.html* and *www.mtsu.edu/~pmccarth/work_fam.htm.*

CAUSES OF STRESS IN THE WORKPLACE

Many aspects of the work environment can induce stress. Some of these are work overload, work underload, organizational change, role conflict, and role ambiguity.

Work Overload and Work Underload

Psychologists use the term **work overload** to describe the common condition of overwork. They have identified two types: quantitative overload and qualitative overload.

Quantitative overload is the condition of having too much work to do in the time available. It is an obvious source of stress and has been linked to stress-related ailments such as coronary heart disease. The key factor seems to be the degree of control workers have over the rate at which they work rather than the amount of work itself. In general, the less control employees have over their work pace, the greater the stress. *Qualitative* overload involves work that is too difficult. Having insufficient ability to perform a job is stressful. Even employees with considerable ability can find themselves in situations in which they cannot cope with the job's demands.

A questionnaire survey of 418 employees in 143 different jobs in 65 organizations found that employees in complex jobs who believed their abilities were not high enough to meet the demands of their jobs experienced significantly higher stress than did employees who believed that their abilities matched their job's demands. In other words, employees in a situation of work overload who did not feel competent to cope with the required tasks reported a high level of stress (Xie & Johns, 1995).

This positive correlation between work overload and stress is not unique to business in the United States. A 5-year study of 1,100 factory workers in China found that increased pressure on the job (in the form of extended working hours and bonuses for extra production), combined with job insecurity during a period of layoffs, led to significant increases in the workers' blood pressure and cholesterol levels (Siegrist, 1996).

Another study of approximately 100 middle managers from 21 countries found higher levels of work overload in non-Western countries such as India, Indonesia, Korea, and Nigeria. These managers believed they had been given so much work that it was impossible to do it well (Peterson, et al., 1995). In other words, they believed that their workloads and levels of responsibility were excessive, a belief not shared to the same extent by middle managers from Western countries. The difference may relate to the greater focus on individual effort that characterizes Western cultures. Non-Western cultures tend to be more oriented toward collective efforts. Thus, the organizational climate forces non-Western managers to depend more on the abilities of their colleagues to solve work problems rather than on their own individual efforts. This, in turn, can increase the perceived demands and complexity of their jobs.

The opposite condition, **work underload**—having work that is too simple or is insufficient to fill one's time or challenge one's abilities—is also stressful. A study of 63 musicians in a symphony orchestra found that they sometimes faced both overload and underload—overload when the job tasks were too difficult and underload when the tasks did not make full use of the musicians' skills (Parasuraman & Purohit, 2000).

A study of blue-collar workers in Israel found that ratings of job satisfaction and psychological distress, as well as absences due to illness, were directly related

Work overload Too much work to perform in the time available or work that is too difficult for the employee to perform.

Work underload Work that is too simple or insufficiently challenging for one's abilities.

to the self-reported monotony of the work. The higher the monotony (the work underload), the lower the job satisfaction, the higher the psychological distress, and the greater the absences due to sickness (Melamed, Ben-avi, Luz, & Green, 1995). A survey of 5450 blue-collar workers in Finland also found a significant relationship between job monotony and increased psychological distress, such as anxiety and worry, as well as greater physiological symptoms of that stress. These relationships were strongest in men under the age of 35 and in women over the age of 35 (Kivimäki & Kalimo, 1996).

NEWSBREAK

It Gets Worse After Work

Susan R. is a manager at AT&T in Basking Ridge, New Jersey, and she is a daily victim of stress caused by work overload, both on and off the job. When she leaves her office at five o'clock, the workday is far from over. For many women like Susan, the most difficult part of the day is just beginning.

She must leave precisely at five, not a minute later, even if she's in the middle of a meeting. "It's a frantic rush to get out of the office," she said. "It's so stressful." What's her hurry? She has to pick up her 4-year-old son from his day-care center, then drive across town at the height of rush-hour traffic to collect her 7-year-old daughter from her after-school program. If she's not on time, she'll be met by a fretting child and a harried teacher (who's probably late picking up her own kids), and then docked for a late fee.

A quick stop at the grocery store to buy food for dinner, a dash home to let the dog out, prepare the meal, referee fights between the children, pay attention to her husband (who doesn't do much to help), supervise the children's homework, do the laundry, and so it goes. . . .

By the time she's gotten the kids to bed, Susan has put in more than a 12-hour workday. No wonder she's exhausted and stressed out. And she's not alone. Even for wives whose husbands share more of the child-care and household duties, the primary responsibility still falls on the woman. And if she's a single working mom, it can be worse.

How do they do it all? Where do they find the time and energy? "They steal it from themselves," said a sociologist who studied the lives of 300 mothers who had jobs outside the home. In order to spend time with their children, these women cut down on sleep and on their own free time. Today, working mothers sleep nearly 6 hours less per week and have 12 fewer hours for their own activities than do mothers who do not have outside jobs. "There's no time for hobbies or socializing," one woman said. "I can't tell you the last time I went out."

Having it all—a family and a job—is not always so terrific. There's a lot of stress along the way.

Sources: A. L. Kelly. For employed moms, the pinnacle of stress comes after work ends. *New York Times,* June 13, 1999; Working moms don't shirk times with kids. *St. Petersburg (FL) Times,* March 28, 2000.

Thus, an absence of challenge in the workplace is not necessarily beneficial. A certain level of job stress can be stimulating, invigorating, and desirable. Our goal should be to find the optimum level under which we can function and remain in good health and to avoid the extremes of work overload and work underload.

Organizational Change

Another stressor is change. Employees who see change as exciting and challenging are less vulnerable to stress than are those who view change as a threat. It is the way we perceive or respond to change, rather than the change itself, that is the source of the stress. Many people resist change, preferring the familiar so that they will know what to expect.

Consider the relationship between employees and supervisors. Once that relationship has been established, assuming it is positive, all parties feel comfortable with it because each knows what to expect from the other. The situation is predictable, safe, and secure. When the supervisor leaves and employees face a new boss, they no longer know what behaviors will be tolerated, how much work will be expected, or how their job performance will be evaluated. Such changes in the work environment can be stressful. Other stressful changes include revised work procedures, required training courses, and new workplace facilities. Company mergers can lead to concerns about job security, new managers, and different organizational policies.

A 3-year study of 397 employees of a regional water authority agency in Britain, which was changing from public to private ownership, showed how stressful such an upheaval and reorganization can be. Three levels of employees were studied: administrative, management, and manual workers. All groups displayed declines in job satisfaction and in measures of mental and physical health. Those affected most by the change (who evidenced the greatest signs of stress) were the manual workers, the group that could exercise the least control over the situation (Nelson, Cooper, & Jackson, 1995).

A stressful change for many older employees is the presence of younger workers, women workers, and workers of diverse ethnic backgrounds who bring to the workplace unfamiliar attitudes, habits, and cultural values. Employee participation in decision-making and other changes in the organizational culture can be stressful for higher-level managers.

Role Ambiguity and Role Conflict

An employee's role in the organization can be a source of stress. **Role ambiguity** arises when the scope and responsibilities of the job are unstructured or poorly defined. The employee is not sure what is expected or even what to do. This is particularly crucial for new employees, whose job guidelines may be unclear. Adequate orientation and socialization programs for new employees can reduce role ambiguity.

A study of 102 accountants revealed that they considered role ambiguity (as well as work overload) to be a high job stressor because it threatened their reputations with their supervisors. With this sample of subjects, the stress of role ambiguity was also found to generate anxiety at home as well on the job (Doby & Caplan, 1995).

Role ambiguity A situation that arises when job responsibilities are unstructured or poorly defined.

I-O psychologists have proposed three components of role ambiguity (Breaugh & Colihan, 1994):

- Performance criteria ambiguity—uncertainty about the standards used to evaluate a worker's job performance
- Work method ambiguity—uncertainty about the methods or procedures appropriate to the successful performance of the job
- Scheduling ambiguity—uncertainty about the timing or sequencing of work

You can readily see how for most jobs it would not be too difficult for supervisors to alleviate role ambiguity by establishing and promoting consistent standards and procedures.

Role conflict A situation that arises when there is a disparity between job demands and the employee's personal standards.

Role conflict arises when a disparity exists in job requirements or between the job's demands and the employee's values and expectations. For example, when a supervisor is told to allow subordinates to participate in decision making and at the same time is pressured to increase production, the supervisor faces an obvious conflict. To meet production goals immediately may require authoritarian behavior, yet meeting participation goals requires democratic behavior.

When the job requires behaviors that contradict an employee's moral code, such as when a salesperson is asked to sell a product known to be inferior or dangerous, role conflict can develop. The salesperson can quit, but the threat of unemployment may be a greater stressor than the role conflict.

Other Stressors

Supervisors and managers can be major sources of stress to their subordinates. Research confirms that poor leadership behaviors—such as when supervisors fail to be supportive of their employees or refuse to allow participation in decision making—can lead to stress.

Problems of career development—such as when an employee fails to receive an anticipated promotion—may also lead to stress. If career aspirations are not satisfied, frustration can be intense. Overpromotion can be stressful when employees are advanced beyond their level of competence to positions with which they cannot cope, leading to qualitative overload. The fear of failure on the job can induce considerable stress. Performance appraisal is a source of stress. Few people like being evaluated relative to others. Also, a poor evaluation can have a significant impact on one's career.

Taking responsibility for subordinates can be a stressor for supervisors and managers. Evaluating employees for salary, promotion, or termination decisions; providing incentives and rewards; and managing their output on a daily basis can lead to stress. Managers are much more likely to report stress-related physical complaints than are employees such as accountants whose daily responsibilities do not include supervising others.

A study of 800 hospital patients who had been employed at the time of their heart attacks found that two conditions had put them at high risk: working under a deadline and having to fire a subordinate. Making the decision to lay off an employee more than doubled a manager's risk of having a heart attack within a week (Wells, 1998).

College professor is one of the least stressful jobs.

A person otherwise free of stress on the job can be adversely affected by a boss or co-worker who is experiencing stress (a so-called stress carrier). The anxiety exhibited by one stressed employee can easily affect other people.

Assembly-line work is associated with stress because it is repetitious, monotonous, noisy, and lacks challenge and control. A study of 662 blue-collar workers in The Netherlands found that the percentage of workers in factory jobs, farming, and highway transport dealing with physical stressors, such as excessive noise, is as high as 30% (Houtman & Kompier, 1995). Other physical working conditions that are common sources of job stress are temperature extremes, poor lighting, shift work, and indoor pollution.

Computer-controlled performance monitoring can be stressful. Machine pacing of mail sorting and other repetitive keyboard tasks increases stress and is related to absenteeism, poor performance, and muscle fatigue. Automated monitoring of keystrokes and keyboard time is stressful, like having an ever-vigilant supervisor constantly looking over one's shoulder.

EFFECTS OF STRESS IN THE WORKPLACE

We have noted some of the long-term health consequences of stress, those psychosomatic disorders that arise from prolonged exposure to stressful conditions. In addition, there are long-term psychological consequences, such as tension, depression, irritability, anxiety, low self-esteem, resentment, psychological fatigue, and neuroticism. Research has also linked high work-related stress to spouse abuse, child abuse, and aggressive behavior on the job, such as overt hostility and sabotage. Other effects of work stress include mass psychogenic illness, burnout, and some types of workaholism.

Mass Psychogenic Illness

Mass psychogenic illness A stress-related disorder manifested in a variety of physical symptoms that spreads rapidly among a group of workers; popularly called assembly-line hysteria.

A stress-related disorder among assembly-line workers is **mass psychogenic illness,** popularly known as assembly-line hysteria. This stress-induced malady typically affects greater numbers of women than men. It strikes suddenly, spreading so quickly throughout a production facility that the line may have to be shut down.

Consider the case of an electronics plant in Ohio. One morning, an assembly-line worker complained of dizziness, nausea, muscular weakness, and difficulty breathing. Within minutes, nearly 40 employees went to the company health clinic with the same symptoms. The illness spread, and the plant had to be closed. Managers speculated that something was wrong with the air—perhaps some chemical, gas, virus, or other infectious agent. Physicians, toxicologists, and industrial hygienists were called in to investigate. They found nothing in the factory to explain the problem. The cause was determined to be mass psychogenic illness, a stress-related disorder that has no physical origin and that spreads by contagion.

On another assembly line, employees were packing frozen fish in boxes for shipping. One employee remarked about a strange odor. Suddenly, workers began to choke, experiencing dizziness, nausea, and trouble breathing. The plant was closed, and investigators were summoned to search the building. They found nothing, no toxic agent in the air, in the drinking water, or in the fish that the workers were processing. There was no apparent physical cause for the illness, yet there was no denying that the workers were physically sick.

Although there is no physical cause, such as a virus in the air-conditioning system or a contaminant in the drinking water, physical stressors in the workplace have been found to trigger the onset of mass psychogenic illness. For example, the noise, speed, poor lighting, variable temperatures, unpleasant odors, and work overload conditions common to assembly lines can lead to mass psychogenic illness. Often, pressure to increase production on the line may contribute to the phenomenon. This situation may involve considerable overtime work, which most employees are not in a position to refuse. Poor relations with supervisors can also be a factor. If management has not established formal grievance procedures or if communication and feedback between employees and management are poor, then the resulting friction will be a source of stress.

Another stressor related to mass psychogenic illness is social isolation. Employees who are unable to communicate with one another because of the noise and the rapid work pace can experience feelings of isolation and a lack of social support from co-workers. Work-family conflict, especially for women, can be a source of stress, which may help explain why more women than men fall victim to assembly-line hysteria.

ONLINE!

For information about mass psychogenic illness, including details of actual cases, see *www.indiana.edu/~engs/articles/ hysteria.htm* and *www.mhsource.com/pt/p000463.html.*

Burnout

The effects of job stress that result from overwork can be seen in the condition called **burnout.** Employees suffering from burnout become less energetic and less interested in their jobs. They are emotionally exhausted, apathetic, depressed, irritable, and bored. They tend to find fault with all aspects of their work environment, including co-workers, and react negatively to the suggestions of others. The quality of their work deteriorates but not necessarily the quantity.

Employees suffering from burnout tend to become rigid about their work, following rules and procedures compulsively because they are too exhausted to be flexible or to consider alternative approaches. In time, the burned-out employee will have an impact on the emotional health and efficiency of co-workers and subordinates. Advanced burnout is characterized by even lower energy, self-esteem, self-efficacy, and job involvement, as well as an increase in physical stress symptoms and social withdrawal at the very time social support is most needed. Deterioration in job performance becomes noticeable, and poor performance appraisals are usually the result.

Three components of the burnout syndrome have been described (Maslach, 1982):

1. Emotional exhaustion—the feeling of being drained and empty that is caused by excessive psychological and emotional demands, often brought about by work overload or unrealistically high expectations
2. Depersonalization—a feeling of callousness and cynicism and a reduced sensitivity toward others
3. Reduced sense of personal accomplishment—the feeling that one's actions and efforts are wasted and worthless

The Maslach Burnout Inventory was developed to measure this condition (Maslach & Jackson, 1986). It consists of four subscales to assess the components of emotional exhaustion, depersonalization, and personal accomplishment, and a related factor called personal involvement. Studies show the test to have high reliability and validity. High scores on the burnout scale have been related to exhaustion and to work overload in various occupations.

Sample items from the Burnout Inventory include the following. Do they apply to anyone you know?

- I feel emotionally drained by my work.
- I feel used up at the end of the workday.
- I feel like I'm at the end of my rope.
- I worry that this job is hardening me emotionally.

Women managers show more frequent and intense effects from the emotional exhaustion component of burnout than do men managers. Single and divorced persons have been found to be more likely than married persons to experience emotional exhaustion. Emotional exhaustion has also been related to lack of opportunity for promotion. Burnout typically strikes employees who are highly dedicated and committed to their work—those who put in overtime, take work home, or come to the office on weekends. An early sign of burnout is

Burnout A condition of job stress that results from overwork.

when these employees spend more time at work but accomplish less because of their exhaustion.

Burnout victims may feel insecure and have unfulfilling personal lives. Because they lack self-esteem and recognition off the job, they try to find it on the job. By working hard and making significant contributions to the company, they earn esteem and tangible rewards and also prove to themselves that they are worthwhile. The price for prolonged overwork is an accumulation of stress and the depletion of the body's energy. This condition, in turn, leads to physical and psychological problems.

A comparison of 241 Mexican women factory workers and 729 U.S. human services workers (teachers, police officers, and nurses) found that burnout was experienced in different ways and for different reasons. The most significant predictors of burnout for the factory workers were a low level of control over life events and high economic concerns. The most significant predictors of burnout for the human services workers were work overload and role conflict (Pines & Guendelman, 1995).

Nurses who work in intensive care units of hospitals, a highly stressful work environment, have a high likelihood of burnout. A study of 508 ICU nurses in The Netherlands (57% women, 43% men) confirmed significantly higher burnout symptoms than shown by nurses working in other parts of the hospital. The results also showed that qualitative overload was significantly related to burnout (Schaufeli, Keijsers, & Miranda, 1995).

Workaholism

Workaholism So-called addiction to work because of anxiety and insecurity or because of a genuine liking for the job.

Burnout victims are sometimes described as **workaholics,** employees who are addicted to their work. However, not all workaholics strive to perform well because they are driven by anxiety and insecurity. Some workaholics genuinely like their work and derive satisfaction from it. To them, work is not an unhealthy compulsion that gradually wears them down. Rather, work provides a healthy, enriching, and stimulating focus for their lives. These workaholics are happy, well-adjusted people who enjoy their jobs. They seldom take vacations because they feel no need to escape from their work. However, because of their intense sense of commitment, they can be a source of stress to others.

Psychologists estimate that 5% of all employees are workaholics and that the majority of these are content. These healthy workaholics are likely to have supportive families, autonomy and variety on the job, and tasks that match their levels of knowledge, skills, and abilities. Workaholics who lack these qualities tend to be discontent and dissatisfied. They are more susceptible to burnout and to the negative effects of stress.

We have a distinction, then, between healthy and unhealthy workaholism. Healthy workaholics, or work enthusiasts, are highly committed to and involved with their work and derive great enjoyment from it. Unhealthy workaholics are also highly involved with their work but derive little satisfaction from it. Unhealthy workaholics have been found to be compulsive and driven to perform their job tasks. They also score significantly higher than healthy workaholics on measures of stress and significantly lower on measures of health.

Unhealthy workaholics may have an undesirable effect on their company and their co-workers. Their compulsive addiction to work can lead to negative situations such as rigidity in thinking and analyzing problems, setting unrealistically high work hours and performance standards for colleagues and subordinates, and attempting to maintain total control over the work procedures. As a result, these workaholics find it difficult to delegate authority, request help, or function as team players. For all their effort and hard work, true workaholics may do more harm than good for their organizations.

ONLINE!

Are you a workaholic? To find out more, try *www.focus-asia.com/home/samvak/nm36.html.*

TREATING STRESS IN THE WORKPLACE

Organizational stress-management interventions include altering the organizational climate and providing treatment under employee assistance programs (EAPs). Individual techniques for dealing with stress include relaxation training, biofeedback, and behavior modification.

Organizational Techniques

Controlling the Organizational Climate.   Because one of the stressors of modern organizational life is planned change, the organization should provide sufficient support to enable employees to adapt to change. Stress can be prevented or reduced by allowing employees to participate in decisions about changes in work practices and in the organizational structure. Participation helps employees accept change and allows them to express their opinions and air their complaints.

Providing Control.   The belief that we can exercise some control over our work greatly reduces the effects of stress. Organizations can improve employees' sense of control by enriching, enlarging, and expanding jobs to provide greater responsibility and decision-making authority.

Defining Employee Roles.   To reduce the stress caused by role ambiguity, managers should tell subordinates clearly what is expected of them and what their job responsibilities are.

Eliminating Work Overload and Work Underload.   Appropriate employee selection and training programs, equitable promotion decisions, fair distribution of work, and proper matching of job requirements with employee abilities can help eliminate the stress of work overload and work underload.

Providing for Social Support.   Social support networks can reduce personal vulnerability to stress effects. Organizations can enhance social support by promoting cohesive work groups and by training supervisors to show empathy and concern for subordinates.

Research on social support shows that an increase in social support can alleviate many of the harmful effects of stress. One hypothesis is that social support moderates the impact of stressors on a person's perception of being under strain, especially in situations of work overload and role conflict. Another view is that social support enhances a person's overall ability to cope with stress. Some researchers suggest that the first-line supervisor, as the personification of the organization's social support network, is the most important buffer against job stress.

Providing Stress-management Programs.   EAPs can include in-house counseling programs on managing stress. Evaluative research has been conducted on EAPs that teach individual stress control and inoculation techniques such as relaxation, biofeedback, and cognitive restructuring. Studies show that these programs can reduce the level of physiological arousal associated with high stress. Participants who master behavioral and cognitive stress-relief techniques report less tension and fewer sleep disturbances, and an improved ability to cope with workplace stressors. A meta-analysis of 37 studies involving 1,837 participants showed that stress-inoculation techniques significantly reduced anxiety and enhanced job performance (Saunders, Driskell, Johnston, & Salas, 1996).

A study of 130 employees in The Netherlands who participated in a corporate stress-management training program found significant reductions in anxiety and psychological distress, and improvements in assertiveness. These effects lasted up to 6 months. Social workers and other employees who received two days of training in managing stress were found to be just as effective in helping other employees reduce stress as were highly trained clinical psychologists (de-Jong & Emmelkamp, 2000). Obviously, using trained employees rather than clinical psychologists as instructors would greatly reduce the cost of a stress management program.

Providing Fitness Programs.   The number of organizations offering wellness or physical fitness programs to promote occupational health is now well over 80%. By enhancing physical and emotional well-being, employees may become less vulnerable to the effects of stress. The focus is on counseling employees to change or modify unhealthy behaviors and to maintain a healthy lifestyle. Although such programs are sponsored by the organization, the responsibility for healthful behaviors—such as exercise, proper diet, and stopping smoking—rests with the employee.

Some corporate stress management programs are directed toward Type A executives in the hope of reducing the incidence of coronary heart disease. Xerox estimates that the cost to the company of the loss of an executive is $600,000. Stress reduction and behavioral change techniques are considerably less expensive. Exercises to alter Type A behaviors include speaking more slowly and learning not to interrupt others when they are talking. Executives can be trained in such management practices as delegating responsibility, establishing daily goals, setting priorities, and avoiding stress-producing situations.

Individual Techniques

Some individual techniques for dealing with stress can be taught in company-sponsored EAPs or stress reduction programs. Others can be adopted personally, such as a program of physical exercise. Exercise can increase stamina

NEWSBREAK

Take a Vacation! But Will It Work?

It happens twice a month at S. C. Johnson & Company in Racine, Wisconsin. The corporate conference room is closed, sealed by order of the "No Meeting Day Police." It's the company's way of trying to get their employees to back off, slow down, and recharge to help avoid overload and burnout.

Intel encourages its managers to avoid phoning employees after hours or sending e-mails and faxes to their homes. At Southwest Airlines, managers take an occasional "thinking day" to brainstorm by themselves—no phones, no meetings, unless it's an emergency. Other organizations suggest that employees turn off the company-provided cell phones, pagers, and e-mail on evenings and weekends, to escape the demands of work.

Radio Shack, expressing concern about employee burnout, tried a different approach. The company adopted a guilt-free vacation program, giving employees one simple rule: Don't call the office while you're on vacation! Other companies insist that employees at all levels actually take their vacations instead of accumulating the time for extra pay.

Does it work? Is a forced vacation the best way to relieve stress and prevent burnout? Dr. Dov Eden, a management professor at Tel Aviv University in Israel, studied 76 clerical workers before and after their vacations. The results were not encouraging. The benefits from the break dissipated after only 3 weeks. Employees quickly returned to their prevacation levels of stress. It was as if they had never been away.

Dr. James Quick, a professor of organizational behavior at the University of Texas at Arlington, discovered that the incidence of heart attacks rises on Monday mornings, when people return to work from their weekend break. He suggested that a longer vacation brings an even greater risk.

So what's the choice? Your work may be stressful, but now it appears that your vacation can also be harmful to your health!

Sources: D. Galant. Now for the hard part: It's over. *New York Times,* July 12, 2000; Bosses beg workers to get away. *St. Petersburg (FL) Times,* July 7, 2000.

and endurance, reduce risk factors for coronary heart disease, and dissipate excess energy and tension. Many companies sponsor physical fitness programs and provide exercise facilities and running tracks at the workplace. Other individual techniques for reducing stress are relaxation training, biofeedback, and behavior modification.

Relaxation Training.   As early as the 1930s, **relaxation training** was promoted as a way to reduce stress. Patients were taught to concentrate on one part of the body after another, systematically tensing and relaxing the muscles. By focusing on the sensations produced by the relaxed state, they could achieve progressively deeper relaxation.

Relaxation training A stress-reduction technique that concentrates on relaxing one part of the body after another.

Psychologists have proposed several refinements of this basic technique. In autogenic training, subjects learn to relax by imagining that their limbs are growing warm and heavy. In meditation, subjects concentrate on deep, regular breathing and the repetition of a phrase or sound. The relaxation-response approach combines these two techniques. The quieting reflex technique teaches subjects to achieve the relaxed state more quickly. Feedback on muscle tension can be combined with these approaches, along with self-measurement of blood pressure before and after relaxation exercises.

Biofeedback A stress-reduction technique that involves electronic monitoring of physiological processes, such that people can learn to control muscle tension, blood pressure, and brain waves.

Biofeedback.   **Biofeedback** is a popular technique for dealing with stress effects. It involves the electronic measurement of physiological processes such as heart rate, blood pressure, and muscle tension. These measurements are converted into signals, such as flashing lights or beeps, which provide feedback on how a bodily process is operating.

Using the feedback, people then learn to control their internal states. For example, suppose that a light is activated on a monitor whenever your heart is beating at a relaxed rate. With practice, you can learn to keep the light on by maintaining that relaxed heart rate. Precisely how you learn to do this has not been established, but with enough practice, you can control your heart rate and soon will no longer need feedback from the light to do so.

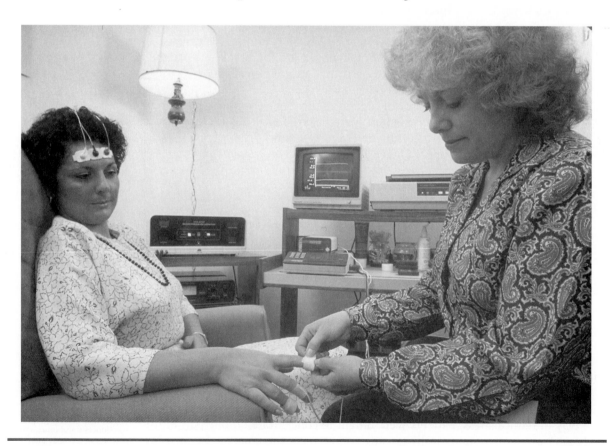

Biofeedback, a popular stress-reduction technique, involves electronic measurement and control of bodily processes such as heart rate and muscle tension.

Biofeedback can be used to control muscle tension, blood pressure, body temperature, brain waves, and stomach acid. By reducing the physiological changes that accompany stress, people can reduce the incidence of stress-related disorders.

Behavior Modification. Behavior modification techniques are effective in rendering Type A persons less vulnerable to stress. Characteristics that can be altered by behavior modification include intense drive, self-imposed deadlines, and a high rate of activity. Behavior modification involves the conditioning of positive emotional responses to stressful events.

Work, Family, and Psychological Well-Being

Conflicts between work and family are a source of stress for many working parents. In dual-earner families, the woman usually has the greater share of responsibility for childrearing and household management. Thus, she essentially has two full-time jobs.

To investigate how stress at work and at home affects the psychological well-being of dual-earner couples, a questionnaire survey was administered to 94 employed mothers and 48 employed fathers; all were from different households. The questionnaires were distributed to 350 elementary school children in a suburban New York school system, who were asked to give them to their parents. Half the fathers and one third of the mothers were in professional, technical, or management positions. The rest held clerical, service, or blue-collar jobs.

The questionnaires assessed the following factors:

- Depression and self-esteem
- Job-home interference, defined as the conflict between the demands of work and the demands of home
- Work stress: role ambiguity, work overload, lack of autonomy, nonchallenging work, work role insignificance, lack of resources on the job, and work environment discomfort
- Family stress: family role insignificance, family role overload, conflicting home demands, family role ambiguity, nonchallenge at home, lack of emotional support from spouse, lack of task sharing at home, and lack of emotional support from children

No significant differences between men and women were found on levels of work stress, family stress, job-home interference, and depression/self-esteem. However, there were significant differences in some of the dimensions of family stress.

Source: N. S. Schwartzberg and R. S. Dytell (1996). Dual-earner families: The importance of work stress and family stress for psychological well-being. *Journal of Occupational Health Psychology, 1,* 211–223.

Mothers reported higher levels of lack of task sharing at home, and fathers reported greater lack of challenge from their family role. On specific dimensions of work stress, fathers reported greater stress than mothers arising from dependency on others (a lack of autonomy).

The researchers found that for both men and women self-esteem was more affected by work stress, whereas depression was more affected by family stress. They concluded that the employees derived pride from their accomplishments at work rather than at home. However, their emotional states of happiness or depression depended more on family relationships.

The results confirm other research findings showing that mothers employed outside the home experience higher levels of time pressure and time shortage than do fathers employed outside the home. As a result, these women seem greatly concerned about the amount of assistance they receive, or fail to receive, from their spouses. The researchers referred to this effect as "Don't tell me I'm terrific. Tell me you'll do the laundry."

Think About It

1. Given the greater demands on women in dual-earner families, why do you think this and similar studies reported no gender differences in work-family conflicts?
2. Is it possible that women might be more reluctant than men to admit conflicts between their jobs and their families? If so, how would you explain this?
3. Why do you think work-family conflicts are greater among women with blue-collar jobs than among women managers and professionals?
4. How do the emotional and physical health of women who work outside the home compare with the emotional and physical health of women who are full-time homemakers?
5. What steps can employers take to reduce the stress of their employees' work-family conflicts?

SUMMARY

Occupational health psychology is concerned with the effects of stress in the workplace. **Stress** lowers productivity, increases absenteeism and turnover, and causes physiological changes. Prolonged stress can be a factor in the psychosomatic origins of illnesses, including heart disease, gastrointestinal distress, arthritis, skin diseases, allergies, headaches, and cancer. Factors that can reduce stress include high job satisfaction, control, high autonomy and power, social support, good health, job skills, and certain personality characteristics.

People identified as **Type A** may be more prone to heart attacks. They have a high competitive drive, a sense of time urgency, and high levels of hostility, aggression, anger, and impatience. **Type B** persons lack these characteristics and may be less vulnerable to stress effects. People high in **hardiness** (a belief that they can control life events, a commitment to work, and a view that change is stimulating) are less vulnerable to stress effects. Similarly, people high in self-efficacy, internal **locus of control** and self-esteem are less vulnerable to stress.

Causes of stress include work-family conflicts, **work overload, work underload,** change, **role ambiguity, role conflict,** career development problems, supervision, contact with stress carriers, machine-paced jobs, and physical conditions of the workplace. Consequences of stress include long-term effects of psychosomatic disorders and short-term effects on health, behavior, and job performance.

Mass psychogenic illness affects more women than men and is spread quickly among co-workers. It is related to physical and psychological stressors. **Burnout** is related to prolonged overwork and results in lower productivity, exhaustion, irritability, rigidity, and social withdrawal. Burnout victims are often **workaholics** who are compulsively driven to work hard out of insecurity and lack of fulfillment in their personal lives. Healthy workaholics derive satisfaction from work and are free of the stress effects of burnout.

Organizational techniques for coping with stress include emotional climate control, social support, redefinition of employee roles, and elimination of work overload and underload. Individual techniques include physical exercise, **relaxation training, biofeedback,** behavior modification, vacations, and quitting a highly stressful job.

KEY TERMS

biofeedback

burnout

hardiness

locus of control

mass psychogenic illness

negative affectivity

occupational health psychology

organization-based self-esteem

relaxation training

role ambiguity

role conflict

stress

Type A/Type B personalities

work overload

work underload

workaholism

ADDITIONAL READING

Allen, D. (2001). *Getting things done: The art of stress-free productivity.* New York: Viking. Offers advice on decision-making to minimize stress and maximize productivity. Suggests dividing tasks into categories: do it yourself, delegate it, defer action on it, or drop it.

Maslach, C., Schaufeli, W. B., & Leiter, M. P. (2001). Job burnout. *Annual Review of Psychology, 52,* 397–422. Burnout, the prolonged response to chronic emotional and interpersonal job stressors, is described in terms of exhaustion, cynicism, and inefficacy. Describes recent research on "engagement," the antithesis of burnout, which suggests possible interventions to alleviate the burnout syndrome.

Nelson, D. B., & Burke, R. J. (2000). Women executives: health, stress, and success. *Academy of Management Executive, 14*(2), 107–121. Explores the unique health issues of women with high-level paying jobs outside the home. Describes stressors, ways of coping, and effects on organizational effectiveness.

Wright, T. A., & Cropanzano, R. (2000). The role of organizational behavior in occupational health psychology. *Journal of Occupational Health Psychology, 5,* 5–10. Introduces a special section of 9 articles highlighting the effects on organizations of employee health and psychological well-being.

Engineering Psychology

Engineering psychologists are involved in the design of comfortable, safe, and efficient workplaces. From the adjustability of office chairs and the brightness level of the data displayed on your computer monitor to the controls on your fax machine, psychologists study many aspects of working life to make jobs less stressful and employees more productive. Chapter 13 describes the contributions of engineering psychologists to the design of tools, equipment, and work areas to ensure that these are compatible with the needs and abilities of employees.

Engineering
Psychology

CHAPTER 13

HISTORY AND SCOPE OF ENGINEERING PSYCHOLOGY

We have discussed various ways in which I-O psychologists contribute to the organizational goals of increasing employee efficiency, productivity, and job satisfaction. We have seen how employees with the best abilities can be recruited and selected, trained for their jobs, and supervised and motivated effectively. We have also described techniques that can be applied to optimize the quality of work life and the conditions of the work environment. But we have mentioned only briefly a factor as influential as any of those discussed—the design of the machinery and equipment employees use to do their jobs and the workspaces in which those tasks are performed.

Tools, equipment, and work stations must be compatible with the workers who use them. We may think of this as a team operation, a person and a machine functioning together to perform a task that could not be accomplished by either working alone. If the person and the machine are to work smoothly in this person-machine system, they must be compatible so that each makes use of the strengths of the other and, where necessary, compensates for the weaknesses of the other.

Engineering psychology
The design of machines and equipment for human use, and the determination of the appropriate human behaviors for the efficient operation of the machines. The field is also called human factors, human engineering, and ergonomics.

This pairing of operator and machine is the province of **engineering psychology,** also called human factors, or human engineering. British psychologists use the term *ergonomics,* which is derived from the Greek word *ergon,* meaning work, and *nomos,* meaning natural laws. In conjunction with engineers, engineering psychologists apply their knowledge of psychology to the formulation of natural laws of work. Thus, engineering psychology is the science of designing or engineering machines and equipment for human use and of engineering human behavior for the efficient operation of the machines.

Until the 1940s, the design of machinery, equipment, and industrial plants was solely the responsibility of engineers. They made design decisions on the basis of mechanical, electrical, space, and size considerations. They paid little attention to the workers who would have to operate the machines. The machine was a constant factor, incapable of being changed to meet human needs. It was the employee who would have to adapt. No matter how uncomfortable, tiring, or unsafe the equipment, the operators—the only flexible part of the person-machine system—had to adjust, to make the best of the situation and fit themselves to the machine's requirements.

Adapting the worker to the machine was accomplished through time-and-motion study, a forerunner of engineering psychology, in which jobs were analyzed to determine how they could be simplified. Of course, this approach to designing machines while ignoring the needs of the people who operated them could not be maintained. Machines were becoming too complex, requiring levels of speed, skill, and attention that threatened to exceed human capacities to monitor and control them.

The weapons developed for use in World War II placed greater demands on human abilities, not only muscle strength but also sensing, perceiving, judging, and making decisions. For example, pilots of sophisticated fighter aircraft were allowed little time to react to a dangerous situation, to determine a course of action, and to initiate the appropriate response. Radar and sonar operators also required high levels of skill. In general, the wartime equipment worked well, but mistakes were frequent. The most precise bombsight ever developed was not leading to accurate bombing. Friendly ships and aircraft were being misidentified and fired upon. Whales were mistaken for submarines. Although the machinery seemed to be functioning properly, the system—the interaction of the person and the machine—clearly was not.

It was this wartime need that spurred the development of engineering psychology, similar to the way the screening and selection needs of the army in World War I gave rise to mass psychological testing. Authorities recognized that human abilities and limitations would have to be taken into account while designing machines if the overall system was to operate efficiently. Psychologists, physiologists, and physicians soon joined engineers to design aircraft cockpits, submarine and tank crew stations, and components of military uniforms.

An example of this early work involved helping American pilots stay alive. At the time, there was no consistent or standard arrangement of displays and controls within the cockpits of different models of aircraft. A pilot used to one type of plane who was suddenly assigned to another would be confronted by a different set of displays and controls. The lever to raise the wheels in the new plane might be in the same place as the lever to operate the flaps in the old plane. Imagine trying to drive a car in which gas pedal and brake pedal are reversed. In an emergency you would probably step on what you thought was the brake pedal but would be stepping on the gas instead.

There was also no consistency in the operating characteristics of aircraft controls. Within the same cockpit, one control might be pushed upward to turn something on and another switched downward to turn something on. A number of separate controls with identical knobs were often placed close together so that a pilot whose attention was diverted would not be able to distinguish among the controls by touch alone. As these problems were recognized, they were corrected, but many pilots were killed because their machines had been designed poorly from the reference point of the pilot, whose job was to direct and control the aircraft's power.

Poor design has also led to other kinds of accidents. In 1979, a disastrous situation occurred at the nuclear power plant at Three Mile Island, Pennsylvania. The accident occurred during the night shift when the operators were less alert, but part of the problem involved a lack of attention to human needs. In the power plant's control room, instrument dials and controls had been placed too far apart. When operators detected a dangerous reading on one of the displays, valuable time was lost because the employees had to run to another part of the room to activate controls to correct the malfunction. To prevent a recurrence, the Nuclear Regulatory Commission ordered modification of nuclear power plant control rooms to consider the abilities of the human operators.

To deal with human factors in aircraft accidents, 66% of which can be traced to pilot error, the National Transportation Safety Board added engineering psychologists to its staff. Their job is to investigate pilot and crew fatigue, shift work schedules, health issues, stress, and equipment design, all of which can contribute to accidents.

Much human factors research has been conducted on passenger vehicles in an effort to make them safer. Variables studied include the brightness of automobile and motorcycle headlights; the position, color, and brightness of brake lights; and the layout of dashboard controls and displays. Since 1985, passenger cars driven in the United States must have a brake light mounted in the rear window.

This requirement is a result of human factors research on 8,000 vehicles that showed that a high-mounted brake light reduced the incidence of rear-end collisions by 50%.

Engineering psychologists are studying ways to make license plates and traffic signs more legible and noticeable at night. They investigate the effects of alcohol on driver behavior and conduct research on driver reaction time—how drivers perceive and comprehend risky situations and make decisions about responding.

Another problem engineering psychologists are tackling is the effect on visibility of tinting or solar film on car windows. Research results show that the detection of objects, such as pedestrians or other cars, through the rear window while backing up is significantly reduced when that window is tinted. In some cases, a tinted window admits only half of the available light, a finding that has led many states to regulate the use of solar film for safe visibility.

Research by engineering psychologists has demonstrated that using cell phones while driving reduces reaction time, particularly among older drivers, and can lead to a higher accident risk among drivers of all ages. These and similar research findings are instigating state regulation of cell phone use.

A study of 298 drivers in Britain found that drivers identified as being aggressive were more likely to make driving errors while trying to overtake and pass other cars. They also became irritable and confrontational when forced to deal with controls that were awkwardly placed or difficult to operate. The psychologists conducting this research concluded that poor design and layout of the car's dashboard and instrument panel could increase the risk of an accident (Matthews, Dorn, Hoyes, Davies, Glendon, & Taylor, 1998).

Engineering psychologists contribute to the design of a variety of other products, including dental and surgical implements, cameras, toothbrushes, and bucket seats for cars. They have been involved in the redesign of the mailbags used by letter carriers. Why? Because more than 20% of letter carriers suffer from musculoskeletal problems such as low back pain from carrying mailbags slung over their shoulders. A mailbag with a waist-support strap and a double bag that requires the use of both shoulders have been shown to reduce muscle fatigue.

Because the field of engineering psychology is a hybrid, it is not surprising that its practitioners have diverse backgrounds. The membership of the Human Factors and Ergonomics Society consists primarily of psychologists and engineers but also includes professionals from medicine, sociology, anthropology, computer sciences, and other behavioral and physical sciences. Over the last decade there has been a substantial increase in the number of masters-level psychologists undertaking careers in engineering psychology. The growth of the field remains dynamic, and its work extends to many types of organizations.

TIME-AND-MOTION STUDY

Time-and-motion study An early attempt to redesign work tools and to reshape the way workers performed routine, repetitive jobs.

Time-and-motion study was an early attempt to redesign work tools and equipment and to reshape the way workers performed their jobs. It stemmed from the efforts of three pioneers who focused on ways to make physical labor more efficient.

The first systematic attempt to study the performance of specific job tasks began in 1898 when Frederick W. Taylor, the promoter of scientific management, undertook an investigation of the nature of shoveling at the request of a large U.S. steel manufacturer. Taylor observed the workers and found that they were using shovels of many sizes and shapes. As a result, the loads being lifted by each man ranged from 3 1/2 pounds to 38 pounds. By experimenting with different loads, Taylor determined that the optimum shovel—the one with which workers were most efficient—held 21 1/2 pounds. Lighter or heavier loads resulted in a decrease in total daily output. Taylor introduced shovels of different sizes for handling different materials—for example, a small one for heavy iron ore and a larger one for ashes. These changes may sound trivial, but Taylor's work saved the company more than $78,000 a year, an enormous sum at that time. With the new shovels, 140 men could accomplish the same amount of work that previously required 500 men. By offering an incentive of higher pay for greater productivity, the company allowed workers to increase their wages by 60% (Taylor, 1911).

Taylor's work was the first empirical demonstration of the relationship between work tools and worker efficiency. The next pioneers in the field were Frank Gilbreth, an engineer, and Lillian Gilbreth, a psychologist, who did more than anyone else to promote time-and-motion study. Whereas Taylor had been concerned primarily with tool design and incentive wage systems, the Gilbreths were interested in the mechanics of job performance. Their goal was to eliminate all unnecessary motion (Gilbreth, 1911).

It began when Frank Gilbreth at age 17 was working as an apprentice bricklayer. During his first day on the job, he noticed that the bricklayers made many unnecessary motions in doing their work. He thought he could redesign the job to make it faster and easier, and within a year he was the fastest bricklayer on the job. Once he persuaded his co-workers to try his methods, the entire crew was accomplishing far more work without becoming exhausted.

Gilbreth designed a scaffold that could be raised or lowered so that the worker would always be at a height convenient to the task. By analyzing the hand and arm movements involved in laying bricks and changing to the most efficient ones, he found that workers could lay 350 bricks an hour instead of 120. This increase in productivity was not brought about by forcing men to work faster but by reducing the number of motions needed for laying each brick from 18 to 4 1/2.

Frank and Lillian Gilbreth organized their household and their personal lives around the principles of time-and-motion economy. Every activity was scrutinized for wasted motion. For example, Frank Gilbreth always buttoned his vest from the bottom up because it took 4 seconds less than buttoning it from the top down. He used two brushes, one in each hand, to lather his face for shaving, a savings of 17 seconds. He tried shaving with two razors simultaneously but lost more time bandaging cuts than he had saved in shaving. The efforts to schedule the activities of the 12 Gilbreth children were recounted in the popular book and movie, *Cheaper by the Dozen.*

ONLINE!

For more about the life and work of Frederick Taylor, see *www.eldritchpress.org/fwt/taylor.html.* For much, much more about Frank and Lillian Gilbreth, and about the THERBLIG (which is Gilbreth spelled backward—well, almost), go to *www.gilbrethnetwork.tripod.com.*

NEWSBREAK

World's Greatest Woman Engineer

Lillian Moller thought she was so plain that no one would ever marry her, so she decided to have a career. This was an unpopular notion for a 22-year-old woman in the year 1900. She graduated from the University of California at Berkeley that year and was the first woman ever to be chosen as the school's commencement speaker. She stayed on at Berkeley to study for her PhD in English literature with a minor in psychology. In 1904, her plans were upset when she met a handsome, charismatic, wealthy owner of a construction company.

Frank Gilbreth was 10 years older than Lillian. He lived in Boston, where Lillian and some friends had stopped on their way to Europe. When they returned, Frank was waiting at the dock with flowers. Before long, he traveled to California to meet her parents and set the date for the wedding. Frank wanted a wife, children, and all the pleasures of domesticity, but he also desired a partner for his work. At his urging, Lillian changed her major to psychology and enrolled in graduate school at Brown University. She started working alongside him at construction sites, climbing ladders and striding across steel girders high in the sky. A fearless and fast learner, Lillian was soon helping Frank with decisions that would make construction work more efficient. She encouraged Frank to give up the construction business and become a management consultant, so they could apply their ideas about work performance and efficiency to a broad range of jobs.

But the times decreed that women couldn't do such things. That was made clear to Lillian in many ways. In 1911, for example, Lillian and Frank wrote a book, *Motion Study*, but the publisher refused to list her as co-author, claiming that a woman's name would detract from the book's credibility. The same thing happened a year later with their next book. In 1914, Lillian completed her PhD in psychology, but when she tried to publish her dissertation in book form, the publisher would not let her use her first name, insisting that hardheaded businessmen would never buy a book on the psychology of management that was written by a woman. (Consequently, the title page listed the author as L. M. Gilbreth.)

Twenty years later, with a thriving consulting business to run and 12 children to raise, Lillian Moller Gilbreth found herself a widow. She tried to carry on their work, but most of the business executives for whom she and Frank had done consulting work for many years now cut her off. They had been willing to tolerate her as a wife helping her husband but wanted nothing to do with her on her own.

If she could no longer apply time-and-motion study in the workplace, the business she and Frank had built, she decided to teach others how to do it. She organized workshops on industrial management, which attracted participants from many countries. These workshops, and the quality of the trainees she turned out, enhanced her reputation so that, eventually, business and industrial organizations began to seek her advice.

Over the years, Lillian Gilbreth became immensely successful and influential. She was awarded several honorary degrees, received appointments to presidential commissions, and won accolades from the male-dominated engineering community. One business leader called her "the world's greatest woman engineer." She and Frank earned an additional measure of fame when the movie *Cheaper by the Dozen* was made about how they reared their 12 children according to the principles of time-and-motion study.

Lillian Gilbreth died in 1972, in her nineties, still working in the field of scientific management. She applied her ideas to problems of efficient work at home as well as in the factory. The next time you open your refrigerator, notice the shelves on the inside of the door. That was her idea. Does your trash can have a foot-pedal to operate the lid? That's easier to use than having to bend down to lift the lid, isn't it? That was her idea, too. Although these may seem like trivial examples to us today, Lillian Gilbreth's contributions in applying the principles of time-and-motion economy were so extensive that they touched everyday tasks not only at home, but in factories, shops, and offices, making work for everyone a little easier.

Source: R. M. Kelly & V. P. Kelly (1990). Lillian Moller Gilbreth (1878–1972). In A. N. O'Connell & N. F. Russo (Eds.), *Women in psychology: A bio-bibliographic sourcebook* (pp. 117–124). New York: Greenwood Press.

Time-and-motion engineers (sometimes called efficiency experts) have applied the Gilbreths' techniques to many types of jobs, with the goal of reducing the number of motions required. The familiar operating room procedure of having nurses place each tool in the surgeon's hand is an outgrowth of time-and-motion analysis. Previously, surgeons sought out tools themselves, a practice that greatly increased operating time.

The next time you see a United Parcel Service truck stop to make a delivery, watch how the driver behaves. Every move has been dictated by time-and-motion analysis to ensure a fast delivery. Drivers carry packages only under their left arm, step out of the truck with their right foot, cover 3 feet per second when they walk, and hold their truck's keys with the teeth face up. Unnecessary and wasteful motions have been eliminated. These procedures allow the drivers to work faster and more efficiently without creating extra work and stress.

The most significant results of time-and-motion analysis have been with routine and repetitive work. In a typical motion study the worker's movements are recorded on videotape and analyzed with a view to modifying or eliminating inefficient and wasteful motions. (The same technique is applied by sports psychologists and coaches to analyze the performance of athletes.)

From years of research, psychologists have developed guidelines for efficient work. Some rules for increasing the ease, speed, and accuracy of manual jobs include the following:

1. Minimize the distance workers must reach to get tools and supplies or to operate machines.
2. Both hands should begin and end their movement at the same time. Movements should be as symmetrical as possible. The right hand should

reach to the right for one item as the left hand reaches to the left for another item.

3. The hands should never be idle except during authorized rest breaks.
4. The hands should never do tasks that can be performed by other parts of the body, particularly legs and feet. A foot control can often be used, thus relieving the hands of one more operation.
5. Whenever possible, work materials should be held by a mechanical device, such as a vise, instead of being held by hand.
6. The work bench or table should be of sufficient height that the job can be performed when standing or when sitting on a high stool. Alternating positions relieves fatigue.

You might think that these guidelines for simplifying jobs would be received with enthusiasm. After all, the company reaps a greater output and employees' jobs are made easier. Although management has generally been pleased with the results of time-and-motion study, workers and labor unions have been suspicious, even hostile. They have argued that the only reason for time-and-motion study is to force employees to work faster. This would lead to lower pay and to dismissals because fewer workers would be needed to maintain production levels. These concerns do have some validity. Other worker complaints are that job simplification leads to boredom, to a lack of challenge and responsibility, and to low motivation, which is manifested in lower productivity.

Many satires have been written about attempts to reduce wasted motion and impose efficiency. One offers a time-and-motion analysis of a symphony orchestra performance:

> For considerable periods the four oboe players had nothing to do. The number should be reduced and the work spread more evenly over the whole of the concert. All twelve violins were playing identical notes; this seems unnecessary duplication. The staff of this section should be drastically cut. There seems to be too much repetition of some musical passages. No useful purpose is served by repeating on the horns a passage which has already been handled by the strings. It is estimated that if all redundant passages were eliminated the whole concert time of 2 hours could be reduced to 20 minutes ("How to be efficient," 1955, pp. 454–455).

Time-and-motion analysis is most applicable today for routine tasks such as assembly-line jobs. When operations, equipment, and functions are more complex and the total relationship between person and machine must be considered, a more sophisticated approach to the person-machine interaction is needed.

PERSON-MACHINE SYSTEMS

Person-machine system A system in which human and mechanical components operate together to accomplish a task.

A **person-machine system** is one in which both components work together to accomplish a task. Neither part is of value without the other. A person pushing a lawnmower is a person-machine system. A person driving a car or operating a word processor is a more complex person-machine system. At a more sophisti-

An airplane cockpit is a complex person-machine system. Displays present information on the machine's status. The flight engineer processes the information and initiates action by operating the appropriate controls.

cated level, the Concorde supersonic airliner and its crew of specialists, each responsible for a different operation, is a person-machine system. An air traffic control network includes a number of separate person-machine systems, each an integral part of the whole. If one part—mechanical or human—fails, all other parts of the system will be affected.

In all person-machine systems, the human operator receives input on the status of the machine from the displays. On the basis of this information, the operator regulates the equipment by using the controls to initiate some action (see Figure 13–1). Suppose you are driving a car on a highway at a constant speed. You receive input from the speedometer (a display), process this information mentally, and decide that you are driving too fast. Through the control action of easing your foot off the accelerator, you cause the computer-aided fuel injection system to reduce the flow of gasoline to the engine, which slows the speed of the car. This decrease in speed is displayed on the speedometer for your information, and so the process continues.

Drivers also receive information from the external environment, such as a sign noting a change in the speed limit or a slow car blocking your lane. You

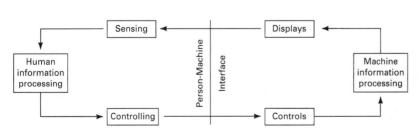

FIGURE 13–1. A person-machine system. (Adapted from "Human Factors in the Workplace" by W. C. Howell, 1991. In M. D. Dunnette and L. M. Hough (Eds.), *Handbook of Industrial and Organizational Psychology,* 2nd ed., vol. 2, p. 214. Palo Alto, CA: Consulting Psychologists Press.)

process this information and dictate a change in speed to the machine. Verification of the altered status of the machine—the new speed—is displayed on the speedometer. The principle is the same for even the most sophisticated person-machine systems. It is the total system that is the starting point for the engineering psychologist's job.

Person-machine systems vary in the extent to which the human operator is actively and continuously involved. In flying an airplane or controlling traffic at a busy airport, operators are necessary most of the time. Even when an airplane is on automatic pilot, the flight crew must be prepared to assume control in an emergency. In other person-machine systems, humans interact less extensively. Many large-scale production processes, such as those in oil refineries, are highly automated. Some products and components can be assembled entirely by industrial robots. Although this automated equipment can operate itself, it cannot design, build, or maintain itself, or replace its own light bulb. Humans remain important components of such automated manufacturing systems even when they are not directly or continuously operating the equipment.

Automation has complicated the task of engineering psychologists. Employees who are required to monitor automated equipment find that task to be more fatiguing and boring than the job of actually running a machine. Engineering psychologists must design monitoring equipment to keep observers alert and vigilant so that they can detect errors and malfunctions and respond immediately and appropriately.

In general, the definition and requirements of person-machine systems are the same, regardless of the degree of involvement of the worker with the machine. No one has yet developed a machine that can design, build, and maintain other machines. Humans are still vital to the system.

Allocating Functions

The initial step in the design of a person-machine system involves making decisions about the division of labor between the human operator and the machine. To do that, each step or process in the functioning of the total system must be analyzed to determine its characteristics: the speed, accuracy, and frequency with which it is performed; and the stress under which it occurs. When this information is evaluated, the engineering psychologist can proceed to match the requirements of the system with the abilities of the person and of the machine. Each component—person and machine—has its advantages and its limitations.

Research by psychologists, physiologists, and physicians has provided considerable information about human strengths and weaknesses, revealing those functions for which humans are superior or inferior to machines. In general, machines are better than humans in performing the following functions:

1. Machines can detect stimuli such as radar wavelengths and ultraviolet light that are beyond human sensory capacities.
2. Machines can monitor reliably for lengthy periods as long as the stimulus in question is programmed or specified in advance for the machine.
3. Machines can make large numbers of rapid, accurate calculations.
4. Machines can store and retrieve huge amounts of information with a high level of accuracy.

5. Machines can apply greater physical force continuously and rapidly.
6. Machines can engage in repetitive activities with no performance deterioration as long as proper maintenance is applied.

Of course, machines are not perfect. They have several weaknesses and limitations.

1. Machines are not very flexible. Even the most sophisticated computer can do only what it is programmed to do. When the system requires the ability to adapt to changing circumstances, machines are at a disadvantage.
2. Machines cannot learn from errors or modify their behavior on the basis of past experience. Any change in operation must be built into the system or initiated by the human operator.
3. Machines cannot improvise. They are unable to reason or to examine unprogrammed alternatives.

It seems naïve to talk, as some futurists do, about designing the human component out of the system. People can perform many vital functions that machines cannot. In other cases, people can perform functions at least as well as, and often cheaper than, machines. As long as machines lack flexibility and responsiveness, people remain necessary to the operation of the system.

Some engineers believe that they should automate every possible function in a person-machine system, relegating the operator to a peripheral role. However, fully automated systems can fail, sometimes with disastrous results.

Consider modern mass transit systems. In some subway lines, drivers do not control the train's speed, nor do they bring it to a stop at station platforms. Those functions are computer controlled. In a study of the Metrorail system in Miami, Florida, trains fail to stop at stations 10% of the time, forcing the drivers to press an emergency button to stop the train quickly, usually overshooting the station platform. Without the driver to intercede, the train proceeds automatically to the next station, delivering its passengers to the wrong place.

Drivers in this system have been reduced to being little more than monitors, acting only when the machine malfunctions. They say they find it hard to remain alert when they have so little to do. The job is boring, lacking challenge and responsibility, and it rarely requires the drivers to use their skills. As the operators become more dependent on the computer-controlled equipment, they become less capable of making crucial decisions in emergencies. No matter how thoroughly they have been trained, if their job skills are rarely used, those skills will deteriorate.

A similar problem has been found in passenger aircraft. Consider the different philosophies behind the design of the European-built Airbus and the U.S.-built Boeing 777. The Airbus is largely computer controlled and limits the actions pilots are allowed to take in flying the plane. In general, Airbus pilots are unable to override the computer. In the Boeing airplane, pilots can take the controls themselves at any time to negate or override the onboard computer. Nevertheless, all large passenger aircraft today have such efficient flight computers, navigational equipment, and automatic pilots that much of the human pilot's time is spent merely monitoring the informational displays rather than actively controlling and flying the plane. As a result, pilots can easily become bored and inattentive. The Federal Aviation Administration (FAA) has officially expressed concern that pilots' basic flying skills are deteriorating because they rely so much on automation. One could say that too many functions in modern aircraft are being allocated to the machine component of the system and not enough to the human.

ONLINE!

These Web sites offer information on a variety of issues in engineering psychology, including the design of office furniture, back safety, and computer use: *www.ergonomics.ucla.edu* and *www.office-ergo.com*.

WORKSPACE DESIGN

The harmful effects of poor workspace design can be seen in the U.S. Army's M-1 Abrams tank. The interior of a tank is the crew's workspace, and its design can influence job performance—in this case, the tank crew's fighting efficiency. The tank was designed without benefit of engineering psychology research and thus without regard for the needs and abilities of the crew. When the tank was tested, 27 of the 29 test drivers developed such severe neck and back pains that they required medical attention. Also, the drivers were unable to see the ground in front of the tank for a distance of 9 yards, making it difficult to avoid obstacles or to cross trenches.

When the engine and turret blowers were operating, more than half the tank's gunners, loaders, and drivers reported that they could not hear one another well enough to communicate because the noise of the machinery was too loud. All crew members reported visibility problems at their work stations. When drivers and tank commanders rode with an open hatch, they found that the front fenders had been so poorly designed that they did not protect the crew from rocks, dirt, and mud churned up by the tank's treads. It was obvious that the designers of the M-1 tank had given no consideration to the human factor, to the people who would have to operate the machine.

The effective design of the human operator's workspace, whether it is a bench for an electronic parts assembler, a display screen for a newspaper copywriter, or a locomotive cab for a driver, involves the following established principles from time-and-motion study and engineering psychology research.

1. All materials, tools, and supplies needed by the workers should be placed in the order in which they will be used so that the paths of the workers' movements will be continuous. Knowing that each part or tool is always in the same place saves the time and annoyance of searching for it.
2. Tools should be positioned so that they can be picked up ready for use. For example, for a job requiring the repeated use of a screwdriver, that tool can be suspended just above the work area on a coil spring. When the tool is needed, the worker can reach up without looking and pull it down ready for use.

3. All parts and tools should be within a comfortable reaching distance (approximately 28 inches). It is fatiguing for workers to change positions frequently to reach beyond the normal working area.

As an example of good workspace design, see Figure 13–2, which illustrates the workstation of a radar operator or power plant monitor. Typically, the worker is seated before a panel or console of lights, dials, and switches. The job involves monitoring and controlling the operation of complex equipment. The monitoring console is designed so that operators can see and reach everything necessary to successful job performance without leaving their chair or reaching excessively beyond normal seated posture.

Sometimes it is necessary to alter a workspace design to accommodate workers' special needs. Consider the case of pregnant women employees working at standup desks or worktables. In the latter stages of pregnancy, the enlarged abdomen forces these women to stand farther away from the table or to twist sideways, putting unusual pressure on the muscles of the back. A survey of 875 pregnant women workers in France revealed that more than half were required to perform their jobs in a standing position. A study of pregnant women workers in The Netherlands assigned to a manual assembly-line task showed that women in the late months of pregnancy were more comfortable and efficient when their work table was in a lower position (Paul, Frings-Dresen, Sallé, & Rozendal, 1995). The psychologists who conducted the study recommended that heights of all working surfaces be fully adjustable, not only to accommodate conditions such as pregnancy or overweight, but also to suit employees of different heights.

Another important consideration in workspace design is the size and shape of individual hand tools that must be used repeatedly. Applying engineering psychology principles can improve even basic tools such as hammers to make them easier, safer, and less tiring to use. Hand tools should be designed so that workers can use them without bending their wrists. Hands are less vulnerable to injury

44 in.
Will Allow the Operator
to Reach the Corners

18 in.

FIGURE 13–2. Monitoring console work arrangement. (From *Human Engineering Guide for Equipment Designers* (p. 1:37) by W. Woodson, 1954, Berkeley, CA: University of California Press. Copyright © 1954 & 1964 by The Regents of the University of California. Reprinted by permission of the University of California Press.)

FIGURE 13–3. Application of human factors principles to the design of pliers. (From "Ergonomics," 1986, *Personnel Journal*, 65(6), p. 99.)

Avoid short tool handles that press into the palm of the hand. The palm is very soft and easily damaged.

Avoid narrow tool handles that concentrate large forces onto small areas of the hand.

Tools and jobs should be designed so that they can be performed with straight wrists. Hands are stronger and less vulnerable to injury when the wrists are kept straight.

when the wrists can be kept straight. Research comparing the standard straight hammer with hammers that have handles angled at 20 degrees and 40 degrees found that for 3-minute sessions of continuous hammering the angled hammers decreased the incidence of wrist injuries, reduced muscle fatigue, and lessened workers' subjective judgments of discomfort (Schoenmarklin & Maras, 1989a, 1989b). Engineering psychology principles applicable to the design of pliers are shown in Figure 13–3.

The proper design of hand tools affects productivity, satisfaction, and physical health. The continuous use of tools that require bending the wrist while working can lead to nerve injuries, such as carpal tunnel syndrome, caused by the repetitive motion. Carpal tunnel syndrome can be painful and debilitating. It is also prevalent among people who spend a great deal of time playing the piano, knitting, or playing video games, a finding that may influence your choice of hobbies. Even the basic ballpoint pen has been redesigned to reduce stress on the tendons of the hand and wrist that can lead to carpal tunnel syndrome (Chen, 1999). The so-called Ergo Pen has a thick barrel that keeps the user from clenching the fist. Grooves in the barrel fit the index and middle fingers, and a leather thumb pad keeps the pen from slipping.

ONLINE!

Check out the ergonomic pen at *www.ergopen.com*.

Human anthropometry A branch of engineering psychology concerned with the measurement of the physical structure of the body.

A branch of engineering psychology called **human anthropometry** is concerned with the measurement of the physical structure of the human body. Complete sets of body measurements have been compiled from a large, representative sample of the population in the performance of various activities. Specific data include height (standing and sitting), shoulder breadth, back height,

FIGURE 13–4. Typical postures used in gathering body measurements (anthropometric data). (From "Engineering Anthropometry" by K. H. E. Kroemer, 1987. In G. Salvendy (Ed.), *Handbook of Human Factors*, p. 160. New York: Wiley.)

chest depth, foot and hand length, knee angle, and so on (see Figure 13–4). These measurements are applied to the design of work areas to determine, for example, normal and maximum reaching distances, tool and desk height and arrangement, size and shape of seats, and viewing angles for video display terminals.

For the millions of people who work at a desk or work bench, the seats we use, if improperly designed, can cause back and neck pain and lead to fatigue, which, in turn, reduces productive efficiency. Research has been conducted on every conceivable aspect of the design of workplace seating, and guidelines are available for various kinds of jobs. Recent studies have shown that seats are getting larger and wider—because *we* are! With the notable exception of seats in airplanes, the seats in stadiums, movie theaters, and subway cars have become roomier. The ferries crossing Puget Sound in Washington State used to hold 250 people in seats 18 inches wide. Because the operators had to install wider seats, each boat now carries only 230 people.

ONLINE!

For a fascinating, fun-filled look at bad human factors design—of everything from maps to toothbrushes—log on to *www.baddesigns.com.*

We don't buy just any seats. We design them.

GM begins with detailed studies of the human body. Biomedical research. The kind of comprehensive investigation of anatomy da Vinci undertook in the 1500s.

As a leader in the field of Human Factors Engineering, we design interiors scientifically to minimize the possible distractions from your driving.

It may take us two years and countless clay models to arrive at a more comfortable, durable seat for new GM cars and trucks. But we think it's worth it.

And we believe old Leonardo would have thought so, too.

We believe in taking the extra time, giving the extra effort and paying attention to every detail. That's what it takes to provide the quality that leads more people to buy GM cars and trucks than any other kind. And why GM owners are the most loyal on the road.

That's the GM commitment to excellence.

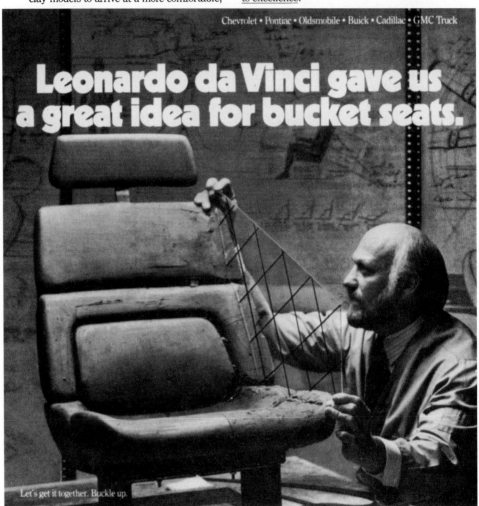

Engineering psychologists help design components for various workspaces. (Reproduced by permission of General Motors Corporation.)

DISPLAYS: PRESENTING INFORMATION

In person-machine systems, operators receive inputs from the machine through the physical senses. For example, in driving a car you receive information on the operating status of the machine from visual displays (speedometer, temperature indicator, gas gauge) and from auditory displays (the chime alerting you to fasten your seat belt or remove the ignition key). More informally, you receive inputs tactually, such as when a balky engine causes the car to vibrate.

One of the earliest decisions to be made about the presentation of information in the design of a person-machine system is to select the most effective means of communication. Visual presentation of information, the mode most frequently used, is more appropriate in the following instances:

- The message is long, difficult, and abstract.
- The environment is too noisy for auditory messages.
- The auditory channels of communication are overloaded.
- The message consists of many different kinds of information that must be presented simultaneously.

The auditory presentation of information is more effective in the following instances:

- The information is short, simple, and straightforward.
- The message is urgent; auditory signals typically attract attention more readily than visual ones do.
- The environment is too dark or otherwise does not allow for visual communication.
- The operator's job requires moving to different locations. The ears can receive messages from all directions, whereas the eyes must be focused on the display to receive messages.

Visual Displays

A common error made in the visual presentation of information is to provide more input than the operator needs to run the system. For example, most drivers do not need a tachometer to indicate engine rpm. Although this may not be a major concern in a passenger car, in an airplane, where large amounts of vital information must be displayed, any useless input adds to the display problem and is potentially confusing for the pilot. The engineering psychologist must ask: Is this information necessary to the operation of the system? If the system can function without it, then that is one less item for the busy human operator to confront. If the information *is* vital to the operation of the equipment, what is the most effective way to display it?

Three types of visual displays commonly used in person-machine systems are quantitative, qualitative, and check reading.

Quantitative Displays.   **Quantitative displays** present a precise numerical value. In situations dealing with speed, altitude, or temperature, for example, the operator must know the precise numerical value of a condition of the system. A pilot must know if the altitude is, say, 10,500 feet, as dictated by the flight

Quantitative visual displays Displays that present a precise numerical value, such as speed, altitude, or temperature.

Visual displays in an air traffic control tower present information in words, symbols, and graphics.

plan. An approximate indication of altitude instead of an exact one could lead the plane into the path of another aircraft or into a mountain in fog.

Five displays for presenting quantitative information and their relative reading accuracy are shown in Figure 13–5. You can see that the open-window display was read with the fewest errors. The vertical display was misread more than one third of the time. These results, from a now-classic research study, were ob-

FIGURE 13–5. Percentage of errors in reading five types of quantitative display. (From "The Effect of Instrument Dial Shape on Legibility" by R. Sleight, 1948, *Journal of Applied Psychology, 32,* p. 177. Copyright 1948 by the American Psychological Association. Reprinted by permission.)

tained from a laboratory experiment on instrument dial shapes in which subjects were required to read displays in a brief fixed time period.

A quantitative display that is easier to read than the open-window type is the digital display, or counter, in which actual numbers are shown. The familiar digital clock or wristwatch is an example of this type of display. Digital displays are common in electronic consumer products such as videocassette players and microwave ovens.

Although digital displays can be read faster and with fewer errors than any other type of display, they cannot be used in all situations. If the information being presented changes rapidly or continuously, a set of numbers may not remain in place long enough to be read and processed by the human operator. Digital displays are also unsuitable when it is important to know the direction or the rate of change—for example, whether temperature is rising or falling, or whether it is rising rapidly or slowly.

Qualitative Displays.   **Qualitative displays** can be used when a precise numerical reading is not necessary. For example, most drivers do not need to know the precise temperature of their car's engine. All most of us want to know is whether the temperature is in the safe operating range. With many components of person-machine systems, the operator needs to know only whether the system is functioning within the proper range and whether the values are increasing or decreasing over time.

Qualitative visual displays Displays that present a range rather than a precise numerical value. They are frequently used to show whether components, such as engine temperature, are operating in the safe or unsafe range.

A typical qualitative display is shown in Figure 13–6. The operating ranges are often color coded with the dangerous, or hot, portion in red and the safe portion in green. Such a display permits quick, accurate verification of the system's status and reduces the amount of technical information the operator must absorb.

When several qualitative displays must be checked frequently, consistent patterning makes them easier to read accurately (see Figure 13–7). Placing the dials so that they always face the same way in the normal operating range makes it easier to scan the display and detect an abnormal reading. Unpatterned displays force the operator to read each dial separately. Patterned displays are used in aircraft cockpits, power plant control rooms, and automated manufacturing plants.

Check Reading Displays.   **Check reading visual displays** are the simplest kind of visual display. They tell the operator whether the system is on or off, safe or unsafe, or operating normally or abnormally. For example, with the engine temperature gauge in your car, a warning light is sufficient to indicate whether

Check reading visual displays Displays that tell the operator whether the system is on or off, safe or unsafe, or operating normally or abnormally.

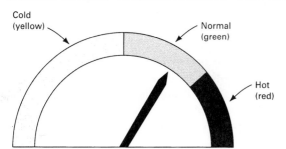

Cold (yellow)

Normal (green)

Hot (red)

FIGURE 13–6.   A qualitative visual display. (Adapted from *Human Factors in Engineering and Design* (p. 76) by E. J. McCormick, 1976, New York: McGraw-Hill.)

Unpatterned Dial Display   Patterned Dial Display

FIGURE 13–7. Patterned and unpatterned dial displays. (From *Applied Experimental Psychology* (p. 151) by A. Chapanis, W. Garner, and C. Morgan, 1949, New York: Wiley. Reprinted by permission.)

you can continue to drive safely or should stop because the engine is in danger of overheating. This kind of display is sometimes referred to as "go/no go." Either the system is in condition to operate (to go) or it is not.

The most common check reading display is the warning light. When the light is not illuminated, the system is functioning satisfactorily. When the light comes on, it indicates a system malfunction serious enough to require the operator to take immediate corrective action.

Among the considerations in the design of warning lights is level of brightness. On a display panel that contains several sources of light, it is vital that a warning light be at least twice as bright as the background to get the operator's attention. Location of warning lights is also important. They should be centrally located within the operator's field of vision. Warning lights too far to one side of a console may not be noticed when the worker is paying attention to more centrally located displays and controls. Also, flashing lights attract attention more quickly than continuous warning lights.

Visual displays today include more than the familiar lights, dials, and gauges. Much information is displayed on video screens and in words, symbols, and graphics. The electronic flight information system used in aircraft and in air traffic control radar screens combines lines, numbers, and pictorial symbols to present precise information about location. Adding color to cockpit displays reduces errors and response times for aircraft crew members in reading and processing information.

The U.S. Air Force and U.S. Navy use a different type of visual display in some of their jet fighters. These aircraft travel at such high speeds that saving even a fraction of a second in the movement of a pilot's eyes can be crucial to a mission's success. At these speeds, it is difficult for pilots to watch a target through the windscreen and simultaneously scan the instrument panel for information. The new approach enables pilots to project the required data—such as fuel level or target display—directly onto the windscreen so that they do not have to shift their eyes from place to place. This is popularly called a "heads-up" display because it allows pilots to keep their heads up while looking through the windscreen instead of glancing down to scan instruments. A similar system is available in some new cars.

Not all visual displays are so high-tech or intended for such limited use. For example, the common push/pull door signs are used every day by millions of people entering and exiting stores, factories, and office buildings. Some doors need to be pushed, others pulled. To find out how best to display this basic information visually, so that users would follow directions accurately, a study was conducted using 60 subjects under laboratory conditions and 1,100 subjects in the real world. Eleven different kinds of signs were tested. The most effective signs (those quickly identified or eliciting the greatest compliance) combined a drawing of a hand with an arrow and the word *push* or *pull* displayed horizontally (see Figure 13–8). Even a simple visual display can be improved through engineering psychology research.

Auditory Displays

An **auditory display** can be more compelling than a visual display for the following reasons: (1) Our ears are always open, but our eyes are not; (2) We can receive auditory information from all directions; and (3) Our visual sense is often taxed to capacity. Table 13–1 presents the major types of auditory alarms.

An evaluation by engineering psychologists of the auditory warning signals used in U.S. Air Force planes revealed several potential problems from the standpoint of the human operator (Doll & Folds, 1986). These findings are still relevant today as examples of poor human engineering design. First, auditory warning signals were found to be poorly standardized and inconsistent among aircraft, even among planes with similar combat roles. This violates a basic principle of engineering psychology: that displays and controls among similar types of machines be consistent.

Auditory displays Alarms or warning signals in person-machine systems. Auditory displays can be more compelling than visual displays.

Most effective (word plus symbol)

FIGURE 13–8.   Most effective and least effective door pull signs. (Adapted from T. J. B. Kline & G. A. Beitel, "Assessment of push/pull door signs: A laboratory and a field study." *Human Factors,* 1994, *36,* 688.)

Least effective (symbol only)

Let Jack Do It

"In his 15 years on the job," wrote a reporter for the *New York Times*, "Jack has been trapped in coal mines and forced to lift and carry objects that could break his back, and once while pregnant—yes, pregnant—was stuffed into a car to see if he could fit behind the wheel and reach the pedals. Jack never complains, however, because Jack is a piece of software, a virtual reality representation of a person who can take on various forms. Jack can walk, avoid obstacles, reach, and lift. But if he cannot perform a certain task, an image of the character will signal a problem, sometimes by turning a body part a different color on a computer screen. Jack rolls with the punches so that we don't have to."

By wearing virtual reality helmets, real people, like designers of cars or aircraft cockpits or workstations, can see through Jack's eyes as he becomes a driver or pilot, a factory worker or office manager. Thus, the engineering psychologists or human factors engineers can see how something works—or fails to work—before they actually build it.

For example, they might find out whether by reaching to change a radio station in your sports car, you could accidentally nudge the gear shift lever into neutral. Or whether the farmer driving the redesigned tractor has a clear view of the blades that are tilling the soil behind it. When the John Deere company learned that Jack couldn't see those blades from the new tractor cab, it was no big deal to change the design at that stage. But had the tractors already started rolling off the assembly line, it would have been tremendously expensive to redesign them.

Good ol' Jack never fails. And never gets tired or cranky or comes in late or stays home with the flu. And he costs only $25,000. In today's market, Jack's a bargain.

Source: D. Sorid. Jack is put through the wringer, so you won't be. *New York Times*, May 11, 2000.

Second, too many auditory warning signals were being used. For example, the F-15 fighter plane had 11 auditory signals (tones at various frequencies and with different numbers of repetitions). Each tone signified a separate condition, such as external threat, low altitude, or landing gear engaged. During combat missions, it would be easy for the pilot to confuse these signals and initiate the wrong control action. Many of the auditory signals sounded so similar that they would lead to confusion even under noncombat conditions.

Third, the auditory warning signals did not provide any indication of the urgency of the situation. If two signals were activated close in time, the pilot would not necessarily know quickly enough which problem was the more important.

Sometimes, even the most carefully designed person-machine system does not work as intended because the human operator violates the conditions under which the system is supposed to function. On the night of May 17, 1987, aboard the navy frigate *USS Stark* on duty in the Persian Gulf, a radar operator was mon-

TABLE 13–1 Characteristics of Auditory Alarms

Alarm	Intensity	Attention-Getting Ability
Foghorn	Very high	Good
Horn	High	Good
Whistle	High	Good, if intermittent
Siren	High	Very good, if pitch rises and falls
Bell	Medium	Good
Buzzer	Low to medium	Good
Human voice	Low to medium	Fair

Note. Adapted from "Auditory and Other Sensory Forms of Information Presentation" by B. H. Deatherage, 1972, *Human Engineering Guide to Equipment Design,* Washington, DC: U.S. Government Printing Office.

itoring a complex system that was tracking all nearby radar signals. The system had visual and auditory warning devices to alert the operator if hostile radar was detected. The system designers believed that with both visual and auditory displays, there was no way the operator could miss a warning. If the operator was looking away from the visual display screen, the auditory signal—a rapid beeping—would surely be noticed.

Yet, when hostile radar was detected that night and the visual warning signal flashed on the screen, the operator was looking away and the auditory signal failed to sound. That operator, or an operator from an earlier shift, had disconnected the auditory alarm because he found it to be annoying. Because the ship was in enemy territory, the alarm was beeping frequently, and the sailor had decided that it was bothersome.

With the auditory alarm disabled and the visual warning signal unseen, a jet fighter plane from Iraq fired an Exocet missile at the *USS Stark,* killing 37 American sailors. In this case the equipment portion of the person-machine system functioned satisfactorily, but the human operator did not.

Auditory signals may be used to transmit complex information. One example is the shipboard use of sonar for detecting underwater objects. A high-frequency sound is transmitted from beneath the ship through the water. When it strikes a large enough object, the signal is reflected back to the ship and reproduced as the familiar pinging sound heard in old war movies. The job of interpreting the message or information that the sound conveys can be difficult. Extensive training is required to be able to discriminate among the sound's various qualities. With sonar, if the detected object is moving away from the ship, the reflected sound is of a lower frequency than is the transmitted sound. An object moving toward the ship provides a higher frequency of returning sound.

Humans can receive and interpret a variety of information through the auditory sense. We are capable of responding to formal signaling procedures (warning horns, whistles, and buzzers) and to informal cues (the misfire of a car engine, the wail of a mis-wound audiotape, or the beep of the computer that lost your term paper).

CONTROLS: TAKING ACTION

In person-machine systems, once the human operators receive input through the displays and mentally process that information, they must communicate some control action to the machine. They transmit their control decisions through such devices as switches, pushbuttons, levers, cranks, steering wheels, mouses, trackballs, and foot pedals. Human factors decisions must be made about the choice, location, and shape of the controls. These decisions are based on the task's requirements; different tasks dictate different types of controls.

Engineering psychologists analyze the nature of the task to determine whether it involves, for example, turning on a light or activating some other system component. Does the task involve a fine adjustment, such as selecting one radio frequency from the spectrum of frequencies? Does it require frequent and rapid readjustment of a control, or is a single setting sufficient? How much force must the operator exert to accomplish the job? If the control must be activated in cold temperatures, will the wearing of gloves interfere with proper operation? If the control must be activated under low lighting conditions, can it be easily identified by shape alone?

Guidelines for Controls.   After system designers have answered these questions, they select the best control for the task. Engineering psychology research offers general guidelines. For a task that requires two discrete settings of a control, such as "on" and "off," a hand or foot pushbutton is a suitable on/off switch. For four or more discrete settings, a group of finger pushbuttons or a rotary selector switch is preferred. For continuous settings, knobs or cranks are the best choice. For selecting elements on a computer display, devices such as a mouse, light pen, or touch pad can be used. A selection of controls and the actions for which they are appropriate are shown in Figure 13–9. In addition, controls should satisfy the following two criteria:

1. *Control-body matching.* Although some controls could be activated with the head or the elbow, most of them use hands and feet. It is important that no one limb be given too many tasks to perform. The hands are capable of greater precision in operating controls, and the feet are capable of exerting greater force.
2. *Control-task compatibility.* A control action should imitate the movements it produces. For example, pulling an airplane's control column to the right pulls the plane to the right; the control movement and the machine's response are parallel. To lower aircraft flaps or landing gear, the control should move downward. Typically, we turn a control knob to the right (clockwise) to turn a machine on. Most people would have difficulty adjusting to a knob that turned to the left to activate a machine.

Combining Related Controls.   Wherever possible, it is more efficient to combine controls that perform similar or related operations. For example, simple radios have three control functions—on/off, volume, and station selection—yet there are only two controls. The on/off and volume controls, which perform related functions, are combined to reduce the number of separate actions required of the human operator and to save space on the control panel.

For transmitting discrete information

Hand push button	Foot push button	Toggle switch 2-position	Toggle switch 3-position	Rotary selector switch

For transmitting traditional continuous information

Knob	Crank	Wheel	Lever	Pedal

For transmitting cursor positioning information

Mouse	Trackball	Digitizing tablet	Light pen

FIGURE 13–9. Control devices and the type of information they best transmit. (From M. S. Sanders & E. J. McCormick, *Human factors in engineering and design,* 6th ed., p. 261. New York: McGraw-Hill, 1987. Copyright 1987, McGraw-Hill Book Co. Used with permission.)

Identification of Controls. Controls must be clearly marked or coded to assure their correct and rapid identification. Automobile manufacturers code instrument panels by using pictorial symbols to represent control functions (for example, a miniature wiper blade identifies the windshield wiper switch). On a crowded instrument panel, easily identifiable controls can minimize errors caused by activating the wrong control.

Shape coding means designing each knob on a console or control panel in a recognizably different shape. This allows for rapid visual identification of the correct control and permits identification by touch in low-lighting conditions or when the eyes must focus elsewhere. Sometimes the control's shape symbolizes its function. In U.S. Air Force planes the landing flap control looks like a landing flap, and the landing gear control looks like a tire. Each control is unique in touch and appearance, and the control functions can be learned quickly. Standardizing the controls on all aircraft reduces the opportunity for pilot error.

Shape coding Designing knobs for control panels in recognizably different shapes so that they can be identified by touch alone.

Placement of Controls.   Once the kind and shape of the controls have been selected, engineering psychologists determine their placement on the control panel. They also consider the control's relationship to an informational display. A primary requisite for control location is consistency or uniformity of placement. For example, we expect the gas pedal to be located to the right of the brake pedal on automobiles, and for the Enter key to be on the right side of the keyboard. The greater the standardization of control arrangement, the easier and safer it is for people to work with different models of the same system. This sounds like common sense, but it took many years before engineering psychology research was accepted and for aircraft instrument panels to be standardized. This basic design principle is still being ignored in many consumer products.

Consider the kitchen range. Typically, there are four burners on top and four knobs on a panel to control the burners. However, there is little consistency in the relationship between control knobs and burners. A survey of 49 electric and gas ranges revealed six different knob-burner operating linkages. Although this does not create as serious a problem as lack of standardization in an airplane, it can lead to burns and other accidents. With a gas range, we receive immediate feedback when we turn a knob to activate a burner, but with an electric range, we could touch a burner, thinking it was cold, to find out it had been turned on.

In the global marketplace, where a product manufactured in one country may be sold in many others, human engineers must be aware of cultural differences that may influence the product's use, such as the linkage between displays and controls. For example, research subjects in Taiwan preferred a different burner-control link when operating a 4-burner stove than subjects in the United States. They automatically reached for different knobs than the American subjects to operate the same burners. The researchers suggested that this finding reflected the Taiwanese practice of reading characters vertically and from right to left, whereas English-speaking people read horizontally and from left to right. Thus, the so-called natural approach to the use of these controls differed for people in the two cultures (Hsu & Peng, 1993).

Controls that are associated with emergency functions must be placed in the normal line of sight where they can be distinguished from other controls. The operator should be able to reach emergency controls quickly. The controls should be protected with a cover or shield so that they cannot be activated accidentally.

When displays are associated functionally with controls—such as a dial that must be set by turning a knob—they should be placed as close together as possible. It is desirable to group related displays and controls according to function. For example, in an aircraft cockpit displays and controls involving engine performance are grouped. When the order of operation is consistent, displays and controls can be grouped sequentially.

Design of Controls for People with Disabilities.   Human engineers must also consider whether the controls on consumer products can be operated easily and efficiently by persons who have physical limitations. Just as visual displays have been altered to accommodate visually impaired people (by presenting information in braille or in auditory formats, for example), so controls can be modified for use by people who are deficient in strength or in the ability to make precise muscle movements.

To determine the difficulty of operating the controls found on ordinary consumer products, 34 adults in The Netherlands were videotaped in their homes. Some 109 control operations were studied. The subjects were afflicted with arthritis or muscular disorders and all had difficulty manipulating objects with both hands. They attempted to operate washing machines, radios, stoves, alarm clocks, watches, refrigerators, coffee grinders, telephones, and kitchen and bathroom faucets. The primary difficulty detected was the amount of force required to push, pull, turn, or otherwise manipulate the controls. Often, the exertion of force was accompanied by pain.

The researcher offered the following control design recommendations to make consumer products easier to use by persons with physical disabilities (Kanis, 1993):

- Controls should operate with the least amount of force possible.
- A physically impaired person should not have to perform simultaneous operations, such as pushing and turning at the same time (the kind of manipulation required to open safety caps on pill bottles).
- Pushing a control is better than having to turn or rotate it; turning or rotating a control requires manipulations with the fingers whereas pushing can be done with the whole hand.
- A control should not have to be held down for any length of time.
- If a control has to be gripped, it should be possible to do so with the whole hand or with both hands rather than with the fingers.
- There should be no obstructions that could interfere with reaching for and operating a control.

As the U.S. population ages, engineering psychologists are beginning to consider the motor, cognitive, visual, and general health changes that are characteristic of the normal aging process. A series of focus group interviews with 59 healthy, active adults, ages 65 to 88, who were living independently, found that their major complaint was related to transportation. Specific problems included getting on and off buses, using stairs and escalators in subway stations, and driving at night (because of problems with glare and difficulty reading traffic signs). The researchers concluded that more than half of these problems encountered by elderly persons could be eliminated by the proper redesign of everyday items from a human engineering perspective (Rogers, Meyer, Walker, & Fisk, 1998).

COMPUTERS

Millions of employees use computer terminals on the job. When the human engineering aspects of the design of computer terminals and computer furniture are ignored, the result is physical strain and discomfort. Concern about the effects of prolonged computer use on employee health began in the 1970s when two employees of the *New York Times* reportedly developed cataracts, which they attributed to working at video display terminals. Many computer users have since complained of blurred vision, eyestrain, and changes in color perception.

The organization Nine to Five, the National Association of Working Women, established a telephone hotline to take complaints from computer users. In a 2-month period, it received more than 3,000 calls, 17% of which concerned eye

Don't Take Your Laptop to Lunch

NEWSBREAK

It happens every day. You've probably done it yourself. You're leaning over your computer, intent on surfing the Web or sending an e-mail, and you drop food on the keyboard. Chocolate chip cookie crumbs, pizza, cheese curls. Or worse, coffee or soda. The high-tech wonders of the workplace, which have so transformed the way we live and do our jobs—these marvels of design and engineering—can be totally ruined by a diet cola. No joke! This is a serious problem as more and more people stay at their desks to eat lunch or take their laptops to the cafeteria.

All that food and drink is messing up today's sensitive electronics. At the Execuspace company in Chicago, a woman trashed a $1000 digital telephone when she spilled iced tea on it. Sticky liquids with sugar are the worst. They jam keys and pushbuttons, clog openings, and also attract bugs. An exterminator in Chicago, whose business is obviously increasing, was quoted as saying "We're seeing more and more cockroach, mice, and ant problems in [office] cubicles." To solve this growing problem, the Amherst-Merritt International company of Dallas, Texas, is marketing a computer condom. A simple plastic sheath, called the Safeskin, keeps those nasty crumbs out of your keyboard.

But suppose you've already done the damage. Is it too late to save the mechanism? An official from Gateway advises, "Take the keyboard into the shower [unplugged, of course]. Give it a good going over with warm water. Let it sit upside down for two weeks. There's a slight possibility it will work again."

Source: Desk dining may be hazardous to office's health. *St. Petersburg (FL) Times,* April 18, 2000.

problems. However, the National Academy of Sciences concluded that there is no scientific evidence that computers caused visual damage. A study of computer users and non-users performing similar tasks found no differences between the two groups in visual complaints (Howarth & Istance, 1986).

Based on these and similar findings, engineering psychologists have suggested that most employee complaints about visual disturbances result not from the terminals but from equipment components and from the design of the work station. Equipment factors identified as potential hazards include the color of the phosphor in the cathode ray tube, the size of the screen, the degree of flicker of the characters on the screen, and the rate at which characters are generated.

In addition, level of illumination and glare in the workplace can be sources of eyestrain. Antiglare coatings and shields can be applied to reduce the problems. The overall lighting of the work area can be reduced and walls can be painted in darker colors. Fluorescent overhead lights can be replaced by indirect lighting. All these changes can enhance visual comfort for computer users.

There is evidence that people read more slowly from computer screens than from paper. Research has not identified specific factors in the display or the user—

such as length of time spent at the terminal—to explain this phenomenon, but psychologists suggest that slower reading speed may be related to the quality of the image on the screen (size, type style, clarity, and contrast with background).

Many people have a better understanding of what they read on paper than what they read on the screen. This was shown in a study of 113 college students who read and answered questions about two magazine articles. One group was presented with the material on paper; the other group read the articles on a computer. More readers of the paper version reported that the articles were interesting and persuasive than did the readers of the computer version. The readers of the paper version also showed a higher degree of comprehension of the content of the articles (Greenman, 2000).

Other complaints from computer users are fatigue and pain in wrists, hands, shoulders, neck, and back, all of which can be related to a lack of attention to human engineering concerns. For example, desks and chairs used with computer equipment are often poorly designed for jobs that involve sitting for long periods. The best chair is adjustable, enabling computer operators to adapt it to their height, weight, and posture. Periodically changing position can reduce fatigue, and this is easier to do with an adjustable chair.

Cultural differences are important in furniture design. Chairs for computer users in the United States and in European countries were found to be unsuitable for employees in Singapore. Asian workers were, on average, shorter in height and had shorter elbow-to-fingertip measurements. Also, they preferred a different seated posture (Ong, Koh, Phoon, & Low, 1988).

Desks with split and adjustable tops that hold keyboard and display screen components at different heights can increase user comfort. If the keyboard angle can be adjusted to individual needs, fatigue and back pain can be reduced (see Figure 13–10). Typically, the comfort range for keyboard operation is an angle of 7 to 20 degrees, which minimizes bending the wrists.

FIGURE 13–10. Guidelines for the design of computer work stations. (Adapted from M. S. Sanders & E. J. McCormick, *Human factors in engineering and design*, 6th ed., p. 358. New York: McGraw-Hill, 1987. Copyright 1987, McGraw-Hill Book Co. Used with permission.)

Experimental comparisons of the standard flat keyboard and the split adjustable keyboard, using experienced typists as subjects, found no differences between the two designs in terms of their causing musculoskeletal pain. However, people who used a padded wrist rest reported less pain in elbows and forearms than people who did not use a wrist rest (Smith, et al., 1998).

Finally, in the continuing effort to combat carpal tunnel syndrome, considerable attention has been paid to variations of the mouse. One, called Dr. Mouse, is essentially a joystick similar to those used in computer games. Designed in Norway, in small and large versions to fit different size hands, Dr. Mouse's buttons are on the top and front. Its manufacturer claims that it reduces stress on the nerves and arm muscles (Brier, 1999). Another mouse, called The Whale, can be stretched up to two inches longer than the standard mouse and is designed to keep the fingers flat. According to studies conducted at Cornell University, The Whale decreases the angle of the wrist and requires arm rather than hand movement to operate (Guernsey, 2000).

> ONLINE!
>
> For a report on the ergonomic advantages of The Whale, see *www.ergo.human.cornell.edu/cuehnews.html.*

The most unusual alternative to the mouse may be the FootRat, a black plastic shell that fits over the standard mouse. The FootRat attaches to one shoe with an elastic strap and is moved over a pad called a RatMat. A pedal for the other foot substitutes for the mouse's click buttons.

INDUSTRIAL ROBOTS

The use of robots to perform industrial jobs formerly done by humans has caused significant alterations in the work environment for many manufacturing jobs. Whereas computers affect jobs at all organizational levels from assembly line to corporate office, robots have changed the nature of blue-collar jobs. Workers most affected are mechanics, assemblers, welders, painters, assembly-line workers, and other semiskilled and unskilled industrial employees. According to the *Handbook of Industrial Robotics,* the number of industrial robots in the workplace has increased from 35,000 to 950,000 over the last two decades.

One fourth of the robots in U.S. companies are used in the automobile industry for welding and painting car bodies. The second largest use is in the manufacture of consumer appliances such as refrigerators and dishwashers. Robots are valuable in jobs that involve exposure to hazardous chemicals, such as spray painting epoxies on booster rockets.

Robots consistently perform better than humans do in routine, repetitive work. They are capable of producing more products of higher quality in a shorter time. In one locomotive plant a team of eight unskilled workers and their robots can produce a locomotive frame in 1 day. Previously, it took 68 skilled machinists 16 days to produce a locomotive frame.

At this automobile plant, welding and car body assembly tasks are performed by industrial robots.

Industrial robots are also superior to humans in finding defects in components or products while these items are moving rapidly along a conveyor belt. Some robots have been designed to inspect fruit, accurately detecting acceptable colors, shapes, and bruises. Other machines inspect sheets of steel or aluminum, faultlessly checking for defects in appearance and thickness.

Robots work under difficult conditions, including extremes of noise and temperature, without any deterioration in performance. They are cheaper than human labor at an average cost of approximately one third that of the typical industrial employee. Robots can be programmed to run 24 hours a day, 7 days a week, without fatigue or errors.

Aside from freeing employees from dangerous and uncomfortable work environments, most of the advantages of industrial robots accrue to management. Workers fear losing their jobs and being replaced by machines, and they are concerned about having to match their work habits to the robot's pace.

Consider the situation at a General Motors automobile assembly plant in New Jersey. In modernizing the production facility, management installed more than 200 industrial robots for welding, painting, and sealing windows. The assembly-line work force was reduced by 26%, and the number of first-line supervisors by 42%. However, an increase of 80% in the number of skilled electricians, machinists, and carpenters was required to maintain the new robots. Interviews with these skilled workers revealed that they experienced greater challenge and responsibility and more opportunities to upgrade their skills. The production workers who remained on the job reported a downgrading of responsibility and a reduction in the skills required to perform their jobs. They expressed the belief that they had become subordinate to the new equipment.

Thus, when robots are introduced into the workplace, the nature of the employees' jobs necessarily changes. In a robotized plant, it is also likely that employees will be separated by greater physical distance. This separation reduces their opportunity for social contact and group cohesiveness because more of the workday is spent alone. Some workers feel so threatened that they have engaged in sabotage. In a Russian industrial plant, high metal barricades had to be erected around the robots to protect them from angry workers.

At first glance it may appear that industrial robots are solely machines, but they are in fact person-machine systems. Once designed, built, programmed, and maintained, robots work with little human contact or intervention. But first, people are necessary to the system to design, manufacture, program, and maintain the machines.

Engineering psychologists are involved in the design of hardware and software for industrial robots. Hardware includes control panels (knobs, dials, warning signals), workspace features, operator seating, illumination, and other physical attributes of the person-machine system. Software aspects include computer programs, computer language, and the means of presenting information on the display screen.

A critical issue for engineering psychologists is the division of labor (the allocation of functions) between industrial robots and human operators. Factors affecting this decision include the cost of developing the robot, the complexity of the task, safety concerns, space limitations, and the degree of accuracy required.

The growing use of industrial robots presents continuing challenges for engineering psychologists. Robots perform detailed and skilled factory jobs such as assembling computer components and undertaking maintenance operations in nuclear power plants. In Japan, a tiny ant-size robot weighing 1/100th of an ounce has been programmed to move at 6 inches per minute. It has been designed to crawl through the smallest gaps around bundles of pipes in electric and nuclear power plants to inspect for cracks and other defects, as well as to make certain repairs.

Robots are also appearing in service industries, operating in plants and offices as tireless, vigilant security guards to patrol buildings at night and summon human guards when they sense intruders. Robot janitors clean office buildings, programmed (we hope) to avoid bumping into the robot security guards. The HelpMate Robotics company in Connecticut is marketing two-armed 5-foot-tall robots to hospitals, where they deliver medications and charts to the staff.

Fast-food chains are experimenting with robot-operated restaurants. A robot has been developed to make pizza. Activated by voice commands and programmed to recognize spoken words such as "cheese" and "pepperoni," the machine was created to assist physically disabled workers operating franchise pizza restaurants. And a machine called McRobot has been developed to flip hamburgers.

ONLINE!

For the latest information about robots of all types, plus links to related Web sites, log on to *www.fullcoverage.yahoo.com/fc/tech/robots_and_robotics*.

Reducing Physical Discomfort Through Ergonomics

We have described the discomfort that can result from a lack of attention to human engineering details and human capacities in the design of office furniture, factory equipment, and workspaces. Physical complaints are particularly common among people who work at computers. Poorly designed desks, chairs, and worktables lead not only to pain but also to employee dissatisfaction, absenteeism, and reduced productivity.

To test the effects of human engineering design principles as applied to computer workspaces, psychologists studied 577 office workers at the Department of Labor and Industries in Washington State. The research focused on musculoskeletal discomfort in workers' hands, arms, necks, shoulders, and backs. The subject group represented approximately 40% of the agency's workforce. Subjects currently worked in several offices but were soon to be brought together in a new building. They completed questionnaires prior to the move and again 7 months after relocation.

In the old workplaces, no attention had been given to human needs, but in the new building, individual modular workstations were designed with adjustable work surfaces, adjustable-height keyboards, and optimum illumination.

Ergonomic chairs were provided in three sizes, for different body types, with adjustable seat heights and back-angle tilt controls. Arm rests could be raised and lowered, and seat backs had adjustable lumbar supports. Employees were given a 1-hour ergonomics awareness training session to teach them the proper use of the new chairs and work surfaces.

Source: N. A. Nelson & B. A. Silverstein (1998). Workplace changes associated with a reduction in musculoskeletal symptoms in office workers. *Human Factors, 40,* 337–350.

The questionnaires administered to the employees assessed the following factors:

- Desk comfort: satisfaction with desk, arm rests, computer monitor and keyboard, and telephone handset
- Physical satisfaction: satisfaction with workstation, privacy, amount of space, and overall physical environment
- Glare: satisfaction with control of glare relating to lights, computer screens, and windows
- Chair comfort: satisfaction with chair adjustment and comfort

The results showed a substantial reduction in physical complaints in the workspaces designed on human engineering principles. For nearly 12% of the employees, hand and arm pain improved, and 20% reported reduced discomfort in necks, shoulders, and backs. Keep in mind that the job tasks had not changed. The employees were doing the same work in the new facility as in the old ones. The only difference was in the equipment design.

Think About It

1. What factors other than the ones described could have influenced the employees' responses in this study?
2. What criticisms would you make of this experiment? What suggestions can you make to improve it?
3. Describe other ways that proper human factors design can reduce the physical strain of computer use.
4. What does engineering psychology research show about the design of chairs, keyboards, and display screens for people who work at computers?
5. Do you think that job enrichment programs could affect the physical complaints of computer users? Why or why not?

SUMMARY

Engineering psychology is concerned with the design of tools, equipment, and workspaces to make them compatible with the abilities of employees. Psychologists consider the limitations and capacities of workers as well as the characteristics of the equipment to produce an efficient **person-machine system.** A precursor to engineering psychology was **time-and-motion study,** pioneered by Frederick Taylor and Frank and Lillian Gilbreth, which attempted to redesign tools and wage-incentive systems and to eliminate wasted motions on the job. Time-and-motion study is applied to routine jobs, whereas engineering psychology focuses on higher level jobs involving more complex systems.

The initial step in designing a person-machine system is allocating functions between human operators and machines. Humans are superior in detecting a range of stimuli, detecting rare or low-level stimuli from a confusing background, sensing and recognizing unusual or unexpected stimuli, recalling relevant information, using past experiences in making decisions, responding quickly to diverse situations, using inductive reasoning, and showing flexibility in problem solving. Machines are superior to humans in detecting stimuli beyond human sensory powers, monitoring for long periods, calculating rapidly and accurately, storing and retrieving large amounts of data, applying physical force, and engaging in repetitive tasks with no performance deterioration.

Workspace design involves principles of motion economy as well as data from **human anthropometry** (measurements of the body's physical structure). Three types of visual informational display are quantitative, qualitative, and check reading. **Quantitative displays** provide a precise numerical value. **Qualitative displays** provide an indication of relative operating conditions. **Check reading displays** tell whether a system is operating normally or abnormally or whether it is on or off. **Auditory displays** can attract attention more readily than can visual displays because the ears receive sound from all directions.

Controls to initiate action must be compatible with the task and the worker's abilities. Controls should be combined for similar or related operations and must be easily identifiable. Control identification can be aided by pictorial symbols or by **shape coding.** Controls may have to be modified for users from different cultures and for users with physical disabilities.

Computers are person-machine systems that may cause problems for the human operator. Computer use can lead to a downgrading of human skills, job dissatisfaction, boredom, and physical complaints. Robots can perform better than humans can in routine, repetitive work. Robots can produce more products of higher quality without any deterioration in job performance.

KEY TERMS

auditory displays	qualitative visual displays
check reading visual displays	quantitative visual displays
engineering psychology	shape coding
human anthropometry	time-and-motion study
person-machine systems	

ADDITIONAL READING

Carroll, J. M. (1997). Human-computer interaction. *Annual Review of Psychology, 48,* 61–83. Reviews research and applications in the field of human-computer interaction focusing on the development of user-centered systems.

Nelson, N. A., & Silverstein, B. A. (1998). Workplace changes associated with a reduction in musculoskeletal symptoms in office workers. *Human Factors, 40,* 337–350. Identifies workplace factors associated with hand/arm and neck/shoulder/back complaints among office workers.

O'Brien, T. G., & Charlton, S. G. (Eds.) (1996). *Handbook of human factors testing and evaluation.* Hillsdale, NJ: Erlbaum. A sourcebook on assessing the components of a person-machine system.

Shih, H. M., & Goonetilleke, R. S. (1998). Effectiveness of menu orientation in Chinese. *Human Factors, 40,* 569–576. An example of cultural differences in human factors applications. Studies reading and writing flow (for example, vertical versus horizontal) in the effectiveness of computer menus.

Consumer Psychology

Not everyone works for an organization, but all of us are consumers of the products and services of many organizations. We buy cars, cosmetics, clothing, and cell phones. We vote for political candidates and express our opinions on issues in public opinion polls. We respond to appeals from charities and special interest groups.

We are bombarded by communications from all these organizations—messages from business, government, and other groups urging us to behave in one way or another. These thousands of advertising appeals appear on television and computer screens and billboards, and in the pages of our magazines and newspapers.

Consumer psychologists are concerned with the interactions between consumers and organizations. Advertisers spend billions of dollars to influence our choices, and many of their persuasive techniques were devised by psychologists. Consumer psychology is also important to you as an employee. If people do not buy what your company produces, then it will not be in business for long.

Chapter 14 deals with the major facets of the producer-consumer interaction—the ways of studying consumer behavior and preferences; the nature of advertising; the importance of packaging, trademarks, and product images; and the assessment of reactions to television programs.

Consumer Psychology

CHAPTER 14

THE SCOPE OF CONSUMER PSYCHOLOGY

There is no escaping the influence of consumer psychology. Pick up a magazine, turn on the radio or TV, go online, or drive down a billboard-lined road, and almost everywhere you will be bombarded by thousands of advertising messages every day. Your phone company sends advertising flyers with your monthly bill. The supermarket prints ads on the back of your cash register receipt. Videotapes of popular films contain commercials. Public buildings post ads on the inside of the stall doors in the rest rooms.

Banks run ads on their ATMs and spew out money-saving coupons with your cash. Office buildings install high-resolution color monitors in elevators to beam ads to the captive audience. Cable TV presents a running band across the bottom of the screen to show news headlines, sports scores, weather and traffic reports, and—you guessed it—ads! Supermarket checkout lines, gas pumps, the post office, doctors' offices—you'll find high-tech ads running wherever people have to wait.

Scented paper forces us to smell a product, even if we do not look at the ad for it. Aromas of perfumes, chocolates, detergents, and the leather upholstery of the Rolls-Royce automobile fill the glossy pages of our magazines. More than a billion scent strips a year are distributed, creating severe problems for people who suffer from allergies. Thanks to microchips the size of a grain of salt, it is possible to hear advertisements in print. Several years ago, a popular brand of vodka spent $1 million on a Christmastime ad that played "Jingle Bells" when readers turned the page. The company claimed that the ad produced the largest holiday season sales in its history.

It is not possible for us to pay attention to or respond adequately to all the messages directed toward consumers, nor should we, if we want to maintain our sanity. We do not consciously perceive the majority of the messages around us, but even if we remain unaware of the details of many ads, we are certainly aware that the process of advertising is ongoing.

Consumer behavior has been of interest to I-O psychologists since the beginning of the field. In fact, it was the study of consumer behavior that launched I-O psychology. Industrial psychology dates from the early twentieth-century work of Walter Dill Scott on advertising and selling. In 1921, John B. Watson, founder of the behaviorist school of psychology, began to apply his ideas about human behavior to problems in the business world. He proposed that consumer behavior could be conditioned—and, therefore, predicted and controlled—just like any other kind of behavior. He brought the experimental and survey methods to marketing and he insisted that advertisements should focus on style and image rather than substance and fact. He also pioneered the use of celebrity endorsements.

RESEARCH METHODS

Most consumer psychology research relies on the techniques described in Chapter 2, such as laboratory experiments and surveys. Women and children are surveyed more often than are men. Consumer research is conducted in various settings, such as university laboratories, downtown intersections, homes, shopping centers, and the offices of manufacturers and advertising agencies.

Surveys and Public Opinion Polls

The premise underlying the use of surveys is simple—that is, most people can and will express their feelings, reactions, opinions, and desires when somebody asks them. This assumption holds whether we are trying to determine reactions to a new brand of peanut butter or to a presidential candidate. We have only to recall how accurately most preelection polls have predicted election results or how successfully new products have been introduced on the basis of market testing to know that the survey method often works well. However, there have also been spectacular failures to predict election results or to forecast a product's success.

Part of the difficulty is the complex and changeable nature of human behavior. Some people will tell a pollster on Friday that they intend to vote Republican and then will change their mind and vote Democratic on Tuesday. Respondents may tell an interviewer that they drink expensive imported beer, but a glance inside their refrigerator would reveal cans of some generic "lite" brand. They may have claimed to drink the imported brand because they thought it would make them appear sophisticated.

Searches of trash cans have revealed that on the average people drink twice the amount of beer and liquor than they report in consumer surveys. Survey respondents consistently underreport the amount of junk food they consume and overreport the amount of fresh fruit and diet soft drinks they eat. People tend to respond to surveys and polls with statements they believe will enhance their status, and on such vagaries elections are lost and manufacturers go bankrupt.

Focus Groups

A widely used type of survey involves **focus groups,** which are small samples of consumers who meet in groups of 8 to 12 to describe their reactions to a product, package, or ad, or to the ideas and issues being promoted by a political candidate. Members of focus groups are usually paid for their participation and are selected to match the profile of the average voter or consumer of a particular type of product. For example, only pet owners would be selected for a focus group to test an ad for dog food. Only mothers of infants would be chosen to evaluate a new disposable diaper. Focus groups can be structured on the basis of age, income, educational level, or any other variable relevant to the product.

Focus groups A method of surveying public opinion through the paid participation of 8 to 12 group members who meet to describe their reactions to a product, or advertisement, or to specific issues.

The focus group sessions are observed through one-way mirrors and videotaped for later analysis. The data produced by the focus groups—the comments and responses of the participants—are more qualitative than are those obtained from questionnaires in large-scale empirical surveys. Sometimes, focus group members are not asked direct questions but are observed as they try to use a new product. In a session to evaluate a disposable razor, observers found that many men cut themselves while shaving because the package directions were not clear.

As in surveys, focus group participants may distort their answers, saying what they think others want to hear—or what they want others to hear. Consider the focus group that was discussing ads for a company that performed surgical hair replacements (Lauro, 2000). The men in the group all insisted that they were not bothered, personally, by losing their hair. Yet they were all wearing hats—on a hot day in Atlanta, Georgia! Their behavior may have been more truly reflective of their attitude about hair loss than what they said to others in the group, but how could we know for sure?

NEWSBREAK

Are You a Minivan or an SUV?

Consumer researchers tell us that different products attract different kinds of people. This seems particularly true for the kinds of automobile we drive. A survey of 5,400 owners of minivans and sport utility vehicles revealed that what you drive tells the world a lot about your personality. And maybe that's why you chose it.

The research showed that SUV owners tend to be more restless, more devoted to pleasurable pursuits, less social, and more fearful of crime than are people who purchased minivans. Minivan owners tend to be more self-confident and sociable and more comfortable with the idea of being married and having children than are SUV drivers.

Both groups said they wanted to be "in control" of their vehicle, but they don't mean the same thing by that phrase. Minivan people want to be in control in terms of safety, the ability to maneuver well in traffic, and to park easily. SUV people want to be in control in the sense of dominating everyone around them.

It is not surprising, then, that SUV drivers have been found to be more aggressive and less concerned with behaving courteously to drivers of other vehicles. A French anthropologist who is a consultant to Ford, General Motors, and DaimlerChrysler said, "Sport utilities are designed to be masculine and assertive, often with hoods that resemble those on 18-wheel trucks and vertical metal slats across the grilles to give the appearance of a jungle cat's teeth. Sport utilities are designed to appeal to Americans' deepest fears of violence and crime."

SUVs are like weapons, he concluded, "armored cars for the battlefield." Their message is *"Don't mess with me."*

What do you drive? Hmmmmm?

Source: K. Bradsher. Was Freud a minivan or an SUV kind of guy? *New York Times,* July 17, 2000.

Virtual focus groups conducted online function in a similar way as face-to-face groups and offer the advantages of lower cost and greater efficiency. They can sample a more diverse group of people, including elderly or disabled persons, full-time homemakers and mothers with young children, all of whom might lack the time and transportation to come to a central meeting place for the focus group session.

The responses of members of actual and virtual focus groups may differ. Usually, in a face-to-face meeting, one person at a time expresses an opinion. Sometimes, one individual will dominate the group. In an online meeting, all participants have the chance to speak simultaneously and thus will tend to be less influenced by the opinions of others. When dealing with sensitive topics such as health issues, the privacy and anonymity of an online session enables people to speak more candidly (Collins, 2000).

Projective Techniques

We cannot uncover all human motivations by asking questions that permit people to mask or distort their true intentions and feelings. To probe these deeper motivations, psychologists recommend in-depth procedures such as projective techniques.

We described projective techniques in Chapter 4—for example, the Rorschach Inkblot Test, the Thematic Apperception Test, and the sentence completion test. Additional projective techniques used in market and motivation research are listed in Table 14–1. The theory behind the use of projective techniques is the same whether they are applied to employee selection or to consumer behavior. When people are presented with an ambiguous stimulus, such as an inkblot, it is assumed that they will project their needs, fears, and values onto the stimulus in the act of interpreting it.

An example of the use of projective techniques to study consumer behavior involved the reaction of low-income Southern women to a new brand of roach killer packaged in small plastic trays. Surveys showed that consumers *said* they believed the plastic trays were far more effective than the old-style sprays, yet they continued to buy the sprays. To determine the reasons for this inconsistency, groups of women were asked to draw pictures of roaches and to write stories about them. The researchers reported the following about the possible motivation of the female consumers:

> The results were very informative—all the roaches in the pictures were male, "symbolizing men who the women said had abandoned them and left them feeling poor and powerless." The women were said to be expressing their built-up hostility by spraying the roaches and watching them squirm and die! (Foxall & Goldsmith, 1994, p. 162).

Direct questioning would not have revealed this motivation.

In theory, the projective approach offers the same advantages as projective tests for employee selection, namely, the ability to reach deeper levels of motivation and to uncover feelings and desires that cannot be assessed by objective tests and questionnaires. However, projective tests are low in reliability and validity.

TABLE 14–1 Projective Techniques for Market Research

Technique	Instructions to Consumers
Role Playing	Imagine you are the manufacturer of this brand of athletic shoe . . .
Analogies	Describe yourself as a corn flake . . . Describe this brand of deodorant as a kind of flower . . .
Psychodrawings	Draw brown bread as compared with white bread.
Personifications	If jeans came to life as a person, who would it be?
Obituaries	Write an obituary for roach killer.

Adapted from J. Lannon. Asking the right questions: What do people do with advertising? In D. A. Aaker & A. L. Biel (Eds.), *Brand Equity and Advertising.* Hillsdale, NJ: Erlbaum, 1993, p. 169.

Even the most highly trained and experienced psychologists can disagree on the interpretation of projective test results. If the method is of doubtful validity in a clinical setting, it may be more questionable in consumer research where the practitioner may not even be a trained psychologist. There have been successful uses of projective techniques to study consumer behavior, but because the advertising industry does not publicize its failures, it is difficult to determine the extent of that success.

Observations of Shopping Behavior

Consumer surveys and projective techniques share a basic weakness. They reveal only what people *say* they believe or will do. These expressed intentions do not always coincide with behavior. Because of this discrepancy, some consumer psychologists prefer behavioral observation as the most accurate way to investigate consumer behavior—that is, to watch what people do when purchasing a product or when expressing their preference by selecting one brand over another.

Common sense suggests that acceptance of a new product or advertising campaign will be reflected in subsequent sales figures. For example, if sales of a toothpaste brand double in the 6 months following an ad campaign, then the campaign must have been successful. However, unless all other variables capable of influencing sales were controlled, we cannot conclude with certainty that the new advertising program was solely or even partially responsible for the boost in sales.

Suppose the company's aggressive sales staff arranged for more prominent shelf display of the toothpaste during the 6-month period. That increased visibility could have contributed to higher sales, independent of the ad campaign. Or suppose the company's leading competitor was faulted in a government report for adding an allegedly harmful ingredient to its toothpaste formula. That criticism could contribute to higher sales for all other toothpaste manufacturers. Thus, sales data can reflect factors other than the one being evaluated, and without adequate control over all possible influencing variables, we cannot determine precisely what caused any increase or decrease in sales.

Would you have guessed that the kind of music played in a supermarket can influence a shopper's choice of wine, regardless of any advertising campaign? At a market in England over a period of 2 weeks, French music and German music were played over the loudspeakers on alternate days. French wines accounted for more sales on the French music days, and German wines sold best when German music was played. Yet when the shoppers were questioned after they had made their purchases, most were unaware of the influence of the music (North, Hargreaves, & McKendrick, 1999).

A direct way to investigate purchasing behavior is to place observers in stores. Researchers have watched mothers with young children as they shopped for cereals and snack foods. More than 65% of the time, children ask for a particular product. And more than half the time, the mothers buy the products their children demand. This kind of data is especially valuable because it indicates that children, not adults, should be the target of ads for cereals and snack foods. Had the mothers been questioned directly in a survey, however, they might have said that *they* were the ones to choose these products, not wanting to appear to be dominated by their children—or perhaps not realizing the extent of their children's influence.

Another observation of purchasing behavior resulted in a change in how a product was stocked. Supermarket observers noted that while adults purchased dog food, dog treats were more often selected by children or older persons. However, dog treats were usually stocked on the upper shelves. Hidden cameras caught children climbing on the shelves to reach the dog cookies. Elderly women were observed using boxes of foil or other long objects to knock down a favorite brand of dog biscuit. By moving the dog treats to lower, more accessible shelves, sales improved almost overnight (Underhill, 1999).

Although observations of actual purchasing behavior can be useful, they are costly and time-consuming. There are other problems as well. One relates to adequate sampling of shopping behavior. Stores in different locations (such as inner city versus suburban) attract customers with different needs and income levels. For example, a 3-year study of 1,215 households found that city shoppers were more likely to be single, separated, divorced, or widowed, retired or unemployed. They typically had less education and lower annual income than did suburban shoppers (Smith, 1999). As you might expect, then, city and suburban shoppers preferred different kinds of stores, chose different types of products, and had differing amounts of disposable income for shopping.

Various types of shoppers can be found in the same store at different times of the day or week. People who shop in the evenings and on weekends may have different buying habits from those of people who shop during the day. The research design must compensate for this problem by providing for observations at an adequate sample of locations and shopping hours, but this increases the cost of the research.

Another problem with behavioral observations of purchasing behavior is the lack of experimental control over other influencing variables; this is a weakness of all types of observational research studies. In observing supermarket shopping patterns in urban and suburban locations, for example, it is difficult to determine whether the differences found are a function of socioeconomic level, ethnic composition, shelf arrangement, or inventory. All these factors could affect the outcome of the research.

A study of 87 consumers shopping for dishes and microwave ovens found that a significant influencing factor was the country of origin of the company making the product (Knight, 1999). These shoppers preferred U.S.-made items over Japanese-made products and were willing to pay higher prices for them. However, they were not willing to pay a higher price for a product of the same quality from a Japanese company, even if it was assembled in the United States.

Brand Identification and Preference Research

Consumer psychologists are also interested in how well shoppers recognize, identify, or recall specific product brands. Much of this research focuses on the ability to discriminate among competing brands of a product. When all recognizable cues are removed—such as product name and distinctive packaging—can consumers truly distinguish, say, one brand of cola from another? Studies consistently demonstrate that many people cannot discriminate among brands of products such as soft drinks, cigarettes, beer, and margarine. Researchers have concluded that many consumer preferences and loyalties are based on factors other than the product's taste or other intrinsic qualities.

Testing Reactions to Advertising

A major research activity of consumer psychologists is testing the effectiveness of advertising and promotional campaigns. The most direct approach is to ask people for their reactions to an ad. Does the ad make them want to buy the product? Do they believe the ad? Which of two ads for a product do they find more interesting? It is necessary that the respondents be a representative sample of the population for whom the product is intended. Using single men or elderly women to pretest an ad for baby food is not likely to yield useful results.

Aided Recall.   The most popular technique to test advertising effectiveness is **aided recall,** which is used to determine the extent to which the contents of an ad can be remembered.

> **Aided recall technique**
> A test of advertising effectiveness to determine the extent to which ad content can be recalled. The interviewer aids the recall by asking specific questions.

Once an ad has appeared in a magazine or broadcast on radio or television, a sample of consumers is questioned, usually the following day, about whether they read the magazine or heard or saw the program in which the commercial appeared. If so, they are asked to tell as much of the selling message as they can recall. The interviewer asks specific questions about the nature of the ad; this aids the recall. However, a high rate of recall for an ad's message did not necessarily lead the consumer to purchase the product.

Recognition.   Another technique for testing the effectiveness of ads is **recognition.** People who have seen a particular television program or magazine are shown copies of the ads and are questioned about them.

> **Recognition technique**
> A technique for testing advertising effectiveness by asking people if they recognize a particular ad, where they saw it, and what they can recall about it.

Do the consumers recognize the ad and remember where they saw it? Do they recall the name of the product? Had they read the message? Unfortunately, people may say that they have seen an ad or commercial even when they have not. When researchers showed people ads that had not yet appeared in the media, some respondents claimed to have seen them. A comparison of aided recall and recognition techniques showed that recognition was the more sensitive measure of memory for TV commercials.

Physiological Measures.   Because TV commercials are designed to elicit an emotional response in viewers, physiological measures of those emotions are an effective way to measure a commercial's usefulness. This hypothesis was supported by research on 49 adult subjects (25 women and 24 men) who were exposed to 17 30-second commercials for a variety of consumer products and services, including automobiles, soft drinks, foods, beauty aids, movies, and telecommunication companies (Hazlett & Hazlett, 1999). The subjects rated each ad on its likability and the intensity of emotion (such as pleasure) that it aroused. Recall tests were given 4 days later.

While the subjects were viewing the commercials, their physiological responses were measured by electromyography (EMG), which detects changes in the electrical activity of the muscles. When applied to certain facial muscles, it measures a person's reaction to emotional stimuli. The results showed that facial EMG data correlated strongly and positively with measures of recall for the content of the ads. In other words, the more intense the emotional response, the greater the recall, and thus, the researchers suggested, the greater the effectiveness of the TV commercial.

Sales Tests. Some psychologists argue that the only meaningful test of advertising effectiveness is whether it results in higher sales. However, we have noted the limitations of using sales data as a measure of advertising success. The **sales test technique** is designed to reduce those problems because it permits experimental control of extraneous variables. Sales tests have been found to be a highly accurate way of assessing the impact of advertising on sales.

In a sales test, an advertising campaign is introduced in selected test markets, such as a specific neighborhood, city, or other geographical area. Other locations, chosen to be as similar as possible to the test markets, serve as controls; the new advertising is not presented in these control areas. If the test and control areas are comparable, then any change in sales within the test areas can be attributed to the advertising campaign. The control over possible influencing variables is the major advantage of sales tests. The researcher is not measuring interest in an ad or what subjects say they remember, but whether they actually buy the product on the basis of the ad.

The use of sales tests for studying advertising effectiveness also has limitations. An adequate sales test is costly. It takes time to arrange, and it requires precise accounting of the purchasing behavior of a large number of people. Another problem involves the areas selected for the control group. By not exposing people in the control markets to the new ad campaign, the company risks losing sales to its competitors.

Coupon Returns. The effectiveness of magazine and newspaper advertising can be tested by evaluating coupon returns. When coupons are returned to the manufacturer to obtain a product sample or to enter a contest, they provide a measure of reader interest. When coupons are used to purchase a product or receive a discount (cents-off coupons), they measure actual buying behavior. However, if the inducement to return the coupon is attractive, such as when a West Coast mail-order retailer offered a free pair of sweat socks to introduce a house brand, there is the danger that people will respond even though they have no interest in the product. Many people just want to get something free. There are also people who will return virtually any coupon because they like to get mail. It is difficult to determine how many coupon returns come from habitual coupon clippers and how many come from people genuinely interested in the product.

Coupon returns may indicate the attention-getting value of an ad, but they do not provide a direct measure of the ad's impact on sales. When coupons offer a reduced price for a product, they are effective in inducing people to change brands, at least temporarily. A price reduction obtained by redeeming a coupon at the supermarket promotes greater sales than an equivalent price markdown given at the store.

Sales test technique A way of testing the effectiveness of an advertising campaign by introducing the new advertising in selected test markets.

ONLINE!

For access to free coupons, log on to *www.coupons.yahoo.com/; www.qponz.com/;* and *www.bigcoupons.com/.*

Coupons Make a Lot of Cents

It started in 1895, more than a hundred years ago, when Asa Chandler, of Atlanta, Georgia, distributed coupons for a free glass of Coca-Cola at his soda fountain. Today, an estimated 270 billion cents-off, free-product, and rebate coupons are distributed annually, an average of almost 3,000 for every U.S. household. We cut them out of newspapers and magazines or download them from the Internet and take them to stores to redeem for our purchases of toothpaste, headache remedies, cookies, and breakfast cereal. Pharmacies give them out for discounts on prescription drugs, department stores offer them for special sales, and cemeteries have dollars-off coupons for gravesites.

Coupons can save real money. The average family that uses coupons can count on saving approximately $700 a year, a substantial hourly payback rate for the time required to clip, assemble, and organize the coupons. Hard-core coupon users, who have been known to purchase several copies of the Sunday newspaper to get additional coupons, save even more money.

Most people obtain their coupons from the Sunday newspapers and use them primarily at the supermarket. Grocery store surveys have shown that 9 out of every 10 shoppers said that they had used at least one coupon during the previous 6 months. However, most of the coupons made available in newspapers and magazines are never redeemed. Although sufficient research data are not yet available, it can be suggested that this low redemption rate will change because of the Internet. Consumers can now download and print coupons at home and also receive e-mail alerts about new coupons for particular brands and products. If this type of distribution becomes popular, companies can save money by no longer printing coupons for an audience that largely ignores them. Faithful shoppers who want a certain cents-off coupon can obtain it through their computers. Thus, the redemption rate and use of coupons should increase dramatically.

Sources: No more clipping. *Newsweek,* April 1, 1996. It all started with a coupon for a free coke. *St. Petersburg (FL) Times,* January 11, 1996. D. R. Fortin, Clipping coupons in cyberspace. *Psychology and Marketing, 17*(6), 515–534.

TELEVISION PROGRAMMING RESEARCH

Millions of dollars are spent annually to develop television programs that will attract and hold a sizable portion of the viewing audience. Networks compete keenly for the advertising dollar. The fact that the majority of new programs are canceled before the viewing season is half over attests to the frequency with which television executives are unable to select winning programs. Several techniques are available to help predict the likelihood of success for a program or series, as well as audience size and composition.

Predicting Audience Response to New Programming. Before a program is aired, samples of potential viewers are invited to screen previews or pilot programs. The usual procedure is for viewers to communicate their reactions continuously throughout the show. They are given a control device with two pushbuttons. When they like a particular scene, they press one button; when they dislike a scene, they press the other button. When they are indifferent or neutral, they do not press either button.

These studies of audience reaction can be an excellent way of predicting program acceptance, assuming the subjects are a representative sample of the intended viewing audience. Unfortunately, most viewer samples selected by television networks are composed of people chosen at random off the street. People who happen to be walking past a TV studio in New York or Los Angeles at a particular time of day can hardly be considered typical of the viewer population as a whole.

Determining Audience Size and Composition. Viewership ratings determine which programs remain on the air. These data are then used as a basis for determining how much networks and stations can charge advertisers for broadcasting their commercials. In telephone surveys to gauge audience size and composition, interviewers ask respondents about their television viewing during a recent period, such as the previous day or week, and inquire about the programs that were seen and the family members who watched each program. Interviewers may also ask what program, if any, is being watched at the moment of the telephone call.

Nielsen Ratings. Nielsen Media Research uses mechanical devices to assess audience size and composition. These devices eliminate the errors inherent in telephone surveys. A recorder called the Audimeter, installed in the houses of a viewer sample, notes the times the television set is on and the channels to which it is tuned. Although the Audimeter provides an accurate record of channel choice for all programming periods, it does not tell who is watching a particular program, or whether anyone is watching. Some people leave a TV set on much of the day as a babysitter for infants or because they like the sound.

Nielsen uses a diary system during periods of ratings sweeps in which 250,000 households are asked to record viewing choices. Critics of this approach argue that it fails to reflect the way people use TV nowadays. Many people channel-surf rapidly from one station to another; this behavior is rarely recorded in the viewer diaries. Other people multitask, doing two or three things at once and thus not paying close attention to whatever program (and whatever commercial) happens to be on.

Nielsen executives admit to other problems with the diary system. Most people fill out their diaries at the end of the week, rather than nightly, and so rely on their memory of what programs they watched. Often, they will report that they watched their favorite programs out of habit, even if it was not shown that week. Further, Nielsen reports that the cooperation rate of their target households has fallen to a low of 30% (Carter, 2000).

The bulk of the Nielsen ratings data comes from the People Meter, which looks like a standard remote control device. Each member of the sample of 5,000 households is assigned a personal code to enter when he or she is watching television. Thus, the People Meter registers who is watching what channel. When the viewer leaves the room, he or she is supposed to push appropriate buttons to tell the People Meter, but some viewers fail to do so. Some viewers will enter another family member's code as a joke. Further, few people in the Nielsen sample bother to push the appropriate buttons on the People Meter to indicate age and sex data. Viewers most likely to follow instructions on using the device are older persons who have only one television set. Nielsen concedes that only half of their randomly selected families accept the offer of a People Meter, and it is not known how these families might differ from those who do not participate. Despite such criticisms, Nielsen continues to dominate the television ratings industry.

Nielsen ratings are used by TV programmers and sponsors throughout North America, Europe, and Asia. The company also offers a Hispanic ratings service in the United States, with the Telemundo and Univision networks, to help advertisers evaluate the audience for Spanish-language programming. Nielsen monitors television viewing in bars, truck stops, college dormitories, airports, health clubs, and medical offices. In a joint venture with Netratings, Inc., Nielsen tracks Web surfers to tally the number of hits on various Internet advertising banners, along with the demographics of the users.

> **ONLINE!**
> For current ratings on your favorite TV program, go to *www.ytv.yahoo.com/nielsen/*. For more about how Nielsen conducts its ratings, log on to *www.nielsenmedia.com/*. To learn about Internet ratings, see *www.nielsen-netratings.com/*.

THE NATURE AND SCOPE OF ADVERTISING

Let us examine some of the techniques the sellers of goods and services use to encourage, persuade, stimulate, or manipulate you, the consumer, to buy their products. There are several different types of advertising. Although the most frequently used is the direct sell type, designed to elicit an immediate response from the consumer, other advertising is created for different purposes.

Consumer Awareness. Another type of advertising is designed to create consumer awareness of a new product, an improved product or package, or a price change. This advertising also tries to reinforce the brand name. Because so much purchasing behavior is linked to brand names, companies spend considerable sums creating and maintaining public awareness of company and product names.

Product Image. Some advertising tries to establish an image for a product or service. Many products cannot be distinguished from one another on the basis of ingredients or quality, so advertisers try to create differences in terms of images, symbols, or feelings. For example, an automobile must do more than provide transportation; a lipstick must provide more than color. It must, through its

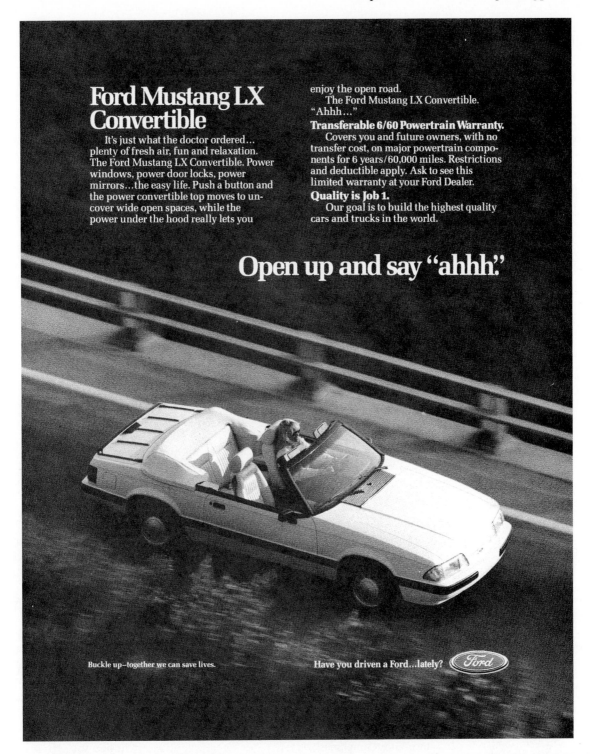

This direct-sell ad promotes consumer awareness of the product and tries to establish an image of luxury and fun. (Courtesy of Ford Motor Company.)

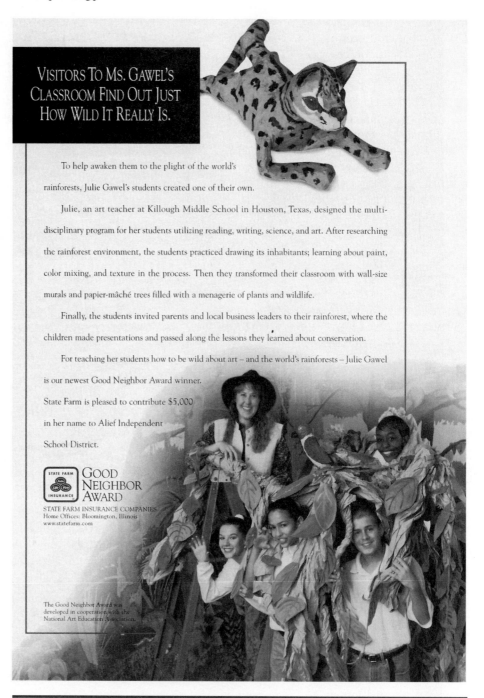

Institutional advertising promotes the idea that the company is a good neighbor and community benefactor. (Reproduced by permission of State Farm Insurance Companies.)

image, make the owners feel younger, sportier, or more attractive, or enhance their prestige and economic status. As the president of a firm that makes men's and women's fragrances said, "In the factory we make cosmetics. In the store we sell hope."

Institutional Advertising.   The goal of institutional advertising is to persuade the public that the company is a good neighbor and community benefactor. An example is the campaign conducted by an oil company to promote highway safety rather than simply to sell its brand of gasoline. Companies advertise that their products are good for the environment, that they contribute a share of their profits to charities, or that they support Little League baseball teams. Institutional advertising can build public good will, boost sales, help recruit employees, improve employee morale, and drive up the price of the company's stock.

Informational Advertising.   Some advertising comes under the heading of informational advertising when it enables consumers to make more intelligent purchasing decisions. The type of information provided in such an ad can include price, quality, performance data, components or contents, availability, nutritional information, warranties, and safety record. The use of informative advertising has increased from an average of 20% of all ads a decade ago to more than 65% today. Magazine ads tend to be more informative than television ads. More cable television commercials than network television commercials are of the informative type.

ONLINE!   Want to see some really bad ads? Check out *www.absurdgallery.com.*

Types of Advertising Appeals

The major way in which an ad campaign can persuade you to buy a product is through its appeal—that is, what it promises to do for you. Look at some magazine ads. Which human needs or motivations does the product promise to satisfy? Psychologists have identified many human needs: the innate or primary needs, such as food, water, shelter, security, and sex; and the learned or secondary needs, such as power, status, achievement, esteem, and affiliation. These secondary motivations depend on our personal experiences and thus will vary from one person to another and one culture to another.

To sell their products and services, advertisers must identify the relevant needs and direct their messages toward the appropriate segment of the population. Most ads attempt to satisfy more than one need. For example, an ad for imported beer can promise to quench thirst (a primary need) and to satisfy the desires for status and belonging (secondary needs). Ads for mouthwash and deodorant promise to help us avoid embarrassing situations and thus be more likeable. If we use the right cologne, we are assured by advertisers that we will find love and thus fulfill the needs for social support and self-esteem. Driving the right car can provide power, prestige, and achievement, along with the hope of attracting a mate. Advertisers use several techniques to appeal to these diverse human needs.

Celebrity Endorsements.   A product endorsed by a celebrity entertainer or sports figure invites the audience to identify with that person's success. Celebrities are often used to sell products, although there is little published evidence of the impact of such endorsements on actual purchasing unless the celebrity is believed to be qualified to promote that product. A study of college students investigated the influence of celebrity status, attractiveness, trustworthiness, and perceived expertise on their expressed intentions to purchase particular items. Only the perceived expertise of the celebrities was positively related to buying intentions. For example, a tennis pro was considered to be a believable endorser of tennis rackets, a good-looking male movie star was an effective promoter of men's cologne, and a fashion model an appropriate spokesperson for a line of designer jeans.

Some celebrities endorse more than one product. Basketball star Michael Jordan has appeared in ads for more than a dozen different products. Does multiple endorsement affect a celebrity's credibility or effectiveness in selling a product? To answer that question, nearly 500 college undergraduates participated in a study in which some students were shown up to eight ads featuring a movie star endorsing products such as cameras, toothpaste, breath mints, and a major credit card. Under other experimental conditions, the subject groups viewed a single ad, two ads, or four ads featuring the same celebrity endorsing the products (Tripp, Jensen, & Carlson, 1994).

The results showed that as the number of products endorsed by the celebrity increased, the subjects' ratings of the celebrity's credibility decreased significantly. In addition, the students' attitudes toward the ads became significantly less favorable.

Positive and Negative Appeals.   Advertising appeals can be positive or negative. The message can suggest that something good will happen to you if you use the product or that something unpleasant will happen if you don't use the product. An ad for deodorant soap can show a room full of happy people who are obviously desirable because they use the featured soap, or it can show a person sitting at home alone, dateless and dejected because he or she failed to bathe with the soap. A related approach is to make the person feel guilty for not buying the product, a tactic that is particularly effective with mothers of young children.

Negative appeals are effective for certain types of products, but they do not work when the consequences are overly unpleasant. Pictures of gruesome automobile accidents to promote safe driving or depictions of diseased lungs in anti-smoking campaigns have been shown to be ineffective. Such fear-laden appeals distract people from the message.

The same holds true for guilt appeals. Research has shown that strong appeals are significantly less effective than moderate appeals in inducing feelings of guilt. A strong guilt appeal can easily generate anger toward the ad and the company that sponsored it. A frequently used approach combines both types of

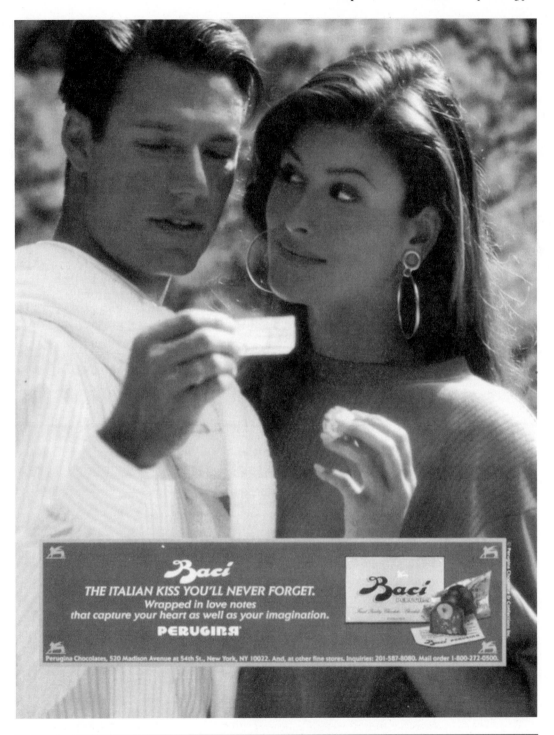

Some advertisers attempt to appeal to emotional needs and feelings such as affection, romance, and beauty. (Reproduced by permission of Perugina Chocolates.)

appeal, first showing the negative consequences of not using the product and then showing the positive consequences of using the product.

Implied Superiority.   A widely used appeal is implied superiority, in which the superiority of one product over its competitors is not stated directly but is inferred by the consumer. For example, if all headache remedies take the same amount of time to bring relief, one company may claim that no competitor provides faster relief than its product. The claim is true—no one product is faster than another—but the phrasing may lead people to conclude that this brand is superior because it sounds as if it works faster. The ad also suggests indirectly that its claim is based on scientific research.

Trademarks

A familiar trademark can facilitate advertising effectiveness because it serves as a shorthand symbol of the feelings and images associated with the product (see Figure 14–1). Key aspects of the product come to be identified with and exemplified by the trademark. Most trademarks are brand names—for example, Coca-Cola, Kleenex, and Xerox. When a trademark is well established in the marketplace, it alone, without any other advertising message, can stimulate consumers to recall the product.

A recent survey of brand names and trademarks asked executives to rate them on the reputation, management strength, and investment potential of their companies. A second survey asked a random sample of more than 10,000 people

---

FIGURE 14–1.   Trademarks. (Reproduced by permission of Chevron Corporation; AT&T Corporation; and Toyota Motor Sales USA, Inc.)

to rate the brand names on product quality, corporate vision, and leadership. The rankings are shown in Table 14–2, in descending order of popularity. Only three names—Coca-Cola, Walt Disney, and Johnson & Johnson—appear on both lists. Otherwise, the companies selected by the executives are different from those selected by the random sample of consumers. Thus, it is clear that the "best" brand names depend on who is being asked to pick them.

Companies spend a great deal of time and money on the development of product trademarks and brand names. Identity consultants specialize in naming and renaming products and companies. For example, California Airlines changed its name to AirCal when focus-group interviews revealed that the new name had greater consumer impact. Allegheny Airlines changed its name to USAir (now US Airways) to make it sound more like a national than a regional carrier.

Research can also tell manufacturers how recognizable their product name is to the consuming public and what it means to the target audience. This is especially crucial for U.S. companies marketing products in other countries. Sometimes a trademark can have an unintended, or unfavorable, meaning in another language. The Chevrolet Nova, named for a star that suddenly increases in brightness and energy, became in Spanish "no va," which means "doesn't go,"—not a very good name for a car. Coca-Cola changed its product name in China when the company discovered that in Chinese, Coca-Cola meant "bite the wax tadpole." Pepsi had a similar problem. "Come alive with the Pepsi generation" translated into Chinese as "Pepsi will bring your ancestors back from the dead." Remember Kentucky Fried Chicken's "finger-lickin' good"? In Chinese it became "eat your fingers off." Oops. One U.S. airline boasted in Spanish-language magazines about the leather upholstery on its seats; in translation the message meant "sit naked." The Scandinavian vacuum cleaner company, Electrolux, pulled an ad that promised, "Nothing sucks like an Electrolux," when informed by their American distributors that this was not quite the image they wanted associated with their brand.

TABLE 14–2 Rank Order of U.S. Companies by Reputation and Brand Name Recognition

By Executives	By Random Sample
Coca-Cola	**Johnson & Johnson**
Microsoft	**Coca-Cola**
Walt Disney	Hewlett-Packard
Campbell Soup	Intel
Johnson & Johnson	Ben & Jerry's
General Electric	Wal-Mart
Fedex	Xerox
Procter & Gamble	Home Depot
Hershey Foods	Gateway
Harley-Davidson	**Walt Disney**

A trademark can be so effective that it comes to stand for all brands of a product. For example, kleenex is now used to mean any kind of facial tissue, xerox any type of photocopier, and fedex any express mail carrier. When this occurs, the company can lose its identifiability and its exclusive share of the market.

Trademarks that have worked successfully for years may have to be altered to reflect changes in the culture of the marketplace. The image of Betty Crocker, the fictional woman trademark for many General Mills's food products, was updated in 1996 to reflect the greater racial and ethnic diversity of the American population. The new Betty Crocker is a computer-generated hybrid of 75 real American faces. Designed to represent many races, she now looks multicultural, in an attempt to depict more accurately American society.

Product Image

Often allied with a product's trademark is its image—the ideas, thoughts, and feelings associated with the product's personality. The development of a successful product image, one with which consumers will want to identify, can bring a company from obscurity to prosperity. Indeed, the image can be more important than the qualities of the product itself.

Sometimes product image is transmitted by a symbol, such as the tiny alligator on some popular knit shirts. This symbol is supposed to convey the image of the person wearing the product. A classic study compared consumer perceptions of a person wearing a plain knit shirt and wearing shirts with alligator, fox, and polo player logos. The person wearing the plain shirt was judged to be self-confident, tolerant, satisfied, and friendly. The same person in the fox emblem shirt was described as self-confident, enthusiastic, and a leader. In the polo player shirt he was perceived as less self-confident, tolerant, enthusiastic, satisfied, and friendly than in any of the other shirts. In the alligator shirt, the same person was described as preppy but neither a leader nor a follower. The shirt was identical in all cases; the only difference was the logo (Swartz, 1983).

The most difficult problem in developing a product image is determining the qualities that will attract potential buyers. One technique for studying product image involves group interviews with selected samples of consumers in which they are questioned about their perceptions of various products. This in-depth approach attempts to elicit positive and negative feelings about the products.

A more objective approach involves the adjective checklist, which is what was used in the study of the shirts with the logos. Consumers are given a list of descriptive adjectives and phrases and are asked to select those that characterize their feelings about the product or their conception of the person who would buy the product.

Product Packaging

Another important aspect of an advertising campaign is the product's package, the part of the product that consumers see at the critical point of sale, the moment of deciding whether to purchase. Shoppers looking for a box of crackers on a supermarket shelf who are confronted by an array of competing brands may not remember the TV commercial they saw last night or the magazine ad they read last week. At the instant of purchase, the packaging may be the deciding factor.

There is an old saying about not judging a book by its cover, but many people make various decisions on just that basis. We often evaluate people by their clothing or their car, and we make similar judgments about the products we purchase. Consumer attitudes are often shaped not by the quality of an item but by the wrapping in which it is offered.

The most famous example is an early consumer study on the taste of coffee. Two groups of people were questioned. For one group, the coffee was poured from an ordinary electric coffeemaker. For the other group, the coffee was served from an ornately engraved antique silver urn. You guessed it. The consumers rated the taste of the coffee poured from the silver urn much higher than the coffee from the electric coffeemaker, though the coffee was the same in both cases. It was the container—the package—that accounted for the difference in the way people perceived the taste.

In other research on this concept, pills of two sizes were shown to groups of patients and physicians, who were asked to rate the potency of each drug. Both groups reported that they believed that the larger pill was the more potent. In fact, the larger pill was less than half as strong as the smaller pill.

Overall, the package must reinforce the product's image or personality as established by its advertising campaign. For example, a men's hair gel should not be packaged in a pink bottle with letters in script but in a sturdy box with bold stripes and colors. The design and matching of product and package can be determined through consumer research. Consumers may be asked to free-associate to the designs of current or proposed packaging, telling researchers the positive or negative images elicited by the designs. Surveys and projective techniques can also be used to determine packaging impact and preference.

Packaging is an expensive part of the manufacturing and marketing process, accounting for more than one third of the cost of most supermarket items. For every dollar you spend on food, drugs, cosmetics, clothing, and electronics, approximately 35 cents goes for the container, not for what is in it.

Sex in Advertisements

The use of attractive and scantily clad models of both sexes is popular in advertising, so we might assume that their effectiveness is beyond question. However, the value of sexy images in ads has been accepted on faith, with little empirical research support. Sex appeal does have a high attention-getting value. Studies using the eye camera show that most consumers reading magazines, when confronted with several ads on a page, will immediately look at the ad that contains an element of sex. But what then? In general, the information in the ad that features provocative pictures of women is read more often by women than by men. Men look at the pictures, but women read the message, which usually means that the ad is communicating with the wrong audience. Similar results have been found with ads featuring pictures of attractive men; the messages are read more often by men than by women, again attracting the wrong audience.

More discouraging is research evidence suggesting a very low rate of recall for information that accompanies sexy illustrations. One company published two versions of a magazine ad, each containing a mail-in coupon for additional information. One ad showed a bikini-clad young woman; the other ad did not. Coupon returns were significantly higher for the ad without the sexy model.

Laboratory research supports these field observations. In one study, male subjects viewed several ads; some of the ads had sexy illustrations and some did not. The subjects were then shown the same ads with the brand names deleted and were asked to identify the product or advertiser. They were questioned again 24 hours later. There was no difference in the rate of recall for the sexy and non-sexy ads. After 7 days, the subjects had forgotten significantly more of the sexy ads than the non-sexy ads.

It appears, then, that the wrong audience reads the messages accompanying sexy ads, and although many people enjoy looking at the ads, they are not likely to remember the product. However, advertisers continue to rely on the shock value, and their promotions—especially for fragrances, underwear, and jeans—grow more daring every year.

Women in Advertisements

Women are often depicted in print ads and TV commercials as sex objects, housewives, and mothers—people implied to be inferior and subordinate to men. And though many ads continue to show women in traditional roles, others feature them in the business world and in positions of authority.

Growing numbers of women are heads of households responsible for purchasing items formerly bought almost exclusively by men, such as automobiles, home repair products, and travel services. There has also been an increase in the number of men purchasing products for cooking, housecleaning, and child care. Some advertisers have recognized these changes in the social climate and have responded accordingly, designing their media campaigns for different segments of the male and female buying public.

Effectiveness of Advertising Campaigns

The most important question for the seller is whether its advertising campaign is effective in increasing the sales of its product or service. In many cases, neither the advertising agency nor the company knows the answer, because effectiveness is difficult to determine. Further, companies are reluctant to go public with their failures and are apt to exaggerate their successes.

Research on television ad campaigns consistently shows that most people dislike commercials. Television viewers watch fewer than half the commercials broadcast. They leave the room during commercial breaks, turn off the sound or switch channels with the remote control device, and erase or fast-forward through commercials on video recorded programs.

Advertising agencies usually assume that most people are not sitting through or paying attention to television ads. They describe viewers as "nomads," because they wander or surf from one channel to another. Consumer psychologists have described three types of viewers:

1. *Channel nomads:* people who surf from channel to channel looking for a program of interest. In New York City, viewers change channels on the average of every 3 minutes 26 seconds.
2. *Mental nomads:* people multitasking, concerned with other activities such as preparing dinner, talking on the phone, or playing with their children. Only occasionally do they glance at the TV set.

Some advertisers recognize the buying power of women for products that are beyond the scope of the traditional homemaker role. (Reproduced by permission of Samsonite Corporation.)

3. *Physical nomads:* people busy in other parts of the house who watch snatches of programs and commercials when they pass through the room containing the television set.

In laboratory test situations, where people watching TV commercials were unable to tune them out, channel surf, or leave the room, subjects typically misunderstood or forgot approximately one third of what they had seen when questioned immediately after viewing the ads. A day later, the subjects had forgotten or misunderstood three fourths of what they had seen. The figures were higher for magazine ads.

The trend toward briefer TV commercials (15-second spots instead of 30-second spots) may render advertising even less effective. In one laboratory study, 78 college students watched a television program with three commercial breaks. One of the breaks featured two 15-second commercials and one 30-second ad. When questioned after the program, the subjects demonstrated consistently lower recall for the 15-second commercials than for the 30-second ad (Ward, Oliva, & Reibstein, 1994).

Several other factors can influence ad recall. For example, a telephone survey of 418 adults found that they were significantly more likely to remember an ad they had liked than an ad they had disliked. Whereas 65% of the subjects were able to describe ads they had disliked (which in itself is a respectable level of recall), more than 90% were able to describe ads they had liked (Stone, Besser, & Lewis, 2000).

How we feel about commercials in general can affect how well we remember them. In one study, the attitudes of 1914 adults toward ads were measured first. Although 45% of the subjects believed that advertising was informative, 77% believed that ads were annoying and manipulative and that many products failed to live up to their claims. These results tell advertisers that even people who think ads can be useful may also hold negative attitudes toward them. When these subjects were shown a series of magazine ads and asked on the following day to recall them, people with highly favorable attitudes toward advertising recalled significantly more of the ads they had seen than did people with highly unfavorable attitudes toward advertising (Mehta, 2000).

The effectiveness of advertising campaigns may depend on the context in which an ad appears. Some 200 college students were shown either a violent or a nonviolent film clip containing two commercials. Those who saw the violent film were significantly less able to recall the ads than were those who saw the nonviolent film. Further study of these subjects found that the televised violence increased their anger, which, in turn, decreased their memory for the ads (Bushman, 1998).

Some research on advertising effectiveness has focused on other media, including billboards. One study found that billboard ads for a local science museum at which attendance had been declining were able to reverse that trend significantly. After a 1-month period, a billboard ad for the facility was shown to have increased attendance by 58% (Bhargava & Donthu, 1999).

Another effective advertising medium for supermarkets is sales flyers in local newspapers. A study of 582 shoppers who were questioned when leaving the store found that people who paid attention to sales flyers purchased more of the advertised products, spent more money on those products, and bought more items overall on that shopping trip than did people who disregarded the sales flyers (Burton, Lichtenstein, & Netemeyer, 1999).

A factor that reduces the effectiveness of all types of print ads is the national literacy rate. In the United States today, more than 30% of the population cannot fully comprehend advertising copy written at an 8th-grade level. Thus, it is unlikely that they will respond to the information in the way that advertisers and sellers expect.

Advertising on the Web

The Internet is providing a new way for advertisers to spread their messages, although the effectiveness of their banner ads is still undetermined. To date, the effort is small, but it has the potential to grow. One survey reported that 40% of the people who use the Internet do so primarily for shopping. Even consumers who do not actually make purchases from Internet sites find it a good source of consumer information. Popular purchases include computers, books, flowers, music, travel services, and investment products.

Yet for all the success stories, particularly around the Christmas shopping season, many companies have been disappointed by the response to their Web sites. A great deal more research is needed to identify the characteristics of potential Internet shoppers and the best ways to attract them. One such study involved a telephone survey of 790 adults. Of these, 122 said that they were Internet shoppers; 668 said that they were not. How did the two groups differ? Internet shoppers were, on the average, older, more affluent, more innovative, more impulsive, and less risk-aversive than were non-Internet shoppers. Internet shoppers were also less brand and price conscious, and they expressed more positive attitudes toward advertising. No differences in gender or educational level were noted between the two groups (Donthu & Garcia, 1999).

Interviews with 401 Web users confirmed that older people with higher incomes were more likely to make purchases on the Internet than were younger people with lower incomes. It is interesting that older, high-income users spent the least amount of time on the Internet—typically less than an hour a day—and most of that time was devoted to business (Korgaonkar & Wolin, 1999).

One consumer researcher sought to identify the types of direct mail print ads that were likely to draw customers to commercial Web sites. Five different ads for a company that manufactured antique reproductions were mailed to 2,000 antique dealers, interior decorators, and designers. A Web address was included. The ads that produced the greatest number of hits were those that mentioned the Web address the greatest number of times. The ad that drew the fewest responses was the one that listed the Web address only once, at the end of the ad. The ad designed to look like a Web page, with a line of Web-like graphics across the top, drew the highest response rate (Bellizzi, 2000).

Research with groups of employed adults and college students on the design of Web pages has shown that complexity has a negative influence on advertising effectiveness. The simpler the Web page design, the higher was the stated intent to purchase the product displayed. Also, simpler Web pages engendered more favorable attitudes toward the company and the ad (Bruner & Kumar, 2000; Stevenson, Bruner, & Kumar, 2000).

It is too soon to draw more than tentative conclusions about the effectiveness of Internet advertising. Although it is possible to count the number of times a specific Web site has been accessed, it is not yet possible to determine the characteristics of the person who visited that site (age, level of education, or income, for example). Nor can a company tell how long a potential shopper may have browsed. In time, surveys of regular online users will provide this demographic data.

CONSUMER BEHAVIOR AND MOTIVATION

Consumers can be influenced by marketplace factors other than advertising when they make their purchasing decisions. A store's atmosphere and cleanliness, the ease of parking, the length of the aisles—all these things can affect buyer behavior. For example, research on supermarket shopping behavior found that people will look down short aisles rather than walk down them. They are much more likely to walk down long aisles and to make more impulse buys as a result. In addition, the products more likely to be purchased on impulse are those displayed at the ends of the aisles and around the checkout lanes. You can readily see where manufacturers would want to shelve their products for maximum visibility.

Personal factors that affect consumer behavior include the standard biographical variables—age, sex, educational level, socioeconomic status, and ethnic origin—along with cognitive variables such as perceived time available for shopping, attitudes toward shopping, purpose of the shopping trip, and the shopper's mood and personality. For example, people who are self-conscious in public (overly concerned about the impression they make on others and what others think of them) tend to be concerned about the labels on the products they buy. Perhaps they believe that people will think more highly of them if they purchase national brands rather than store brands or generic brands of the same product.

NEWSBREAK

Here's a Tip for You

Consumer psychologists try to amass as much information as possible about human behavior and motivation—where we shop, what we purchase, why we buy it, what ads we like, what ads turn us off. There's not much that escapes the scrutiny of consumer psychologists, even leaving a tip in a restaurant. To the people who serve meals and clear tables, the tips make up the bulk of their income. Therefore, the amount you decide to leave for their service is vital to them.

The money left on restaurant tables as tips totals more than $12 billion a year. Researchers have found that tipping has little to do with your opinion of the quality of the service you received and much more to do with the waiter's opinion of you! In other words, so researchers claim, we tip to please the waiter because we believe he or she is judging us. Do you buy that?

How do you decide on the size of the tip you leave at a restaurant? Do you tend to tip excessively? Do you tip only a token amount and hurry to leave before the waitperson notices? Here are several other factors that may influence the size of your tips:

- *How big was your bill?* The size of the tab you run up is the single best predictor of tip size. The larger the bill, the larger the tip.
- *How friendly was your server?* This should be the first thing a new server learns. The friendlier they are, the larger tip they receive. Waiters who smile and introduce themselves by name tend to make more money than those who do not. Also, waiters who crouch or bend down to your level while taking your order get better tips than those who remain standing. Women servers who draw smiley faces on the bill get higher tips than those who do not, but men servers who draw smiley faces get lower tips.
- *How professional was the service?* Studies show a weak relationship between customer evaluations of the quality of service and the size of the tip. Thus, friendliness may compensate for making a mistake with the order.
- *How attractive was the server?* As with many social activities, more attractive people fare better than less attractive people. In this case, they tend to receive somewhat larger tips, although the difference is not significant.
- *How many in your party?* Do you expect to leave a bigger tip when you are eating alone than when you're with a group? Tip size seems to decrease with the size of the party. Single diners leave an average of 20% of the bill. Two diners tip an average of 17% apiece. But when the group includes four or more, tip size drops to around 13%.
- *How often do you eat there?* Regulars at a restaurant tend to tip more than first-time customers or people who eat there only occasionally. Apparently, people feel differently about tipping when they expect to patronize the restaurant again.
- *Cash or charge?* People who charge meals leave larger tips than those who pay cash. Perhaps it doesn't seem like "real money" when you're using plastic.
- *What's the weather like?* Hotel room-service waiters receive larger tips on pleasant days when they can tell customers that the weather is sunny than on cloudy days when they say it is raining.

One final point about tipping, though there's no psychological research to back it up. Bartenders at establishments around the Capitol Hill area of Washington, D.C., whose bars are frequented by members of Congress and their staffs, report that Republicans are bigger tippers than Democrats!

Sources: S. Daley, Hey, big spender. *Washingtonian Magazine*, May 1996, p. 194. W. Grimes, Tips: Check your insecurity at the door. *New York Times*, February 3, 1999. M. McCall, & H. J. Belmont (1996). Credit card insignia and restaurant tipping, *Journal of Applied Psychology, 81*, 609–613. B. Rind (1996). Evidence of beliefs about weather conditions for tipping. *Journal of Applied Social Psychology, 26*, 137–147.

Other aspects of consumer behavior of interest to psychologists are buying habits, brand loyalty, and the effect of product pricing.

> **ONLINE!**
>
> To learn more about the art of tipping and how much to leave in different situations, see *www.tipping.org/tipping/tipping.html.*

Buying Habits and Brand Loyalty

Many of the stores in which we shop and the products we select are chosen on the basis of habit. Once we find a product we like, it is simpler to continue to buy it than to find a new one. To demonstrate the strength of shopping habits, one supermarket rearranged its display of canned soups. The soups had been grouped by brand name but were changed to alphabetical order by type of soup, thus intermixing all the different brands. Although signs were posted to explain the new arrangement, more than 60% of the customers were fooled. Habit led them to the space on the shelf where they had previously gotten the desired soups. When questioned, customers said that the soups had been stocked in their usual order. They were amazed to find the wrong cans in their shopping cart. When consumers shop in new stores, where habit does not automatically lead them to the shelf locations of their preferred products, they tend to buy many more different brands than in the past.

The design of an ad campaign to change persistent buying habits presents a challenge. Studies show that consumer loyalty to major brands can remain unchanged up to 8 years. Sixteen brands that were top sellers in their product category in 1923 retained their primacy 60 years later: these included Campbell soup, Lipton tea, Kodak cameras, and Wrigley chewing gum. These findings reinforce the importance to advertisers of establishing brand preferences in childhood. Once committed, consumers tend to remain loyal to a particular brand for many years and to pass that loyalty on to their children.

It is sometimes difficult for researchers to distinguish between buying habits and brand loyalty. Both can be defined in terms of repeat purchase behavior, with the result that the consumer is relatively impervious to ads for competing brands.

Product Pricing

The price of a product can be an important influence on buying behavior, independent of advertising and product quality. Consumers frequently use price as an index of quality on the assumption that the more an object costs, the better it must be. Some manufacturers capitalize on this belief and charge a higher price than their competitors do for a product of equal quality. Identical products, differing only in price, are often judged solely by their cost, with the more expensive product rated higher in quality.

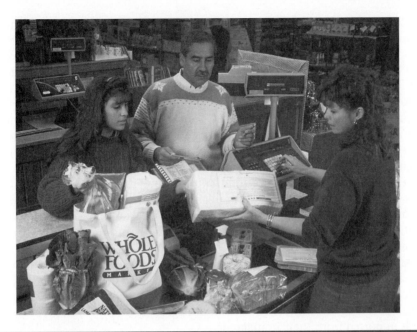

Supermarket shoppers may judge certain products to be superior solely on the basis of price.

Some consumers do not consider price when shopping for certain items. Observations of supermarket shoppers reveal that most do not pay attention to price information when shopping for staples such as breakfast cereal, coffee, and soft drinks, and they cannot accurately report current prices. Because of different package weights and sizes, shoppers are often unable to make the calculations necessary to determine which of several brands is the best buy. When supermarkets provide unit pricing information, such as cost per serving or cost per item, shoppers use this information extensively in making purchasing decisions.

A popular technique to gain sales for a new product or package is to charge a low price as an introductory offer. The idea is that once shoppers purchase the product, they will continue to do so out of habit, even when the price is raised to the level of competing products. Research does not support this notion. Sales are usually high during the introductory price period but drop when the price is raised. In stores that do not lower the price during the introductory period, sales typically remain stable. Rebates are a more effective way of offering a price reduction as an inducement to purchase. A price decrease in the form of a rebate usually produces higher sales than an equal point-of-sale price reduction.

Advertising to Ethnic Groups

Research has identified important differences in consumer values, attitudes, and shopping behavior among people of different ethnic groups. Studies of whites, blacks, Hispanic Americans, and Asian Americans have documented preferences for various products. In many large cities, blacks and Hispanics account for the majority of the residents, forming sizable markets with considerable purchasing power.

Blacks tend to spend more money than whites with comparable incomes for clothing but less for food, housing, and medical care. Research also shows that blacks purchase more milk and soft drinks but less coffee and tea. They favor national brands over private label house brands. Black spokespersons in ads are more effective than white spokespersons in reaching black consumers.

Advertising expenditures for the Spanish-speaking consumer market have increased significantly in the past decade. National brand advertising is being targeted at Spanish-language publications and cable television networks. Publications such as *Newsweek* and *People* are producing Spanish-language editions, and bilingual magazines such as *Latina* are developing significant readership. Other advertising outlets are the more than 400 Hispanic radio stations in the United States and two major TV networks, which have seen a 14% increase in viewership over the past few years. Major corporations such as MasterCard, AT&T, Sprint, Coca-Cola, McDonald's, and General Motors produce Spanish-language ads for these networks.

Among neighborhood businesses, which are preferred by the majority of Mexican American shoppers, there is a greater reliance on word-of-mouth communication and in-store advertising posters than on larger media ad campaigns. Spanish-speaking consumers show a high degree of brand loyalty, especially to brands imported from their homelands.

The degree of assimilation into mainstream U.S. culture has been found to affect decision-making behavior in Hispanic families with regard to major consumer purchases such as automobiles and houses. In general, the more assimilated a family becomes, the greater the influence of the wife in making consumer decisions. In more traditional families, the husband's decision is dominant.

Asian Americans are a fast-growing segment of the U.S. population. What makes this ethnic group so appealing to advertisers is that Asian Americans are typically affluent, well educated, and likely to hold high-tech jobs. They far outspend other ethnic groups in categories such as computers, insurance, and international long-distance telephone calls.

ONLINE!

The Internet has become a thriving marketplace for ethnic minority groups in the United States. African-American Web sites include *www.nationalbcc.com*, the National Black Chamber of Commerce, which offers discounts from major corporations and other benefits. *www.blackplanet.com* offers college databases, financial tools, and technology classes. Hispanic-American Web sites include *www.starmedia.com*, which offers shopping services, travel services, classified ads, and chat rooms in Spanish. *www.zonafinanciera.com* provides banking, insurance, auto, and real estate services in English, Spanish, and Portuguese for 21 countries. Asian-American Web sites include *www.aonline.com*, focusing on culture and lifestyle, and *www.click2asia.com* for links to shopping, business, and travel in Japan, Taiwan, Korea, and the United States.

Advertising to Children and Adolescents

The 4-to-12 age group contains 35 million children with control over approximately $15 billion in disposable income. The fastest-growing spending categories for these young consumers are shoes and clothing. One explanation psychologists have advanced for the children's high degree of purchasing power is parental guilt. Consumer psychologists suggest that in single-parent families, in families with both parents employed outside the home, and in families in which parents have postponed childbearing until their thirties, the children have been indulged with more money to spend and more influence over family purchasing decisions.

Marketing to children uses techniques such as placing products on lower supermarket shelves, airing cartoon commercials on children's TV programs, and distributing in schools pencils, magazines, and book covers featuring a product's name or logo.

A substantial portion of the advertising directed toward children appears on television. It is estimated that preteens watch 25,000 TV commercials a year. In the 2- to 7-year age group, the average time spent watching TV is 2 hours a day, making them an easy target for advertisers. So powerful is the influence of television advertising that children as young as 2 have been found to hold firmly established brand name preferences. Other research shows that advertising is an important source of information for children and makes a strong impact on their thinking (McClain, 1999; Moore & Lutz, 2000).

Adolescents are also a favorite target for advertisers. Teenagers spend an estimated $30 billion a year on clothing, cosmetics, and other personal items such

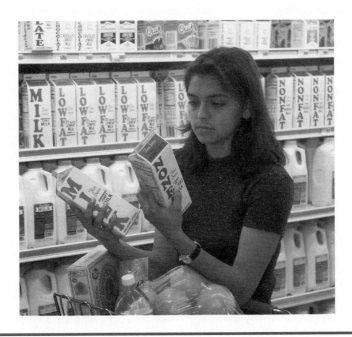

Many teenage shoppers are responsible for household grocery purchases.

Should Psychologists Help Deceive Children?

Here's an ethical question for you: Is it proper for psychologists to use their expertise to help advertisers develop techniques to persuade children to buy their products? Psychologists are very good at this job, which, of course, is why organizations hire them. But are there valid ethical concerns about the goal of manipulating, or even deceiving, young consumers through the ads they design?

There seems to be no question that commercials do exploit children. Even advertisers admit that. The head of one ad agency said, "Advertising at its best is making people feel that without their product, you're a loser. Kids are very sensitive to that. If you tell them to buy something, they are resistant. But if you tell them they'll be a dork if they don't, you've got their attention. You open up emotional vulnerabilities, and it's easy to do that with kids."

Advertisers refer to a product's "nag factor"—how much they can get kids to nag their parents before they give in and purchase the product. One clinical psychologist reported that parents experience considerable emotional turmoil over how they should respond to such nagging. They feel guilty about surrendering and buying their children the junk food or violent video games the kids want, because the parents believe these things are bad for their children. And the parents feel guilty if they don't agree, thinking that maybe their decision will lead to a child's depression or anxiety or lowered self-esteem if he or she doesn't get the right shoes or backpack.

Advertisers also like to develop materialistic attitudes as early as possible, which, critics say, can lead children to grow up defining their self-worth in terms of their possessions instead of their personal qualities.

Now, how about that manipulation and deception, which critics charge is done on a massive scale? Psychologists admit, "The fake promise of popularity, success, and attractiveness that marketers routinely make for their products are such common lies that we have become inured to their dishonesty. Yet we know that when adults chronically deceive and manipulate a child it erodes the youngster's ability to trust others and to feel secure in the world."

Is this controversy real, or is it moral posturing blown out of proportion? Do children learn from a young age that advertising is not like real life and that they shouldn't take it seriously? Is this part of growing up—learning who and what to trust? And even if no consumer psychologists were involved, wouldn't advertisers be doing the same thing anyway? Here's the bottom line: If companies didn't use advertising ploys to sell their products, they'd go out of business, firing hundreds of thousands of employees, most of whom have kids. Where do you stand on this issue?

Sources: R. A. Clay. Advertising to children: Is it ethical? *Monitor on Psychology,* August 2000, 52–53. A. D. Kanner & T. Kasser (2000). Stuffing our kids: Should psychologists help advertisers manipulate children? *The Industrial-Organizational Psychologist, 38*(1), 185–187.

as videotapes, audiotapes, and CDs. They have also assumed responsibility for much household spending. Many adolescents compile the household grocery list, make decisions about specific brands, and do the family marketing. More than 60% of teenage girls and 40% of teenage boys are believed to do routine grocery shopping.

A study of nearly 200 teenagers found that half reported spending up to 3 hours a day watching television, and one third spent the same amount of time listening to the radio (LaFerle, Edwards, & Lee, 2000). Teenagers are also increasing their use of the Internet. Some 72% spent up to an hour a day surfing the Web from their home computers. At school, 92% spent up to an hour a day on the Internet. Thus, these activities make them available to advertisers in several media.

Advertisements oriented toward children under 18 have generated a great deal of controversy, and complaints have been voiced by parents and consumer groups. Surveys reveal highly negative opinions about child-oriented advertising. The majority of adults tend to believe that advertising stifles creativity, promotes materialism, and encourages poor nutritional habits.

Advertising to Older Persons

Changing demographic trends have produced another important market for advertisers: working people over the age of 50. This consumer segment, growing in numbers and affluence, will, by the year 2020, constitute more than one third of the population. The over-50 group now includes the first of the baby boomers, a market of 76 million consumers with a large disposable income that they are used to spending freely. People over 50 have half the discretionary income in the United States, and people over 65 have twice that of people between 25 and 34, in their prime earning years.

The over-50 age group represents a multi-billion-dollar market for goods and services. Advertisers have responded to this trend by revising their image of older people in ads and by eliminating stereotypes about the older consumer. Ads featuring attractive older models now promote cosmetics, hair care products, luxury travel, automobiles, clothing, jewelry, health clubs, and investments.

Retired people over age 65 constitute a large market for clothing, home furnishings, travel, entertainment, and health care products and services. They tend to read more newspapers and magazines, and their television preferences include news and sports programs. Thus, they rely on mass media advertising and also use the Internet for shopping. They are critical of ads suggesting that young people are the only ones who have any fun.

Some older consumers resent being treated as a separate segment of the marketplace on the basis of their age. They resist participating in programs that use terms such as "golden years" or "senior citizen," even when it would save them money. A study of 113 people over age 50 delineated the following levels of age segregation (Tepper, 1994):

- Ages 50–54: highly unlikely to use a senior citizen's discount, because doing so would mean admitting to being old.
- Ages 55–64: more likely than the previous group to use a senior discount.
- Ages 65 and older: totally accepting of a senior discount and of the label "senior citizen."

Consumer researchers suggest that people in these categories will respond to different kinds of ads and advertising appeals, based on their rejection or acceptance of their age status.

Advertising to the Gay Community

A vocal and visible consumer group, gay persons are better educated and more affluent than the general population. A survey of 20,000 homosexuals that was conducted by a Chicago opinion polling firm found that approximately 60% of gay men and women were college graduates, compared to about 20% of the U.S. population as a whole. As a large potential market of people with high discretionary incomes, they are increasingly coming to the attention of advertisers.

Interviews with 44 gay men in Canada found that they preferred making consumer purchases only from companies that were perceived as "gay positive." These were companies that advertised in gay media, supported gay and lesbian employee groups, and offered same-sex domestic-partnership benefits. These companies also supported the gay community at large—for example, by making corporate contributions to AIDS charities. In addition, the survey showed that these gay consumers actively boycotted companies perceived as being homophobic or practicing discrimination in hiring (Kates, 2000).

Another survey of 372 homosexuals in the United States confirmed their status as a better-educated and more affluent segment of the population, but these upscale characteristics applied more often to men than to women. The questionnaire responses indicated that these gay consumers preferred to read the *Wall Street Journal, Business Week, Fortune, Money, The New Yorker, Sports Illustrated,* and *National Geographic;* they were less likely to read *TV Guide* or *Readers' Digest.* Television preferences included network news programs, CNN, "Late Night with David Letterman," and "60 Minutes." They rarely watched game shows, soap operas, or talk shows. This information tells companies where to target their ads. However, the survey also reported that these subjects claimed to have little use for advertising in making their purchasing decisions. They tended not to believe advertising in general and described most of it as condescending to homosexuals (Burnett, 2000).

> ONLINE!
>
> The Web sites *www.gay.com* and *www.planetout.com* offer chat rooms, personal ads, shopping, HIV information, investment opportunities, news, and links to gay-owned businesses.

Advertising to Persons with Disabilities

Another substantial consumer group with financial clout is the 43 million people in the United States who are disabled. Advertisers now use disabled persons as models in catalog ads, print ads, and television commercials. Companies such as McDonald's and retailers such as Target, Lands' End, and Kmart have shown people in wheelchairs, persons with artificial limbs, and children with Down's syndrome. The companies report that such advertising has a positive effect on sales and enhances their public image.

This awareness of disabled persons was heightened by the Americans with Disabilities Act that mandated accessibility of public places, including stores, restaurants, and shopping centers. As a result, more disabled persons are becoming active shoppers. Also, more companies are responding to the needs of disabled persons with products to extend their strength and mobility and to compensate for their limitations. These items range from easy-to-fasten clothing to easy-to-grasp kitchen utensils. One popular mail-order catalog calls its products "designs for independent living."

> **ONLINE!**
>
> *www.wemedia.com* offers at-home shopping and information about health assistance, finances, education, sports, wheelchair-accessible housing, and links to employment services that specialize in jobs for persons with disabilities.

Let us conclude by noting that manufacturers and advertisers respond to changing markets with new products and marketing techniques. Consumers should be aware of the varied nature of advertising—sometimes valuable and informative and sometimes manipulative and deceptive. As a consumer, you should remember one of history's oldest lessons: *caveat emptor.* Let the buyer—whether of ideas, political philosophies, values, theories, research findings, and even psychology textbooks—beware.

Guilt Appeals In Advertising

CASE IN POINT

Advertisements are designed to appeal to many human needs. Some ads appeal to the needs for sex, status, power, or achievement. Others to esteem and affiliation. Many ads appeal to more than one need at the same time. Some advertising messages use positive appeals, promising that something good will happen to you if you use the right product. Others threaten terrible consequences—such as never having a date—if you are foolish enough to reject what they are selling. And some ads use guilt appeals to try to persuade you that you are a worthless person and a failure if you do not follow the advertiser's advice.

The major target audience for guilt appeals is mothers who have jobs outside the home, some of whom may already feel guilty because they are not staying full time with their children. To investigate the effect of guilt appeals on these working mothers, two marketing professors conducted a study in three phases.

In Phase 1, 80 undergraduates identified three ads they believed were intended to create guilt. They described the ads in terms of components they perceived to be guilt-inducing, such as facial expressions, postures, and the wording of the ad copy.

In Phase 2, the two professors and a research assistant analyzed ads in women's and parents' magazines, identifying copy and pictures they believed were capable of inducing various levels of guilt. They based their judgments on the guilt-inducing components identified by the subjects in Phase 1.

Using the data from Phases 1 and 2, the researchers wrote advertising copy for two fictitious products (bread and dental floss) at three levels of guilt. For example, the Phase 3 ads for bread are as follows:

- Low guilt appeal: Whoever said "children will eat anything" had to be joking. Children have taste too!
- Moderate guilt appeal: Moms who don't teach their children to eat good meals have children who don't always learn. You shape your child's eating habits, so don't let your family down.
- High guilt appeal: It's YOUR responsibility to make sure that your kids have healthy eating habits. The pressure is on YOU, so don't make any mistakes. DO IT RIGHT!

Next, the researchers matched appropriate photographs with each of the guilt appeals. They selected 12 photos of a mother and son, depicting various facial expressions and postures, and asked 10 working mothers to judge the photos that seemed appropriate for each of the three ads for each product. The picture-ad combinations were pretested to determine whether they induced the appropriate level of guilt.

A new sample of 20 working mothers rated the three ads on a 5-point scale as to how much guilt they induced. The results confirmed that the high guilt ad copy and picture induced the most guilt, the low guilt ad induced the least guilt, and the moderate guilt ad was rated midway between the other two.

A sample of 60 mothers with jobs outside the home was shown the three ads and asked to complete questionnaires assessing their emotional responses to the ads, their attitudes toward the company promoting the product, and their intention to purchase the brand advertised. The results showed that the moderate guilt appeal elicited significantly more guilt than the high and low guilt appeals. The high guilt appeal generated significantly more negative feelings (anger and irritation) and a lower intent to purchase the product, than did the other two levels of guilt appeals.

The researchers concluded that the high guilt appeal was counterproductive, leading to anger and negative feelings toward the company. It reduced the consumers' intention to purchase the product and did not induce as high a level of guilt as did the moderate appeal.

Source: R. H. Coulter, & M. B. Pinto (1995). Guilt appeals in advertising: What are their effects? *Journal of Applied Psychology, 80,* 697–705.

Think About It

1. With what kinds of products, and with what kinds of people, do you think guilt appeals would be most effective?
2. Why do you think the high guilt appeal ads generated so much anger among the subjects while engendering less guilt than the moderate appeal?
3. What are the advantages and disadvantages of questionnaire and survey data in consumer psychology research?
4. What weaknesses can you find in the research methodology of this study? What strengths?
5. How would you design an advertising campaign to induce guilt feelings sufficient to motivate people to donate to a charitable cause? Give examples using both positive and negative appeals.

SUMMARY

Consumer psychology studies consumer behavior through surveys, **focus groups,** in-depth procedures, and behavioral observations. Testing for advertising effectiveness is done through direct questioning, **aided recall** and **recognition,** physiological measures, **sales tests,** and coupon returns. Television programming research uses viewer panels to screen programs, and Nielsen ratings to estimate audience size and composition. Advertising types include direct sell, product image, consumer awareness, and institutional. Advertising appeals can be positive, negative, or mixed. Many ads involve claims of implied superiority, which consumers tend to believe.

Trademarks can be effective advertising aids, as can the product image. Packaging can also be influential at the point of purchase. Sexy images are commonly used in ads; they attract people to the ads but do not seem to influence how much of the advertising message is recalled. The image of women in advertising has changed somewhat; although women are increasingly shown in positive roles outside the home, they are still portrayed in traditional homemaker roles and as sex objects. Most people dislike TV commercials, avoid watching them, and fail to remember three fourths of the ads they see. Internet advertising has increased; simpler Web page design is effective in getting people to purchase the advertised products. Brand loyalty can render buyers immune to advertising for competing products. Product price is often used as an indication of quality.

Child-oriented commercials are effective in persuading children to want the products advertised. Ethnic groups, older persons, disabled persons, and gay persons are being targeted as market segments with specific needs and preferences.

KEY TERMS

aided recall technique	recognition technique
focus groups	sales test technique

ADDITIONAL READING

Lewis, D., & Bridger, D. (2000). *The soul of the new consumer: Authenticity—What we buy and why in the new economy.* London: Nicholas Breakley. Market researchers present findings from consumer surveys on shopping experiences and television commercials. They describe the modern consumer as individualistic and well-informed.

Longinotti-Buitoni, G. L. (1999). *Selling dreams: How to make any product irresistible.* New York: Simon & Schuster. The CEO of Ferrari North America describes his research on the emotional link between a product's image and its function. He applies his ideas to cars, hotels, magazines, beauty products, wines, clothing, and electronics.

Simonson, I., Carmon, Z., Dhar, R., Drolet, A., & Nowlis, S. M. (2001). Consumer research. *Annual Review of Psychology, 52,* 249–275. Reviews theories of consumer behavior, social and cognitive influences, and research methods (including online behaviors, field experiments, and laboratory research).

Twitchell, J. B. (2001). *20 ads that shook the world: The century's most groundbreaking advertising and how it changed us all.* New York: Crown. A look back at classic ad campaigns for Coca-Cola, Volkswagen, Listerine, Nike, and Lydia E. Pinkham's Vegetable Compound, showing how a market can be created for a products we never knew we needed.

Underhill, P. (1999). *Why we buy: The science of shopping.* New York: Simon & Schuster. An urban geographer presents his findings based on 20 years of observations of shoppers in supermarkets, bookshops, and department stores.

References

Adams, J. S. (1965). Inequity in social exchange. In L. Berkowitz (Ed.), *Advances in experimental social psychology* (vol. 2). New York: Academic Press.

Adkins, C. L. (1995). Previous work experience and organizational socialization. *Academy of Management Journal, 38,* 839–862.

Akbar-Khanzadeh, F., Bisesi, M. S., & Rivas, R. D. (1995). Comfort of personal protective equipment. *Applied Ergonomics, 26*(3), 195–198.

Alderfer, C. (1972). *Existence, relatedness and growth.* New York: Free Press.

Antonioni, D. (1994). The effects of feedback accountability on upward appraisal ratings. *Personnel Psychology, 47,* 349–356.

Aquino, K., Grover, S. L., Bradfield, M., & Allen, D. G. (1999). The effects of negative affectivity, hierarchical status, and self-determination on workplace victimization. *Academy of Management Journal, 42,* 260–272.

Ashford, S. J., & Black, J. S. (1996). Proactivity during organizational entry. *Journal of Applied Psychology, 81,* 199–214.

Ashforth, B. E., & Saks, A. M. (1996). Socialization tactics. *Academy of Management Journal, 39,* 149–178.

Atkinson, J. W., & Feather, N. T. (1996). *A theory of achievement motivation.* New York: Wiley.

Atwater, L., Roush, P., & Fischthal, A. (1995). The influence of upward feedback on self- and follower ratings of leadership. *Personnel Psychology, 48,* 35–59.

Atwater, L., Waldman, D. A., Atwater, D., & Cartier, P. (2000). An upward feedback field experiment. *Personnel Psychology, 53,* 275–295.

Baker, K., Olson, J., & Morisseau, D. (1994). Work practices, fatigue, and nuclear power plant safety performance. *Human Factors, 36,* 244–257.

Baltes, B. B., Briggs, T. E., Huff, J. W., Wright, J. A., & Neuman, G. A. (1999). Flexible and compressed workweek schedules. *Journal of Applied Psychology, 84,* 496–513.

Bamberger, P., Admati-Dvir, M., & Harel, G. (1995). Gender-based wage and promotion discrimination in Israeli high-technology firms. *Academy of Management Journal, 38,* 1744–1761.

Barber, A. E., Wesson, M. J., Roberson, Q. M., & Taylor, M. S. (1999). A tale of two job markets. *Personnel Psychology, 52,* 841–867.

Barling, J., Zacharatos, A., & Hepburn, C. G. (1999). Parents' job insecurity affects children's academic performance through cognitive difficulties. *Journal of Applied Psychology, 84,* 437–444.

Barnum, P., Liden, R. C., & Ditomaso, N. (1995). Double jeopardy for women and minorities. *Academy of Management Journal, 38,* 863–880.

Barrick, M. R., & Mount, M. K. (1993). Autonomy as a moderator of the relationship between the Big Five personality dimensions and job performance. *Journal of Applied Psychology, 78,* 111–118.

Barrick, M. R., Mount, M. K., & Strauss, J. P. (1993). Conscientiousness and performance of sales representatives. *Journal of Applied Psychology, 78,* 715–722.

Barton, J. (1994). Choosing to work at night. *Journal of Applied Psychology, 79,* 449–454.

Becker, T. E., Billings, R. S., Eveleth, D. M., & Gilbert, N. L. (1996). Foci and bases of employee commitment. *Academy of Management Journal, 39,* 464–482.

Behling, O. (1998). Employee selection. *Academy of Management Executive, 12*(1), 77–86.

Bellizzi, J. A. (2000). Drawing prospects to E-commerce Websites. *Journal of Advertising Research, 40,* 43–53.

Bennett, R. J., & Robinson, S. L. (2000). Development of a measure of workplace deviance. *Journal of Applied Psychology, 85,* 349–360.

Bhargava, M., & Donthu, N. (1999). Sales response to outdoor advertising. *Journal of Advertising Research, 39*(4), 7–18.

Bishop, J. W., & Scott, K. D. (2000). An examination of organizational and team commitment in a self-directed team environment. *Journal of Applied Psychology, 85,* 439–450.

Bobko, P., Roth, P. L., & Potosky, D. (1999). Derivation and implications of a meta-analytic matrix incorporating cognitive ability, alternative predictors, and job performance. *Personnel Psychology, 52,* 561–589.

Bogg, J., & Cooper, C. (1995). Job satisfaction, mental health, and occupational stress among senior civil servants. *Human Relations, 48,* 327–341.

Booth-Kewley, S., & Friedman, H. S. (1987). Psychological predictors of heart disease. *Psychological Bulletin, 101,* 343–362.

Borman, W. C., White, L. A., & Dorsey, D. W. (1995). Effects of rater task performance and interpersonal factors on supervisor and peer performance ratings. *Journal of Applied Psychology, 80,* 168–177.

Bosma, H., Stansfeld, S. A., & Marmot, M. G. (1998). Job control, personal characteristics, and heart disease. *Journal of Occupational Health Psychology, 3,* 402–409.

Breaugh, J. A., & Colihan, J. P. (1994). Measuring facets of job ambiguity. *Journal of Applied Psychology, 79,* 191–202.

Broad, W., & Wade, N. (1982). *Betrayers of the truth.* New York: Simon & Schuster.

Bruner, G. C., II, & Kumar, A. (2000). Web commercials and advertising hierarchy-of-effects. *Journal of Advertising Research, 40,* 35–42.

Budd, J. W., Arvey, R. D., & Lawless, P. (1996). Correlates and consequences of workplace violence. *Journal of Occupational Health Psychology, 1,* 197–210.

Burnett, J. J. (2000). Gays: Feelings about advertising and media used. *Journal of Advertising Research, 40,* 75–84.

Burnfield, J. L., & Medsker, G. J. (1999). Income and employment of SIOP members in 1997. *The Industrial-Organizational Psychologist, 36*(4), 19–30.

Burton, S., Lichtenstein, D. R., & Netemeyer, R. G. (1999). Exposure to sales flyers and increased purchases in retail supermarkets. *Journal of Advertising Research, 39*(5), 7–14.

Bushman, B. J. (1998). Effects of television violence on memory for commercial messages. *Journal of Experimental Psychology: Applied, 4,* 291–307.

Bycio, P., Hackett, R. D., & Allen, J. S. (1995). Further assessments of Bass's (1985) conceptualization of transactional and transformational leadership. *Journal of Applied Psychology, 80,* 468–478.

Cable, D. M., & Gilovich, T. (1998). Looked over or overlooked? Prescreening decisions and postinterview evaluations. *Journal of Applied Psychology, 83,* 501–508.

Caldwell, D. F., & Burger, J. M. (1998). Personality characteristics of job applicants and success in screening interviews. *Personnel Psychology, 51,* 119–136.

Caligiuri, P. M. (2000). The Big Five personality characteristics as predictors of expatriates' desire to terminate the assignment and supervisor-rated performance. *Personnel Psychology, 53,* 67–88.

Callister, R. R., Kramer, M. W., & Turban, D. B. (1999). Feedback seeking following career transitions. *Academy of Management Journal, 42,* 429–438.

Carlopio, J. R. (1996). Construct validity of a Physical Work Environment Satisfaction Questionnaire. *Journal of Occupational Health Psychology, 1,* 330–344.

Carlson, K. D., Scullen, S. E., Schmidt, F. L., Rothstein, H., & Erwin, F. (1999). Generalizable biographical data validity can be achieved without multiorganizational development and keying. *Personnel Psychology, 52,* 731–755.

Cartwright, S. (2000). Taking the pulse of executive health in the U.K. *Academy of Management Executive, 14*(2), 16–23.

Cascio, W. F. (1998). The virtual workplace. *The Industrial-Organizational Psychologist, 35*(4), 32–36.

Cascio, W. F. (2000). Managing a virtual workplace. *Academy of Management Executive, 14*(3), 81–90.

Cavanaugh, M. A., Boswell, W. R., Roehling, M. V., & Boudreau, J. W. (2000). An empirical examination of self-reported work stress among U.S. managers. *Journal of Applied Psychology, 85,* 65–74.

Cawley, B. D., Keeping, L. M., & Levy, P. E. (1998). Participation in the performance appraisal process and employee reactions. *Journal of Applied Psychology, 83,* 615–633.

Chad, K. E., & Brown, J. M. M. (1995). Climatic stress in the workplace. *Applied Ergonomics, 26,* 29–34.

Chandler, A. D., Jr. (1988). Origins of the organization chart. *Harvard Business Review, 66*(2), 156–157.

Chen, X-P., Hui, C., & Sego, D. J. (1998). The role of organizational citizenship behavior in turnover. *Journal of Applied Psychology, 83,* 922–931.

Clay, R. A. (2000). Advertising to children. *Monitor on Psychology, 31*(8), 52–53.

Collins, J. M., & Gleaves, D. H. (1998). Race, job opportunities, and the five-factor model of personality. *Journal of Applied Psychology, 83,* 531–544.

Coulter, R. H., & Pinto, M. B. (1995). Guilt appeals in advertising. *Journal of Applied Psychology, 80,* 697–705.

Crant, J. M. (1995). The Proactive Personality Scale and objective job performance among real estate agents. *Journal of Applied Psychology, 80,* 532–537.

Daniels, K., & Guppy, A. (1994). Occupational stress, social support, job control, and psychological well-being. *Human Relations, 47,* 1523–1544.

Davidson, O. B., & Eden, D. (2000). Remedial self-fulfilling prophecy. *Journal of Applied Psychology, 85,* 386–398.

Davis, B. L., & Mount, M. K. (1984). Design and use of a performance appraisal feedback system. *Personnel Administrator, 29*(3), 91–97.

Day, S. X., & Rounds, J. (1998). Universality of vocational interest structure among racial and ethnic minorities. *American Psychologist, 53,* 728–736.

DeAngelis, T. (2000). Is Internet addiction real? *Monitor on Psychology, 31*(4), 24–26.

DeFrank, R. S., Konopaske, R., & Ivancevich, J. M. (2000). Executive travel stress. *Academy of Management Executive, 14*(2), 58–71.

DeFruyt, F., & Mervielde, I. (1999). RIASEC types and big five traits as predictors of employment status and nature of employment. *Personnel Psychology, 52,* 701–727.

DeGroot, T., & Motowidlo, S. J. (1999). Why visual and vocal interview cues can affect interviewers' judgments and predict job performance. *Journal of Applied Psychology, 84,* 986–993.

de Jong, G. M., & Emmelkamp, P. M. G. (2000). Implementing stress management training. *Journal of Occupational Health Psychology, 5,* 309–320.

Dembowski, J. M., & Callans, M. C. (2000, April). *Comparing computer and paper forms of the Wonderlic Personnel Test.* Paper presented at the meeting of the Society for Industrial and Organizational Psychology, New Orleans, LA.

DeNisi, A. S., & Kluger, A. N. (2000). Feedback effectiveness. *Academy of Management Executive, 14*(1), 129–139.

DeReamer, R. (1980). *Modern safety and health technology.* New York: Wiley.

Dessler, G. (1999). How to earn your employees' commitment. *Academy of Management Executive, 13*(2), 58–67.

Doby, J. J., & Caplan, R. D. (1995). Organizational stress as threat to reputation. *Academy of Management Journal, 38,* 1105–1123.

Doll, T. J., & Folds, D. J. (1986). Auditory signals in military aircraft. *Applied Ergonomics, 17,* 257–264.

Donovan, J. J., & Radosevich, D. J. (1999). A meta-analytic review of the distribution of practice effect. *Journal of Applied Psychology, 84,* 795–805.

Donovan, M. A., Drasgow, F., & Probst, T. M. (2000). Does computerizing paper-and-pencil job attitude scales make a difference? *Journal of Applied Psychology, 85,* 305–313.

Donthu, N., & Garcia, A. (1999). The Internet shopper. *Journal of Advertising Research, 39*(3), 52–58.

Dougherty, T. W., Turban, D. B., & Callender, J. C. (1994). Confirming first impressions in the employment interview. *Journal of Applied Psychology, 79,* 659–665.

Dreher, G. F., & Cox, T. H., Jr. (1996). Race, gender, and opportunity. *Journal of Applied Psychology, 81,* 297–308.

Driskell, J. E., Copper, C., & Moran, A. (1994). Does mental practice enhance performance? *Journal of Applied Psychology, 79,* 481–492.

Duffy, M. K., Ganster, D. C., & Shaw, J. D. (1998). Positive affectivity and negative outcomes. *Journal of Applied Psychology, 83,* 950–959.

Dunn, W. S., Mount, M. K., Barrick, M. R., & Ones, D. S. (1995). Relative importance of personality and general mental ability in managers' judgments of applicant qualifications. *Journal of Applied Psychology, 80,* 500–509.

Dvir, T., Eden, D., & Banjo, M. L. (1995). Self-fulfilling prophecy and gender. *Journal of Applied Psychology, 80,* 253–270.

Eagly, A. H., Karau, S. J., & Makhijani, M. G. (1995). Gender and the effectiveness of leaders. *Psychological Bulletin, 117,* 125–145.

Eklund, J. A. E. (1995). Relationships between ergonomics and quality in assembly work. *Applied Ergonomics, 26*(1), 15–20.

Ellemers, N., de Gilder, D., & van den Heuvel, H. (1998). Career-oriented versus team-oriented commitment and behavior at work. *Journal of Applied Psychology, 83*, 717–730.

Ellingson, J. E., Gruys, M. L., & Sackett, P. R. (1998). Factors related to the satisfaction and performance of temporary employees. *Journal of Applied Psychology, 83*, 913–921.

Ely, R. J. (1995). The power in demography. *Academy of Management Journal, 38*, 589–634.

Evans, G. W., & Johnson, D. (2000). Stress and open-office noise. *Journal of Applied Psychology, 85*, 779–783.

Fiedler, R. E. (1978). The contingency model and the dynamics of the leadership process. In L. Berkowitz (Ed.). *Advances in experimental social psychology.* New York: Academic Press.

Fiedler, F. E., & Garcia, J. E. (1987). *New approaches to effective leadership.* New York: Wiley.

Fiedler, F. E., Murphy, S. E., & Gibson, F. W. (1992). Inaccurate reporting and inappropriate variables. *Journal of Applied Psychology, 77*, 372–374.

Finkelstein, L. M., Burke, M. J., & Raju, N. S. (1995). Age discrimination in simulated employment contexts. *Journal of Applied Psychology, 80*, 652–663.

Fleishman, E. A., & Harris, E. F. (1962). Patterns of leadership behavior related to employee grievances and turnover. *Personnel Psychology, 15*, 43–56.

Florey, A. T., & Harrison, D. A. (2000). Responses to informal accommodation requests from employees with disabilities. *Academy of Management Journal, 43*, 224–233.

Foxall, G. R., & Goldsmith, R. E. (1994). *Consumer psychology for marketing.* London: Routledge.

Frame, J. H., & Beaty, J. C., Jr. (2000, April). *An investigation of high-technology survey methods at Hewlett-Packard.* Paper presented at the meeting of the Society for Industrial and Organizational Psychology, New Orleans, LA.

Frayne, C. A., & Geringer, J. M. (2000). Self-management training for improving job performance. *Journal of Applied Psychology, 85*, 361–372.

Frese, M. (1999). Social support as a moderator of the relationship between work stressors and psychological dysfunctioning. *Journal of Occupational Health Psychology, 4*, 179–192.

Fried, Y., & Tiegs, R. B. (1995). Supervisors' role conflict and role ambiguity differential relations with performance ratings of subordinates and the moderating effect of screening ability. *Journal of Applied Psychology, 80*, 282–291.

Friedman, M., & Rosenman, R. H. (1974). *Type A behavior and your heart.* New York: Knopf.

Frone, M. (1998). Predictors of work injuries among employed adolescents. *Journal of Applied Psychology, 83*, 565–576.

Frone, M., Russell, M., & Barnes, G. M. (1996). Work-family conflict, gender, and health-related outcomes. *Journal of Occupational Health Psychology, 1*, 57–69.

Fullagar, C. J. A., Gallagher, D. G., Gordon, M. E., & Clark, P. F. (1995). Impact of early socialization on union commitment and participation. *Journal of Applied Psychology, 80*, 147–157.

Gallupe, R. B., Cooper, W. H., Grisé, M. L., & Bastianutti, L. M. (1994). Blocking electronic brainstorms. *Journal of Applied Psychology, 79,* 77–86.

Ganzach, Y. (1998). Intelligence and job satisfaction. *Academy of Management Journal, 41,* 526–539.

Gilbreth, F. B. (1911). *Motion study.* Princeton, NJ: Van Nostrand.

Gladwell, M. (2000). *The tipping point: How little things can make a big difference.* Boston: Little, Brown.

Glomb, T. M., Munson, L. J., Hulin, C. L., Bergman, M. E., & Drasgow, F. (1999). Structural equation models of sexual harassment. *Journal of Applied Psychology, 84,* 14–28.

Goldenhar, L. M., Swanson, N. G., Hurrell, J. J., Ruder, A., & Deddens, J. (1998). Stressors and adverse outcomes for female construction workers. *Journal of Occupational Health Psychology, 3,* 19–32.

Goldstein, H. W., Yusko, K. P., Braverman, E. P., Smith, D. B., & Chung, B. (1998). The role of cognitive ability in the subgroup differences in incremental validity of assessment center exercises. *Personnel Psychology, 51,* 357–374.

Goodstein, J. (1994). Institutional pressures and strategic responsiveness. *Academy of Management Journal, 37,* 350–382.

Gopher, D., Weil, M., & Baraket. T. (1994). Transfer of skill from a computer game trainer to flight. *Human Factors, 36,* 387–405.

Gowan, M. A., Riordan, C. M., & Gatewood, R. D. (1999). Test of a model of coping with involuntary job loss following a company closing. *Journal of Applied Psychology, 81,* 75–86.

Graen, G., & Schliemann, W. (1978). Leader-member agreement. *Journal of Applied Psychology, 63,* 206–212.

Greguras, G. J., & Robie, C. (1998). A new look at within-source interrater reliability of 360-degree feedback ratings. *Journal of Applied Psychology, 83,* 960–968.

Griffin, M. A., & Neal, A. (2000). Perceptions of safety at work. *Journal of Occupational Health Psychology, 5,* 347–358.

Grover, S. L., & Crooker, K. J. (1995). Who appreciates family-responsive human resources policies? *Personnel Psychology, 48,* 271–288.

Hackman, J. R., & Oldham, G. R. (1976). Motivation through the design of work. *Organizational Behavior and Human Performance, 16,* 250–279.

Hackman, J. R., & Oldham, G. R. (1980). *Work redesign.* Reading, MA: Addison-Wesley.

Hancock, E. (1996, Feb.). High control at work makes for a healthy heart. *Johns Hopkins Magazine,* p. 31.

Harris, M. M., Smith, D. E., & Champagne, D. (1995). A field study of performance appraisal purpose. *Personnel Psychology, 48,* 151–160.

Hart, P. M. (1999). Predicting employee life satisfaction. *Journal of Applied Psychology, 84,* 564–584.

Hazlett, R. L., & Hazlett, S. Y. (1999). Emotional response to television commercials. *Journal of Advertising Research, 39*(2), 7–23.

Healy, M. C., Lehman, M., & McDaniel, M. A. (1995). Age and voluntary turnover. *Personnel Psychology, 48,* 335–345.

Heaney, C. A., Israel, B. A., & House, J. S. (1994). Chronic job insecurity among automobile workers. *Social Science and Medicine, 38,* 1431–1437.

Herzberg, F. (1966). *Work and the nature of man.* Cleveland: World.

Herzberg, F. (1974). Motivator-hygiene profiles. *Organizational Dynamics, 3*(2), 18–29.

Highhouse, S., Stierwalt, S. L., Bachiochi, P., Elder, A. E., & Fisher, G. (1999). Effects of advertised human resource management practices on attraction of African-American applicants. *Personnel Psychology, 52,* 425–442.

Hill, E. J., Miller, B. C., Weiner, S. P., & Colihan, J. (1998). Influences of the virtual office on aspects of work and work/life balance. *Personnel Psychology, 51,* 667–683.

Hormann, D. A., & Morgeson, F. P. (1999). Safety-related behavior as a social exchange. *Journal of Applied Psychology, 84,* 286–296.

Hofmann, D. A., & Stetzer, A. (1996). A cross-level investigation of factors influencing unsafe behaviors and accidents. *Personnel Psychology, 49,* 307–339.

Hofmann, D. A., & Stetzer, A. (1998). The role of safety climate and communication in accident interpretation. *Academy of Management Journal, 41,* 644–657.

Hogan, R., Curphy, G. J., & Hogan, J. (1994). What we know about leadership. *American Psychologist, 49,* 493–504.

Hollenbeck, G. P., & McCall, M. W., Jr. (1999). Leadership development. In A. I. Kraut & A. K. Korman (Eds.), *Evolving practices in human resource management* (pp. 172–200). San Francisco: Jossey-Bass.

Hollingworth, H. L. (1929). *Vocational psychology and character analysis.* New York: Appleton.

Hom, P. W., Griffeth, R. W., Palich, L. E., & Bracker, J. S. (1998). An exploratory investigation into theoretical mechanisms underlying realistic job previews. *Personnel Psychology, 51,* 421–451.

Hough, L. M., & Oswald, F. L. (2000). Personnel selection. *Annual Review of Psychology, 51,* 631–664.

House, R. J. (1971). A path-goal theory of leader effectiveness. *Administrative Science Quarterly, 16,* 321–338.

House, R. J., & Mitchell, T. (1974). Path-goal theory of leadership. *Journal of Contemporary Business, 3,* 81–97.

Houtman, I. L. D., & Kompier, M. A. J. (1995). Risk factors and occupational risk groups for work stress in the Netherlands. In S. L. Sauter & L. R. Murphy (Eds.), *Organizational risk factors for job stress* (pp. 209–225). Washington, DC: American Psychological Association.

How to be efficient with fewer violins. (1955). *American Association of University Professors Bulletin, 41,* 454–455.

Howarth, P. A., & Istance, H. O., (1986). The validity of subjective reports of visual discomfort. *Human Factors, 28,* 347–351.

Howell, J. M., & Hall-Merenda, K. E. (1999). The ties that bind. *Journal of Applied Psychology, 84,* 680–694.

Hsu, S. H., & Peng, Y. (1993). Control/display relationship of the four-burner stove. *Human Factors, 35,* 745–749.

Huffcutt, A. I., & Roth, P. L. (1998). Racial group differences in employment interview evaluations. *Journal of Applied Psychology, 83,* 179–189.

Hunt, S. T. (1996). General work behavior. *Personnel Psychology, 49,* 51–83.

Huseman, R. C., Hatfield, J. D., & Miles, E. W. (1987). A new perspective on equity theory. *Academy of Management Review, 12,* 222–234.

Hyde, J. S., Klein, M. H., Essex, M. J., & Clark, R. (1995). Maternity leave and women's mental health. *Psychology of Women Quarterly, 19,* 257–285.

Ingram, P., & Simons, T. (1995). Institutional and resource dependence determinants of responsiveness to work-family issues. *Academy of Management Journal, 38,* 1466–1482.

Janssens, M., Brett, J. M., & Smith, F. J. (1995). Confirmatory cross-cultural research. *Academy of Management Journal, 38,* 364–382.

Jex, S. M., & Bliese, P. D. (1999). Efficacy beliefs as a moderator of the impact of work-related stressors. *Journal of Applied Psychology, 84,* 349–361.

Johns, G., & Xie, J. L. (1998). Perceptions of absence from work. *Journal of Applied Psychology, 83,* 515–530.

Johnson, J. W., & Ferstl, K. L. (1999). The effects of interrater and self-other agreement on performance improvement following upward feedback. *Personnel Psychology, 52,* 271–303.

Jones, R. G., & Whitmore, M. D. (1995). Evaluating developmental assessment centers as interventions. *Personnel Psychology, 48,* 377–388.

Judge, T. A., & Bono, J. E. (2000). Five-factor model of personality and transformational leadership. *Journal of Applied Psychology, 85,* 751–765.

Judge, T. A., Bono, J. E., & Locke, E. A. (2000). Personality and job satisfaction. *Journal of Applied Psychology, 85,* 237–249.

Judge, T. A., Thoresen, C. J., Pucik, V., & Welbourne, T. M. (1999). Managerial coping with organizational change. *Journal of Applied Psychology, 84,* 107–122.

Judiesch, M. K., & Lyness, K. S. (1999). Left behind? The impact of leaves of absence on managers' career success. *Academy of Management Journal, 42,* 641–651.

Kane, J. S., Bernardin, H. J., Villanova, P., & Peyrefitte, J. (1995). Stability of rater leniency. *Academy of Management Journal, 38,* 1036–1051.

Kanis, H. (1993). Operation of controls on consumer products by physically impaired users. *Human Factors, 35,* 305–328.

Kanner, A. D., & Kasser, T. (2000). Stuffing our kids. *The Industrial-Organizational Psychologist, 38*(1), 185–187.

Karau, S. J., & Hart, J. W. (1998). Group cohesiveness and social loafing. *Group Dynamics, 2,* 185–191.

Kates, S. M. (2000). Out of the closet and out on the street! *Psychology and Marketing, 17,* 493–513.

Kelley, P. L., Jacobs, R. R., & Farr, J. L. (1994). Effects of multiple administrations of the MMPI for employee screening. *Personnel Psychology, 47,* 575–591.

Kelly, R. M., & Kelly, V. P. (1990). Lillian Moller Gilbreth (1878–1972). In A. N. O'Connell & N. F. Russo (Eds.), *Women in psychology* (pp. 117–124). New York: Greenwood.

Kilduff, M., & Day, D. V. (1994). Do chameleons get ahead? *Academy of Management Journal, 37,* 1047–1060.

King, W. C., Jr., & Miles, E. W. (1995). A quasi-experimental assessment of the effect of computerizing noncognitive paper-and-pencil measurements. *Journal of Applied Psychology, 80,* 643–651.

Kinicki, A. J., Prussia, G. E., & McKee-Ryan, F. M. (2000). A panel study of coping with involuntary job loss. *Academy of Management Journal, 43,* 90–100.

Kirkman, B. L., & Rosen, B. (1999). Beyond self-management. *Academy of Management Journal, 42,* 58–74.

Kivimäki, M., & Kalimo R. (1996). Self-esteem and the occupational stress process. *Journal of Occupational Health Psychology, 1,* 187–196.

Klein, H. J., & Kim, J. S. (1998). A field study of the influence of situational constraints, leader-member exchange, and goal commitment on performance. *Academy of Management Journal, 41,* 88–95.

Klein, H. J., & Weaver, N. A. (2000). The effectiveness of an organizational level orientation training program in the socialization of new hires. *Personnel Psychology, 53,* 47–66.

Klein, H. J., Wesson, M. J., Hollenbeck, J. R., & Alge, B. J. (1999). Goal commitment and the goal-setting process. *Journal of Applied Psychology, 84,* 885–896.

Kluger, A. N., & De Nisi, A. (1996). The effects of feedback interventions on performance. *Psychological Bulletin, 119,* 254–284.

Knight, G. A. (1999). Consumer preferences for foreign and domestic products. *Journal of Consumer Marketing, 16,* 151–162.

Kobasa, S. C. (1979). Stressful life events, personality, and health. *Journal of Personality and Social Psychology, 37,* 1–11.

Kobasa, S. C. (1982). The hardy personality. In G. Sanders & J. Suls (Eds.), *Social psychology of health and illness* (pp. 3–32). Hillsdale, NJ: Erlbaum.

Korgaonkar, P. K., & Wolin, L. D. (1999). A multivariate analysis of Web usage. *Journal of Advertising Research, 39*(2), 53–68.

Kossek, E., & Nichol, V. (1992). The effects of on-site child care on employee attitudes and performance. *Personnel Psychology, 45,* 485–509.

Kossek, E., & Ozeki, C. (1998). Work-family conflict, policies, and the job-life satisfaction relationship. *Journal of Applied Psychology, 83,* 139–149.

Kossek, E., Roberts, K., Fisher, S., & Demarr, B. (1998). Career self-management. *Personnel Psychology, 51,* 935–962.

Kraut, R., Patterson, M., Lundmark, V., Kiesler, S., Mukopadhyay, T., & Scherlis, W. (1998). Internet paradox. *American Psychologist, 53,* 1017–1031.

Kravitz, D. A., & Klineberg, S. L. (2000). Reactions to two versions of affirmative action among Whites, Blacks, and Hispanics. *Journal of Applied Psychology, 85,* 597–611.

LaFerle, C., Edwards, S. M., & Lee, W.-N. (2000). Teens' use of traditional media and the Internet. *Journal of Advertising Research, 40*(3), 55–65.

Lawler, E. E., III. (1986). *High-involvement management.* San Francisco: Jossey-Bass.

Lefkowitz, J. (1970). Effect of training on the productivity and tenure of sewing machine operators. *Journal of Applied Psychology, 54,* 81–86.

Liden, R. C., Wayne, S. J., Judge, T. A., Sparrowe, R. T., Kraimer, M. L., & Franz, T. M. (1999). Management of poor performance. *Journal of Applied Psychology, 84,* 835–850.

Liden, R. C., Wayne, S. J., & Sparrowe, R. T. (2000). An examination of the mediating role of psychological empowerment on the relations between the job, interpersonal relationships, and work outcomes. *Journal of Applied Psychology, 85,* 407–416.

Locke, E. A. (1968). Toward a theory of task motivation and incentives. *Organizational Behavior and Human Performance, 3,* 157–189.

Locke, E. A., & Latham, G. P. (1990). *A theory of goal setting and task performance.* Upper Saddle River, NJ: Prentice Hall.

Long, B. C. (1998). Coping with workplace stress. *Journal of Counseling Psychology, 45*, 65–78.

Lundberg, U. (1996). Influence of paid and unpaid work on psychophysiological stress responses of men and women. *Journal of Occupational Health Psychology, 1*, 117–130.

Lundberg, U., & Frankenhaeuser, M. (1999). Stress and workload of men and women in high-ranking positions. *Journal of Occupational Health Psychology, 4*, 142–151.

Lyness, K. S., & Thompson, D. E. (2000). Climbing the corporate ladder. *Journal of Applied Psychology, 85*, 86–101.

Macan, T. H. (1994). Time management. *Journal of Applied Psychology, 79*, 381–391.

Mael, F. A., & Ashforth, B. E. (1995). Loyal from day one. *Personnel Psychology, 48*, 309–333.

Magley, V. J., Hulin, C. L., Fitzgerald, L. F., & DeNardo, M. (1999). Outcomes of self-labeling sexual harassment. *Journal of Applied Psychology, 84*, 390–402.

Manning, M. R., Jackson, C. N., & Fusilier, M. R. (1996a). Occupational stress and health care use. *Journal of Occupational Health Psychology, 1*, 100–109.

Manning, M. R., Jackson, C. N., & Fusilier, M. R. (1996b). Occupational stress, social support, and the cost of health care. *Academy of Management Journal, 39*, 738–750.

Markham, S. E., & McKee, G. H. (1995). Group absence behavior and standards. *Academy of Management Journal, 38*, 1174–1190.

Marlowe, C. M., Schneider, S. L., & Nelson, C. E. (1996). Gender and attractiveness biases in hiring decisions. *Journal of Applied Psychology, 81*, 11–21.

Marras, W. S., Marklin, R. W., Greenspan, G. J., & Lehman, K. R. (1995). Quantification of wrist motion during scanning. *Human Factors, 37*, 412–423.

Martocchio, J. J. (1994). Effects of conceptions of ability on anxiety, self-efficacy, and learning in training. *Journal of Applied Psychology, 79*, 819–825.

Maslach, C. (1982). *Burnout.* Upper Saddle River, NJ: Prentice Hall.

Maslach, C., & Jackson, S. E. (1986). *Maslach Burnout Inventory manual* (2nd ed.). Palo Alto, CA: Consulting Psychologists Press.

Maslow, A. (1970). Motivation and personality (2nd ed.). New York: Harper & Row.

Matthews, G., Dorn, L., Hoyes, T. W., Davies, D. R., Glendon, A. I., & Taylor, R. G. (1998). Driver stress and performance on a driving simulator. *Human Factors, 40*, 136–149.

Maurer, T. J., Raju, N. S., & Collins, W. C. (1998). Peer and subordinate performance appraisal measurement equivalence. *Journal of Applied Psychology, 83*, 693–702.

May, D. R., & Schwoerer, C. E. (1994). Employee health by design. *Personnel Psychology, 47*, 861–876.

Mayer, R. C., & Davis, J. H. (1999). The effect of the performance appraisal system on trust for management. *Journal of Applied Psychology, 84*, 123–136.

Mays, V. M., Coleman, L. M., & Jackson, J. S. (1996). Perceived race-based discrimination, employment status, and job stress in a national sample of Black women. *Journal of Occupational Health Psychology, 1*, 319–329.

McCall, M., & Belmont, H. J. (1996). Credit card insignia and restaurant tipping. *Journal of Applied Psychology, 81*, 609–613.

McClelland, D. C. (1961). *The achieving society.* New York: Free Press.

McClelland, D. C. (1975). *Power*. New York: Irvington.

McClelland, D. C., Atkinson, J. W., Clark, R. A., & Lowell, E. L. (1953). *The achievement motive*. New York: Appleton-Century-Crofts.

McFarlin, S. K., Fals-Stewart, W., Major, D. A., & Justice, E. M. (2000, April). *Alcohol use and workplace aggression*. Paper presented at the meeting of the Society for Industrial and Organizational Psychology, New Orleans, LA.

McGregor, D. (1960). *The human side of enterprise*. New York: McGraw-Hill.

McLain, D. L. (1995). Responses to health and safety risk in the work environment. *Academy of Management Journal, 38*, 1726–1743.

McNatt, D. B. (2000). Ancient Pygmalion joins contemporary management. *Journal of Applied Psychology, 85*, 314–322.

McNeely B. L., & Meglino, B. M. (1994). The role of dispositional and situational antecedents in prosocial organizational behavior. *Journal of Applied Psychology, 79*, 836–844.

Mehta, A. (2000). Advertising attitudes and advertising effectiveness. *Journal of Advertising Research, 40*(3), 67–72.

Meijman, T. F., Ulenbelt, P., Lumens, M. E. J. L., & Herbert, R. F. M. (1996). Behavioral determinants of occupational exposure to chemical agents. *Journal of Occupational Health Psychology, 1*, 85–91.

Melamed, S., Ben-Avi, I., Luz, J., & Green, M. S. (1995). Objective and subjective work monotony. *Journal of Applied Psychology, 80*, 29–42.

Mellor, S. (1995). Gender composition and gender representation in local unions. *Journal of Applied Psychology, 80*, 706–720.

Mellor, S., Mathieu, J. E., & Swim, J. K. (1994). Cross-level analysis and the influence of local union structure on women's and men's union commitment. *Journal of Applied Psychology, 79*, 203–210.

Meyer, J. P., & Allen, N. J. (1991). A three-component conceptualization of organizational commitment. *Human Resource Management Review, 1*, 61–98.

Milliken, F. J., & Martins, L. L. (1996). Searching for common threads. *Academy of Management Review, 21*, 402–433.

Milliken, F. J., Martins, L. L., & Morgan, H. (1998). Explaining organizational responsiveness to work-family issues. *Academy of Management Journal, 41*, 580–592.

Moore, E. S., & Lutz, R. J. (2000). Children, advertising, and product experiences. *Journal of Consumer Research, 27*, 31–48.

Morrison, E. W., & Phelps, C. C. (1999). Taking charge at work. *Academy of Management Journal, 42*, 403–419.

Morrow, C. C., Jarrett, M. Q., & Rupinski, M. T. (1997). An investigation of the effect and economic utility of corporate-wide training. *Personnel Psychology, 50*, 91–119.

Mount, M. K., Barrick, M. R., & Strauss, J. P. (1994). Validity of observer ratings of the big five personality factors. *Journal of Applied Psychology, 79*, 272–280.

Mount, M. K., Sytsma, M. R., Hazucha, J. F., & Holt, K. E. (1997). Rater-ratee race effects in developmental performance ratings of managers. *Personnel Psychology, 50*, 51–69.

Mount, M. K., Witt, L. A., & Marrick, M. R. (2000). Incremental validity of empirically keyed biodata scales over GMA and the five-factor personality constructs. *Personnel Psychology, 53*, 299–323.

Mulvey, P. W., Veiga, J. F., & Elsass, P. M. (1996). When teammates raise a white flag. *Academy of Management Executive, 10*(1), 40–49.

Munson, L. J., Hulin, C., & Drasgow, F. (2000). Longitudinal analysis of dispositional influences and sexual harassment. *Personnel Psychology, 53,* 21–46.

Münsterberg, H. (1913). *The psychology of industrial efficiency.* Boston: Houghton Mifflin.

Nelson, A., Cooper, C. L., & Jackson, P. R. (1995). Uncertainty amidst change. *Journal of Occupational and Organizational Psychology, 68,* 57–71.

Nelson, D. L., & Burke, R. J. (2000). Women executives. *Academy of Management Executive, 14*(2), 107–121.

Nelson, N. A., & Silverstein, B. A. (1998). Workplace changes associated with a reduction in musculoskeletal symptoms in office workers. *Human Factors, 40,* 337–350.

Neuman, G. A., & Wright, J. (1999). Team effectiveness. *Journal of Applied Psychology, 84,* 376–389.

North, A. C., Hargreaves, D. J., & McKendrick, J. (1999). The influence of in-store music on wine selections. *Journal of Applied Psychology, 84,* 271–276.

Nutt, P. C. (1999). Surprising but true: Half the decisions in organizations fail. *Academy of Management Executive, 13*(4), 75–90.

Oldham, G. R., Cummings, A., Mischel, L. J., Schmidke, J. M., & Zhou, J. (1995). Listen while you work. *Journal of Applied Psychology, 80,* 547–564.

Ones, D. S., & Viswesvaran, C. (1998). Gender, age, and race differences in overt integrity tests. *Journal of Applied Psychology, 83,* 35–42.

Ong, C. N., Koh, D., Phoon, W. O., & Low, A. (1988). Anthropometrics and display station preferences of VDU operators. *Ergonomics, 31,* 337–347.

Organ, D. W., & Ryan, K. (1995). A meta-analytic review of attitudinal and dispositional predictors of organizational citizenship behavior. *Personnel Psychology, 48,* 775–802.

Overton, R. C., Taylor, L. R., Zickar, M. J., & Harms, H. J. (1996). The pen-based computer as an alternative platform for test administration. *Personnel Psychology, 49,* 455–464.

Oz, S., & Eden, D. (1994). Restraining the Golem. *Journal of Applied Psychology, 79,* 744–754.

Parasuraman, S., & Purohit, Y. S. (2000). Distress and boredom among orchestra musicians. *Journal of Occupational Health Psychology, 5,* 74–83.

Parker, S. K. (1998). Enhancing role-breadth self-efficacy. *Journal of Applied Psychology, 83,* 835–852.

Paul, J. A., Frings-Dresen, M .H. W., Sallé, H. J. A., & Rozendal, R. H. (1995). Pregnant women and working surface height and working surface areas for standing manual work. *Applied Ergonomics, 26*(2), 129–133.

Peirce, E., Smolinski, C. A., & Rosen, B. (1998). Why sexual harassment complaints fall on deaf ears. *Academy of Management Executive, 12*(3), 41–54.

Peterson, M. F., et al. (1995). Role conflict, ambiguity, and overload. *Academy of Management Journal, 38,* 429–452.

Pfeffer J. (1995). Producing sustainable competitive advantages through the effective management of people. *Academy of Management Executive, 9*(1), 55–70.

Phillips, J. M. (1998). Effects of realistic job previews on multiple organizational outcomes. *Academy of Management Journal, 41,* 673–690.

Pieper, K. F. (2000). The latest on state licensure and activities of the state affairs committee. *The Industrial-Organizational Psychologist, 37*(4), 134–136.

Pines, A., & Guendelman, S. (1995). Exploring the relevance of burnout to Mexican blue-collar women. *Journal of Vocational Behavior, 47,* 1–20.

Prewett-Livingston, A. J., Feild, H. S., Veres, J. G., III, & Lewis, P. M. (1996). Effects of race on interviewer ratings in a situational panel interview. *Journal of Applied Psychology, 81,* 178–186.

Probst, T. M. (2000). Wedded to the job. *Journal of Occupational Health Psychology, 5,* 63–73.

Probst, T. M., & Brubaker, T. L. (2000, April). Cross-sectional and longitudinal explorations of the effects of job insecurity on employee safety motivation and compliance. Paper presented at the meeting of the Society for Industrial and Organizational Psychology, New Orleans, LA.

Quiñones, M. A. (1995). Pretraining context effects. *Journal of Applied Psychology, 80,* 226–238.

Ragins, B. R., & Cotton, J. L. (1999). Mentor functions and outcomes. *Journal of Applied Psychology, 84,* 529–550.

Ragins, B. R., Townsend, B., & Mattis, M. (1998). Gender gap in the executive suite. *Academy of Management Executive, 12*(1), 28–42.

Ramsey, J. D. (1995). Task performance in heat. *Ergonomics, 38,* 154–165.

Redman, T., & Snape, E. (1992). Upward and onward. *Personnel Review, 21*(7), 32–46.

Reilly, R. R., Smither, J. W., & Vasilopoulos, N. L. (1966). A longitudinal study of upward feedback. *Personnel Psychology, 49,* 599–612.

Richman, W. L., Kiesler, S., Weisband, S., & Drasgow, F. (1999). A meta-analytic study of social desirability distortion in computer-administered questionnaires, traditional questionnaires, and interviews. *Journal of Applied Psychology, 84,* 754–775.

Rind, B. (1996). Effects of beliefs about weather conditions on tipping. *Journal of Applied social Psychology, 26,* 137–147.

Ringenbach, K. L., & Jacobs, R. R. (1995). Injuries and aging workers. *Journal of Safety Research, 26*(3), 169–176.

Robinson, S. L., Kraatz, M. S., & Rousseau, D. M. (1994). Changing obligations and the psychological contract. *Academy of Management Journal, 37,* 137–152.

Robinson, S. L., & O'Leary-Kelly, A. M. (1998). Monkey see, monkey do. *Academy of Management Journal, 41,* 658–672.

Roethlisberger, F. J., & Dickson, W. J. (1939). *Management and the worker.* Cambridge, MA: Harvard University Press.

Rogelberg, S. G., Luong, A., Sederburg, M. E., & Cristol, D. S. (2000). Employee attitude surveys. *Journal of Applied Psychology, 85,* 284–293.

Rogers, W. A., Meyer, B., Walker, N., & Fisk, A. D. (1998). Functional limitations to daily living tasks in the aged. *Human Factors, 40,* 111–125.

Rosenthal, R., & Jacobson, L. (1968). *Pygmalion in the classroom.* New York: Holt.

Roth, P. L., & Bobko, P. (2000). College grade point average as a personnel selection device. *Journal of Applied Psychology, 85,* 399–406.

Rothausen, T. J., Gonzalez, J. A., Clarke, N. E., & O'Dell, L. L. (1998). Family-friendly backlash. *Personnel Psychology, 51,* 685–706.

Rotundo, M., & Sackett, P. R. (1999). Effect of rater race on conclusions regarding differential prediction in cognitive ability tests. *Journal of Applied Psychology, 84,* 815–822.

Rousseau, D. M., & Tijoriwala, S. A. (1999). What's a good reason to change? *Journal of Applied Psychology, 84,* 514–528.

Saks, A. M. (1995). Longitudinal field investigations of the moderating and mediating effects of self-efficacy on the relationship between training and newcomer adjustment. *Journal of Applied Psychology, 80,* 211–225.

Salgado, J. F. (1997). The five factor model of personality and job performance in the European community. *Journal of Applied Psychology, 82,* 30–43.

Sarchione, C. D., Cuttler, M. J., Muchinsky, P. M., & Nelson-Gray, R. O. (1998). Prediction of dysfunctional job behavior among law enforcement officers. *Journal of Applied Psychology, 83,* 904–912.

Saunders, T., Driskell, J. E., Johnston, J. H., & Salas, E. (1996). The effect of stress inoculation training on anxiety and performance. *Journal of Occupational Health Psychology, 1,* 170–186.

Schaubroeck J., Ganster, D. C., Sime, W. E., & Ditman, D. (1993). A field experiment testing supervisory role clarification. *Personnel Psychology, 46,* 1–25.

Schaubroeck, J., Lam, S. S. K., & Xie, J. L. (2000). Collective efficacy versus self-efficacy in coping responses to stressors and control. *Journal of Applied Psychology, 85,* 512–525.

Schaufeli, W. B., Keijsers G. J., & Miranda, D. R. (1995). Burnout, technology use, and ICU performance. In S. L. Sauter & L. R. Murphy (Eds.), *Organizational risk factors for job stress* (pp. 259–271). Washington, DC: American Psychological Association.

Schliefer, L. M., Galinski, T. L., & Pan, C. S. (1995). Mood disturbance and musculoskeletal discomfort effects of electronic performance monitoring in a VDT data-entry task. In S. L. Sauter & L. R. Murphy (Eds.), *Organizational risk factors for job stress* (pp. 195–203). Washington, DC: American Psychological Association.

Schmidt, F. L., & Hunter, J. E. (1998). The validity and utility of selection methods in personnel psychology. *Psychological Bulletin, 124,* 262–274.

Schmidt, F. L., Law, K., Hunter, J. E., Rothstein, H. R., Pearlman, K., & McDaniel, M. (1993). Refinements in validity generalization methods. *Journal of Applied Psychology, 78,* 3–12.

Schmidt, F. L., & Rader, M. (1999). Exploring the boundary conditions for interview validity. *Personnel Psychology, 52,* 445–464.

Schminke, M., Ambrose, M. L., & Cropanzano, R. S. (2000). The effect of organizational structure on perceptions of procedural fairness. *Journal of Applied Psychology, 85,* 294–304.

Schneider, B., Smith, D. B., Taylor, S., & Fleenor, J. (1998). Personality and organizations. *Journal of Applied Psychology, 83,* 462–470.

Schneider, K. T., Hitlan, R. T., & Radhakrishnan, P. (2000). An examination of the nature and correlates of ethnic harassment experiences in multiple contexts. *Journal of Applied Psychology, 81,* 3–12.

Schoenmarklin, R. W., & Marras, W. S. (1989a, 1989b). Effects of handle angle and work orientation on hammering. *Human Factors, 31,* 397–411, 413–420.

Schriesheim, C. A., Neider, L. L., & Scandura, T. A. (1998). Delegation and leader-member exchange. *Academy of Management Journal, 41,* 298–318.

Schwartzberg, N. S., & Dytell, R. S. (1996). Dual-earner families. *Journal of Occupational Health Psychology, 1,* 211–223.

Schweitzer, M. E., & Kerr, J. L. (2000). Bargaining under the influence. *Academy of Management Executive, 14*(2), 47–57.

Scott, W. D. (1903). *The theory and practice of advertising.* Boston: Small.

Seashore, S. E., & Bowers D. G. (1970). Durability of organizational change. *American Psychologist, 25,* 227–233.

Seibert, S. E., Crant, J. M., & Kraimer, M. L. (1999). Proactive personality and career success. *Journal of Applied Psychology, 84,* 416–427.

Settoon, R. P., Bennett, N., & Liden, R. C. (1996). Social exchange in organizations. *Journal of Applied Psychology, 81,* 219–227.

Shah, P. P. (2000). Network destruction. *Academy of Management Journal, 43,* 101–112.

Shalley, C. E., Gilson, L. L., & Blum, T. C. (2000). Matching creativity requirements and the work environment. *Academy of Management Journal, 43,* 215–223.

Shaw, J. D., Delery, J. E., Jenkins, G. D., Jr., & Gupta, N. (1998). An organizational-level analysis of voluntary and involuntary turnover. *Academy of Management Journal, 41,* 511–525.

Shore, T. H., Shore, L. M., & Thornton, G. C., III. (1992). Construct validity of self- and peer-evaluations of performance dimensions in an assessment center. *Journal of Applied Psychology, 77,* 42–54.

Siegrist, J. (1996). Adverse health effects of high-effort/low-reward conditions. *Journal of Occupational Health Psychology, 1,* 27–41.

Smith, M. F. (1999). Urban versus suburban consumers. *Journal of Consumer Marketing, 16,* 58–73.

Smith, M. J., Karsh, B. T., Conway, F. T., Cohen, W. J., James, C. A., Morgan, J. J., Sanders, K., & Zehel, D. J. (1998). Effects of a split keyboard design and wrist rest on performance, posture, and comfort. *Human Factors, 40,* 324–336.

Smith-Jentsch, K. H., Jentsch, F. G., Payne, S. C., & Salas, E. (1996). Can pre-training experiences explain individual differences in learning? *Journal of Applied Psychology, 81,* 110–116.

Spector, P. E., Chen, P. Y., & O'Connell, B. J. (2000). A longitudinal study of relations between job stressors and job strains while controlling for prior negative affectivity and strains. *Journal of Applied Psychology, 85,* 211–218.

Stajkovic, A. D., & Luthans, F. (1998). Self-efficacy and work-related performance. *Psychological Bulletin, 124,* 240–261.

Stanton, J. M. (1998). An empirical assessment of data collection using the Internet. *Personnel Psychology, 51,* 709–725.

Stanton, J. M. (1999). Validity and related issues in Web-based hiring. *The Industrial-Organizational Psychologist, 36*(3), 69–77.

Steel, R. P., & Rentsch, J. R. (1995). Influence of cumulative strategies on the long-range prediction of absenteeism. *Academy of Management Journal, 38,* 1616–1634.

Steiner, D. D., & Gilliland, S. W. (1996). Fairness reactions to personnel selection techniques in France and the United States. *Journal of Applied Psychology, 81,* 134–141.

Stevens, C. K. (1998). Antecedents of interviewer interactions, interviewers' ratings, and applicants' reactions. *Personnel Psychology, 51,* 55–85.

Stevens, C. K., & Kristof, A. L. (1995). Making the right impression. *Journal of Applied Psychology, 80,* 587–606.

Stevenson, J. S., Bruner, G. C., II, & Kumar, A. (2000). Web page background and viewer attitudes. *Journal of Advertising Research, 40,* 29–34.

Stewart, G. L. (1999). Trait bandwidth and stages of job performance. *Journal of Applied Psychology, 84,* 959–968.

Stewart, G. L., Carson, K. P., & Cardy, R. L. (1996). The joint effects of conscientiousness and self-leadership training on employee self-directed behavior in a service setting. *Personnel Psychology, 49,* 143–164.

Stone, G., Besser, D., & Lewis, L. E. (2000). Recall, liking, and creativity in TV commercials. *Journal of Advertising Research, 40*(3), 7–18.

Sutton, R. I., & Rafaeli, A. (1998). Untangling the relationship between displayed emotions and organizational sales. *Academy of Management Journal, 31,* 461–487.

Swartz, T. A. (1983). Brand symbols and message differentiation. *Journal of Advertising Research, 23*(5), 59–64.

Taylor, F. W. (1911). *Scientific management.* New York: Harper.

Taylor, S. E., Klein, L. C., Lewis, B. P., Gruenewald, T. L., Gurung, R. A. R., & Updegraff, J. A. (2000). Biobehavioral responses to stress in females. *Psychological Review, 107,* 411–429.

Tenopyr, M. L. (1992). Reflections of a pioneering woman in industrial psychology. *Professional Psychology, 23,* 172–175.

Tepper, K. (1994). The role of labeling processes in elderly consumers' responses to age segmentation cues. *Journal of Consumer Research, 20,* 503–519.

Thomas, L. T., & Ganster, D. C. (1995). Impact of family-supportive work variables in work-family conflict and strain. *Journal of Applied Psychology, 80,* 6–15.

Tierney, P., Farmer, S. M., & Graen, G. B. (1999). An examination of leadership and employee creativity. *Personnel Psychology, 52,* 591–620.

Toterdell, P., Spelten, E., Smith, L., Barton, J., & Folkard, S. (1995). Recovery from work shifts. *Journal of Applied Psychology, 80,* 43–57.

Tracey, J. S., Tannenbaum, S. I., & Kavanagh, M. J. (1995). Applying trained skills on the job. *Journal of Applied Psychology, 80,* 239–252.

Tripp, C., Jensen, T. D., & Carlson, S. (1994). The effects of multiple product endorsements by celebrities on consumers' attitudes and intentions. *Journal of Consumer Marketing, 20,* 535–547.

Truxillo, D. M., & Bauer, T. N. (1999). Applicant reactions to test score banding in entry-level and promotional contexts. *Journal of Applied Psychology, 84,* 322–339.

Turban, D. B., Campion, J. E., & Eyring, A. R. (1995). Factors related to job acceptance decisions of college recruits. *Journal of Vocational Behavior, 47,* 193–213.

Turban, D. B., & Dougherty, T. W. (1994). Role of protégé personality in receipt of mentoring and career success. *Academy of Management Journal, 37,* 688–702.

Underhill, P. (1999). *Why we buy.* New York: Simon & Schuster.

Valacich, J. S., Dennis, A. R., & Connolly, T. (1994). Idea generation in computer-based groups. *Organizational Behavior and Human Decision Processes, 57,* 448–467.

van Velsor, E., & Leslie, J. B. (1995). Why executives derail. *Academy of Management Executive, 9*(4), 62–72.

Van Vianen, A. E. M. (2000). Person-organization fit. *Personnel Psychology, 53,* 113–149.

Vecchio, R. P. (1990). Theoretical and empirical examination of cognitive resource theory. *Journal of Applied Psychology, 75,* 141–147.

Vecchio, R. P. (1992). Cognitive resource theory. *Journal of Applied Psychology, 77,* 375–376.

Vroom, V. H., & Jago, A. G. (1998). *The new leadership.* Upper Saddle River, NJ: Prentice Hall.

Waclawski, J., & Church, A. H. (2000). The 2000 SIOP member survey results are in! *The Industrial-Organizational Psychologist, 38*(1), 59–68.

Walker, A. G., & Smither, J. W. (1999). A five-year study of upward feedback. *Personnel Psychology, 52,* 393–423.

Wanberg, C. R., & Banas, J. T. (2000). Predictors and outcomes of openness to changes in a reorganizing workplace. *Journal of Applied Psychology, 85,* 132–142.

Wanberg, C. R., Bunce, L. W., & Gavin, M. B. (1999). Perceived fairness of layoffs among individuals who have been laid off. *Personnel Psychology, 52,* 59–84.

Wanberg, C. R., & Kammeyer-Mueller, J. D. (2000). Predictors and outcomes of proactivity in the socialization process. *Journal of Applied Psychology, 85,* 373–385.

Wanberg, C. R., Kanfer, R., & Rotundo, M. (1999). Unemployed individuals. *Journal of Applied Psychology, 84,* 897–910.

Ward, S., Oliva, T. A., & Reibstein, D. J. (1994). Effectiveness of brand-related 15-second commercials. *Journal of Consumer Marketing, 1*(2), 38–44.

Warr, P., & Bunce, D. (1995). Trainee characteristics and the outcomes of open learning. *Personnel Psychology, 48,* 347–375.

Waung, M. (1995). The effects of self-regulatory coping orientation on newcomer adjustment and job survival. *Personnel Psychology, 48,* 633–650.

Wayne, S. J., & Liden, R. C. (1995). Effects of impression management on performance ratings. *Academy of Management Journal, 38,* 232–260.

Weber, M. (1947). *The theory of social and economic organization.* New York: Oxford University Press.

Weekley, J. A., & Jones, C. (1999). Further studies of situational tests. *Personnel Psychology, 52,* 679–700.

Weisband, S. P., Schneider, S. K., & Connolly, T. (1995). Computer-mediated communication and social information. *Academy of Management Journal, 38,* 1124–1151.

Wright, T. A., & Cropanzano, R. (2000). Psychological well-being and job satisfaction as predictors of job performance. *Journal of Occupational Health Psychology, 5,* 84–94.

Xie, J. L., & Johns, G. (1995). Job scope and stress. *Academy of Management Journal, 38,* 1288–1309.

Yang, N., Chen, C. C., Choi, J., & Zou, Y. (2000). Sources of work-family conflict. *Academy of Management Journal, 43,* 113–123.

Yukl, G., & Taber, T. (1983). The effective use of managerial power. *Personnel, 60*(2), 37–44.

Zohar, D. (2000). A group-level model of safety climate. *Journal of Applied Psychology, 85,* 587–596.

Glossary

Accident proneness   The idea that some people have personality traits that predispose them to have accidents, and that most accidents are caused by or involve these same few people. This theory is not supported by research.

Achievement motivation   The theory of motivation that emphasizes the need to accomplish something, to do a good job, and to be the best.

Adverse impact   When a minority group of job applicants or employees is treated markedly worse than the majority group in staffing decisions.

Aided recall technique   A test of advertising effectiveness to determine the extent to which ad content can be recalled. The interviewer aids the recall by asking specific questions.

Apprenticeship   A training method for skilled crafts and trades involving classroom instruction and on-the-job experience.

Aptitude tests   Psychological tests to measure specific abilities, such as mechanical or clerical skills.

Assessment center   A method of selection and training that involves a simulated job situation in which candidates deal with actual job problems.

Attribution   A source of error in performance appraisal in which raters attribute or assign positive or negative explanations to an employee's behavior.

Auditory displays   Alarms or warning signals in person-machine systems. Auditory displays can be more compelling than visual displays.

Authoritarian leadership   A leadership style in which a leader makes all decisions and tells followers what to do.

Average rating error   A source of error in performance appraisal in which a rater is unwilling to assign very good or very poor ratings. Consequently, most ratings fall in the middle of the rating scale.

Banding   A controversial practice of grouping test scores for minority job applicants to equalize hiring rates.

Behavior modification   A training program of positive reinforcement to reward employees for displaying desirable job behaviors.

Behavioral observation scales (BOS)   A performance appraisal technique in which appraisers rate the frequency of critical employee behaviors.

Behaviorally anchored rating scales (BARS)   A performance appraisal technique in which appraisers rate critical employee behaviors.

Biofeedback   A stress-reduction technique that involves electronic monitoring of physiological processes, such that people can learn to control muscle tension, blood pressure, and brain waves.

Biographical inventory   An employee selection technique covering an applicant's past behavior, attitudes, preferences, and values.

Bureaucracy   A formal, orderly, and rational approach to organizing business enterprises.

Burnout   A condition of job stress that results from overwork.

Business games   A training method that simulates a complex organizational situation to encourage the development of problem-solving and decision-making skills.

Carpal tunnel syndrome   A repetitive motion disorder that may involve numbness, tingling, or pain in fingers, hands, and forearms.

Case studies   A method of executive training in which trainees analyze a business problem and offer solutions.

Change agents   Organization development facilitators who work with business groups to implement change and develop group confidence and effectiveness.

Charismatic leadership   A leadership style characterized by a self-promoting personality, a high energy level, and a willingness to take risks. Charismatic leaders stimulate their followers to think independently.

Check reading visual displays   Displays that tell the operator whether the system is on or off, safe or unsafe, or operating normally or abnormally.

Cognitive resource theory   A leadership theory that focuses on the interaction among the following factors: a leader's cognitive resources (intelligence, technical competence, and job-related knowledge), job performance, and level of stress.

Computer-assisted instruction (CAI)   A computer-based training method in which trainees learn material at their own pace and receive immediate feedback on their progress.

Computerized adaptive tests   A means of administering psychological tests in which an applicant's response to an item determines the level of difficulty of succeeding items.

Concurrent validity   A way to establish criterion-related validity that involves administering a test to employees on the job and correlating their scores with job performance data.

Consideration leadership functions   Leadership behaviors that involve awareness of and sensitivity to the feelings of subordinates.

Constant bias   A source of error in performance appraisal based on the different standards used by raters.

Construct validity   A type of validity that attempts to determine the psychological characteristics measured by a test.

Content validity   A type of validity that assesses test items to ensure that they adequately sample the skills the test is designed to measure.

Contingency theory   A leadership theory in which a leader's effectiveness is determined by the interaction between the leader's personal characteristics and the characteristics of the leadership situation.

Control group   In an experiment, this is the group of research participants that is not exposed to the independent variable.

Correlation   The relationship between two variables. The strength and direction of the relationship is expressed by the correlation coefficient.

Criterion-related validity   A type of validity concerned with the relationship between test scores and subsequent job performance.

Critical-incidents technique   A means of identifying specific activities or behaviors that lead to desirable or undesirable consequences on the job.

Democratic leadership   A leadership style in which a leader and followers discuss problems and make decisions jointly.

Dependent variable   In an experiment, this is the resulting behavior of the subjects, which depends on the manipulation of the independent variable.

Descriptive statistics   Ways of describing or representing research data in a concise, meaningful manner.

Dysfunctional turnover   The situation that arises when good employees quit their jobs. This type of turnover can be harmful to the organization.

Employee assistance programs (EAPs)   Counseling and rehabilitative services for various employee problems, notably alcohol and drug abuse.

Engineering psychology   The design of machines and equipment for human use, and the determination of the appropriate human behaviors for the efficient operation of the machines. The field is also called human factors, human engineering, and ergonomics.

Environmental psychology   The study of the effect of workplace design on behavior and attitudes.

Equity theory   The theory of motivation that states that our motivation on the job is influenced by our perception of how fairly we are treated.

Equivalent-forms method   A way to determine test reliability that involves administering similar forms of a new test to the same group of subjects and correlating the two sets of scores.

ERG theory   The theory of motivation based on three types of needs: existence needs, relatedness needs, and growth needs.

Experimental group   In an experiment, this is the group of research participants exposed to the independent variable.

Experimental method   The scientific way to determine the effect or influence of a variable on the subjects' performance or behavior.

Face validity   A subjective impression of how well test items seem to be related to the requirements of a job.

Fixed-alternative questions   Survey questions to which respondents limit their answers to the choices or alternatives presented. They are similar to multiple-choice questions on college exams.

Flextime   A system of flexible working hours combining core mandatory work periods with elective work periods at the beginning and end of the workday.

Focus groups   A method of surveying public opinion through the paid participation of 8 to 12 group members who meet to describe their reactions to a product, or advertisement, or to specific issues.

Forced-choice technique   A performance appraisal technique in which raters are presented with groups of descriptive statements and are asked to select the phrase in each group that is most descriptive or least descriptive of the worker being evaluated.

Forced-distribution technique   A performance appraisal technique in which supervisors rate employees according to a prescribed distribution of ratings, similar to grading on a curve.

Frequency distribution   A graphic representation of raw data that shows the number of times each score occurs.

Functional turnover   The situation that arises when poor employees quit their jobs. This type of turnover is not necessarily detrimental to the organization.

Goal-setting theory   The theory of motivation based on the idea that our primary motivation on the job is defined in terms of our desire to achieve a particular goal.

Group tests   Psychological tests designed to be administered to a large number of people at the same time.

Halo effect   The tendency to judge all aspects of a person's behavior or character on the basis of a single attribute.

Hardiness   A personality variable that may explain individual differences in vulnerability to stress. So-called hardy persons believe they can control the events in their lives and thus may be more resistant to stress.

Hawthorne studies   A long-term research program at the Hawthorne, Illinois, Western Electric Company plant. It documented the influence of a variety of managerial and organizational factors on employee behavior.

High performance cycle   The theory of motivation and job satisfaction that suggests that goals affect job performance, depending on the kind of task and the abilities of the worker.

Human anthropometry   A branch of engineering psychology concerned with the measurement of the physical structure of the body.

Impression management   Acting deliberately to make a good impression, to present oneself in the most favorable way.

Inadequate information error   A source of error in performance appraisal in which supervisors rate their subordinates even though they may not know enough about them to do so fairly and accurately.

In-basket technique   An assessment center exercise that requires job applicants to process memos, letters, and directives found in a typical manager's in-basket.

Independent variable   In an experiment, this is the stimulus variable that is manipulated to determine its effect on the subjects' behavior.

Individual tests   Psychological tests designed to be administered to one person at a time.

Inferential statistics   Methods for analyzing research data that express relationships in terms of probabilities.

Initiating structure leadership functions   Leadership behaviors concerned with organizing, defining, and directing the work activities of subordinates.

Interest tests   Psychological tests to assess a person's interests and preferences. These tests are used primarily for career counseling.

Interpersonal affect   Our feelings or emotions toward another person. In performance appraisal, the emotional tone of the relationship between manager and employee, whether positive or negative, can influence the assigned ratings.

I-O psychology   The application of the methods, facts, and principles of the science of psychology to people at work.

Job analysis   The study of a job to describe in specific terms the nature of the component tasks performed by the workers.

Job congruence   The match between our abilities and the requirements of our jobs.

Job enrichment   An effort to expand the scope of a job to give employees a greater role in planning, performing, and evaluating their work.

Job rotation   A management training technique that assigns trainees to various jobs and departments over a period of a few years.

Job satisfaction   Our positive and negative feelings and attitudes about our jobs.

Job simplification   The reduction of manufacturing jobs to the simplest components that can be mastered by unskilled or semiskilled workers.

Job-characteristics theory   The theory of motivation that states that specific job characteristics lead to psychological conditions that can increase motivation, performance, and satisfaction in employees who have a high growth need.

Leaderless group discussion   An assessment center exercise in which job applicants meet to discuss an actual business problem under the pressure of time. Usually, a leader emerges from the group to guide the discussion.

Leader-member exchange   A leadership theory that focuses on how the leader-follower relationship affects the leadership process.

Locus of control   One's belief about the source of one's rewards. People with an internal locus of control believe that job performance, pay, and promotion are under their control and dependent on their own behavior. People with an external locus of control believe such events depend on outside forces such as luck.

Management by objectives (MBO)   A performance appraisal technique that involves a mutual agreement between employee and manager on goals to be achieved in a given period.

Mass psychogenic illness   A stress-related disorder manifested in a variety of physical symptoms that spreads rapidly among a group of workers; popularly called assembly-line hysteria.

Matched group design   A method for ensuring similarity between experimental and control groups that matches subjects in both groups on characteristics, such as age, job experience, and intelligence, that could affect the dependent variable.

Mean   The arithmetic average; a way of describing the central tendency of a distribution of data.

Median   The score at the midpoint of a statistical distribution; half the scores fall below the median and half above.

Merit pay   A wage system in which pay is based on level of performance.

Merit rating   Objective rating methods designed to provide an objective evaluation of work performance.

Meta-analysis   The large-scale reanalysis of the results of previous research studies.

Mode   The most frequently obtained score in a distribution of data.

Most-recent-performance error   A source of error in performance appraisal in which a rater tends to evaluate a worker's most recent job behavior rather than behavior throughout the period since the last appraisal.

Motivator-hygiene (two-factor) theory   The theory of motivation that explains work motivation and job satisfaction in terms of job tasks and workplace features.

Naturalistic observation   The scientific observation of behavior in its natural setting, without any experimental manipulation of the independent variable.

Needs assessment   An analysis of corporate and individual goals undertaken before designing a training program.

Needs hierarchy theory   The theory of motivation that encompasses physiological, safety, belonging, esteem, and self-actualization needs.

Negative affectivity   A personality dimension characterized by a generalized life and job dissatisfaction and by a focus on negative aspects of life events.

Nominal working hours   The prescribed number of hours employees are supposed to spend on the job; not all of these hours are actually spent performing job tasks.

Normal distribution   A bell-shaped distribution of data in which most scores fall near the center and few fall at the extreme low and high ends.

Normative decision theory   A leadership theory that focuses on the correct norms or standards of behavior for leaders to follow.

Objective tests   Tests for which the scoring process is free of personal judgment or bias.

Occupational health psychology   The field of study dealing with the health effects of job stress and other aspects of employee well-being.

On-the-job training   Training that takes place directly on the job for which the person has been hired.

Open-end questions   Survey questions to which respondents state their views in their own words. They are similar to essay questions on college exams.

Organizational culture   The organization's pattern of beliefs, expectations, and values as manifested in company and industry practices.

Organizational development (OD)   The study and implementation of planned organizational changes.

Organization-based self-esteem   A personality dimension relating to our assessment of our adequacy and worth with regard to our place in the employing organization.

Paired-comparison technique   A performance appraisal technique that compares the performance of each worker with that of every other worker in the group.

Path-goal theory   A leadership theory that focuses on the kinds of behaviors leaders should exercise to allow their subordinates to achieve personal and organizational goals.

Peer rating   A performance appraisal technique in which managers or executives at the same level assess one another's abilities and job behaviors.

Performance appraisal   The periodic, formal evaluation of employee performance for the purpose of making career decisions.

Personality tests Psychological tests that assess personal traits and feelings.

Person-machine system A system in which human and mechanical components operate together to accomplish a task.

Person-organization fit The congruence between an employee's values and the organization's values.

Power tests Tests that have no time limit. Applicants are allowed as much time as they need to complete the test.

Predictive validity An approach to establishing criterion-related validity in which a new test is administered to all job applicants, and all applicants are hired, regardless of test scores. Later, when a measure of job performance can be obtained, test scores are correlated with job performance to see how well the test predicted job success.

Probability The idea that the differences between the means of experimental and control groups could have occurred by chance.

Probability sampling A method for constructing a representative sample of a population for surveys or polls. Each person in the population has a known probability or chance of being included in the sample.

Projective techniques A personality assessment technique in which test-takers project their feelings onto an ambiguous stimulus such as an inkblot.

Prosocial behavior Behaviors directed toward supervisors, co-workers, and clients that are helpful to an organization.

Protective exclusion The practice of barring certain groups of employees, such as women of childbearing age, from potentially hazardous jobs because of fear of lawsuits.

Pygmalion effect A self-fulfilling prophecy in which managers' expectations about the level of their employees' job performance can influence that performance.

Qualitative visual displays Displays that present a range rather than a precise numerical value. They are frequently used to show whether components, such as engine temperature, are operating in the safe or unsafe range.

Quality control circles Employee groups organized to deal with specific production problems.

Quality-of-work-life (QWL) programs Organizational programs based on active employee participation in decision and policy making.

Quantitative visual displays Displays that present a precise numerical value, such as speed, altitude, or temperature.

Quota sampling A method for constructing a representative sample of a population for surveys or polls. Because the sample must reflect the proportions of the larger population, quotas are established for various categories such as age, gender, and ethnic origin.

Race norming A controversial practice, now outlawed, of boosting test scores for minority job applicants to equalize hiring rates.

Random group design A method for ensuring similarity between experimental and control groups that assigns subjects at random to each condition.

Ranking technique A performance appraisal technique in which supervisors list the workers in their group in order from highest to lowest or best to worst.

Rating scales A performance appraisal technique in which supervisors indicate how or to what degree a worker possesses each relevant job characteristic.

Rational validity The type of validity that relates to the nature, properties, and content of a test, independent of its relationship to job performance measures.

Realistic job previews A recruitment technique that acquaints prospective employees with positive and negative aspects of a job.

Recognition technique A technique for testing advertising effectiveness by asking people if they recognize a particular ad, where they saw it, and what they can recall about it.

Relaxation training A stress-reduction technique that concentrates on relaxing one part of the body after another.

Reliability The consistency or stability of a response on a psychological test.

Reverse discrimination The phenomenon that may occur when recruiting, hiring, promotion, and other human resources decisions in favor of members of a minority group result in discrimination against members of the majority group.

Role ambiguity A situation that arises when job responsibilities are unstructured or poorly defined.

Role conflict A situation that arises when there is a disparity between job demands and the employee's personal standards.

Sales test technique A way of testing the effectiveness of an advertising campaign by introducing the new advertising in selected test markets.

Scientific management A management philosophy concerned with increasing productivity that regarded workers as extensions of the machines they operated.

Scientific method A controlled, objective, and systematic approach to research.

Selection ratio The relationship between the number of people to be hired (the number of jobs) and the number available to be hired (the potential labor supply).

Self-managing work groups Employee groups that allow the members of a work team to manage, control, and monitor all facets of their work, from recruiting, hiring, and training new employees to deciding when to take rest breaks.

Self-ratings A performance appraisal technique in which managers assess their own abilities and job performance.

Self-report personality inventories Personality assessment tests that include questions dealing with situations, symptoms, and feelings. Test-takers are asked to indicate how well each item describes themselves or how much they agree with each item.

Shape coding Designing knobs for control panels in recognizably different shapes so that they can be identified by touch alone.

Situational interviews Interviews that focus not on personal characteristics or work experience but on the behaviors needed for successful job performance.

Situational testing An early term for the assessment-center technique for employee selection and performance appraisal. Employees are placed in a simulated job setting so that their behavior under stress can be observed and evaluated.

Skewed distribution   An asymmetrical distribution of data with most scores at either the high or the low end.

Social loafing   The idea that people do not work as hard in a group as they do when working alone.

Socialization   The adjustment process by which new employees learn their role in the organizational hierarchy, their company's values, and the behaviors considered acceptable by their work group.

Speed tests   Tests that have a fixed time limit, at which point everyone taking the test must stop.

Split-halves method   A way to determine test reliability that involves administering a new test to a group of subjects, dividing in half the total number of items, and correlating the two sets of scores.

Standard deviation   A measure of the variability of a distribution, the standard deviation is a precise distance along the distribution's baseline.

Standardization   The consistency or uniformity of the conditions and procedures for administering a psychological test.

Standardization sample   The group of subjects used to establish test norms. The scores of the standardization sample serve as the point of comparison for determining the relative standing of the persons being tested.

Statistical significance   The level of confidence we can have in the results of an experiment. Significance is based on the calculation of probability values.

Stress   Physiological and psychological responses to excessive and usually unpleasant stimulation and to threatening events in the environment.

Structured interviews   Interviews that use a predetermined list of questions that are asked of every person applying for a particular job.

Subjective tests   Tests that contain items such as essay questions. The scoring process can be influenced by the personal characteristics and attitudes of the scorer.

Survey research method   Interviews, behavioral observations, and questionnaires designed to sample what people say about their feelings or opinions, or how they say they will behave in a given situation.

Test norms   The distribution of test scores of a large group of people similar in nature to the job applicants being tested.

Test-retest method   A way to determine test reliability that involves administering a new test twice to the same group of subjects and correlating the two sets of scores.

Theory X/Theory Y   The Theory X approach to management assumes that people are lazy and dislike work and therefore must be led and directed. Theory Y assumes that people find satisfaction in their work and function best under a leader who allows them to participate in working toward both personal and organizational goals.

Time-and-motion study   An early attempt to redesign work tools and to reshape the way workers performed routine, repetitive jobs.

Transactional leadership   A leadership style that focuses on the social interactions between leaders and followers, based on followers' perceptions of and expectations about the leader's abilities.

Transformational leadership A leadership style in which leaders are not constrained by their followers' perceptions but are free to act to change or transform their followers' views.

Type A/Type B personalities Personality patterns related to one's ability to tolerate stress; Type A persons have been associated with heart disease, anger, hostility, time urgency, and depression; Type B persons may work as hard as Type As but show fewer stress effects.

Unstructured interviews Interviews in which the format and questions asked are left to the discretion of the interviewer.

Valence-instrumentality-expectancy (VIE) theory The theory of motivation that states that people make choices that are based on their perceived expectations that certain rewards will follow if they behave in a particular way.

Validity The determination of whether a psychological test or other selection device measures what it is intended to measure.

Validity generalization The idea that tests valid in one situation may also be valid in another situation.

Vestibule training Training that takes place in a simulated workspace.

Wage-incentive system The primary pay system for production workers, in which the more units produced, the higher the wage.

Work analysis The study of certain tasks and skills that workers can transfer from one job to another.

Work overload Too much work to perform in the time available or work that is too difficult for the employee to perform.

Work underload Work that is too simple or insufficiently challenging for one's abilities.

Workaholism So-called addiction to work because of anxiety and insecurity or because of a genuine liking for the job.

Photo Credits

Author Index

Subject Index

A

Abrams tank design, 396
Absenteeism, 247–248
Accident proneness, 332
Accidents, 324–337
Achievement motivation, 225–226
Active practice, 167–168
Activity logs, 78
Adolescent consumers, 453–455
Adverse impact, 69, 163
Advertising, 430–431, 434–448
Age discrimination, 70–72, 128
Age Discrimination in Employment Act, 72
Agreeableness, 118
Aided recall, 430
Alcohol abuse, 329, 340–343
American Psychological Association (APA), 19
American Psychological Society, 19
Americans with Disabilities Act (ADA), 72–73
Anonymity in rating, 146
Anthropometry, 398–399
Appearance, discrimination based on, 74
Application blanks, 69–70, 79–82
Applied Experimental and Engineering Psychologists division (APA), 19
Apprenticeships, 172–173
Aptitude tests, 114–115
Army Alpha test, 10
Army Beta test, 10
Asian-American consumers, 451–452
Assembly-line hysteria, 372
Assembly-line work, 371–372
Assessment-center technique, 91–93, 144
Attribution error, 151

Auditory displays, 405–407
Authoritarian leaders, 201
Average rating error, 149–150

B

Banding of test scores, 105
Beautyism, 74
Behavior modeling, 177, 179
Behavior modification, 174, 379
Behavioral observation scales (BOS), 143
Behaviorally anchored rating scales (BARS), 142–143
Bennett Mechanical Comprehension Test, 114
Beta-II test, 111–112
Big Five personality factors, 118–119
Biofeedback, 378–379
Biographical data, 78–82, 135–136
Biographical inventories, 81–82
Black consumers, 451–452
Black managers, 218–219
Boredom, 312
Brand loyalty, 450
Brand names, 429, 440–442
Bureaucracy, 195, 258–261
Burnout, 373
Business games, 175–176

C

California Psychological Inventory, 117–118
Career development issues, 180–183, 370
Carpal tunnel syndrome, 328, 347–348, 398, 414
Case studies, 175
Celebrity endorsements, 438